THE MOSAIC WAY
FIELD
GLOSSARY

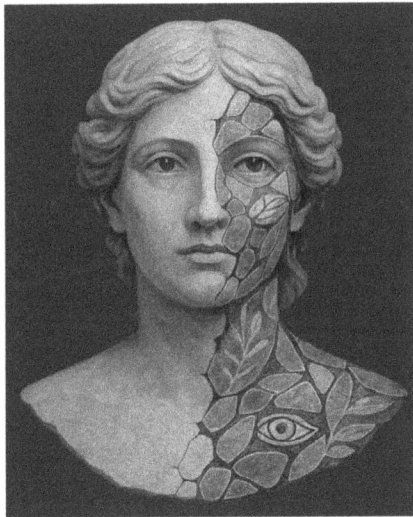

*Language for Leading with Identity,
Inclusion, and Cultural Intelligence*

DR. KARISSA THOMAS

The Mosaic Way Field Glossary
Language for Leading with Identity, Inclusion, and Cultural Intelligence

First Edition

Library of Congress Control Number 2025914809
Published by Mosaic Intelligence Publishing
www.MosaicIntelligenceMethod.com

ISBN 978-1-968277-33-8

Interior and Cover design by Marigold Emal

Printed in the United States of America

The Mosaic Intelligence Method™, The Mosaic Way™, and Mosaic Question™ are trademarks of Dr. Karissa Thomas. All other trademarks are the property of their respective owners.

For permissions, speaking engagements, or licensing inquiries, please contact info@MosaicIntelligenceMethod.com

DEDICATION

For every leader who lingered after the meeting to listen, for every voice overlooked yet still daring to rise, for the educators, coaches, healers, adjusters, facilitators, bridge-builders, and culture-shapers weaving belonging quietly when no one is watching. For those asked to translate, tolerate, or fold themselves small to fit, yet who chose truth even when it cost them comfort. For the next generation who will inherit our language and decide how to use it. This work is for you, this language yours to carry, this future ours to build—together.

TABLE OF CONTENTS

AUTHOR'S NOTE
The Journey Behind the Glossary

This glossary was not created in isolation. It draws from years of experiencing the emotional struggles of leadership, understanding the unspoken language of identity, and observing the everyday moments where inclusion, trust, and clarity either take root or quietly fade away.

My journey began in classrooms, leadership offices, claim centers, and cross-cultural education spaces. I have led DEI (Diversity, Equity, and Inclusion) conversations in corporate boardrooms, listened to educators on the edge of burnout, and partnered with executives striving to balance profit with people. Across industries and borders, I have heard leaders share their unseen stories—of race and displacement, pressure and loss, hope and aspiration.

My doctoral research explored identity conflict and belonging through social identity theory. This work evolved into a multidimensional leadership model now called the Mosaic Intelligence Method™—a practical, identity-aware approach emphasizing emotional integrity, cultural fluency, and identity agility in leadership.

This glossary complements that method. It strives to be practical and reflective because leadership language should not only be found in academic journals—it should also be vibrant in boardrooms, classrooms, and communities. Every entry is based on lived experience, field observation, and coaching sessions.

If you've ever struggled to find the right word in an tense meeting, or wished someone could reveal the truth you've been holding inside, this guide is for you.

Call to Action Build with Us, Study with Us, Invest in the Work

The Mosaic Way™ is more than just a brand—it is a method, a movement, and a growing framework designed to address the emotional and cultural needs of modern leadership. This glossary is only the beginning.

If you are an educator, executive, or change agent

- Incorporate this glossary into trainings, classrooms, or boardrooms.
- Weave it into leadership programs or DEI strategies.
- Use the Mosaic Question™ prompts to enhance reflection and increase cultural fluency in your teams.

If you're involved in the research or philanthropic community

- Partner with us to advance the study of the Mosaic Intelligence Method™ as a peer-reviewed global leadership framework.
- Fund pilot programs, cross-sector training initiatives, or comparative studies on how emotional integrity, cultural flexibility, and identity agility enhance retention, trust, and organizational resilience.

If you are someone quietly repairing culture—whether you're leading after a crisis, reshaping inclusion in your school, or simply trying to lead without losing yourself—this work is for you.

Let it fuel your next courageous conversation.

Let it give voice to what you've always known but couldn't name.

Let it become part of your daily leadership practice.

Visit www.mosaicintelligencemethod.com to explore

- Full training and certification programs
- CEU pathways and licensing opportunities
- Research collaborations and publications

Together, we can lead differently. Let's make language part of the solution—not part of the silence.

— Dr. Karissa Thomas

Founder, The Mosaic Way™

PREFACE
From Emotional Intelligence to Cultural Fluency

Why Language Evolves in The Mosaic Way™

For decades, emotional intelligence (EI) has given leaders a framework for understanding relationships, boosting self-awareness, and managing emotions. It has provided language for truths we've always known but found difficult to express that feelings influence leadership, that empathy matters, and that how we communicate emotionally directly impacts how others respond. EI remains an essential foundation—but in today's global, high-stakes settings, it alone is no longer enough.

That's where *Cultural Fluency* steps in.

Cultural Fluency builds on the strengths of emotional intelligence while adding the often unspoken layers—identity, context, history, and power. EI mainly focuses on individual awareness and interpersonal skills; Cultural Fluency expands the perspective.

- How do systems influence whose emotions are acknowledged and whose are ignored?
- Who is supposed to regulate, and who is allowed to respond?
- How do unfamiliar or misunderstood cultural codes change meaning in a conversation?

- How do race, gender, language, and history shape our understanding of "empathy" or "self-awareness" in real-life situations?

In diverse, high-pressure settings, emotional intelligence alone can unintentionally support the idea that sameness is the ideal. It might reward tone over truth and conformity over authenticity. Cultural Fluency equips leaders to navigate not just emotional realities but also the cultural, systemic, and historical forces that influence them. It focuses on awareness of differences, power dynamics, and dignity across all facets of identity.

This glossary—and The Mosaic Way™ as a whole—does not reject emotional intelligence. It redefines it, broadening its scope to align with today's realities. EI asks, *"How am I feeling, and how do I respond?"* Cultural Fluency asks, *"What am I missing, and how do I adapt—with respect, curiosity, and courage?"*

As you explore the terms in this Field Glossary, you'll notice shifts in vocabulary—not as a loss of depth, but as growth. Language that reflects current complexity. Models that mirror real-life experiences, not just theory. Leadership tools that don't just seem effective—but genuinely do good—because they are grounded in culture, identity, and emotional integrity.

Cultural Fluency is more than just a concept.

It's a discipline, a daily practice, and the foundation of The Mosaic Way™.

ABOUT THE TERMS IN
THIS GLOSSARY

The terms in *The Mosaic Way*™ *Field Glossary* are a carefully curated blend of established concepts, adapted cultural language, and newly created vocabulary—each chosen to emphasize the emotional, cultural, and identity-based aspects of modern leadership and communication.

Some concepts—such as *psychological safety* or *implicit bias*—are well known in academic and organizational literature. Here, they are reinterpreted through the three core pillars of the Mosaic Intelligence Method™ **Emotional Integrity, Cultural Flexibility, and Identity Agility.**

Other entries—such as *tone policing, youth tokenism,* or *x-factor bias*—emerge from contemporary cultural discourse. While not originally coined within this framework, they are redefined and expanded into practical tools for organizational strategy, equity development, and relational leadership.

A third category includes original terms and conceptual pairings developed specifically for this framework, such as *trust leakage* and *zones of proximal identity,* along with reframed practices like *mirror work.* These ideas draw from Dr. Karissa Thomas's applied research, coaching, and consulting in high-pressure environments where identity, belonging, and leadership intersect.

Each glossary entry is crafted to transition smoothly from definition to application, including

- **A practical definition** for shared understanding
- **A Business Application** relevant to teams, leadership, or systems
- **A reflective leadership Insight** rooted in lived organizational realities
- **A culturally grounded caution** to honor nuance and prevent harm
- **A signature Mosaic Question**™ to spark dialogue and prompt action
- **A Mosaic in Action vignette** illustrating the concept in practice

This is not a static glossary. It is purposely evolving—reflecting how language changes through culture, community, and honest conversation. You are encouraged to view these terms not as strict rules, but as starting points for deeper learning, rethinking, and building relationships.

Use it to name what has gone unnamed, clarify misunderstandings, and spark informed, identity-aware communication that changes not only how we speak but also how we lead.

Note on Entry Length and Variation

Entries in *The Mosaic Way*™ *Field Glossary* are intentionally varied in length and depth. Some terms require added context, real-world examples, or leadership applications to fully convey their significance. Others can be captured more directly with concise definitions.

Readers will notice that

- **Expanded entries** include layered applications and longer *Mosaic in Action* vignettes. These highlight terms that often spark deeper reflection in training, coaching, and organizational strategy.

- **Concise entries** provide essential definitions and guidance without extensive elaboration—serving as quick, practical tools.

This variation reflects the nature of language itself some words carry centuries of cultural weight, while others are sharper instruments designed for immediate clarity. Both are valuable.

Leaders and teams are encouraged to use this glossary flexibly— drawing on detailed entries for deeper study and discussion, while turning to concise entries for quick reference and decision-making.

Sorting Note

For consistency, all glossary terms are alphabetized using the following rules:

- Sort case-insensitively.
- Treat hyphens as spaces (e.g., "White-Passing" sorts as "White Passing").
- Ignore diacritics and punctuation (e.g., "X-Leadership").
- Sort by the first differing word for "vs." and parenthetical clarifiers (e.g., "Appropriation vs. Appreciation" files under "Appropriation").

This mirrors how the glossary is already structured and provides a reference point for future updates.

INTRODUCTION
Why Language Matters Now
More Than Ever

We are living through a time of quick and deep change—culturally, politically, emotionally, and spiritually. Systems once trusted are being questioned. Cultural norms are evolving. Communities are breaking apart, reforming, and trying to heal. In this moment of urgency and redefining, language is no longer just a professional tool—it becomes a way of leading. The words we pick are not random; they influence our choices, our relationships, and our ability to connect across differences.

In high-stakes settings—such as corporate leadership, education, healthcare, nonprofit work, disaster response, and government—language can no longer be an afterthought. It is not just about "saying the right thing." It's about whether people feel seen, respected, protected, and included. Words can affirm or erase, repair or retraumatize, inspire trust or shatter it. In a world increasingly shaped by identity-based harm, emotional labor, and cultural disconnect, emotionally intelligent communication has become essential rather than optional.

This is why *The Mosaic Way™ Field Glossary* was created. It is not a static list of textbook definitions. It is a living, breathing leadership tool—designed for those who lead in the tension of identity, belonging, power, and perception. It is for facilitators navigating transformation in charged environments. For leaders crossing generational, cultural, and geopolitical lines. For those unwilling to simply "manage diversity" but committed to leading humans—with care, clarity, and conscience.

What makes this glossary unique is not just what it defines, but how it does so. Each entry is crafted to be emotionally aware, practically relevant, and culturally grounded. Every term includes

> **Definition** – A clear, understandable explanation based on modern usage.
>
> **Business Application** – How and where the term usually appears in organizational or team settings.
>
> **Leadership Insight** – Why the concept is important for emotionally intelligent and culturally responsive leadership.
>
> **Cultural Caution** – How the term can be misused, misunderstood, or weaponized, and what to watch out for.
>
> **Mosaic Question** – A reflective prompt designed to spark dialogue, promote self-examination, or deepen awareness.
>
> **Mosaic in Action** – A brief real-world example illustrating the term's impact and potential leadership responses.

This guide is rooted in decades of lived experience—not just theory. From international classrooms to post-disaster recovery zones, from corporate DEI consultations to one-on-one executive coaching, these terms reflect the realities of navigating identity, culture, and trust under pressure. The language here is sharp yet compassionate, bold yet accessible, honoring the vital work of leading across differences.

Who This Is For

This guide is for leaders working at the intersection of language and leadership. Whether you're a coach, consultant, manager, educator,

DEI leader, Human Resources (HR) professional, clinician, facilitator, or an executive leading culture change—this glossary is your essential resource.

You might be the person people turn to when communication fails. You may hold space for pain while remaining centered yourself. Or you could lead from within systems that aren't built for you, doing the emotional and intellectual work of translation every day. If so, this book was created with you in mind.

You don't need to be an expert in cultural studies or DEI strategy to use this glossary. All that's required is the willingness to lead with empathy, clarity, and presence.

Why This Glossary Matters Now

What makes *The Mosaic Way™ Field Glossary* unique is not just what it defines—it's how it defines it. Every term is rooted in lived experience from various sectors and cultures from executive boardrooms to post-disaster recovery zones, from restorative justice circles to frontline coaching sessions. This language has been tested in real-world conditions by people navigating high-stakes, culturally complex, and emotionally charged environments.

This glossary honors that work—and prepares you to carry it forward. Because the truth is this: how we communicate either maintains the status quo or drives transformation. The way we lead through language will decide whether we simply respond to change or actively heal and reimagine the spaces we share.

How to Use This Guide

Think of this glossary as a tool to foster deeper connection, enhance reflection, and build trust in real time. It can be incorporated into leadership training, curriculum development, crisis recovery, equity assessments, and coaching sessions. You might refer to one term during a team check-in or review several entries to guide a strategic initiative.

Professionals use this glossary to

- Break the ice at leadership retreats, equity trainings, or onboarding.
- Assist in resolving conflicts when communication breaks down.
- Serve as a coaching framework for identity growth and emotional understanding.
- Enhance cultural intelligence across global or cross-functional teams.
- Offer daily reflection prompts for those dedicated to wielding power with mindfulness and presence.

The **Mosaic Question** in each entry is not accidental—it's a deliberate practice. These prompts encourage pause, dialogue, and repair, guiding teams from mere checkbox inclusion toward relational, responsive leadership.

The **Mosaic in Action** example connects each term to real-life experience, highlighting both the difficulty and the chance to learn. These snapshots can inspire discussion, support case study work, and help link theory with practice in real time.

A Closing Invitation

We are in a season where language can no longer be reactive—it must be restorative. Too often, words are used to perform rather than transform, to protect reputations rather than relationships. But there is another way. *The Mosaic Way™ Field Glossary* is a guide for that path—built on lived insight, courageous clarity, and a steadfast commitment to cultural and emotional integrity.

This glossary will not provide you with scripts; it will broaden your awareness. It will not eliminate discomfort; it will help you handle it wisely. It will not give quick fixes; it will support you in staying present during difficult conversations without avoiding what truly matters.

Let it guide your next courageous conversation. Let it shape your next policy draft, your next team huddle, your next act of repair. Let it serve not only as a glossary of terms but also as a declaration of leadership. Because how we speak reflects what we value—and how we lead with our words reveals the truth about who we are.

PHILOSOPHY, ORIGIN & APPLICATION OF THE MOSAIC INTELLIGENCE METHOD™

The Philosophy

The Mosaic Intelligence Method™ is a leadership framework based on the idea that effective communication and inclusion require more than just empathy. They also need **emotional integrity, cultural flexibility, and identity agility.** These three pillars form a versatile set of skills for navigating today's diverse and emotionally intense environments. The method encourages leaders to move beyond passive awareness toward deliberate alignment, where values, voice, and visibility work together to create lasting impact.

The Origin Story

The Mosaic Intelligence Method™ developed from the clash between traditional leadership theories and the realities of today's organizations. As workplaces and communities change faster than most leaders can keep up, a clearer and more human-focused language became necessary—one that respects complexity, recognizes harm, and encourages understanding across differences.

This framework draws from the real experiences of professionals who switch between cultures, lead from underrepresented positions, or handle invisible labor. It is built on decades of observation, cross-sector coaching, global leadership development, and hands-on work in culturally complex settings—from classrooms in the United Arab Emirates (UAE) to corporate boardrooms, from DEI strategy meetings to post-disaster response teams. In these environments, the same gaps kept appearing identity mistaken for resistance, culture misunderstood as conflict, and emotion ignored as weakness.

The Mosaic Intelligence Method™ bridges these gaps through language, storytelling, and intentional leadership design—empowering leaders to lead with clarity, connection, and courage.

Application Areas

The Mosaic Intelligence Method™ is used across education, healthcare, non-profits, technology, disaster response, and government. Its tools are especially helpful in

- Leadership training and coaching
- Organizational DEI strategy
- Onboarding and HR development
- Crisis communication and conflict resolution
- Curriculum design and culturally responsive pedagogy
- Mentoring, succession planning, and cross-cultural teamwork

This glossary serves as your introduction to the method—arming you with the language, insights, and frameworks to lead inclusively, communicate clearly, and foster cultures where everyone can belong without losing their true selves.

The Mosaic Intelligence Method™

A proprietary leadership and identity framework developed and trademarked by Dr. Karissa Thomas

At the core of the Mosaic Intelligence Method™ are three interconnected pillars. Collectively, they enable leaders to manage complexity
with clarity, trust, and authenticity.

1. Emotional Integrity

The connection between your feelings, your values, and how you
present yourself in the world. Emotional integrity involves honoring
your inner experience and expressing it through actions that show
honesty, accountability, and respect.

- **Focus:** Wholeness of inner and outer self
- **Risk without it:** Manipulation, disconnection, or performance
- **Strength with it:** Trustworthy and authentic leadership

2. Cultural Flexibility

The ability to connect across cultural, generational, and social differences while maintaining your identity. Cultural flexibility blends
empathy, adaptability, and curiosity to handle unfamiliar or evolving
situations.

- **Focus:** Connection across difference
- **Risk without it:** Rigidity, misunderstanding, or exclusion
- **Strength with it:** Inclusive, adaptive leadership that hon-
  ors complexity

3. Identity Agility

The ability to adjust one's sense of self and role in various settings
without sacrificing core values or authenticity. Identity agility enables
leaders to adapt in diverse and high-pressure environments with confidence and integrity.

- **Focus:** Dynamic self-expression
- **Risk without it:** Burnout, fragmentation, or inauthenticity

- **Strength with it:** Grounded adaptability and resilient presence

Together, the Three Pillars Create:

- **Trust** (through Emotional Integrity)
- **Belonging** (through Cultural Flexibility)
- **Resilience** (through Identity Agility)

The Mosaic Intelligence Method™ asserts that leadership is not about inflexible certainty but about adaptable alignment — being grounded enough to stand firm, yet flexible enough to grow with people and situations.

How to Use This Glossary

This glossary is not a checklist to master or a test of correctness. It's not about memorizing terms or aiming for an ideal culture. Culture, leadership, and identity aren't fixed — they are always changing, adapting, and growing. The language we use should mirror that movement.

Think of this glossary like a compass, not a map. The words here won't give you exact directions, but they'll help you stay oriented when you need to:

- elevate a conversation beyond surface talk,
- deepen trust and belonging in your team or community,
- build bridges across differences,
- evaluate systems with sharper clarity,
- stretch your own thinking and imagination, or
- grow into a fuller version of your leadership.

This is the language of possibility. It is the vocabulary you can turn to when you want to disrupt old habits of thought, when you want to give a name to what has gone unnamed, or when you want to expand the way you show up for yourself and others.

It's not about perfection. Knowing every definition here won't make you the "ideal" leader. But learning to use language with care, curiosity, and courage will. Words help us shape meaning, and meaning helps us change behavior. With the right language, leaders can transform conversations, and transformed conversations can change cultures.

If you feel overwhelmed by the vastness of these terms, take a moment and remember: you're not expected to know all of them. You are encouraged to work with them. Let the glossary be a resource you revisit as needed—a living guide that provides you with the words to match the leadership you practice or the culture you build.

The Mosaic Way™ reminds us that we are always in motion—learning, unlearning, integrating, and growing. This glossary is not the end; it's part of the journey. Each term serves as a doorway to reflection, conversation, and change.

Use it to stretch, question, reframe, and imagine. Use it to build a culture where integrity, flexibility, and agility are more than just values — they are lived practices.

This is not just terminology; it's a language for change.

Note: Entries vary in length and depth; some are expanded, while others remain concise, depending on the concept.

A – Accountability, Allyship, Assimilation, and the Architecture of Authenticity

A signals the beginning—not only of the alphabet but also of the shift from intention to action. It marks the point where aspirational language must become everyday practice. It asks leaders not only what they believe but what they are building.

A manager allows only three voices to dominate while others stay strategically silent. A team member points out bias and is dismissed as "miscommunicating." A company posts a diversity statement online, but its leadership, pay equity, and decision-making tell a different story. These contradictions show that inclusion spoken but not practiced erodes trust.

Words like allyship, authenticity, and accountability are easy to say. But what do they truly mean when power remains unchallenged and sameness is rewarded as "fit"? A forces us to face the gap between story and system—between what we promise and what we actually practice.

A asks us to examine the foundation of our leadership values

- Are new perspectives embraced—or merely reshaped to fit existing frameworks?
- Are lived experiences respected—or used as optics to check a box?

1

- Is harm acknowledged—or glossed over to preserve comfort?
- Is accountability performed—or structurally embedded?

This section explores deeper truths about belonging, leadership, and design. Accountability is a practice, not just a policy. Allyship is earned, not self-appointed. And assimilation, often mistaken for inclusion, erodes authenticity until belonging becomes just survival.

A is not a checklist — it is a mirror. It reveals the toll of conformity, the exhaustion from code-switching, and the erosion of trust when language is performative but systems remain unchanged.

A calls on leaders to turn aspiration into architecture to make allyship a daily practice, to protect authenticity even when it disrupts norms, and to measure accountability not by statements but by repair. Because leadership does not start with belief—it starts with building.

A

Accent Bias

Definition: Prejudice against a speaker based on how their accent differs from a perceived linguistic norm. Accent bias is often implicit—operating below conscious awareness—and can distort perceptions of intelligence, competence, and credibility, regardless of the speaker's actual expertise.

Business Application: In professional settings, accent bias can appear in hiring, promotions, and client placements. Leaders may unconsciously prefer individuals with an accent they see as "neutral" or "standard," associating it with competence. This limits the talent pool and reduces diversity of thought and experience within the organization.

Leadership Insight: When leaders judge a person's ideas by how they sound rather than what they contribute, they risk overlooking valuable insights. Identity-aware leaders deliberately separate delivery style from the worth of the message and actively create space for all voices to be heard.

Cultural Caution: Accent-based judgments often reflect colonial, classist, or regional hierarchies. Without awareness, leaders can unintentionally reinforce these hierarchies even in multicultural settings where inclusion is a stated goal.

Mosaic Question: Whose voice are you unintentionally ignoring — and what might you be missing because of it?

Mosaic in Action: During a cross-departmental meeting, a logistics coordinator presents a supply chain solution, but her strong regional accent makes it difficult for some colleagues to understand. The project lead, aware of potential bias, invites her to elaborate on her points in a follow-up session and ensures the solution is documented in writing. The final plan—mainly based on her proposal—saves the organization significant costs and delays.

Access Equity

Definition: The fair and purposeful distribution of resources, opportunities, and tools so individuals and groups can fully participate, regardless of their starting point or systemic barriers. Access equity recognizes historical and structural disadvantages and aims to actively address them.

Business Application: In organizations, access equity involves customizing resources to serve diverse needs instead of using a one-size-fits-all approach. Examples include targeted mentorship for underrepresented groups, adaptive technology for employees with disabilities, or tailored onboarding for those shifting from different industries.

Leadership Insight: Equity-focused leaders recognize that fairness is not the same as equality. They view resource distribution as a way to address systemic disparities, not as a luxury. By meeting people where they are, leaders foster not only retention but also innovation and sustainable growth.

Cultural Caution: Equity initiatives can encounter resistance from those who equate fairness with equal treatment. Without careful framing, efforts may be misunderstood as favoritism. Leaders must explain how equitable practices benefit everyone and support organizational health.

Mosaic Question: What structural changes could you implement so that everyone on your team can genuinely access the same level of opportunity?

Mosaic in Action: A mid-sized tech company notices that employees from rural areas struggle with internet connectivity during remote work. Rather than expecting them to "find a solution," leadership provides high-speed mobile hotspots and covers the costs. Within months, collaboration improves, new product ideas emerge from previously less vocal employees, and overall retention rates climb.

Access Inequity

Definition: The unequal distribution of resources, opportunities, or participation caused by systemic barriers, discrimination, or oversight. Access inequity is often maintained by intersecting factors such as geography, socioeconomic status, language, or disability.

Business Application: In corporate and institutional settings, access inequality can occur in who receives leadership training, budget support, or visibility in high-profile projects. It can also exist in digital divides, where individuals lack the technology or tools to fully participate in meetings, learning, or decision-making.

Leadership Insight: Leaders who recognize inequity—and take action to eliminate it—show that fairness is more important than convenience. This requires humility, data-driven awareness, and ongoing effort to stop inequities from reappearing in new forms.

Cultural Caution: Quick fixes like short-term grants or one-time accommodations might create a false sense of progress but fail to tackle the root causes. Without systemic change, inequality will continue and keep disadvantaging the same groups over time.

Mosaic Question: Where in your organization are talented people unable to fully participate—not because of skill, but due to barriers you have the power to eliminate?

Mosaic in Action: For years, an international conference only offered keynote sessions in English, leaving attendees who spoke other languages on the sidelines. Many participants quietly skipped these sessions. When simultaneous translation was introduced, attendance grew, cross-cultural connections improved, and speakers began receiving more diverse feedback that shaped future events.

Accountability Culture

Definition: A workplace environment where people are expected to take responsibility for their actions, decisions, and results, with this behavior being encouraged and reinforced at all levels. In an accountability culture, individuals own both successes and mistakes, and feedback is given and received in a constructive manner.

Business Application: An accountability culture fosters trust, boosts productivity, and aligns teams around common goals. It makes sure that projects advance smoothly without constant oversight because each member recognizes their role and the significance of fulfilling commitments. This culture minimizes blame-shifting and encourages problem-solving when issues occur.

Leadership Insight: Leaders shape an accountability culture not by micromanaging every detail but by setting clear expectations, demonstrating follow-through, and acknowledging ownership when it's present. Accountability without fear fosters resilience; accountability tied to punishment breeds silence and disengagement.

Cultural Caution: In some cultural settings, openly pointing out mistakes can cause someone to lose face or harm relationships. Effective leaders adjust their accountability strategies to align with cultural norms—focusing on responsibility while safeguarding dignity.

Mosaic Question: How can you model accountability in a way that builds trust instead of creating fear?

Mosaic in Action: A marketing team misses a major campaign deadline. Instead of blaming each other in a tense meeting, the team leader brings everyone together to discuss what went wrong and how to improve. Each member commits to one step they will take to prevent similar issues. Within three months, deadlines are consistently met, and the team's reputation improves across the company.

Accountability Leadership

Definition: A leadership style that focuses on responsibility, transparency, and follow-through. Accountability leadership makes sure commitments are kept and that leaders and teams take responsibility for the results.

Business Application: Organizations succeed when accountability and strong leadership establish the tone. Clear expectations, open communication, and ongoing evaluation build cultures of trust and dependability.

Leadership Insight: Accountability is not punishment — it's taking ownership with honesty. Leaders who demonstrate accountability encourage others to do the same.

Cultural Caution: Not all cultures value individual accountability equally; some emphasize collective accountability. Leaders must clarify expectations while respecting cultural norms.

Mosaic Question: Do you hold yourself accountable with the same rigor you expect of others?

Mosaic in Action: A CEO publicly admits a strategic mistake, describes corrective measures, and demonstrates accountability to the whole organization.

Acculturation

Definition: The process of cultural exchange and adaptation that happens when individuals or groups are in sustained contact with a different culture. Acculturation involves adopting certain values, behaviors, and norms from the new culture while still maintaining aspects of one's original identity.

Business Application: In global teams, acculturation influences how quickly employees integrate into the workplace culture, adapt to communication norms, and manage expectations. Effective acculturation supports retention, morale, and cross-cultural collaboration; poor acculturation can lead to misunderstandings and identity strain.

Leadership Insight: Leaders who understand acculturation know that adaptation is not the same as assimilation. They make room for team members to share their genuine cultural perspectives while learning the norms of the new environment. This balance boosts creativity and problem-solving.

Cultural Caution: Acculturation is not one-way—dominant cultures can also change. Not recognizing this can lead to expecting only newcomers to adjust, which can reinforce power imbalances and undermine inclusion.

Mosaic Question: How can you promote cultural adaptation while respecting the uniqueness of the people involved?

Mosaic in Action: A multinational company brings in engineers from another country for a two-year project. Instead of expecting them to immediately adapt to the existing office culture, leadership provides cultural orientation for both the newcomers and the existing team. Over time, workplace norms evolve to include greetings, holiday observances, and collaboration styles from multiple cultures, strengthening the team's cohesion and innovation.

Achievement Gap

Definition: The ongoing gap in performance or outcomes between different groups, often related to inequities in resources, access, or opportunities. Achievement gaps can occur in education, career advancement, pay, or other measurable results.

Business Application: In organizational settings, achievement gaps can appear between departments, demographic groups, or regions. These gaps usually indicate systemic issues rather than ability differences—such as inconsistent mentorship, unequal access to development programs, or bias in promotion processes.

Leadership Insight: Closing achievement gaps requires leaders to address the root causes, not just the symptoms. This means analyzing data, seeking direct input from affected groups, and designing interventions that remove barriers while maintaining performance standards.

Cultural Caution: Highlighting achievement gaps without context can unintentionally reinforce stereotypes. Leaders must present gaps as systemic challenges rather than flaws in individuals or groups.

Mosaic Question: Where do performance disparities occur within your sphere of influence, and what systemic changes could help reduce them?

Mosaic in Action: A school district observes a notable difference in math scores between schools in high-income and low-income neighborhoods. Instead of concentrating solely on student results, district leaders invest in teacher training, updated learning materials, and family engagement initiatives in under-resourced schools. Within two years, the gap diminishes, and overall district performance improves.

Adaptive Capacity

Definition: The ability of individuals, teams, and organizations to adapt effectively to change, uncertainty, or disruption. Adaptive capacity combines resilience, flexibility, and creativity.

Business Application: Adaptive capacity enables companies to adapt in volatile markets, maintain performance during crises, and innovate under pressure.

Leadership Insight: Adaptive capacity increases when leaders encourage learning and

experimentation, not perfection. Leaders who invest in adaptive capacity help future-proof their organizations.

Cultural Caution: Some cultures value stability more than change. Leaders need to present adaptation in a way that respects continuity while supporting growth.

Mosaic Question: How does your leadership enhance — or restrict — your team's ability to adapt?

Mosaic in Action: During a rapid market shift, a regional director reallocates resources and promotes cross-functional teamwork, helping the company stay competitive.

Adaptive Leadership

Definition: A leadership approach that focuses on navigating change, uncertainty, and complexity by inspiring people to address challenges without clear or technical solutions. Adaptive leadership emphasizes experimentation, learning, and strategy adjustment while staying aligned with the core purpose.

Business Application: In rapidly changing environments—whether driven by technology, market disruption, or cultural shifts— adaptive leadership enables teams to respond creatively. It helps organizations differentiate between technical problems, which can be solved with existing expertise, and adaptive challenges, which require cultural shifts, new learning, and broader participation.

Leadership Insight: Adaptive leaders don't claim to have all the answers. They focus on building others' capacity to respond effectively, guiding teams to reframe problems, test approaches, and grow through uncertainty. Flexibility is not indecisiveness— it's a deliberate strategy for long-term resilience.

Cultural Caution: In cultures that value authoritative guidance, adaptive leadership might be seen as weak or unclear. Leaders should present adaptability as intentional, not as a sign of lacking direction, while still communicating a clear vision.

Mosaic Question: What obstacle in your current job demands adaptive thinking instead of a quick technical solution?

Mosaic in Action: During a sudden market downturn, a retail company's sales drop sharply. Instead of enforcing strict cost-cutting, the Chief Executive Officer (CEO) forms cross-functional teams to explore new sales channels, partnerships, and digital strategies. Within a year, the company stabilizes—not by returning to old methods but by developing new ones through collective problem-solving.

Adaptive Resilience

Definition: The ability to recover from setbacks, adapt to change, and grow stronger throughout the process. Adaptive resilience combines endurance with flexibility, enabling individuals and organizations to adjust in real time without losing sight of values and purpose.

Business Application: In volatile industries, adaptive resilience allows teams to pivot quickly— whether reorganizing workflows after staffing changes, shifting product lines based on customer feedback, or developing new systems during crises.

Leadership Insight: Resilient leaders do not romanticize hardship; they recognize challenges and lead teams toward solutions that enhance capacity. They see disruption not as a threat, but as an opportunity to innovate, repair, and rebuild.

Cultural Caution: "Resilience" is sometimes misused to justify harmful conditions by shifting the burden of adaptation to individuals instead of addressing systemic causes. True adaptive resilience requires structural change along with personal and team flexibility.

Mosaic Question: When disruption happens, are you aiming to restore the old normal—or to create something stronger for the future?

Mosaic in Action: After a major storm damages a regional office, leadership moves operations online within 48 hours. Instead of treating it as temporary, they experiment with flexible work policies and digital tools. Employee satisfaction increases, and the company adopts a permanent hybrid model.

Additive Identity

Definition: A process of identity development where new cultural, social, or personal layers are added without removing existing ones. Additive identity enhances depth and complexity, enabling individuals to hold multiple aspects of their identity at the same time.

Business Application: In workplaces, additive identity encourages employees to bring their whole selves to work—integrating professional roles with cultural heritage, passions, and lived experiences. This fosters richer perspectives and stronger team engagement.

Leadership Insight: Leaders who embrace additive identity create environments where authenticity is preserved rather than compromised. When individuals can fully integrate all parts of themselves, creativity, problem-solving, and trust improve across teams.

Cultural Caution: Assimilationist environments often undervalue additive identity by expecting conformity to dominant norms. Such cultures risk erasing diversity instead of leveraging it for collective strength.

Mosaic Question: How can your workplace create room for people to add new layers to their identity without losing what came before?

Mosaic in Action: A first-generation immigrant consultant initially hides her bilingual skills, fearing stereotypes. After a company initiative encourages cultural sharing, she begins to incorporate her language abilities into client projects, opening new markets and enhancing her sense of belonging.

Addressing Bias

Definition: The intentional process of recognizing, challenging, and reducing the impact of prejudiced attitudes, stereotypes, or discriminatory behaviors—whether conscious or unconscious—on decision-making and relationships. Addressing bias requires both personal awareness and systemic change.

Business Application: In professional settings, addressing bias improves decision-making, talent retention, and workplace fairness. This may include structured hiring methods, bias-awareness strategies in meetings, or regular equity reviews to ensure fair access to opportunities.

Leadership Insight: Effective leaders recognize that bias cannot be eliminated through a single training session. Addressing bias requires ongoing self-reflection, feedback, and structural changes. Leaders demonstrate this by seeking critique, exploring their own blind spots, and integrating accountability into organizational systems.

Cultural Caution: In some situations, discussions about bias may lead to defensiveness or denial, especially when linked to cultural or historical injustices. Leaders should present these efforts as part of organizational growth rather than personal attacks.

Mosaic Question: What systems in your organization can help prevent individual bias from turning into institutional practice?

Mosaic in Action: A hiring panel notices that most of their top candidate choices come from the same universities. After reviewing their process, they remove school names during résumé screening and implement structured interview questions. Within a year, new hires demonstrate a wider range of educational and cultural backgrounds, and team innovation grows.

Aesthetic Labor

Definition: The work employees do to meet an organization's desired appearance, style, or personal presentation—often beyond their job-specific skills. Aesthetic labor may include grooming standards, dress codes, mannerisms, and vocal tone.

Business Application: Retail, hospitality, and client-facing industries often emphasize aesthetic labor to strengthen brand identity. While this can improve customer experiences, it might also create obstacles for employees who don't meet narrow appearance standards, reducing diversity and inclusion.

Leadership Insight: Leaders should critically evaluate whether aesthetic expectations genuinely support the brand or merely mirror subjective, culturally biased preferences. Broadening acceptable standards can attract a larger pool of talent and promote a more authentic workplace culture.

Cultural Caution: Aesthetic labor demands can unintentionally uphold classist, racist, sexist, or ableist standards. Overemphasizing appearance can overshadow skills and lead to discriminatory hiring and evaluation practices.

Mosaic Question: Do your organization's presentation standards truly reflect your brand values, or are they influenced by outdated cultural biases?

Mosaic in Action: A luxury hotel chain realizes its strict grooming policy excludes employees with natural hairstyles and some cultural dress. After revising its policy to embrace broader expressions of professionalism, the company sees an increase in employee satisfaction and a more genuine connection with diverse guests.

Aesthetic Politics

Definition: The use of style, visual symbols, and cultural expression to convey political or social messages. Aesthetic politics influences how movements, leaders, and ideas are perceived and remembered, often shaping public opinion as much as policy.

Business Application: Organizations participate in aesthetic politics when they select certain colors, symbols, or branding to reflect specific values or social causes. This can boost visibility and deepen emotional connections with stakeholders, but it also demands genuine authenticity to prevent accusations of performative acts.

Leadership Insight: Leaders who understand aesthetic politics recognize the power of visual and symbolic choices to communicate values. They make sure these choices are supported by concrete actions so that symbols strengthen credibility instead of undermining trust.

Cultural Caution: Using powerful symbols without a real commitment to the underlying cause can lead to backlash, especially from communities whose struggles are being represented. Cultural appropriation in aesthetic politics can cause serious harm.

Mosaic Question: What visual or symbolic choices in your organization genuinely reflect the values you claim—and which ones might require deeper alignment?

Mosaic in Action: A nonprofit adopts a rainbow logo during

Pride Month but faces criticism for lacking Lesbian, Gay, Bisexual, Transgender, Queer/Questioning, and others (LGBTQ+) leadership and programs. In response, they partner with advocacy organizations, update policies to protect LGBTQ+ staff, and launch year-round initiatives. The logo becomes more than just a symbol—it becomes a sign of real change.

Affinity Bias

Definition: The unconscious tendency to prefer people who share similar backgrounds, interests, experiences, or identities as our own. Affinity bias can impact hiring, promotions, team assignments, and relationship-building, often without explicit intent.

Business Application: In the workplace, affinity bias can cause teams to become homogeneous, result in missed talent opportunities, and reinforce the perspectives of dominant groups. Leaders who recognize affinity bias can counteract it by diversifying hiring panels, using structured evaluation criteria, and intentionally seeking out perspectives different from their own.

Leadership Insight: Leaders who actively challenge affinity bias

broaden the organization's ability for innovation and problem-solving. By deliberately including people outside their comfort zone, they demonstrate fairness, adaptability, and the belief that value extends beyond familiarity.

Cultural Caution: In some cultures, strong affinity networks are a vital survival strategy. Efforts to reduce affinity bias should be balanced with respect for the positive role trust-based networks play, especially in marginalized communities.

Mosaic Question: Where could your feeling of connection be clouding your judgment about someone's ability or potential?

Mosaic in Action: A manager consistently promotes team members who attended the same university as she did. After learning about affinity bias, she implements blind résumé reviews and structured interview rubrics. Within a year, promotions more accurately reflect the diversity of the team's overall talent pool.

Affirmative Action

Definition: A policy or set of practices aimed at addressing historical and systemic discrimination by actively promoting opportunities for underrepresented groups. Affirmative action often emphasizes hiring, education, and contracting decisions.

Business Application: Organizations may use affirmative action to ensure fairer access to jobs, promotions, or training programs. This can include targeted outreach, establishing diversity goals, or giving priority to qualified candidates from historically excluded groups.

Leadership Insight: Effective leaders see affirmative action not as lowering standards but as broadening the pool of qualified candidates considered. They understand that merit must be evaluated in context and that systemic barriers have historically limited opportunities for many talented individuals.

Cultural Caution: Affirmative action is often politicized and misunderstood, with critics framing it as reverse discrimination. Leaders must clearly communicate the purpose and results of these initiatives to foster understanding and trust.

Mosaic Question: How can you ensure your recruitment and promotion practices actively combat systemic exclusion without introducing new inequities?

Mosaic in Action: A construction company implements an affirmative action plan to boost the number of women in project management roles. Through targeted recruitment, mentorship, and training, the share of female project managers doubles in three years—without sacrificing performance or safety standards.

Affirmative Space

Definition: An environment intentionally created to validate, support, and celebrate the identities, experiences, and contributions of marginalized or underrepresented groups. Affirmative spaces go beyond neutrality, actively promoting belonging and psychological safety.

Business Application: In organizations, affirmative spaces can include employee resource groups, mentorship programs, or inclusive policy environments. These spaces enhance retention, morale, and engagement for employees who might otherwise feel isolated.

Leadership Insight: Leaders who create positive environments send a clear message people are valued not despite their identities but because those identities enhance the collective. This builds trust and encourages innovation.

Cultural Caution: Creating affirmative spaces without sufficient resources, influence, or leadership support risks tokenism—these spaces must be empowered to create real change, not just serve as symbolic gestures.

Mosaic Question: What intentional actions can you take to shift your workplace from passive tolerance to active support?

Mosaic in Action: A global tech company launches a mentorship program for LGBTQ+ employees, pairing them with senior leaders. Within two years, LGBTQ+ representation in management roles increases, and employee surveys show a significant boost in feelings of belonging and support.

Afrocentrism

Definition: A worldview and cultural perspective that focuses on African history, heritage, and values as key reference points for understanding the experiences and contributions of people of African descent. Afrocentrism challenges Eurocentric narratives and affirms African cultural identity as a source of knowledge and pride.

Business Application: In organizational settings, Afrocentric perspectives can influence diversity initiatives, leadership development, and cultural programs that acknowledge the historical and cultural impacts of African peoples worldwide. This can enhance authenticity in inclusion efforts and broaden cultural understanding across teams.

Leadership Insight: Leaders who engage with Afrocentrism do more than recognize African heritage; they incorporate it into decision-making, curriculum, or brand identity when appropriate. This shows respect for cultural specificity and opposes the tendency to see "diversity" as a generic, one-size-fits-all idea.

Cultural Caution: Afrocentrism is sometimes mischaracterized as exclusionary. In fact, it serves as a positive correction to historical silencing. Leaders should present Afrocentric efforts as ways to enrich everyone's understanding rather than as ways to diminish other perspectives.

Mosaic Question: How can highlighting African perspectives enhance the inclusivity and accuracy of your work?

Mosaic in Action: A publishing company reviews its history textbooks and finds that African civilizations are only mentioned in the context of colonialism. Partnering with Afrocentric historians, they revise the curriculum to include pre-colonial African innovations, trade networks, and cultural achievements. Teachers report that students engage more deeply and critically with the material.

Afrofuturism

Definition: A cultural movement that combines African heritage, history, and philosophy with science fiction, technology, and imaginative stories to envision liberated futures for people of African descent. Afrofuturism contests oppressive histories by imagining empowered and innovative possibilities.

Business Application: Afrofuturism can spark innovation in design, branding, media, and technology by drawing on African diasporic aesthetics and storytelling. Organizations that incorporate Afrofuturistic themes into their creative work can connect with audiences looking for fresh, culturally meaningful visions of the future.

Leadership Insight: Leaders embracing Afrofuturism encourage teams to think beyond current limitations—using creativity, culture, and speculative thinking to reimagine what equity, justice, and prosperity could be. This mindset drives breakthroughs across industries, from entertainment to urban planning.

Cultural Caution: Afrofuturism is deeply tied to specific historical and cultural backgrounds. Using its imagery without recognizing its origins or purpose risks turning it into a superficial trend instead of a transformative vision.

Mosaic Question: What future can you envision if African and diasporic perspectives are central to its design?

Mosaic in Action: A film production company creates a sci-fi series that features African scientists, explorers, and inventors shaping interplanetary society. The project is guided by African historians, artists, and futurists to ensure the storytelling respects cultural authenticity while exploring bold new possibilities.

Agency

Definition: The ability of individuals or groups to act independently, make decisions, and influence their own situations. Agency encompasses both internal empowerment and the external factors that enable action.

Business Application: Agency in the workplace empowers employees to take initiative, solve problems, and innovate without waiting for constant approval. Building agency can involve decentralizing decision-making, offering professional development, and creating psychologically safe environments for risk-taking.

Leadership Insight: Leaders who foster agency trust their teams to make significant decisions and learn from the results. They eliminate unnecessary obstacles, provide resources, and recognize proactive efforts. Agency boosts engagement and builds a sense of ownership.

Cultural Caution: Agency is influenced by systemic and cultural factors; not everyone has equal access to it. Leaders must address structural barriers—such as discriminatory policies or rigid hierarchies—that restrict some individuals' ability to act.

Mosaic Question: Where can you increase people's ability to act on their ideas without needing permission first?

Mosaic in Action: In a nonprofit organization, junior staff previously had to get approval for even small budget changes. Leadership revises policy so managers can authorize adjustments up to a set amount. Staff begin launching community initiatives more quickly, improving responsiveness and impact.

Age Diversity

Definition: The presence and integration of people from different age groups within a team, organization, or community. Age diversity values the unique perspectives, skills, and experiences that come from a multigenerational mix.

Business Application: Age-diverse teams can integrate innovation and institutional knowledge, combining emerging technologies with proven practices. Leveraging age diversity can improve decision-making, enhance customer service for different demographics, and increase organizational adaptability.

Leadership Insight: Leaders who value age diversity avoid stereotyping younger workers as inexperienced or older workers as resistant to change. They intentionally foster opportunities for cross-generational mentoring, skill-sharing, and project collaboration.

Cultural Caution: Some cultures emphasize seniority, while others prioritize youth and fresh ideas. Navigating these differences involves respecting experience while staying open to change.

Mosaic Question: How can you build environments where all generations view themselves as contributors to innovation and success?

Mosaic in Action: A marketing firm pairs early-career staff with veteran account managers to co-lead client projects. The younger employees bring fresh digital strategies, while seasoned staff contribute relationship-building expertise. Clients benefit from both innovation and continuity, and internal trust between generations increases.

Ageism

Definition: Prejudice, discrimination, or stereotyping based on a person's age. Ageism can target both older and younger individuals, influencing assumptions about competence, adaptability, or value.

Business Application: In workplaces, ageism can influence hiring, promotion, training opportunities, and daily interactions. This might lead to talent loss, lower morale, and damage to reputation. Combating ageism requires making sure policies, language, and practices are free from age-based bias.

Leadership Insight: Leaders must recognize that ageism often hides in "culture fit" language or unexamined assumptions.

Confronting these biases requires clear anti-discrimination policies, training, and active modeling of respect for contributions at every career stage.

Cultural Caution: In some societies, devaluing older workers goes against cultural norms that respect elders; in others, neglecting younger voices can reinforce outdated hierarchies. Leaders must tailor their strategies to the cultural context while promoting fairness.

Mosaic Question: Where could unspoken age-related assumptions be affecting your decisions?

Mosaic in Action: A startup initially dismisses an applicant in his 50s, assuming he wouldn't adapt to their fast-paced tech environment. After reevaluating their criteria, they hire him for his industry expertise and discover he quickly masters the necessary tools—while also mentoring junior staff on project management.

Ally Development

Definition: The deliberate process of developing skills, awareness, and behaviors to actively support and advocate for marginalized individuals or groups. Ally development extends beyond empathy to ongoing, informed action.

Business Application: Organizations can promote ally development through training, resource groups, and mentorship programs. Allies contribute to building inclusive cultures by addressing microaggressions, challenging bias, and elevating underrepresented voices.

Leadership Insight: Leaders who focus on developing allies uphold accountability and demonstrate that inclusion is a collective responsibility. They build structures that enable allies to act consistently, even in difficult circumstances.

Cultural Caution: Allyship without education or follow-through can result in performative actions that do more harm than good. Genuine ally development requires humility, listening, and a willingness to share power.

Mosaic Question: How can you transition from passive support to active, ongoing allyship in your daily work?

Mosaic in Action: A company launches an allyship program to help employees support colleagues with disabilities. After attending workshops and participating in accessibility audits, allies successfully advocate for software updates and building modifications that enhance workplace inclusion for everyone.

Allyship

Definition: A consistent and active practice of using one's privilege, position, or influence to support and advocate for marginalized or underrepresented individuals and communities. Allyship involves listening, learning, and taking meaningful action to challenge injustice.

Business Application: In organizational settings, allyship appears when employees speak up against discriminatory practices, amplify marginalized voices in meetings, and ensure policies are inclusive. Incorporating allyship into company culture builds trust, improves retention, and enhances overall performance.

Leadership Insight: Leaders practicing allyship show that inclusion is not just the job of those who are marginalized. They create systems that make it easier for others to be allies, sharing the workload of advocacy in a way that can last.

Cultural Caution: Performative allyship—symbolic gestures without ongoing action—can erode trust and hurt the very groups it aims to support. Genuine allyship needs accountability, humility, and a readiness to be uncomfortable.

Mosaic Question: How are you leveraging your influence to advocate for others when they are not present?

Mosaic in Action: During a strategy meeting, a woman of color's idea is ignored until a white male colleague repeats it. A senior leader interrupts, recognizes the original contributor by name, and invites her to expand on it. This small act changes the tone of the discussion and shows a cultural expectation of giving credit where it's due.

Ally Fatigue

Definition: The exhaustion that occurs when individuals or organizations show temporary or performative allyship without a lasting commitment to equity and justice.

Business Application: Ally fatigue harms credibility. Employees become disengaged when leaders support diversity initiatives during crises or public pressure but don't maintain their efforts over time.

Leadership Insight: True allyship demands perseverance. Leaders who prevent ally fatigue see equity as a continuous effort, not a temporary display.

Cultural Caution: In cultures where allyship is developing,

fatigue might be seen as resistance. Leaders need to balance perseverance with rest and collective responsibility.

Mosaic Question: Is your allyship a fleeting reaction or an ongoing commitment?

Mosaic in Action: After initial diversity pledges fade, a company reaffirms its equity commitments by integrating them into strategic planning and leadership assessments.

Ambiguity Culture

Definition: An organizational or societal environment where uncertainty, open interpretation, and lack of clear rules are common. In an ambiguity culture, success often depends on managing incomplete information and changing expectations.

Business Application: Ambiguity culture can promote innovation and flexibility by providing multiple paths to success. However, if not intentionally managed, it can also lead to stress, miscommunication, and decision-making difficulties for employees who prefer clear guidance.

Leadership Insight: Leaders in ambiguity-tolerant cultures thrive by providing strategic direction while allowing space for experimentation. They help teams manage uncertainty by setting priorities, communicating often, and demonstrating flexibility in the face of change.

Cultural Caution: Not all individuals or cultures cope well with ambiguity. In some contexts, vague expectations might be seen as disorganization or a lack of competence. Leaders need to assess their team's comfort level and strike the right balance between clarity and flexibility.

Mosaic Question: How can you support your team in staying grounded when there is not a single "right" way forward?

Mosaic in Action: A startup in a rapidly changing market shifts its product direction three times in six months. The CEO maintains high morale by explaining the reasons for each pivot, emphasizing shared goals, and encouraging staff to see ambiguity as an opportunity to innovate instead of a sign of instability.

Amplification

Definition: The intentional act of making someone's voice, contribution, or perspective more visible and influential, especially when that person is overlooked or marginalized. Amplification ensures that credit is properly given and ideas receive the attention they deserve.

Business Application: Amplification can occur during meetings, public forums, or digital platforms. Colleagues may repeat and credit someone's idea, invite them to present their work, or use organizational channels to showcase their contributions.

Leadership Insight: Leaders who strategically use amplification can change cultural norms, ensuring that good ideas are recognized no matter who presents them. This approach fosters psychological safety and promotes equitable participation.

Cultural Caution: Amplifying without giving credit risks appropriation, where the original contributor is overlooked. True amplification always acknowledges and credits the source.

Mosaic Question: Who on your team consistently provides valuable input that others might overlook— and how will you amplify it?

Mosaic in Action: During a cross-functional project meeting, a junior analyst suggests a data visualization approach that initially goes unnoticed. The project manager revisits the idea, highlights the analyst's name, and encourages the team to explore her proposal in detail. The approach is adopted, and the analyst's credibility increases across departments.

Amplification Network

Definition: A structured method for making sure marginalized voices are heard by repeatedly confirming, validating, and strengthening their input in decision-making processes.

Business Application: Amplification networks prevent erasure in meetings, projects, and leadership settings. They promote fairness by making sure credit is given where it is deserved.

Leadership Insight: Leaders who promote amplification networks shift culture from hierarchy to collaboration, ensuring diverse perspectives influence decisions.

Cultural Caution: Amplification should steer clear of tokenism. Relying too much on marginalized voices without sharing power risks exploitation.

Mosaic Question: Who is amplified in your organization — and who stays unheard?

Mosaic in Action: A leadership team commits to highlighting contributions from women and BIPOC colleagues during meetings, making sure their ideas are credited to their creators.

Anchor Bias

Definition: A cognitive bias where people rely too much on the first piece of information presented (the "anchor") when making decisions. This anchor can unfairly influence judgments, even if it's irrelevant or outdated.

Business Application: In hiring, sales negotiations, and project planning, anchor bias can distort decisions. A salary negotiation might be influenced by the first figure mentioned, or a project's timeline may be anchored by an initial, overly optimistic estimate. Recognizing and adjusting for this bias enhances accuracy and fairness in decision-making.

Leadership Insight: Leaders who recognize anchor bias deliberately seek diverse perspectives and data points before making final decisions. They promote teams to question initial assumptions and evaluate whether the anchor is genuinely relevant to the current situation.

Cultural Caution: In societies that respect authority, a leader's influence may remain unquestioned, deepening bias. Leaders need to foster psychological safety for questioning and adjusting.

Mosaic Question: What "first number" or "first idea" might be influencing your decisions more than it should?

Mosaic in Action: A department head sets an impractical deadline for a cross-functional project, and the team struggles to meet it. After learning about anchor bias, she asks team members to reevaluate and suggest a more realistic timeline. The updated schedule results in higher quality work and less burnout.

Ancestral Knowledge

Definition: The collective wisdom, practices, and cultural understandings passed down through generations, often rooted in lived experience, oral tradition, and community memory. Ancestral knowledge can include agriculture, medicine, storytelling, spirituality, and conflict resolution.

Business Application: Organizations engaging with Indigenous or culturally rooted communities benefit from integrating ancestral knowledge into sustainability, wellness, and leadership practices. It can guide environmental stewardship, ethical sourcing, and community-based problem-solving.

Leadership Insight: Leaders who respect ancestral knowledge see it as a living resource—one that remains relevant in modern innovation. Valuing this knowledge requires humility, cultural collaboration, and acknowledgment of intellectual property rights.

Cultural Caution: Extracting ancestral knowledge without permission or fair reciprocity is cultural exploitation. Any use must be based on consent, respect, and fair benefit-sharing.

Mosaic Question: What lessons or traditions from the past could provide solutions to your current challenges?

Mosaic in Action: A city government dealing with repeated flooding consults with Indigenous elders whose community has lived on the land for generations. The elders share water management techniques that inspire a sustainable flood-control plan, combining ancestral practices with modern engineering.

Ancestral Land

Definition: Territory that holds cultural, spiritual, and historical importance for a specific community, often related to identity, heritage, and traditional practices. Ancestral land is more than just property—it represents relationships, responsibilities, and intergenerational continuity.

Business Application: For organizations in sectors like construction, mining, or agriculture, understanding the concept of ancestral land is crucial for ethical dealings, legal compliance, and maintaining trust with local communities. Recognizing ancestral land rights can help prevent conflicts and build long-term partnerships.

Leadership Insight: Leaders who recognize ancestral land show respect for community sovereignty and cultural heritage. They view land use as stewardship rather than exploitation, aligning development goals with community well-being.

Cultural Caution: Ignoring ancestral land claims can cause reputational harm, legal conflicts, and damage to communities. Token acknowledgment without real action is often viewed as disrespectful or superficial.

Mosaic Question: How does your work honor or challenge the bond between people and their ancestral lands?

Mosaic in Action: A renewable energy company collaborates with a First Nations community before installing wind turbines on their ancestral land. Together, they develop a project that safeguards sacred sites, creates jobs for local residents, and directs a portion of profits to community-led initiatives.

Ancestral Resilience

Definition: The lasting ability of individuals and communities to adapt, survive, and thrive despite adversity, rooted in the strength, strategies, and values passed down through generations. Ancestral resilience relies on cultural heritage, collective memory, and support systems across generations.

Business Application: Organizations serving diverse communities can benefit from recognizing ancestral resilience as a source of strength rather than pathology. This awareness can influence leadership development, wellness programs, and community partnerships that honor lived histories.

Leadership Insight: Leaders who recognize ancestral resilience affirm the ways people have overcome systemic challenges over time. They make room for stories and traditions that embody endurance and resourcefulness, turning heritage into a strength for solving modern problems.

Cultural Caution: Romanticizing resilience can mask the systemic inequalities that create it. Leaders should acknowledge community resilience without justifying the conditions that necessitated it.

Mosaic Question: What inherited strengths or practices can you draw on to face today's challenges?

Mosaic in Action: A health clinic serving refugee populations integrates traditional healing practices with Western medicine into its care model. Patients report feeling more understood and engaged, and health outcomes improve through this combined approach.

Anger as Information

Definition: Viewing anger not just as an emotion to suppress or avoid, but as a signal that a boundary has been crossed, a value has been violated, or a need has gone unmet. This perspective redefines anger as a tool for insight and purposeful action.

Business Application: In workplace settings, viewing anger as a form of communication can help leaders identify systemic problems—such as unfair workloads or exclusionary practices—before they become major issues. It supports conflict resolution strategies that target root causes instead of just addressing symptoms.

Leadership Insight: Leaders who can listen to anger without defensiveness open pathways for trust and meaningful change. They recognize that anger, when channeled constructively, can highlight priorities for improvement and innovation.

Cultural Caution: Cultural norms influence how anger is shown and understood. In some settings, open displays of anger are frowned upon, while in others they might be expected. Leaders need to approach these differences with cultural awareness.

Mosaic Question: What might someone's anger be revealing about the conditions, values, or relationships in your environment?

Mosaic in Action: An employee expresses frustration about being left out of key meetings. Instead of dismissing the complaint as an emotional reaction, the manager investigates and finds that decision-making processes are unintentionally leaving out several team members. The process is then revised to promote inclusivity and build trust.

Anti-Oppression Practice

Definition: A conscious and continuous effort to identify, challenge, and dismantle systemic inequities, discrimination, and power imbalances. Anti-oppression practice focuses on how various forms of marginalization intersect and impact people's lives.

Business Application: In organizations, anti-oppression practices can be integrated through fair hiring processes, inclusive policy development, leadership accountability measures, and training that addresses bias, privilege, and systemic discrimination.

Leadership Insight: Leaders dedicated to anti-oppression work go beyond just diversity statements. They integrate equity into strategic plans, track progress, and include marginalized voices in decision-making at every level.

Cultural Caution: Token actions—such as one-time trainings or symbolic gestures—are inadequate and can even harm credibility. Anti-oppression work must be consistent, measurable, and integrated into daily operations.

Mosaic Question: How are you actively working to break down barriers to equity within your sphere of influence?

Mosaic in Action: A social services organization reviews its intake process and finds that language barriers are excluding immigrant clients. They hire multilingual staff, translate materials, and adjust procedures. The number of clients from immigrant communities served doubles within a year.

Anti-Racist Practice

Definition: An intentional, ongoing commitment to actively identify, challenge, and dismantle racism at individual, institutional, and systemic levels. Anti-racist practice requires sustained action, self-reflection, and the redistribution of power and resources to promote equity.

Business Application: In organizations, anti-racist practice can include revising recruitment and promotion systems to address racial bias, implementing transparent pay equity measures, and incorporating equity metrics into performance evaluations. It also involves creating safe channels for reporting racism and ensuring consistent, visible follow-up actions.

Leadership Insight: Leaders practicing anti-racism understand that remaining silent or neutral in the face of racism reinforces the status quo. They hold themselves accountable, set clear equity goals, and recognize that progress requires discomfort, humility, and persistent effort.

Cultural Caution: Anti-racist practice is not a one-time effort or a PR stunt. Superficial actions that lack clear and measurable results may be seen as tokenism or opportunism, which can damage trust with employees and communities.

Mosaic Question: What concrete steps are you taking to eliminate racial inequities in your work?

Mosaic in Action: A healthcare organization reviews patient outcomes by race and discovers significant disparities. Leadership invests in bias training for medical staff, hires community health advocates, and updates treatment protocols. Within two years, disparities in patient outcomes start to decrease.

Antibias Education

Definition: An approach to teaching and learning that actively challenges prejudice, stereotypes, and discrimination while promoting critical thinking, empathy, and inclusion. Antibias education helps individuals identify and stop bias in themselves, others, and systems.

Business Application: In workplace training, antibias education can enhance fairness in hiring, customer service, and team collaboration. It emphasizes practical skills—such as bias intervention techniques, inclusive communication, and cross-cultural awareness—rather than just abstract theory.

Leadership Insight: Leaders who incorporate antibias education recognize that awareness is just the beginning. They support training with policy changes, accountability measures, and modeling inclusive behavior to make bias reduction a part of the organization's culture.

Cultural Caution: If presented as a mandatory "check the box" activity without proper context or leadership support, antibias education may lead to resistance or resentment. Framing it as a shared investment in team strength and fairness boosts engagement.

Mosaic Question: How can you transform awareness of bias into ongoing, bias-interrupting actions?

Mosaic in Action: A retail chain adopts antibias training for all frontline employees, teaching them how to greet and serve customers without making assumptions based on appearance. Customer satisfaction scores improve, especially among groups that previously reported negative experiences.

Anticolonial Lens

Definition: A perspective that examines and challenges the legacies of colonialism in systems, relationships, and knowledge production. An anticolonial lens emphasizes Indigenous sovereignty, cultural self-determination, and the dismantling of exploitative structures.

Business Application: Using an anticolonial lens, organizations may revise land use policies, intellectual property agreements, or supply chains to ensure they do not perpetuate extraction or displacement. This approach also guides curriculum design, marketing narratives, and community engagement strategies.

Leadership Insight: Leaders who apply an anticolonial perspective recognize both historical and ongoing harms caused by colonialism. They commit to making structural changes that restore agency and resources to affected communities. They ensure that engagement is founded on partnership, reciprocity, and respect.

Cultural Caution: Applying an anticolonial lens requires more than symbolic gestures like land acknowledgments. Without tangible action—such as returning decision-making authority, profits, or land—acknowledgments risk being empty statements.

Mosaic Question: Where in your work could colonial legacies still influence decisions, resources, or narratives?

Mosaic in Action: An international conservation NGO updates its project approach after receiving feedback from Indigenous leaders. Instead of managing programs from abroad, they shift funding and decision-making power to local governance councils, leading to more sustainable and culturally aligned results.

Antidiscrimination Policy

Definition: A formal organizational commitment to prevent and address unfair treatment based on protected characteristics such as race, gender, age, disability, religion, sexual orientation, or other legally recognized categories. An antidiscrimination policy outlines rights, responsibilities, and procedures for reporting and resolving incidents.

Business Application: An effective antidiscrimination policy not only ensures legal compliance but also communicates to employees, customers, and partners that the organization values equity and respect. It should be clear, accessible, and supported by training, transparent reporting channels, and consistent enforcement.

Leadership Insight: Leaders set the tone by holding themselves accountable to the policy and addressing violations quickly and visibly. They know that a policy only works when it's supported by a culture of trust where people feel safe reporting issues without fear of retaliation.

Cultural Caution: Policies that are only on paper—lacking real enforcement—damage credibility and can cause ongoing harm. Cultural differences in how discrimination is understood also mean that policies need to be tailored and communicated in ways that are relevant locally.

Mosaic Question: How effectively does your organization's antidiscrimination policy work in real practice—not just on paper?

Mosaic in Action: A midsize firm updates its antidiscrimination policy to clearly protect gender identity and expression. Within a few months, employees feel more confident in speaking up about concerns, and managers start applying inclusive practices in daily team activities.

Antiracism

Definition: A proactive approach and set of actions aimed at dismantling racism at all levels—personal, institutional, and systemic. Antiracism requires both opposing discriminatory behaviors and building systems that promote racial equity.

Business Application: Antiracism in organizations can include revising hiring pipelines, auditing pay and promotion practices, diversifying leadership, and integrating equity metrics into strategic plans. It also involves creating forums for dialogue and learning that address race directly and constructively.

Leadership Insight: Antiracist leaders understand that remaining neutral in the face of racism sustains inequality. They respond quickly to racist incidents, ensure their teams grasp the principles of equity, and commit to long-term cultural change.

Cultural Caution: Antiracism must be continuous, not one-time. Public statements without consistent, measurable efforts can cause doubt, especially among those most affected by racial inequalities.

Mosaic Question: What are you actively doing today to dismantle racial inequities where you have influence?

Mosaic in Action: After discovering a racial pay gap, a publishing house conducts a comprehensive equity audit, adjusts salaries accordingly, and implements a transparent pay band system. They complement this with ongoing leadership training focused on antiracist decision-making to prevent the gap from reemerging.

Antiracist Leadership

Definition: A leadership approach dedicated to breaking down racism in structures, policies, and cultures. Antiracist leadership demands courage, accountability, and ongoing learning.

Business Application: Antiracist leaders carry out equity audits, reform hiring practices, and redesign systems to eliminate barriers for marginalized groups. They make sure that equity becomes a structural norm, not just a one-time initiative.

Leadership Insight: Antiracism in leadership involves shifting from passive non-racism to actively dismantling racist norms. Silence sustains inequality; action drives change.

Cultural Caution: Antiracism manifests in various ways around the world. Leaders must adapt their efforts to the context while remaining committed to the fundamental principle of justice.

Mosaic Question: Do your leadership choices dismantle inequity — or leave racism unchallenged?

Mosaic in Action: A school superintendent revises district policies that unfairly penalize Black students, integrating antiracist leadership into systemic reform.

Anti-Blackness

Definition: Systemic, cultural, and interpersonal practices that specifically devalue, marginalize, or harm Black individuals and communities. Unlike general racism, it targets Blackness as an identity.

Business Application: Anti-Blackness can manifest in hiring, promotions, policy enforcement, and workplace culture. Recognizing it helps organizations confront inequities that often go unnoticed under broad "diversity" initiatives.

Leadership Insight: Leaders must explicitly identify anti-Blackness to dismantle it. Avoiding specificity continues harm by ignoring the unique experiences Black employees face.

Cultural Caution: Across the world, anti-Blackness manifests in various ways — from colorism in South Asia to anti-African bias in Europe. Leaders need to understand local dynamics.

Mosaic Question: Where does anti-Blackness appear in your leadership decisions — and how do you confront it?

Mosaic in Action: A university replaces the generic "diversity statement" with targeted commitments to address anti-Black hiring practices and curriculum gaps following feedback from Black faculty.

Appearance Privilege

Definition: The unearned advantages given to individuals whose physical appearance, style, or presentation match culturally dominant standards of beauty or professionalism. These privileges can influence hiring, promotions, credibility, and social mobility.

Business Application: Appearance privilege can subtly influence perceptions of who appears "polished," "leadership material," or "customer-friendly." Recognizing this enables organizations to reevaluate dress codes, grooming standards, and implicit expectations that may exclude or disadvantage qualified individuals.

Leadership Insight: Leaders who recognize appearance privilege actively question whether judgments based on presentation are relevant to performance. They advocate for definitions of professionalism that emphasize skill, reliability, and respect instead of conforming to narrow aesthetic standards.

Cultural Caution: Appearance privilege is shaped by culture and can differ greatly. Standards in one area or industry may be exclusive in another. Leaders must evaluate whose norms are being applied and who bears the cost.

Mosaic Question: How much of your perception of someone's competence is based on appearance rather than ability?

Mosaic in Action: A financial services firm realizes that its grooming policy excludes employees with natural Black hairstyles. After updating the policy to support hair texture and style diversity, they see more applications from underrepresented groups and higher retention rates.

Appreciative Inquiry

Definition: A strengths-based approach to change and problem-solving that emphasizes identifying what works well, envisioning desired futures, and building on existing successes rather than focusing only on deficits or problems.

Business Application: In organizations, appreciative inquiry can be used in strategic planning, team building, and leadership development. By focusing conversations on successes and opportunities, teams generate momentum, increase engagement, and co-create innovative solutions.

Leadership Insight: Leaders who use appreciative inquiry ask questions that uncover potential and possibilities. They understand that focusing only on problems can restrict creativity, while emphasizing strengths can motivate people toward common goals.

Cultural Caution: An excessive focus on the positive can unintentionally suppress critical feedback or overlook systemic issues. Appreciative inquiry should be combined with honest acknowledgment of what needs to change.

Mosaic Question: What strengths are already present in your team or community that could be amplified to drive change?

Mosaic in Action: A nonprofit facing declining donations conducts an appreciative inquiry summit with staff, volunteers, and donors. Instead of focusing on loss, they identify the campaigns and partnerships that achieved the most success in the past. These insights help shape a new strategy that surpasses fundraising goals within the year.

Appropriation vs. Appreciation

Definition: The difference between cultural appropriation—using elements of a culture without permission, understanding, or respect—and cultural appreciation, which involves honoring, learning from, and giving credit to the culture of origin.

Business Application: In branding, design, or product development, understanding this distinction helps organizations avoid harm and foster authentic cultural connections. Cultural appreciation often involves collaboration, fair pay, and storytelling led by members of the original culture.

Leadership Insight: Leaders who prioritize cultural appreciation actively build relationships with cultural stakeholders, ensuring that engagement is mutual, respectful, and benefits the originating community.

Cultural Caution: Appropriation can cause serious harm by reinforcing stereotypes, erasing original creators, or profiting from marginalized cultures without giving back. Appreciation requires humility, consent, and transparency.

Mosaic Question: How can you demonstrate appreciation of cultural elements rather than exploiting them?

Mosaic in Action: A fashion label inspired by Indigenous beadwork collaborates with artisans from that community, paying fair wages and featuring the artists in marketing campaigns. The partnership boosts both brand revenue and the artisans' economic sustainability.

Archetype Disruption

Definition: The deliberate act of challenging and redefining widely accepted cultural archetypes—universal character types, narratives, or roles—especially those that restrict identity, leadership, or representation.

Business Application: In media, marketing, and leadership, archetype disruption can increase diversity and challenge stereotypes. For example, showcasing women leaders in unconventional industries or portraying men in nurturing roles helps broaden public perception.

Leadership Insight: Leaders who challenge archetypes allow people to see themselves beyond limiting stories. This can transform organizational culture, draw in diverse talent, and create new opportunities for innovation.

Cultural Caution: Disrupting archetypes without understanding their cultural or historical importance can backfire, making you seem disrespectful or inauthentic. It's crucial to combine disruption with cultural research and intentional storytelling.

Mosaic Question: Which deeply rooted archetypes in your field need to be challenged—and how can you help rewrite them?

Mosaic in Action: A STEM outreach program for youth intentionally highlights women scientists, engineers with disabilities, and Black inventors in its promotional materials. This challenges the traditional image of who works in science and motivates broader participation.

Assigned Identity

Definition: An identity category—such as race, gender, religion, or social role—imposed on an individual by external systems, institutions, or cultural norms, often without the individual's consent. Assigned identity can influence how others perceive and treat someone, regardless of their self-identification.

Business Application: In workplaces, assigned identity can influence hiring decisions, promotion opportunities, and daily interactions. Understanding assigned identity helps leaders see when employees are being labeled with stereotypes or assumptions that restrict their contributions and growth.

Leadership Insight: Leaders who recognize assigned identities create space for individuals to define themselves on their own terms. This fosters authenticity, boosts engagement, and prevents talent from being overlooked because of external labels.

Cultural Caution: Assigned identities can overlap with systemic discrimination. Ignoring the difference between assigned and chosen identity risks reinforcing oppression by not recognizing the lived experience of imposed labels.

Mosaic Question: Whose role or identity in your organization is more influenced by assumptions than by their own voice?

Mosaic in Action: A woman at a tech company is consistently asked to take notes during meetings, even though she is a lead engineer. After the team discusses the concept of assigned identity, responsibilities are redistributed fairly, allowing her expertise to influence key project decisions.

Assimilation

Definition: The process by which individuals or groups adopt the customs, values, and norms of another (often dominant) culture, sometimes at the expense of their own cultural identity. Assimilation can be voluntary or forced, and it often involves unequal power relationships.

Business Application: In global organizations, assimilation pressures can arise when employees feel they must downplay accents, alter appearance, or suppress cultural traditions to be seen as "professional." Addressing this can enhance retention and psychological safety.

Leadership Insight: Leaders who challenge assimilationist expectations foster workplaces where diversity is appreciated. They promote integration—where multiple identities coexist—rather than conformity to a single cultural standard.

Cultural Caution: Assimilation might be presented as inclusion but can genuinely erase cultural diversity. Leaders should differentiate between shared organizational values and unnecessary conformity that diminishes individuality.

Mosaic Question: What unspoken rules in your environment might be causing people to hide parts of themselves?

Mosaic in Action: A multinational law firm notices employees from minority backgrounds adopting more "neutral" speech patterns during meetings. Leadership responds by organizing cross-cultural dialogue sessions, emphasizing that genuine communication styles are appreciated.

Assimilation Fatigue

Definition: The emotional, mental, and physical exhaustion caused by the ongoing effort to conform to dominant cultural norms, often in environments that devalue or stigmatize difference. Assimilation fatigue can result in burnout, disengagement, and loss of identity.

Business Application: Employees who experience assimilation fatigue may withdraw, reduce their contributions, or leave the organization entirely. Recognizing and addressing this dynamic helps leaders foster environments where authenticity can be maintained.

Leadership Insight: Leaders who reduce assimilation fatigue remove barriers that cause constant self-editing. This includes reviewing policies, broadening definitions of professionalism, and ensuring diversity is reflected in leadership roles and organizational storytelling.

Cultural Caution: Failing to address assimilation fatigue can lead to high turnover among underrepresented groups, damaging organizational trust and reputation. Addressing it requires both cultural and structural changes.

Mosaic Question: Where might members of your team be working harder to "fit in" than to contribute fully?

Mosaic in Action: An employee resource group for first-generation professionals reports high levels of assimilation fatigue caused by dress codes and speech expectations. Leadership updates policies, expands acceptable attire, and emphasizes diverse role models, leading to improved morale and retention.

Assimilation vs. Integration

Definition: The difference between assimilation—which involves individuals fully conforming to the dominant culture, often sacrificing their own identity—and integration, which promotes participation and a sense of belonging while allowing people to keep and express their cultural heritage.

Business Application: In organizations, this distinction influences how diversity and inclusion policies are experienced. Assimilation-focused environments may reward "fitting in," while integration-focused environments value multiple cultural perspectives and practices as part of the organizational identity.

Leadership Insight: Leaders who embrace integration foster cultures where people don't have to choose between authenticity and belonging. They clarify shared goals and values while welcoming different ways of expressing them, ensuring true inclusion rather than conditional acceptance.

Cultural Caution: If "integration" is used as a euphemism for subtle assimilation—where diversity is only celebrated when convenient—it erodes trust. Genuine integration demands structural and cultural willingness to embrace difference.

Mosaic Question: Does your team culture require people to conform, or does it enable them to truly belong?

Mosaic in Action: A multinational engineering firm updates its onboarding process. Instead of expecting international hires to conform to all existing workplace customs, the company encourages them to share practices from their home cultures, many of which are later adopted as standard team rituals.

Asset Mapping

Definition: A process of identifying and organizing the strengths, skills, resources, and relationships within a community, team, or organization. Asset mapping shifts the focus from deficits to existing capacities that can be leveraged for growth and problem-solving.

Business Application: Organizations use asset mapping to identify internal expertise, uncover untapped resources, and strengthen networks. This can guide strategic planning, build resilience, and promote collaboration across departments or stakeholders.

Leadership Insight: Leaders who use asset mapping understand that solutions often already exist within the community. By identifying and connecting assets, they empower people to contribute from their strengths, boosting both engagement and innovation.

Cultural Caution: Asset mapping that ignores historical inequities might overlook who has been excluded from resources initially. It should be combined with an equity lens to guarantee assets are accessible to everyone.

Mosaic Question: What strengths or resources already exist in your environment that could be linked to address current challenges?

Mosaic in Action: A local government facing budget cuts maps out community resources instead of cutting services outright. They identify overlapping programs among nonprofits and coordinate them, maintaining service coverage while lowering costs.

Asset-Based Leadership

Definition: A leadership approach that centers on recognizing, developing, and utilizing the strengths and potential of individuals, teams, and communities instead of focusing mainly on weaknesses or deficiencies.

Business Application: Asset-based leadership can boost morale, retention, and performance by fostering a culture where people's skills and contributions are recognized, valued, and strategically developed. It is especially effective in change management and capacity-building initiatives.

Leadership Insight: Leaders who practice asset-based leadership view talent as something to be unlocked rather than controlled. They invest in skill development, promote autonomy, and align individuals' strengths with organizational needs.

Cultural Caution: Focusing only on strengths without tackling systemic barriers can hide inequities. Asset-based leadership must also confront the structures that restrict how those assets are utilized or acknowledged.

Mosaic Question: How can you align people's strengths with your organization's mission to achieve mutual success?

Mosaic in Action: A school principal recognizes leadership qualities in student volunteers and assigns them roles in peer mentoring. The initiative boosts student engagement, decreases behavioral problems, and enhances the overall school climate.

Assumed Competence

Definition: The assumption that a person is capable, skilled, or knowledgeable without verification, often based on stereotypes, status, appearance, or perceived credibility markers. Assumed competence can be either helpful or harmful depending on its accuracy and context.

Business Application: In the workplace, assumed competence can foster greater trust and opportunities for some—while others may face increased scrutiny for the same tasks. This dynamic often sustains inequities, as those who are already privileged are given more space to lead, innovate, or make mistakes without facing penalties.

Leadership Insight: Leaders who recognize assumed competence evaluate performance based on evidence rather than superficial impressions. They intentionally offer equal chances for skill demonstration, ensuring that trust and responsibility are earned and allocated fairly.

Cultural Caution: Assuming competence can overlap with affinity bias and appearance privilege, unintentionally excluding capable individuals whose skills are undervalued because they do not "look the part" according to mainstream norms.

Mosaic Question: Who on your team might be more likely to be given the benefit of the doubt— and why?

Mosaic in Action: During a board meeting, a senior consultant's suggestions are accepted without question, while a newer employee's similar idea is overlooked. After noticing this pattern, the chair begins evaluating all proposals based on their merit, regardless of who presents them or their tenure.

Assumed Incompetence

Definition: The assumption that a person lacks skill, knowledge, or ability—often without proof— based on stereotypes, bias, or social status. Assumed incompetence can restrict access to important opportunities, damage confidence, and sustain systemic inequalities.

Business Application: In professional settings, assumed incompetence often appears when individuals from marginalized backgrounds are over-supervised, excluded from decision-making, or assigned less challenging work despite their qualifications.

Leadership Insight: Leaders who question assumed incompetence ensure that skill assessments are based on actual performance. They create fair opportunities for growth and leadership, making sure responsibility is not withheld due to bias or assumptions.

Cultural Caution: Assuming incompetence can be internalized by those who experience it repeatedly, leading to self-doubt or disengagement. Leaders must address not only the external behaviors but also the systems that reinforce those assumptions.

Mosaic Question: Who in your environment might have hidden potential because others underestimate them?

Mosaic in Action: A project manager observes that a colleague with a disability is consistently assigned only administrative tasks. After advocating for their involvement in core project work, the colleague's contributions significantly enhance team performance and client satisfaction.

Attribution Bias

Definition: A cognitive bias where people focus too much on personal traits and too little on the situation when explaining others' actions.

Business Application: Attribution bias fosters inequality when underperformance is blamed on

"lack of talent" instead of lack of support or systemic barriers.

Leadership Insight: Leaders who examine attribution bias focus on systems rather than just individuals. This shift promotes fairness and structural improvements.

Cultural Caution: Attribution styles differ across cultures. Some emphasize situational explanations, while others focus on personal responsibility. Leaders need to adjust their approach accordingly.

Mosaic Question: Do you think failure is related to the person or the system they're part of?

Mosaic in Action: Instead of labeling staff as "unmotivated," a school district examined workload and identified structural inequities, which were then corrected through adjusted policies.

Attunement Leadership

Definition: A leadership approach rooted in deep listening, empathy, and alignment with the needs, emotions, and dynamics of individuals and teams. Attunement leadership involves being present, responsive, and adaptable in real time.

Business Application: Attunement leadership builds trust, minimizes conflict, and enhances decision-making by helping leaders notice subtle changes in morale, engagement, and relationships. This approach is especially valuable in high-stakes or fast-changing settings.

Leadership Insight: Leaders who practice attunement understand that connection multiplies performance. They observe unspoken concerns, validate experiences, and adjust strategy or tone to maintain strong relationships while advancing goals.

Cultural Caution: Attunement requires genuine curiosity and care; without sincerity, it can be seen as manipulation. In some cultures, overt emotional inquiry from leaders might be unusual, so adapting to the context is essential.

Mosaic Question: How attentively are you listening to what your team is telling you—both verbally and nonverbally?

Mosaic in Action: During a high-pressure product launch, a department head notices subtle signs of burnout—quieter meetings, shorter emails, and increased errors. She temporarily adjusts deadlines, brings in additional support, and holds small-group check-ins. The team's morale and performance bounce back quickly.

Authentic Engagement

Definition: A true connection between individuals or groups based on sincerity, mutual respect, and shared purpose. Authentic engagement goes beyond simple transactions to foster trust, openness, and long-term collaboration.

Business Application: In organizational settings, genuine engagement involves actively listening to stakeholders, incorporating their feedback into decisions, and consistently showing up in ways that align with stated values. It can enhance customer loyalty, improve employee retention, and foster stronger community partnerships.

Leadership Insight: Leaders who foster genuine engagement prioritize relationships as much as results. They dedicate time to understanding needs, concerns, and aspirations, and ensure communication is clear and responsive.

Cultural Caution: What is considered "authentic" differs across cultures. In some settings, being direct is appreciated; in others, it may be seen as rude. Leaders need to adjust their approach to match cultural expectations without losing sincerity.

Mosaic Question: How can you make sure that your engagement efforts are based on authentic connection instead of obligation or managing appearances?

Mosaic in Action: A city council hosts community forums on proposed zoning changes not only to meet legal requirements but also to listen to and incorporate residents' concerns. The final plan reflects community priorities, fostering increased public trust in local government.

Authentic Leadership

Definition: A leadership style marked by self-awareness, transparency, and alignment between values, words, and actions. Authentic leaders act with integrity, building trust and loyalty by being consistent and true to themselves.

Business Application: Authentic leadership fosters engagement and improves performance by creating psychologically safe environments where people feel valued for who they are. It also boosts decision-making by ensuring that choices align with long-term principles, not just short-term gains.

Leadership Insight: Authentic leaders are not performatively vulnerable; they share appropriately while maintaining focus on collective goals. They balance honesty about challenges with confidence in their ability to handle them.

Cultural Caution: Authenticity should be balanced with emotional intelligence. Over-sharing or using "that's just who I am" to justify harmful behavior damages credibility and trust.

Mosaic Question: Where might your leadership style be influenced more by expectations than by your true values?

Mosaic in Action: A CEO navigating a company restructuring communicates openly about the reasons, the challenges, and the plan forward. Employees appreciate the candor and rally around the vision, reducing turnover during a difficult transition.

Authenticity Paradox

Definition: The tension leaders experience when being "authentic" conflicts with cultural, organizational, or situational expectations. The authenticity paradox demonstrates that authenticity is not fixed but must adapt to the context.

Business Application: Leaders who rigidly hold onto "being authentic" might hinder growth, alienate colleagues, or clash with cultural norms. Navigating this paradox requires balancing personal truth with relational intelligence.

Leadership Insight: Authenticity doesn't give license for unfiltered expression. Leaders develop when they combine self-expression with empathy and adaptability.

Cultural Caution: Cultures differ in expectations for self-disclosure and expression. What seems genuine in one setting might feel wrong in another.

Mosaic Question: Do you hold onto authenticity as self-expression — or practice it as adaptive integrity?

Mosaic in Action: A new manager, encouraged to be "authentic," avoids oversharing personal struggles during a high-stakes presentation. Instead, she communicates openly while respecting professional boundaries.

Authenticity Gap

Definition: The gap between what an organization or leader claims to value and what their actions, policies, or culture actually show. This authenticity gap breaks trust and can harm reputation.

Business Application: In the workplace, authenticity gaps often occur when diversity is promoted in marketing but not reflected in leadership, or when customer service values are advertised but not consistently upheld. Closing these gaps enhances brand integrity and stakeholder trust.

Leadership Insight: Leaders who address authenticity gaps take responsibility for alignment, acknowledge shortcomings, and make tangible changes to close the divide. This builds credibility even in moments of imperfection.

Cultural Caution: An authenticity gap is more apparent in the digital age, where stakeholders can rapidly spot inconsistencies between statements and actions. This makes performative behaviors more risky than ever.

Mosaic Question: Where might there be a gap between your stated values and your actions, and how can you bridge it?

Mosaic in Action: A retail brand promotes itself as environmentally sustainable but uses non-recyclable packaging. After public feedback highlights the inconsistency, leadership switches to fully recyclable materials and publishes a transparent sustainability report, restoring trust.

Authenticity Work

Definition: The ongoing effort individuals—particularly those from marginalized or underrepresented groups—make to align their self-presentation with their true identity while navigating environments that may expect conformity. Authenticity work involves balancing self-expression with strategic adaptation to the context.

Business Application: In professional environments, authenticity work can show in how employees choose to share parts of their identity, values, or life experiences. Organizations that minimize the need for constant self-correction allow employees to focus more on innovation, teamwork, and performance.

Leadership Insight: Leaders who understand authenticity create conditions where employees feel safe expressing themselves without fear of career penalties. This includes challenging narrow definitions of professionalism and amplifying diverse role models.

Cultural Caution: Not everyone has the same freedom to "bring their whole self to work." Promoting authenticity without recognizing systemic risks can leave some employees vulnerable.

Mosaic Question: How can you foster a culture that encourages authenticity without pressuring people to disclose or expose themselves?

Mosaic in Action: At a global media company, an employee initially conceals their cultural background to prevent bias. After leadership launches inclusive storytelling initiatives and diverse leadership panels, they feel comfortable sharing culturally informed perspectives—resulting in a successful campaign that connects with new markets.

Authoritative Knowledge

Definition: Information, expertise, or ways of knowing that are valued more highly or deemed more legitimate within a specific context, often to the exclusion of other viewpoints. Authoritative knowledge is influenced by social, institutional, and cultural power structures.

Business Application: In organizations, authoritative knowledge may come from senior leadership, industry experts, or certain departments whose insights are prioritized in decision-making. Recognizing this dynamic allows leaders to diversify whose voices and expertise are valued.

Leadership Insight: Leaders who understand how authoritative knowledge works can expand decision-making to include lived experience, frontline expertise, and nontraditional forms of insight. This broadens solutions and boosts buy-in.

Cultural Caution: Overreliance on narrowly defined authoritative knowledge can silence valuable contributions from individuals without formal credentials or positional power. In multicultural settings, different ways of knowing may hold equal validity.

Mosaic Question: Whose knowledge do you automatically trust in your environment—and whose do you overlook?

Mosaic in Action: A healthcare organization consistently prioritizes physician input in patient care planning. After patient advocates identify gaps, the leadership team includes nurses, social workers, and patient representatives in care design meetings, enhancing both treatment outcomes and patient satisfaction.

Authority Bias

Definition: The tendency to assign excessive importance to opinions or decisions from authority figures, regardless of their accuracy or fairness.

Business Application: Authority bias leads to unsafe practices when employees follow senior voices without question, even if they have better data. It also distorts promotion and evaluation systems.

Leadership Insight: Strong leaders welcome challenge and avoid being shielded by their own authority. They foster cultures where dissent is safe and appreciated.

Cultural Caution: Cultures with high power distance may see questioning authority as disrespect. Leaders must demonstrate that constructive dissent is allowed.

Mosaic Question: Do you suppress your own judgment when authority is present — and what does it cost?

Mosaic in Action: During a safety review, a junior engineer voiced a concern that others ignored because the VP dismissed it. Later, leadership restructured the process to include all voices.

Authority Gradient

Definition: The gap in perceived or actual power between individuals in a hierarchy, which can affect communication, decision-making, and risk-taking. A steep authority gradient may discourage speaking up, while a flat one can encourage open dialogue.

Business Application: In industries like aviation, healthcare, and engineering, an overly steep authority gradient can prevent critical feedback from reaching decision-makers in time, leading to errors or safety issues. Balanced authority gradients promote collaboration while maintaining clarity of roles.

Leadership Insight: Leaders who effectively manage authority gradients encourage input from all levels, demonstrate openness to challenge, and establish structures that make it safe to raise concerns—especially in high-pressure situations.

Cultural Caution: Cultural norms greatly influence authority dynamics. In some settings, questioning a superior might be viewed as disrespectful. Leaders need to adjust communication methods to minimize harmful silence while honoring cultural values.

Mosaic Question: How can you modify the authority gradient in your team to promote constructive challenge while maintaining clarity?

Mosaic in Action: In an operating room, a nurse hesitates to question a surgeon's decision because of hierarchy. After team training on reducing authority gradients, the nurse feels confident to raise a concern during a procedure, avoiding a potential complication.

◈ LETTER A CALLOUT

"Accountability is not punishment; it is the practice of repair and integrity."

Reflection Questions

- How do accountability and blame differ in your own leadership or learning context?
- What does "repair" look like in a classroom, office, or team?
- Where have you seen accountability build trust instead of fear?

Practical Move

In your next group setting, name one commitment out loud and invite peers to hold you accountable — then check in on it at the close of the project or meeting.

B – Bias, Belonging, Burnout, and the Boundaries That Hold Us Together

B begins with the body—where culture is felt before it is spoken. It enters the workplace through instinct the racing heart of a high performer nearing exhaustion, the tightening chest of a colleague interrupted yet again, the silent voice whispering, *"This doesn't feel right."*

A quiet team member offers insight but is overshadowed by louder voices. A high achiever is praised for pushing through exhaustion—yet they're never asked about the toll. Inclusion is printed on posters, but late-night emails, blurred boundaries, and unspoken expectations remain ingrained in daily practice.

B is where visibility and viability intersect—where visibility should never compromise sustainability.

B asks us to confront the human conflicts shaping our work lives

- Bias disguised as instinct.
- Belonging that disappears when performance slips.
- Burnout praised as dedication.
- Boundaries dismissed as weakness instead of wisdom.

These are not superficial issues—they are structural. They shape the emotional and energetic contracts that determine whether people simply survive or truly thrive. They raise deeper questions

- Who is protected within this culture?

47

- Who is rewarded for endurance while denied balance?
- What is tolerated that quietly corrodes trust?

B links individual well-being to institutional responsibility. It rejects the myth that success requires self-sacrifice, and it exposes how results without care weaken the very people organizations depend on.

B calls leaders to redefine productivity by focusing on preservation, using boundaries as cultural tools, and rejecting the idea that exhaustion equals excellence. When bias is addressed and burnout is prevented, genuine belonging emerges, and no one needs to choose between success and survival.

B

Backlash Effect

Definition: The backlash effect describes the social or professional penalties faced by individuals—often women or marginalized leaders—when they exhibit behaviors that challenge stereotypical expectations, such as assertiveness or authority.

Business Application: This effect can appear in performance reviews, hiring decisions, or promotion processes, where assertive leadership is praised in some groups but penalized in others.

Leadership Insight: Leaders should assess whether their evaluations reward certain behaviors only when displayed by specific demographics, and ensure fair recognition.

Cultural Caution: In cultures with strict gender or status norms, the backlash effect can suppress talent and discourage authentic leadership.

Mosaic Question: Who on your team risks being "punished" for leading with their full potential?

Mosaic in Action: A woman engineer leads a high-profile project with decisiveness, but her style is labeled "abrasive" in feedback—while a male peer with similar behaviors is praised as "strong and visionary."

Balanced Leadership

Definition: Balanced leadership involves integrating various leadership styles—such as task focus and relationship building, short-term results and long-term vision—to achieve sustainable outcomes.

Business Application: Balanced leadership enhances both performance and morale, ensuring teams meet goals without compromising well-being.

Leadership Insight: Leaders who deliberately balance conflicting demands—authority with empathy, decisiveness with openness—demonstrate adaptability and resilience.

Cultural Caution: The idea of "balance" differs across cultures; in some settings, relational warmth may be preferred over efficiency, or vice versa.

Mosaic Question: Which part of your leadership is overdeveloped—

and which needs more development?

Mosaic in Action: A CEO combines data-driven decision-making with regular employee town halls, maintaining strong financial results and high staff engagement.

Bamboo Ceiling

Definition: The bamboo ceiling refers to the obstacles that limit career advancement for Asian professionals, often due to cultural stereotypes, leadership biases, and underrepresentation in executive roles.

Business Application: This obstacle can prevent organizations from fully leveraging the skills and perspectives of Asian leaders.

Leadership Insight: Organizations can overcome the bamboo ceiling by creating leadership pathways that recognize diverse communication styles and expanding mentorship opportunities.

Cultural Caution: Avoid assuming that all Asian professionals face the same challenges—barriers vary widely by ethnicity, gender, and region.

Mosaic Question: How are your leadership pipelines addressing

cultural bias as well as skill development?

Mosaic in Action: A global tech firm implements a sponsorship program pairing Asian mid-level managers with senior leaders, resulting in a measurable increase in executive diversity.

Banished Words

Definition: Banished words are terms or phrases intentionally removed from an organization's vocabulary due to their harmful, outdated, or exclusionary connotations.

Business Application: Reviewing and updating language signals cultural awareness and helps foster a more inclusive environment.

Leadership Insight: Leaders should not only ban harmful words but also provide alternative language that aligns with the organization's values.

Cultural Caution: Some words carry layered meanings in different cultural or regional contexts; banning them without discussion may alienate stakeholders.

Mosaic Question: What everyday terms in your organization should be retired to promote inclusion?

Mosaic in Action: An NGO replaces "at-risk youth" with

"youth with untapped potential," reframing community programs with a strengths-based approach.

Barriers to Belonging

Definition: Barriers to belonging are systemic, cultural, or interpersonal factors that prevent individuals from feeling accepted, valued, and included within a group, organization, or society.

Business Application: These barriers can include exclusionary hiring practices, biased leadership styles, inaccessible spaces, or cultural norms that silence diverse perspectives. Addressing them boosts retention, innovation, and trust.

Leadership Insight: Belonging is not a "soft" concept—it is a critical driver of engagement and performance. Leaders must identify and dismantle structural and cultural obstacles to belonging at every level.

Cultural Caution: What fosters belonging in one culture may not translate to another; leaders must listen locally before implementing global strategies.

Mosaic Question: What silent rules or norms in your space might unintentionally push people out?

Mosaic in Action: A company replaces its unspoken "culture fit"

hiring model with a "culture add" approach, leading to a measurable increase in diverse leadership hires and cross-team collaboration.

Base Rate Neglect

Definition: Base rate neglect is a cognitive bias where people ignore general statistical information (base rates) in favor of specific but less relevant details when making decisions.

Business Application: In recruitment, leaders might focus on one candidate's compelling story instead of considering broader performance data from the entire talent pool—leading to biased or less effective hiring.

Leadership Insight: Good decision-making balances data and story. Leaders who ignore base rates risk costly mistakes in strategy, hiring, or resource allocation.

Cultural Caution: Attitudes toward statistics vary; some regions may prioritize personal testimony or trust over data, requiring culturally aware decision-making.

Mosaic Question: Where are you letting a "good story" overshadow the full truth of the numbers?

Mosaic in Action: A nonprofit invests heavily in a program after hearing a single powerful success story, only to later find that the overall data shows limited impact compared to other initiatives.

Belonging

Definition: Belonging is a fundamental human need to feel accepted, valued, and connected within a group or system. It is not about assimilation but about recognizing one's authentic self as part of the whole.

Business Application: Organizations that prioritize belonging enhance retention, creativity, and well-being. Belonging promotes psychological safety, where employees share ideas without fear of exclusion or dismissal.

Leadership Insight: Leaders who foster belonging understand that it is created daily through consistent trust, recognition, and relational presence. Belonging cannot be forced — it must be nurtured.

Cultural Caution: Belonging manifests differently across cultures. In some, it is rooted in group identity; in others, it is based on individual recognition. Leaders must respect both communal and personal aspects.

Mosaic Question: Do people feel they truly belong in your leadership spaces — or just that they are permitted to stay?

Mosaic in Action: A manager starts each meeting by inviting input from those who are often overlooked, fostering small but meaningful moments of inclusion.

Belonging Fatigue

Definition: The fatigue felt when people—often from marginalized groups—are required to repeatedly justify or navigate their position in organizations that claim to be inclusive but do not actually deliver on that promise.

Business Application: Belonging fatigue weakens retention and trust when employees receive messages about inclusion but feel excluded in practice. Fixing it needs systemic change, not just symbolic gestures.

Leadership Insight: Leaders must understand that belonging is an ongoing effort, not a one-time accomplishment. Fatigue occurs when the responsibility of belonging falls unevenly on underrepresented staff.

Cultural Caution: The language of "belonging" may be warmly embraced in some settings but can feel empty in cultures or communities where systemic inequalities are still unaddressed.

Mosaic Question: Do your belonging initiatives foster true inclusion — or cause fatigue by keeping systems the same?

Mosaic in Action: A company updates its "belonging campaign" after employees say that messaging without accountability feels superficial. Leadership redirects resources toward structural equity reforms.

Belief Perseverance

Definition: Belief perseverance is the tendency to hold onto an initial belief even after new evidence proves it wrong. Business Application This bias can hinder change management, innovation, and diversity efforts when leaders or teams refuse to update outdated assumptions.

Leadership Insight: Leaders should demonstrate intellectual humility—admitting when evidence calls for a change in direction. This helps build credibility and trust.

Cultural Caution: In cultures that value decisiveness or "saving face," changing a stance might be seen as weakness unless it's framed as adaptive leadership.

Mosaic Question: What belief are you clinging to that no longer benefits your team or mission?

Mosaic in Action: A senior manager resists implementing remote work policies despite clear productivity improvements, insisting "collaboration only happens in the office." Over time, staff turnover rises due to inflexibility.

Belonging Cues

Definition: Belonging cues are verbal and nonverbal signals that convey acceptance, inclusion, and value within a group or relationship.

Business Application: These cues can be as simple as maintaining consistent eye contact, facilitating inclusive meetings, or explicitly inviting diverse perspectives. They foster psychological safety and trust.

Leadership Insight: Belonging is reinforced through small, everyday interactions. Leaders who intentionally use belonging cues shape cultures where people feel empowered to contribute fully and authentically.

Cultural Caution: A gesture indicating belonging in one culture (e.g., physical touch, humor) may be uncomfortable or exclusionary in another; leaders should adapt cues to align with cultural norms.

Mosaic Question: What small signals are you sending that either invite people in—or leave them out?

Mosaic in Action: A project leader rotates meeting facilitation among team members, signaling that every voice matters and encouraging stronger engagement across departments.

Belonging Gap

Definition: The belonging gap is the measurable or perceived difference between groups who feel fully included in a community or organization and those who do not.

Business Application: This gap can appear in career advancement, participation rates, retention, and psychological safety scores, often revealing inequities that diversity statistics alone cannot show.

Leadership Insight: Closing the belonging gap requires more than demographic diversity — it demands intentional practices, resource allocation, and leadership accountability to ensure fair inclusion.

Cultural Caution: In some cultures, belonging is more closely tied to shared history or kinship than to organizational policies, making relationship-building essential to narrowing the gap.

Mosaic Question: Who feels at home here — and who is still on the threshold?

Mosaic in Action: After implementing employee-led resource groups, a tech firm notices an increase in engagement scores for underrepresented employees, reducing a multi-year belonging gap.

Belonging Uncertainty

Definition: The ongoing doubt about whether someone truly belongs in a space, often caused by exclusion, stereotype threat, or underrepresentation.

Business Application: Belonging uncertainty hinders performance and retention, especially for first-generation, marginalized, or new employees.

Leadership Insight: Leaders must lower ambiguity by sending firm, consistent belonging signals. One-time gestures are insufficient.

Cultural Caution: In some contexts, signals of belonging can be subtle (like shared meals or rituals). Leaders need to understand the different ways belonging manifests across cultures.

Mosaic Question: Do your teams question if they belong — and what signals do you send daily?

Mosaic in Action: A STEM company implemented structured mentorship for women engineers, lowering uncertainty and boosting retention rates.

Belonging vs. Fitting In

Definition: Belonging means being valued for who you truly are, while fitting in involves adjusting yourself to meet a group's expectations—often at the cost of authenticity.

Business Application: Cultures that prioritize fitting in over belonging can hinder innovation, authenticity, and retention, especially among marginalized groups.

Leadership Insight: Leaders need to demonstrate that authenticity is an advantage, not a weakness. Promoting belonging instead of fitting in unlocks the creative and relational potential of diverse teams.

Cultural Caution: In collectivist cultures, "fitting in" may be seen as harmony; in individualist settings, belonging without conformity might be valued—leaders must find a balance.

Mosaic Question: Are you creating a space where people are appreciated for who they are—or for how well they conform to the majority?

Mosaic in Action: A new manager modifies team rituals to incorporate various cultural traditions instead of expecting everyone to adhere to a single dominant norm.

Belongingness Theory

Definition: Belongingness theory, rooted in social psychology, states that humans have a core need to form and sustain meaningful, lasting relationships.

Business Application: Applying this theory at work involves designing systems that focus on relationships, trust, and inclusion as key to performance.

Leadership Insight: Productivity without belonging doesn't last; leaders who understand belongingness theory can foresee and address turnover risks early.

Cultural Caution: People's ways of seeking and expressing belonging differ—some cultures prefer group activities, while others value one-on-one connections; leaders should adjust accordingly.

Mosaic Question: How is your leadership helping people feel they truly matter here?

Mosaic in Action: A healthcare team redesigns shift schedules to ensure peer overlap, boosting both camaraderie and patient care coordination.

Benevolent Sexism

Definition: A paternalistic belief system that frames women as needing protection or special treatment, while reinforcing gender inequality.

Business Application: Benevolent sexism often limits women's advancement under the guise of "care" — e.g., excluding them from demanding assignments "for their own good."

Leadership Insight: Good intentions don't erase harm. Leaders must see how "protective" practices disempower.

Cultural Caution: In some cultural settings, chivalry is normalized. Leaders must carefully distinguish cultural courtesy from systemic exclusion.

Mosaic Question: Are your "protections" of others truly empowering — or limiting?

Mosaic in Action: A supervisor who routinely excluded women from late travel "to protect them" shifted to providing safety resources, not restrictions.

Bias Amplification

Definition: The process where small biases are amplified by group dynamics, algorithms, or institutional systems, causing disproportionate harm.

Business Application: In technology, bias amplification happens when algorithms mirror and magnify inequalities present in their training data. In organizations, it occurs when subtle biases build up into exclusionary norms.

Leadership Insight: Bias amplification demonstrates that small unchecked biases can develop into systemic harm. Leaders must step in early to stop escalation.

Cultural Caution: Bias amplification varies across situations — sometimes it's driven by technology; other times, it appears in social hierarchies. Leaders need to pinpoint where amplification causes the most harm.

Mosaic Question: Where are small biases in your system quietly getting worse?

Mosaic in Action: A tech company updates its recruitment algorithm after discovering it favors historically male-dominated résumés, increasing gender bias.

Bias Awareness

Definition: Bias awareness is the conscious recognition of personal and systemic biases that shape perceptions, decisions, and interactions.

Business Application: Without bias awareness, even well-intentioned leaders can perpetuate inequities in hiring, promotions, and performance evaluations.

Leadership Insight: Bias awareness is the first step toward equitable action—but awareness without commitment can become performative. Leaders must pair insight with systemic change.

Cultural Caution: What is seen as bias in one context may be seen as fairness in another; cross-cultural bias training must include cultural nuance.

Mosaic Question: Which of your "neutral" judgments might actually be shaped by unseen bias?

Mosaic in Action: A school district uses anonymous resume reviews in its hiring process after discovering that names perceived as ethnic were linked to lower interview callback rates.

Bias Blind Spot

Definition: The bias blind spot is the tendency to recognize biases in others while failing to see them in oneself.

Business Application: This blind spot can weaken diversity and inclusion efforts when leaders assume bias awareness applies to others but not to themselves.

Leadership Insight: Admitting personal vulnerability to bias is not a weakness—it's a sign of emotional maturity and leadership credibility.

Cultural Caution: In cultures with strong hierarchy, leaders may be less willing to acknowledge personal bias, which calls for subtle, trust-based interventions.

Mosaic Question: When was the last time you questioned your own "objective" decision?

Mosaic in Action: A hiring panel reviews past decisions and realizes they consistently rated candidates from certain universities higher—despite having equal qualifications to others.

Bias for Similarity

Definition: Bias for similarity, also called similarity-attraction bias, is the tendency to favor people who share your own traits, background, or worldview.

Business Application: This bias can result in homogenous teams, which can hinder innovation, limit market reach, and reduce the ability to serve diverse stakeholders.

Leadership Insight: Recognizing and addressing this bias can help expand talent pools and broaden decision-making perspectives.

Cultural Caution: What is considered "similar" varies across cultures—leaders need to stay aware of subtle signs of in-group membership in different settings.

Mosaic Question: Who might you be overlooking simply because they aren't "like you"?

Mosaic in Action: A nonprofit leader rotates mentoring assignments so that staff work with leaders outside their usual affinity groups, which expands networks and insights.

Bias Fatigue

Definition: The fatigue that builds up when employees repeatedly participate in anti-bias initiatives, trainings, or discussions without witnessing real systemic change.

Business Application: Bias fatigue causes disengagement and cynicism. Organizations should combine training with policy updates, clear accountability, and leadership example to prevent fatigue.

Leadership Insight: Bias fatigue indicates that education alone is insufficient. Leaders need to link awareness to tangible results.

Cultural Caution: In situations where discussions about bias are starting, fatigue might be seen as resistance. Leaders need to distinguish between resistance and genuine exhaustion.

Mosaic Question: Does your workplace stop at awareness — or turn it into systemic change?

Mosaic in Action: After years of bias training, employees call for policy reform. The leadership team reacts by linking promotions to fair hiring and evaluation methods.

Bias Interruption

Definition: Bias interruption involves identifying and actively preventing bias in real time before it influences outcomes or decisions.

Business Application: Incorporating bias interruption protocols into meetings, hiring, and promotions promotes fairness and can enhance representation.

Leadership Insight: Successful bias interruption requires preparation—leaders must have both the authority and the language to intervene without provoking defensiveness.

Cultural Caution: In some cultures, public correction may cause loss of face; bias interruption might be more effective when done privately or with neutral language.

Mosaic Question: Do you have a plan for how you will intervene when bias occurs?

Mosaic in Action: In a board meeting, a member repeatedly interrupts a colleague; the chair redirects the conversation to ensure the original point is fully heard.

Bias Literacy

Definition: Bias literacy is the ability to recognize, name, and explain different forms of bias in oneself, others, and systems.

Business Application: Teams with high bias literacy are better equipped to challenge inequities and redesign processes that sustain them.

Leadership Insight: Bias literacy is not just about knowing definitions—it's about applying them in decision-making, policy reviews, and daily interactions.

Cultural Caution: Bias language must be tailored to local contexts; words used to describe bias in one region may not resonate—or could even offend—in another.

Mosaic Question: How skilled are you at identifying the biases that influence your workplace?

Mosaic in Action: A marketing team with strong bias literacy identifies gender stereotypes in a campaign and revises it before launch, preventing reputational damage.

Bias of Crowds

Definition: The bias of crowds happens when individual biases are magnified through group interactions, leading to collective decisions that reflect and reinforce prejudice or flawed assumptions.

Business Application: In hiring committees, jury panels, or leadership teams, crowd bias can solidify discriminatory patterns under the illusion of consensus.

Leadership Insight: Recognizing this effect helps leaders implement safeguards—such as anonymous feedback, structured decision-making criteria, and diverse representation—that reduce groupthink and bias reinforcement.

Cultural Caution: Cultural norms that prioritize harmony over dissent can make it harder for individuals to speak up against a crowd's biased direction.

Mosaic Question: How do you ensure group consensus is based on fairness rather than shared bias?

Mosaic in Action: A project selection board votes unanimously for a proposal; a post-review reveals their decision was influenced by assumptions about "cultural fit" that excluded innovative but unfamiliar approaches.

Bias of Urgency

Definition: The bias of urgency is the tendency to prioritize speed over accuracy or fairness, which often leads to snap decisions that overlook equity and long-term effects.

Business Application: During crisis timelines, leaders tend to fall back on familiar patterns, hiring or promoting those already in their networks rather than seeking diverse candidates.

Leadership Insight: Urgency should be managed, not used as an excuse to bypass due diligence; slowing down during critical decision moments can prevent costly or unjust outcomes.

Cultural Caution: In fast-paced business cultures, questioning urgency may be seen as resistance; framing it as "ensuring quality" can create space for better decisions.

Mosaic Question: How often do you trade inclusion for speed?

Mosaic in Action: During a product launch crunch, a marketing team rushes approval of copy; later, customer feedback reveals cultural missteps that could have been avoided with a brief review pause.

Bias Saturation

Definition: Bias saturation happens when individuals or teams see so many examples or discussions of bias that they start to disengage or feel numb to its importance.

Business Application: Overloading employees with bias training without connecting it to real-world change can cause fatigue and cynicism.

Leadership Insight: Effective leaders introduce bias concepts gradually and focus on turning them into real actions instead of overwhelming people with abstract lists.

Cultural Caution: In environments with frequent conversations about identity and equity, it's important to frame bias education with hope and a sense of agency, not just problems.

Mosaic Question: Are your equity conversations building capacity— or draining it?

Mosaic in Action: A university department reduces mandatory bias seminars and instead includes bias reflection in everyday faculty meetings, boosting engagement and practical application.

Bias Tax

Definition: Bias tax refers to the additional mental, emotional, or procedural burden placed on marginalized individuals due to bias within systems or interactions.

Business Application: This can manifest as employees of color being asked to educate colleagues about diversity issues—on top of their existing workload—without extra pay or recognition.

Leadership Insight: Reducing bias tax requires shifting responsibility for equity work to the entire organization, not just those most affected by inequities.

Cultural Caution: In some cultures, refusing to take on these extra burdens may be misunderstood as lacking team spirit; leaders must actively promote shared responsibility.

Mosaic Question: Who bears the cost of bias in your workplace?

Mosaic in Action: A company reorganizes its diversity committee so participation rotates among staff of all backgrounds, ensuring equity work is valued and shared.

Bias Toward Action

Definition: Bias toward action is the tendency to favor immediate movement or decision-making over reflection, often at the expense of long-term strategy or inclusive outcomes.

Business Application: In fast-moving industries, leaders may encourage teams to "just do something" rather than pause to assess the impact on stakeholders, especially those not present.

Leadership Insight: While decisiveness can be a strength, bias toward action must be balanced with intentional listening and scenario planning to avoid costly mistakes.

Cultural Caution: In cultures that value speed and visible productivity, slowing down can be misunderstood as hesitancy; leaders must reframe reflection as a form of strategic readiness.

Mosaic Question: What could happen if you gave your decision the time it truly needs?

Mosaic in Action: A non-profit director delays launching a campaign by two weeks to gather community feedback, resulting in a more relevant and well-received initiative.

Bias Training

Definition: Bias training consists of structured programs designed to help individuals recognize, understand, and reduce their unconscious and conscious biases.

Business Application: Common in corporate Diversity, Equity, and Inclusion (DEI) efforts, bias training can shape hiring practices, promotions, and daily interactions—especially when paired with systemic change initiatives.

Leadership Insight: Training alone rarely changes behavior unless supported by accountability measures, ongoing practice, and leadership modeling.

Cultural Caution: Poorly designed bias training can cause defensiveness or fatigue; culturally relevant content and skilled facilitation are essential.

Mosaic Question: How is your organization making sure bias training leads to real action?

Mosaic in Action: After implementing bias training, a tech company monitors hiring patterns quarterly and observes measurable increases in candidate diversity over a year.

Bias-Proof Processes

Definition: Bias-proof processes are systems and workflows intentionally designed to reduce the impact of bias in decision-making.

Business Application: Examples include blind résumé reviews, structured interview questions, and equity checks in performance evaluations.

Leadership Insight: Leaders who develop bias-proof processes eliminate the need for constant oversight by embedding fairness into the system itself.

Cultural Caution: Over-standardization can unintentionally eliminate cultural nuance; processes must be both fair and flexible.

Mosaic Question: Where in your workflow can you incorporate fairness by design?

Mosaic in Action: A publishing house removes author names from manuscript submissions during the initial review stage, increasing opportunities for underrepresented voices.

Bias-Resilient Leadership

Definition: Bias-resilient leadership is the practice of leading in ways that recognize, resist, and actively oppose personal and systemic biases.

Business Application: Leaders who are bias-resilient anticipate where bias might influence decisions, seek diverse input, and are ready to course-correct when inequities appear.

Leadership Insight: This type of leadership is not about being bias-free—it's about being bias-aware and bias-accountable.

Cultural Caution: In hierarchical cultures, challenging bias at the leadership level can be risky; creating safe feedback channels helps bring issues to light without retaliation.

Mosaic Question: How do you make your leadership safe for truth-telling?

Mosaic in Action: A senior manager invites an external equity advisor to review promotion decisions annually, ensuring transparency and trust within the organization.

Bias Stacking

Definition: Bias stacking happens when multiple biases build up in a decision, policy, or interaction—making inequality worse and harder to identify.

Business Application: A hiring process might unintentionally combine gender bias, educational elitism, and accent prejudice, leading to the systematic exclusion of certain candidates.

Leadership Insight: Bias stacking is rarely done on purpose; leaders need to examine each stage of decision-making to find where these combined biases gather.

Cultural Caution: In cross-cultural settings, bias stacking can go unnoticed because each bias might seem culturally "normal" on its own.

Mosaic Question: What layered biases could be influencing this decision without you realizing?

Mosaic in Action: An NGO adjusts its funding criteria after discovering rural applicants face three main disadvantages—limited internet, language barriers, and fewer personal connections to decision-makers.

Biased Innovation

Definition: Biased innovation refers to the creation of products, services, or systems that unintentionally perpetuate inequality due to unexamined assumptions in the design process.

Business Application: From AI algorithms that misidentify darker skin tones to medical devices calibrated only for male physiology, biased innovation can cause real-world harm.

Leadership Insight: True innovation requires as much attention to equity as to creativity; diversity in design teams helps prevent blind spots.

Cultural Caution: Market-tested solutions in one region may reinforce bias in another if cultural contexts differ.

Mosaic Question: Whose needs were invisible when this solution was designed?

Mosaic in Action: A tech startup consults Indigenous community leaders before finalizing a water purification device, ensuring it meets cultural and environmental priorities.

Bigotry Fatigue

Definition: Bigotry fatigue is the exhaustion felt by individuals and communities who must continually face, explain, or defend against prejudice and discrimination.

Business Application: Employees experiencing bigotry fatigue may withdraw from meetings, limit contributions, or avoid roles with public visibility.

Leadership Insight: Leaders must recognize that fatigue is not disengagement—it's a sign that systemic inequalities remain unaddressed.

Cultural Caution: Well-meaning "allyship" efforts can increase fatigue if they require marginalized people to repeatedly educate others without systemic follow-through.

Mosaic Question: How are you reducing—not adding to—the emotional labor of those most affected?

Mosaic in Action: A school district implements peer-led learning circles on bias, relieving teachers of color from having to serve as the default educators on racism.

Bilingual Advantage

Definition: The bilingual advantage refers to the cognitive, cultural, and professional benefits gained from fluency in two or more languages.

Business Application: Bilingual employees often bridge cultural gaps, expand market reach, and improve negotiation skills in global operations.

Leadership Insight: Encouraging multilingualism can boost team creativity and problem-solving, while showing the value of cultural diversity.

Cultural Caution: Avoid tokenizing bilingual staff or assuming their role is only to translate without proper recognition or compensation.

Mosaic Question: How is your organization using multilingual skills to build trust and access new opportunities?

Mosaic in Action: A healthcare network hires bilingual patient navigators, reducing miscommunication and improving care outcomes for immigrant communities.

Bilingual Favoritism

Definition: The tendency of leaders or team members to favor those who speak their language, whether consciously or unconsciously, leading to unequal access to trust, opportunities, and influence.

Business Application: Bilingual favoritism often appears in promotions, project assignments, and informal trust networks. Addressing it promotes fairer collaboration and helps leaders prevent unintentionally reinforcing inequalities within multicultural teams.

Leadership Insight: Inclusive leadership involves leveraging bilingual skills to expand engagement, not limit it. Recognizing and addressing favoritism enhances credibility and promotes equity within teams.

Cultural Caution: Language-based favoritism can be subtle but harmful. Colleagues left out of conversations or decision-making because of language preference might feel overlooked or undervalued, even if unintentional.

Mosaic Question: How can speaking multiple languages promote inclusion instead of creating hidden barriers?

Mosaic in Action: A bilingual director at a multinational company intentionally holds informal team talks in both French and English, making sure all employees—regardless of their main language—stay equally involved and informed.

Bilingual Naïveté

Definition: The assumption that a person's intelligence, competence, or worth can be judged by their fluency—or lack of fluency—in a specific language. Bilingual naïveté can show as undervaluing those who are less fluent or overestimating bilinguals without considering the depth of their skills or their broader contributions.

Business Application: In multinational settings, naivety about bilingual abilities can distort hiring, promotions, and credibility. Leaders might overlook highly skilled individuals who are less fluent in the dominant workplace language or assume bilingual speakers are automatically cultural experts. Both misunderstandings decrease organizational effectiveness.

Leadership Insight: True global leadership involves distinguishing linguistic fluency from intellectual capacity or cultural depth. A leader aware of bilingual naïveté avoids the mistake of equating accent or grammar with ability and instead judges colleagues based on substance, skills, and contributions.

Cultural Caution: Bilingual naïveté can easily lead to microaggressions—such as mocking accents, dismissing slower speakers, or over-praising bilingual colleagues in ways that feel tokenizing. Leaders must avoid equating "linguistic ease" with "professional worth."

Mosaic Question: When you hear someone struggling in your dominant language, do you focus on understanding them—or do you unconsciously judge their intelligence?

Mosaic in Action: A project lead recognizes that a team member has limited English fluency but offers valuable engineering expertise. Instead of sidelining them, she arranges translation support and ensures their insights remain central to decision-making, challenging assumptions of incompetence.

Bilingualism in Leadership

Definition: Leaders' ability to fluently operate in two or more languages uses linguistic versatility to build trust, navigate cultural differences, and expand influence. Beyond just translating words, bilingualism allows leaders to embody multiple cultural perspectives and communicate with emotional nuance that strengthens connections.

Business Application: Bilingual leaders can negotiate across markets, lead diverse teams with greater empathy, and tailor messages for cultural resonance. They often boost global business growth by connecting with customer bases, forming regional partnerships, and reducing reliance on intermediaries. In internal settings, bilingual leaders enhance team cohesion by making sure all members feel recognized and understood in their native language.

Leadership Insight: Bilingualism is more than just a communication tool—it's a mindset centered on flexibility, empathy, and perspective-taking. Leaders who switch between languages also learn to navigate different cultural logics, which makes them more adaptable in conflict resolution, decision-making, and identity-sensitive conversations. This flexibility improves relational leadership and boosts credibility across various contexts borders.

Cultural Caution: Avoid presenting bilingualism as just a new skill or token gesture. It should be recognized as a strategic leadership competency, not merely a personal asset. Be mindful of the risk of bilingual favoritism—where leaders unconsciously favor those who speak their language. Genuine linguistic inclusion requires intentional efforts to ensure equal access and prevent exclusion. (See also Bilingual Favoritism.)

Mosaic Question: How does your leadership voice shift when switching languages, and what strengths emerge in each? How can you ensure both voices remain authentic and inclusive?

Mosaic in Action: A CEO holds stakeholder meetings in both English and Spanish, ensuring Latin American partners feel directly involved rather than filtered through translation. Later, she updates internal communications for staff in Mandarin, Spanish, and English, highlighting that linguistic diversity is a strategic driver of belonging and global impact.

Bipartisan Collaboration

Definition: The intentional effort to work across political boundaries to find common solutions, based on mutual respect rather than ideological agreement.

Business Application: Bipartisan approaches can stabilize policy-driven industries, enhance advocacy efforts, and promote inclusive decision-making.

Leadership Insight: Successful bipartisan collaboration requires skill in reframing problems so they transcend party identities and appeal to shared values.

Cultural Caution: Collaboration is not about compromising at all costs—leaders must protect core principles while seeking consensus.

Mosaic Question: How can you frame this issue so it invites—rather than alienates—opposing perspectives?

Mosaic in Action: A nonprofit leader gathers lawmakers from both parties to co-sponsor education reform, focusing on shared goals like literacy and workforce readiness.

BIPOC Solidarity

Definition: The intentional alliance among Black, Indigenous, and People of Color communities to address intersecting oppressions and promote collective liberation.

Business Application: In organizations, BIPOC solidarity can lead to more effective DEI coalitions, cross-community mentorship, and unified advocacy.

Leadership Insight: Solidarity flourishes when leaders respect differences within BIPOC identities rather than reducing them to a single narrative.

Cultural Caution: Be cautious of tokenistic "unity" efforts that overlook internal power dynamics or historical tensions among marginalized groups.

Mosaic Question: How can you show up for another community's fight without making it about yourself?

Mosaic in Action: Asian American, Latinx, and Black employee resource groups work together to advocate for fair parental leave policies that recognize cultural caregiving norms.

Black Excellence

Definition: A celebration of the achievements, creativity, and resilience of Black individuals and communities in the face of systemic inequities.

Business Application: Showcasing Black excellence in leadership pipelines, marketing, and thought leadership counters deficit-based narratives and inspires broader innovation.

Leadership Insight: Supporting Black excellence means creating environments where talent thrives without the burden of overperformance to prove worth.

Cultural Caution: Avoid commodifying Black excellence as a diversity "brand" while ignoring structural inequities that limit opportunity.

Mosaic Question: Are you celebrating individual achievement without addressing the systems that demand resilience in the first place?

Mosaic in Action: A corporation features Black innovators in a global campaign while simultaneously funding scholarships and mentorship programs for Black students in STEM.

Black Joy

Definition: The unapologetic celebration of happiness, creativity, and fulfillment by Black individuals and communities, often as a form of resistance against narratives focused solely on struggle.

Business Application: Emphasizing Black joy in workplace culture, branding, and storytelling humanizes diversity initiatives and challenges negative stereotypes.

Leadership Insight: Leaders who create space for Black joy foster environments that prioritize holistic well-being rather than just survival under systemic pressure.

Cultural Caution: Do not romanticize joy as a replacement for addressing inequalities—celebration must go hand in hand with systemic change.

Mosaic Question: How can your leadership make joy a sustainable, everyday reality for those who have been historically excluded?

Mosaic in Action: A company hosts a storytelling series where Black employees share moments of joy and creativity, amplifying diverse narratives beyond resilience alone.

Black Tax

Definition: The extra financial, emotional, or social burden placed on Black individuals, often due to systemic inequities or expectations to support extended networks disproportionately affected by discrimination.

Business Application: Understanding the Black tax can help develop fair compensation, benefits, and wellness policies.

Leadership Insight: Recognizing invisible burdens enables leaders to create policies that foster equality in both opportunity and pay.

Cultural Caution: Do not frame the Black tax only as a personal responsibility—it highlights systemic failures, not individual faults.

Mosaic Question: Are your policies recognizing and addressing the hidden costs that some employees carry?

Mosaic in Action: An organization offers targeted financial wellness programs and flexible benefits after employee feedback emphasizes the impact of the Black tax on long-term career advancement.

Blame Culture

Definition: A workplace environment where mistakes, failures, or setbacks are met with finger-pointing, punishment, or shame rather than constructive analysis and collective problem-solving. Blame culture thrives on fear, erodes trust, and discourages employees from taking risks or speaking up about challenges.

Business Application: Organizations trapped in blame culture often experience low morale, high turnover, and stagnation in innovation. By contrast, replacing blame with a culture of accountability and learning builds psychological safety, where employees feel free to share mistakes and propose improvements without fear of retaliation. This shift accelerates problem-solving, drives continuous improvement, and positions the organization for sustainable growth.

Leadership Insight: Leaders set the emotional temperature of the workplace. When leaders respond to mistakes with transparency, humility, and a forward-looking mindset, they model resilience and foster collective trust. By focusing on "What can we learn?" instead of "Who's at fault?" leaders create an environment where teams grow stronger from setbacks. Leaders who normalize honest reflection rather than defensiveness transform errors into strategic advantages.

Cultural Caution: Blame culture is not equally distributed. Marginalized employees—whether due to race, gender, language, disability, or cultural background—are often scrutinized more harshly and may bear disproportionate consequences for organizational failures. Without intentional safeguards, blame culture reinforces systemic inequities, undermining inclusion efforts and driving away valuable talent.

Mosaic Question: When things go wrong, do your responses promote learning, or do they prevent it?

Mosaic in Action: After a failed project launch, a leader gathers the team for a no-blame debrief. Instead of asking "Who dropped the ball?" the leader facilitates a structured reflection What went well? What broke down? What safeguards will prevent this in the future? The result is a team that feels trusted, learns quickly, and is more willing to innovate the next time around.

Blind Recruitment

Definition: Hiring practices that remove identifying information, such as names, schools, or addresses, from applications to reduce bias.

Business Application: Blind recruitment can boost diversity by focusing on skills and experience rather than demographic details.

Leadership Insight: This is an effective but partial solution—bias can still occur in later stages if not actively monitored.

Cultural Caution: Blind recruitment should not be a one-time tactic; ongoing systemic bias requires continuous equity efforts.

Mosaic Question: Once candidates reach the interview stage, how will you continue to reduce bias?

Mosaic in Action: A company uses blind screening for all initial applications and trains hiring managers to recognize and interrupt bias during interviews.

Blind Spot Bias

Definition: The tendency to see bias in others more easily than in oneself, often leading to overconfidence in one's own objectivity.

Business Application: This bias can weaken DEI efforts when leaders assume they are immune to the same prejudices they criticize.

Leadership Insight: Effective leaders deliberately seek feedback and establish systems that uncover blind spots, understanding that no one is completely free of bias.

Cultural Caution: Ignoring your own blind spots risks reinforcing the very inequities you want to eliminate.

Mosaic Question: Who in your circle has the power to tell you when you've overlooked something important?

Mosaic in Action: A senior executive believes their promotion process is fair until an internal audit—driven by employee feedback—exposes patterns of gender bias in advancement.

Bloom's Taxonomy for Equity

Definition: An adaptation of Bloom's educational framework that applies its hierarchy of cognitive skills to equity-centered learning, emphasizing critical consciousness alongside knowledge and application.

Business Application: Using this model in training encourages organizations to move beyond awareness into systemic action on equity issues.

Leadership Insight: Leaders can use equity-centered Bloom's Taxonomy to design learning experiences that deepen analysis, synthesis, and transformation of inequitable structures.

Cultural Caution: Avoid treating equity learning as a linear checklist—cultural and systemic contexts may require cyclical or iterative learning.

Mosaic Question: How are you ensuring that your team's equity learning evolves from knowing to doing?

Mosaic in Action: A university's faculty development program uses Bloom's Taxonomy for Equity to design progressive workshops—from identifying bias to redesigning curriculum for cultural relevance.

Board Diversity

Definition: The deliberate inclusion of individuals from diverse backgrounds—such as race, gender, culture, expertise, and lived experience—on an organization's governing board.

Business Application: Diverse boards provide broader perspectives, which can enhance governance, foster innovation, and earn public trust.

Leadership Insight: Board diversity is most effective when paired with equitable participation, not just representation.

Cultural Caution: Token appointments without real influence can backfire, damaging trust and credibility.

Mosaic Question: Does your board reflect the people your organization serves—and do those members have genuine decision-making power?

Mosaic in Action: A nonprofit expands its board recruitment beyond personal networks, bringing in younger leaders and those with community organizing experience to help shape strategic priorities.

Boardroom Allyship

Definition: The active support of marginalized groups by board members, using their influence to challenge inequality and advocate for systemic change.

Business Application: Boardroom allyship transforms equity from a mere statement to a governance priority, affecting budgets, hiring practices, and policies.

Leadership Insight: Genuine allyship in the boardroom involves risk—speaking out when it's unpopular and using positional power to create systemic impact.

Cultural Caution: Don't reduce allyship to silent agreement; it requires consistent, visible, and strategic actions.

Mosaic Question: When equity issues arise, do you lend your voice—or just your vote?

Mosaic in Action: During a budget review, a board member challenges a proposal that would cut funding to a program serving immigrant communities, advocating for alternative cost-saving measures.

Boardroom Cultural Competence

Definition: The ability of board members to understand, respect, and effectively engage with cultural differences when making governance decisions.

Business Application: Culturally competent boards are better equipped to oversee global operations, serve diverse communities, and minimize cultural risks.

Leadership Insight: Genuine cultural competence at the board level requires ongoing learning, not just occasional diversity briefings.

Cultural Caution: A lack of cultural awareness in the boardroom can lead to tone-deaf decisions that harm reputation and stakeholder trust.

Mosaic Question: How does your board ensure cultural competence is reflected in every decision?

Mosaic in Action: A global nonprofit board incorporates cultural briefings into each quarterly meeting to ensure decisions reflect local contexts in their operating regions.

Boardroom Power Dynamics

Definition: The formal and informal distribution of influence among board members, shaped by authority, tenure, relationships, and resource control.

Business Application: Understanding power dynamics helps leaders ensure fair participation and prevents decision-making from being dominated by a small group of members.

Leadership Insight: Skilled chairs and governance leaders use their roles to balance voices, stopping positional power from blocking new perspectives.

Cultural Caution: Overlooking hidden power structures can let systemic biases continue, even with diverse representation.

Mosaic Question: Whose voices carry the most weight in your boardroom—and whose are overlooked or silenced?

Mosaic in Action: A board chair purposely rotates agenda-setting duties among members to share influence and broaden discussion priorities.

Body Neutrality

Definition: A perspective that emphasizes valuing bodies for their functionality instead of their appearance, shifting away from appearance-based judgments.

Business Application: Including body neutrality in workplace wellness programs can promote inclusivity for people of all sizes, abilities, and physical conditions.

Leadership Insight: Leaders can demonstrate body neutrality by focusing conversations on health, capability, and access rather than physical looks.

Cultural Caution: Do not confuse body neutrality with indifference; it's an active decision to move focus away from appearance-based bias.

Mosaic Question: How might your organization's policies change if body functionality was prioritized over aesthetics?

Mosaic in Action: A marketing firm updates its wellness campaign to showcase diverse body types engaging in everyday activities, emphasizing capability rather than appearance.

Body Positivity

Definition: A movement and mindset that promotes acceptance and appreciation of all body types, challenging societal beauty standards and appearance-based discrimination.

Business Application: Body-positive messaging in branding and HR practices can expand market reach, boost employee morale, and reduce appearance bias.

Leadership Insight: Body positivity becomes transformative when it influences hiring, performance evaluation, and workplace culture—not just public campaigns.

Cultural Caution: Avoid using body positivity as a marketing tool without genuine organizational commitment, as tokenism can damage credibility.

Mosaic Question: Does your organizational culture promote body positivity beyond surface-level messaging?

Mosaic in Action: A retail company updates its uniform policy to be size-inclusive, comfortable, and reflective of diverse body shapes and needs.

Bold Leadership

Definition: A leadership style that involves taking calculated risks, making decisive moves, and having the courage to challenge deep-rooted norms in pursuit of meaningful change.

Business Application: Bold leadership fosters innovation and transformation, especially when organizations face disruption or uncertainty.

Leadership Insight: True boldness is not reckless; it's grounded in preparation, ethical clarity, and the ability to handle opposition with composure.

Cultural Caution: Without cultural awareness, bold actions can alienate stakeholders or reinforce harmful power dynamics.

Mosaic Question: What would you dare to try if you weren't afraid of professional risk?

Mosaic in Action: A CEO commits to transparent pay equity reporting despite pushback, setting a new industry standard and earning long-term trust.

Bonding Capital

Definition: The trust, loyalty, and shared identity developed within a closely connected group, often based on common backgrounds or experiences.

Business Application: Strong bonding capital can encourage deep collaboration, team resilience, and high morale—especially during crises.

Leadership Insight: While bonding capital boosts internal cohesion, leaders must ensure it doesn't create exclusionary groups that resist new ideas.

Cultural Caution: Relying too much on bonding capital can hinder innovation by discouraging dissent or shunning outsiders.

Mosaic Question: How can you utilize deep trust within teams without shutting out new voices?

Mosaic in Action: A nonprofit team with solid internal bonds brings in an external facilitator to challenge assumptions and inspire new strategies.

Border Identity

Definition: A complex sense of self shaped by living between or navigating across geographic, cultural, or social boundaries.

Business Application: Leaders with border identities often offer unique insights into cross-cultural negotiations, policy-making, and community engagement.

Leadership Insight: Managing multiple worlds can enhance empathy and adaptive thinking—traits vital for global leadership.

Cultural Caution: Border identities can be romanticized or tokenized, obscuring the complexity and emotional labor of living between worlds.

Mosaic Question: How has moving between different worlds influenced the way you lead?

Mosaic in Action: A cross-border project manager bridges regulatory differences and cultural expectations to launch a bi-national education initiative.

Boundary Leadership

Definition: A leadership style centered on bridging divides across silos, disciplines, and cultural boundaries. Boundary leadership excels in complexity by linking groups that might otherwise stay separate.

Business Application: Boundary leaders are essential in cross-sector collaborations, mergers, and international partnerships. They help organizations to innovate by connecting diverse perspectives.

Leadership Insight: Boundary leadership is not about eliminating differences but about integrating them. Leaders who embrace this approach broaden opportunities by fostering trust at the crossroads.

Cultural Caution: Boundary leadership is often misunderstood as disloyalty to one's "home group." Leaders need to clarify their role as connectors, not defectors.

Mosaic Question: Are you protecting boundaries — or guiding beyond them?

Mosaic in Action: A healthcare leader facilitates collaboration among hospital staff, government agencies, and community organizations to ensure fair vaccine distribution.

Boundary Management

Definition: The deliberate establishment, communication, and maintenance of boundaries to protect personal well-being, productivity, and role clarity.

Business Application: Effective boundary management helps prevent burnout, reduces role conflicts, and promotes healthier workplace cultures.

Leadership Insight: Leaders who demonstrate healthy boundaries set an example for sustainable performance and mutual respect.

Cultural Caution: Boundary expectations differ across cultures—what is considered healthy in one context might be viewed as distant or disengaged elsewhere.

Mosaic Question: Where do you need to establish stronger boundaries to maintain your ability to lead effectively?

Mosaic in Action: A department head refuses non-essential evening meetings, encouraging their team to set similar boundaries for work-life balance.

Boundary Spanning Leadership

Definition: A leadership practice that focuses on bridging divides—across teams, sectors, cultures, or industries—to promote collaboration and shared outcomes.

Business Application: Boundary-spanning leaders break down silos, incorporate diverse perspectives, and align resources toward common goals in complex, multi-stakeholder settings.

Leadership Insight: The ability to move smoothly between groups builds trust, fosters innovation, and speeds up problem-solving.

Cultural Caution: Crossing boundaries without cultural sensitivity can cause misunderstandings, territorial conflicts, or perceived overreach.

Mosaic Question: Which boundaries in your organization should you bridge to achieve the next level of impact?

Mosaic in Action: A university dean forms partnerships between engineering, public health, and local government to tackle a community water crisis.

Brave Space

Definition: A collaborative environment where participants are encouraged to engage in honest, challenging dialogue while respecting one another's dignity.

Business Application: Brave spaces foster innovation, inclusion, and growth by enabling difficult truths to be voiced and heard.

Leadership Insight: Unlike "safe spaces," which focus on comfort, brave spaces emphasize learning and transformation—often requiring leaders to handle discomfort effectively.

Cultural Caution: Without facilitation and clear agreements, a brave space can devolve into defensiveness or harm.

Mosaic Question: How do you cultivate an environment where truth-telling and respect coexist?

Mosaic in Action: A nonprofit board begins meetings with a "bravery round," inviting members to name hard issues that need addressing before decisions are made.

Bridge-Building Leadership

Definition: A leadership style focused on connecting people, groups, or ideas that might otherwise stay separate or conflict.

Business Application: Bridge-building leaders are vital in mergers, cross-cultural partnerships, and coalition-based advocacy efforts.

Leadership Insight: Effective bridge building requires patience, empathy, and the ability to find shared values beneath different perspectives.

Cultural Caution: Superficial bridge-building—without addressing underlying inequities—can reinforce power imbalances instead of dismantling them.

Mosaic Question: Who in your network could benefit from being connected—and what's stopping you from making the introduction?

Mosaic in Action: A city council leader hosts joint town halls for historically divided neighborhoods, sparking new collaborations for local economic development.

Bridging Capital

Definition: The relationships and trust built between different groups or communities, enabling the exchange of resources, ideas, and support across boundaries.

Business Application: Bridging capital promotes innovation and resilience by broadening access to diverse networks and perspectives.

Leadership Insight: Leaders who develop bridging capital improve their organization's flexibility in shifting markets or social environments.

Cultural Caution: Building bridging capital without ongoing relationship upkeep can create an appearance of connection without true depth.

Mosaic Question: How can you strengthen the bonds between groups that rarely collaborate but share a common interest?

Mosaic in Action: An international NGO creates cross-country mentorship programs to connect emerging leaders from different regions facing similar climate issues.

Broken Rung

Definition: The systemic barrier in career advancement where the initial step into management is disproportionately inaccessible to certain groups—often women and marginalized professionals.

Business Application: Addressing the broken rung requires equitable promotion processes, targeted leadership development, and transparent career pathways.

Leadership Insight: If the first rung of the ladder is broken, diversity at senior levels will remain out of reach regardless of later-stage efforts.

Cultural Caution: Focusing only on visible leadership positions without fixing entry-level advancement gaps can reinforce inequities.

Mosaic Question: What's preventing equal access to the first step into leadership in your organization?

Mosaic in Action: A corporation implements mentorship, sponsorship, and bias checks for all first-time manager promotions, resulting in a 40 percent increase in diverse leadership candidates.

Brokering Diversity

Definition: The practice of intentionally bringing together diverse individuals, groups, and perspectives to foster innovation, trust, and cross-cultural understanding.

Business Application: Diversity brokers amplify underrepresented voices, create inclusive collaborations, and bridge decision-making gaps in multicultural environments.

Leadership Insight: Being a diversity broker is not just about representation—it's about strategically linking people to opportunities, resources, and influence.

Cultural Caution: Without structural change, diversity brokering can become tokenistic, placing the labor of inclusion disproportionately on underrepresented leaders.

Mosaic Question: Who in your network is missing from critical conversations—and how can you bring them in?

Mosaic in Action: A team lead pairs product designers from different cultural markets to co-create a global campaign, resulting in a product launch with broader appeal.

Burnout Awareness

Definition: The aware recognition of physical, emotional, and mental exhaustion caused by prolonged stress—often linked to workload, lack of control, or values mismatch.

Business Application: Burnout awareness helps organizations create preventive strategies, from workload adjustment to leader training in emotional resilience.

Leadership Insight: Spotting early burnout signs—both in oneself and in teams—is a sign of emotionally intelligent leadership.

Cultural Caution: Viewing burnout as an individual weakness instead of a systemic problem damages trust and increases staff turnover.

Mosaic Question: What signs of burnout are you overlooking in yourself or your team?

Mosaic in Action: A nonprofit CEO starts quarterly "well-being check-ins" and flexible weeks, resulting in a clear reduction in staff turnover.

Burnout Culture

Definition: A workplace environment where overwork, constant availability, and self-sacrifice are normalized—and often rewarded—at the expense of well-being.

Business Application: Addressing burnout culture requires redefining success metrics, modeling healthy boundaries, and fostering psychological safety around rest.

Leadership Insight: Cultures that elevate exhaustion over effectiveness risk losing their best talent and stifling creativity.

Cultural Caution: Rebranding burnout culture without addressing the underlying incentives for overwork results in performative wellness.

Mosaic Question: How does your organization unintentionally reward burnout behaviors?

Mosaic in Action: A law firm shifts from billable-hour targets to value-based project metrics, reducing after-hours work and boosting client satisfaction.

Burnout Equity Gap

Definition: The uneven impact of burnout on underrepresented or marginalized employees resulting from compounded workplace stressors, exclusion, and cultural taxation.

Business Application: Closing the burnout equity gap requires addressing both workload and the hidden labor involved in navigating bias, representation pressures, and lack of psychological safety.

Leadership Insight: Not all burnout affects groups equally— leaders who ignore disparities in workload and emotional demands risk increasing attrition among diverse talent.

Cultural Caution: Wellness initiatives that overlook systemic inequities may unintentionally benefit the most privileged employees while leaving others behind.

Mosaic Question: Whose burnout is your organization most likely to overlook—and why?

Mosaic in Action: An engineering firm reviews team assignments and meeting loads, discovering that women of color are carrying 40 percent more unpaid committee work. Redistributing responsibilities helps reduce inequitable burnout patterns.

Burnout Prevention

Definition: Proactive strategies, structures, and cultural practices that prevent chronic workplace exhaustion from developing into disengagement or departure.

Business Application: Prevention involves sustainable workloads, flexible work arrangements, manager training in emotional resilience, and regular recovery periods.

Leadership Insight: Preventing burnout is not just about avoiding harm—it's about creating environments where people can work at high energy levels without draining themselves.

Cultural Caution: Viewing burnout prevention as an optional benefit rather than an essential operational practice keeps high performers at risk.

Mosaic Question: How does your team's daily routine actively shield against burnout?

Mosaic in Action: A global NGO adopts "focus weeks" without meetings once each quarter, leading to increased productivity and fewer sick days.

Business Case for Diversity

Definition: The strategic belief that diversity in teams, leadership, and decision-making boosts innovation, performance, and market relevance.

Business Application: A compelling business case for diversity connects inclusion to measurable results—such as profitability, customer reach, and flexibility to adapt.

Leadership Insight: While metrics are important, leaders must ensure that the case for diversity is based on values, fairness, and cultural integrity, not just numbers.

Cultural Caution: Focusing only on financial ROI without addressing systemic inequalities risks turning diversity into a mere numbers game.

Mosaic Question: Is your commitment to diversity motivated by profit margins or a sincere vision for fairness?

Mosaic in Action: A retail chain increases leadership diversity and complements it with local market listening tours, resulting in a 22 percent increase in sales in multicultural regions.

Bystander Apathy

Definition: The passive inaction of individuals who witness harmful, unethical, or unsafe behavior but choose not to respond, often due to fear, uncertainty, or a sense of irrelevance.

Business Application: In workplaces, bystander apathy allows harassment, microaggressions, and safety issues to continue unchecked.

Leadership Insight: Cultures that normalize silence when harm occurs lose moral standing and create environments where misconduct is quietly tolerated.

Cultural Caution: Inaction is often seen as neutrality, but silence during harmful moments signals complicity to those harmed.

Mosaic Question: When was the last time you saw something wrong and stayed silent—what held you back?

Mosaic in Action: During a meeting, a senior leader ignores a sexist joke. A team member later points it out privately, leading the leader to apologize publicly and commit to intervention training.

Bystander Effect

Definition: A psychological phenomenon where the presence of others decreases an individual's likelihood of offering help, as responsibility is spread across the group.

Business Application: In organizational crises, the bystander effect can delay critical responses, especially when multiple departments assume "someone else" will intervene.

Leadership Insight: Overcoming the bystander effect requires clear role assignments and accountability norms that promote immediate action.

Cultural Caution: Diverse and inclusive teams can still experience bystander paralysis if they lack trust or clarity about who has the authority to act.

Mosaic Question: How does your organization make it easier for people to act quickly when something is wrong?

Mosaic in Action: A manufacturing floor implements a "red flag" protocol—any employee can stop production if safety is compromised, bypassing hierarchical delays.

Bystander Fatigue

Definition: The exhaustion faced by individuals who are expected to consistently intervene in bias, harassment, or exclusion, especially without systemic support from leadership.

Business Application: Bystander fatigue undermines safety and fairness at work. When organizations depend only on bystanders to intervene, they risk causing disengagement and retraumatization.

Leadership Insight: Bystander fatigue indicates system failure, not individual failure. Leaders

need to establish structures that share responsibility and support interventions.

Cultural Caution: In certain cultures, stepping in as a bystander can pose significant social or professional risks. Leaders should tailor intervention strategies to fit the cultural context.

Mosaic Question: Do you expect bystanders to shoulder the burden of intervention—or to create systems that share responsibility?

Mosaic in Action: A university establishes formal reporting channels and accountability procedures, lessening the burden on bystanders to handle misconduct on their own.

Bystander Intervention

Definition: The proactive decision to speak up, step in, or take action when witnessing harm, discrimination, or dangerous behavior.

Business Application: Bystander intervention training helps employees recognize harmful situations and respond in a safe, direct, and effective manner.

Leadership Insight: Effective intervention is not just about bravery—it's about skill, timing, and cultural support that make speaking up a normal practice.

Cultural Caution: Intervention methods need to be culturally aware; what seems assertive in one setting may come off as confrontational in another.

Mosaic Question: What tools or language could you use to step in without escalating the conflict?

Mosaic in Action: An employee overhears a client making derogatory comments about a colleague's accent. They steer the conversation in a different direction, support the colleague's expertise, and report the incident privately to HR.

◈ LETTER B CALLOUT

"Belonging is not a feeling you wait for — it is a practice you create."

Reflection Questions

- What signals tell you that you truly belong in a space?
- How does bias, explicit or subtle, erode belonging for others?
- Who might be doubting their belonging in your team, class, or community right now?

Practical Move

In a meeting or classroom discussion, invite a quieter voice to share and affirm their contribution — reinforcing that difference is not just welcomed but valued.

C – Code-Switching, Cognitive Dissonance, Cultural Competence, and the Cost of Navigation

C takes us into the delicate intersection where identity meets adaptation—where every interaction is filtered through both personal truth and cultural expectation. It's an ongoing balancing act of how much of myself is safe to reveal here, and how much I need to change to be accepted.

Consider everyday examples A leader writes a "neutral" hiring email but unknowingly includes bias in the wording. Two colleagues review the same policy—yet only one feels protected by it. A meeting meant to be "inclusive" leaves some participants silent, not because they lack insight, but because speaking up feels too risky in a space not designed for them.

Culture is not just a checkbox, a heritage month on the calendar, or a single training session to complete. It is the atmosphere that shapes who speaks and who stays silent, how risk is perceived, how feedback is given, and how listening is received. It resides in tone, timing, phrasing, and the hidden signals of credibility what is praised, what is ignored, what is punished.

C asks us to notice the realities often hidden beneath the surface

- The daily effort of code-switching—reshaping speech, tone, or expression just to survive.

- The strain of cognitive dissonance when organizational values clash with lived realities.
- The importance of cultural competence, often dismissed until crisis makes its absence undeniable.
- The quiet erosion of trust caused by cross-cultural misunderstandings left unaddressed.

The cost of this constant adaptation is significant. It involves mental and emotional rewiring that depletes focus, creativity, and resilience. It includes the exhaustion from being told to "be yourself" in environments that punish authenticity. It also involves the erosion of belonging when safety depends on silence or conformity.

C reminds us that inclusion is not about perfecting words — it's about broadening perspective. The most urgent question for leaders *is not "Did I say it correctly?" but "Did I create space for meaning beyond my own view?"*

C challenges leaders to become fluent in the invisible to see nuance not as complication but as the essence of ethical leadership. Because when you can navigate the unseen with clarity and courage, you foster cultures where authenticity is not sacrificed for survival but embraced as strength.

C

Calling-In

Definition: A practice of addressing harmful or problematic behavior through private, respectful conversations aimed at fostering understanding and repair rather than public shaming.

Business Application: Calling-in helps leaders address misconduct in ways that preserve dignity, strengthen relationships, and maintain trust while still holding individuals accountable.

Leadership Insight: Effective calling-in requires emotional attunement, good timing, and trust-building so the conversation feels constructive rather than punitive.

Cultural Caution: In some cultures, public accountability is valued more than private correction; adapt the approach to fit community norms and organizational values.

Mosaic Question: How do you decide when to handle an issue privately instead of publicly?

Mosaic in Action: A manager notices an employee repeatedly using outdated terminology for a marginalized group. Instead of calling them out in a meeting, the manager schedules a one-on-one conversation, offers updated language, and shares resources — resulting in immediate change.

Calling-Out

Definition: The act of publicly identifying and confronting harmful, discriminatory, or unethical behavior to emphasize its unacceptability.

Business Application: Calling out can establish firm boundaries, protect vulnerable individuals, and show zero tolerance for certain behaviors when immediate action is needed.

Leadership Insight: While calling out can be necessary, excessive use without offering paths for resolution risks alienating potential allies and provoking defensiveness.

Cultural Caution: Cultural norms around confrontation differ; in some settings, public criticism can irreparably harm relationships or credibility.

Mosaic Question: When has public accountability been the only effective option in your leadership?

Mosaic in Action: During a company town hall, a leader hears a discriminatory comment from another executive. They immediately address it, making it clear that such language is unacceptable and reaffirming the company's equity commitments.

Cancel Culture

Definition: A social phenomenon where individuals, organizations, or brands are collectively shunned or boycotted—often online—due to perceived harmful actions, words, or beliefs.

Business Application: Cancel culture can affect brand reputation, talent attraction, and stakeholder trust, compelling organizations to handle public relations quickly and transparently.

Leadership Insight: Leaders must distinguish between reactive mob justice and genuine accountability, ensuring responses are appropriate and restorative.

Cultural Caution: In global settings, "canceling" can be seen either as necessary social accountability or as culturally inappropriate ostracism, depending on local norms.

Mosaic Question: How can your organization respond to public criticism in a way that preserves

integrity without falling into fear-based decisions?

Mosaic in Action: A nonprofit is accused of discriminatory hiring practices. Instead of ignoring the backlash, leadership conducts an independent audit, shares the results, and commits to a transparent equity plan.

Capitalism and Equity

Definition: The conflict between profit-focused economic systems and efforts to promote fairness, inclusion, and justice within organizations and markets.

Business Application: Leaders within capitalist systems must find ways to pursue growth and profit while addressing inequalities that capitalism may sustain.

Leadership Insight: Long-term sustainability depends on integrating equity into business models instead of viewing it as a cost or charity.

Cultural Caution: In some areas, criticizing capitalism can be politically delicate; discussions should focus on economic resilience, shared prosperity, and human dignity.

Mosaic Question: How does your organization define success beyond just financial gains?

Mosaic in Action: A global apparel company reconfigures its supply chain to ensure fair wages, worker safety, and environmental health—showing that equity and profitability can go hand in hand.

Caste Dynamics

Definition: The social, cultural, and economic power structures formed by hereditary or identity-based hierarchies, often influencing access to resources, opportunities, and status.

Business Application: In global organizations, caste dynamics can impact recruitment, promotion, and workplace relationships—whether officially recognized or operating as unspoken bias.

Leadership Insight: Leaders need to understand how caste-based privilege and exclusion function both openly and subtly, especially within multinational teams, to develop fair pathways for growth.

Cultural Caution: Discussions around caste can be politically sensitive; approach with cultural humility and ensure policies safeguard anonymity for those sharing their experiences.

Mosaic Question: How might inherited social structures quietly shape opportunities within your organization?

Mosaic in Action: A multinational tech company implements an anonymous feedback system that enables employees in caste-sensitive contexts to report discrimination without fear of retaliation, resulting in targeted policy changes.

Care-Centered Leadership

Definition:: A leadership philosophy that focuses on relational well-being, empathy, and human dignity as key to decision-making and organizational success.

Business Application: Care-centered leaders create systems that balance productivity with belonging, making sure policies and practices address the overall needs of employees.

Leadership Insight:: Leading with care is not about sentimentality—it's about understanding that sustainable performance and innovation develop in environments where people feel valued and safe.

Cultural Caution:: In certain situations, centering care might be dismissed as "weak" or "unprofessional." Leaders need to communicate its strategic importance in building resilience and trust.

Mosaic Question:: How can you show care in a way that lifts both individuals and performance?

Mosaic in Action:: A CEO managing layoffs establishes a transparent process with strong support services, hosting open forums where employees can ask difficult questions. By focusing on care, the organization maintains dignity and trust during a challenging transition.

Centering

Definition: The act of prioritizing a person, group, identity, or perspective in attention, decision-making, or storytelling.

Business Application: Focusing on underrepresented voices in strategic planning ensures policies and practices reflect diverse experiences instead of defaulting to dominant norms.

Leadership Insight: Genuine centering is not just symbolic—it's about reallocating time, resources, and influence so that marginalized perspectives influence core decisions.

Cultural Caution: Centering one group without considering intersectional needs can inadvertently marginalize others.

Mosaic Question: Whose voices are always prioritized in your leadership spaces—and whose are often left on the sidelines?

Mosaic in Action: During a product redesign, a health tech company prioritizes feedback from patients with disabilities, changing both usability features and marketing language.

Challenger Safety

Definition: A cultural condition where individuals feel safe to question the status quo, propose new ideas, or challenge authority without fear of negative consequences.

Business Application: Challenger safety drives innovation, enhances problem-solving, and helps address risks early.

Leadership Insight: Leaders should model openness to critique and actively reward constructive dissent to maintain this safety.

Cultural Caution: In hierarchical cultures, challenging authority may be taboo; create structured opportunities where dissent is encouraged and legitimized.

Mosaic Question: How do you signal to your team that respectful disagreement is both welcome and valued?

Mosaic in Action: A project leader asks all team members to submit anonymous "challenge questions" before strategy meetings, leading to sharper decisions and fewer blind spots.

Change Fatigue

Definition: The physical, emotional, and cognitive exhaustion that results from continuous or poorly managed change.

Business Application: Change fatigue can diminish morale, lower productivity, and increase turnover, especially during extended transformation efforts.

Leadership Insight: Successful change management involves pacing, transparency, and consistent communication to avoid burnout and resistance.

Cultural Caution: Some cultures might see resistance to change as disloyalty; leaders need to distinguish between fatigue and unwillingness.

Mosaic Question: How might your pace of change impact the trust and capacity of your team?

Mosaic in Action: After a year of rapid restructuring, a nonprofit pauses new initiatives to allow teams to stabilize, reassess workloads, and rebuild trust before moving forward.

Change Readiness

Definition: The organizational and individual ability to foresee, adapt to, and successfully execute change initiatives without significant drops in performance or morale.

Business Application: Leaders who evaluate and develop change readiness can reduce the time from strategic decisions to successful implementation, lowering resistance and boosting competitive advantage. This often requires reviewing systems, aligning leadership, and fostering employee adaptability before major changes.

Leadership Insight: True change readiness is less about motivational speeches and more about creating psychological safety, transparent communication, and trust in leadership competence.

Cultural Caution: What is considered "readiness" in one cultural or regional context might be seen as premature or disruptive in another. Make sure readiness evaluations include cross-cultural and intersectional viewpoints to prevent excluding marginalized voices.

Mosaic Question: When preparing your team for change, whose readiness are you assuming—and whose are you overlooking?

Mosaic in Action: Before a major platform migration, the CIO conducts a readiness audit (surveys and focus groups), pilots the change with "ambassador" teams in three regions, and then gates the global rollout based on specific adoption and psychological safety metrics.

Change Management

Definition: A structured approach leaders use to guide individuals, teams, and organizations through transitions from their current state to a desired future state. Change management balances strategy, processes, and human factors to reduce resistance and increase adoption.

Business Application: Organizations depend on change management during mergers, restructures, technology rollouts, and cultural transformations. Leaders who implement consistent change frameworks, such as communication strategies, phased deployment, and stakeholder engagement, reduce disruption and boost performance.

Leadership Insight: Effective change management requires both a clear vision and emotional understanding. Leaders who explain the "why," acknowledge fears, and recognize uncertainty build trust — making people more likely to embrace the "what" and "how."

Cultural Caution: Changing strategies that overlook cultural context or dismiss employees' lived experiences often intensifies resistance. A one-size-fits-all approach can alienate diverse groups, causing more dissonance than unity.

Mosaic Question: When implementing change, do you focus more on process efficiency or people's feelings?

Mosaic in Action: A school district superintendent launching a new curriculum spends the first month holding listening sessions with teachers and parents before finalizing timelines — ensuring both buy-in and easier adoption.

Civic Inclusion

Definition: The fair participation of all individuals and communities in the political, social, and economic aspects of society, regardless of identity, status, or background.

Business Application: Organizations operating in diverse markets gain from civic inclusion strategies by building genuine stakeholder relationships, enhancing brand trust, and increasing their license to operate in complex social and political settings.

Leadership Insight: Civic inclusion goes beyond charity—it requires actively breaking down structural barriers and investing in systems that empower marginalized communities to exercise agency.

Cultural Caution: Inclusion efforts can seem superficial if they only appear during public events or crises; consistent, behind-the-scenes structural work is what truly builds trust.

Mosaic Question: If your organization claims to value civic inclusion, how often is that value visible beyond your annual report?

Mosaic in Action: A bank provides paid civic time, partners with community groups to host multilingual voter registration and ID clinics, and collaborates with local leaders to co-design neighborhood lending criteria.

Civic Responsibility

Definition: The duty of individuals and institutions to actively support the health, equity, and sustainability of the communities where they operate.

Business Application: Civic responsibility can be integrated into corporate governance through Environmental, Social, and Governance (ESG) initiatives, social impact programs, and policies that connect profitability with long-term societal well-being.

Leadership Insight: For leaders, civic responsibility serves as a measure of legacy—how your decisions influence communities long after quarterly results are forgotten.

Cultural Caution: Civic responsibility frameworks must adjust to local understandings of "responsibility" and "community," which differ significantly across cultures and governance systems.

Mosaic Question: In what ways does your leadership decision-making extend care to those without direct power or influence within your organization?

Mosaic in Action: A utilities company signs a community-benefits agreement that funds green jobs training and air-quality sensors in frontline neighborhoods, tying executive bonuses to progress.

Clarity

Definition: The state of being emotionally and mentally clear. Clarity helps leaders make well-grounded decisions based on alignment rather than reaction or confusion.

Business Application: In high-pressure environments, clarity helps leaders cut through noise, prioritize effectively, and clearly communicate their vision. Organizations that emphasize clarity promote transparent communication, decrease errors, and ensure alignment across teams.

Leadership Insight: Clarity is not about having all the answers — it's about understanding what matters most and sharing it simply. Leaders who embody clarity ease uncertainty and build confidence even in complex situations.

Cultural Caution: In some cultures, directness is appreciated; in others, clarity needs to be balanced with relational nuance to prevent coming across as blunt or dismissive. Leaders must adapt their communication to the context.

Mosaic Question: When confronted with complexity, do you tend to seek more information or clearer guidance?

Mosaic in Action: A disaster-response leader pauses before giving instructions, filters information into three clear priorities, and communicates them precisely, helping the team stay focused amid chaos.

Class Privilege

Definition: The unearned advantages and opportunities given to individuals based on their socio-economic class, often unnoticed by those who receive them.

Business Application: Class privilege influences recruitment processes, professional networks, and informal decision-making, potentially excluding talented candidates from lower socio-economic backgrounds without intention.

Leadership Insight: Leaders who recognize and actively address class privilege can foster more innovative and resilient teams by valuing lived experience alongside academic achievements or elite connections.

Cultural Caution: Class privilege appears differently in collectivist versus individualist societies, and assumptions about social mobility may not apply across different countries.

Mosaic Question: How do class-based assumptions affect who gets heard, hired, or promoted in your leadership environment?

Mosaic in Action: HR eliminates unpaid internships, removes elite-school filters from ATS settings, adds travel stipends for interviews, and weights lived experience equally with pedigree in hiring rubrics.

Co-Creation

Definition: A collaborative leadership practice where solutions, strategies, and cultures are designed together with stakeholders rather than imposed from the top down.

Business Application: Co-creation enhances innovation by drawing from collective intelligence. Companies use it in product development with customers, NGOs in program design with communities, and leaders in culture-building with employees.

Leadership Insight: Leaders who co-create empower others as partners, not passive recipients. This fosters ownership, long-term sustainability, and resilience because people support what they helped shape.

Cultural Caution: Inviting people to "co-create" without genuinely sharing decision-making power can backfire, creating cynicism and eroding trust. Symbolic inclusion is worse than no invitation at all.

Mosaic Question: When was the last time you let your team shape the solution instead of only the execution?

Mosaic in Action: A nonprofit director redesigns volunteer training by hosting co-creation workshops with both staff and volunteers, leading to more relevant content and stronger commitment.

Co-Regulation

Definition: A relational process where two or more people help each other stabilize their emotional states through presence, tone, and responsiveness. Co-regulation is essential for building trust and resilience within teams.

Business Application: In workplaces, co-regulation appears in how leaders create the emotional environment. A calm, steady leader can de-escalate tense meetings, while teams practicing co-regulation help manage stress during crises. It directly influences morale, collaboration, and productivity.

Leadership Insight: Leaders who model co-regulation demonstrate emotional integrity. By staying attuned to others' cues and managing their own energy, they create an environment where people feel safe to contribute and grow.

Cultural Caution: In some cultural contexts, emotional expression might be subdued or indirect. Assuming co-regulation always appears as visible comfort can overlook subtler practices — like respectful silence, tone shifts, or shared rituals.

Mosaic Question: When stress increases in your team, do you escalate the tension — or help calm the room?

Mosaic in Action: A project manager observes growing frustration within a cross-functional team. By lowering her voice, recognizing the tension, and encouraging one perspective at a time, she helps the group shift from reactiveness to collaboration.

Code-Switching

Definition: The conscious or unconscious practice of changing one's language, behavior, appearance, or communication style to fit different cultural, social, or professional environments.

Business Application: In leadership settings, code-switching helps individuals manage power dynamics, access networks, and build credibility in spaces where their identity markers might otherwise limit their influence.

Leadership Insight: Although it can be a survival tool and enhance influence, frequent code-switching may cause identity strain and emotional exhaustion. Leaders should foster environments where genuine self-expression is appreciated rather than punished.

Cultural Caution: Promoting assimilation under the guise of "professionalism" can pressure underrepresented employees to hide their cultural identities. It's important to distinguish between voluntary adaptation and coercion.

Mosaic Question: Does your workplace value authenticity, or does it favor those who best imitate the norms of the dominant culture?

Mosaic in Action: The Chief Operating Officer (COO) updates performance criteria to separate "professionalism" from accent and style, trains managers on linguistic bias, and encourages clear-language meetings where multiple speech styles are accepted.

Collaborative Leadership

Definition: A leadership style that focuses on shared authority, teamwork in solving problems, and open communication across departments, sectors, or stakeholder groups.

Business Application:
Collaborative leadership is
used in cross-functional teams,
international projects, and inter-
agency partnerships. It breaks
down barriers, sparks innovation,
and helps organizations adjust in
quickly changing environments.

Leadership Insight: Collaboration
requires humility and shifts from
"my team" to "our ecosystem."
Leaders who share credit and
actively seek diverse input unlock
broader solutions than any
individual or department could
achieve.

Cultural Caution: Collaboration
can fail if roles, accountability,
or decision-making rights are
unclear. In cultures that emphasize
hierarchy, collaborative leadership
might be misunderstood as
weakness unless expectations are
clearly established.

Mosaic Question: How do you
manage shared ownership and clear
responsibility when leading across
boundaries?

Mosaic in Action: A hospital
system introduces a new patient-
safety initiative by forming a
collaborative leadership council
that includes nurses, physicians,
administrators, and patients to
co-develop protocols.

Collective Agency

Definition: The shared ability of
a group to influence decisions,
take action, and create change that
reflects its common interests and
values.

Business Application: Collective
agency is essential in stakeholder
coalitions, employee-led initiatives,
and cross-sector partnerships,
facilitating distributed leadership
and coordinated efforts.

Leadership Insight: Effective
leaders understand how to
nurture collective agency without
overshadowing it—ensuring power
is genuinely shared rather than just
symbolically assigned.

Cultural Caution: Collective
agency can manifest differently
in hierarchical versus egalitarian
cultures; strategies must consider
whether authority is centralized or
distributed.

Mosaic Question: When your
team accomplishes something
significant, how much of the credit
is truly shared—and how much is
still attributed to a single leader?

Mosaic in Action: A cross-
functional team agrees on shared
OKRs (Objectives and Key
Results), a goal-setting framework
that translates broad objectives into
measurable outcomes so everyone is
aligned on what success looks like.

Each department contributes part of its budget, and the team uses consent-based decision-making to ensure no single leader can block progress on equity initiatives.

Collective Care

Definition: A cultural and organizational ethic where members actively share responsibility for each other's well-being, safety, and resilience.

Business Application: In leadership practice, collective care can be implemented through policies such as flexible work arrangements, peer support programs, and trauma-informed management.

Leadership Insight: Collective care is not a "soft" skill—it is a structural choice that sustains productivity, prevents burnout, and reinforces trust in leadership.

Cultural Caution: Without intentional design, collective care initiatives risk overburdening already marginalized employees who often serve as informal emotional labor providers.

Mosaic Question: Does your leadership model treat care as an optional perk or as a core operational principle?

Mosaic in Action: A hospital implements peer-support rotations, protected decompression hours following critical incidents, and a relief fund that automatically covers shifts for caregivers without penalties.

Collective Efficacy

Definition: The team-wide belief in its shared ability to organize and carry out actions that reach desired goals, especially during tough times.

Business Application: High collective efficacy links to better teamwork, innovation, and resilience when facing crises. It can be built through small successes, visible skills, and mutual responsibility.

Leadership Insight: Leaders play a key role in shaping collective efficacy by presenting challenges as solvable, reinforcing a shared identity, and demonstrating solution-focused behavior.

Cultural Caution: In cross-cultural settings, the idea of "efficacy" might relate more to community harmony or long-term relationship building rather than immediate, measurable outcomes.

Mosaic Question: How do you evaluate your team's health—by individual talent or by the strength of their collective belief in what they can accomplish together?

Mosaic in Action: During a turnaround, the general manager (GM) breaks goals into 30-day sprints, publicly tracks small wins on a shared board, and narrates how each team's actions influence key indicators.

Collective Healing

Definition: A process where communities or groups actively work to repair harm, rebuild trust, and restore social cohesion after shared trauma, systemic injustice, or organizational crises.

Business Application: Leaders can incorporate collective healing into organizational recovery plans through facilitated dialogues, restorative justice practices, and policies that target both the structural and emotional sources of harm.

Leadership Insight: Healing on a large scale requires more than just empathy—it calls for accountability, systemic repair, and ongoing cultural change.

Cultural Caution: Collective healing may be obstructed if leadership seeks quick fixes without addressing the deeper historical or cultural wounds affecting the group.

Mosaic Question: Are your efforts at "moving forward" based on

genuine repair, or on the hope that people will simply forget?

Mosaic in Action: Following a harm report, leadership facilitates restorative circles, publishes a repair plan with timelines, and funds ongoing counseling alongside policy changes.

Collective Identity

Definition: The shared feeling of belonging and mutual recognition that unites members of a group, organization, or movement, based on common goals, values, or experiences.

Business Application: Developing a strong collective identity enhances organizational culture, boosts engagement, and fosters resilience during times of uncertainty or change.

Leadership Insight: Leaders foster a strong group identity by connecting daily actions to a shared purpose that feels both personal and transcendent, while keeping the "we" open and flexible.

Cultural Caution: Collective identity can become exclusive or rigid when it emphasizes who is excluded rather than what is shared. To avoid falling into tribalism or conformity, leaders should keep identity narratives adaptable, inclusive, and rooted in shared values rather than boundaries.

Mosaic Question: Whose voices contribute to your collective identity—and whose are left out of the story?

Mosaic in Action: Staff collaboratively create a one-page "We Are/We Aren't" charter that highlights shared purpose and clarifies what the group rejects. The charter is reviewed during onboarding, town halls, and recognition rituals to keep the identity inclusive and lively.

Collective Intelligence

Definition: The increased ability of a group to learn, adapt, and solve complex problems together—generating insights and innovations that go beyond what any individual member can accomplish.

Business Application: Organizations harness collective intelligence through cross-functional teams, crowdsourced solutions, and inclusive decision-making platforms that democratize access to ideas and expertise.

Leadership Insight: Collective intelligence flourishes when leaders blend diverse perspectives with psychological safety, ensuring not just that all voices are heard

but that they genuinely shape outcomes.

Cultural Caution: Without fair participation, collective intelligence can become a refined form of groupthink. Instead of encouraging innovation, it may strengthen existing hierarchies and give prominence only to the loudest or most influential voices. Genuine intelligence emerges when dissent, nuance, and minority perspectives are valued equally.

Mosaic Question: Does your team's process genuinely expand the circle of insight, or does it subtly promote conformity and prioritize quantity over quality?

Mosaic in Action: A strategy platform collects anonymous proposals, includes expert commentary, and uses weighted feedback mechanisms. The final decision memo doesn't just summarize inputs but clearly shows how various contributions influenced the final choice, promoting transparency and trust.

Collective Leadership

Definition: A leadership approach where authority, responsibility, and influence are intentionally shared among multiple people, promoting more adaptable, inclusive, and sustainable decision-making.

Business Application:
Collective leadership models are increasingly adopted in complex environments—such as NGOs, social movements, and innovation-driven companies—where flexibility, distributed expertise, and shared accountability are essential for resilience and impact.

Leadership Insight: Collective leadership is not the absence of leadership but a redistribution of it. It thrives when individuals excel at facilitation, clarify roles, and manage conflict—turning shared power from a risk of fragmentation into a force for unity and innovation.

Cultural Caution: In highly hierarchical environments, collective leadership may be perceived as a loss of control, unclear authority, or even organizational weakness. Leaders must communicate the reasons clearly, define authority boundaries, and establish structures that promote credible collaboration instead of chaos.

Mosaic Question: Is leadership in your organization viewed as a collaborative effort that grows stronger when shared, or as a protected role reserved for a few?

Mosaic in Action: A nonprofit adopts a triad governance model—operations, programs, and community—with rotating facilitation. To strengthen accountability, leaders use RACI charts (outlining who is Responsible, Accountable, Consulted, and Informed) for every major decision. Quarterly 360-degree feedback sessions (gathering input from supervisors, peers, and subordinates) then assess how well power is being shared and identify areas for adjustment, ensuring that authority remains transparent and balanced.

Collective Memory

Definition: The collective body of knowledge, stories, and experiences that a group or society keeps over time, shaping identity, guiding decisions, and influencing responses to current challenges.

Business Application:
Organizations rely on collective memory to preserve institutional knowledge, maintain cultural continuity, and avoid repeating past mistakes—especially during leadership changes, periods of innovation, or when recovering from setbacks.

Leadership Insight: Leaders act as stewards of collective memory. Their role is to respect past lessons while preventing nostalgia, trauma, or selective storytelling from distorting the present. Effective stewardship involves creating space for multiple narratives and transforming memory into a source of resilience rather than division.

Cultural Caution: Collective memory can be misused to justify exclusion, reinforce bias, or oversimplify complex histories. When only one version of memory prevails, others are disregarded. Leaders need to create channels where suppressed, overlooked, or uncomfortable truths can coexist with celebrated traditions.

Mosaic Question: Which memories does your organization hold onto—and which ones should be re-examined, reframed, or expanded to tell a more complete story?

Mosaic in Action: An organization gathers oral histories from diverse staff, develops a "lessons learned" wiki that highlights both successes and failures, and adds a quarterly "memory check" to leadership meetings to ensure decisions are informed by history but not constrained by it.

Colonial Legacy

Definition: The lasting political, economic, cultural, and psychological impacts of colonial rule that influence modern institutions, relationships, and power structures.

Business Application: Understanding colonial legacy is crucial in global leadership, especially when engaging in international partnerships, development initiatives, or cross-border markets.

Leadership Insight: Leaders who acknowledge colonial legacies are better equipped to address inequalities embedded in trade, governance, and workplace practices.

Cultural Caution: Attempts to tackle inequality without recognizing colonial legacy risk superficial changes that leave core issues unaddressed.

Mosaic Question: How do historical power dynamics shape your leadership today?

Mosaic in Action: A consumer-goods company reorganizes sourcing through fair-trade agreements, benefit-sharing for traditional knowledge, and local governance councils that can veto extractive practices.

Color Blindness

Definition: The belief that ignoring racial or ethnic differences leads to equity, often erasing lived realities and systemic disparities.

Business Application: While meant to promote fairness, color blindness in hiring, promotions, or team dynamics can sustain inequality by denying how race influences opportunities.

Leadership Insight: Genuine equity work involves seeing, naming, and addressing racial realities—rather than bypassing them in the name of neutrality.

Cultural Caution: Color blindness can dismiss the experiences of marginalized individuals and hinder efforts to challenge structural racism.

Mosaic Question: Are you trying to make race irrelevant, or are you pretending it already is?

Mosaic in Action: Leadership breaks down engagement, pay, and promotion data by race, implements targeted solutions, and trains managers to discuss race explicitly (and skillfully) during reviews.

Colorism

Definition: Prejudice or discrimination based on skin tone, often favoring lighter skin over darker skin within the same racial or ethnic group.

Business Application: Colorism influences hiring, promotion, and public representation, affecting brand perception, employee morale, and market engagement.

Leadership Insight: Confronting colorism requires leaders to critically evaluate internal culture, marketing choices, and representation beyond just racial diversity metrics.

Cultural Caution: The roots of colorism in colonial and class hierarchies mean it is deeply embedded and often harder to recognize—especially in communities that share an ethnic identity.

Mosaic Question: In your organization's visuals, leadership, and language—whose skin tone is considered most acceptable?

Mosaic in Action: Marketing audits on-screen representation, updates casting and lighting guidelines to prevent light-skin favoritism, and adds anti-colorism training and reporting channels.

Comfort with Discomfort

Definition: The ability to stay engaged and thoughtful when facing uncertainty, conflict, or emotional challenges, rather than avoiding or rushing to solve them.

Business Application: Leaders who are comfortable with discomfort foster deeper dialogue, innovation, and better conflict resolution. They resist the urge to prematurely "fix" problems, allowing more sustainable solutions to develop.

Leadership Insight: Comfort with discomfort is not about liking tension; it's about tolerating ambiguity long enough for meaningful change to happen.

Cultural Caution: In some cultures, prolonged tension is viewed as harmful or disrespectful; leaders need to balance patience with responsiveness.

Mosaic Question: How do you usually respond when dialogue gets tense or unclear?

Mosaic in Action: During a cross-cultural merger meeting, two department heads argue over decision-making authority. Instead of stepping in to resolve the disagreement quickly, the CEO asks both to share their perspectives. By creating space without rushing to resolve, underlying values and structural issues come to light—leading to a stronger long-term governance plan.

Command-and-Control Leadership

Definition: A top-down leadership style where decision-making authority is centralized, and compliance is expected through directives rather than collaboration.

Business Application: While effective in emergencies or military operations, this style can hinder innovation and engagement in knowledge-based or creative industries.

Leadership Insight: Relying too much on command-and-control can create dependence rather than developing capabilities in teams.

Cultural Caution: In cultures that highly respect hierarchy, moving away from this model requires careful framing to prevent perceptions of weakness.

Mosaic Question: When does your need for control limit the growth of others?

Mosaic in Action: A nonprofit director who is used to making all final decisions recognizes that younger staff members are disengaged. By gradually shifting from giving orders to setting shared goals and asking for proposed solutions, the director maintains clear direction while enhancing collective problem-solving.

Communication Competence

Definition: The ability to clearly convey ideas, adapt to various contexts, and promote mutual understanding. Communication competence combines message clarity with awareness of audience, culture, and emotional tone.

Business Application:
Organizations depend on communication skills for successful leadership, customer interaction, and resolving conflicts. Leaders who communicate effectively minimize misunderstandings, foster alignment, and boost trust among departments and stakeholders.

Leadership Insight:
Communication competence goes beyond just speaking well; it includes listening actively, adjusting your style, and recognizing when brevity, detail, or storytelling will best serve the situation.

Cultural Caution: What counts as "competent" varies among cultures. In some settings, direct communication demonstrates professionalism; in others, it can seem harsh. Leaders need to adjust their communication style to respect cultural norms while staying genuine.

Mosaic Question: When you communicate, do you focus more on delivering your message or on making sure it's truly received?

Mosaic in Action: An executive presenting to a global team pauses to check for understanding, adjusts language to avoid jargon, and follows up with a summary memo — ensuring all voices remain aligned.

Community Accountability

Definition: A practice where groups collaboratively share responsibility for addressing harm, healing, and repair outside of punitive or hierarchical systems.

Business Application: In organizations, community accountability can replace blame cycles with shared problem-solving and collective learning.

Leadership Insight: Accountability is most effective when spread out. Leaders should encourage cultures where teams hold each other — and themselves — accountable with care.

Cultural Caution: Community accountability can seem unfamiliar in cultures that depend heavily on formal authority. Leaders need to build support gradually.

Mosaic Question: How do you make sure accountability spreads across, not just downward?

Mosaic in Action: After a harmful remark at a retreat, staff worked together on a restorative process, forming agreements for repair instead of relying solely on HR.

Community Agreements

Definition: Clear, collaboratively developed rules that set shared expectations for behavior, interaction, and accountability within a group.

Business Application: These agreements help align diverse stakeholders, prevent misunderstandings, and establish a foundation for psychological safety.

Leadership Insight: When agreements are co-created instead of imposed, they increase buy-in and shared ownership.

Cultural Caution: The language in agreements must be accessible and culturally relevant; overly formal or legalistic wording might alienate participants.

Mosaic Question: What agreements would make your team feel safe enough to take creative risks?

Mosaic in Action: A cross-departmental team creates agreements on meeting etiquette, decision-making, and communication channels. When conflict occurs later, members refer back to these agreements—solving issues without escalation or disengagement.

Community Capacity Building

Definition: The process of enhancing a community's abilities, resources, and leadership to handle its own challenges and opportunities.

Business Application: Capacity building provides communities with sustainable skills and structures instead of relying on external aid.

Leadership Insight: Genuine capacity building involves collaborating with communities, not for them—focusing on local knowledge and leadership.

Cultural Caution: Imposing external frameworks without adaptation can unintentionally displace local practices or erode trust.

Mosaic Question: How can you transition from being the problem-solver to the capability-builder?

Mosaic in Action: An urban development project starts by asking residents to identify their own priorities. Instead of offering ready-made programs, facilitators train local leaders in project management and grant writing—enabling them to maintain improvements long after the initial funding has run out.

Community of Practice

Definition: A group of people who share a common concern, passion, or profession and deepen their expertise through ongoing interaction, shared learning, and collaborative problem-solving.

Business Application: In leadership settings, a well-nurtured community of practice can accelerate organizational learning, maintain institutional memory, and support innovation by connecting diverse perspectives.

Leadership Insight: Leaders who invest in communities of practice cultivate self-sustaining ecosystems of growth where peers learn from each other without heavy top-down management.

Cultural Caution: Be aware of unspoken membership barriers. Geographic, linguistic, and cultural gatekeeping can unintentionally exclude valuable voices.

Mosaic Question: Who is missing from your professional learning spaces, and what structural changes could make participation more accessible?

Mosaic in Action: A nonprofit director organizes a cross-border virtual community of practice for youth program leaders. By including real-time translation and rotating facilitation among members from different countries, the group's shared insights become scalable, culturally adaptable models adopted across regions.

Community Resilience

Definition: The ability of a community to anticipate, adapt to, and recover from adversity while maintaining its core values, identity, and functions.

Business Application: Organizations embedded in communities—such as schools, local businesses, and NGOs— benefit from creating resilience networks that support coordinated responses to crises and long-term recovery.

Leadership Insight: Leaders can bolster resilience by fostering trust-based relationships before crises happen, providing a foundation for quick mobilization and resource sharing.

Cultural Caution: Do not frame resilience as simply "bouncing back." Some communities may prefer transformation rather than restoration, especially if pre-crisis conditions were unequal.

Mosaic Question: How can your leadership help communities not just survive disruptions but also emerge more just and inclusive?

Mosaic in Action: After a devastating flood, a city mayor partners with local cultural centers and mutual aid groups to coordinate relief efforts. Instead of only restoring pre-flood infrastructure, they collaboratively create a more flood-resistant housing plan—integrating cultural spaces into the design to preserve community identity.

Community Wealth Building

Definition: An economic and organizational approach that emphasizes local ownership, shared prosperity, and reinvestment in communities instead of extractive models.

Business Application: Community wealth building redirects procurement, hiring, and investment efforts to uplift marginalized neighborhoods and promote equity in organizational outcomes.

Leadership Insight: Leaders increase their influence when they recognize success not only in profit but also in how value flows back into communities.

Cultural Caution: What qualifies as "wealth" varies across different cultures — whether it's financial assets, land, kinship, or cultural continuity. Leaders should respect local definitions.

Mosaic Question: How does your organization's success benefit its community as a whole?

Mosaic in Action: A hospital system redirected contracts to minority-owned businesses, reinvesting millions into the local economy and boosting patient trust.

Comparative Privilege

Definition: The understanding that privilege exists on a spectrum, where an individual or group might have advantages in some situations but face disadvantages in others.

Business Application: In leadership, recognizing comparative privilege helps teams manage complex power relations and move beyond simple notions of privilege and oppression.

Leadership Insight: Recognizing your own comparative privilege can enhance empathy and improve negotiation skills during cross-cultural and interdisciplinary teamwork.

Cultural Caution: Conversations about privilege can cause defensiveness if seen as accusations; instead, treat them as chances for mutual understanding and societal change.

Mosaic Question: Where might you have advantages in one setting but encounter obstacles in another, and how does that dual experience influence your leadership?

Mosaic in Action: During an international project, a female executive from a high-income country acknowledges her influence in obtaining resources but also faces gender bias during negotiations. She leverages her positional privilege to support herself and colleagues who experience other forms of exclusion.

Compassion Fatigue

Definition: Emotional and physical exhaustion caused by extended exposure to others' suffering, leading to a decreased ability to empathize and care.

Business Application: Leaders in healthcare, education, social services, and crisis response must recognize compassion fatigue as an occupational hazard and establish systems for emotional recovery and workload management.

Leadership Insight: Tackling compassion fatigue is not a sign of personal weakness—it's essential for maintaining long-term leadership effectiveness and ethical care.

Cultural Caution: In some cultures, admitting to compassion fatigue may be stigmatized as a lack of dedication; leaders should model vulnerability to normalize seeking support.

Mosaic Question: What structures in your leadership environment help restore emotional reserves for yourself and your team?

Mosaic in Action: A school principal observes teachers showing signs of burnout after a series of student crises. She reorganizes the schedule to include peer support circles, mental health check-ins, and rotating "low-intensity" teaching days, resulting in renewed energy and lower turnover.

Compassionate Accountability

Definition: A leadership approach that blends empathy with a commitment to clear expectations, ensuring individuals are supported while staying accountable for their actions and impact.

Business Application: In performance reviews, compassionate accountability balances honest feedback with an understanding of personal circumstances, fostering growth without undermining dignity.

Leadership Insight: Leaders who practice compassionate accountability build trust; people know they will be treated fairly while being held to meaningful standards.

Cultural Caution: Compassion without accountability can lead to complacency, while accountability without compassion can create fear. Achieving the right balance requires ongoing self-awareness and situational sensitivity.

Mosaic Question: How do you create space for humanity while ensuring commitments are met?

Mosaic in Action: A department lead notices a project manager struggling to meet deadlines due to a family crisis. Instead of excusing missed deliverables entirely, the leader works with them to reprioritize tasks, adjust timelines, and set achievable milestones—keeping the project moving forward while showing care.

Compassionate Leadership

Definition: A leadership approach based on empathy, understanding, and profound respect for others' experiences, guiding decisions that value people as much as results.

Business Application: In organizational change, compassionate leadership ensures

communication acknowledges the human side of transitions, not just operational details.

Leadership Insight: Compassion is active; it means actively seeing and valuing people, even when making tough decisions.

Cultural Caution: Too much compassion without boundaries can blur the lines between personal and professional roles, risking burnout.

Mosaic Question: When facing difficult choices, how do you make sure compassion is part of the process?

Mosaic in Action: During a corporate downsizing, a CEO holds small group meetings to explain the situation, answer questions honestly, and connect departing employees with support services—dignity preserved during difficult times.

Competency Framework

Definition: A structured model that outlines the skills, behaviors, and knowledge necessary for effective performance within a role, organization, or sector.

Business Application: Used in recruitment, training, and succession planning, competency frameworks help ensure that evaluation criteria are transparent and aligned with organizational goals.

Leadership Insight: Well-designed frameworks create clarity, but they need to evolve to reflect changing cultural, technological, and market conditions.

Cultural Caution: Over-reliance on rigid frameworks can unintentionally exclude diverse talents or undervalue non-traditional expertise.

Mosaic Question: How does your competency model consider cultural intelligence and adaptability?

Mosaic in Action: An NGO develops a competency framework for field leaders that includes cultural agility, local partnership-building, and trauma-informed practices—ensuring technical skills are balanced with relational capacity.

Confidential Leadership

Definition: The practice of handling sensitive information with integrity, safeguarding privacy, and making decisions that uphold trust and ethical responsibility.

Business Application: In executive roles, HR management, or coaching relationships, confidentiality maintains trust. Leaders who safeguard what is shared in confidence build credibility and psychological safety within their organizations.

Leadership Insight: Confidentiality is not secrecy — it's stewardship. Leaders who practice it wisely know when to safeguard information, when to escalate responsibly, and when to communicate openly with stakeholders.

Cultural Caution: In some cultures, confidentiality might be confused with exclusion or favoritism. Not clarifying what can and cannot be shared could hurt credibility.

Mosaic Question: Do the people under your care trust you enough to share things they wouldn't risk telling others?

Mosaic in Action: A senior manager receives anonymous employee feedback about harassment, keeps identities protected, and ensures a safe investigation process — signaling that confidentiality safeguards privacy, not silence.

Conflict Agility

Definition: The ability to quickly, effectively, and constructively navigate and resolve disputes by adapting communication and strategies to the situation.

Business Application: In cross-functional teams, conflict agility allows for faster decision-making by addressing tensions before they escalate.

Leadership Insight: Conflict is not inherently harmful; when handled with agility, it can foster innovation, deepen trust, and strengthen team bonds.

Cultural Caution: In cultures that prefer indirect communication, rushing to resolve conflicts can seem aggressive. Being aware of the context is crucial.

Mosaic Question: Do you view conflict as a threat to avoid or a resource to use?

Mosaic in Action: During a product development meeting, two senior engineers clash over design priorities. The project leader steps in to clarify common goals, asks each to share concerns, and reframes the disagreement as complementary perspectives— resulting in a hybrid solution that enhances the final product.

Conflict Avoidance

Definition: The tendency to sidestep, delay, or ignore conflicts, often to preserve short-term harmony at the cost of long-term resolution.

Business Application: In workplace cultures where dissent is discouraged, conflict avoidance can delay problem-solving, hinder innovation, and erode trust.

Leadership Insight: Leaders should demonstrate healthy confrontation by fostering environments where concerns are raised early, respectfully, and without fear of retaliation.

Cultural Caution: In some cultures, avoiding direct conflict is seen as respectful; in others, it's regarded as evasive. Knowing these norms helps prevent misunderstandings.

Mosaic Question: Which conversation have you been putting off, and how could addressing it now improve your relationships?

Mosaic in Action: In a nonprofit team, two members repeatedly clash over resource allocation but avoid direct discussion. A project lead organizes a structured dialogue with ground rules, resulting in a solution that satisfies both parties and enhances mutual respect.

Conflict Competence

Definition: The ability to recognize, manage, and resolve disputes effectively, transforming potential tension into opportunities for growth and collaboration.

Business Application: Organizations with high conflict competence can adapt more quickly, sustain productivity, and boost morale during disagreements.

Leadership Insight: Conflict competence is developed through emotional regulation, active listening, and skillful reframing of disagreements as shared problem-solving.

Cultural Caution: Not all forms of conflict expression are the same; silence can be as meaningful as open argument in certain cultural settings.

Mosaic Question: How can you approach conflict in a way that both addresses the issue and strengthens the relationship?

Mosaic in Action: In a cross-department meeting, a manager notices increasing tension over a policy change. They pause the discussion to acknowledge concerns, invite each side to express their needs, and collaboratively create a revised rollout plan that everyone supports.

Conflict Literacy

Definition: The knowledge and understanding of conflict dynamics, sources, styles, and resolution strategies.

Business Application: Teams with conflict literacy can quickly diagnose underlying issues and select resolution methods suited to the situation.

Leadership Insight: Conflict literacy helps reactive leaders become proactive by anticipating friction points and preventing escalation.

Cultural Caution: What is labeled as "conflict" in one workplace might be seen as healthy debate in another; shared definitions are important.

Mosaic Question: Do you know your own conflict style and how others perceive it?

Mosaic in Action: Before starting a multi-country project, a team leader conducts a workshop on conflict styles and cultural norms. As a result, team members approach disagreements with mutual understanding, reducing misunderstandings.

Conflict Transformation

Definition: An approach to conflict that aims not only to resolve immediate issues but also to address root causes and transform relationships and systems for the better.

Business Application: Used in peacebuilding, organizational change, and community work, conflict transformation promotes long-term stability and fairness.

Leadership Insight: Leaders who practice conflict transformation focus on restoring trust, changing mindsets, and building structures that prevent future issues.

Cultural Caution: Deep transformation often requires disrupting long-standing power dynamics—expect discomfort and resistance.

Mosaic Question: How might you turn a recurring conflict into a driving force for systemic improvement?

Mosaic in Action: After repeated disputes over promotions, a company conducts a bias audit, redesigns its evaluation criteria, and introduces mentorship programs— transforming years of tension into a fairer system for advancement.

Consensus Building

Definition: A collaborative decision-making process aimed at reaching an agreement acceptable to all participants, focusing on mutual understanding and shared ownership of outcomes.

Business Application: In cross-functional projects, consensus building promotes alignment by ensuring diverse stakeholders have a say in shaping strategies, reducing resistance to implementation.

Leadership Insight: Leaders who prioritize consensus build trust and commitment but need to balance inclusivity with timely decisions to avoid stagnation.

Cultural Caution: In some cultures, open disagreement is discouraged, which can lead to false consensus where concerns go unspoken.

Mosaic Question: How do you create space for genuine agreement without silencing dissent?

Mosaic in Action: During a nonprofit's strategic planning session, facilitators use a round-robin approach so each participant—board members, volunteers, and staff—can share their priorities. A shared mission statement is created that includes language from all groups, boosting buy-in throughout the organization.

Consent Culture

Definition: A social norm where individuals actively seek and respect permission in interactions within personal, organizational, and community settings.

Business Application: In workplace collaboration, a consent culture guarantees that roles, workloads, and boundaries are mutually agreed upon instead of assumed, boosting morale and trust.

Leadership Insight: Consent culture enhances psychological safety by making it normal that saying "no" or setting boundaries is respected rather than penalized.

Cultural Caution: In some hierarchical settings, individuals might feel pressured to agree even if they are uncomfortable; leaders need to actively mitigate this pressure.

Mosaic Question: How do you demonstrate and promote active consent in your leadership approach?

Mosaic in Action: A project manager asks each team member to opt in to additional responsibilities rather than assigning them without discussion, leading to higher-quality work and less burnout.

Consequence Equity

Definition: The principle that consequences for actions—positive or negative—should be applied fairly and proportionally to all

individuals, regardless of status or identity.

Business Application: HR policies based on consequence equity sustain trust by ensuring misconduct is addressed consistently, whether involving junior staff or senior executives.

Leadership Insight: Consistent accountability builds credibility; selective enforcement damages it quickly.

Cultural Caution: In some organizational cultures, informal hierarchies shield certain individuals from consequences, harming morale and inclusion.

Mosaic Question: Are consequences in your organization applied fairly or with favoritism?

Mosaic in Action: In a multinational company, both an executive and an entry-level employee are held to the same standards in a harassment case, showing staff that no one is above accountability.

Conscious Bias

Definition: Prejudice or favoritism that individuals are aware of, whether or not they act on it.

Business Application: Recognizing conscious biases in hiring, promotions, and client selection helps organizations make intentional choices to reduce inequities.

Leadership Insight: Awareness of one's own conscious biases enables leaders to address them before they lead to harmful decisions.

Cultural Caution: In some environments, bias may be openly acknowledged yet still accepted, making genuine change difficult.

Mosaic Question: What conscious biases affect your leadership, and how are you working to address them?

Mosaic in Action: A department head notices a tendency to assign stretch tasks to staff who share their alma mater. They implement a transparent rotation system to ensure fair access to opportunities.

Conscious Leadership

Definition: A leadership style rooted in self-awareness, intention, and alignment between values, actions, and impact. Conscious leaders are intentional in their choices and take responsibility for the ripple effects they create.

Business Application: In organizations, conscious leadership fosters trust, encourages transparency, and aligns business goals with ethical and social responsibilities. It prompts leaders to make decisions that benefit both the bottom line and the greater good.

Leadership Insight: Leadership without self-awareness can lead to harm. Conscious leaders actively reflect on how their behavior influences team dynamics and results.

Cultural Caution: What is considered "ethical" or "responsible" might vary across cultures; a leader must understand cultural differences before applying universal principles.

Mosaic Question: Where do your intentions and your impact align— and where do they diverge?

Mosaic in Action: During a major restructuring, a senior executive holds open forums where employees can ask honest questions, shares the financial reasons clearly, and explains exactly how severance packages will be handled—earning trust even during tough times.

Conscious Uncoupling (Organizational)

Definition: The deliberate, respectful ending of a partnership, team, or organizational relationship with minimal harm and dignity preserved for all parties.

Business Application: This method is useful during mergers, contract terminations, or leadership changes, where the goal is to maintain professionalism and honor past contributions.

Leadership Insight: An organization's reputation depends not only on how it forms relationships but also on how it concludes them. Conscious uncoupling helps prevent lingering resentment and safeguards future collaboration.

Cultural Caution: In cultures where saving face is vital, public acknowledgment of the separation may need to be carefully managed to avoid embarrassment.

Mosaic Question: How can you honor what was built together while parting with care?

Mosaic in Action: When ending a five-year vendor relationship, a nonprofit hosts a small appreciation event, publicly thanks the vendor team, and offers references for their future contracts.

Conscious Use of Power

Definition: The intentional and ethical use of authority or influence to produce positive and fair results.

Business Application: Leaders who intentionally use power are open about their goals, ask for consent when possible, and stay aware of how power relationships influence decisions and participation.

Leadership Insight: Unchecked power creates fear; conscious use of power fosters trust.

Cultural Caution: Power may be understood differently across cultures—what appears as confident leadership in one setting might be viewed as domineering in another.

Mosaic Question: When have you used your influence in a way that built trust rather than fear?

Mosaic in Action: A department head finds out that junior staff feel left out of project decisions. She changes meeting formats so everyone has a chance to share before final choices are made.

Constructive Disruption

Definition: The intentional act of challenging systems, norms, or processes to foster innovation, equity, or positive change without causing unnecessary harm.

Business Application: Leaders may use constructive disruption to pivot strategy, break stagnation, or spark creativity within an organization.

Leadership Insight: Disruption is not chaos — it's clarity with a purpose. It aims for transformation, not destruction.

Cultural Caution: Disruption without cultural awareness can trigger backlash, alienate stakeholders, or deepen divides.

Mosaic Question: Where in your leadership is disruption overdue — and how can it be channeled to serve the greater good?

Mosaic in Action: In a long-standing nonprofit board, a new member respectfully questions a decades-old policy that excludes virtual participation. By presenting research, offering alternative solutions, and inviting dialogue, they spark a unanimous vote to allow hybrid meetings — making decision-making more inclusive.

Constructive Dissent

Definition: The open, respectful expression of disagreement aimed at improving ideas, policies, or decisions.

Business Application:
Constructive dissent helps teams avoid groupthink, recognize blind spots, and foster innovation by testing ideas from diverse perspectives.

Leadership Insight: While agreement can feel comfortable, it is dissent—when expressed respectfully—that sharpens strategy and prevents costly mistakes.

Cultural Caution: In hierarchical or high-context cultures, dissent may need to be conveyed indirectly to be heard and accepted.

Mosaic Question: How do you create an environment where disagreement strengthens rather than fractures your team?

Mosaic in Action: During a product development meeting, a junior designer respectfully questions the timeline as unrealistic. The project lead asks the team to re-map milestones, leading to a more achievable—and ultimately more successful—launch schedule.

Constructive Marginality

Definition: The ability to thrive and contribute meaningfully while positioned between multiple cultural, professional, or identity groups.

Business Application: Employees who embody constructive marginality can connect diverse teams, interpret perspectives, and act as trusted bridges.

Leadership Insight: Being "in-between" can be a position of influence if you embrace both listening and leading.

Cultural Caution: The in-between role can be draining—leaders must ensure these individuals aren't overwhelmed as cultural interpreters.

Mosaic Question: How can you support those navigating multiple worlds without expecting them to carry all the connection burden?

Mosaic in Action: A bilingual project manager facilitates communication between headquarters in New York and a partner organization in Mexico City. By translating not only language but also workplace norms, they resolve tensions early and promote mutual respect in collaboration.

Constructive Rest

Definition: Purposeful, intentional rest that replenishes emotional, cognitive, and physical capacity for high-performance work.

Business Application: Leaders can embed constructive rest into team culture through quiet rooms, flexible schedules, or recovery days after major projects.

Leadership Insight: Rest is not a reward; it's a prerequisite for sustained excellence.

Cultural Caution: In "always-on" cultures, rest may be stigmatized— leaders must normalize and model it for it to be effective.

Mosaic Question: How can your organization reframe rest as an investment in collective performance?

Mosaic in Action: After a high-stakes product launch, a tech CEO blocks the following Friday for a "team reset day," encouraging staff to recharge and return on Monday ready to innovate again.

Contested Space

Definition: A physical, social, or ideological space where different groups with varying interests, values, or power dynamics compete for recognition, influence, or control. Contested spaces can be tangible—such as disputed territories—or symbolic, like debates over curriculum, workplace culture, or public narratives.

Business Application: In organizations, contested spaces arise when departments, teams, or stakeholders have conflicting priorities, limited resources, or different visions of success. Navigating these spaces requires clear communication, negotiated agreements, and processes that respect multiple perspectives while maintaining momentum toward shared goals.

Leadership Insight: Strong leaders see contested spaces as chances for growth instead of just conflicts. By being honest with stakeholders and setting up shared decision-making structures, leaders can turn disputes into teamwork that builds long-term trust.

Cultural Caution: What one group sees as "healthy debate" might feel like erasure or hostility to another, especially when historical inequalities or cultural trauma influence the situation. Leaders need to recognize existing power imbalances and avoid the urge to "neutralize" conflict by silencing marginalized voices.

Mosaic Question: When stepping into a contested space, do you strive to win or to make sure every voice is truly heard?

Mosaic in Action: During the redesign of a city park, planners face conflicting demands one community wants open sports fields, while another desires quiet garden spaces. Instead of imposing a single solution, the lead facilitator hosts bilingual community forums, combines both visions into the final design, and transforms the park into a shared symbol of collaborative effort.

Context Collapse

Definition: The merging or loss of clear boundaries between different social, cultural, or professional settings—often sped up by digital platforms.

Business Application: Context collapse influences brand messaging, leadership communication, and employee privacy in the social media era.

Leadership Insight: Being able to understand and adapt to multiple contexts now represents a key leadership skill.

Cultural Caution: What works well in one setting might backfire in another—especially when audiences blend without shared norms.

Mosaic Question: When your message moves from its original environment, will it still reflect your core values?

Mosaic in Action: A school principal posts a motivational speech for the faculty on the district's internal portal. It goes viral outside the school community, earning both praise and criticism. The principal then uses this moment to hold a public Questions and Answers (Q&A),

explaining their intentions and building trust with unexpected audiences.

Continuous Learning Culture

Definition: An organizational environment where curiosity, adaptability, and skill development are integrated into daily operations. Learning is not limited to formal training; it is part of feedback cycles, experimentation, and knowledge-sharing.

Business Application: A culture of continuous learning fosters innovation and resilience. Organizations that invest in skill development, cross-training, and peer learning respond more quickly to change, meet market demands, and retain top talent who value growth.

Leadership Insight: Leaders influence the culture by demonstrating their own learning—admitting when they don't know something, actively seeking input, and celebrating lessons learned from both successes and failures. This turns learning from an occasional event into a shared cultural habit.

Cultural Caution: Not all employees have equal access to learning opportunities due to budget constraints, time limitations, or digital gaps. A culture of ongoing learning must prioritize equity—making sure that professional development is not just a privilege for a few.

Mosaic Question: Does your learning culture broaden access to opportunity or reinforce existing hierarchies?

Mosaic in Action: A global nonprofit introduces a monthly "Skill Share" where staff from various regions lead short, virtual sessions on skills they've mastered—from data visualization to cross-cultural negotiation. Over time, these sessions foster cross-team collaborations and uncover hidden talent within the organization.

Courage to Lead

Definition: The personal resilience to face risk, conflict, or uncertainty in pursuit of values, vision, and justice — even when the outcome is uncertain or support is limited.

Business Application: Leaders demonstrate courage when they confront toxic behaviors, advocate for equity in boardrooms, or stand firm on ethical decisions despite short-term costs.

Leadership Insight: Courage does not mean fearlessness; it means acting in line with your values despite fear. Leaders who demonstrate courage make vulnerability acceptable and encourage others to act with honesty.

Cultural Caution: In collectivist or high-power-distance cultures, "courage" might be shown through subtle resistance, quiet perseverance, or safeguarding harmony instead of public confrontation.

Mosaic Question: When was the last time you chose courage over compliance?

Mosaic in Action: A millennial manager challenges industry-wide hiring bias by advocating for candidates from non-traditional backgrounds — understanding it may slow approvals but aligns with equity values.

Courageous Conversation

Definition: A dialogue where participants address difficult, high-stakes, or emotionally charged topics with honesty, respect, and a shared goal of understanding. These conversations often reveal hidden tensions, systemic inequities, or personal grievances that affect trust and collaboration.

Business Application: In workplaces, courageous conversations are crucial for resolving conflict, giving meaningful feedback, and breaking down harmful norms. Structured methods—such as setting clear intentions, practicing active listening, and establishing ground rules—help prevent defensiveness from derailing progress.

Leadership Insight: Leaders who avoid difficult conversations often maintain short-term comfort at the cost of long-term trust. Courage in dialogue is not about being confrontational; it's about creating conditions where truth can be spoken, heard, and acted upon for the greater good.

Cultural Caution: The concept of "speaking up" varies across cultures. In some settings, direct confrontation might be viewed as disrespectful; in others, silence could imply complicity. Leaders need to tailor their approach to promote cultural safety while still promoting honesty.

Mosaic Question: When was the last time you entered a conversation knowing it might be uncomfortable—but necessary?

Mosaic in Action: A university department faces long-standing complaints about a lack of diversity in hiring. Instead of dismissing concerns, the dean invites faculty, staff, and student representatives to a facilitated session where the hiring process is openly examined. Although uncomfortable at times, the process results in a new, more inclusive hiring framework.

Courageous Followership

Definition: The practice of supporting a leader's mission while also holding them accountable through constructive challenge, ethical pushback, and principled dissent when necessary. Courageous followership requires both loyalty to the vision and commitment to integrity.

Business Application: In complex projects, courageous followers contribute not only by completing tasks but also by sharing essential insights when they spot risks, blind spots, or ethical issues. This improves decision-making and helps avoid preventable crises.

Leadership Insight: Effective leaders welcome courageous followership because it strengthens—not threatens—their leadership. By encouraging team members to challenge assumptions and voice dissent, leaders foster a healthier balance of power and build a culture where integrity outweighs mere compliance.

Cultural Caution: In hierarchical cultures, challenging authority can lead to social or career repercussions. Organizations aiming for courageous followership must establish clear protections and reward systems that prevent followers from being penalized for principled disagreement.

Mosaic Question: Are you fostering an environment where followers feel safe to speak truth to power?

Mosaic in Action: During a high-stakes product launch, a junior engineer notices a safety flaw. Instead of remaining silent, she raises the issue with her manager, who reports it to the executive team. The product is delayed for adjustments, but the company avoids a costly recall and maintains credibility with its customers.

Courageous Leadership

Definition: The practice of leading with integrity and moral clarity, even when it risks personal reputation, professional standing, or short-term gains. Courageous leadership focuses on people and principles rather than convenience, popularity, or compliance.

Business Application: In organizational settings, courageous leadership appears during critical moments—such as whistleblowing on unethical practices, opposing discriminatory policies, or taking an unpopular stance to safeguard team well-being. This type of leadership fosters loyalty and trust, reinforcing long-term credibility for the organization.

Leadership Insight: Courageous leaders are not reckless; they assess risk carefully while staying true to their core values. They blend conviction with emotional awareness, making sure their actions serve both justice and the common good.

Cultural Caution: In some cultures, leaders are expected to preserve harmony at all costs. Acts of courage might be misunderstood as disruptive or insubordinate. Being sensitive to the context is essential to avoid alienating allies or unintentionally strengthening resistance to change.

Mosaic Question: When the right choice is the toughest choice, what guides you?

Mosaic in Action: A regional director learns that cost-cutting measures will disproportionately harm staff in under-resourced offices. She refuses to implement them as proposed and instead presents a reallocation plan that protects vulnerable teams. The move sparks tense negotiations but ultimately gains board approval.

Critical Consciousness

Definition: A deep, reflective awareness of systemic forces— such as racism, sexism, classism, and colonialism—that shape individual and collective realities. Coined by educator Paulo Freire, critical consciousness goes beyond awareness to include action aimed at dismantling oppression.

Business Application: In organizations, critical consciousness guides inclusive hiring practices, fair pay structures, and culturally responsive policies. Leaders who develop it are better at recognizing and addressing the root causes of inequality rather than just applying superficial solutions.

Leadership Insight: Developing critical consciousness needs ongoing learning, humility, and the bravery to examine one's own biases and participation. Leaders who do this create environments where justice and belonging are essential parts of strategy, not optional extras.

Cultural Caution: Critical consciousness can trigger defensiveness in environments that value neutrality or "colorblindness." Leaders need to anticipate resistance and present the work as mutually beneficial rather than a zero-sum redistribution of power.

Mosaic Question: What inequalities in your environment have you learned to recognize—and what will you approach differently now?

Mosaic in Action: A corporate Vice President (VP) initiates a pay equity audit after discovering that longstanding salary gaps mirror industry-wide gender disparities. Besides making adjustments, she implements transparent pay bands and conducts annual reviews to prevent inequities from recurring.

Critical Hope

Definition: An active, justice-focused belief in the possibility of transformation, based on an honest evaluation of current realities. Critical hope rejects blind optimism and instead blends realistic assessment with ongoing commitment to change.

Business Application: Critical hope sustains teams during long-term change initiatives or after crises. Leaders who embody it acknowledge difficulties openly while reinforcing a shared belief that improvement is possible through collective effort.

Leadership Insight: Hope without critical thinking can be naive; critical thinking without hope can be paralyzing. Leaders who

combine both inspire resilience, mobilize action, and prevent burnout in themselves and others.

Cultural Caution: In areas where distrust runs high, messages of hope might be ignored if they are not backed by clear, tangible actions. Leaders need to show that their optimism is justified through consistent and visible follow-through.

Mosaic Question: How do you maintain hope when signs of change take a long time to appear?

Mosaic in Action: After a failed policy reform, a community coalition reorganizes to analyze what went wrong. The leader acknowledges setbacks while presenting a revised strategy based on lessons learned, inspiring members to keep fighting.

Critical Humility

Definition: The ability to recognize the limits of one's knowledge and perspective, especially about complex social and cultural realities, while staying open to learning from others. Critical humility combines self-awareness with an understanding of systemic complexity.

Business Application: In high-stakes decision-making, critical humility helps leaders consider different viewpoints, avoid overconfidence, and update strategies when new evidence appears. This method lowers costly mistakes and builds trust with stakeholders.

Leadership Insight: Critical humility doesn't weaken authority—it enhances it. Leaders who demonstrate vulnerability and a willingness to learn establish a cultural tone where admitting mistakes and updating approaches are seen as signs of maturity, not failure.

Cultural Caution: Some leadership cultures value certainty more than openness. Showing humility might be misunderstood as indecision unless it's paired with a clear plan for action and decision-making authority.

Mosaic Question: When was the last time you let someone else's insight change your mind?

Mosaic in Action: During an international merger, a CEO recognizes her limited understanding of local labor customs. She forms regional advisory councils to guide policy integration, preventing missteps that could damage employee trust.

Critical Leadership Studies

Definition: An interdisciplinary field that questions traditional, leader-focused approaches by exploring the social, political, and cultural contexts where leadership takes place. Critical Leadership Studies (CLS) analyzes how power, privilege, and ideology influence both the theory and practice of leadership.

Business Application: CLS prompts leadership development programs to consider whose voices are prioritized, whose experiences are overlooked, and what cultural assumptions are embedded in organizational leadership models. Applying CLS principles can assist organizations in creating more equitable leadership pipelines and governance structures.

Leadership Insight: Leaders influenced by CLS look beyond personality traits or competencies to examine the systemic conditions that enable or restrict leadership. This change encourages distributed, collective, and context-aware forms of leadership that are more adaptable in different environments.

Cultural Caution: CLS often questions deeply held beliefs about leadership effectiveness. In hierarchical cultures or legacy institutions, this might be seen as threatening authority or tradition. Framing CLS insights as a way to build resilience and foster innovation can help reduce resistance.

Mosaic Question: Whose view of leadership are you embracing—and who gains from it?

Mosaic in Action: A multinational company implements a CLS-informed leadership review process. Instead of focusing solely on top executives, it assesses how leadership is demonstrated across all levels, showing that mid-level managers and community liaisons are causing the most significant change.

Critical Listening

Definition: A leadership practice of actively examining the meaning, assumptions, and intent behind both what is said and what is left unsaid.

Business Application: Critical listening enhances negotiations, conflict resolution, and team trust. It aids leaders in detecting underlying issues, anticipating risks, and developing genuine solutions instead of superficial fixes.

Leadership Insight: Listening with discernment is not about judgment but understanding. Leaders

who listen for both facts and feelings demonstrate respect while uncovering blind spots that lead to better decisions.

Cultural Caution: Some cultures value silence and indirectness; pushing for verbal disclosure might overlook subtle cues. Leaders should expand "listening" to include body language, tone, and context.

Mosaic Question: Do you listen only for agreement — or also for discomfort, dissent, and nuance?

Mosaic in Action: A CEO observes frustration behind an employee's polite feedback during a town hall, encourages deeper dialogue, and uncovers systemic workload issues that needed attention.

Critical Race Theory (CRT)

Definition: An academic and legal framework that examines how laws, policies, and social systems maintain racial inequality—often in ways that appear neutral but produce unequal outcomes. Originating in United States (U.S.) legal scholarship, CRT emphasizes that racism is not only a matter of individual bias but is also embedded within institutional and structural practices.

Business Application: CRT can assist in organizational audits of hiring practices, promotion criteria, and policy enforcement to identify systemic biases. It can also support diversity and equity training that goes beyond surface-level awareness to address the underlying causes of racial inequity.

Leadership Insight: Leaders who draw on CRT principles understand that achieving equity requires systemic change, not just individual good intentions. They also recognize that race intersects with other identities—such as gender, class, and ability—shaping people's lived experiences at work.

Cultural Caution: CRT is often politically contested and misrepresented. Leaders must approach discussions with clarity, grounding the work in evidence and organizational values, while ensuring psychological safety for all participants.

Mosaic Question: How do your policies and practices reveal or oppose racial inequities?

Mosaic in Action: A school district uses CRT to examine discipline data and finds that students of color are disproportionately suspended for minor infractions. This results in policy changes, staff training, and restorative justice programs that help reduce disparities.

Critical Reflexivity

Definition: A disciplined process of examining one's own assumptions, values, positionality, and potential biases in relation to a specific context or relationship. Critical reflexivity goes beyond self-awareness by exploring how one's identity and power intersect with larger systems.

Business Application: Critical reflexivity can be incorporated into project planning, policy development, and leadership assessments. For example, teams can use reflexive questioning to evaluate how their decisions might affect marginalized groups or uphold systemic inequities.

Leadership Insight: Leaders who practice critical reflexivity avoid the ease of unquestioned certainty. They hold ongoing conversations with themselves and others to ensure their decisions are ethically and contextually sound.

Cultural Caution: Reflexive practices can be uncomfortable, especially in cultures that prioritize action over reflection. Without intentional integration into organizational processes, reflexivity may be dismissed as self-indulgent or irrelevant.

Mosaic Question: When was the last time you paused to consider how your own perspective influences what you notice—and what you overlook?

Mosaic in Action: Before finalizing a major restructuring plan, an executive team conducts a reflective review, recognizing that proposed changes would disproportionately affect single parents. They adjust timelines and offer flexible arrangements to reduce unintended harm.

Critical Whiteness Studies

Definition: An academic field that studies whiteness as a social construct and source of power, rather than as a default or neutral identity. Critical Whiteness Studies (CWS) explores how whiteness functions systematically to uphold racial hierarchies and privilege.

Business Application: CWS can highlight how organizational norms—such as "professionalism" standards—may be implicitly based on white cultural values. This awareness can help create more inclusive practices in recruitment, evaluation, and team culture.

Leadership Insight: Leaders who collaborate with CWS understand that addressing racial inequity requires changing norms, policies, and assumptions that focus on whiteness. They also

realize that this work benefits the entire organization by expanding definitions of excellence and belonging.

Cultural Caution: Discussions of whiteness may trigger defensiveness or guilt, especially when people confuse systemic critique with personal blame. Leaders should present CWS as a tool for collective growth, not as an attack on individuals.

Mosaic Question: What unspoken "defaults" in your organization reflect whiteness—and how could they be reimagined?

Mosaic in Action: A consulting firm reviews its dress code and presentation standards, discovering they implicitly favor Eurocentric grooming and speech norms. The firm updates policies to embrace diverse cultural expressions while maintaining professional standards.

Cross-Cultural Agility

Definition: The ability to quickly and effectively adapt to different cultural norms, values, and communication styles while staying authentic and building trust across various settings. Cross-cultural agility goes beyond awareness — it is a flexible skill that allows for smooth navigation of changing cultural environments.

Business Application: In multinational teams or global markets, cross-cultural agility enables leaders and employees to adapt strategies, adjust language, and modify engagement approaches to meet local expectations while maintaining organizational goals. It is essential for product launches, stakeholder negotiations, and crisis management in multicultural settings.

Leadership Insight: Leaders with cross-cultural agility avoid rigid playbooks. They combine cultural intelligence with situational awareness, reading both verbal and nonverbal cues to respond in ways that maintain relationships and achieve results.

Cultural Caution: Agility should not be confused with opportunism or superficial adaptation. Over-adjusting to "fit in" without grasping deeper cultural meanings can damage credibility and trust.

Mosaic Question: When the cultural context changes mid-conversation, how do you respond?

Mosaic in Action: A project manager at a global NGO quickly adjusts a virtual meeting agenda upon realizing that a partner team in East Africa values building relationships before discussing business. This change enhances rapport and accelerates later decisions.

Cross-Cultural Competence

Definition: The knowledge, skills, and attitudes that enable effective and respectful interaction across cultures. Cross-cultural competence involves understanding one's own cultural lens, recognizing differences and similarities, and applying strategies that bridge gaps in communication and expectations.

Business Application: Organizations with culturally competent staff reduce misunderstandings, enhance collaboration, and boost market success. This skill can be developed through structured training, immersive experiences, and continuous reflection.

Leadership Insight: Competence is not fixed—it demands ongoing learning. Leaders who show this exemplify curiosity, active listening, and a willingness to adapt while staying true to their core values.

Cultural Caution: Having knowledge of a culture doesn't ensure competence. Relying too much on stereotypes or "dos and don'ts" lists can oversimplify complex cultural realities.

Mosaic Question: Does your cultural knowledge lead to meaningful connection?

Mosaic in Action: A healthcare administrator implements bilingual signage and culturally relevant patient care protocols after staff training uncovers language and cultural gaps that were impacting service for immigrant patients.

Cross-Cultural Negotiation

Definition: The process of reaching agreements between parties from different cultural backgrounds, where differences in communication styles, decision-making approaches, and values influence negotiation dynamics.

Business Application: In global supply chains, joint ventures, or international partnerships, cross-cultural negotiation is essential for aligning expectations, building trust, and preventing costly misunderstandings. Preparation involves researching cultural norms and identifying potential areas of agreement and contention.

Leadership Insight: Successful negotiators understand that cultural differences influence not only what is negotiated but also how the process unfolds— such as the role of hierarchy, the importance of building

relationships, and attitudes toward time.

Cultural Caution: Using a single negotiation style across different cultures can backfire. For example, direct confrontation might work in some environments but be considered disrespectful in others.

Mosaic Question: In negotiations, do you adjust to your counterpart's cultural style, or do you expect them to adjust to yours?

Mosaic in Action: An American executive in the tech industry discovers that her Japanese counterpart prefers to build consensus before making formal offers. She dedicates extra time to relationship-building before meetings, resulting in a smoother negotiation process.

Cross-Cultural Sensitivity

Definition: An awareness of and respect for cultural differences, along with the ability to respond appropriately in intercultural interactions. Cross-cultural sensitivity involves empathy, openness, and understanding how one's actions may be perceived through different cultural perspectives.

Business Application: In service industries, marketing campaigns, and internal communications, cross-cultural sensitivity helps prevent unintentional offenses, enhances brand reputation, and boosts employee engagement across diverse teams.

Leadership Insight: Sensitivity is a leadership asset—it builds trust, shows respect, and promotes cooperation. Leaders who practice it proactively seek feedback from culturally diverse stakeholders before making decisions that affect them.

Cultural Caution: Sensitivity without action can seem insincere. Focusing too much on avoiding offense might result in superficial involvement instead of genuine inclusion.

Mosaic Question: Do your actions demonstrate sincere cultural respect or are they just performative politeness?

Mosaic in Action: A tourism company updates its advertising after realizing that an image meant to convey "local authenticity" actually misrepresented a sacred cultural site. They consult community leaders to produce accurate, respectful materials that boost both cultural pride and customer trust.

Cross-Generational Leadership

Definition: The ability to lead teams composed of multiple generations—each with distinct communication styles, work values, and expectations—while transforming these differences into strategic advantages. Cross-generational leadership requires adaptability and a nuanced understanding of generational identity as a cultural factor.

Business Application: In today's multigenerational workplaces, leaders must bridge differences in values, communication preferences, and career priorities. Cross-generational leadership fosters collaboration, reduces friction, and enables knowledge transfer across age groups. This can involve tailoring feedback approaches, adjusting meeting formats, and designing flexible career pathways. As new generations continue to enter the workforce, these adaptive strategies remain essential for sustaining engagement, innovation, and organizational growth.

Leadership Insight: Effective cross-generational leaders emphasize shared purpose over stereotypes. They act as cultural translators, helping team members interpret and value each other's perspectives, strengths, and work styles.

Cultural Caution:
Overgeneralizing traits of a generation can backfire. Not everyone fits their generational stereotype, and differences within generations can be as significant as those across generations.

Mosaic Question: Do you approach generational diversity as a problem to solve or an advantage to leverage?

Mosaic in Action: A hospital department head pairs senior nurses nearing retirement with younger staff for co-led training sessions. This cross-generational mentorship boosts morale, accelerates skill transfer, and improves patient care outcomes.

Cultural Add

Definition: A hiring and organizational development philosophy that focuses on recruiting individuals whose diverse backgrounds, experiences, and perspectives broaden the organization's cultural capacity—rather than just matching existing norms ("culture fit").

Business Application:
Recruitment processes that value cultural add promote innovation and help avoid groupthink. Instead of screening candidates solely for similarity to existing staff, organizations evaluate how a candidate's differences can expand capabilities and improve decision-making.

Leadership Insight: Shifting from "culture fit" to "cultural add" requires intentional change management. Leaders need to prepare teams to see difference as an asset rather than a disruption.

Cultural Caution: If onboarding and workplace culture aren't inclusive, the advantages of cultural add can be lost as new hires feel pressured to conform rather than contribute authentically.

Mosaic Question: Does your hiring process grow your culture—or keep it the same?

Mosaic in Action: A startup intentionally recruits a product designer from a market they aim to enter, knowing her lived experience will help the team develop more relevant offerings for that region.

Cultural Agility

Definition: The ability to effectively work across various cultural settings with adaptability, respect, and strategic awareness. Cultural agility merges understanding of cultural differences with the flexibility to modify behavior and communication in real time.

Business Application:
Culturally agile leaders excel in

mergers, global expansions, and international partnerships. They can interpret nuanced cues, adapt decision-making processes, and build trust among culturally diverse stakeholders.

Leadership Insight: Cultural agility is not about abandoning your own identity—it's about connecting with others where they are while remaining true to your core values.

Cultural Caution: Overemphasizing adaptability without critical awareness can result in compromising key ethical standards or unintentionally supporting harmful practices.

Mosaic Question: When you enter a new cultural setting, do you adapt instinctively—or intentionally?

Mosaic in Action: A nonprofit leader changes facilitation methods during a workshop after noticing that small-group discussions connect better with participants from a collectivist culture than direct Q&A formats.

Cultural Appropriation

Definition: The adoption or use of elements from one culture—such as dress, language, art, or rituals—by members of another culture, especially when the source culture

is marginalized and the exchange occurs without understanding, respect, or mutual benefit.

Business Application: In branding, marketing, and product design, avoiding cultural appropriation safeguards the organization's reputation and prevents harm to communities whose traditions are being commodified or misrepresented. Authentic collaboration with cultural originators can transform potential appropriation into respectful exchange.

Leadership Insight: Leaders must proactively identify appropriation risks. This involves establishing review processes for campaigns, events, and partnerships that involve cultural expressions.

Cultural Caution: Intent doesn't erase impact. Even well-meaning uses of cultural symbols can reinforce stereotypes or exploit histories of oppression if they lack consent and proper context.

Mosaic Question: Are you respecting a culture's contributions—or taking from them?

Mosaic in Action: A fashion brand collaborates with Indigenous artisans before launching a collection inspired by traditional patterns. They co-create designs, credit the source culture, and share profits directly with the community.

Cultural Assimilation

Definition: The process by which individuals or groups adopt the language, norms, values, and behaviors of another culture—often the dominant one—sometimes at the expense of their original cultural identity. Assimilation may be voluntary, strategic, or a result of systemic pressure.

Business Application: In workplaces, cultural assimilation can happen when employees from underrepresented backgrounds feel forced to hide parts of their identity to "fit in." While it may temporarily ease integration, it can also reduce diversity of thought and lower employee engagement.

Leadership Insight: Inclusive leaders recognize the hidden costs of assimilation and work to create environments where people can fully contribute without sacrificing their cultural identity. This encourages innovation and psychological safety.

Cultural Caution: Assimilation is often presented as positive integration, but when it happens unilaterally or under pressure,

it reinforces inequalities and diminishes cultural diversity.

Mosaic Question: Are people thriving in your organization because they belong—or because they've learned to blend in?

Mosaic in Action: A marketing firm replaces its "neutral dress code" with guidelines that permit cultural attire. As a result, employees feel more comfortable expressing themselves, and the company's public-facing materials reflect greater authenticity.

Cultural Attunement

Definition: The ability and expertise to respond to cultural differences with humility, curiosity, and emotional presence. Cultural attunement goes beyond mere awareness; it requires leaders to adjust tone, language, and behavior in ways that respect others' lived experiences.

Business Application: Cultural attunement enhances cross-cultural teams, international negotiations, and intergenerational collaboration. Leaders who practice attunement decrease miscommunication, promote inclusion, and create environments where diverse voices can flourish.

Leadership Insight: Being attuned means listening beneath the surface — to values, histories, and unspoken dynamics. Leaders who practice cultural attunement recognize both what is said and what is left unsaid, building trust across differences.

Cultural Caution: Attunement doesn't mean losing your own identity or over-adapting. Leaders should balance openness with integrity, making sure that adaptation doesn't turn into performative behavior or inauthenticity.

Mosaic Question: When entering a new cultural space, do you assume you already understand — or do you pause to attune?

Mosaic in Action: A university dean meets with international students and, instead of jumping straight into policy updates, listens attentively to how students describe their challenges, modifying language and examples to connect with their cultural backgrounds.

Cultural Audit

Definition: A systematic review of an organization's policies, practices, communications, and culture to assess how well they align with stated values of diversity, equity, and inclusion. A cultural audit uncovers gaps, strengths, and opportunities for improvement.

Business Application: Cultural audits can reveal patterns—such as unequal promotion rates, biased language in job postings, or informal networks that exclude certain groups—and offer a roadmap for meaningful change.

Leadership Insight: Conducting a cultural audit shows a commitment to transparency and accountability. Leaders who implement the findings prove that equity and inclusion are practical priorities, not just ideals.

Cultural Caution: Audits without follow-up can damage trust and increase skepticism, especially among marginalized employees. Recommendations need proper resources and ongoing tracking.

Mosaic Question: If you audited your culture today, what truths might you uncover?

Mosaic in Action: A university's cultural audit reveals that students with disabilities face barriers in accessing campus services. The school invests in training, infrastructure upgrades, and a new accessibility office to close the gaps.

Cultural Awareness

Definition: An awareness that cultural differences exist and impact beliefs, behaviors, and interactions. Cultural awareness forms the basis for cross-cultural communication, promoting respect even when values or practices vary.

Business Application: Cultural awareness training can help employees interpret behaviors in culturally diverse teams, reducing miscommunication and building rapport with clients or partners from different backgrounds.

Leadership Insight: Awareness alone is not enough—leaders must turn it into action by adjusting processes, policies, and communication styles to meet diverse needs.

Cultural Caution: Superficial awareness—limited to facts or holidays—risks turning cultures into checklists or stereotypes. Genuine awareness involves curiosity, humility, and understanding of context.

Mosaic Question: Do you notice cultural differences only when they cause conflict, or do you try to understand them proactively?

Mosaic in Action: A sales team modifies its pitch process after discovering that in certain cultures, establishing trust before discussing contracts is crucial. Deals close more quickly when relationships are prioritized.

Cultural Blind Spots

Definition: Unrecognized biases or gaps in awareness that cause individuals or organizations to overlook the importance of cultural differences in decisions, policies, or interactions.

Business Application: Blind spots can lead to missed opportunities, misunderstandings, or unintentional offense. Recognizing and addressing them enhances service delivery, product design, and team cohesion.

Leadership Insight: Leaders must proactively seek feedback from diverse perspectives to uncover blind spots. Establishing channels where employees can voice concerns without fear of retaliation is essential.

Cultural Caution: Blind spots are unavoidable—ignoring them after they are highlighted shows a lack of inclusion and respect.

Mosaic Question: What cultural perspectives are absent from the rooms where decisions are made?

Mosaic in Action: A health app launches with meal plans that assume access to certain Western foods. Feedback from users worldwide prompts the company to add culturally diverse options, expanding its market and increasing relevance.

Cultural Broker

Definition: An individual who helps improve understanding, communication, and collaboration between people or groups from different cultural backgrounds. Cultural brokers interpret not only language but also social norms, values, and expectations, helping to bridge gaps that might otherwise interfere with relationships or outcomes.

Business Application: In global organizations, cultural brokers can serve as mediators between headquarters and regional teams, ensuring strategies are tailored for local relevance while maintaining alignment with organizational goals. They can also play a key role in negotiations, conflict resolution, and community engagement.

Leadership Insight: Leaders who identify and empower cultural brokers enhance organizational agility and trust-building ability. Brokers typically have strong relational capital and contextual knowledge that formal authority cannot replicate.

Cultural Caution: Overreliance on a single cultural broker without organizational learning can lead to dependency and impose disproportionate emotional labor on one individual—especially if they belong to a marginalized group.

Mosaic Question: Who in your network naturally connects different cultures—and how are you supporting them?

Mosaic in Action: A city council hires a bilingual community organizer to act as a bridge between municipal agencies and immigrant residents. By framing policies in culturally relevant ways, she boosts civic participation and trust in public services.

Cultural Capital

Definition: The non-financial social assets—such as education, language proficiency, aesthetic preferences, and cultural knowledge—that can give individuals advantages in social mobility, influence, and opportunity.

Business Application: In hiring and promotion, cultural capital often plays an unacknowledged role. Employees who share the dominant group's cultural capital (e.g., communication style, dress, hobbies) may be perceived as a "better fit," even when qualifications are equal.

Leadership Insight: Recognizing how cultural capital works enables leaders to create fairer systems that appreciate a wider variety of experiences and credentials. This change can broaden talent pools and reveal hidden potential.

Cultural Caution: When organizations define professionalism or competence too narrowly, they unintentionally favor certain types of cultural capital while excluding others.

Mosaic Question: Whose cultural capital is valued in your organization—and whose is ignored?

Mosaic in Action: A law firm reevaluates its recruitment process after recognizing that traditional networking events tend to favor candidates from elite schools. They implement community-based recruitment strategies to expand the pool of successful applicants.

Cultural Competence

Definition: The ability to interact effectively and respectfully with people from diverse cultural backgrounds by applying knowledge, skills, and attitudes that foster mutual understanding.

Business Application: Cultural competence allows teams to navigate global markets, serve diverse clients, and create inclusive workplaces. It involves not only learning about other cultures but

also reflecting on one's own cultural perspective and biases.

Leadership Insight: Competent leaders go beyond "awareness" by adapting their behaviors—changing processes, communication, and decision-making to foster equity and inclusion.

Cultural Caution: Cultural competence is an ongoing process, not a one-time achievement; it requires continuous learning and self-reflection. Viewing it as a single training completion can lead to complacency.

Mosaic Question: How do you turn cultural understanding into meaningful action?

Mosaic in Action: A healthcare system implements mandatory interpreter services and culturally tailored care plans after identifying gaps in patient outcomes caused by language and cultural barriers.

Cultural Continuity

Definition: The preservation and continued practice of cultural traditions, values, and knowledge across generations, even amid migration, modernization, or outside pressures to assimilate.

Business Application: Organizations serving Indigenous or diasporic communities can build trust by supporting cultural continuity—such as integrating traditional knowledge into programming, services, or product design.

Leadership Insight: Leaders who respect and protect cultural continuity understand that honoring heritage enhances identity, resilience, and ongoing community involvement.

Cultural Caution: Ignoring or undermining cultural continuity can lead to identity loss, community division, and intergenerational tension.

Mosaic Question: How does your work honor the cultural legacies of the people you serve?

Mosaic in Action: A school district partners with tribal elders to include Indigenous language classes in the curriculum, helping younger generations stay connected to their linguistic heritage.

Cultural Curiosity

Definition: A mindful approach to engaging cultural differences with openness, humility, and inquiry instead of assumption or judgment.

Business Application: Cultural curiosity drives cross-border negotiations, global teamwork, and intergenerational leadership. It turns differences into opportunities

for learning, encouraging creativity and mutual respect.

Leadership Insight: Curiosity is the key to cultural intelligence. Leaders who ask questions instead of making assumptions, and explore rather than dismiss, create bridges of trust across differences.

Cultural Caution: Curiosity must be genuine. Viewing cultures as "exotic" or exploring them disrespectfully can seem intrusive or performative.

Mosaic Question: When encountering cultural differences, do you rush to explain — or pause to explore?

Mosaic in Action: A corporate leader entering a new market takes time to learn local customs by participating in community gatherings, showing genuine curiosity and respect.

Cultural Displacement

Definition: The experience of being physically or socially uprooted from one's cultural environment, leading to a loss or disruption of familiar norms, practices, and community ties. Displacement can occur through migration, gentrification, war, economic forces, or systemic exclusion.

Business Application: Organizations working in

communities experiencing rapid change need to understand how cultural displacement affects consumer behavior, workforce stability, and trust. Being sensitive to these issues can help guide fair relocation support, hiring practices, and community engagement strategies.

Leadership Insight: Leaders who recognize and address cultural displacement show empathy and a long-term perspective. Supporting displaced individuals involves more than just logistical help—it includes creating opportunities for belonging and cultural expression in new settings.

Cultural Caution: Well-meaning integration programs can unintentionally pressure displaced people to assimilate rather than honor their cultural heritage.

Mosaic Question: When people are displaced, do your actions support their adaptation without erasing their identity?

Mosaic in Action: A tech company opening a new campus in a historically working-class neighborhood provides free cultural space for local artists and funds community heritage programs to help preserve local identity amid economic change.

Cultural Dominance

Definition: The systemic favoring of one culture's norms, values, and worldview over others, often upheld through institutions, media, laws, and economic structures. Cultural dominance influences what is regarded as "normal," "professional," or "high value" in a specific context.

Business Application: Recognizing cultural dominance helps organizations see where policies, branding, and decision-making might unintentionally favor one worldview and marginalize others. Making adjustments can create more inclusive services, marketing, and leadership pipelines.

Leadership Insight: Leaders must critically assess how their own cultural perspective influences authority, influence, and decision-making. Tackling cultural dominance requires intentionally sharing voice, resources, and recognition.

Cultural Caution: Challenging cultural dominance can trigger resistance from those who gain from the current system. Strategic framing and coalition-building are crucial to maintaining progress.

Mosaic Question: What cultural assumptions influence your organization—and who established them?

Mosaic in Action: A global advertising agency shifts away from "neutral" beauty standards in campaigns, replacing them with diverse representations after realizing its imagery mostly reflected Western ideals.

Cultural Dissonance

Definition: The psychological discomfort or conflict experienced when personal cultural values and practices clash with those of the surrounding environment or dominant culture. Cultural dissonance can occur in workplaces, educational settings, or social spaces.

Business Application: In organizations, cultural dissonance can lead to decreased engagement, high turnover, or miscommunication. Addressing it with inclusive policies, flexible work arrangements, and cross-cultural dialogue can enhance retention and productivity.

Leadership Insight: Effective leaders view cultural dissonance not just as a challenge but as a signal for where systems and norms might need adjustment. Listening carefully to those experiencing dissonance can reveal systemic blind spots.

Cultural Caution: Ignoring cultural dissonance risks normalizing exclusion and reinforcing unjust power structures.

Mosaic Question: Where could cultural dissonance in your organization indicate a need for change?

Mosaic in Action: An international student at a U.S. university struggles with classroom participation norms that emphasize quick, outspoken debate. Faculty adjust participation grading to allow for reflective contributions, reducing stress and boosting engagement.

Cultural Durability

Definition: The resilience and adaptability of cultural practices, beliefs, and values over time, allowing them to withstand external pressures, environmental shifts, and generational changes.

Business Application: Organizations working with long-standing communities can align initiatives with cultural durability by incorporating traditional knowledge into modern solutions—such as sustainable business models grounded in local practices.

Leadership Insight: Supporting cultural durability involves valuing heritage as a living resource rather than a relic. Leaders can encourage it by creating space for cultural evolution while safeguarding core identity markers.

Cultural Caution: Preserving cultural resilience should avoid romanticizing tradition in ways that overlook the community's ability to adapt and innovate.

Mosaic Question: What cultural strengths in your community or organization have lasted— and why?

Mosaic in Action: A coastal town integrates centuries-old fishing techniques into its marine conservation plan, maintaining ecological balance while supporting local livelihoods.

Cultural Erosion

Definition: The gradual decline or disappearance of cultural traditions, languages, values, and practices, often caused by external pressures such as globalization, assimilation policies, economic migration, or dominant cultural influence. Cultural erosion can happen over generations or within a single lifetime.

Business Application: Organizations operating in culturally diverse regions need to be aware of how their products,

services, or practices may contribute to or help prevent cultural erosion. This awareness is especially important in sectors like tourism, media, and education, where representation and narrative control influence cultural preservation.

Leadership Insight: Leaders can combat cultural erosion by incorporating heritage knowledge into organizational strategies, fostering intergenerational exchange, and working with community leaders to maintain identity and pride.

Cultural Caution: Efforts to combat cultural erosion must avoid tokenism or superficial preservation, ensuring that cultural practices stay meaningful and relevant rather than being frozen in time.

Mosaic Question: Are your efforts unintentionally harming the cultures you want to connect with?

Mosaic in Action: A development agency funds community-led language revitalization programs after realizing that its earlier projects had focused only on dominant national languages in educational materials.

Cultural Essentialism

Definition: The oversimplification of a culture by assuming that all members share fixed, homogeneous traits, values, or behaviors. Essentialism often overlooks internal diversity, change over time, and the impact of intersecting identities.

Business Application: In training, marketing, or recruitment, cultural essentialism can cause stereotyping, missed opportunities, and alienation. Recognizing the complexity within cultures enables more nuanced engagement and innovation.

Leadership Insight: Effective leaders avoid essentialist narratives by listening to various voices within a cultural group. This strategy enhances credibility and helps prevent exclusionary decisions.

Cultural Caution: Even positive stereotypes can be harmful—they turn people into cultural caricatures and ignore individual differences in experience.

Mosaic Question: Are you relating to people as individuals—or as representatives of a simplified idea of their culture?

Mosaic in Action: An international aid organization stops creating "one-size-fits-all" programs for rural women in a region after realizing that needs vary greatly between villages, age groups, and economic backgrounds.

Cultural Fit (Critical View)

Definition: The traditional hiring and leadership framework that evaluates individuals based on their conformity to an existing culture — often reinforcing sameness and bias.

Business Application: Overemphasizing "fit" perpetuates inequalities by excluding those with different lived experiences, communication styles, or cultural backgrounds.

Leadership Insight: The future of leadership focuses on culture add instead of culture fit. Leaders need to move from gatekeeping sameness to valuing differences as an asset.

Cultural Caution: In certain situations, "fit" is linked to loyalty. Leaders need to distinguish between commitment to shared values and conformity to prevailing norms.

Mosaic Question: Are you hiring for someone who feels familiar — or for someone who expands your vision?

Mosaic in Action: A law firm updated its hiring criteria, replacing "fit" with "value add," resulting in a more diverse and innovative team.

Cultural Flexibility

Definition: The ability to connect across cultural, generational, and social differences without losing your identity. Cultural flexibility combines empathy, adaptability, and curiosity to navigate unfamiliar or changing situations. It is the second pillar of the Mosaic Intelligence Method™, developed and trademarked by Dr. Karissa Thomas, and it allows leaders to stay authentic while respecting differences.

Business Application: In global and diverse organizations, cultural flexibility enables leaders to work effectively across borders, time zones, and perspectives. It facilitates mergers, strengthens international partnerships, and promotes inclusive teamwork by decreasing conflict and fostering mutual understanding.

Leadership Insight: Cultural flexibility is not about giving up your identity but about broadening your range of responses. Leaders who practice this stay true to their values while adapting language, tone, and practices to show respect and build connections with others.

Cultural Caution: Flexibility without boundaries can lead to people-pleasing or performative adaptation. Over-adapting might damage credibility. True cultural flexibility balances openness with emotional honesty and self-awareness.

Mosaic Question: Do you navigate cultural tension as a survival strategy — or as a way to build deeper connection and trust?

Mosaic in Action: A regional director leading a cross-country project adjusts meeting protocols to accommodate both local customs and corporate expectations, establishing a rhythm that respects different work styles while keeping the team focused on shared goals.

Cultural Fluency

Definition: The ability to communicate and collaborate effectively across cultures by combining cultural knowledge with adaptive skills, emotional intelligence, and contextual awareness. Cultural fluency goes beyond competence to achieve seamless, respectful interaction in complex settings.

Business Application: Culturally fluent teams excel in negotiations, global partnerships, and engaging diverse customers. This skill supports conflict resolution, builds brand trust, and enhances organizational adaptability in changing markets.

Leadership Insight: Cultural fluency is built through consistent exposure, reflective practice, and a willingness to learn from mistakes. Leaders who demonstrate cultural fluency foster psychologically safe environments for experimentation and growth.

Cultural Caution: Fluency is not the same as mimicry. Imitating surface traits without grasping their deeper significance can harm trust and credibility.

Mosaic Question: Do your cross-cultural interactions come across as natural—or do they feel forced?

Mosaic in Action: A senior diplomat effectively mediates a conflict between two nations by adjusting communication styles on the spot—balancing straightforwardness with politeness based on each side's cultural norms.

Cultural Framework

Definition: A structured model or set of concepts used to understand, analyze, and compare cultural patterns, values, and behaviors. Cultural frameworks help identify similarities, differences, and potential areas of conflict or synergy.

Business Application: Organizations use cultural frameworks—such as Hofstede's dimensions or the Lewis model— to inform strategy, training, and global project planning. When applied effectively, frameworks help guide adaptation and prevent cultural missteps.

Leadership Insight: Leaders should view frameworks as starting points rather than rigid formulas. The aim is to guide decision-making while allowing room for local nuances and changing realities.

Cultural Caution: Relying too much on one framework can cause oversimplification and strengthen stereotypes if not balanced with firsthand experience and diverse viewpoints.

Mosaic Question: Do you use cultural frameworks to limit people—or to expand possibilities?

Mosaic in Action: A global marketing team uses a cultural framework to tailor a product campaign for three regions and then adjusts the messaging after in-market feedback reveals distinct local priorities.

Cultural Gatekeeping

Definition: The act of controlling or restricting access to cultural knowledge, practices, spaces, or representation, often by individuals or groups who decide what is considered authentic, acceptable, or worthy of visibility. Cultural gatekeeping can either preserve integrity or uphold exclusion, depending on how it is practiced.

Business Application: In industries such as publishing, fashion, and media, gatekeeping influences who gets to tell stories and whose voices are heard. Organizations can review gatekeeping systems to make sure they promote inclusion without sacrificing cultural authenticity.

Leadership Insight: Leaders must distinguish between protective gatekeeping—which defends cultural traditions from misappropriation—and restrictive gatekeeping—which can silence innovation or exclude marginalized voices within the culture.

Cultural Caution: Completely removing gatekeeping can lead to exploitation, while too much rigidity can hinder cultural growth. Finding the right balance is essential.

Mosaic Question: Who controls access to cultural participation in your community—and why?

Mosaic in Action: An arts council reviews its grant criteria after realizing that community-led projects by newer immigrant groups are consistently overlooked due to narrow definitions of "traditional" art forms.

Cultural Harmony

Definition: A state of respectful coexistence between individuals or groups from different cultural backgrounds, characterized by mutual understanding, shared values, and fair participation in shared spaces.

Business Application: In multinational corporations, cultural harmony enhances collaboration, decreases workplace conflict, and builds trust. It involves active dialogue, fair policies, and creating an environment where diversity is valued as an asset.

Leadership Insight: Cultural harmony is not passive—it demands intentional effort to address inequities and ensure all groups have equal voice and influence. Leaders who foster harmony do so by integrating inclusion into daily decision-making.

Cultural Caution: Superficial displays of harmony can hide underlying tensions if power imbalances are not addressed.

Mosaic Question: Is your idea of harmony rooted in equality or in conforming to the dominant culture?

Mosaic in Action: A regional office of an international NGO hosts monthly cultural exchange lunches where employees share food and stories from their heritage, fostering connections that enhance cross-team problem-solving.

Cultural Heirlooms

Definition: Physical objects, artifacts, or symbols passed down through generations that hold cultural, familial, or historical importance. Cultural heirlooms represent collective memory and identity, often telling stories of resilience, migration, or tradition.

Business Application: Museums, heritage organizations, and brands working with cultural heirlooms must ensure respectful handling, proper attribution, and community involvement in interpretation and display.

Leadership Insight: Leaders in heritage preservation recognize that cultural heirlooms are more than just aesthetic objects—they hold emotional and identity-related significance that can strengthen community bonds.

Cultural Caution: Taking heirlooms out of their cultural context without permission can be seen as appropriation or erasure.

Mosaic Question: How do you safeguard the tangible symbols of cultural memory in your work?

Mosaic in Action: A public library partners with local elders to digitize photographs and documents stored in private homes, making them accessible to the community while preserving the originals.

Cultural Heritage

Definition: The traditions, practices, languages, artifacts, and knowledge systems passed down from previous generations and preserved for the benefit of current and future communities. Cultural heritage includes both physical elements (monuments, art, artifacts) and intangible ones (oral traditions, rituals, music).

Business Application: Heritage-informed initiatives can boost brand authenticity, improve tourism strategies, and increase community engagement. Partnering with cultural custodians ensures respectful integration of heritage elements into programs or products.

Leadership Insight: Leaders who engage with cultural heritage understand its importance in shaping identity, building social bonds, and connecting generations. They make sure preservation efforts support—rather than overshadow—the living culture that sustains it.

Cultural Caution: Monetizing heritage for commercial purposes without permission risks cultural exploitation and losing significance.

Mosaic Question: Does your use of cultural heritage honor its origin—or dilute its meaning?

Mosaic in Action: A hospitality group partners with Indigenous communities to craft guest experiences based on local storytelling, with profits invested back into cultural education programs for youth.

Cultural Heterogeneity

Definition: The presence of various cultural backgrounds, identities, and perspectives within a group, organization, or society. Cultural heterogeneity shows variation in language, traditions, beliefs, and lived experiences.

Business Application: Heterogeneous teams have greater potential for creativity and innovation because they draw from a wider range of viewpoints. However, they require intentional facilitation to navigate differences and prevent miscommunication.

Leadership Insight: Leaders who embrace cultural diversity foster inclusive decision-making processes that view diversity as a competitive strength rather than a management obstacle.

Cultural Caution: Diversity without inclusion can lead to tension or alienation. Heterogeneity needs to be paired with fair structures for participation and influence.

Mosaic Question: Do you view cultural diversity in your environment as a challenge or as an asset?

Mosaic in Action: A product development team from five different countries creates a globally successful app by incorporating feedback from various cultural markets during the design phase.

Cultural Heuristics

Definition: Cognitive shortcuts or mental rules of thumb shaped by cultural norms, values, and experiences that influence how people interpret information, make decisions, and solve problems. These heuristics are learned through socialization and often operate unconsciously.

Business Application: Understanding cultural heuristics helps organizations design products, communications, and policies that match how different groups process information and evaluate risk. This insight is especially useful in marketing, customer service, and cross-cultural negotiations.

Leadership Insight: Leaders who understand cultural heuristics can predict decision-making patterns in diverse teams and adjust processes to overcome differences. They also recognize when their own heuristics might restrict perspectives or cause bias.

Cultural Caution: Heuristics can be effective, but they might also reinforce stereotypes or overlooked biases if not examined. Cross-cultural work requires verifying assumptions before taking action.

Mosaic Question: How could your decision-making habits be influenced by cultural shortcuts you haven't yet questioned?

Mosaic in Action: A U.S.-based manager discovers that in a partner culture, avoiding direct refusals helps maintain harmony. She adjusts contract discussions to interpret indirect signals of disagreement, avoiding misunderstandings.

Cultural Homogeneity

Definition: The condition of a group, organization, or society where members share similar cultural backgrounds, values, and practices, leading to a high level of consistency in norms and behaviors.

Business Application: While cultural homogeneity can enable smoother communication and quicker consensus, it may also restrict creativity, adaptability, and the ability to serve diverse markets. Recognizing when homogeneity is beneficial and when it poses a risk is crucial for strategy.

Leadership Insight: Leaders in uniform environments must intentionally seek outside perspectives to prevent insular thinking and blind spots that can impede innovation and responsiveness.

Cultural Caution: Overvaluing homogeneity can sustain exclusionary practices, deepen bias, and undermine resilience in changing settings.

Mosaic Question: Is cultural sameness in your organization aiding your focus or limiting your perspective?

Mosaic in Action: A family-owned business with a long history of hiring exclusively from the local community starts bringing in talent from other regions, sparking new approaches to marketing and operations.

Cultural Humility

Definition: A lifelong commitment to self-evaluation, self-critique, and openness to learning from others about their cultural experiences. Cultural humility emphasizes curiosity, respect, and an awareness of power imbalances, rather than assuming expertise based solely on knowledge acquisition.

Business Application: Cultural humility in leadership builds stronger relationships with clients, employees, and communities by emphasizing listening, co-creation, and shared authority. It is especially important in healthcare, education, and international development.

Leadership Insight: Unlike cultural competence, which can suggest mastery, cultural humility recognizes that fully understanding another's experience is never attainable. Leaders who demonstrate humility foster psychological safety for ongoing dialogue and development.

Cultural Caution: Humility without action can lead to passivity. It needs to be combined with concrete steps to address inequalities and change systems.

Mosaic Question: How often do you set aside your expertise to learn directly from those you serve or lead?

Mosaic in Action: A hospital administrator invites community health workers to collaborate on designing patient care protocols, incorporating local cultural practices into treatment plans to enhance trust and outcomes.

Cultural Imposition

Definition: The act of imposing the norms, values, beliefs, or practices of one culture onto another, often ignoring or undermining the traditions and autonomy of the recipient culture. Cultural imposition can be obvious, like through laws or policies, or subtle, through institutional norms and "best practices" presented as universal.

Business Application: In global operations, cultural imposition can happen when headquarters enforces policies or workflows that reflect the preferences of the dominant culture without adjusting them to fit local contexts. This can lead to employee disengagement, low adoption rates, or damage to reputation.

Leadership Insight: Leaders dedicated to equity assess whether their strategic choices unintentionally reflect dominant cultural norms. They build systems for collaborative design and local tailoring to promote shared ownership.

Cultural Caution: Even well-meaning "standardization" can wipe out valuable local practices and knowledge, undermining trust and sustainability.

Mosaic Question: Are your systems supporting local culture or replacing it?

Mosaic in Action: A nonprofit revises its international program guidelines after discovering that its mandatory meeting schedule conflicts with community religious observances, making adjustments to respect local customs.

Cultural Inclusivity

Definition: An intentional and ongoing effort to create environments where people of all cultural backgrounds feel valued, respected, and able to participate fully. Cultural inclusivity involves adjusting structures, policies, and practices to reflect and address diverse needs.

Business Application: Inclusive organizations enhance talent retention, broaden market reach, and promote innovation by removing barriers to participation and integrating equity into decision-making processes.

Leadership Insight: Leaders who practice cultural inclusivity go beyond just representation; they create feedback loops, measure inclusion outcomes, and address systemic inequities that affect participation and belonging.

Cultural Caution: Inclusivity without accountability can be just surface-level actions. True inclusivity demands structural change, not only celebratory gestures.

Mosaic Question: Does your inclusion strategy foster genuine belonging or merely showcase visible diversity?

Mosaic in Action: A media company forms an inclusion review board with members from diverse cultural backgrounds to evaluate scripts and campaigns, leading to increased audience engagement and fewer mistakes.

Cultural Intelligence (CQ)

Definition: The ability to connect with and work effectively across different cultures by combining cognitive, motivational, and behavioral skills. Cultural intelligence involves understanding cultural norms, handling uncertainty, and adjusting communication and leadership styles to fit various contexts.

Business Application: High CQ is linked to improved performance in international assignments, global negotiations, and multicultural team leadership. Organizations can evaluate and enhance CQ through training, mentorship, and experiential learning.

Leadership Insight: Leaders with high CQ anticipate cultural dynamics before they turn into challenges, using diversity as a strategic strength instead of a complication.

Cultural Caution: High CQ can be diminished by overconfidence— believing that success in one cultural setting guarantees success in another.

Mosaic Question: Do you approach new cultural contexts with open adaptability or with assumptions?

Mosaic in Action: A global project lead rotates team members through regional offices to gain firsthand experience and boost CQ, enhancing collaboration and problem-solving across time zones.

Cultural Intersectionality

Definition: The interconnected and overlapping aspects of cultural identities—such as ethnicity, language, religion, nationality, and heritage—and how these intersections influence individual experiences, opportunities, and challenges within social systems.

Business Application: Applying an intersectional lens to culture enables organizations to develop more nuanced policies and programs. For instance, recruitment efforts that consider cultural intersectionality may reveal barriers unique to individuals with multiple marginalized identities.

Leadership Insight: Leaders who understand cultural intersectionality see that experiences of inclusion or exclusion vary, even within the same cultural group. They use this understanding to avoid one-size-fits-all strategies.

Cultural Caution: Failing to consider intersectionality can make inclusion efforts ineffective or even harmful, as they might only address the needs of the most visible subgroup.

Mosaic Question: How do intersecting cultural identities influence how people experience your organization?

Mosaic in Action: An education nonprofit refines its scholarship program after recognizing that first-generation immigrant women encounter unique cultural and economic barriers compared to their male counterparts, resulting in more targeted support.

Cultural Legitimacy

Definition: The recognition and validation of a culture's practices, narratives, and authority by influential institutions, communities, or audiences— often determining which cultural expressions are considered credible, valuable, or worth preserving.

Business Application: In media, education, and policy, cultural legitimacy shapes which voices are highlighted and which contributions are ignored. Organizations can build cultural legitimacy by promoting marginalized perspectives and challenging limited standards of authority.

Leadership Insight: Leaders who deliberately expand cultural legitimacy help break down gatekeeping systems that have traditionally excluded specific groups. This work often involves confronting established power structures.

Cultural Caution: Cultural legitimacy is often linked to dominant culture standards, meaning that gaining "recognition" may require conformity instead of authenticity. Leaders should be careful not to reinforce this pattern.

Mosaic Question: Whose culture is validated in your sphere—and who makes that call?

Mosaic in Action: A national arts festival uses a community-led jury to choose featured performances, making sure local cultural forms get equal recognition along with globally recognized genres.

Cultural Literacy

Definition: The ability to understand, interpret, and engage meaningfully with cultural references, norms, values, and communication styles. Cultural literacy includes both knowledge of one's own culture and awareness of others.

Business Application: High cultural literacy improves marketing, negotiation, and team collaboration by reducing miscommunication and encouraging respectful engagement across cultural differences. It also helps organizations respond effectively to cultural events and social movements.

Leadership Insight: Leaders with cultural literacy can read between the lines—understanding subtext, symbolism, and context in diverse environments. This ability enhances decision-making and relationship-building.

Cultural Caution: Superficial familiarity with a culture can lead to overconfidence and mistakes. Cultural literacy should be combined with humility and a willingness to learn.

Mosaic Question: Do you genuinely understand the cultural signals around you — or just recognize them?

Mosaic in Action: A global HR director updates onboarding materials after recognizing that certain idioms and humor in the original text were confusing to international staff, replacing them with culturally neutral language.

Cultural Mapping

Definition: The process of identifying, documenting, and analyzing both tangible and intangible cultural resources of a community, organization, or region. Cultural mapping can uncover heritage assets, identity markers, and patterns of cultural engagement.

Business Application: Organizations use cultural mapping to guide urban planning, tourism strategies, and community development initiatives. By engaging local stakeholders, they make sure the map reflects lived experiences instead of outsider assumptions.

Leadership Insight: Leaders who adopt cultural mapping view it as both a tool for gathering data and building relationships. The process can strengthen trust while guiding strategic decisions.

Cultural Caution: Mapping without community consent can result in cultural exploitation, especially if the information is used for commercial purposes without fair benefit sharing.

Mosaic Question: Whose cultural assets are you mapping, and for whom are they intended?

Mosaic in Action: A regional development agency partners with local elders and youth to create an interactive cultural map, which becomes both a planning resource and an educational tool for schools.

Cultural Memory

Definition: The shared memory of a community's history—maintained through stories, rituals, art, monuments, and traditions—that shapes collective identity and influences current values.

Business Application: Organizations can utilize cultural memory to establish brand authenticity, develop meaningful community partnerships, or design programs that connect with local identity. Respecting and incorporating cultural memory ensures that initiatives are relevant and well-received.

Leadership Insight: Leaders who engage with cultural memory recognize its influence in shaping resilience, belonging, and intergenerational ties. They create safe spaces where memory can be expressed and passed down.

Cultural Caution: Misusing or selectively presenting cultural memory for political or commercial gain can harm trust and continue historical trauma.

Mosaic Question: How does your past memory influence your current relationships with the community?

Mosaic in Action: A city museum works with neighborhood residents to create an exhibit on local civil rights history, making sure that firsthand accounts shape the story.

Cultural Narratives

Definition: The shared stories, myths, and interpretations that a community or society uses to explain its values, history, and identity. Cultural narratives shape collective memory, influence

behavior, and determine which voices and events are remembered or forgotten.

Business Application: In branding, leadership communication, and policy development, understanding dominant and countercultural narratives helps organizations craft messages that resonate authentically while highlighting underrepresented perspectives.

Leadership Insight: Leaders who critically engage with cultural narratives can reshape them to be more inclusive, challenging stories that exclude or stereotype marginalized groups.

Cultural Caution: Narratives can be powerful tools for unity, but they also risk perpetuating bias or erasing complex truths if oversimplified or controlled by a narrow group.

Mosaic Question: Whose stories shape your organization's narrative—and whose are missing?

Mosaic in Action: A university updates its campus tours to include the history of Indigenous stewardship of the land, reframing the institution's origin story to honor voices that were previously excluded.

Cultural Navigation

Definition: The ability to navigate different cultural settings effectively by understanding norms, building trust, and adjusting strategies while staying true to personal integrity.

Business Application: Cultural navigation is crucial for leaders managing international teams, entering new markets, or mediating between different community groups. It blends emotional intelligence, active listening, and strategic flexibility.

Leadership Insight: Culturally skilled leaders recognize differences in decision-making, hierarchy, and communication styles, and they adapt their approach to foster mutual understanding.

Cultural Caution: Overemphasizing adaptation at the expense of authenticity may cause perceptions of insincerity or opportunism.

Mosaic Question: Do you navigate cultures by blending in—or by building genuine connection?

Mosaic in Action: A project director at a humanitarian NGO adjusts her leadership style in each country office, balancing direct task management in some cases with relationship-first approaches in others.

Cultural Norms

Definition: The shared expectations, rules, and standards that guide behavior within a cultural group. These norms influence communication styles, decision-making processes, and social etiquette.

Business Application: Awareness of cultural norms helps organizations avoid unintentional offense, improve negotiation outcomes, and strengthen global partnerships. It is essential in onboarding, training, and policy development.

Leadership Insight: Leaders who understand cultural norms can better interpret behaviors and avoid misjudging competence or intent. They also know when to respectfully challenge norms that conflict with equity or inclusion goals.

Cultural Caution: Norms are not fixed—they change over time and can differ within the same cultural group. Assuming they are uniform risks stereotyping and oversimplifying.

Mosaic Question: Which cultural norms in your environment promote inclusion—and which should be reconsidered?

Mosaic in Action: A global sales team adjusts meeting times to honor cultural norms around religious observances, boosting participation and morale.

Cultural Ownership

Definition: The right of a community or group to control how its cultural knowledge, symbols, and practices are used, represented, and shared. Cultural ownership includes decision-making authority over intellectual property, interpretation, and benefit sharing.

Business Application: In industries like fashion, media, and tourism, respecting cultural ownership helps prevent exploitation and builds genuine partnerships. This can include licensing agreements, joint ventures, or community-led content creation.

Leadership Insight: Leaders who respect cultural ownership see it as both an ethical duty and a strategic edge, fostering long-term trust with cultural stakeholders.

Cultural Caution: Ignoring cultural ownership can lead to reputational harm, legal issues, or the loss of important relationships.

Mosaic Question: Are you using cultural elements with permission or just with access?

Mosaic in Action: A design firm partners with a tribal council to create a product line featuring traditional motifs, ensuring profits are shared and designs are approved by cultural representatives.

Cultural Permission

Definition: The explicit or implicit consent given by a cultural group or its recognized representatives to share, adapt, or use its cultural expressions, knowledge, or symbols. Cultural permission ensures that engaging with a culture is respectful, ethical, and mutually beneficial.

Business Application: In industries such as marketing, publishing, and product design, gaining cultural permission helps prevent appropriation and boosts credibility. This may include formal agreements, licensing arrangements, or community-led approval processes.

Leadership Insight: Ethical leaders see cultural permission as a way to build relationships, not as a bureaucratic obstacle. Asking for permission shows respect, builds trust, and creates opportunities for genuine collaboration.

Cultural Caution: Assuming permission from an individual or subgroup can cause conflict if they are not recognized by the community as having the authority to grant it.

Mosaic Question: Do you truly have permission to use cultural elements, or do you just have convenient access?

Mosaic in Action: A documentary filmmaker collaborates with a Māori council to obtain permission to film sacred rituals, agreeing to cultural guidelines on what can be shown and how the footage will be used.

Cultural Preservation

Definition: The active effort to protect and sustain a culture's language, traditions, artifacts, and practices so they can be handed down to future generations. Preservation can be led by the community or supported by institutions.

Business Application: Organizations involved in heritage tourism, education, and the arts can collaborate with cultural communities to develop preservation initiatives that also generate economic benefits— such as cultural festivals, archival projects, or language revitalization programs.

Leadership Insight: Leaders who invest in cultural preservation understand that protecting heritage enhances identity, community strength, and intergenerational continuity.

Cultural Caution: Preservation should prevent culture from becoming rigid, letting it evolve organically within its community.

Mosaic Question: Are you maintaining culture as an active part of life—or as a fixed display?

Mosaic in Action: A community center starts an oral history project to record elders' stories, making sure they are preserved for future generations while inspiring current cultural activities.

Cultural Proficiency

Definition: The highest level of cultural capability, where individuals and organizations not only understand and respect cultural differences but also actively incorporate cultural knowledge into leadership, decision-making, and policy to promote equity and excellence.

Business Application: Culturally proficient organizations design systems, services, and products with diverse communities—not just for them—ensuring that inclusion is integrated into every stage of development.

Leadership Insight: Cultural proficiency demands ongoing learning, advocacy, and responsibility. Leaders demonstrate it by shaping policy, influencing organizational culture, and promoting systemic change.

Cultural Caution: Claiming proficiency without proof of impact can damage trust. Proficiency must be shown through measurable actions, not just self-declaration.

Mosaic Question: Does your organization's cultural capability stop at awareness or go beyond to transformation?

Mosaic in Action: A school district moves from isolated diversity workshops to integrating culturally responsive teaching into curriculum development, hiring practices, and community involvement.

Cultural Relativism

Definition: The principle that a culture's beliefs, practices, and values should be understood within that culture's own standards, rather than judged by the norms of another culture.

Business Application: In international business, cultural relativism aids leaders in understanding behaviors and decisions without letting their own cultural biases influence them. This approach can enhance negotiation success, conflict resolution, and international partnerships.

Leadership Insight: Cultural relativism promotes humility by encouraging leaders to understand the "why" behind practices before assuming they need to be changed.

Cultural Caution: Relativism is not moral absolution—leaders must balance cultural respect with universal human rights and ethical standards.

Mosaic Question: Do you aim to understand a culture on its own terms before deciding how to respond?

Mosaic in Action: An NGO developing health programs in rural communities consults local healers to incorporate traditional practices into medical outreach, ensuring cultural acceptance and program success.

Cultural Representation

Definition: The depiction and inclusion of different cultural groups, identities, and experiences in media, policies, organizational leadership, and public conversations. Cultural representation influences how groups are viewed by others and how they view themselves.

Business Application:
In marketing, publishing, entertainment, and leadership pipelines, accurate and diverse representation can expand reach, build brand trust, and promote social equity. Representation choices impact hiring, storytelling, and customer engagement strategies.

Leadership Insight: Leaders dedicated to cultural representation ensure portrayals are authentic, multidimensional, and community-informed, advancing beyond tokenism toward true inclusion.

Cultural Caution:
Misrepresentation or underrepresentation can reinforce stereotypes, invisibility, and cultural erasure. Representation should be accompanied by access to decision-making power.

Mosaic Question: Who embodies your organization's values and audiences — and who makes the decisions?

Mosaic in Action: A streaming service partners with Indigenous filmmakers to create original content, keeping creative control in the hands of the storytellers.

Cultural Responsiveness

Definition: The ability to recognize, understand, and adapt to the cultural needs, preferences, and values of individuals and groups in real time, ensuring interactions and services are relevant and respectful.

Business Application: In healthcare, education, customer service, and product design, cultural responsiveness enhances engagement, satisfaction, and outcomes by aligning approaches with the lived experiences of diverse populations.

Leadership Insight: Culturally responsive leaders listen carefully, adapt strategies swiftly, and create systems that proactively address diversity instead of just reacting to it.

Cultural Caution: Responsiveness without structural change risks remaining temporary rather than becoming systemic. Leaders must integrate responsiveness into policies, training, and operations.

Mosaic Question: Do you adapt to cultural needs only when prompted, or do you do so proactively?

Mosaic in Action: A hospital updates meal services after patient feedback exposes the lack of culturally appropriate food options, boosting satisfaction and recovery outcomes.

Cultural Retention

Definition: The ongoing practice and preservation of cultural traditions, languages, values, and knowledge within individuals or communities, especially in contexts of migration, globalization, or assimilation pressures.

Business Application: Organizations serving multicultural communities can strengthen relationships by supporting cultural retention—such as providing bilingual services or creating spaces for traditional practices.

Leadership Insight: Leaders who promote cultural retention recognize that preserving cultural identity can boost well-being, resilience, and creativity. They foster environments where authenticity is celebrated.

Cultural Caution: Retention efforts must be community-driven; imposing which elements "should" be retained risks undermining cultural agency.

Mosaic Question: How does your work support people in preserving their culture without compromise?

Mosaic in Action: A corporation sponsors employee resource groups that host cultural events, enabling

staff to share traditions while promoting organizational learning.

Cultural Revitalization

Definition: The deliberate effort to restore and revitalize cultural practices, languages, and traditions that have been weakened or disrupted by colonization, displacement, or assimilation.

Business Application: Organizations can promote revitalization through funding, partnerships, and infrastructure—such as language immersion programs, artisan cooperatives, or heritage festivals—that emphasize community leadership.

Leadership Insight: Leaders involved in cultural revitalization respect community authority and focus on building capacity so that cultural practices can sustain themselves over time.

Cultural Caution: Revitalization efforts should avoid romanticizing the past or ignoring current cultural expressions that show natural growth.

Mosaic Question: Are you helping revive culture in a way that sustains it for future generations?

Mosaic in Action: An education nonprofit collaborates with tribal elders to create a digital archive of oral histories and traditional songs, incorporating them into school curricula to promote cultural pride and preserve language.

Cultural Rituals

Definition: Symbolic actions or ceremonies, often performed in a prescribed way, that express and reinforce the values, beliefs, and identity of a cultural group. Cultural rituals can be religious, seasonal, communal, or personal, serving both social and spiritual purposes.

Business Application:
In organizational settings, understanding and respecting cultural rituals—such as holidays, life events, or rites of passage—can boost employee engagement, customer loyalty, and community ties. This involves adjusting schedules, policies, or communications to honor these traditions.

Leadership Insight: Leaders who recognize and incorporate cultural rituals into the workplace show respect for diversity and promote a sense of belonging.

Cultural Caution:
Commercializing or modifying sacred rituals for marketing or entertainment can offend people and damage trust.

Mosaic Question: Do you create space for cultural rituals in ways that honor their significance?

Mosaic in Action: A company with a large Muslim workforce adjusts meeting times during Ramadan and hosts an optional Iftar gathering, promoting inclusivity and team bonding.

Cultural Safety

Definition: An environment where individuals feel respected, valued, and able to express their cultural identity without fear of discrimination, marginalization, or harm. Cultural safety goes beyond tolerance by actively addressing power imbalances and systemic inequities.

Business Application: In healthcare, education, and service delivery, cultural safety guarantees that policies and practices enable clients or employees from diverse backgrounds to participate fully and confidently.

Leadership Insight: Leaders who promote cultural safety invest in building trust, reviewing policies, and implementing accountability measures that tackle both interpersonal and structural barriers.

Cultural Caution: A space might seem welcoming but still be unsafe if hidden biases, microaggressions, or inequities are left unaddressed.

Mosaic Question: Is your environment safe for people to fully express their cultural selves— or only the parts that conform?

Mosaic in Action: A university implements a reporting system for cultural bias incidents, combined with restorative dialogue sessions to ensure safety is actually maintained, not just promised.

Cultural Scripts

Definition: Implicit, culturally specific rules that guide how people communicate, behave, and interpret social interactions. These scripts affect everything from greetings and conflict resolution to expressions of emotion.

Business Application: Understanding cultural scripts helps organizations prevent miscommunication in global teams and develop marketing that genuinely connects with target audiences.

Leadership Insight: Leaders who understand cultural scripts can tailor their messages and methods to ensure clarity and respect, particularly in cross-cultural negotiations or managing diverse teams.

Cultural Caution: Assuming everyone follows the same script can cause misunderstandings or unintentional offense, especially in multicultural settings.

Mosaic Question: What unspoken cultural scripts influence your interactions—and how do they compare to others'?

Mosaic in Action: An American manager learns that in a partner culture, declining an invitation indirectly is a politeness script. She adjusts her interpretation of "maybe" responses to prevent misreading them as indecision.

Cultural Signaling

Definition: The conscious or unconscious use of symbols, language, behaviors, or affiliations to express one's cultural identity, values, or group membership to others. Cultural signaling can reinforce belonging, demonstrate alignment, or show solidarity.

Business Application: Brands and leaders use cultural signaling— through imagery, language choice, or event participation—to connect with specific audiences. Effective signaling builds trust, while misaligned or inauthentic signals can harm credibility.

Leadership Insight: Leaders need to ensure that cultural signals are genuine, supported by actions and commitments that align with the values they express.

Cultural Caution: Performative signaling—where messages aren't backed by action—can cause backlash and erode trust.

Mosaic Question: Does your cultural signaling truly reflect your commitments, or just the image you want to project?

Mosaic in Action: A company publicly celebrates Pride Month while also offering year-round benefits and policies that support LGBTQ+ employees, ensuring its actions align with its values.

Cultural Sovereignty

Definition: The inherent right of a cultural group—especially Indigenous or historically marginalized communities—to govern, protect, and control its own cultural knowledge, language, traditions, and resources without outside interference.

Business Application: In areas like education, tourism, and intellectual property, honoring cultural sovereignty involves securing formal agreements, respecting self-determination, and making sure communities control how their heritage is shared or represented.

Leadership Insight: Leaders who uphold cultural sovereignty recognize that genuine partnerships involve sharing power, distributing benefits fairly, and committing for the long term.

Cultural Caution: Ignoring cultural sovereignty can sustain colonial patterns, leading to exploitation, mistrust, and damage to reputation.

Mosaic Question: Are your cultural collaborations based on partnership—or on control?

Mosaic in Action: An environmental nonprofit collaborates with a tribal council to restore a sacred river, ensuring the community itself sets both cultural and ecological priorities.

Cultural Stewardship

Definition: The responsible care, preservation, and transmission of cultural heritage—both tangible and intangible—so that it remains meaningful and accessible to future generations.

Business Application: Organizations involved in cultural stewardship may operate museums, archives, festivals, or digital repositories, ensuring that cultural materials are protected and interpreted with integrity.

Leadership Insight: Effective cultural stewardship balances preserving traditions with fostering cultural vitality, allowing traditions to evolve while maintaining their core meaning.

Cultural Caution: Stewardship without community involvement can lead to paternalism, taking away communities' control over their own heritage.

Mosaic Question: Whose culture are you guiding—and are they guiding the process?

Mosaic in Action: A regional arts council supports community-led documentation of traditional music, making sure recordings and ownership stay with local artists.

Cultural Sustainability

Definition: The practice of keeping cultural traditions, expressions, and systems lively, flexible, and meaningful over time, even amid social, economic, and environmental shifts.

Business Application: Cultural sustainability can be incorporated into corporate social responsibility initiatives, urban development projects, and education programs to ensure that economic growth does not erase cultural identity.

Leadership Insight: Leaders promoting cultural sustainability

invest in both preservation and innovation—supporting cultural expression as a dynamic, evolving resource.

Cultural Caution: Focusing only on preservation without permitting adaptation can hinder cultural growth and alienate younger generations.

Mosaic Question: Does your work support culture as a vibrant, ongoing force—or does it trap it in the past?

Mosaic in Action: A coastal city integrates traditional fishing practices into modern marine management policies, preserving both livelihoods and heritage.

Cultural Symbolism

Definition: The use of objects, colors, gestures, or imagery to express cultural meanings, values, or beliefs. Cultural symbolism often reflects deep historical and emotional importance, varying across and within cultures.

Business Application: Brands and organizations use cultural symbolism in logos, campaigns, and events to connect with target audiences—though improper use can cause cultural misrepresentation or offense.

Leadership Insight: Leaders who responsibly engage with

cultural symbolism ensure that symbols are used in ways that honor their origins and meanings, often through consulting cultural custodians.

Cultural Caution: Symbols can carry different meanings in various cultures; misuse may harm relationships or unwittingly convey conflicting values.

Mosaic Question: Do the symbols you use match the values you want to communicate?

Mosaic in Action: An apparel company collaborates with Indigenous artists to include traditional patterns in its designs, ensuring proper representation and direct financial support for the artists.

Cultural Trauma

Definition: The collective emotional and psychological harm experienced by a cultural group due to systemic oppression, displacement, violence, colonization, or other events that threaten its survival or identity. Cultural trauma is passed down through generations, shaping beliefs, behaviors, and community well-being.

Business Application: In sectors like healthcare, education, and community development,

understanding cultural trauma helps design programs that address current needs and historical harm. Trauma-informed approaches enhance trust, participation, and outcomes.

Leadership Insight: Leaders who recognize cultural trauma foster healing, resilience, and restoration in their engagement strategies. They avoid dismissing historical context as irrelevant to current performance or relationships.

Cultural Caution: Ignoring cultural trauma can cause ongoing harm, especially when policies or messages dismiss the validity of lived experiences.

Mosaic Question: Do your policies recognize the histories that influence people's realities today?

Mosaic in Action: A school district incorporates Indigenous history and perspectives into its curriculum, alongside community-led healing circles to address the intergenerational impacts of boarding school systems.

Cultural Translation

Definition: The process of adapting ideas, messages, or content from one culture to another in a way that maintains meaning, relevance, and emotional impact, rather than just translating words literally.

Business Application: In global marketing, diplomacy, and product design, cultural translation ensures that communications align with local values, humor, symbolism, and social norms. This minimizes misunderstandings and enhances impact.

Leadership Insight: Leaders who prioritize cultural translation invest in expertise that surpasses linguistic fluency—understanding that meaning relies on cultural context and lived experience.

Cultural Caution: Literal translation without cultural adjustment can distort meaning or lead to offense, damaging trust and credibility.

Mosaic Question: Are your cross-cultural messages understood as you intend—or only as you phrase them?

Mosaic in Action: A nonprofit adjusts its environmental conservation campaign for multiple countries by customizing slogans and imagery to reflect local cultural symbols and priorities.

Cultural Translator

Definition:: A person who bridges cultural gaps by interpreting meanings, behaviors, and values across groups to promote mutual understanding.

Business Application: Cultural translators help worldwide organizations prevent expensive mistakes by adapting communication to connect with diverse teams.

Leadership Insight:: Leaders who recognize and empower cultural translators lessen conflict, speed up collaboration, and broaden inclusion.

Cultural Caution:: Translators should not be overburdened as token representatives; their role demands recognition and shared responsibility.

Mosaic Question:: Who on your team quietly navigates differences—and how can you support their efforts?

Mosaic in Action:: In a multinational project, a bilingual team member rephrases a leader's directive that came across as harsh in translation. By adjusting tone and context, she rebuilds trust and ensures the project stays on track.

Cultural Validity

Definition: The extent to which a practice, policy, program, or assessment accurately reflects and respects the values, norms, and lived experiences of the cultural group it aims to serve. Cultural validity ensures that interventions are relevant and meaningful to the target community.

Business Application: In research, education, and program design, applying cultural validity helps prevent the use of metrics or frameworks that misrepresent or marginalize certain groups. It enhances accuracy, trust, and adoption.

Leadership Insight: Leaders dedicated to cultural validity involve community input during the design process and make sure evaluation measures align with culturally grounded definitions of success.

Cultural Caution: Using "universal" standards without cultural adaptation can undermine experiences and exclude important voices from decision-making.

Mosaic Question: Whose standards determine success in your work—and are they culturally appropriate?

Mosaic in Action: An education board updates its student assessment tools after community consultations show that current measures undervalue bilingual skills and culturally specific problem-solving abilities.

Cultural Wealth

Definition: The collection of cultural knowledge, skills, relationships, traditions, and resilience strategies that individuals and communities possess—often developed in response to systemic marginalization. The concept redefines culture as a source of strength and capital instead of a deficiency.

Business Application: Recognizing and leveraging cultural wealth in hiring, leadership development, and community partnerships can unlock innovation, expand networks, and boost organizational adaptability.

Leadership Insight: Leaders who recognize cultural wealth shift the narrative from "helping disadvantaged groups" to collaborating on opportunities that appreciate what these groups already contribute.

Cultural Caution: Recognizing cultural wealth by tokenizing it—without establishing systems to utilize and reward it—can seem exploitative.

Mosaic Question: Do you view cultural differences as an asset to leverage or as a gap to address?

Mosaic in Action: A startup speeds up its entry into immigrant communities by partnering with local entrepreneurs whose cultural ties and bilingual abilities help build trust-based customer channels.

Culture Add

Definition: A recruitment and organizational development approach that focuses on candidates whose unique backgrounds, perspectives, and experiences will help grow and enhance the organization's culture—rather than simply matching existing norms ("culture fit").

Business Application: Hiring for culture add encourages innovation, decreases groupthink, and boosts adaptability by including voices that challenge assumptions and expand problem-solving strategies. It is especially valuable for organizations aiming to grow or enter new markets.

Leadership Insight: Leaders who embrace culture intentionally create space for diversity and develop systems that incorporate new perspectives into decision-making, rather than expecting assimilation.

Cultural Caution: If onboarding systems lack inclusivity, culture add hires might feel forced to conform, which undermines the value of their unique contributions.

Mosaic Question: Does your hiring process grow your culture or keep it the same?

Mosaic in Action: A tech company hires a community organizer with extensive grassroots experience to help create an outreach plan for underserved markets, resulting in a successful new customer segment.

Culture Fit

Definition: The alignment between a candidate's values, behaviors, and work style and those of the existing organizational culture. Historically, culture fit has been used to select individuals who seamlessly integrate into current norms and practices.

Business Application: When thoughtfully defined, culture fit can promote cohesion and decrease friction within teams. However, if used too narrowly, it can unintentionally reinforce biases and restrict diversity.

Leadership Insight: Leaders should redefine culture fit as alignment with mission and values—not as similarity in background, personality, or worldview.

Cultural Caution: Overemphasizing "fit" can

lead to homogeneity, exclude nontraditional talent, and reinforce inequalities.

Mosaic Question: Are you hiring to ensure alignment with values or to promote comfort with sameness?

Mosaic in Action: A nonprofit adjusts its interview process to emphasize alignment with its equity mission instead of personal rapport, leading to more diverse and mission-focused hires.

Culture of Belonging

Definition: An organizational environment where everyone feels accepted, respected, and valued for who they truly are, with equal opportunities to contribute and influence results.

Business Application: A culture of belonging boosts retention, engagement, and performance by promoting psychological safety and connection across teams. This involves policies, leadership actions, and daily practices that focus on inclusion.

Leadership Insight: Leaders foster belonging by actively confronting bias, promoting open dialogue, and acknowledging contributions from everyone—not just those who align with dominant norms.

Cultural Caution: Belonging should not be confused with

conformity; genuine belonging embraces individuality and dissent within a shared purpose.

Mosaic Question: Do people in your organization feel they belong because they can be themselves—or because they've learned to blend in?

Mosaic in Action: A global company implements mentorship programs that pair employees across regions and levels, fostering cross-cultural connections and strengthening a sense of belonging.

Culture of Care

Definition: An organizational ethos that prioritizes the well-being, dignity, and humanity of employees, clients, and communities alongside performance and productivity.

Business Application: A culture of care manifests in policies like flexible scheduling, mental health support, equitable pay, and transparent communication. It boosts loyalty, prevents burnout, and improves reputation.

Leadership Insight: Leaders demonstrate a culture of care by showing empathy, listening attentively, and making decisions that balance results with human needs.

Cultural Caution: Care must be systemic, not situational—sporadic acts of kindness cannot replace structural policies that support well-being.

Mosaic Question: Is care in your organization practiced consistently or is it just an occasional gesture?

Mosaic in Action: An education nonprofit offers paid sabbaticals for long-term staff, lowering turnover and encouraging renewed energy and innovation.

Culture of Compliance

Definition: An organizational environment that emphasizes following rules, regulations, and established procedures—mainly to ensure legal, ethical, and operational integrity. While crucial for managing risk, a culture of compliance can be empowering or restrictive depending on how it is applied.

Business Application: In regulated industries like finance, healthcare, or manufacturing, a strong compliance culture reduces legal risks and builds trust with stakeholders. It involves clear policies, consistent enforcement, and training that links compliance to organizational values.

Leadership Insight: Effective leaders balance compliance with innovation, ensuring that rules protect integrity without stifling adaptability or creativity.

Cultural Caution: When compliance is overly strict and punitive, it can discourage initiative, lower morale, and promote a "check-the-box" mentality.

Mosaic Question: Does compliance in your organization safeguard integrity—or hinder progress?

Mosaic in Action: A pharmaceutical company redefines compliance training to focus on patient safety outcomes, transforming it from a bureaucratic duty into a purpose-driven commitment.

Culture of Excellence

Definition: An organizational ethos that emphasizes high standards, ongoing improvement, and outstanding performance at all levels of work. In a healthy form, it fosters pride, innovation, and long-term success.

Business Application: A culture of excellence fosters quality assurance, customer satisfaction, and competitive advantage. It succeeds when high expectations are met with resources, recognition, and opportunities for growth.

Leadership Insight: Leaders promote excellence by establishing clear benchmarks, demonstrating accountability, and celebrating milestones without instilling a fear of failure.

Cultural Caution: If not carefully managed, a culture of excellence can turn into perfectionism, leading to burnout and discouraging calculated risk-taking.

Mosaic Question: Does your drive for excellence motivate people—or wear them out?

Mosaic in Action: A software company launches a "fail forward" initiative, encouraging teams to share lessons from unsuccessful experiments as part of their journey toward innovation.

Culture of Fear

Definition: An organizational climate where employees feel unsafe to voice concerns, take risks, or challenge decisions because of fear of negative consequences like retaliation, exclusion, or harm to their careers.

Business Application: A culture of fear weakens innovation, damages trust, and raises turnover. Identifying its causes—such as punitive leadership, opaque decision-making, or lack of psychological safety—is crucial for organizational health.

Leadership Insight: Leaders should replace fear-driven control with trust-based accountability, making sure concerns are heard and addressed without punishment.

Cultural Caution: Fear might produce immediate compliance, but it damages engagement, creativity, and long-term loyalty.

Mosaic Question: Are people silent in your organization because they're aligned—or because they're afraid?

Mosaic in Action: A manufacturing plant reduces high turnover rates by replacing authoritarian supervision with collaborative problem-solving teams, boosting morale and productivity.

Culture of Feedback

Definition: An organizational environment where open, constructive feedback is encouraged, valued, and acted upon as a driver of growth, collaboration, and continuous improvement.

Business Application: A strong culture of feedback enhances performance, builds relationships, and speeds up professional growth.

It needs clear guidelines, effective facilitation, and leaders who demonstrate receptivity.

Leadership Insight: Leaders in a feedback-rich culture view feedback as a two-way conversation, welcoming critique of their own performance just as much as they give it to others.

Cultural Caution: Feedback without follow-up can weaken trust; feedback given without skill can lead to defensiveness or damage.

Mosaic Question: Is feedback in your organization a tool for growth or just a compliance task?

Mosaic in Action: A retail chain conducts quarterly 360-degree feedback sessions, pairs them with action plans and visible leadership updates to demonstrate responsiveness.

Culture of Innovation

Definition: An organizational climate that actively promotes creativity, experimentation, and the development of new ideas, products, or processes. A culture of innovation recognizes problem-solving and values adaptability when facing change.

Business Application: In competitive markets, a culture of innovation helps organizations to anticipate trends, respond quickly to challenges, and stand out. It often involves cross-functional collaboration, a tolerance for calculated risks, and structures that make experimentation accessible to all staff levels.

Leadership Insight: Leaders promote innovation by creating safe environments for sharing ideas, providing resources for experimentation, and acknowledging contributions regardless of results.

Cultural Caution: Without clear boundaries or strategic alignment, innovation initiatives can become unfocused and resource-draining, failing to produce meaningful results.

Mosaic Question: Do you see innovation as everyone's responsibility—or just the role of specialists?

Mosaic in Action: A logistics company introduces monthly "solution sprints," where employees propose and test process improvements, many of which reduce costs and enhance client satisfaction.

Culture of Learning

Definition: An environment where ongoing growth, knowledge sharing, and skill development are integrated into daily activities. A learning-focused culture values both formal and informal learning as key drivers of organizational success.

Business Application: Organizations with a strong learning culture adapt more quickly to industry changes, retain talent, and develop leadership pipelines. Learning opportunities can include mentoring, training programs, and peer knowledge exchanges.

Leadership Insight: Leaders in a learning culture demonstrate curiosity, admit what they don't know, and view mistakes as learning opportunities rather than failures.

Cultural Caution: A learning environment lacking equitable access to opportunities can strengthen existing hierarchies. Leaders must guarantee inclusion in all development pathways.

Mosaic Question: Is learning in your organization available to everyone—or only a select few?

Mosaic in Action: A global nonprofit runs a "teach-back" program where employees who attend conferences share key insights with the whole organization, multiplying the value of each learning opportunity.

Culture of Safety

Definition: An organizational commitment to prioritize physical, psychological, and cultural safety in every decision and process. A safety culture goes beyond mere compliance to foster an environment where people feel safe to speak up, take action, and care for one another.

Business Application: In healthcare, manufacturing, and education, a strong safety culture lowers accidents, prevents harm, and builds trust with stakeholders. It also encourages accountability and shared responsibility for safety.

Leadership Insight: Leaders foster a safety culture by demonstrating safe practices, encouraging hazard reporting without fear, and embedding safety into planning and performance metrics.

Cultural Caution: If safety is seen as a separate function instead of an integrated value, its effectiveness will be restricted.

Mosaic Question: Does safety in your organization feel like a shared value or just a compliance checklist?

Mosaic in Action: A construction company gives workers the authority to stop work without penalty if they find unsafe conditions, resulting in fewer accidents and greater employee trust.

Culture Shift

Definition: A major change in the shared values, behaviors, and norms of an organization or community. Culture shifts can be intentional—driven by leadership and strategy—or organic, resulting from demographic, technological, or societal changes.

Business Application: Culture shifts are necessary when existing norms hinder innovation, inclusion, or alignment with evolving market demands. Successful shifts require a clear vision, consistent communication, and reinforcement through systems and incentives.

Leadership Insight: Leaders must serve as visible advocates for the desired culture while removing structural obstacles to change.

Cultural Caution: Culture shifts fail when they are superficial or when leadership behavior conflicts with the intended change.

Mosaic Question: Is your culture change supported by both words and actions?

Mosaic in Action: A financial institution transitions from a competitive, siloed culture to a collaborative one by redesigning

performance metrics to incentivize cross-departmental achievements.

Clarity

Definition: The state of being emotionally and mentally clear. Clarity helps leaders make grounded decisions based on alignment instead of reactivity or confusion.

Business Application: In high-pressure environments, clarity helps leaders cut through noise, prioritize effectively, and communicate vision. Organizations that value clarity promote transparent communication, minimize errors, and align teams.

Leadership Insight: Clarity is not about knowing all the answers — it's about identifying what matters most and expressing it clearly. Leaders who demonstrate clarity ease uncertainty and build confidence, even in complex situations.

Cultural Caution: In some cultures, directness is appreciated; in others, clarity must be balanced with relational nuance to prevent seeming blunt or dismissive. Leaders need to adapt their communication to the context.

Mosaic Question: When encountering complexity, do you lean toward providing more information or offering clearer guidance?

Mosaic in Action: A disaster-response leader pauses before giving instructions, channels information into three non-negotiable priorities, and communicates them clearly, helping the team stay focused amid chaos.

Curiosity-Driven Leadership

Definition: A leadership style grounded in genuine inquiry, active listening, and a willingness to learn. Curiosity-driven leaders focus on exploration rather than assumptions, viewing uncertainty as an opportunity instead of a threat.

Business Application: In fast-changing industries, curiosity-driven leadership fosters innovation, identifies hidden opportunities, and builds stronger relationships by showing genuine interest in diverse perspectives.

Leadership Insight: Curiosity-driven leaders ask better questions, challenge the status quo constructively, and foster cultures where discovery is valued as much as decision-making.

Cultural Caution: Curiosity without empathy can seem intrusive or superficial; leaders must make sure questions are respectful and purposeful.

Mosaic Question: Do your questions create possibilities—or just reaffirm what you already believe?

Mosaic in Action: A CEO hosts quarterly "ask me anything" sessions with employees at all levels, using their questions to inform strategy and policy adjustments.

◈ LETTER C CALLOUT

"Culture is the ground beneath every decision; ignore it, and the foundation cracks."

Reflection Questions

- Which cultural assumptions shape how you give or receive feedback?
- How do cultural norms influence leadership styles you admire — or resist?
- What does cultural flexibility look like in your daily interactions?

Practical Move

Review one everyday practice (a hiring process, grading policy, or meeting structure) and ask: Whose culture does this reflect? Who might it unintentionally exclude?

D – Disruption, Disparity, and Dissonance

D is where the air shifts. What once felt smooth becomes fractured; what was politely unspoken rises to the surface. D is the sound of harmony straining, the crack in the façade where truth begins to leak through. Language itself feels unsettled here—words no longer glide; they stumble, resist, or demand to be redefined.

The terms in this section reveal the hidden currents of inequality and contradiction that often lie beneath polished institutions disparities in pay and acknowledgment, the disconnect between promises and actions, and the harm endured in silence because speaking up feels risky.

Disruption is not always loud. Sometimes it whispers. It's the resignation letter no one saw coming. The innovation that was never pitched. The burnout dismissed as "low engagement." These quiet moments expose how fragile power can be—and they serve as the crossroads where leaders choose maintain comfort or risk the fracture that sparks growth.

D asks us to notice what is easy to overlook

- The defensiveness masked as fear.
- The distance mistaken for professionalism.
- The dominance hidden as efficiency.
- The quiet resignations that speak louder than protests.

However, disruption for its own sake is superficial. The aim is not to destroy what exists but to expose what has been hidden so that equity, healing, and true alignment can take shape. Leadership here demands restraint as much as courage to listen without defensiveness, to respond promptly, and to proceed without damaging what is fragile.

Because naming dissonance is just the start. The real test is who we become after the break—whether we retreat into denial or rise into repair.

D

Data Colonialism

Definition: The extraction and control of individuals' and communities' personal data by powerful entities, often without consent, reflecting colonial exploitation.

Business Application: Data colonialism happens when companies make money from community data without sharing the benefits. This damages trust and worsens inequality.

Leadership Insight: Ethical leaders view data stewardship as a matter of justice, ensuring transparency, consent, and fair return of value.

Cultural Caution: In certain situations, data is considered communal property rather than individual. Leaders need to respect cultural views on data ownership.

Mosaic Question: Who has control over the data in your organization — and who gains from it?

Mosaic in Action: An NGO established data-sharing agreements with Indigenous communities, ensuring local control and mutual benefits.

Data Sovereignty

Definition: The principle that data is subject to the laws, governance, and control of the nation, community, or cultural group from which it originates. In Indigenous and marginalized communities, data sovereignty asserts the right to determine how information about the group is collected, stored, accessed, and used.

Business Application: For organizations working with community-generated data—such as in research, education, or public health—respecting data sovereignty involves obtaining consent, respecting local governance protocols, and ensuring fair access to data outcomes.

Leadership Insight: Leaders who uphold data sovereignty build trust, safeguard privacy, and align their efforts with ethical and legal responsibilities that surpass mere compliance to respect cultural rights.

Cultural Caution: Failing to respect data sovereignty can lead to exploitation, misuse, or cultural harm, especially in communities that have been historically oppressed.

Mosaic Question: Who manages the data in your projects—and whose interests does it benefit?

Mosaic in Action: A university research team collaborates with an Indigenous council to store health data on servers within tribal lands, with access and use controlled by the community.

Decentering

Definition: A process of shifting focus away from a dominant perspective, identity, or framework to make room for other voices, experiences, and ways of knowing. Decentering questions the idea that one viewpoint is universal.

Business Application: In leadership, decentering might include adjusting meeting formats to promote fair participation, revising policies to accommodate diverse needs, or inviting marginalized voices to influence strategy.

Leadership Insight: Decentering is not about removing your own perspective but about recognizing its boundaries and intentionally creating space for others to lead and contribute.

Cultural Caution: Decentering requires more than symbolic inclusion—it must be combined with structural changes that shift influence and decision-making power.

Mosaic Question: What would your work look like if another perspective defined the terms?

Mosaic in Action: A museum updates its exhibit planning process by inviting community representatives to serve as co-curators, ensuring narratives reflect multiple viewpoints.

Decentering Whiteness

Definition: The deliberate practice of shifting cultural, institutional, and narrative focus away from white norms, values, and perspectives as the default standard, to make space for multiple racial and cultural frameworks to lead and define meaning.

Business Application: Organizations can decenter whiteness by revising hiring criteria, communication styles, or "professionalism" standards that disproportionately favor white cultural norms, creating more inclusive and equitable workplaces.

Leadership Insight: Leaders involved in decentering whiteness actively challenge how their own assumptions and systems reinforce racial hierarchies, and they encourage racially diverse leadership to participate in strategic decision-making roles.

Cultural Caution: Decentering whiteness can cause defensiveness if seen as an attack instead of an expansion. It should be presented as a step toward equity, shared power, and more diverse perspectives.

Mosaic Question: What would leadership, success, or professionalism be like without whiteness as the default?

Mosaic in Action: A publishing house removes Eurocentric style requirements from author guidelines, enabling global writers to keep their own linguistic and narrative elements.

Decision-Making Under Cultural Complexity

Definition: The ability to make choices in environments where multiple cultural values, priorities, and norms intersect—often with competing or unclear expectations.

Business Application: In global teams, multicultural markets, and cross-border negotiations, leaders must balance efficiency with cultural respect. What seems decisive in one culture may feel reckless in another; what feels inclusive in one setting may seem

slow or indecisive elsewhere. Strong decision-making here produces outcomes that are both effective and trustworthy.

Leadership Insight: Skilled leaders adapt by embracing diverse perspectives, balancing short-term results with long-term relationships, and understanding that clarity often comes from accepting ambiguity. Effective decision-making in complex environments is not just about speed; it's about sustainability and building trust.

Cultural Caution: Depending on a single approach—whether directive, consensus-driven, or data-only—can alienate stakeholders. Even well-intentioned leaders may unintentionally reinforce exclusion if they assume their cultural "norm" is universal.

Mosaic Question: How do you modify your decision-making when no single cultural perspective defines the "right" choice?

Mosaic in Action: A humanitarian organization planning a relief effort consults local leaders from different ethnic and religious groups. Instead of enforcing a one-size-fits-all approach, they work together to develop a solution that addresses immediate needs while honoring cultural priorities—building both impact and trust.

Decolonial Design

Definition: A design approach that actively challenges and dismantles colonial power structures, narratives, and aesthetics in creative processes. Decolonial design centers the knowledge, priorities, and leadership of historically marginalized communities, ensuring that design solutions reflect their cultural contexts and sovereignty.

Business Application: In architecture, product development, and service design, decolonial design involves collaborating with communities as co-creators, valuing traditional knowledge alongside modern methods, and opposing extractive design practices.

Leadership Insight: Leaders applying decolonial design principles transition from designing for communities to designing with them, integrating reciprocity and equity into the process.

Cultural Caution: Decolonial design is not just about superficially adding cultural motifs — it requires a fundamental shift in who sets the agenda, owns the outcome, and reaps the benefits.

Mosaic Question: Who determines the problem, process, and product in your design work— and who gains from it?

Mosaic in Action: An urban planning firm collaborates with Indigenous leaders to create public spaces that incorporate traditional ecological knowledge, promoting cultural and environmental sustainability.

Decolonial Healing

Definition: The process of addressing and transforming the harms caused by colonization at individual, community, and systemic levels. Decolonial healing includes cultural renewal, intergenerational trauma work, and practices based on community knowledge and traditions.

Business Application: In education, healthcare, and community development, decolonial healing guides program design that prioritizes cultural practices, land relationships, and community-led solutions instead of applying external models.

Leadership Insight: Leaders involved in decolonial healing recognize past harm, foster spaces for truth-telling, and support restorative systems that empower impacted communities.

Cultural Caution: Decolonial healing should be led by those directly affected; external actors should support without taking control or shifting the focus.

Mosaic Question: Are your healing efforts empowering the communities they serve—or fostering dependency?

Mosaic in Action: A regional health authority funds Indigenous-led wellness retreats incorporating traditional medicine, storytelling, and land-based practices as part of a trauma recovery initiative.

Decolonial Leadership Practice

Definition: A leadership style that challenges colonial hierarchies and emphasizes equity, self-determination, and collective well-being. Decolonial leadership redefines authority as relational rather than exploitative, valuing diverse knowledge systems and shared power.

Business Application: Organizations practicing decolonial leadership alter decision-making structures, incorporate cultural governance models, and challenge mainstream ideas of efficiency, success, and authority.

Leadership Insight: Decolonial leaders focus on listening, consent, and reciprocity, and they evaluate success based on community-

defined outcomes rather than just institutional metrics.

Cultural Caution: Without structural change, decolonial leadership risks being just symbolic gestures or superficial inclusion.

Mosaic Question: Does your leadership shift power or just rebrand the same hierarchy with new words?

Mosaic in Action: A nonprofit board uses a co-leadership model where decisions are made together by elected community representatives and executive leadership, ensuring equal authority.

Decolonization

Definition: Decolonization is the active process of dismantling colonial systems of power, knowledge, and control. It involves returning land, rights, and decision-making authority to Indigenous and local communities, while also breaking down the cultural and institutional legacies of colonization.

Business Application: In corporate and institutional settings, decolonization can involve revising procurement processes to prioritize Indigenous-owned businesses, restructuring governance to distribute power, or reforming curricula to incorporate historically excluded knowledge.

Leadership Insight: Leaders dedicated to decolonization understand that it is not just a metaphor or a branding exercise—it's about real material, political, and relational power shifts.

Cultural Caution: Using "decolonization" as a symbolic concept without genuine change risks co-opting the term and diluting its radical intent.

Mosaic Question: Are your decolonization efforts truly transferring power, or just changing the story?

Mosaic in Action: A national park shifts stewardship of ancestral lands to tribal governance, establishing co-managed conservation efforts based on Indigenous ecological knowledge.

Deconstructing Whiteness

Definition: The critical study of whiteness as a social construct, including the norms, values, and power structures that maintain it as the default cultural standard. Deconstructing whiteness involves analyzing how it influences institutions, narratives, and interpersonal relationships, and actively challenging its dominance.

Business Application: Organizations can work on deconstructing whiteness by reviewing hiring criteria, leadership pipelines, and communication norms to identify where white cultural standards are embedded and privilege certain groups.

Leadership Insight: Leaders dedicated to this work foster an environment where diverse cultural perspectives can take the lead, appreciating multiple ideas of professionalism, success, and authority.

Cultural Caution: This process can cause defensiveness if it is presented as personal blame instead of systemic analysis. Clear communication that emphasizes equity and shared benefits is crucial.

Mosaic Question: What would your organization's culture be like if whiteness were no longer the default?

Mosaic in Action: A university's faculty hiring committee removes requirements that disproportionately benefit candidates from elite Western institutions, expanding its pool of applicants and perspectives.

Deep Cultural Competence

Definition: A level of cultural competence that exceeds awareness and basic skills by integrating cultural knowledge into all aspects of decision-making, leadership, and strategy. Deep cultural competence demands continuous immersion, reflection, and accountability.

Business Application: In multinational organizations, strong cultural competence ensures that strategy, product design, and communication are based on nuanced, context-specific understanding rather than generic assumptions.

Leadership Insight: Deeply competent leaders approach cross-cultural engagement with humility, a willingness to be corrected, and systems that incorporate learning into daily practice.

Cultural Caution: Claiming deep cultural competence without personal experience or ongoing involvement can weaken credibility and trust.

Mosaic Question: Is your cultural competence superficial or embedded in every decision you make?

Mosaic in Action: A humanitarian agency trains leaders to collaborate with cultural liaisons at every project site, ensuring program design aligns with local customs, needs, and decision-making processes.

Default Leadership Norms

Definition: The implicit and often unexamined beliefs about how leaders should behave, communicate, and make decisions—usually influenced by dominant cultural, gender, or class norms.

Business Application: Recognizing default leadership norms helps organizations broaden their definitions of leadership, allowing for diverse styles that may be more effective in specific situations or with particular teams.

Leadership Insight: Challenging default norms helps leaders embrace adaptability, authenticity, and equity while dismantling bias in performance evaluations and promotion pathways.

Cultural Caution: If left unchecked, default leadership norms can reinforce exclusion by favoring those who naturally fit the dominant models.

Mosaic Question: What unspoken leadership norms exist in your organization—and who benefits from them?

Mosaic in Action: A global company updates its leadership assessment to include collaborative, community-focused leadership alongside traditionally valued assertive styles.

Deficit Framing

Definition: The portrayal of individuals, groups, or communities mainly in terms of their perceived shortcomings, needs, or problems, rather than their assets, strengths, and potential.

Business Application: In education, social services, and community development, shifting from deficit framing to asset-based approaches fosters more empowering narratives, increased engagement, and sustainable solutions.

Leadership Insight: Leaders who reject deficit framing focus on building capacity and amplifying resources, making sure that language and policies reflect the strengths of the people they serve.

Cultural Caution: Even well-meaning efforts can unintentionally reinforce deficit framing if they focus on 'fixing" communities without recognizing their existing strengths and resources.

Mosaic Question: Do your strategies define people by what they lack—or by what they contribute?

Mosaic in Action: A youth mentoring program shifts its mission from "helping at-risk youth" to "partnering with emerging leaders," shaping both program design and participant results.

Defensive Leadership

Definition: A leadership style characterized by self-protection, resistance to feedback, and prioritizing image or control over growth. Defensive leadership often arises in environments of insecurity or fear of failure.

Business Application: Defensive leaders foster cultures of blame and rigidity, which hinder innovation and trust. Organizations that recognize and tackle defensive leadership patterns can transition toward openness and adaptability.

Leadership Insight: Defensiveness often stems from fear. Leaders who go beyond it — welcoming feedback with curiosity — increase credibility and resilience.

Cultural Caution: In certain situations, defending one's status or authority is considered honorable. Leaders need to differentiate between cultural norms of respect and harmful defensiveness.

Mosaic Question: When faced with challenges, do you protect your image — or focus on growth?

Mosaic in Action: A senior manager, initially defensive during an employee survey debrief, pauses, admits discomfort, and reframes feedback as a chance to build trust.

Deliberative Leadership

Definition: A leadership approach that focuses on thoughtful dialogue, inclusive participation, and consensus-building prior to making decisions.

Business Application: Deliberative leadership is particularly effective in diverse teams and cross-sector coalitions. By taking the time to gather perspectives, leaders create stronger and more sustainable solutions.

Leadership Insight: Deliberation demands patience and humility. Leaders who practice it balance urgency with reflection, making decisions that respect both the process and the results.

Cultural Caution: In fast-paced cultures, taking time to consider may be seen as indecisiveness. Leaders need to clarify that the aim is not to delay but to achieve a deeper understanding.

Mosaic Question: Do you prioritize speed over reflection — or do you make room for deliberation?

Mosaic in Action: A city council leader holds community discussions before drafting a policy, making sure voices from marginalized groups influence the final decision.

Dehumanization

Definition: The process of devaluing individuals or groups by stripping away their humanity, reducing them to stereotypes, objects, or threats. Dehumanization justifies discrimination, exclusion, and violence by depicting people as less than fully human.

Business Application: In workplace settings, dehumanization can appear as treating employees only as "resources" or metrics, ignoring their personal experiences, emotional needs, and dignity. Strategies to combat dehumanization—such as empathetic policy development and human-centered leadership—enhance retention and foster trust.

Leadership Insight: Leaders can counteract dehumanization by deliberately affirming the value of every person, especially in stressful or divided settings. This involves demonstrating empathy and establishing systems that prioritize humanity over convenience.

Cultural Caution: Unchecked dehumanization can escalate during times of crisis, change, or conflict. Leaders must recognize early signs, such as demeaning language, systemic neglect, or the erasure of cultural identity.

Mosaic Question: Whose humanity is your system quietly ignoring—and how can you bring it back?

Mosaic in Action: During a labor strike, a manufacturing CEO chooses to meet directly with workers, listening to their concerns and stopping an adversarial Public Relations (PR) campaign. By shifting from image management to collaborative negotiation, the CEO builds trust and begins repairing strained relationships.

Denial Culture

Definition: An organizational or societal environment where inconvenient truths—such as systemic inequities, misconduct, or harmful patterns—are actively ignored, minimized, or rationalized.

Business Application: Denial culture undermines accountability and innovation. Combating it involves creating psychologically safe spaces for truth-telling, protecting whistleblowers and change agents, and integrating transparency into reporting structures.

Leadership Insight: Leaders who break down denial culture create environments where honesty is promoted, data is not twisted to support stories, and performance metrics show the truth instead of hopes.

Cultural Caution: Denial culture can be reinforced by groupthink, power imbalances, or fear of reputational harm. Addressing it often requires bold, visible action from top leadership.

Mosaic Question: What truths is your organization avoiding—and at what costs?

Mosaic in Action: A school district publishes a public report recognizing systemic bias in discipline practices and pairs it with a multi-year equity plan developed with community stakeholders.

Design Justice

Definition: An equity-focused design framework that emphasizes the voices and leadership of those most affected by inequalities in developing solutions.

Business Application: Design justice challenges organizations to co-create systems, products, and policies with marginalized stakeholders, not just for them.

Leadership Insight: Leaders who embrace design justice understand that equity is integrated into systems from the start, not added later as an afterthought.

Cultural Caution: Western design methods might not fit with Indigenous or collectivist knowledge systems. Leaders need to adjust to local ways of knowing.

Mosaic Question: Who was involved in designing your systems — and who was excluded?

Mosaic in Action: A city employed participatory budgeting with community members from underserved neighborhoods to redesign public spaces.

Developmental Trauma

Definition: Chronic or repeated exposure to neglect, abuse, instability, or violence during formative childhood years, often leading to long-term emotional, cognitive, and relational effects.

Business Application: In professional settings, developmental trauma can affect communication styles, stress responses, and interpersonal trust. Trauma-informed leadership understands these dynamics and creates policies that minimize triggers and promote resilience.

Leadership Insight: By understanding developmental trauma, leaders can shift away from punitive responses to challenging behaviors, creating environments that promote healing and equal opportunities.

Cultural Caution: While recognizing trauma is important, avoid labeling or defining individuals only by their trauma history—focus on strengths, resilience, and potential for growth.

Mosaic Question: How can your leadership foster environments where past harm no longer controls current opportunities?

Mosaic in Action: A corporate training program includes trauma-awareness modules that help managers respond to conflict with empathy and adapt communication to reduce escalation.

Dialogic Justice Frameworks

Definition: Approaches to justice that focus on dialogue, repairing relationships, and mutual understanding rather than solely punishment. These frameworks emphasize truth-telling, shared accountability, and collaborative problem-solving.

Business Application: Organizations using dialogic justice frameworks engage in facilitated conversations to tackle workplace harm, restore trust, and reinforce community ties, decreasing dependence on adversarial complaint procedures.

Leadership Insight: Leaders practicing the dialogic justice model emphasize active listening, transparency, and shared power, fostering conditions where diverse voices influence solutions.

Cultural Caution: Dialogic justice is not a replacement for necessary consequences; it must be combined with structures that address harm and prevent recurrence.

Mosaic Question: When conflict occurs, do you pursue resolution through dialogue or through control?

Mosaic in Action: A nonprofit uses facilitated dialogue circles after a public misstep, enabling community members and leadership to collaborate on an action plan that addresses harm and prevents future incidents.

Dialogic Leadership

Definition: A leadership style based on authentic dialogue, co-creation, and shared understanding. Dialogic leadership emphasizes listening, questioning, and embracing diverse viewpoints over authoritative commands.

Business Application: In multicultural teams or fast-changing industries, dialogic leadership promotes agility, trust, and innovation by making space for all voices to influence solutions. It is especially useful in handling complexity when no single leader has all the answers.

Leadership Insight: The power of dialogic leadership resides in its capacity to turn conversations from mere transaction into collaborative exploration, fostering shared ownership of the results.

Cultural Caution: Dialogue without follow-through risks becoming performative. Leaders must combine listening with transparent action to sustain credibility.

Mosaic Question: When you invite dialogue, are you prepared to be influenced by it?

Mosaic in Action: During a cross-functional project crisis, a tech lead facilitates an open forum where engineers, designers, and end users co-create the recovery plan, leading to quicker buy-in and more lasting solutions.

Diaspora Identity

Definition: The complex, layered sense of self shaped by living outside one's ancestral homeland while maintaining cultural, familial, or emotional ties to it. Diaspora identity often involves navigating dual or multiple cultural affiliations.

Business Application: Diaspora perspectives enrich global organizations by connecting markets, cultures, and networks. Leaders who understand diaspora identity can better utilize cross-cultural skills and transnational links for organizational growth.

Leadership Insight: Recognizing diaspora identity in leadership roles affirms the importance of mixed perspectives and can enhance a sense of belonging for those who often feel "in-between" cultures.

Cultural Caution: Avoid assuming a single diaspora experience; identities within diasporic communities differ greatly based on generation, migration history, and context.

Mosaic Question: How does your leadership create space for identities that exist across multiple worlds?

Mosaic in Action: An international nonprofit hires a marketing director from a diaspora community whose insights transform outreach strategies, connecting with global audiences through culturally resonant messaging.

Diasporic Knowledge Systems

Definition: The body of cultural knowledge, practices, and innovations that come from diaspora communities, often blending ancestral traditions with modern experiences.

Business Application: In sectors ranging from design to healthcare, diasporic knowledge systems can provide innovative problem-solving methods that challenge monocultural assumptions and promote inclusive innovation.

Leadership Insight: Leaders who engage with diasporic knowledge systems enhance their ability for adaptive thinking and uncover resources that traditional frameworks might overlook.

Cultural Caution: When drawing from diasporic knowledge, make sure to give proper attribution and reciprocal benefit—avoid extracting knowledge without providing something in return to the communities of origin.

Mosaic Question: What knowledge might you access by looking beyond dominant systems?

Mosaic in Action: A city planning team incorporates urban agriculture practices from diasporic farming traditions, revitalizing underused land and promoting food security.

Digital Colonialism

Definition: The dominance of digital spaces, platforms, and infrastructures by powerful corporations or nations, resulting in the cultural, economic, and data exploitation of less powerful regions.

Business Application: Digital colonialism influences everything from global supply chains to content moderation policies. Leaders must evaluate how their organization's digital footprint promotes or resists exploitative patterns.

Leadership Insight: Resisting digital colonialism involves advocating for fair technology access, local content development, and data sovereignty in the communities you serve or employ from.

Cultural Caution: Global digital expansion can unintentionally reinforce colonial power dynamics when technology is implemented without local consultation or benefit-sharing.

Mosaic Question: Whose digital world are you creating—and for whom?

Mosaic in Action: A global NGO invests in open-source tools and trains local developers to build region-specific apps, avoiding reliance on foreign-owned platforms.

Digital Inclusion Equity

Definition: The principle and practice of ensuring that all individuals—regardless of socioeconomic status, geography, disability, language, or cultural background—have meaningful access to, and the skills to benefit from, digital technologies.

Business Application: In a growing hybrid and remote work environment, promoting digital inclusion equity broadens talent pools, enhances customer outreach, and guarantees fair participation in training, communication, and decision-making.

Leadership Insight: True digital inclusion involves more than just supplying devices; it also requires tackling issues like affordability, literacy, relevance, and cultural fit in technology adoption.

Cultural Caution: Providing "equal" access without considering different needs can reinforce inequities; true equity involves tailoring tools and training to accommodate diverse user contexts.

Mosaic Question: Who is excluded from your digital systems, and what is the impact of their absence?

Mosaic in Action: A multinational company updates its online training platform with offline access options and multilingual audio captions, enabling rural and low-bandwidth employees to participate fully.

Disaggregated Data

Definition: Data divided into detailed subcategories—such as race, ethnicity, gender identity, disability status, or other demographics—to uncover inequities that aggregated data may hide.

Business Application: Organizations use disaggregated data to pinpoint specific gaps in service, representation, or outcomes, allowing for targeted interventions and greater accountability in diversity and equity efforts.

Leadership Insight: Leaders who analyze disaggregated data can make more accurate, justice-focused decisions instead of relying on averages that conceal marginalized experiences.

Cultural Caution: Disaggregation must be combined with safeguards for privacy, cultural sensitivity, and consent to prevent harm or stigmatization.

Mosaic Question: What inequities would be revealed if you broke down your data more specifically?

Mosaic in Action: A school district analyzes disaggregated achievement data and finds that, while overall graduation rates are increasing, Indigenous students' rates are decreasing—leading to targeted support programs.

Disability Justice

Definition: A framework that goes beyond inclusion to achieve collective liberation by centering the leadership, needs, and wisdom of disabled people—especially those who are Black, Indigenous, queer, trans, and people of color.

Business Application: Organizations adopting disability justice design policies, spaces, and systems that recognize disability as a valued aspect of human diversity, not as an exception to accommodate.

Leadership Insight: Disability justice redefines accessibility as a catalyst for innovation and cultural transformation, benefiting all members of the organization.

Cultural Caution: Avoid framing accessibility as charity; paternalistic approaches undermine agency and reinforce ableism.

Mosaic Question: How does your leadership culture change when disabled voices take the lead in the conversation?

Mosaic in Action: A public health department creates a policy advisory council led by disabled community members, shaping city planning decisions that enhance mobility and safety for all residents.

Discourse Power Dynamics

Definition: The ways in which power affects who can speak, how ideas are presented, and whose voices are heard or silenced in conversations, debates, and decision-making.

Business Application: In team settings, understanding discourse power dynamics helps leaders create meetings, training sessions, and policies where contributions are not restricted by hierarchy, language fluency, or social capital.

Leadership Insight: Leaders can alter discourse power relations by proactively sharing speaking opportunities, recognizing different styles of communication, and challenging the standards that determine "credible" speech.

Cultural Caution: Even well-meaning leaders can reinforce dominance by letting familiar voices steer narratives; if unchecked, this can weaken trust and stifle innovation.

Mosaic Question: Whose voices influence the "truth" in your spaces—and whose truths are absent?

Mosaic in Action: During a strategy session, a nonprofit director ensures junior staff speak first before senior leaders respond, reshaping the flow of influence in the room.

Disenfranchised Grief

Definition: Grief that is not socially recognized, validated, or supported—often because the loss is stigmatized, minimized, or unseen in dominant cultural stories.

Business Application: In workplace settings, disenfranchised grief can arise after job loss, changes in professional identity, miscarriages, the death of a pet, or community tragedies. Leaders who recognize it can provide meaningful support that boosts retention and morale.

Leadership Insight: By recognizing and naming disenfranchised grief, leaders demonstrate empathy and foster an environment where unspoken emotional realities can be acknowledged, ultimately influencing performance and culture.

Cultural Caution: Avoid judging grief by its visibility or "legitimacy" within dominant norms; doing so alienates employees and worsens harm.

Mosaic Question: Whose losses are you ignoring—and how might things change if you recognized them?

Mosaic in Action: A manager learns that a colleague is struggling after their estranged parent's death. Instead of ignoring it, she offers flexible deadlines and recommends peer support resources, validating a loss the employee felt unable to share openly.

Disidentification

Definition: A strategy where individuals challenge or reshape imposed identities by partly accepting, rejecting, or altering parts of dominant cultural stories.

Business Application: Disidentification helps employees navigate spaces where full assimilation is expected but harmful, allowing them to maintain self-respect while engaging professionally.

Leadership Insight: Recognizing disidentification in team members can help leaders understand subtle forms of resistance, innovation, and self-preservation within restricted environments.

Cultural Caution: Do not confuse disidentification with disengagement; it is often a creative, adaptive response to systemic exclusion.

Mosaic Question: Where might your leadership enable people to express more of their authentic selves without feeling the need to filter or alter their identity?

Mosaic in Action: An LGBTQ+ employee in a conservative corporate culture chooses to share personal stories in ways that subtly challenge stereotypes while keeping certain aspects of their life private for safety.

Displacement Identity

Definition: A sense of self shaped by involuntary movement— whether through migration, exile, gentrification, or disaster—leading to complex relationships with belonging, memory, and place.

Business Application: Understanding displacement identity can assist leaders in developing more empathetic onboarding, community integration, and employee support programs for individuals adjusting to new cultural or professional environments.

Leadership Insight: People with displacement identities often have unique perspectives on adaptation, resilience, and intercultural problem-solving—valuable assets in globally connected teams.

Cultural Caution: Avoid romanticizing displacement solely as a character-building experience; it frequently entails lasting trauma and structural injustice.

Mosaic Question: How do you recognize the histories of movement and loss that influence the people you lead?

Mosaic in Action: A city council involves displaced residents in redevelopment planning to ensure rebuilding respects the original community values and avoids further exclusion.

Disparity

Definition: A measurable gap in opportunity, access, or outcomes between groups, often along lines of race, gender, class, ability, or other identities.

Business Application: Disparities are evident in pay gaps, promotion rates, healthcare access, and representation in leadership. They reflect not only inequality of outcomes but also systemic inequities that shape those results.

Leadership Insight: Recognizing disparity is the first step toward achieving equity. Leaders should

monitor, analyze, and respond to disparities to prevent confusing representation with fairness.

Cultural Caution: Focusing only on surface disparities (e.g., representation numbers) without addressing structural causes can create an illusion of progress while inequities continue.

Mosaic Question: What disparities are present in your team or organization, and what structures help maintain them?

Mosaic in Action: A tech company notices a disparity in leadership promotions between men and women. In response, it redesigns evaluation criteria to minimize bias and launches sponsorship programs to ensure equal advancement opportunities.

Discretionary Effort

Definition: The level of energy, creativity, and commitment employees decide to contribute beyond the minimum requirement. Discretionary effort indicates trust, motivation, and organizational culture.

Business Application: When leaders promote belonging and psychological safety, discretionary effort rises. Teams willingly go "above and beyond," fueling innovation and resilience without exploitation.

Leadership Insight: Discretionary effort cannot be demanded — it must be earned. Leaders gain it through trust, fairness, and care.

Cultural Caution: In cultures that prioritize collective achievement over individual success, discretionary effort might be seen as group loyalty rather than personal initiative. Leaders need to interpret these signals with cultural humility.

Mosaic Question: Do people give extra because they want to — or because they have to?

Mosaic in Action: A nonprofit staff member stays late to finish a critical report, not out of fear, but due to shared commitment to the mission and trust in leadership.

Disruption (as Leadership Strategy)

Definition: The deliberate interruption of harmful patterns, inequitable systems, or stagnant practices to enable transformation and inclusion.

Business Application: Disruption as a strategy enables leaders to challenge entrenched norms— such as biased hiring pipelines, inequitable pay structures, or exclusionary decision-making processes—and replace them with practices that create new opportunities for belonging and innovation.

Leadership Insight: Disruptive leaders are not reckless; they are purposeful. They blend courage with caution, ensuring disruption is used not to destabilize but to reset and rebuild. They understand that discomfort is often the cost of growth.

Cultural Caution: Disruption without clarity or accountability can lead to confusion, harm, and resistance. When used solely for performance or shock value, disruption loses its integrity and damages trust.

Mosaic Question: When have you decided to disrupt comfort to bring about change?

Mosaic in Action: A school district leader challenges traditional meeting protocols that exclude parent voices, replacing them with community listening forums that shift budget and policy priorities.

Disruptive Innovation in Equity Work

Definition: The process of adopting new frameworks, tools, or practices that replace outdated approaches to diversity and inclusion with models that are more fair, adaptable, and effective.

Business Application:
Organizations that implement disruptive innovation in equity work go beyond superficial training to make structural reforms— altering hiring algorithms, creating equitable leadership pipelines, or introducing pay transparency systems that permanently change the landscape.

Leadership Insight: Disruptive innovation demands leaders to look beyond mere compliance and focus on transformation. It's not about making minor adjustments to old systems but completely rethinking them.

Cultural Caution: Not every new idea is inherently fair. Innovation that overlooks history or ignores community voices risks repeating the same inequalities it aims to fix.

Mosaic Question: What unfair practice in your organization needs a disruptive innovation?

Mosaic in Action: A multinational corporation stops relying on performative diversity metrics and instead develops an AI-driven equity dashboard co-designed with employee resource groups, ensuring the data uncovers systemic gaps rather than hiding them.

Dissonance

Definition: The tension that occurs when expressed values, organizational practices, and lived experiences are not aligned.

Business Application: Dissonance occurs when companies promote an "inclusive culture" but fail to address harassment, or when leaders tout "work-life balance" yet reward overwork. It erodes trust and leads to disengagement.

Leadership Insight: Leaders who recognize and tackle dissonance build credibility. Those who overlook it risk losing talent and moral authority.

Cultural Caution: Unresolved dissonance often leads to burnout, silent resistance, or public backlash. It takes courage to name it, but failing to do so allows harm to continue.

Mosaic Question: Where does your organization's expressed culture differ from how its people actually experience it daily?

Mosaic in Action: An NGO claims to value collaboration discovers that decisions are being made unilaterally by executives. After employees highlight this disconnect, leadership establishes transparent decision-making councils that rebuild alignment and trust.

Distributed Leadership

Definition: A leadership style where responsibility, authority, and decision-making are distributed among multiple people or roles instead of being held by a single individual.

Business Application: Distributed leadership boosts agility, fosters innovation, and strengthens resilience by empowering teams to act freely without bottlenecks.

Leadership Insight: This model depends on trust, transparency, and clear role definitions to avoid confusion and promote accountability.

Cultural Caution: In cultures that value hierarchy, distributed leadership might be misunderstood as a lack of direction unless it is intentionally framed and supported.

Mosaic Question: What decisions can you delegate to others to boost ownership and shared responsibility?

Mosaic in Action: A hospital department implements distributed leadership during a public health crisis by assigning small, cross-functional teams to oversee patient care, logistics, and communications—reducing delays and enhancing outcomes.

Distributive Justice

Definition: A principle of fairness related to how resources, rights, and opportunities are distributed among individuals or groups. Distributive justice is essential to equity efforts.

Business Application: Organizations implement distributive justice in pay equity audits, promotion policies, and workload distribution. Fair resource allocation decreases attrition and fosters trust.

Leadership Insight: Leaders who embrace distributive justice recognize that equality alone is insufficient — true equity demands intentional rebalancing of systems.

Cultural Caution: Fairness varies across cultures. Some emphasize equal shares; others focus on distribution by need, contribution, or relationship. Leaders need to clarify and align these values.

Mosaic Question: How are power, resources, and opportunities allocated in your leadership environments?

Mosaic in Action: A university updates faculty pay scales to correct historic inequities across gender and race, using principles of distributive justice to rebuild trust.

Diversity Fatigue

Definition: A feeling of exhaustion, frustration, or disengagement that results from prolonged exposure to diversity, equity, and inclusion (DEI) efforts—often caused by poor implementation, lack of measurable results, or the emotional strain of repeated discussions without structural change.

Business Application: In organizations, diversity fatigue can cause decreased engagement in DEI initiatives, increased turnover among marginalized employees, and lower trust in leadership commitments.

Leadership Insight: Addressing diversity fatigue requires moving beyond symbolic gestures to implement systemic reforms, measurable goals, and transparent progress reports.

Cultural Caution: Do not dismiss diversity fatigue as merely a sign of "resistance"; sometimes it indicates burnout from being overburdened with DEI labor without enough resources or influence.

Mosaic Question: What structural changes would make your DEI efforts feel sustainable and worth investing in over the long term?

Mosaic in Action: A company notices declining attendance in its DEI sessions. Leadership shifts to targeted, department-specific strategies with clear accountability metrics, revitalizing engagement and trust.

Diversity Theater

Definition: Performative diversity efforts that focus on appearance rather than actual impact, usually emphasizing public image over meaningful structural or cultural change.

Business Application: Diversity theater can involve token representation in marketing campaigns, creating DEI committees without authority, or issuing public statements without internal reform.

Leadership Insight: Employees can quickly recognize when diversity initiatives are superficial, which damages credibility and erodes trust in leadership.

Cultural Caution: Tokenism and superficial representation can cause more harm than no initiative at all, as they reinforce cynicism and marginalization.

Mosaic Question: Are your diversity efforts aimed at the press release—or at the people they are meant to serve?

Mosaic in Action: A tech company faces criticism for its lack of women in leadership roles. Instead of organizing a photo shoot, it invests in leadership development programs for women and transparently monitors promotions over three years.

Dignity Culture

Definition: An organizational or community culture where mutual respect, fairness, and recognition of human worth are core values and guiding principles for decision-making and interactions.

Business Application: Dignity culture emphasizes psychological safety, fair treatment, and the conviction that each role contributes to the organization's success.

Leadership Insight: Leaders who foster a dignity culture demonstrate respect through language, policy, and conflict resolution — often lowering workplace conflicts and boosting collaboration.

Cultural Caution: Be aware that dignity varies across cultures; assumptions about what "respect" means should be discussed openly and inclusively.

Mosaic Question: How does your leadership make sure every person in your organization feels seen, valued, and respected?

Mosaic in Action: A nonprofit board uses dignity-based decision-making, making sure that staff at all levels are consulted before major policy changes.

Dog Whistle Language

Definition: Coded language that communicates a targeted, often exclusionary or discriminatory message to a specific audience while seeming harmless or neutral to outsiders.

Business Application: Dog whistle language can shape hiring practices, political messages, and workplace culture in ways that sustain bias without openly violating policies.

Leadership Insight: Recognizing and addressing dog whistle language is crucial for building trust and promoting fairness; silence in response often indicates implicit approval.

Cultural Caution: Because dog whistle language depends on shared but unspoken understanding, its meaning can be overlooked by those outside the intended audience—making it more difficult to challenge.

Mosaic Question: Where could coded language be hurting trust or inclusivity in your environment?

Mosaic in Action: During a recruitment meeting, a hiring manager uses the phrase "cultural fit" to exclude applicants from certain backgrounds. Another leader rephrases the discussion toward "cultural add" to promote broader inclusion.

Dominant Culture

Definition: The cultural norms, values, language, and behaviors that hold the most power and influence within a society, institution, or organization—often shaping what is considered "normal" or "acceptable."

Business Application: Dominant culture affects hiring practices, communication styles, and decision-making processes. Organizations that do not intentionally examine it risk excluding voices and perspectives that don't match those norms.

Leadership Insight: Effective leaders recognize the influence of dominant culture and actively work to prevent it from silencing or marginalizing those outside its boundaries.

Cultural Caution: Dominant culture often goes unnoticed by those who benefit from it, making it difficult for them to see its exclusionary impacts.

Mosaic Question: What unspoken rules in your organization reflect the dominant culture—and who might those rules be excluding?

Mosaic in Action: A global nonprofit recognizes its "professional dress" policy reflects Western corporate norms. It updates the policy to permit culturally specific attire, demonstrating respect and inclusion.

Double Bind

Definition: A no-win situation where an individual, often from a marginalized background, faces conflicting demands — satisfying one expectation violates another. Double binds frequently impact women, BIPOC, and underrepresented leaders.

Business Application: In workplaces, double binds occur when women leaders are penalized for being "too assertive" but also for being "too accommodating." These dynamics undermine equity and retention.

Leadership Insight: Double binds are systemic issues, not personal failures. Leaders need to identify them and redesign environments to eliminate conflicting expectations.

Cultural Caution: Double binds appear in various forms

across different cultures. In some societies, age or class creates similar dilemmas of "damned if you do, damned if you don't."

Mosaic Question: Where might people in your organization encounter impossible choices — and how can you change the system, not just the individual?

Mosaic in Action: A Black woman executive notes she is criticized as "aggressive" when she voices ideas but considered "uninvolved" when silent. Her board modifies meeting norms to address the double bind.

Double Consciousness

Definition: A term created by W.E.B. Du Bois that describes the internal conflict faced by marginalized individuals as they manage their own identity while also viewing themselves through the perspective of the dominant society.

Business Application: In the workplace, double consciousness can lead employees to modify their speech, behavior, or appearance to fit dominant norms, often at the expense of their emotional health.

Leadership Insight: Leaders can lessen the effects of double consciousness by creating environments that value

authenticity and do not penalize differences.

Cultural Caution: Double consciousness is not the same as adaptability; it reflects a survival strategy under systemic bias, not a voluntary cultural skill.

Mosaic Question: Whose success in your organization still depends on managing two versions of themselves?

Mosaic in Action: A Black executive mentoring program fosters open conversations about the challenges of code-switching, resulting in policy changes that encourage more genuine leadership styles.

Downstream Equity

Definition: Efforts to address inequities after they have happened, aiming to reduce harm instead of preventing it at the source.

Business Application: Downstream equity includes initiatives like diversity scholarships, bias training, or mentoring programs that address disparities without addressing root causes.

Leadership Insight: While downstream equity measures can be helpful, leaders should also implement upstream interventions to prevent inequities from developing.

Cultural Caution: Over-reliance on downstream equity can reinforce inequities by leaving systemic issues unresolved.

Mosaic Question: Are your equity initiatives addressing root causes or just symptoms?

Mosaic in Action: A city funds free coding bootcamps for underrepresented youth (downstream equity) while also reforming its public school tech curriculum to provide earlier access (upstream equity).

◆ LETTER D CALLOUT

"Data can illuminate or distort — what matters is whose story the numbers are telling."

Reflection Questions

- How do you decide which data to trust in shaping policy or leadership decisions?
- Where might your workplace or classroom be using deficit framing rather than highlighting resilience?
- What blind spots emerge when data excludes marginalized voices?

Practical Move

Review one data source (student outcomes, employee surveys, performance metrics). Ask whose voices are missing — then design one way to capture them.

E – Equity, Emotional Labor, and Erasure

E enters through the quiet door—what is often felt but rarely named. It sheds light on the unseen structures that determine who advances, who gets stuck, and who gradually fades away beneath unspoken norms. The terms in this section distinguish between surface-level fairness and the deeper emotional realities of inclusion. They give voice to what many carry but few can find words for.

Equity here is not just a slogan, checkbox, or quick fix. It's an ongoing effort to balance time, power, recognition, and repair. True equity is not just about being in the room; it's about reshaping whose presence matters, whose contributions are valued, and whose wellbeing is protected.

With equity comes often hidden costs emotional labor—the unpaid effort of translating, soothing, absorbing, or self-editing to help others feel comfortable. It is done without acknowledgment, breaks, or reciprocity. Alongside it is erasure the slow, silent disappearance of voices, identities, and contributions when systems fail to recognize them.

E asks us to notice what is easy to dismiss

- The emotional labor that never appears in performance reviews.
- The erasure that happens not with cruelty, but with indifference.

- The inequities masked by policies that look fair but operate unevenly.
- The unrecorded toll of constantly carrying others' comfort.

These are not just abstract ideals but lived experiences. Emotional labor is not always obvious. Erasure is not always intentional. However, both leave lasting marks—on trust, memory, and morale.

E is a call for vigilance and visibility. It reminds leaders that belonging cannot be built on disappearance, and equity cannot thrive on language alone. The true test of leadership is whether equity is demonstrated through daily actions — not just talked about but genuinely lived.

E

Economic Inclusion Index

Definition: A measurement tool that evaluates how fairly individuals and communities can access economic opportunities, resources, and benefits.

Business Application: Organizations can utilize an economic inclusion index to pinpoint obstacles in hiring, pay equity, procurement, and community investment activities, allowing for targeted enhancements.

Leadership Insight: Tracking inclusion through data helps leaders translate intention into measurable progress. It shifts equity work from a moral argument alone to a strategic and accountable business priority.

Cultural Caution: Metrics need context—numbers alone can hide disparities that impact marginalized groups in different ways.

Mosaic Question: If you assessed your organization's economic inclusion today, what truths might emerge—and how would you respond to them?

Mosaic in Action: A multinational company publishes its economic inclusion index each year, monitoring supplier diversity, wage equity, and regional hiring data, then uses the results to modify leadership performance targets.

Economic Justice

Definition: The fair distribution of economic resources, opportunities, and systems, ensuring that everyone can meet their basic needs and thrive without discrimination or exploitation.

Business Application: Economic justice principles guide pay transparency, fair trade practices, equitable investment, and living wage policies in organizations and industries.

Leadership Insight: Leaders dedicated to economic justice recognize that fairness in pay and opportunity drives loyalty, productivity, and sustainable growth.

Cultural Caution: Economic justice requires more than token gestures—structural and systemic change is essential to dismantle inequities.

Mosaic Question: Where in your sphere of influence do economic policies continue to favor some at the expense of others?

Mosaic in Action: A city government implements a living wage ordinance for all contracted workers, resulting in lower turnover and greater economic stability for low-income families.

Elder Wisdom

Definition: The knowledge, insight, and lived experience held by older generations, often rooted in cultural traditions, community memory, and long-term perspective.

Business Application: In organizations, elder wisdom can guide mentoring programs, succession planning, and long-term strategy by grounding decisions in historical patterns and lessons learned.

Leadership Insight: Valuing elder wisdom bridges generational gaps and strengthens cultural continuity, ensuring that progress builds on the lessons of the past.

Cultural Caution: Some societies overlook elders in fast-paced, innovation-driven settings, resulting in loss of institutional memory and intergenerational gaps.

Mosaic Question: Whose wisdom from past generations influences your current choices—and whose is absent?

Mosaic in Action: A community healthcare organization pairs younger staff with retired practitioners in a cross-generational mentorship program, enhancing both cultural understanding and service results.

Emancipatory Leadership

Definition: A leadership style that aims to liberate individuals and groups from oppressive systems, promoting self-determination, equity, and shared power.

Business Application: Emancipatory leadership practices involve dismantling hierarchical barriers, encouraging collaborative decision-making, and advocating for policy reforms that eliminate systemic obstacles.

Leadership Insight: True emancipation in leadership demands courage—challenging entrenched systems even when it risks personal or institutional comfort.

Cultural Caution: If not rooted in cultural humility, emancipation efforts risk forcing one group's idea of "freedom" on others without understanding their lived experiences.

Mosaic Question: Are you maintaining the system in your leadership, or are you empowering people to shape it for themselves?

Mosaic in Action: A school district implements a shared governance model that empowers teachers, parents, and students with decision-making authority over curriculum, discipline policies, and resource allocation.

Embodied Identity

Definition: The lived experience of one's identity expressed through the body—appearance, movement, voice, and presence—shaped by cultural, social, and personal factors.

Business Application: In workplaces, embodied identity affects how individuals are perceived, treated, and included, influencing opportunities, leadership credibility, and team dynamics.

Leadership Insight: Recognizing embodied identity helps leaders challenge appearance-based bias, respect cultural forms of self-expression, and create environments where authenticity is protected.

Cultural Caution: Some cultures regulate bodies through dress codes, grooming standards, or physical behavior, often reinforcing exclusionary norms.

Mosaic Question: How do you interpret and respond to others' embodied identities—and how might bias shape that response?

Mosaic in Action: A company updates its dress code to permit hairstyles, clothing, and accessories that showcase cultural heritage, resulting in higher morale and retention among underrepresented employees.

Embodied Leadership

Definition: A leadership approach that combines physical presence, body language, and emotional awareness to convey authenticity, confidence, and connection.

Business Application: Executives employ embodied leadership techniques—such as grounded posture, deliberate gestures, and mindful breathing—to build trust and influence during negotiations and presentations.

Leadership Insight: Your body shows leadership well before your words do; aligned presence and message boost credibility.

Cultural Caution: Physical signs of authority differ—what shows confidence in one culture might appear as arrogance or aloofness in another.

Mosaic Question: What does your body communicate when you lead under pressure?

Mosaic in Action: During a crisis meeting, a nonprofit director slows their speech, maintains open posture, and makes steady eye contact, calming the room and guiding the team toward solutions.

Emotional Adaptability

Definition: The ability to stay emotionally effective during change, complexity, or ambiguity. Emotional adaptability blends flexibility with a grounded presence, helping leaders respond without losing stability.

Business Application: Organizations constantly facing disruption rely on leaders who demonstrate adaptability. During restructuring, crises, or innovation, emotionally adaptable leaders maintain team morale while managing uncertainty.

Leadership Insight: Adaptability doesn't mean suppressing emotions — it means honoring them while remaining resourceful. Leaders who practice adaptability foster confidence by demonstrating that

uncertainty can be handled with stability.

Cultural Caution: In certain situations, adaptability can be confused with inconsistency. Leaders need to clearly communicate their values so that flexibility is seen as strength, not unpredictability.

Mosaic Question: When everything around you changes, do you fall back on old habits — or adapt with integrity?

Mosaic in Action: A nonprofit director handles sudden funding cuts by acknowledging her team's fears and then guiding them to see challenges as chances for creative problem-solving.

Emotional Agility

Definition: The ability to manage emotions with flexibility, awareness, and purpose—selecting responses that reflect values instead of reacting impulsively.

Business Application: Leaders with emotional agility adapt to changing circumstances, handle conflicts effectively, and keep motivation high in themselves and their teams.

Leadership Insight: Emotional agility transforms emotional awareness into action, enabling leaders to pivot without sacrificing their principles.

Cultural Caution: Not all cultures prioritize overt emotional expression—adapting how you express yourself while staying true to yourself may be necessary.

Mosaic Question: When encountering a triggering situation, do you react out of habit or choose to respond intentionally?

Mosaic in Action: A project manager receives unexpected negative feedback but takes a moment to process it, shifting it into constructive input and modifying the project plan without increasing tension.

Emotional Alignment

Definition: The integration of emotional insight, core values, and outward actions. Emotional alignment guarantees consistency between what leaders feel, believe, and demonstrate.

Business Application: Alignment fosters organizational trust. Teams succeed when leaders' emotional cues align with their declared values — such as showing patience during collaboration or demonstrating openness when seeking feedback.

Leadership Insight: Alignment reflects credibility. When leaders' inner feelings and outward actions

align, people see them as genuine and trustworthy.

Cultural Caution: Different cultures interpret emotional expression differently. What feels aligned in one setting (directness, transparency) may seem abrasive elsewhere. Leaders must align not only internally but also with the context.

Mosaic Question: Do your actions support the values you claim, or do they show contradiction?

Mosaic in Action: A CEO who advocates for work–life balance openly blocks off personal time on her calendar, demonstrating consistency between her values and actions.

Emotional Anchor

Definition:: A stabilizing presence, principle, or practice that keeps individuals and teams focused when emotions are high or uncertainty disrupts normal rhythms.

Business Application: Leaders who develop emotional anchors— through consistent routines, values, or relational stability—become the reference point others turn to in confusion. Anchors soothe chaos by restoring clarity.

Leadership Insight:: Anchors are about reliability, not rigidity. They maintain balance when chaos risks provoking overreaction, helping to make wise decisions instead of reactive ones.

Cultural Caution:: In some cultures, anchoring might be collective (family, faith, ritual); in others, it might be more individual. Leaders must recognize what provides stability to different groups.

Mosaic Question:: What practices or people keep you grounded when the ground shakes?

Mosaic in Action:: During an economic downturn, a department head starts each staff meeting with a simple grounding pause and a shared affirmation. Over time, this ritual becomes the cultural anchor that eases anxiety and helps the team refocus before tough decisions.

Emotional Attunement

Definition:: The refined skill of noticing, interpreting, and accurately responding to others' emotional signals, whether spoken or unspoken.

Business Application: Attuned leaders recognize morale shifts before they lead to conflict or turnover. They adapt their communication styles, prevent missteps, and build trust by demonstrating they "get it."

Leadership Insight:: Attunement establishes credibility not by guessing emotions but by being willing to check, clarify, and respond thoughtfully. It is the foundation of psychological safety.

Cultural Caution:: Emotional signals differ—what's a direct expression in one setting might be a subtle cue in another. Leaders need to understand cultural "emotional dialects" to avoid misunderstandings misreading.

Mosaic Question:: How often do you pause to check your emotional read before responding?

Mosaic in Action:: A project manager notices silence after announcing a new workflow. Instead of pushing forward, she asks open questions and listens. The pause reveals hidden concerns, allowing her to address resistance before it grows.

Emotional Availability

Definition: The ability to be emotionally available, responsive, and engaged with others. Availability indicates openness, accessibility, and care.

Business Application: Leaders who show emotional availability strengthen relationships, boost retention, and enhance psychological safety. A leader's openness encourages people to share concerns or suggest ideas.

Leadership Insight: Availability is more about the quality of attention than constant presence. Leaders who listen without distraction, validate emotions, and follow up on concerns build lasting trust.

Cultural Caution: Some cultures value reserved professionalism. Leaders need to balance availability with boundaries so emotional openness does not lead to overfamiliarity or a loss of authority.

Mosaic Question: Are you emotionally present for your team — or just available on a surface level?

Mosaic in Action: A VP notices her team's anxiety during layoffs and hosts open office hours where employees can share concerns and get transparent answers.

Emotional Capacity

Definition: The energy, bandwidth, and inner space required to process emotions, hold space for others, and respond without becoming overwhelmed.

Business Application: Leaders with strong emotional intelligence handle crises, feedback, and conflict without burning out. They keep people engaged by pacing themselves and setting emotional boundaries.

Leadership Insight: Capacity is like a container—it expands through self-care, reflection, and intentional practice. Leaders who develop capacity avoid reacting impulsively and foster more stable environments for their teams.

Cultural Caution: In cultures that undervalue emotional awareness, leaders with high emotional capacity may be dismissed as "too sensitive." Framing capacity as resilience and strength helps normalize it.

Mosaic Question: When your emotional burden increases, do you expand your capacity — or pass the weight to others?

Mosaic in Action: A project leader pauses a heated meeting, suggests a short break, and then continues with renewed clarity — demonstrating the ability to manage stress for the group.

Emotional Clarity

Definition: The accurate recognition and expression of emotional states. Emotional clarity allows for wise decision-making, self-regulation, and genuine connection.

Business Application: Leaders who communicate clearly prevent misunderstandings by naming emotions directly. For example, distinguishing between frustration and disappointment enables more accurate responses.

Leadership Insight: Clarity turns unclear tension into actionable data. Leaders who recognize emotions accurately can act purposefully instead of reacting on impulse.

Cultural Caution: In cultures where emotions are seldom verbalized, clarity might need to be communicated subtly through tone, behavior, or context instead of explicit labels.

Mosaic Question: Do you confuse emotions with general stress — or do you clearly identify what you truly feel?

Mosaic in Action: A team leader admits, "I'm not angry, I'm concerned about our timeline," helping colleagues adjust responses based on the clarified emotion.

Emotional Contagion

Definition: The unconscious transfer of emotions from one person to another through verbal and nonverbal cues.

Business Application: In team settings, a leader's mood can influence the atmosphere—positive emotions can motivate teamwork, while negativity can foster disengagement.

Leadership Insight: Awareness of emotional contagion enables leaders to intentionally foster environments of calm, optimism, and resilience, even during high-pressure moments.

Cultural Caution: In cross-cultural teams, emotional cues might be interpreted differently, which can cause misunderstandings about intent or tone.

Mosaic Question: What emotional climate are you unintentionally creating?

Mosaic in Action: A customer service manager begins each shift by sincerely appreciating employees and greeting them with a relaxed smile, prompting employees to mirror this behavior—leading to higher client satisfaction scores.

Emotional Depth

Definition:: The ability to connect with emotions on a deep, reflective level—seeking meaning and growth rather than just superficial acknowledgment.

Business Application: Leaders with depth shift teams from transactional responses ("get back to work") to transformative ones ("what does this loss teach us?"). This enhances resilience and innovation.

Leadership Insight:: Emotional depth is not about dramatic intensity; it is about having the patience to sit with discomfort, listen deeply, and extract wisdom from experience.

Cultural Caution:: Depth can be mistaken for weakness in fast-paced or highly competitive cultures. The skill is knowing when to show it and when to hide it.

Mosaic Question:: Do you give enough room for emotions to teach you before moving on?

Mosaic in Action:: After a sudden layoff announcement, a leader organizes not only logistical meetings but also reflection circles. Giving staff space to process grief builds trust and strengthens commitment to shared goals.

Emotional Design

Definition: The deliberate design of environments — physical, relational, or digital — to promote emotional safety, connection, and belonging.

Business Application: Workplaces incorporate emotional design in office setups, onboarding routines, and communication methods. Thoughtful design lessens stress,

boosts engagement, and conveys values beyond words.

Leadership Insight: Leaders who prioritize emotional design understand that culture is shaped not only by policies but also by atmospheres. Emotional design fosters environments where people can flourish.

Cultural Caution: Design choices can carry cultural meanings. A gesture meant to promote openness (e.g., casual dress codes, open offices) might feel awkward or disrespectful in different settings.

Mosaic Question: Does your leadership environment encourage people to relax and connect — or make them brace for survival?

Mosaic in Action: A team leader redesigns weekly check-ins to start with gratitude rounds, reducing stress and strengthening connections among team members.

Emotional Discernment

Definition: The ability to interpret and understand emotions with nuance, enabling informed, empathetic, and wise responses.

Business Application: Leaders who exercise discernment can distinguish surface reactions from underlying causes. For example, they recognize when "anger" conceals fear or when "silence" indicates exclusion.

Leadership Insight: Discernment is emotional wisdom. Leaders who cultivate it prevent overreactions, build deeper trust, and select responses that align with their long-term vision instead of seeking short-term relief.

Cultural Caution: Emotions show differently across cultures. What seems like disengagement in one setting could be a cultural way of showing respect. To understand this, you need awareness of the context.

Mosaic Question: When emotions run high, do you react on the surface — or try to understand what truly lies beneath?

Mosaic in Action: A mediator perceives that frustration in a community meeting comes more from generational distrust than logistics, shifting the conversation to focus on history.

Emotional Fluency

Definition: The ability to recognize, regulate, and respond to emotions — both your own and others' — with presence, nuance, and care. Unlike traditional "emotional intelligence," emotional fluency emphasizes depth, integration, and relational authenticity.

Business Application: Fluency helps leaders handle conflict, motivate teams, and adjust communication for different audiences. It is particularly useful in global or multicultural settings where emotional cues differ.

Leadership Insight: Fluency is not about controlling emotions but about moving with them wisely. Leaders fluent in emotion incorporate honesty, empathy, and strategy in real time.

Cultural Caution: Fluency is influenced by cultural norms. A leader fluent in one cultural setting may need to "relearn" cues in another to prevent misunderstandings.

Mosaic Question: Are you just managing emotions — or truly fluent in the language of emotion?

Mosaic in Action: A global manager notices tension in a cross-cultural team, addresses it respectfully, and fosters dialogue that recognizes different cultural approaches to conflict.

Emotional Granularity

Definition: The ability to recognize and express emotions accurately, differentiating between similar feelings (e.g., frustration vs. disappointment).

Business Application: Emotional granularity enhances communication, lowers conflict, and boosts emotional regulation in high-stress settings.

Leadership Insight: Leaders with high emotional granularity build trust by precisely naming and addressing emotions instead of using vague generalizations.

Cultural Caution: Not all cultures prioritize expressing emotions verbally. Leaders need to honor cultural standards regarding emotional expression.

Mosaic Question: Do you identify emotions clearly — or lump them into broad categories like "stress"?

Mosaic in Action: A manager trained staff to recognize emotions beyond "burnout," which led to tailored support for anxiety, grief, and fatigue.

Emotional Honesty

Definition: The practice of honestly naming one's emotions without distortion or performance. Emotional honesty promotes authenticity, vulnerability, and trust in relationships.

Business Application: In leadership, being honest about

emotions fosters transparency and reduces organizational dissonance. Teams led by emotionally truthful leaders are more likely to raise concerns and address issues early.

Leadership Insight: Honesty doesn't mean oversharing; it means courageously accepting emotions as they are. Leaders who demonstrate this foster cultures where others feel safe to do the same.

Cultural Caution: In some situations, openly sharing emotions might be seen as unprofessional. Leaders need to balance honesty with cultural norms while staying genuine.

Mosaic Question: Do you conceal emotions behind performance — or acknowledge them honestly and compassionately?

Mosaic in Action: A department chair admits, "I feel discouraged about our slow progress, but I also believe we can adjust," modeling honesty while maintaining hope.

Emotional Integrity

Definition: The alignment between what you feel, what you value, and how you show up in the world. Emotional integrity involves honoring your inner experience while expressing it through actions that demonstrate honesty, accountability, and respect. It is the first pillar of the Mosaic Intelligence Method™, developed and trademarked by Dr. Karissa Thomas, and it serves as the foundation of authentic and trustworthy leadership.

Business Application: Emotional integrity fosters organizational trust. Leaders who demonstrate it build cultures of credibility, where words and actions align. This consistency enhances communication, boosts engagement, and promotes psychological safety across diverse teams.

Leadership Insight: True integrity needs consistency, not just performance. Leaders with emotional integrity avoid the urge to manipulate or hide feelings to control others. Instead, they lead with clarity, alignment, and courage — even when feeling vulnerable.

Cultural Caution: Emotional integrity can vary across cultures. Direct expression may indicate authenticity in some settings but be viewed as disruptive in others. Leaders need to demonstrate integrity with cultural awareness while staying true to their values.

Mosaic Question: Do your emotions, values, and actions align — or do they pull in different directions?

Mosaic in Action: A nonprofit leader who values inclusion advocates for marginalized staff during a board meeting, prioritizing honesty and accountability over silence, even at personal or political cost.

Emotional Intelligence (EQ)

Definition: The ability to recognize, understand, and manage one's own emotions while effectively perceiving and influencing the emotions of others. EQ combines self-awareness, self-regulation, empathy, and relationship management into a unified leadership skill.

Business Application: In high-pressure environments, emotionally intelligent leaders defuse conflicts, foster trust across differences, and communicate in ways that support both performance and psychological safety. EQ has become a vital factor in hiring, promotions, and leadership readiness assessments.

Leadership Insight: Technical skill may open the door for you, but emotional intelligence decides how far you'll go. Leaders with high EQ consistently inspire loyalty, navigate complexity, and influence outcomes without relying solely on authority.

Cultural Caution: EQ models based on Western norms may underestimate collective emotional expression or different communication styles found in other cultures.

Mosaic Question: How does your cultural perspective influence how you interpret emotions—both in yourself and others?

Mosaic in Action: During a tense cross-departmental meeting, a senior leader notices increasing defensiveness in the room, pauses the agenda, and invites each participant to share their main concern. This shift in tone leads to breakthroughs that had been stalled for months.

Emotional Labor

Definition: The effort of managing one's emotions—often suppressing genuine feelings—to meet organizational, cultural, or social expectations, especially in service or caregiving roles.

Business Application: From customer-facing staff to senior executives, emotional labor is a key part of work that requires composure, empathy, and conflict resolution. Unrecognized emotional labor can lead to burnout, turnover, and disengagement.

Leadership Insight: Valuing emotional labor involves recognizing it, fairly compensating for it, and distributing it evenly—rather than silently relying on certain people based on their role, identity, or personality.

Cultural Caution: In some cultures, emotional labor becomes so normalized that it remains invisible, especially for women, marginalized groups, and younger workers—hiding systemic inequities in workloads.

Mosaic Question: Who on your team is taking on unspoken emotional labor—and at what personal cost?

Mosaic in Action: After noticing that frontline staff absorb daily client frustration, a healthcare director facilitates debrief circles, rotates coverage to allow recovery time, and includes emotional load in workload planning.

Emotional Legacy

Definition: The emotional patterns, behaviors, and beliefs passed down through generations or organizational cultures. Emotional legacy shapes how people view leadership, conflict, and belonging.

Business Application: Leaders often inherit workplace legacies such as "we don't talk about

221

feelings" or "conflict is avoided." Identifying these legacies helps organizations develop healthier norms and break cycles of dysfunction.

Leadership Insight: Unexamined emotional legacies maintain blind spots. Leaders who examine their inherited emotional frameworks — whether personal or organizational — are more capable of creating new opportunities.

Cultural Caution: Legacies vary among families, communities, and cultures. What is regarded as strength in one legacy (such as stoicism or toughness) can be seen as harmful repression in another.

Mosaic Question: Whose emotional legacy are you carrying into your leadership — and which parts need to be released?

Mosaic in Action: A university president recognizes the school's past reluctance to discuss race and initiates conversations to reshape its emotional legacy toward openness and fairness.

Emotional Literacy

Definition:: The ability to recognize, label, and communicate emotions in ways that promote clarity rather than confusion.

Business Application: Literate leaders use a vocabulary of

feelings that decreases conflict. Naming feelings like "frustration," "uncertainty," or "relief" provides teams with language to handle tension constructively.

Leadership Insight:: Emotional literacy is a leadership asset comparable to financial or technical literacy. Without it, miscommunication often occurs, and silence replaces honest conversation.

Cultural Caution:: Some emotional words carry different significance across cultures. Leaders must stay aware of how certain terms are received in context.

Mosaic Question:: How accurate is your vocabulary when you describe emotions to your team?

Mosaic in Action:: A healthcare CEO introduces a shared emotion framework during feedback sessions. Staff learn to distinguish between "stress," "overload," and "burnout," which enhances support system accuracy and lowers attrition.

Emotional Maturity

Definition: The ability to handle emotional complexity with empathy, accountability, and composure. Emotional maturity involves taking responsibility for one's impact.

Business Application: Mature leaders demonstrate self-control and humility even in high-pressure situations. They admit mistakes without defensiveness and lead teams calmly through conflict and change.

Leadership Insight: Maturity is reflected in how a leader responds rather than reacts. It distinguishes between escalating tension and fostering space for resolution.

Cultural Caution: Different cultures assess maturity in different ways — some by restraint, others by transparency. Leaders need to balance cultural expectations with genuine expression.

Mosaic Question: Do you judge maturity by avoiding emotion — or by responding to it responsibly?

Mosaic in Action: A COO admits an error in rollout planning, apologizes without shifting blame, and invites the team to collaboratively develop solutions — showing maturity through accountability.

Emotional Presence

Definition: The state of being fully present and aware of oneself and others in the moment. Emotional presence shows care and connection that words alone cannot express.

Business Application: Presence is essential in leadership situations like conflict mediation, coaching, or crisis response. Leaders who demonstrate presence foster trust and psychological safety.

Leadership Insight: Presence is a form of influence. Leaders who control distractions and give full attention to others send the message: you matter here.

Cultural Caution: Presence can vary across cultures. In some, silence shows presence; in others, verbal affirmation is necessary. Leaders should pay close attention to contextual cues.

Mosaic Question: When you're with others, are you truly present — or just physically there?

Mosaic in Action: During a board retreat, the chair silences devices, leans forward, and listens intently, demonstrating emotional presence that enhances engagement in dialogue.

Emotional Resonance

Definition: The ability to generate emotional impact through genuine alignment between inner feelings and outward expression. Resonance strengthens connection and influence.

Business Application: Resonant leaders foster loyalty and motivate action. From keynote speeches to team meetings, resonance fuels collective energy by aligning authenticity with communication.

Leadership Insight: Resonance is not about performance; it is about truth expressed clearly enough for others to feel it. Leaders who resonate mobilize hearts as well as minds.

Cultural Caution: What resonates in one culture, such as expressive passion, might appear excessive in another. Resonance demands cultural awareness to prevent misinterpretation.

Mosaic Question: Do your words sound hollow — or do they truly resonate with the emotions you feel?

Mosaic in Action: An educator shares her personal struggle with burnout while launching a wellness initiative, creating resonance that affirms her team's lived experiences.

Emotional Resilience

Definition:: The ability to recover, adapt, and maintain presence and effectiveness despite pressure, disruption, or loss.

Business Application: Organizations with resilient leaders recover quickly from crises, maintaining stability for customers, stakeholders, and staff.

Leadership Insight:: Resilience is not just passive toughness but active renewal—turning stress into strength and getting ready for future challenges.

Cultural Caution:: Overemphasizing resilience can serve as an excuse for systemic neglect, where endurance is praised, but harmful conditions persist.

Mosaic Question:: Do you see resilience as a healthy recovery or silent endurance?

Mosaic in Action:: After a natural disaster, an insurance team rotates work schedules, conducts reflective debriefs, and implements peer-support check-ins. Resilience becomes a collective effort, not solely an individual burden.

Emotional Repression

Definition: The conscious or unconscious act of avoiding, suppressing, or denying emotional expression, often as a way to cope or in response to cultural, family, or organizational norms.

Business Application: While staying composed can be strategic, persistent suppression damages decision-making, affects authenticity, and can result in conflict avoidance or passive resistance within teams.

Leadership Insight: Leaders who suppress emotions send signals that certain feelings are not welcome, which can lead to environments of mistrust or disengagement. Encouraging healthy emotional expression can enhance team cohesion and foster innovation.

Cultural Caution: Some cultures link emotional restraint with professionalism, making it hard to distinguish between strategic control and unhealthy suppression.

Mosaic Question: What emotions do you regularly suppress, and what might they be trying to teach you?

Mosaic in Action: A senior engineer often suppresses frustration until it appears as sarcasm during meetings. After leadership training, she learns to express concerns earlier, improving project timelines and morale.

Emotional Safety

Definition: A workplace or community environment where individuals can openly share emotions, ideas, and identities without fear of judgment, retaliation, or marginalization. Emotional safety is a vital foundation for building trust, collaboration, and well-being.

Business Application: Teams with emotional safety handle feedback, disagreement, and innovation more resiliently, resulting in higher retention and better performance outcomes.

Leadership Insight: Leaders are responsible for setting the tone— emotional safety doesn't happen by accident. It is built through consistent behavior, accountability for harm, and modeling vulnerability.

Cultural Caution: Different cultures have varying ideas of what constitutes 'safe' emotional expression; what seems open to one person may feel invasive to another.

Mosaic Question: What signals— spoken or unspoken—tell your team it's safe to speak and express openly?

Mosaic in Action: In a multinational project team, a manager starts each meeting with a "pulse check" question, creating space for both personal and work-related updates. Over time, less vocal members begin to share more freely, enhancing team innovation.

Emotional Wholeness

Definition: A state of integration where past wounds, present awareness, and future vision coexist in harmony. Emotional wholeness signifies healing, maturity, and authenticity.

Business Application: Organizations led by whole leaders benefit from stability, clarity, and compassion. Wholeness decreases reactive cycles and fosters healthier organizational cultures.

Leadership Insight: Wholeness is the result of resilience. It is not perfection, but the capacity to lead from a healed and grounded self.

Cultural Caution: Not all cultures see emotional wholeness as individual healing. Some interpret it as collective harmony, where leaders connect personal well-being with community thriving.

Mosaic Question: Are you leading from unresolved wounds or from a place of wholeness?

Mosaic in Action: A community leader who has experienced personal loss helps create a grief-support program, turning his own healing into a source of collective strength.

Empathic Leadership

Definition: A leadership approach that actively strives to understand and respond to the emotional experiences, needs, and perspectives of others—while balancing empathy with decisive decision-making and accountability.

Business Application: Empathic leaders foster stronger engagement, reduce turnover, and boost innovation because they create environments where employees feel seen and valued. This is especially important during organizational change, crisis recovery, or high-stress project cycles.

Leadership Insight: Empathy without boundaries can cause emotional fatigue; empathy with judgment builds trust and lasting influence.

Cultural Caution: Cultural norms influence how empathy is shown— some may prefer verbal praise, while others rely on practical help or shared activities.

Mosaic Question: When was the last time you listened for what wasn't said, and how did that shift your perspective?

Mosaic in Action: During a restructuring, a department head notices anxiety among junior staff. Instead of giving generic reassurances, she hosts small group discussions to listen to concerns, clarify timelines, and provide targeted support tailored to individual needs.

Empathy Gap

Definition: A disconnect between the lived experiences or emotions of one group and the understanding—or willingness to understand—those experiences by another group, often leading to miscommunication, inequality, or exclusion.

Business Application: Empathy gaps often occur between leadership and frontline staff, among departments, or across cultural and generational differences. Closing these gaps needs deliberate dialogue, active listening, and shared experiences.

Leadership Insight: An empathy gap is not always due to malice; it can arise from limited exposure, isolated work, or unconscious bias. Leaders need to actively bridge these gaps.

Cultural Caution: Assuming empathy can be developed only through data or reports overlooks the importance of relational and human elements necessary to bridge the gap.

Mosaic Question: Where in your organization are empathy gaps growing—and who is most affected by them?

Mosaic in Action: After a poor employee engagement survey, a retail chain's executives spend a week shadowing store staff, leading to policy changes that directly address overlooked pain points.

Employee Resource Group (ERG) Dynamics

Definition: The formal and informal structures that determine the effectiveness, influence, and sustainability of employee-led groups organized around shared identity, interests, or advocacy goals within an organization.

Business Application: Healthy ERG dynamics can boost retention, improve inclusion, and guide business strategy. Poorly supported ERGs can result in tokenism, burnout, or mistrust among members.

Leadership Insight: ERG success relies on clear purpose, sufficient resources, executive sponsorship, and integration into organizational decision-making—not just ceremonial recognition.

Cultural Caution: Organizations that promote ERGs for branding while ignoring their recommendations risk damaging trust and authenticity.

Mosaic Question: Are your ERGs empowered to drive change—or just to host events?

Mosaic in Action: An LGBTQ+ ERG identifies gaps in healthcare benefits and successfully advocates for inclusive coverage, aligning benefits with company values and attracting top talent.

Empowerment Capital

Definition: The accumulated trust, credibility, and influence that allow individuals or groups to take initiative, challenge norms, and implement change without facing too much resistance.

Business Application: Organizations with high empowerment capital promote innovation and resilience, as people feel confident their contributions will be valued and supported.

Leadership Insight: Empowerment capital increases through regular inclusion in decision-making, visible acknowledgment of contributions, and accountability for following through on commitments.

Cultural Caution: In hierarchical cultures, empowerment capital may be concentrated among senior leaders; in flatter structures, it can be more widely distributed but still unevenly accessible.

Mosaic Question: What steps have you taken lately to boost someone else's empowerment capital?

Mosaic in Action: A mid-level manager nominates a junior colleague to present their project to the executive team, boosting visibility and credibility that accelerate the colleague's career growth.

Environmental Justice

Definition: The principle and practice of making sure that everyone—regardless of race, ethnicity, income, or location—has equal protection from environmental hazards and equal access to decision-making about environmental policies and resources.

Business Application: Organizations that incorporate environmental justice into their strategies address disparities in pollution exposure, resource allocation, and climate resilience. This is especially important for companies in manufacturing, energy, real estate, and global supply chains.

Leadership Insight: Environmental justice is not just about ecology; it is closely linked to social and economic fairness. Leaders need to consider how environmental choices disproportionately affect vulnerable communities.

Cultural Caution: Global environmental priorities differ; a solution praised in one area might be opposed or misunderstood in another because of historical exploitation or sovereignty issues.

Mosaic Question: Whose environment are your decisions protecting, and whose are they sacrificing?

Mosaic in Action: A multinational company adjusts its plant expansion plan after community feedback shows the site would raise asthma rates in a low-income neighborhood, choosing a location with lower health risks.

Environmental Racism

Definition: Policies and practices that unfairly expose marginalized communities to environmental hazards, pollution, or climate risks.

Business Application: Organizations operating globally must evaluate supply chains and site locations to prevent perpetuating environmental racism.

Leadership Insight: Leaders dedicated to justice understand that sustainability without equity still causes harm. True responsibility combines environmental and racial fairness.

Cultural Caution: Environmental justice movements vary around the world. Leaders must adapt strategies to local histories of extraction and exploitation.

Mosaic Question: How does your organization's environmental impact relate to racial and social equity?

Mosaic in Action: A logistics company moved its warehouse location away from heavily burdened low-income neighborhoods, decreasing toxic air exposure.

Epigenetic Trauma

Definition: The biological and psychological transmission of trauma effects across generations through changes in gene expression, often due to systemic oppression, conflict, displacement, or chronic stress.

Business Application: Understanding epigenetic trauma helps leaders develop workplace policies and cultures that address deep-rooted stress responses in employees from marginalized or historically oppressed groups.

Leadership Insight: The visible behaviors you observe—hypervigilance, distrust, difficulty with authority—may stem from generational trauma rather than just individual personality or performance issues.

Cultural Caution: Avoid using the idea of epigenetic trauma to stereotype groups or justify lower expectations; the goal is to create environments where healing and thriving are possible.

Mosaic Question: How could generational history influence the current dynamics in your team or community?

Mosaic in Action: A school district serving refugee families implements trauma-informed practices throughout all classrooms, leading to improved attendance and academic achievement.

Epistemic Humility

Definition:: Recognizing the limits of one's knowledge and being open to perspectives, data, and wisdom beyond one's expertise.

Business Application: Epistemic humility encourages innovation by reducing overconfidence. Leaders who admit "I don't know" foster collaboration and enable collective problem-solving.

Leadership Insight:: Strength increases when leaders show confidence in what they know while also respecting others' contributions.

Cultural Caution:: In certain organizational or cultural settings, humility can be misunderstood as indecisiveness. Presenting it as strategic openness maintains credibility.

Mosaic Question:: When has admitting uncertainty boosted trust in your leadership?

Mosaic in Action:: A global development director relies on local health workers during a crisis, placing their community knowledge at the heart of the strategy. This approach saves time and fosters cultural trust.

Epistemic Injustice

Definition: The unfair treatment of someone because of their role as a knower, often by discrediting their testimony (testimonial injustice) or denying them access to resources needed to understand their experiences (hermeneutical injustice).

Business Application: In organizations, epistemic injustice happens when lived experience is ignored in favor of "expert" opinion, or when decision-making processes exclude those most impacted by the outcomes.

Leadership Insight: Correcting epistemic injustice involves actively validating various forms of knowledge—such as data, lived experience, and cultural wisdom—and making sure they influence policies and strategies.

Cultural Caution: What qualifies as "credible" knowledge is influenced by culture; Western standards often favor written or data-based evidence over oral traditions or communal storytelling.

Mosaic Question: Who is consistently left out of shaping the knowledge that influences your decisions?

Mosaic in Action: A healthcare task force includes community elders in designing patient outreach, recognizing their authority and insights as equal to medical data in addressing public health concerns.

Equality of Opportunity

Definition: A core principle that everyone should have equal opportunities to pursue education, employment, and advancement without discrimination, regardless of identity or background.

Business Application: Equality of opportunity policies focus on recruitment, promotion, training access, and pay fairness, aiming to eliminate systemic barriers while upholding merit-based evaluation.

Leadership Insight: Equality of opportunity doesn't ensure equality of outcome; leaders must make sure the starting line is accessible and support systems are in place for fair participation.

Cultural Caution: In some settings, "equal opportunity" rhetoric can be used to oppose targeted efforts for historically excluded groups, thus maintaining inequalities.

Mosaic Question: What invisible barriers still prevent equal access within your sphere of influence?

Mosaic in Action: A tech company revamps its internship program by partnering with community colleges and offering stipends, expanding access to students from underrepresented backgrounds.

Equitable Access

Definition: Conditions where people from all backgrounds can realistically access and use opportunities, services, and resources—considering historical and current barriers like cost, language, disability, geography, time, technology, and cultural fit. Equitable access differs from equal access by customizing supports so that outcomes are not predictably influenced by identity.

Business Application: Organizations enable equitable access through tiered pricing, multilingual and plain-language communication, accessible technology (captioning, alt text, screen-reader compatibility), flexible scheduling, and distributed locations. Tracking participation with disaggregated data ensures that access is effective for those most affected.

Leadership Insight: Access is a deliberate design choice, not a random side effect. Leaders allocate resources for access (childcare, transportation stipends, assistive tech) and assign owners, timelines, and KPIs to ensure equity is maintained instead of relying on goodwill.

Cultural Caution: "Open to all" often means "optimized for some." Declaring access without addressing trust, cultural safety, or past harm perpetuates exclusion.

Mosaic Question: Who needs to work the hardest to utilize what you provide—and why?

Mosaic in Action: A city workforce program shifts its orientation to evenings and weekends, adds on-site childcare and transit vouchers, and offers materials in five languages. Enrollment and completion rates for immigrant women double within a year.

Equitable Design

Definition: A participatory approach to developing products, services, policies, and environments that focuses on those most impacted by inequity, from defining problems to assessing solutions. Equitable design blends human-centered methods with power-aware practices such as co-creation, shared decision-making, and benefit sharing.

Business Application: Teams utilize equity personas, harm-mapping, and disparate-impact testing along with usability testing. Procurement focuses on vendors with community credibility. Success metrics include distributional effects—who benefits and who bears costs—not just overall averages.

Leadership Insight: Equity arises from who is at the table and who holds the pen. Leaders go beyond "feedback sessions" to foster community co-ownership of scope, budget, and success criteria.

Cultural Caution: Aesthetic inclusion without changing governance is tokenism. If the people most affected can't veto harmful choices, the design is not equitable.

Mosaic Question: Who identified the problem your design addresses—and who has the authority to declare it successful?

Mosaic in Action: A health system co-designs a maternal-care app with Black mothers, doulas, and nurses; features include culturally responsive content, on-demand lactation support, and transportation integration. Post-launch, ER visits decrease for the target population.

Equity Audit

Definition: A structured, time-limited assessment of policies, practices, culture, and outcomes to identify inequities, their root causes, and corrective actions. It combines quantitative data (representation, pay, advancement, attrition, service outcomes) with qualitative evidence (focus groups, climate surveys, artifact review).

Business Application: An equity audit produces an action plan with designated owners, milestones, and resources across talent, operations, customer experience, and community impact. Regular re-audits monitor progress and prevent regression.

Leadership Insight: Audits serve as credibility tests. Leaders publish topline findings, safeguard participants, and link compensation to remediation goals so that results translate from report to reality.

Cultural Caution: Audits that extract stories without providing repairs can retraumatize communities. Obtain consent, reduce identification risks, and

showcase visible wins early to build trust.

Mosaic Question: What honest insights would an audit reveal that your dashboards currently conceal?

Mosaic in Action: A university audit uncovers pay compression affecting women faculty of color. The board allocates funds for a multi-year adjustment, revises promotion criteria, and implements transparent pay bands with annual equity reviews.

Equity Debt

Definition: The accumulated shortfall between current organizational practices and the level needed to achieve equity—similar to technical debt. Equity debt grows "interest" as disparities build, leading to turnover, reputational harm, legal risks, missed opportunities, and burnout among marginalized employees.

Business Application: Organizations address equity debt through targeted investments such as retroactive pay corrections, accessible infrastructure, leadership diversification, supplier diversity, and policy redesign. They also establish a "debt register" that measures backlog and plans pay-down schedules.

Leadership Insight: Ignoring equity debt is a strategic liability. Leaders allocate funds for principal and interest immediate harm mitigation plus upstream redesign to prevent new debt from forming.

Cultural Caution: Performative fixes (such as one-time trainings) conceal debt without lowering the principal. Transparent costing and sequencing help prevent "equity insolvency."

Mosaic Question: What equity or debt are you carrying, how quickly is the interest compounding, and what's your pay-down plan?

Mosaic in Action: A global firm develops a three-year equity and debt plan $6M for pay equity and parental leave parity, $2M for accessibility upgrades, and policy changes that halve biased hiring drop-offs—saving more in attrition costs than the program's cost.

Equity Fatigue

Definition: The physical, emotional, and mental exhaustion experienced by individuals—often those from marginalized groups or diversity-focused roles—when repeatedly facing inequities, bias, or systemic barriers without seeing lasting change.

Business Application: In organizations, equity fatigue can develop when initiatives stall, responsibility for equity work is disproportionately placed on underrepresented staff, or leadership does not act on collected feedback. It often causes disengagement, burnout, and attrition among key talent.

Leadership Insight: Recognizing equity fatigue is not about lowering expectations—it's about balancing urgency with sustainability. Leaders who emphasize pacing, visible wins, and shared responsibility can prevent demoralization that comes when meaningful change constantly feels out of reach.

Cultural Caution: Equity fatigue is different from resistance to change. Calling it "lack of buy-in" risks dismissing real concerns and alienating those who have worked hardest for progress.

Mosaic Question: How can you redistribute the weight of equity work so it doesn't fall on the same few voices?

Mosaic in Action: At a midsize tech company, the only Black woman on the leadership team notices she's been asked—again—to lead the company's annual diversity report. She shares her concern that her advocacy is overshadowing her actual job responsibilities. The CEO responds by creating a rotating equity leadership council, making sure accountability for progress is shared across all departments.

Equity Lens

Definition: A deliberate approach to decision-making that assesses policies, practices, and outcomes for their impact on marginalized groups, with the goal of identifying and dismantling inequities before they become reinforced.

Business Application: Using an equity lens can guide strategic planning, hiring practices, budget distribution, and product development. It helps ensure that systemic biases are not repeated in organizational decisions and that resources are allocated fairly.

Leadership Insight: Using an equity lens is more than a checklist—it's a mindset that prompts leaders to ask "Who benefits? Who is harmed? Who is missing?" at every stage of a decision.

Cultural Caution: An equity lens is ineffective if used only at the end of a process. Adding equity considerations after important decisions are already made can result in token changes that fail to address root causes.

Mosaic Question: At what point in your decision-making process

can you introduce an equity lens earlier, so inclusion is built in—not patched on?

Mosaic in Action: During budget planning, a nonprofit director pauses the discussion to ask how the proposed cuts might impact programming for immigrant youth. The team recognizes that these services are disproportionately affected and reallocates funds to protect them, altering the organization's trajectory for the year.

Equity vs. Equality

Definition: Equality means giving everyone the same resources or opportunities. Equity involves acknowledging that people start from different positions and may need different resources or opportunities to reach fair outcomes.

Business Application: In workplace training, providing identical onboarding sessions to all employees (equality) may overlook the unique needs of first-generation college graduates, neurodivergent employees, or those working in a second language. Equity-focused onboarding would tailor content to remove those barriers.

Leadership Insight: Leaders who understand equity versus equality shift from "same for everyone" to "fair for everyone." This change often decides whether diversity initiatives succeed or stall.

Cultural Caution: Framing efforts solely as "equality" can unintentionally reinforce privilege, as those with systemic advantages gain more quickly from the same resources.

Mosaic Question: How might "treating everyone the same" unintentionally widen a gap?

Mosaic in Action: A city government introduces a new online permitting process for all residents. After feedback shows that residents without home internet access are left out, the city establishes in-person assistance centers at public libraries—shifting from equality to equity in service delivery.

Erasure

Definition: The systematic exclusion, dismissal, or rewriting of a group's presence, contributions, or identity in cultural, historical, or institutional narratives.

Business Application: Erasure can happen in marketing campaigns that exclude certain demographics, in company histories that omit contributions from marginalized staff, or in policies that fail to address the needs of specific communities.

Leadership Insight: Addressing erasure demands that leaders do more than just acknowledge it—actively recovering and amplifying the stories, data, and contributions that have been ignored or misrepresented.

Cultural Caution: Erasure is not always obvious; it can occur through well-meant "neutral" policies or narratives that make the dominant group the default.

Mosaic Question: Which voices or histories have been excluded from your organization's story—and how will you include them moving forward?

Mosaic in Action: A museum preparing a new exhibit on local history finds that its materials mostly omit Indigenous narratives. The curator collaborates with tribal historians to develop sections that highlight Indigenous perspectives, permanently transforming the institution's storytelling methods.

Ethical AI Leadership

Definition: The practice of guiding the development and deployment of artificial intelligence with a focus on fairness, transparency, accountability, and social responsibility. Ethical AI leadership recognizes that technological progress must be balanced with safeguards to protect human dignity and fairness.

Business Application: Leaders in organizations using AI must establish clear ethical guidelines, ensure compliance with data privacy laws, and address bias in algorithms. This role includes encouraging collaboration among engineers, ethicists, and community stakeholders to make sure AI tools benefit the public.

Leadership Insight: Without intentional ethical oversight, AI systems can sustain or worsen social inequalities. Leaders need to be proactive in creating policies and promoting responsible innovation, rather than reacting after harm occurs.

Cultural Caution: AI can reflect the biases of its creators and the data it's trained on. It's important to consider global contexts and marginalized voices to prevent systemic discrimination from being reinforced at a large scale.

Mosaic Question: How will your leadership guarantee that AI acts as a tool for fairness rather than exploitation?

Mosaic in Action: A city's public housing authority uses an AI-driven tenant application review system. When early results show applicants from certain zip codes being unfairly denied, the agency's director halts the program, brings together a review board with community advocates, and retrains the system with bias-reduced data—restoring fairness to the process.

Ethical Leadership

Definition: A leadership style based on moral values, integrity, and accountability, emphasizing doing what is right rather than what is merely convenient or profitable. Ethical leadership fosters trust and stability within organizations and communities.

Business Application: Ethical leaders create codes of conduct, demonstrate transparency in decision-making, and protect whistleblowers. They incorporate ethics into performance measures and reward systems to promote long-term trust over immediate gains.

Leadership Insight: Trust is delicate and can take years to build but seconds to destroy. Leaders who make morally sound decisions—even if unpopular—strengthen the organization's culture and resilience.

Cultural Caution: "Ethics" are not universally understood; cultural standards and values differ across regions. What is considered ethical in one setting might be seen differently elsewhere.

Mosaic Question: When stakes are high, how do you ensure your decisions reflect both your values and your community's trust?

Mosaic in Action: A multinational company faces pressure to buy cheaper materials from a supplier accused of labor exploitation. The CEO refuses, opting instead to support sustainable local partnerships—gaining criticism for higher costs but earning loyalty from ethically conscious clients.

Ethical Relativism

Definition: The belief that moral standards and ethical judgments are shaped by cultural, societal, or situational contexts rather than fixed universal principles.

Business Application: Leaders working across borders may need to navigate ethical differences, such as acceptable business practices, labor standards, or data privacy norms. Awareness of ethical relativism helps prevent ethnocentric decision-making.

Leadership Insight: Understanding ethical relativism does not mean abandoning personal or organizational values—

it means recognizing the diversity of moral frameworks and finding respectful, fair ways to operate within them.

Cultural Caution: Overemphasizing relativism can be used to justify harmful practices as cultural respect. Leaders must discern when to adapt and when to stand firm.

Mosaic Question: How do you uphold your values while respecting ethical perspectives that differ from your own?

Mosaic in Action: A global health nonprofit partners with a rural clinic in a country where informal payments to staff are common. Instead of condemning the practice outright, the project leader collaborates with local leaders to transition toward transparent wages while maintaining community trust.

Ethical Tech Leadership

Definition: The practice of guiding technological innovation with a strong moral compass, emphasizing human rights, equity, and environmental sustainability alongside business success.

Business Application: Ethical tech leaders manage the development of products and platforms with user safety, privacy, and long-term societal impact in mind. They create oversight systems and promote inclusive representation within design teams.

Leadership Insight: Technology is never neutral — it reflects the intentions, biases, and values of those who create it. Ethical tech leaders design with future generations in mind, not just immediate profits.

Cultural Caution: Technologies that succeed in one market may cause harm in another if cultural, political, or economic differences are overlooked.

Mosaic Question: How can your technology leadership ensure that innovation benefits the many without exploiting the few?

Mosaic in Action: A wearable tech company develops a health-monitoring device for global markets. Before launch, the CTO leads an ethics review that uncovers potential misuse of biometric data by authoritarian governments. The company incorporates decentralized data storage and opt-in privacy controls, even if it reduces profit margins.

Ethnic Identity

Definition: The feeling of belonging to a specific ethnic group, influenced by shared ancestry, cultural traditions, language, and historical experiences. Ethnic identity can be adaptable, growing stronger or changing throughout different life stages, migrations, and generations.

Business Application: Recognizing ethnic identity in the workplace helps with recruitment, retention, and employee engagement — especially in international teams where heritage impacts communication styles, leadership expectations, and problem-solving methods.

Leadership Insight: Leaders who foster authentic ethnic expression — through storytelling, cultural celebrations, or inclusive policies — build greater trust and spark innovation within diverse teams.

Cultural Caution: Overemphasizing ethnic identity without nuance may lead to tokenism or essentialism, reducing individuals to stereotypes instead of recognizing their complex, multifaceted identities.

Mosaic Question: How can you create spaces where ethnic identity is celebrated without it becoming a limitation?

Mosaic in Action: During a product design meeting, an engineer mentions a traditional weaving pattern from their ethnic

239

background as inspiration for a sustainable materials prototype. The project leader encourages them to share the story behind the design with the larger team, fostering cultural appreciation and encouraging innovation.

Ethnic Tourism

Definition: Travel experiences focused on engaging with the traditions, heritage, and lifestyles of specific ethnic groups—often marketed for cultural immersion or authenticity.

Business Application: Organizations involved in travel, hospitality, or cultural events can utilize ethnic tourism to promote sustainable economic growth while safeguarding cultural heritage. This involves forming partnerships with community members to ensure fair benefits.

Leadership Insight: Leaders in this industry can transition from extractive approaches to community-led tourism, making sure that the narrative, profits, and cultural representation stay in the hands of those whose heritage is being showcased.

Cultural Caution: Poorly managed ethnic tourism can commodify culture, distort traditions for entertainment, or reinforce

stereotypes—undermining, rather than preserving, cultural integrity.

Mosaic Question: How can cultural tourism be designed to protect both heritage and dignity for the communities involved?

Mosaic in Action: A travel company collaborates with an Indigenous community to create an immersive cooking experience. Community members set the prices, control the storytelling, and manage visitor numbers to ensure respect and fair compensation.

Ethnocentrism

Definition: The belief that one's own ethnic group or culture is inherently superior, which often leads to judging other cultures through one's own cultural lens.

Business Application: In global organizations, ethnocentrism can obstruct cross-cultural teamwork, restrict market access, and alienate talent. Leaders need to actively challenge ethnocentric biases in hiring, product development, and customer service.

Leadership Insight: Replacing ethnocentric beliefs with cultural humility boosts adaptability, empathy, and market understanding—crucial qualities for sustainable leadership.

Cultural Caution: Ethnocentrism is not always obvious; it can subtly show up in "best practices" that assume one cultural approach fits all.

Mosaic Question: Where might unexamined ethnocentric assumptions be influencing your decisions—and at whose expense?

Mosaic in Action: A U.S.-based marketing team initially rejects a packaging color for an Asian market because of "low appeal" in U.S. focus groups. After consulting local experts, they learn the color represents prosperity in the target culture, leading to a successful product launch.

Ethnography

Definition: A qualitative research method centered on the systematic study of people and cultures through immersive observation, participation, and contextual analysis.

Business Application: Ethnography helps organizations understand customer behavior, workplace dynamics, and cultural trends—offering insights beyond what surveys or analytics can provide.

Leadership Insight: Leaders who include ethnographic methods in their strategies can develop policies, products, and services that reflect the real experiences of diverse stakeholders.

Cultural Caution: When conducted by outsiders, ethnography can unintentionally misinterpret or exploit communities if not done with consent, transparency, and shared benefits.

Mosaic Question: How might ethnographic insights change the way you engage with your audience, team, or community?

Mosaic in Action: A tech company places researchers within rural farming communities to observe daily irrigation challenges. The insights from this immersion help develop an affordable, solar-powered pump co-designed with local farmers.

Euphemistic Language

Definition: The use of mild, vague, or indirect expressions to soften or hide the impact of difficult, offensive, or uncomfortable truths. While it can make language more acceptable, it can also hide systemic issues or reduce harm.

Business Application: Organizations often use euphemisms in official communications—saying "rightsizing" instead of layoffs, or "opportunities for improvement" instead of "failures"—to reduce backlash and keep morale high. However, this practice can damage trust if stakeholders feel deceived.

Leadership Insight: Leaders who depend too much on euphemistic language risk damaging their credibility. Clear and compassionate communication fosters more trust than vague wording.

Cultural Caution: Euphemisms depend on culture—what seems polite in one setting might appear dismissive or even deceptive in another. Overusing them can make marginalized groups feel gaslit about real issues.

Mosaic Question: Where might your choice of words comfort you but confuse others?

Mosaic in Action: During a workplace town hall, a leader mentions an upcoming "restructuring" but does not explain that entire departments will be eliminated. Employees leave the meeting feeling uncertain and anxious. The next day, the leader holds a follow-up session using plain language, explaining the changes and available support resources—restoring some of the trust that had been lost.

Exclusionary Practices

Definition: Actions, policies, or cultural norms—formal or informal—that intentionally or unintentionally hinder individuals or groups from fully participating in opportunities, decision-making, or community life.

Business Application: This can show up as hiring bias, inaccessible facilities, informal decision-making cliques, or cultural traditions that alienate certain employees. Even unspoken norms, like after-hours networking at bars, can become exclusionary.

Leadership Insight: Leaders need to go beyond written policies to uncover hidden barriers that prevent talented individuals from contributing fully.

Cultural Caution: What feels "standard" or "neutral" to one group may be exclusionary to another. Inclusion requires awareness of both visible and invisible gatekeeping mechanisms.

Mosaic Question: Who could be excluded from your processes—and what unseen barriers keep them there?

Mosaic in Action: A leadership team recognizes that their promotion criteria heavily favor employees who can travel internationally, which creates a barrier for caregivers. They revise the criteria to include remote project leadership experience, opening advancement opportunities for a more diverse group of employees.

Exhaustion Culture

Definition:: A workplace norm that celebrates overwork, exhaustion, and "busyness" as signs of loyalty or excellence.

Business Application: Exhaustion culture damages productivity, increases burnout, and speeds up attrition, costing organizations both talent and reputation.

Leadership Insight:: Wise leaders avoid exhaustion as a badge of honor. They see productivity as achievable through sustainable impact, not through endless hours.

Cultural Caution:: In industries where overwork is normalized, challenging exhaustion culture may face resistance or ridicule.

Mosaic Question:: Does your workplace mistake exhaustion for dedication?

Mosaic in Action:: A tech firm's CEO removes mandatory late-night hours and establishes clear "no-email zones." Performance increases because staff energy remains intact, and morale boosts.

Experiential Equity

Definition: The fair and intentional design of experiences so that people from different backgrounds have equal opportunities to learn, grow, and thrive—not just access the same resources.

Business Application: Besides providing consistent training materials, organizations practicing experiential equity adapt environments, facilitation styles, and engagement methods to accommodate diverse needs. For example, ensuring both introverts and extroverts have opportunities to contribute during brainstorming sessions.

Leadership Insight: Equity is more than what is given; it's about how people perceive and experience it. Leaders should evaluate success based on participation quality, not just numbers.

Cultural Caution: In some cultures, participation norms vary—silence can indicate respect rather than disengagement. Experiential equity involves adjusting interpretations, not just actions.

Mosaic Question: How can you assess whether everyone's experience—not just their access—is fair and equal?

Mosaic in Action: A global nonprofit runs a leadership program in multiple countries. Instead of translating materials exactly, they collaborate with local facilitators to customize examples, pacing, and discussion formats to match cultural norms—leading to more meaningful learning results.

Experiential Learning in Leadership

Definition: A leadership development method that focuses on learning through direct, hands-on experience combined with reflection, feedback, and real-world application.

Business Application: This might include job rotations, shadowing senior leaders, leading special projects, or simulated crisis management exercises. The goal is to cultivate adaptability, decision-making skills, and emotional intelligence in real-world situations.

Leadership Insight: Experiential learning speeds up growth because it reinforces lessons through action. Leaders who include reflection in these experiences enhance learning results and better apply them to new situations.

Cultural Caution: Leadership "experiments" may be viewed differently in various cultures; in some environments, failure during experiential learning might carry more stigma than growth. Adjust approaches accordingly.

Mosaic Question: How can you develop leadership experiences that challenge people without damaging their confidence?

Mosaic in Action: A mid-sized company launches a leadership program where participants rotate through cross-departmental projects. After each rotation, they participate in peer coaching circles to reflect on lessons learned, building both skills and relationships that last beyond the program.

Exploitative Inclusion

Definition: A form of inclusion that seems to welcome underrepresented individuals but primarily uses their presence for optics, public relations, or token compliance—without providing real influence, decision-making power, or equitable resources.

Business Application: This occurs when organizations showcase diverse faces in marketing but exclude them from high-level strategy, pay equity, or promotion tracks. Leaders need to recognize when inclusion is being used to boost brand image rather than achieve genuine change.

Leadership Insight: True inclusion is measured by shared authority and the removal of systemic barriers—not just by the diversity of a photo on the company website. Leaders who mistake representation for empowerment risk damaging trust.

Cultural Caution: Communities that have been historically excluded can spot performative gestures quickly. Exploitative inclusion can increase cynicism and disengagement, undermining even sincere future efforts.

Mosaic Question: Are the people you include also shaping the rules—or only following them?

Mosaic in Action: A major company celebrates hiring a record number of women executives but quietly assigns them to low-impact roles with no budget authority. Months later, several resign, citing burnout and lack of decision-making power, prompting an internal review that uncovers systemic gatekeeping in leadership pipelines.

Exponential Leadership

Definition:: Leadership that harnesses networks, technology, and distributed ownership to scale influence and results.

Business Application: Exponential leaders go beyond incremental gains, quickly scaling solutions through collective intelligence and digital reach.

Leadership Insight:: Influence increases when leaders let go of control, empower others, and utilize systems thinking.

Cultural Caution:: Rapid scaling without focusing on equity can worsen exclusion just as much as it promotes inclusion.

Mosaic Question:: Where could exponential leadership take the place of gradual, step-by-step progress?

Mosaic in Action:: A grassroots climate group launches a digital training platform. Instead of focusing on one community at a time, hundreds of micro-leaders emerge, expanding the movement's reach across continents.

Expressive Freedom

Definition: The right and ability to share ideas, perspectives, and identities without fear of retribution, suppression, or stereotyping, while respecting others during the exchange.

Business Application: In leadership, expressive freedom is vital for innovation and teamwork. It allows teams to challenge assumptions, suggest new strategies, and voice concerns that might otherwise go unheard.

Leadership Insight: Leaders who promote expressive freedom foster psychological safety, which enhances creativity and helps avoid groupthink. This requires balancing openness with accountability to ensure respectful dialogue.

Cultural Caution: Expressive freedom is not the same everywhere; some cultures or organizations have implicit penalties for speaking honestly. Leaders must recognize differing risks and develop ways to protect vulnerable voices.

Mosaic Question: Who in your environment feels the most free to speak—and who holds back?

Mosaic in Action: During a global strategy meeting, a junior employee questions a proposed marketing slogan for cultural insensitivity. Instead of shutting down the criticism, the leader encourages discussion, resulting in a more inclusive and effective campaign.

External Validation Loop

Definition: A recurring cycle where individuals or organizations base their sense of worth, success, or credibility mainly on recognition, approval, or validation from external sources.

Business Application: This cycle can hinder authentic leadership by encouraging decisions focused on appearance rather than values. For example, a leader might prioritize awards, social media engagement, or client praise over measurable impact.

Leadership Insight: Leaders rooted in internal values and a clear mission can use external validation strategically without becoming reliant on it. The healthiest growth comes from aligning intrinsic purpose with outward recognition.

Cultural Caution: In cultures or industries where prestige is currency, breaking free from the validation cycle may seem risky— but dependence on it can leave leaders vulnerable to manipulation or burnout.

Mosaic Question: If no one clapped, posted, or praised you, would you still lead the same way?

Mosaic in Action: A nonprofit director spends months pursuing a high-profile partnership to gain public prestige, neglecting smaller grassroots collaborations. After reflecting on the organization's mission, they shift focus, rebuild trust within the community, and achieve deeper impact.

Extrinsic vs. Intrinsic Motivation

Definition: Extrinsic motivation is motivated by external rewards like money, recognition, or status. Intrinsic motivation is driven by internal satisfaction, purpose, or personal growth.

Business Application: Understanding these motivations helps leaders create roles, incentives, and recognition programs that foster ongoing engagement. Relying too much on extrinsic motivators may lead to short-term compliance but not lasting commitment.

Leadership Insight: High-performance cultures combine both motivators, making sure external recognition supports—rather than replaces—internal purpose. Leaders who cultivate intrinsic motivation enable people to take action even without an immediate reward.

Cultural Caution: What counts as a motivator varies widely across cultures and individuals. Leaders must avoid assuming that what drives them will motivate everyone else.

Mosaic Question: When was the last time you did something just for the joy of it, without expecting any reward?

Mosaic in Action: A company introduces a "Top Performer" award with cash prizes, but the winner later reveals that their true motivation stemmed from seeing the community impact of their work—leading leadership to incorporate mission-focused recognition into their culture.

◈ LETTER E CALLOUT

"Emotions are not distractions from leadership — they are the signals that guide it."

Reflection Questions

- How do you recognize the difference between emotional clarity and emotional overwhelm?
- What cultural factors shape how emotions are expressed or suppressed?
- How can emotional resilience be cultivated in ways that honor diversity?

Practical Move

At your next decision point, pause and name the emotion underneath your instinct. Share it briefly — then let it inform, not override, your action.

F – Fragility, Feedback, and False Neutrality

F brings us to the tipping point—where power, discomfort, and perception collide. This is the letter where conversations stray from the point, honesty gets watered down, and silence claims to be safety. The terms in this section expose the unspoken rules that shape how truth is received—and who bears the consequences for speaking it.

Fragility—whether emotional, racial, or cultural—often acts as an invisible barrier to progress. Instead of addressing harm, systems shift focus to protecting the comfort of those with the most privilege. Feedback is often coded, softened, or withheld—not to promote growth, but to protect egos. And false neutrality appears to be "above the fray," while in reality, it reinforces the very inequalities it claims to overcome.

F asks us to notice the fragile patterns that halt movement

- The instinct to protect comfort instead of addressing harm.
- The coded feedback that avoids truth to preserve status.
- The neutrality that masks bias and maintains inequity.
- The expectation that the most burdened remain composed.

These dynamics explain why "professionalism" is so often misused as a weapon against honesty, why truth-telling is mislabeled as aggression, and why efforts toward equity stall as soon as discomfort emerges. In such environments, those bearing the heaviest emotional burden are the ones told to stay calm.

F is not an invitation to blame but a call to build capacity the ability to stay present when tension rises, to give and receive feedback without breaking down, and to recognize that neutrality is never truly neutral in an unjust system.

Because lasting change doesn't come from comfort. It is built in clarity—truth spoken with courage, even when it unsettles. The question is not whether tension will show up, but whether you have the resilience to face it without retreat.

F

Facework

Definition: The strategies people use to protect, maintain, or restore their social image ("face") in interactions, especially during conflict, negotiation, or cultural exchange.

Business Application: Leaders navigating high-stakes meetings, cross-cultural partnerships, or customer relations need to understand how face concerns influence communication styles and conflict resolution. Recognizing when to preserve face—both for oneself and others—can reduce defensiveness and build trust.

Leadership Insight: Effective leaders observe subtle cues of embarrassment, pride, or loss of credibility and adjust their responses to protect dignity without avoiding accountability.

Cultural Caution: In collectivist or high-context cultures, direct confrontation can lead to severe face loss and long-term relationship damage. In individualistic cultures, overemphasizing saving face may seem evasive.

Mosaic Question: When have you unintentionally caused someone to lose face, and what did you learn about repairing the relationship?

Mosaic in Action: In a joint venture meeting, a project manager notices her international counterpart struggling to answer a performance question. Instead of pushing for details publicly, she suggests moving that topic to a follow-up call. This preserves the partner's credibility and keeps collaboration on track.

Facial Profiling

Definition: The practice of making judgments, decisions, or assumptions about individuals based on their facial features, expressions, or perceived ethnicity, often resulting in discriminatory treatment.

Business Application: AI-powered facial recognition used in security, hiring, or marketing can unintentionally incorporate racial or gender bias, posing reputational and legal risks. Leaders must ensure the ethical use of such technology and restrict its scope.

Leadership Insight: Bias in facial profiling—whether human or AI-driven—undermines diversity efforts and damages trust. Leaders who challenge surface-level assumptions pave the way for deeper, evidence-based decisions.

Cultural Caution: In many societies, facial features are linked to historical prejudices and stereotypes. Without oversight, facial profiling can reinforce oppressive narratives and institutional discrimination.

Mosaic Question: What systems in your workplace might be making judgments about people's worth or trustworthiness based on appearance?

Mosaic in Action: A company's customer verification system incorrectly flags customers with darker skin tones as potential fraud risks. The operations director immediately stops the process, investigates vendor algorithms, and replaces the system with a bias-checked alternative.

Fair Algorithm Practices

Definition: Policies, protocols, and design principles that guarantee algorithmic systems function without bias, discrimination, or harm to specific groups. This includes transparency in decision-making processes, regular audits, and diverse data sets to prevent the continuation of inequities.

Business Application: Organizations using AI for hiring, promotions, customer targeting, or risk assessment must employ bias detection and mitigation measures to sustain trust and comply with laws. Regular third-party audits and varied testing scenarios can bolster credibility.

Leadership Insight: Leaders who see algorithms as neutral risk ignoring the human biases embedded in their design and training data. By emphasizing fairness in AI, leaders show accountability, digital literacy, and a dedication to equity.

Cultural Caution: Without deliberate oversight, algorithms can intensify systemic discrimination—especially against marginalized groups—quickly and at scale. Never assume automation is objective.

Mosaic Question: If your AI system made a harmful or biased choice, how fast would you find out—and what steps would you take?

Mosaic in Action: A retail company's hiring algorithm starts rejecting significantly more applicants from one postal code. Instead of ignoring it, the HR director stops automated screenings, orders a fairness audit, and updates the algorithm to remove geographic bias, restoring diversity among applicants.

Fairness Heuristic

Definition: A psychological shortcut where people assess whether a decision or system is fair primarily based on the process rather than the outcome.

Business Application: In organizations, transparent and inclusive processes often matter more to employees than just the outcomes. Fairness heuristics influence perceptions of legitimacy and trust in leadership.

Leadership Insight: Leaders who focus on process fairness build credibility, even if their decisions are unpopular. Process integrity is just as important as outcomes.

Cultural Caution: Fairness is understood differently across cultures. In some, equal treatment is seen as fairness; in others, fairness is related to equity or outcomes based on relationships.

Mosaic Question: Do your team members trust the fairness of your process — or do they just judge the outcome?

Mosaic in Action: During layoffs, a company involves employee representatives in the decision-making process. Even affected staff recognize the fairness of the approach.

Fairness Justice

Definition: A principle connecting fairness to equity, stressing that justice requires both transparent processes and fair outcomes. Fairness ensures that systems are judged not only by how decisions are made but also by their actual impact.

Business Application: Organizations that practice fairness and justice go beyond mere compliance to focus on both procedures and outcomes. This might include transparent hiring processes and fair pay scales, ensuring that fairness is demonstrated, not just promised.

Leadership Insight: Fairness without justice risks becoming superficial. Leaders must ensure that fairness is not just about appearances but is based on actions that address inequity.

Cultural Caution: Fairness varies across cultures. In some contexts, it means equal treatment; in others, it focuses on redistribution based on need or relationships. Leaders must clarify which definition of fairness they are using.

Mosaic Question: Does fairness in your leadership include actual results — or does it end at appearances?

Mosaic in Action: A multinational company combines transparent promotion processes with targeted equity programs to ensure women and underrepresented staff not only have access but also achieve advancement at similar rates.

Faith Expression

Definition: The outward expression of personal or group religious beliefs, values, and traditions in workplace, community, or public settings.

Business Application: Leaders managing diverse teams must balance freedom of faith expression with inclusive policies that prevent proselytizing or marginalization of non-adherents. This includes creating spaces for prayer or reflection and accommodating religious holidays.

Leadership Insight: Respecting faith expression doesn't demand personal agreement—it requires the ability to lead inclusively across different belief systems.

Cultural Caution: Over-accommodating one group's

faith expression while ignoring others can lead to perceptions of favoritism or exclusion.

Mosaic Question: How do your policies allow faith expression while avoiding pressure to participate or silencing differences?

Mosaic in Action: A hospital uses a rotating schedule to ensure all employees—Christian, Muslim, Hindu, and non-religious—have access to time and space for spiritual or reflective practices without disrupting patient care.

Familial Obligation

Definition: The cultural, social, or personal expectation to prioritize the needs, responsibilities, and well-being of family members, often above individual desires or professional ambitions.

Business Application: Leaders from collectivist or family-oriented cultures might make career choices, move, or change schedules to fulfill family responsibilities. Organizations that ignore these priorities risk losing key talent.

Leadership Insight: Recognizing family obligation as a motivator and limitation helps leaders create policies—like flexible schedules or leave—that keep talent without penalizing family commitments.

Cultural Caution: Avoid thinking that family obligation only exists in certain ethnic groups; it shows up across cultures, even though the ways it's expressed differ. Overly romanticizing it can also hide the pressures and sacrifices it involves.

Mosaic Question: How does your leadership recognize the unseen responsibilities employees handle outside of work?

Mosaic in Action: A high-performing team member at a multinational company requests a temporary reduction in hours to care for an ailing parent. Instead of questioning her dedication, the manager reassigns certain tasks and pairs her with a partner on key projects—keeping her expertise while respecting her family commitments.

Family-Leave Equity

Definition: Ensuring fair distribution of family leave benefits across genders, roles, and caregiving responsibilities, so all employees can balance work and caregiving.

Business Application: Organizations with unfair leave policies reinforce gender gaps in career advancement. Fair leave policies promote retention and demonstrate that caregiving is a shared responsibility.

Leadership Insight: Leaders who promote family-leave equity break down barriers that force women and caregivers out of leadership pipelines.

Cultural Caution: Norms for parental leave differ greatly. In some cultures, long leave is standard; in others, it might be stigmatized. Leaders must adapt with care.

Mosaic Question: Does your leave policy support all caregivers — or does it place more burden on some than others?

Mosaic in Action: A global company standardized parental leave for all genders, which doubled retention rates for women after childbirth.

False Neutrality

Definition: The act of appearing to be impartial while actually supporting existing power structures, norms, or inequalities.

Business Application: In conflict resolution or policy making, false neutrality can sustain systemic damage by treating unequal positions as if they have equal validity and resources.

Leadership Insight: True neutrality is uncommon in leadership. Leaders need to recognize that neutrality often benefits those already in power and can unintentionally silence marginalized voices.

Cultural Caution: Declaring neutrality during moral or ethical crises might be seen as complicity. Cultural norms regarding confrontation or harmony influence how "neutral" stances are perceived.

Mosaic Question: When you claim neutrality, whose reality are you defending?

Mosaic in Action: During a workplace harassment investigation, a department head insists on remaining "neutral." In reality, this delays necessary action—allowing harassment to persist and signaling to staff that leadership will not intervene against inequalities.

Fatphobia

Definition: Prejudice, discrimination, or bias aimed at individuals based on body size or weight, often reinforced through language, policy, or cultural beauty standards.

Business Application: Hiring practices, workplace wellness programs, and professional dress codes can all reflect and reinforce fatphobic biases, affecting advancement opportunities for employees in larger bodies.

Leadership Insight: Leaders who actively challenge fatphobia contribute to a culture of dignity and respect, where health and ability are not linked to size or appearance.

Cultural Caution: Fatphobia intersects with race, gender, class, and disability—making it crucial to avoid framing it solely as a matter of individual choice or "personal health."

Mosaic Question: In what ways do your policies or culture equate worthiness with thinness?

Mosaic in Action: A company revamps its corporate wellness program after employees raise concerns that weight-loss challenges and "ideal BMI" incentives stigmatize larger-bodied staff. The new approach prioritizes overall well-being and employee-defined health goals.

Faux Inclusion

Definition: Superficial or performative diversity efforts that signal inclusion without making meaningful changes to systems, policies, or culture.

Business Application: Faux inclusion often shows up in marketing campaigns, token hires, or diversity events that lack follow-up actions or measurable results.

Leadership Insight: Genuine inclusion requires redistributing power, not just symbolic gestures. Leaders need to assess whether diversity initiatives truly shift decision-making and resource distribution.

Cultural Caution: Marginalized employees may become disillusioned or leave if promises of inclusion do not lead to real equity. Tokenism can cause more harm than no representation at all.

Mosaic Question: Are your inclusion efforts opening doors—or just polishing windows?

Mosaic in Action: A tech firm showcases women in its promotional materials but maintains an all-male executive team. After employee feedback, leadership commits to succession planning, mentorship programs, and targeted recruitment of women into leadership roles.

Favoritism

Definition: The unfair practice of giving preferential treatment to certain individuals or groups based on personal bias, loyalty, or affinity rather than merit or fairness.

Business Application: Favoritism undermines morale and causes inequality in workplaces. It can show up in promotions, resource distribution, or access to leadership, often damaging trust and the company culture.

Leadership Insight: True leadership depends on fairness. When leaders identify and eliminate favoritism, they foster an environment where merit, equity, and belonging can flourish.

Cultural Caution: What one culture perceives as favoritism might be seen as kinship or obligation in another. Leaders need to differentiate between cultural norms of reciprocity and unfair privileges.

Mosaic Question: Whose opportunities are expanded in your space — and whose are limited?

Mosaic in Action: A manager replaces informal mentorships driven by personal closeness with a transparent, rotating mentorship program that provides all staff with equal access.

Fear-Based Leadership

Definition: A leadership style based on control, intimidation, or punishment, where fear—rather than trust or inspiration—drives performance.

Business Application: Fear-based leadership might temporarily ensure compliance, but it damages morale, hinders innovation, and promotes short-term thinking instead of sustainable results. Organizations guided by fear often face high turnover, low psychological safety, and decreased engagement.

Leadership Insight: True influence arises from trust, not intimidation. Leaders who transition from fear to empowerment foster creativity, loyalty, and resilience within their teams—especially during high-stakes or uncertain times.

Cultural Caution: In some cultural settings, hierarchy is highly valued, and openly challenging leaders is uncommon. It's important to distinguish between genuine respect and compliance driven by fear to ensure fair leadership.

Mosaic Question: What would your leadership look like if people followed you because they wanted to — not because they felt obligated to?

Mosaic in Action: In a multinational company, a department head known for sharp criticism notices declining performance across teams. After leadership coaching, they replace public reprimands with private, constructive feedback sessions. Within six months, employee surveys show a 40 percent increase in trust and collaboration.

Feedback Culture

Definition: A workplace environment where feedback is normalized, safe, and constructive, fostering ongoing dialogue rather than one-off reviews.

Business Application: Strong feedback cultures boost performance, trust, and innovation by promoting continuous growth instead of sporadic improvements.

Leadership Insight: Leaders demonstrate feedback culture by being as open to receive as they are to give. This balance dissolves hierarchies and fosters trust.

Cultural Caution: Feedback norms differ — some cultures value directness, while others prefer subtlety. Leaders need to balance these cultural preferences with clarity in the organization.

Mosaic Question: Do people in your organization feel comfortable providing you with feedback?

Mosaic in Action: A nonprofit used "feedforward" check-ins to lower staff turnover and boost collaboration.

Feedback Fatigue

Definition: A state of emotional or mental exhaustion caused by receiving excessive, poorly timed, or conflicting feedback, often resulting in disengagement or reduced performance.

Business Application: While feedback is crucial for growth, too much feedback—especially without proper context or prioritization—can overwhelm employees. Organizations that streamline feedback processes and align them with development goals experience better retention and productivity.

Leadership Insight: Feedback is only as effective as the space leaders create for it to be processed, understood, and acted upon. Quality and clarity matter more than quantity.

Cultural Caution: In cultures where direct feedback is rare, even well-meaning constructive criticism can seem harsh or aggressive. Adjusting how you deliver feedback to match cultural and personal preferences helps avoid unnecessary tension.

Mosaic Question: Are you providing feedback to help your team grow—or merely to record their errors?

Mosaic in Action: A startup conducts weekly "micro-feedback" check-ins instead of endless Slack comments. Leaders point out one strength and one growth area for each employee. Over time, staff say they feel more focused, less defensive, and more motivated to act on feedback.

Feeling Undervalued

Definition: The feeling of having one's contributions, presence, or worth ignored, minimized, or dismissed in organizational or cultural settings.

Business Application: Employees who feel undervalued tend to disengage, withdraw, or leave. Leaders who do not recognize contributions risk losing talent, creativity, and trust.

Leadership Insight: Recognition is not flattery — it fuels engagement. Leaders who listen, affirm, and credit their teams build loyalty and boost performance.

Cultural Caution: Expressions of value vary. In some cultures, public praise is encouraging; in others, it might cause discomfort. Leaders need to confirm value in culturally appropriate ways.

Mosaic Question: How do you make sure the people you lead feel recognized, respected, and appreciated?

Mosaic in Action: An organization implements a peer-recognition system where employees routinely acknowledge each other's contributions, helping to highlight quiet but essential work.

Feminist Geography

Definition: An academic and applied method that explores how gender, identity, and power influence our experience and understanding of physical and social spaces.

Business Application: Urban planning, workplace design, and event logistics benefit from feminist geography by examining how various genders and identities experience safety, accessibility, and inclusion in physical spaces.

Leadership Insight: Leaders who use this perspective challenge standard designs—whether in office layouts, community planning, or policy-making—ensuring environments are welcoming and safe for everyone.

Cultural Caution: What is seen as a "safe" or "inclusive" space changes based on cultural norms, political situations, and history. Leaders should not assume there is one universal standard.

Mosaic Question: Whose needs are incorporated into the spaces you design—and whose are excluded?

Mosaic in Action: A city council redesigns public transit routes and lighting after surveying women, caregivers, and differently-abled residents about safety and accessibility. Ridership increases, and community satisfaction ratings improve.

Feminist Leadership

Definition: A leadership philosophy and practice that focuses on equity, collaboration, and dismantling oppressive structures, often drawing on feminist theory and intersectional analysis.

Business Application: Feminist leadership promotes shared decision-making, amplifies marginalized voices, and prioritizes well-being alongside results—making it well-suited for organizations navigating complexity and diversity.

Leadership Insight: By fostering transparency, mutual accountability, and collective care, feminist leaders build environments where everyone can thrive without recreating the systems they aim to transform.

Cultural Caution: The term "feminist" has different meanings around the world—ranging from empowerment to political controversy. Leaders should adjust language and framing while keeping core principles intact.

Mosaic Question: If leadership is about power, how are you using yours to make sure others can lead as well?

Mosaic in Action: A nonprofit's executive director reorganizes meetings so that decision-making rotates among team members. This method encourages ideas from those who previously remained silent, resulting in more innovative programming and stronger team cohesion.

Feminist Pedagogy

Definition: An educational and leadership framework that emphasizes equity, critical inquiry, and shared power within learning environments. It questions hierarchical norms and gives priority to marginalized voices.

Business Application: Feminist pedagogy shapes leadership training, team facilitation, and organizational learning. It encourages inclusion, dialogue, and shared knowledge.

Leadership Insight: Leaders using feminist pedagogy share authority, encourage diverse perspectives, and challenge traditional

power dynamics in learning environments.

Cultural Caution: In certain cultural or organizational contexts, feminist pedagogy might be dismissed as political rather than educational. Leaders need to present it in ways that connect locally.

Mosaic Question: How do your learning spaces organize or challenge power?

Mosaic in Action: A leadership development program updates its curriculum to include co-teaching, storytelling, and shared authority, amplifying voices that have been historically excluded.

Feminization of Labor

Definition: The process where industries, sectors, or roles become increasingly dominated by women, often resulting in the devaluation of the work and a decline in wages and status. This shift is not necessarily about achieving gender balance but about the social and economic reclassification of the work.

Business Application: When fields like teaching, nursing, or customer service become mostly female, organizations may unconsciously give them less prestige and fewer resources. This affects recruitment, pay fairness, and career growth.

Leadership Insight: A leader's role is to identify the structural biases that come with the feminization of labor and ensure that the work's value is maintained, adequately resourced, and respected regardless of gender representation.

Cultural Caution: Avoid portraying feminized work as "less skilled" or "less strategic." This bias can alienate talent, widen wage gaps, and reinforce harmful gender norms.

Mosaic Question: When a role becomes more associated with women, how does your organization maintain or enhance its perceived and actual value?

Mosaic in Action: A school district notices that as more men leave teaching, the profession is losing political and financial support. A superintendent launches a campaign highlighting the profession's essential skills, advocates for competitive pay, and develops a mentorship program to raise the role's status across genders.

Fictive Kinship

Definition: A social bond formed between individuals who are not biologically related but consider each other family, often developing in cultural, community, or workplace settings.

Business Application: In workplaces, fictive kinship can foster strong loyalty and mutual support. Teams with this level of trust often show higher resilience and collaboration during crises.

Leadership Insight: While fictive kinship can boost morale, leaders must ensure it doesn't create exclusivity or obstruct accountability. Healthy boundaries maintain both trust and performance.

Cultural Caution: Be aware that fictive kinship is shaped by culture—what seems like genuine care in one culture might feel like overstepping in another. Misinterpreting these dynamics can cause tension or misunderstanding.

Mosaic Question: How do you foster a sense of belonging that feels like "family" while maintaining clear roles and professional standards?

Mosaic in Action: A nonprofit team calls themselves "the village." When a staff member faces a personal loss, colleagues step up to cover her duties and bring meals to her home. The director thanks them publicly while also making sure the workload shift is temporary and fair.

Filter Bubble

Definition: The narrowing of perspective that occurs when algorithms or social patterns reinforce existing beliefs and limit exposure to diverse viewpoints.

Business Application: Filter bubbles impact workplace communication, digital marketing, and public discussion. Leaders need to address them to promote innovation and diverse perspectives.

Leadership Insight: Leaders who recognize filter bubbles proactively foster environments for dissent, alternative perspectives, and open information sharing.

Cultural Caution: Filter bubbles are not just technological; they can also form in social, cultural, or ideological silos. Leaders need to look beyond the digital perspective.

Mosaic Question: What voices or ideas are absent from your leadership "bubble"?

Mosaic in Action: An executive team purposefully involves stakeholders outside its industry bubble to challenge assumptions during strategic planning.

Financial Inclusion

Definition: The effort to ensure individuals and communities, especially marginalized groups, have access to affordable and fair financial services.

Business Application: Financial inclusion grows markets, lowers inequality, and builds stronger communities. It plays a key role in leadership across banking, fintech, and social enterprises.

Leadership Insight: Leaders who promote financial inclusion look past profit to prioritize social impact, balancing business success with fairness.

Cultural Caution: Financial inclusion strategies must adjust to local conditions. Tools that succeed in one area (e.g., microcredit) might be ineffective or even damaging in another.

Mosaic Question: Who in your ecosystem is denied financial access — and what can you do about it?

Mosaic in Action: A fintech startup develops mobile banking for rural communities, lowering barriers for women and farmers who have been historically excluded from traditional finance.

Fiscal Justice Leadership

Definition: A leadership approach that guarantees the fair, transparent, and socially responsible allocation, management, and distribution of financial resources.

Business Application: Organizations practicing fiscal justice incorporate equity into budget planning, vendor selection, and compensation strategies, ensuring resources are allocated in ways that minimize systemic disparities.

Leadership Insight: Fiscal justice leadership goes beyond just managing money; it's about aligning spending with core values and making decisions that foster lasting fairness instead of focusing only on short-term savings.

Cultural Caution: Avoid performative "equity budgeting" that only reallocates funds in appearance. Transparency, stakeholder involvement, and measurable impact are essential.

Mosaic Question: How does your budget align with your organization's stated commitments to fairness, equity, and inclusion?

Mosaic in Action: A university reviews its budget and discovers that diversity initiatives are underfunded compared to other programs. The president reallocates funds, doubles community partnership grants, and publicly shares the budget breakdown to foster trust and accountability.

First-Generation Pressure

Definition: The unique expectations and burdens placed on individuals who are the first in their family to reach certain milestones, such as going to college, starting a professional career, or holding leadership positions.

Business Application: First-generation professionals often feel pressure to succeed not only for themselves but also for their families and communities, which can lead to increased stress and potential burnout.

Leadership Insight: Leaders can support first-generation employees through mentorship, clear advancement pathways, and recognition of the cultural and emotional weight they carry.

Cultural Caution: Avoid assuming all first-generation employees face the same challenges or have similar backgrounds. Overgeneralizing can damage trust and ignore individual needs.

Mosaic Question: What systems are in place to support first-generation leaders and professionals without tokenizing them?

Mosaic in Action: A law firm observes that its first-generation associates consistently work longer hours and experience higher stress levels. In response, leadership starts a mentorship program, encourages mental health days, and hosts workshops on navigating unspoken workplace norms.

Flexibility Stigma

Definition: The bias and negative assumptions aimed at employees who utilize flexible work arrangements, such as remote work or adjusted hours.

Business Application: Flexibility stigma hinders equity and retention, especially for caregivers, parents, and women. Leaders who normalize flexible work help reduce stigma and broaden talent pipelines.

Leadership Insight: Flexibility is not a perk but a strategic equity practice. Leaders who reduce stigma build trust and loyalty.

Cultural Caution: In certain situations, flexibility is seen as a lack of discipline. Leaders need to challenge cultural norms by providing evidence of productivity.

Mosaic Question: Does your workplace view flexibility as a weakness — or as a strength?

Mosaic in Action: A manager openly demonstrates flexible scheduling, establishing a standard

that emphasizes results over physical presence.

Folk Wisdom

Definition:: Informal knowledge, beliefs, and practices passed down through generations in a culture or community, often transmitted orally or through lived experience.

Business Application: Folk wisdom can influence organizational decision-making, especially in family businesses, community enterprises, or organizations rooted in tradition. Leaders who recognize and respect these traditions can connect formal systems with community trust.

Leadership Insight:: When used thoughtfully, folk wisdom can offer nuanced solutions that data alone might miss. It reminds leaders that experience-based knowledge often holds emotional and cultural importance, which can strengthen team cohesion.

Cultural Caution:: Not all folk wisdom aligns with current ethical standards or inclusive practices. Following it blindly without reflection can reinforce bias or exclusion.

Mosaic Question:: How can you honor the cultural significance of folk wisdom while ensuring it promotes fairness and inclusion?

Mosaic in Action:: During a regional project, a nonprofit leader consults a local elder whose folk wisdom about water cycles guides the team to adjust their well-drilling approach—avoiding seasonal flooding and earning deep community trust.

Followership Dynamics

Definition: The patterns of behavior, engagement, and influence among those in subordinate or supportive roles within a leadership structure.

Business Application: Understanding followership dynamics helps leaders foster environments where team members are proactive, accountable, and empowered to influence outcomes.

Leadership Insight: Strong leadership is not only about vision—it's about creating conditions where followers are engaged partners rather than passive workers. Leaders who recognize followership dynamics can unlock collective potential.

Cultural Caution: Cultural norms shape followership differently. In some contexts, openly challenging leadership is seen as disrespectful; in others, it is expected as part of healthy dialogue.

Mosaic Question: What unspoken rules about followership exist in your team, and do they help or hinder progress?

Mosaic in Action: A project manager notices that junior staff rarely voice concerns in meetings. By introducing anonymous input channels and rewarding constructive dissent, she shifts the followership dynamic toward shared responsibility and innovation.

Food and Identity

Definition: The link between culinary traditions, food practices, and a person's sense of cultural, family, or personal identity.

Business Application: In global organizations, food-focused events and inclusive catering can promote belonging, celebrate diversity, and foster cross-cultural understanding.

Leadership Insight: Food can serve as a powerful way to open up conversations about culture, heritage, and values—especially when leaders use it to create inclusive environments.

Cultural Caution: Avoid tokenizing cuisines or reducing cultures to their most popular dishes. Food representation should be genuine and include voices from the communities involved.

Mosaic Question: How can you use food as a way to connect without turning culture into a commodity?

Mosaic in Action: A school district hosting a staff retreat includes a potluck where each participant brings a dish linked to their personal story. Discussions sparked by these dishes deepen relationships across roles and backgrounds.

Forced Assimilation

Definition: The systematic pressure applied to individuals or groups to abandon their cultural identity, language, or traditions in favor of a dominant culture's norms.

Business Application: In organizations, forced assimilation can appear through strict policies, dress codes, or communication styles that erase cultural differences.

Leadership Insight: Genuine inclusion enables individuals to maintain and express their identities while actively participating in shared goals. Leaders who oppose assimilationist practices foster environments where diversity flourishes.

Cultural Caution: Assimilation often benefits the dominant group while marginalizing others. Leaders must distinguish between shared organizational values and conforming to a single cultural norm.

Mosaic Question: What organizational practices might unintentionally enforce assimilation, and how can they be redesigned to promote inclusivity?

Mosaic in Action: A multinational corporation revises its policy requiring all client interactions in English after realizing it discourages talented multilingual staff from using their native languages to connect with local clients.

Forced Migration

Definition: The involuntary movement of individuals or communities from their home regions due to conflict, persecution, environmental disasters, or development projects, often without the chance to return.

Business Application: Organizations serving refugee or displaced populations need to understand the complexities of forced migration to create effective policies, inclusive hiring practices, and trauma-informed services. In global supply chains, leaders should be aware of displacement caused by resource extraction, infrastructure projects, or geopolitical instability.

Leadership Insight: Addressing forced migration is not just about providing aid; it requires long-term integration strategies, acknowledgment of disrupted identities, and advocacy to address systemic causes. Leaders who grasp these dynamics can foster more resilient, equitable communities.

Cultural Caution: Forced migration experiences vary greatly, and assuming a single "refugee narrative" can overlook individual agency. It is important to avoid conflating forced migration with voluntary relocation or economic migration.

Mosaic Question: How can you create spaces for displaced voices to lead—rather than just be recipients of support?

Mosaic in Action: A municipal leader in a European city partners with local refugee-led organizations to co-design housing, language programs, and small-business grants, ensuring displaced residents help shape their own resettlement policies.

Foreignness Bias

Definition: The tendency to see individuals as outsiders or less capable because of perceived differences in nationality, accent, cultural norms, or background.

Business Application: This bias can affect hiring, promotion,

and client trust, resulting in the exclusion of highly skilled professionals. To address it, organizations need fair evaluation systems, culturally inclusive onboarding, and bias-aware leadership development.

Leadership Insight: Leaders who actively combat foreignness bias enhance talent retention, broaden market understanding, and build credibility within diverse communities.

Cultural Caution: Overcompensating with tokenism can be as damaging as exclusion. Avoid framing foreignness solely as a "value add" or "novelty," and instead acknowledge the individual's expertise and humanity.

Mosaic Question: How might your leadership unintentionally signal that some voices are less valuable than others?

Mosaic in Action: A multinational tech company notices that clients tend to listen more to team members with North American accents. The project leader reorganizes presentations so everyone speaks on their areas of expertise, making competence—not accent—the key to credibility.

Formal vs. Informal Power

Definition: The difference between authority granted through official roles, titles, or structures (formal) and influence gained through relationships, expertise, or cultural capital (informal).

Business Application: Leaders who understand and utilize informal power can access hidden networks, improve morale, and encourage grassroots innovation. Ignoring informal power often results in missed opportunities and resistance to formal instructions.

Leadership Insight: Effective leadership combines both types of power—formal authority for establishing structure and informal influence for building trust and cultural alignment.

Cultural Caution: Relying too much on informal power can create cliques or favoritism; relying heavily on formal power can lead to rigidity and alienation.

Mosaic Question: How do you blend authority with influence to build trust rather than dependence?

Mosaic in Action: During a nonprofit merger, the new director maps both the official organizational chart and the informal "influence web," ensuring that community elders and long-standing volunteers are involved alongside department heads in developing integration plans.

Forgiveness Culture

Definition: An organizational or community norm that promotes acknowledgment of harm, accountability, and rebuilding trust, rather than ongoing punishment or avoidance.

Business Application: In workplaces, a forgiveness culture can enhance collaboration after conflicts, decrease turnover, and foster innovation by making it safer to take risks. However, it must be rooted in accountability to prevent enabling harmful behavior.

Leadership Insight: Leaders who demonstrate public accountability and genuine repair set an example that boosts resilience and cohesion within teams.

Cultural Caution: Forgiveness should never be forced, especially on those who are harmed. Norms around forgiveness vary widely—what is considered healing in one setting may seem dismissive in another.

Mosaic Question: How can your leadership foster conditions where repair is possible without erasing the harm done?

Mosaic in Action: After a high-stakes project failure, a senior manager meets privately with affected teams, acknowledges the mistakes, and invites open dialogue about repair steps. Team members report greater trust in leadership and a renewed willingness to collaborate across departments.

Foundational Myths

Definition: Widely accepted stories or origin tales that shape group identity, values, and beliefs, often mixing historical fact with selective memory or cultural symbols.

Business Application: Organizations and institutions frequently operate based on their own "foundational myths," like the story of how they started or a key moment in their history. These myths can motivate loyalty, but they can also hide past mistakes or exclude certain groups from the shared story.

Leadership Insight: Leaders need to examine which myths are being shared, who benefits from them, and who is left out. Unquestioned myths can reinforce blind spots in culture and decision-making.

Cultural Caution: Foundational myths often leave out marginalized viewpoints, replacing complex histories with simplified or romanticized stories that favor dominant groups.

Mosaic Question: Which foundational stories influence your team or community, and whose voices were missing in their telling?

Mosaic in Action: During a company anniversary, the founder's speech highlights only the contributions of early leaders, ignoring the role of frontline employees who kept things running during crises. After employee feedback, leaders rewrite the official history to include multiple perspectives, honoring the full truth of the organization's journey.

Framing Bias

Definition: The tendency to interpret information differently based on how it is presented, even when the underlying facts stay the same.

Business Application: In project proposals, problem statements framed as opportunities often get more support than those framed as threats, despite having identical data.

Leadership Insight: Skilled leaders recognize when framing influences decisions and work to present both opportunities and risks clearly and fairly.

Cultural Caution: Framing can subtly reinforce stereotypes—

such as describing certain markets as "risky" due to cultural unfamiliarity—leading to biased decisions.

Mosaic Question: How might changing the way a challenge is framed alter the actions your team considers possible?

Mosaic in Action: A school district faces declining enrollment. Initially framed as a budget crisis, leaders notice community morale dropping. They reframe it as a chance to redesign programs and build partnerships, which sparks creative ideas and renewed engagement.

Fragility Response

Definition: An emotional defensive reaction—often from members of dominant groups—when faced with information that challenges their worldview, privilege, or identity.

Business Application: In diversity training, a fragility response can show as defensiveness, denial, or emotional withdrawal, slowing progress toward inclusion goals.

Leadership Insight: Leaders who demonstrate self-regulation and curiosity when confronted with uncomfortable truths set a positive tone for open dialogue.

Cultural Caution: Dismissing fragility responses as mere oversensitivity risks increasing resistance; they need to be addressed with accountability and support, not avoidance.

Mosaic Question: How do you respond—both internally and outwardly—when your assumptions are questioned?

Mosaic in Action: After a team member highlights gender bias in meeting facilitation, a manager initially reacts defensively. Recognizing the fragility response, they pause, thank the colleague, and commit to reviewing facilitation patterns—resulting in a more equitable distribution of speaking time.

Freedom Narratives

Definition: Stories or frameworks that define what freedom means for individuals or groups, often shaped by historical, political, and cultural contexts.

Business Application: In organizational culture, freedom narratives influence how autonomy, innovation, and decision-making are valued or restricted.

Leadership Insight: Effective leaders understand that notions of "freedom" vary across cultures and generations; aligning organizational values with multiple perspectives can build trust and cohesion.

Cultural Caution: Freedom narratives can be exploited to justify exclusionary practices or ignore structural inequalities—for example, framing deregulation as freedom while harming vulnerable groups.

Mosaic Question: Whose definition of freedom influences your work environment, and how does it include—or exclude—others?

Mosaic in Action: A nonprofit in a post-conflict region creates youth programs based on a Western narrative of freedom as individual choice. Local leaders highlight the community's view of freedom as collective security. The program is then redesigned to balance personal agency with community resilience.

Frontline Wisdom

Definition: Practical knowledge and situational insight gained from direct, on-the-ground experience, often held by those in frontline roles.

Business Application: Frontline wisdom helps bridge the gap between policy and practice, guiding leaders on operational realities and the human impact of decisions.

Leadership Insight: Leaders who listen to frontline voices are better equipped to make relevant, sustainable changes. These insights often carry urgency and clarity not found in reports.

Cultural Caution: Avoid romanticizing frontline roles as "pure" knowledge without recognizing the risks, burnout, and inequities often associated with them.

Mosaic Question: How often do you incorporate frontline perspectives into your decision-making?

Mosaic in Action: A hospital administrator shadows nurses for a week, discovering how a small procedural change could save hours of unnecessary work. This observation prompts a system-wide update that improves patient care and reduces staff stress.

Functional Diversity

Definition: The presence of diverse skill sets, problem-solving approaches, and cognitive styles within a team or organization.

Business Application: Functional diversity boosts innovation, adaptability, and creative problem-solving, especially in complex or volatile environments.

Leadership Insight: A variety of roles and skills can prevent groupthink and help organizations tackle challenges from multiple perspectives.

Cultural Caution: Functional diversity without relational trust can lead to friction and inefficiency rather than innovation.

Mosaic Question: Are you leveraging functional diversity or just assembling it?

Mosaic in Action: A product team combines engineers, marketers, and customer service reps in its design meetings to ensure the final launch addresses both technical excellence and real user needs.

Future-Belonging

Definition: A forward-looking approach to inclusion that ensures people see themselves as part of the organization's or community's future.

Business Application: This principle helps organizations retain talent, especially from underrepresented groups, by indicating that their voices matter in shaping the path ahead.

Leadership Insight: People stay engaged when they see a place for themselves in what's next—not just in what's now.

Cultural Caution: Future-belonging must be paired with present action; promises about the future are meaningless without progress today.

Mosaic Question: What future do your people believe they are being invited into?

Mosaic in Action: A nonprofit not only recruits diverse interns but also involves them in strategy sessions, showing that their perspectives will influence next year's initiatives.

Future Fluency

Definition: The ability to understand, anticipate, and adapt to emerging trends, technologies, and social changes.

Business Application: Leaders with future fluency can align organizational strategies with likely industry and cultural shifts, avoiding reactive decisions.

Leadership Insight: Anticipating change strengthens resilience; preparing for multiple futures encourages agility.

Cultural Caution: Future fluency without cultural fluency risks making changes that alienate people or deepen inequalities.

Mosaic Question: How effectively do you balance readiness for the future with relevance today?

Mosaic in Action: A school district leader examines global education trends and tests a blended learning model—ensuring both technological preparedness and community trust before applying it district-wide.

Future Literacy

Definition: The ability to "read" and understand the future as a space of possibility, using foresight to guide current decisions.

Business Application: Future literacy enables organizations to innovate proactively instead of just reacting to disruptions.

Leadership Insight: Future literacy reinterprets uncertainty as a resource for creativity rather than a threat to control.

Cultural Caution: Overreliance on predictive models can lead to overconfidence; humility is essential when dealing with the unknown.

Mosaic Question: How do you train your team to engage with uncertainty in a constructive way?

Mosaic in Action: A municipal leader conducts future scenario workshops with citizens, incorporating community ideas into long-term urban planning that considers climate change, migration, and cultural shifts.

Future-Ready Leadership

Definition: A leadership mindset and practice that enable individuals and organizations to anticipate, adapt to, and succeed in uncertain, rapidly changing environments.

Business Application: Future-ready leadership ensures organizations stay resilient amid technological disruption, climate change, and global shifts.

Leadership Insight: Future-ready leaders focus on foresight, agility, and innovation while staying grounded in values and equity.

Cultural Caution: Visions of the "future" are influenced by culture. Leaders should avoid pushing Western ideas of the future and instead encourage a variety of perspectives.

Mosaic Question: Are you getting your organization ready for today's challenges or tomorrow's opportunities?

Mosaic in Action: A global nonprofit trains its leadership team in scenario planning to anticipate climate impacts on vulnerable communities.

◈ LETTER F CALLOUT

"Fairness is not sameness; equity requires context, courage, and continual adjustment."

Reflection Questions

- How do you distinguish between treating people equally and treating them equitably?
- What hidden favoritism can creep into feedback, grading, or promotion decisions?
- How does fragility show up when fairness is challenged?

Practical Move

Choose one policy, assignment, or reward structure. Adjust it slightly to meet an overlooked need — and explain openly why equity, not sameness, guided your choice.

G – Gatekeeping, Gaslighting, and Generational Tension

G symbolizes the quiet barriers and shifting perspectives that determine who enters, who belongs, and whose voice carries weight. Gatekeeping often hides behind words like "standards," "experience," or "culture fit" — but its true aim is exclusion masked as excellence. Gaslighting reinterprets harm as misunderstanding and twists reality until personal truths seem like overreactions. And generational tension, often dismissed as personality conflict, exposes deeper differences in values, communication, and lived experiences.

These dynamics shape the everyday fabric of leadership. They influence hiring decisions, mentorship opportunities, performance reviews, and even the subtle shifts in language during meetings. They determine who is affirmed, who is dismissed, and whose version of events becomes the story everyone accepts.

G asks us to notice the forces that reshape belonging

- The gatekeeping that measures worthiness by bias, not ability.
- The gaslighting that erases harm by rewriting the narrative.
- The generational divides that fracture collaboration into misunderstanding.
- The uneven credibility granted not by merit, but by perception and history.

The G terms do more than diagnose—they reveal how authority is built, how narratives are sustained, and how trust diminishes when these patterns go unchallenged. They remind us that credibility is not always earned fairly but is distributed through unseen hierarchies of bias and tradition.

G urges leaders to slow down before taking charge, listen longer than they speak, and develop empathy strong enough to hold differences without diminishing them. When gatekeeping is dismantled, gaslighting is confronted, and generational voices are respected, leadership grows beyond control—it becomes about creating spaces where more people genuinely belong.

G

Gaslighting

Definition: A form of psychological manipulation where someone or a group causes another person to doubt their own perceptions, memories, or judgment, often to gain power or control.

Business Application: It can happen in workplaces when leaders or peers deny facts, rewrite events, or question colleagues' competence to maintain authority or avoid responsibility.

Leadership Insight: Leaders need to actively create environments where honesty and accountability are prioritized over protecting their image or personal power.

Cultural Caution: In cross-cultural settings, gaslighting may be hidden by politeness norms or hierarchical structures, making it more difficult to identify and address.

Mosaic Question: Whose reality might you be unintentionally dismissing, and how can you rebuild trust?

Mosaic in Action: During a team debrief, a manager claims an employee's concerns were never raised, despite clear meeting notes. A peer steps in, confirms the record, and supports a constructive dialogue—helping to preserve the employee's credibility and trust in the process.

Gate-Opener Leadership

Definition: Leadership that actively removes barriers and creates access to opportunities, networks, and resources for others, especially those who are underrepresented or excluded.

Business Application: This may include making strategic introductions, advocating for someone's inclusion in decision-making spaces, or sharing vital insider knowledge.

Leadership Insight: Gate-openers view influence as a responsibility to multiply opportunity rather than to hoard it.

Cultural Caution: Without cultural sensitivity, efforts to "open gates" can seem paternalistic or self-promoting instead of empowering.

Mosaic Question: Whose career or influence could you support this week by opening a door for them?

Mosaic in Action: A senior executive nominates an early-career professional from an underrepresented background to present at a major conference, while staying in the audience to amplify and support their voice.

Gatekeeping

Definition: The practice of controlling access to opportunities, information, or resources, often in ways that uphold existing hierarchies or power structures.

Business Application: Can show up as informal cliques, selective communication, or setting arbitrary requirements that put certain groups at a disadvantage.

Leadership Insight: Gatekeeping is often unintentional but can reinforce inequalities; leaders should critically assess their own decision-making processes.

Cultural Caution: What one culture sees as "quality control" might be viewed as exclusion in another.

Mosaic Question: What opportunities are you controlling that could be shared more fairly?

Mosaic in Action: A department head refuses to share project leads beyond a trusted few, limiting the growth of other capable team members—until a colleague questions the practice and pushes for a fair rotation system.

Gender Equity

Definition: The process of ensuring fairness in how individuals of all genders are treated, considering their different needs and systemic barriers.

Business Application: Encompasses fair pay systems, inclusive recruiting, and policies that support all gender identities.

Leadership Insight: Achieving gender equity is not about treating everyone exactly the same, but about providing what each person needs to succeed.

Cultural Caution: Gender norms and equity strategies differ greatly across cultures; global leaders must adjust their methods to fit local contexts while maintaining core principles.

Mosaic Question: Where might your policies and practices unintentionally favor one gender over others?

Mosaic in Action: An organization conducts a pay review, finds women in similar roles earn less, and makes immediate salary adjustments along with transparent reporting to ensure accountability.

Gender Expression

Definition: The outward presentation of a person's gender identity through clothing, hairstyle, voice, mannerisms, and other physical or social cues.

Business Application: In workplace culture, policies that support diverse gender expressions—such as inclusive dress codes—signal safety and respect, which can improve employee engagement and retention.

Leadership Insight: Leaders who demonstrate acceptance of different gender expressions create environments where authenticity is accepted rather than punished.

Cultural Caution: Gender expression norms vary across cultures and settings; what is seen as neutral or appropriate in one environment may be viewed as transgressive in another.

Mosaic Question: How does your organization's culture support people in expressing themselves fully without fear of judgment or career consequences?

Mosaic in Action: During a major client presentation, a team member arrives in attire that reflects their authentic gender expression, which differs from traditional expectations. The leader affirms their presence, gives them a central speaking role, and later updates the company dress policy to explicitly protect self-expression.

Gender Norms

Definition: Socially constructed expectations about behaviors, roles, and appearances linked to perceived gender.

Business Application: Gender norms can quietly influence leadership chances, task assignments, and performance reviews, often reinforcing unfairness.

Leadership Insight: Challenging outdated gender norms can unlock hidden potential in teams and broaden the types of leadership that are valued.

Cultural Caution: While some gender norms are deeply rooted in tradition, unexamined adherence can sustain discrimination or restrict participation.

Mosaic Question: Which unspoken gender norms affect decision-making at your workplace—and how could removing them boost fairness?

Mosaic in Action: In a cross-functional project, leadership roles are initially assigned based on outdated ideas about assertiveness and gender. A manager notices this and reorganizes responsibilities based on skills and interests, leading to better performance and morale.

Gender Pronouns

Definition: The words used to refer to someone instead of their name, often reflecting their gender identity (e.g., she/her, he/him, they/them).

Business Application: Including pronouns in introductions, email signatures, and name tags can show respect and help create a culture of belonging.

Leadership Insight: Using pronouns correctly shows cultural understanding and emotional intelligence, building trust in leadership.

Cultural Caution: Pronoun use norms differ around the world; in some places, sharing pronouns publicly may involve risks or need sensitive handling.

Mosaic Question: How does your workplace automatically normalize correct pronoun use without singling people out?

Mosaic in Action: In a company all-hands meeting, the leader models sharing pronouns during their introduction, encourages others to do the same voluntarily,

and makes sure internal profiles are updated to show the selected pronouns.

Gendered Racism

Definition: The intersectional discrimination that happens when both race and gender contribute to unique patterns of bias and inequality.

Business Application: Gendered racism can affect hiring, pay equity, performance reviews, and opportunities for advancement, especially for women of color.

Leadership Insight: Tackling gendered racism requires an intersectional perspective—policies that focus only on race or only on gender may miss the combined experiences of those at the intersection.

Cultural Caution: Experiences of gendered racism differ across regions, industries, and communities; assuming they are the same can overlook important differences.

Mosaic Question: How does your leadership approach consider the combined effects of multiple marginalized identities?

Mosaic in Action: When reviewing promotion data, a director notices women of color are promoted at much lower rates despite performing well. They start an intersectional equity review, introduce mentorship programs, and make structural changes to remove promotion barriers.

Generational Intelligence

Definition: The ability to recognize, respect, and utilize the distinct values, communication styles, and work habits of different generations in a shared environment.

Business Application: Leaders with generational intelligence minimize friction by customizing engagement strategies to bridge age-related differences in motivation, feedback, and decision-making.

Leadership Insight: A multigenerational team is not a difficulty to manage—it's an advantage when differences are viewed as assets.

Cultural Caution: Avoid assuming all members of a generation have identical traits; stereotypes diminish individual identity.

Mosaic Question: How often do you interpret someone's actions through a generational lens without considering their intent?

Mosaic in Action: In a nonprofit board meeting, a Gen Z member

advocates for rapid change while a Baby Boomer board chair recommends a more cautious approach. The director mediates by encouraging each to share the values shaping their pace preference, revealing shared goals and aligning on a phased strategy.

Generational Trauma

Definition: Psychological, emotional, and sometimes physical harm passed down through families or communities, rooted in historical oppression, conflict, or systemic inequities.

Business Application: Recognizing generational trauma can help shape organizational policies that focus on mental health, cultural healing, and inclusive leadership.

Leadership Insight: Healing from generational trauma often requires systemic change, not just individual resilience.

Cultural Caution: Trauma-informed strategies should never stigmatize entire cultures; they should aim to empower agency and voice.

Mosaic Question: What histories shape the fears, motivations, and communication styles of those you lead?

Mosaic in Action: A school district serving Indigenous students incorporates community-led healing circles into policy planning, acknowledging historical harms while fostering pathways for student and family leadership.

Generational Wealth Gap

Definition: The difference in accumulated assets, opportunities, and financial stability among different generations, often influenced by historical privilege or exclusion.

Business Application: Leaders can work to bridge wealth gaps by promoting fair pay, creating career development pathways, and providing access to investment education.

Leadership Insight: Financial inequities are not only personal issues—they are structural and require systemic awareness in leadership choices.

Cultural Caution: Conversations about wealth gaps can cause defensiveness; frame them as opportunities for mutual prosperity rather than assigning blame.

Mosaic Question: How can your leadership help reduce, rather than increase, the financial divides between generations?

Mosaic in Action: A corporate internship program transitions from unpaid to fully paid, allowing participation from candidates who might otherwise be unable to afford it due to financial barriers.

Generative Leadership

Definition: A leadership approach that fosters innovation, growth, and sustainability. Generative leaders focus on empowering others to succeed and advance shared vision.

Business Application: In rapidly evolving industries, generative leadership encourages creativity and develops pools of new talent. Organizations gain when leaders focus on building systems that endure beyond their time in charge.

Leadership Insight: Generativity is about legacy, not control. Leaders who practice it see success not only in outcomes but also in the resilience and capacity they pass on.

Cultural Caution: Generative leadership must steer clear of paternalism — the trap of assuming others need to be "given" capacity rather than trusted to develop it on their own.

Mosaic Question: Do you build systems around yourself — or do you create structures that endure beyond you?

Mosaic in Action: A retiring nonprofit founder passes the torch by coaching emerging leaders and decentralizing authority, ensuring the mission continues with fresh vision.

Generosity Culture

Definition: An organizational environment where giving—of time, resources, knowledge, and recognition—is encouraged and celebrated.

Business Application: A generosity culture enhances trust, loyalty, and collaboration, making it easier to handle high-pressure or uncertain situations.

Leadership Insight: Generosity on a large scale needs boundaries; unstructured giving can lead to burnout.

Cultural Caution: In some cultures, generosity is reciprocal and connected to relationship-building; ignoring this can make giving seem transactional.

Mosaic Question: Does your organization reward generosity as much as productivity?

Mosaic in Action: A senior engineer spends part of her week mentoring junior staff. Leadership recognizes and promotes her not only for her technical contributions but also for her role in strengthening team cohesion.

Gentrification

Definition: The process by which neighborhoods that were historically under-resourced see an influx of wealthier residents, leading to increased property values, cultural displacement, and shifting social dynamics.

Business Application: Organizations moving into revitalized areas need to assess whether they are contributing to displacement or promoting fair community development. Implementing social impact plans, local hiring practices, and investing in cultural preservation can help reduce harm.

Leadership Insight: Leaders can foster economic growth while preserving community character by engaging residents early, respecting local histories, and including their voices in decision-making.

Cultural Caution: Gentrification is not just about buildings—it's about erasure. Overlooking the lived experiences of long-term residents can deepen distrust and inequality.

Mosaic Question: How does your presence in a community change its fabric—for better or worse?

Mosaic in Action: A nonprofit planning to open a new arts center in a "revitalizing" district holds listening sessions with local elders, business owners, and youth. Based on their feedback, they modify their plans to include affordable studio space for existing artists, ensuring the center enhances rather than replaces the neighborhood's cultural identity.

Geographic Bias

Definition: Prejudice or preference based on a person's place of origin, residence, or the perceived status of that location.

Business Application: Geographic bias can appear in hiring, promotions, and partnerships— such as favoring urban over rural candidates or certain regions over others.

Leadership Insight: Leaders who recognize geographic bias actively diversify pipelines and decision-making bodies to include perspectives from different regions.

Cultural Caution: Geography often intersects with class, race, and access to resources. Ignoring this intersection can sustain systemic exclusion.

Mosaic Question: Whose ideas or contributions might you be ignoring because of where they come from?

Mosaic in Action: A global consultancy changes its recruitment process after noticing it mainly hired graduates from a few metropolitan universities. By expanding outreach to rural colleges and regional networks, they attract team members whose local insights help open new markets.

Ghost Structures

Definition: Outdated systems, policies, or cultural norms that remain in place—either formally or informally—despite no longer serving their original purpose.

Business Application: Ghost structures drain resources and hinder innovation. Identifying and removing them can create space for more responsive and future-oriented practices.

Leadership Insight: Naming ghost structures openly encourages teams to question inherited assumptions and rebuild systems that align with current realities.

Cultural Caution: Ghost structures often carry emotional significance for those who created or benefited from them; dismantling them without respecting that history can lead to resistance.

Mosaic Question: What practices or systems in your organization exist only because "that's how we've always done it"?

Mosaic in Action: A school district still requires paper attendance sheets despite having a working digital system. After teachers highlight the inefficiency in a leadership meeting, the superintendent removes the old process, freeing up time and reducing errors.

Glass Ceiling

Definition: An invisible barrier that prevents certain groups—often women and marginalized individuals—from reaching top leadership roles despite their qualifications.

Business Application: Overcoming the glass ceiling requires structural changes, not just individual effort—policies on pay equity, mentorship, and transparent promotion standards are crucial.

Leadership Insight: Leaders can become proactive sponsors, not just mentors, by advocating for overlooked talent and promoting diverse representation in decision-making.

Cultural Caution: The glass ceiling varies; intersecting identities like race, disability, or sexual orientation can deepen or multiply these barriers.

Mosaic Question: How are you ensuring that pathways to leadership are equally visible, accessible, and attainable for everyone?

Mosaic in Action: A corporate vice president observes that women of color are underrepresented in executive training programs. She promotes targeted outreach and sponsorship, leading to a measurable increase in promotions over two years.

Glass Cliff

Definition: The phenomenon where women or members of marginalized groups are placed in leadership roles during times of crisis or instability, when the chance of failure is highest.

Business Application: Organizations under public or financial pressure may select leaders from underrepresented groups to signal change, inadvertently placing them in positions with limited support or insurmountable odds.

Leadership Insight: While such appointments can seem progressive, they often lack the necessary structural backing for success, which can reinforce stereotypes if the leader does not "turn things around."

Cultural Caution: Celebrating representation without tackling systemic barriers can cause harm to continue. Inclusion must be combined with real empowerment and resources.

Mosaic Question: Who is called to lead when stakes are high, and are they being set up to succeed—or to fall?

Mosaic in Action: A nonprofit appoints its first woman of color CEO after a public funding scandal. She inherits a drained staff and broken board. By quickly securing interim funding, establishing transparent reporting, and engaging with stakeholders through listening sessions, she rebuilds trust and stabilizes operations, showing that the decision was about capability—not optics.

Glass Escalator

Definition: The invisible advantage men often have in female-dominated professions is that they advance more quickly into leadership roles.

Business Application: The glass escalator explains why gender gaps

still exist even in fields like nursing, education, or social work where women are the majority.

Leadership Insight: Leaders must identify and confront how privilege speeds up some careers while hindering others.

Cultural Caution: Patterns vary around the world. In some situations, men entering women-majority fields faces stigma instead of benefit.

Mosaic Question: Whose careers are being accelerated — and why?

Mosaic in Action: A school district monitored promotions and found that men in teaching advanced more quickly than women. The district then redesigned leadership pathways.

Global Citizenship

Definition: A sense of identity and responsibility that goes beyond national borders, focusing on participating in global issues and fostering solidarity across cultures.

Business Application: Leaders with a global citizenship mindset promote cross-border collaboration, sustainability, and fair trade practices, acknowledging their organization's role within the global ecosystem.

Leadership Insight: Leading with a global perspective requires humility, cultural understanding, and a readiness to question ethnocentric assumptions.

Cultural Caution: Without meaningful engagement, global citizenship can become a superficial label rather than a genuine practice, disguising privilege instead of promoting equitable change.

Mosaic Question: How do your everyday decisions demonstrate a responsibility to communities you might never meet?

Mosaic in Action: A tech company adjusts its supply chain to source ethically produced materials, partnering with small producers in multiple nations. The CEO shares these efforts directly with customers, framing them as both a moral obligation and a business advantage.

Global Competence

Definition: The knowledge, skills, and attitudes necessary to understand and interact effectively across different cultures, nations, and perspectives. It combines cultural intelligence with global awareness.

Business Application: Global competence is crucial in multinational corporations, diplomatic affairs, and education. Leaders who demonstrate it can navigate international markets, promote cross-border collaboration, and minimize cultural conflicts.

Leadership Insight: Global competence is not just about recognizing differences — it's about having the humility to learn, the flexibility to adapt, and the courage to engage meaningfully across borders.

Cultural Caution: Superficial "global" gestures (like token celebrations) without depth can seem performative. True competence requires immersion, ongoing learning, and respect.

Mosaic Question: Do you see the global stage as a challenge to face — or an opportunity to build connections?

Mosaic in Action: A university president incorporates intercultural exchange into curriculum design, ensuring students graduate with both technical skills and global competence.

Global Health Equity

Definition: The fair and just opportunity for all individuals worldwide to achieve their highest level of health, regardless of geography, income, or identity.

Business Application: Global health equity is relevant to organizations investing in employee wellness, CSR initiatives, and product impact—especially those involved in healthcare, pharmaceuticals, and global supply chains.

Leadership Insight: Health inequities are not accidental; they stem from intersecting systems of policy, economics, and culture. Leaders can address these issues through advocacy and action.

Cultural Caution: Efforts must be community-driven and locally informed; top-down "solutions" can cause harm if they overlook cultural contexts.

Mosaic Question: Whose health outcomes are deprioritized in your area of influence—and how can you change that?

Mosaic in Action: An international nonprofit partners with rural clinics in multiple countries to offer telehealth services and trains local practitioners to incorporate culturally relevant care alongside technological tools.

Global South

Definition: A term used to describe regions—often in Latin America, Africa, Asia, and Oceania—that have historically faced colonial exploitation and still experience structural inequalities in the global system.

Business Application: Understanding the Global South is essential for promoting inclusive market growth, fair partnerships, and preventing exploitative practices in labor and resource use.

Leadership Insight: Leaders must recognize historical inequalities and actively build partnerships based on mutual benefit rather than dependence.

Cultural Caution: Avoid portraying the Global South as a monolith or just a place of need—these regions are also hubs of innovation, resilience, and cultural richness.

Mosaic Question: How can your leadership transition from extractive engagement with the Global South to a co-created, equitable exchange?

Mosaic in Action: A fashion brand sources textiles from artisans in West Africa using a cooperative model, ensuring profit-sharing, skill transfer, and decision-making stay with the community.

Good-Faith Dialogue

Definition: An exchange in which all parties sincerely commit to honesty, understanding, and mutual respect, even when they disagree.

Business Application: In negotiations, policy discussions, or organizational change, good-faith dialogue ensures that different perspectives are heard without manipulation or hidden agendas. It builds trust and encourages solutions that everyone can accept.

Leadership Insight: Leaders who exemplify good-faith dialogue show that transparency and curiosity matter more than winning an argument. This promotes a culture where candor is met with respect rather than retaliation.

Cultural Caution: What is considered "respectful" dialogue can vary widely across cultures. Without cultural awareness, a leader's attempt at openness might seem intrusive, confrontational, or performative.

Mosaic Question: When was the last time you entered a conversation more committed to understanding than persuading?

Mosaic in Action: During a tense budget meeting, two department heads with opposing priorities agree to a brief "listening round" where each speaks without interruption for two minutes. This slows the discussion, reveals shared concerns, and results in

a compromise plan neither had considered before.

Gossiping

Definition: Sharing unverified, personal, or harmful information about others in ways that damage trust and cause division within teams or communities.

Business Application: Gossiping undermines psychological safety. In organizations, it shifts focus away from teamwork, encourages cliques, and harms reputations without accountability. If left unaddressed, it weakens morale and raises turnover.

Leadership Insight: Leaders who ignore gossip risk creating toxicity. Effective leaders steer gossip into open conversations, fostering cultures where issues are dealt with directly instead of whispered about.

Cultural Caution: In some cultural settings, informal storytelling or sharing community knowledge might seem like gossip, but it plays a relational role. Leaders need to identify when talk is damaging and when it fosters connection.

Mosaic Question: When tension arises, do you address it directly to resolve it — or let gossip influence the culture?

Mosaic in Action: A manager noticed gossip dividing a project team. Instead of punishing individuals, she established structured feedback circles, providing staff with safe channels to express concerns openly.

Governance Bias

Definition: Unseen or seen favoritism in decision-making, policies, or leadership that favors certain groups, voices, or perspectives over others.

Business Application: Governance bias influences who is on a board and which communities benefit from resources. Tackling it involves reviewing policies and diversifying decision-making teams.

Leadership Insight: Leaders able to recognize governance bias can step in to restore balance, empowering historically excluded voices to help shape outcomes instead of just reacting to them.

Cultural Caution: Sometimes, token appointments or symbolic acts are mistaken for real change, which can actually reinforce inequalities instead of fixing them.

Mosaic Question: Who really holds decision-making power in your system—and who is missing from that table?

Mosaic in Action: A nonprofit board notices that policies tend to favor urban programs over rural ones. They include rural community leaders on their governance council, changing priorities to promote fair resource distribution.

Governance Equity

Definition: The principle of fairness, transparency, and inclusion guides how organizations, institutions, or societies are governed. Governance equity guarantees that decision-making processes distribute power responsibly.

Business Application: Companies demonstrate governance equity by diversifying boards, enhancing transparency, and integrating equity into accountability frameworks. It boosts legitimacy and stakeholder trust.

Leadership Insight: Governance is not neutral; it embodies values. Leaders who aim for governance equity intentionally allocate decision-making authority and work to remove systemic obstacles in institutional structures.

Cultural Caution: In highly hierarchical cultures, governance equity might be resisted or misunderstood. Leaders need to balance respect for tradition with gradual, meaningful changes.

Mosaic Question: Who has the authority to make decisions in your system — and who is regularly left out?

Mosaic in Action: A corporate board updates bylaws to ensure community representatives have a seat on oversight committees, promoting equity in governance.

Gratitude Fatigue

Definition: Emotional exhaustion caused by the constant pressure to show appreciation—often for basic rights, limited resources, or situations where gratitude may mask deeper inequities.

Business Application: Employees or marginalized groups might feel compelled to remain "grateful" for opportunities, even when those opportunities are unfair or unsustainable.

Leadership Insight: Leaders need to recognize when gratitude is used as a silencing tactic, blocking individuals from speaking out for better conditions. Genuine appreciation exists alongside the freedom to raise concerns.

Cultural Caution: Some cultures emphasize outward gratitude regardless of circumstances, which can make it hard to challenge unfair situations without being seen as ungrateful.

Mosaic Question: Are you fostering genuine appreciation, or are you training people to accept less than they deserve?

Mosaic in Action: A junior employee repeatedly thanks their manager for flexible hours but feels guilty asking for a pay raise. The manager notices this imbalance, starts a salary review, and affirms that gratitude should not replace fair compensation.

Grief Literacy

Definition: The ability to understand, support, and respond to the various ways individuals and communities experience and express grief.

Business Application: Organizations with grief literacy implement policies, training, and cultures that recognize loss beyond bereavement leave—such as layoffs, cultural loss, migration, or systemic injustice.

Leadership Insight: Grief-literate leaders normalize conversations about loss, creating space for emotional realities that, if ignored, can affect morale and productivity.

Cultural Caution: Expressions of grief differ across cultures; misinterpretation can lead to judgments about professionalism or emotional control.

Mosaic Question: How does your leadership create space for grief as a natural part of the human experience at work?

Mosaic in Action: After a major natural disaster impacts employees' families abroad, leadership hosts optional support circles, provides extended leave, and partners with local relief organizations—showing that personal loss is also a concern of the organization.

Grief-Informed Leadership

Definition: A leadership approach that acknowledges the importance of grief—whether personal, communal, or organizational—in influencing behavior, resilience, and capacity. It emphasizes compassion and stability during times of loss.

Business Application: Leaders often help teams cope with grief after layoffs, natural disasters, or collective tragedies. Grief-informed leadership promotes recovery and prevents burnout by acknowledging emotions while offering guidance.

Leadership Insight: Grief is not a detour from leadership — it is part of it. Leaders who can acknowledge loss while holding vision model humanity and inspire resilience.

Cultural Caution: Expressions of grief differ greatly across cultures. In some societies, public mourning is expected; in others, privacy is considered sacred. Leaders must respect these differences with sensitivity.

Mosaic Question: Do you push teams through grief quickly — or guide them with compassion through it?

Mosaic in Action: After a community tragedy, a mayor halts public celebrations, organizes collective vigils, and offers counseling resources, demonstrating grief-informed leadership.

Greenwashing

Definition: The practice of giving a false impression or misleading information about how a company's products, policies, or practices are environmentally friendly.

Business Application: Organizations may use greenwashing to appeal to consumers and stakeholders who value sustainability, even when their actions don't meet genuine environmental standards.

Leadership Insight: Ethical leaders look beyond marketing claims and ensure that sustainability efforts are transparent, measurable, and truly integrated into operations rather than just branded.

Cultural Caution: In some cultures, environmental stewardship is closely tied to identity and history. Greenwashing in such contexts can damage reputation and erode trust more quickly.

Mosaic Question: How can you confirm that your sustainability claims are genuine and impactful?

Mosaic in Action: A multinational clothing brand launches a "green" clothing line made from recycled materials but continues large-scale wasteful production. A sustainability officer advocates for a full audit and publicly shares progress reports—changing the company's reputation from performative to proactive.

Group Belonging Dynamics

Definition: The psychological and social processes that influence how individuals experience inclusion, exclusion, and identity within a group.

Business Application: Leaders who understand belonging dynamics can create team environments where diversity enhances rather than fragments collaboration.

Leadership Insight: Belonging is not just about fitting in—it's about feeling seen, valued, and respected for your authentic contributions.

Cultural Caution: Expectations of group belonging vary worldwide; in some cultures, group harmony is more valued than individuality, while others promote outspoken self-expression.

Mosaic Question: What signals in your team environment encourage or hinder authentic belonging?

Mosaic in Action: During a team project, quieter members hesitate to share ideas. A project manager introduces a rotating "first word" system so each person begins the discussion—boosting engagement and fostering creative solutions.

Groupthink

Definition: The tendency for cohesive groups to prioritize consensus over critical thinking, often resulting in flawed decision-making.

Business Application: Identifying and stopping groupthink can help avoid costly mistakes and promote diverse perspectives.

Leadership Insight: Healthy disagreement is a leadership strength; it indicates intellectual engagement, not disloyalty.

Cultural Caution: In cultures with high power distance, challenging authority may be seen as disrespectful, increasing the likelihood of groupthink if leaders do not actively seek dissent.

Mosaic Question: How can you establish structures that make constructive disagreement safe?

Mosaic in Action: A school board unanimously supports a costly technology upgrade without exploring other options. A board member introduces a "red team" process, prompting a subgroup to critically evaluate the proposal—resulting in a more cost-effective solution without sacrificing quality.

Grounded Awareness

Definition: A state of centered, present-focused attention that combines emotional stability with understanding of the situation. Grounded awareness helps leaders remain balanced in chaos and respond thoughtfully rather than react impulsively.

Business Application: In crisis management or high-pressure negotiations, grounded awareness helps leaders stay calm, evaluate realities accurately, and guide teams with confidence. It lowers the chance of escalation and maintains decision quality under stress.

Leadership Insight: Grounded awareness serves as the core of effective leadership. Leaders who nurture it show more than just mindfulness—they exhibit practical presence—a stability that others rely on during times of uncertainty.

Cultural Caution: Some cultural contexts may interpret "groundedness" differently — as stillness, humility, or control. Leaders must demonstrate awareness in ways that align with the community they serve's expectations.

Mosaic Question: When tension increases, do you lose your grounding — or do you deepen your awareness?

Mosaic in Action: A principal de-escalates a heated parent meeting by pausing, taking deep breaths, and calmly restating shared priorities before reopening dialogue.

Grounded Leadership

Definition: A leadership approach rooted in self-awareness, authenticity, and alignment between values and actions, enabling leaders to stay steady under pressure.

Business Application: Grounded leaders promote stability in their teams, especially during times of uncertainty. Their consistent alignment between words and actions builds trust and resilience within organizational culture.

Leadership Insight: Stability doesn't mean stagnation—leaders who stay grounded can adapt to change without losing their core values.

Cultural Caution: What feels "grounded" to one culture might seem rigid to another; flexibility in applying core principles is crucial in cross-cultural settings.

Mosaic Question: What values keep you steady when external pressures increase?

Mosaic in Action: In a merger between two companies from different sectors, the new department head holds weekly listening sessions to hear employees' concerns. By consistently showing up, addressing feedback transparently, and reaffirming shared values, she reduces tensions and models stability during change.

Growth Mindset (Culturally Applied)

Definition: The belief that abilities can be developed through effort, learning, and feedback—implemented with cultural awareness and sensitivity to diverse learning contexts.

Business Application: Leaders with a culturally aware growth mindset customize development opportunities to respect cultural norms around feedback, collaboration, and risk-taking.

Leadership Insight: Without cultural awareness, growth mindset efforts can unintentionally favor dominant cultural norms and marginalize other voices.

Cultural Caution: In some cultures, public mistakes carry a heavier stigma; leaders must adapt their encouragement of "learning from failure" to prevent shame or loss of face.

Mosaic Question: How can you promote growth while respecting the cultural contexts where learning occurs?

Mosaic in Action: A multinational company's training program shifts from a competitive, individual achievement model to a collaborative approach that values teamwork, respecting collectivist cultural norms while fostering personal growth.

Guerrilla Leadership

Definition: An inventive, unconventional leadership style that utilizes creativity, agility, and strategic risk-taking to reach goals, often in limited or high-pressure environments.

Business Application: Guerrilla leaders thrive in startups, nonprofits, and crisis situations where traditional approaches are too slow or demand too many resources.

Leadership Insight: Being unconventional doesn't mean being reckless—effective guerrilla leadership balances innovation with calculated risks.

Cultural Caution: Bold, disruptive strategies might be praised in some settings but seen as disrespectful or disruptive in others.

Mosaic Question: When have you used unconventional methods to get results, and how were they received?

Mosaic in Action: During a sudden funding cut, a nonprofit director starts a social media campaign that combines compelling storytelling with small community donations. This approach sidesteps formal grant cycles and keeps operations running without compromising the mission.

◈ LETTER G CALLOUT

"Generosity in leadership is not about giving more tasks — it is about giving more trust."

Reflection Questions

- How does gatekeeping limit opportunity in your classroom, office, or community?
- What does it feel like when trust is extended to you without micromanagement?
- Where might governance structures unintentionally reinforce inequity?

Practical Move

This week, delegate one meaningful responsibility — not just busy work — to someone newer or less visible, and affirm your trust in their ability.

H – Harm, Healing, and Historical Amnesia

H brings us to the core of cultural work—where policies end and people remain. Harm seldom announces itself. It enters quietly in whose pain is ignored, whose contributions are overlooked, and whose decisions neglect history and relationships. Left unspoken, these moments do not disappear—they harden, becoming the silent foundation of mistrust.

Healing, in contrast, is not passive. It is a conscious act of honesty without avoidance, repair without rushing, and presence without retreat. True healing demands the courage to stay where others turn away, to face the fracture without glossing it over.

And then there is historical amnesia—more than mere forgetfulness. It is erasure. It disconnects today's norms from the injustices that formed them, removes accountability, and leaves only a polished version of progress. Without memory, repairs are superficial; without honesty, history repeats itself in quieter, more dangerous ways.

H asks us to notice what too often remains buried

- The harm normalized through silence or neglect.
- The healing rushed into performance instead of practice.
- The histories erased in favor of comfort.
- The accountability lost when amnesia replaces truth.

The H terms remind us that leadership is not judged by how harm is prevented, but by how it's addressed when it happens. Healing can't be forced, but it can be fostered. History can't be rewritten, but it can be remembered with honesty.

H calls on leaders to resist performative repair, to acknowledge wounds long ignored, and to foster cultures where truth is not an inconvenience but a foundation. Because leadership is not measured by avoiding pain—it is defined by the courage to face it and the discipline to repair it with honesty.

H

Hair Politics

Definition: The social, cultural, and political influences related to hair texture, style, and grooming—often linked to identity, belonging, and bias.

Business Application: Workplace grooming policies and norms can unfairly impact employees from certain racial or cultural backgrounds, affecting hiring, promotion, and inclusion.

Leadership Insight: Leaders who support hair diversity demonstrate that being authentic matters more than conforming, fostering psychological safety and cultural respect.

Cultural Caution: Avoid policing or exoticizing hair choices; both can reinforce systemic discrimination and lead to feelings of alienation.

Mosaic Question: What unspoken appearance rules might be restricting authenticity in your environment?

Mosaic in Action: A school principal updates the student dress code to remove language banning "distracting hairstyles." She then hosts a cultural hair showcase, inviting families to share the meaning behind different styles—shifting the focus from compliance to celebration.

Harm Accountability

Definition: The process of recognizing, accepting responsibility for, and addressing harm within organizational and leadership contexts. Harm accountability highlights taking ownership rather than deflecting or minimizing.

Business Application: Companies show accountability for harm when they respond transparently to employee complaints, equity violations, or community impact, pairing an apology with concrete action.

Leadership Insight: True accountability needs courage. Leaders who admit mistakes and work to rebuild trust boost credibility and resilience.

Cultural Caution: Some cultures avoid directly acknowledging harm and prefer indirect ways to resolve issues. Leaders must adjust accountability practices to fit cultural norms without avoiding responsibility.

Mosaic Question: When harm happens, do you deflect, minimize, or take responsibility and step forward?

Mosaic in Action: A university recognizes its history of discriminatory admissions practices, issues a public apology, and invests in scholarships for underrepresented groups.

Harm Amplification

Definition: Actions or policies that unintentionally escalate the severity or spread of harm, even when aimed at solving an issue.

Business Application: Excessively punitive workplace policies intended to prevent misconduct can create fear, discourage reporting, and ultimately increase harm.

Leadership Insight: Leaders should evaluate potential unintended consequences and seek input from those most affected before implementing solutions.

Cultural Caution: Well-meaning interventions may backfire without proper cultural and situational awareness, leading to increased inequity.

Mosaic Question: Could your "solution" actually worsen the original problem?

Mosaic in Action: A nonprofit's zero-tolerance attendance policy for volunteers unintentionally discourages single parents from participating. After receiving feedback, the policy is adjusted to include flexible shifts, boosting participation and trust.

Harm Reduction

Definition: Strategies aimed at reducing negative outcomes of risky or harmful behaviors without necessarily eliminating the behavior completely.

Business Application: In corporate wellness programs, providing stress-management tools and flexible schedules can lower burnout risk without requiring employees to leave high-pressure roles.

Leadership Insight: Harm reduction emphasizes compassion, pragmatism, and meeting people where they are, instead of enforcing unrealistic standards.

Cultural Caution: Some may see harm reduction as enabling harmful behavior; leaders must clearly communicate its purpose and measurable benefits.

Mosaic Question: Where might a "less harm" approach be more effective than a "zero tolerance" one?

Mosaic in Action: A city replaces punitive fines for public intoxication with offering transportation to safe shelters, reducing ER visits and public disturbances.

Healing-Centered Engagement

Definition: A framework that focuses on collective healing, resilience, and well-being in communities and organizations, based on relationships, culture, and systemic awareness.

Business Application: Leaders apply healing-centered engagement in schools, nonprofits, and workplaces to foster environments that focus on restoration, cultural identity, and emotional safety.

Leadership Insight: Unlike trauma-informed care, healing-centered engagement emphasizes possibility and wholeness instead of focusing solely on pain. It asks, "What's right with you?" rather than "What's wrong with you?"

Cultural Caution: Healing-centered approaches must avoid applying universal practices. Engagement should be specific to the context and driven by the communities most affected.

Mosaic Question: Do your leadership spaces focus only on past wounds — or do they also nurture future wholeness?

Mosaic in Action: A community center integrates cultural rituals, art, and storytelling into its programs, helping participants reclaim resilience and connection.

Healing-Centered Leadership

Definition: A leadership approach that emphasizes relational trust, emotional attunement, and restorative practices to create environments where people can thrive after experiencing harm or crisis.

Business Application: Leaders in education, healthcare, and corporate sectors use healing-centered leadership to guide teams through change, recovery from burnout, or organizational trauma. They incorporate reflection, emotional check-ins, and restorative dialogues into routine operations.

Leadership Insight: Healing-centered leaders recognize that productivity is closely connected to emotional safety. They address harm by encouraging dialogue, restoring relationships, and demonstrating vulnerability.

Cultural Caution: Do not confuse healing-centered leadership with "soft" leadership. It requires discipline, boundaries, and a commitment to justice, not just kindness or agreeableness.

Mosaic Question: Where can you intentionally create space for repair and relationship rebuilding in your leadership?

Mosaic in Action: After a department-wide conflict, a manager arranges restorative circles where team members discuss concerns, rebuild agreements, and establish new norms for collaboration.

Healing Ecosystems

Definition: Communities, workplaces, or networks intentionally created to promote collective recovery, resilience, and well-being.

Business Application: Trauma-informed leadership models can change workplaces into environments that encourage healing, innovation, and retention.

Leadership Insight: Healing requires leaders to focus on trust, connection, and psychological safety as key priorities, not afterthoughts.

Cultural Caution: Superficial "wellness" programs without real structural support can lead to cynicism.

Mosaic Question: How does your environment actively support collective healing?

Mosaic in Action: A tech company forms a peer-support network for employees affected by layoffs— offering counseling, professional networking, and mentorship— helping both those who stay and those who leave to manage the transition with dignity.

Healing Justice

Definition: A holistic framework that addresses the generational, systemic, and interpersonal harms experienced by marginalized communities, emphasizing cultural, spiritual, and community-based healing practices alongside structural change.

Business Application: In organizational settings, healing justice informs wellness initiatives, conflict resolution, and leadership development by incorporating mental health care, cultural rituals, and systemic advocacy. It extends beyond individual self-care to community care, especially for employees carrying compounded trauma from discrimination or exploitation.

Leadership Insight: Leaders who embrace healing justice recognize that equity work without healing can inadvertently cause harm. They create policies and environments where rest, restoration, and resilience are regarded as vital to performance and belonging.

Cultural Caution: Healing justice approaches must be rooted in the lived experiences of the communities they serve. Imposing practices without cultural relevance—or commodifying them—can damage trust and continue to cause harm.

Mosaic Question: How can you build systems of repair that honor both individual and collective healing needs?

Mosaic in Action: A nonprofit changes its meeting culture by incorporating grounding rituals from the cultures represented among staff, offering mental health stipends, and reducing workload after a major campaign to allow time for restoration and reconnection.

Health Equity

Definition: Ensuring everyone has a fair and just chance to reach their highest health potential by removing barriers like poverty, discrimination, and lack of access to resources.

Business Application: Organizations incorporate health equity principles when creating benefits packages, workplace wellness programs, and supplier diversity efforts that tackle systemic disparities.

Leadership Insight: Leaders dedicated to health equity consider both workplace and community effects—acknowledging how their choices influence health outcomes for employees, customers, and surrounding communities.

Cultural Caution: Achieving health equity does not mean giving the same resources to everyone; it involves targeted strategies that address historical and current inequities.

Mosaic Question: Whose health outcomes are impacted by your organization's decisions—and what inequities could you help reduce?

Mosaic in Action: A company broadens parental leave to include adoptive and non-biological parents, adds mental health coverage for employees in high-stress roles, and partners with local clinics to offer preventive care in underserved neighborhoods.

Hegemony

Definition: The dominance of one group over others, often maintained through cultural norms, institutional structures, and control of ideas, narratives, and resources.

Business Application: Hegemony appears in organizations when dominant cultural norms shape what is considered acceptable behavior, communication styles, or definitions of success—often excluding marginalized voices.

Leadership Insight: Recognizing and disrupting hegemonic structures helps leaders create inclusive decision-making processes, redistribute power, and diversify influence.

Cultural Caution: Challenging hegemony requires courage and strategic coalition-building; direct confrontation without support can backfire or reinforce existing power imbalances.

Mosaic Question: Where might invisible power structures be influencing your leadership environment without your awareness?

Mosaic in Action: A university department reviews its promotion criteria to eliminate biases toward Western publication standards, valuing diverse forms of scholarship and community-based research equally.

Heritage Language

Definition: The original language connected to a person's cultural or ethnic background, often spoken at home or within a community, even if it is not the dominant language of the surrounding society.

Business Application: In diverse workplaces, supporting the use of heritage languages—such as allowing multilingual meetings or offering translations—can improve communication, inclusion, and market reach.

Leadership Insight: Valuing heritage language helps preserve cultural identity and builds trust with employees or clients from those communities. Leaders who promote linguistic diversity show respect for both personal and collective history.

Cultural Caution: Treating heritage language as "less professional" can alienate employees and send an unintended message of assimilation over authenticity. Avoid tokenism—true support means integration, not just celebration days.

Mosaic Question: How might valuing someone's heritage

language strengthen your team's innovation and cohesion?

Mosaic in Action: A city department produces key safety announcements in English, Spanish, and Somali—the top three languages spoken locally. When Somali-speaking residents receive emergency alerts in their native language, compliance with safety measures goes up, and trust in the department increases.

Heritage Month Fatigue

Definition: The exhaustion felt by individuals and communities when cultural or heritage months are regarded as the only time to recognize their contributions, resulting in superficial engagement or performative inclusion.

Business Application: Relying solely on heritage month celebrations without ongoing integration can lead to disengaged employees and weaken diversity initiatives. Genuine acknowledgement should be integrated into policies, hiring practices, and everyday culture.

Leadership Insight: Real inclusion involves consistently celebrating heritage, not just during isolated periods. Leaders who incorporate cultural learning throughout the year sustain engagement and build trust.

Cultural Caution: Avoid turning heritage months into marketing opportunities without meaningful internal efforts—this can increase cynicism.

Mosaic Question: How do you ensure recognition of cultural heritage goes beyond just a calendar event?

Mosaic in Action: A global company pairs its Asian American and Pacific Islander Heritage Month celebrations with year-round mentorship programs led by AAPI leaders, ensuring the acknowledgment connects to long-term opportunities and visibility.

Heritage Resilience

Definition: The ability of cultural traditions, languages, and practices to survive and adapt despite displacement, colonization, or systemic oppression.

Business Application: Using heritage resilience in branding, product development, or community partnerships helps organizations project authenticity, especially when serving culturally rooted markets.

Leadership Insight: Leaders who acknowledge and respect

heritage resilience inspire teams to draw strength from their cultural histories during times of change or crisis.

Cultural Caution: Do not romanticize resilience—recognize the systemic challenges that created it, and avoid suggesting that enduring hardship is inherently positive.

Mosaic Question: What practices from your heritage could help your team overcome today's challenges?

Mosaic in Action: A nonprofit serving refugee communities incorporates traditional farming methods into its urban agriculture program, combining cultural heritage with local food access and climate resilience.

Heteronormativity

Definition: The belief that heterosexuality is the default or "normal" sexual orientation, which often leads to the marginalization of LGBTQ+ identities.

Business Application: Heteronormative policies or language in hiring, benefits, and marketing can exclude LGBTQ+ employees and customers, limiting talent retention and market reach.

Leadership Insight: Inclusive leaders address heteronormativity by reviewing benefits, policies, and language to make sure they support diverse sexual orientations and family structures.

Cultural Caution: Merely adding rainbow branding without systemic inclusion efforts can be viewed as "rainbow-washing."

Mosaic Question: Where might your workplace or leadership unintentionally prioritize heterosexual norms?

Mosaic in Action: A healthcare system updates intake forms to include various gender and relationship options. Patients feel more seen and respected, which leads to higher satisfaction scores among LGBTQ+ communities.

Hidden Curriculum

Definition: The unwritten, unofficial lessons, values, and perspectives conveyed through a group's or institution's culture, routines, and norms, rather than through formal teaching.

Business Application: In workplaces, hidden curricula can be seen in unspoken expectations about attire, communication, meeting manners, or decision-making. Leaders who clarify these expectations help reduce barriers for newcomers and marginalized team members.

Leadership Insight: By revealing hidden curricula, leaders can replace gatekeeping with clarity—creating fair access to influence, advancement, and participation.

Cultural Caution: What is "common sense" in one setting might be entirely unfamiliar in another. Assuming everyone "just knows" can unintentionally exclude people based on background, language, or culture.

Mosaic Question: What unspoken rules in your setting might someone from another culture or generation overlook—and how could identifying them improve inclusion?

Mosaic in Action: In a global nonprofit, a new project manager misses deadlines because no one informed her that informal pre-meetings—where key decisions are made—happen at a local café each morning. Once a senior colleague explains this practice and invites her to join, her projects progress, and her confidence grows.

Hidden Harm

Definition: Damage or disadvantage that occurs out of sight, often unnoticed by those not directly affected, yet carrying significant long-term effects.

Business Application: In organizations, hidden harm might show as burnout among overworked staff, reputational damage from unchecked microaggressions, or silent disengagement of employees whose contributions are undervalued.

Leadership Insight: The most dangerous harms are often invisible to those in power. Leaders who actively listen, gather anonymous feedback, and monitor long-term impacts foster safer, more resilient environments.

Cultural Caution: In some cultures, openly discussing harm is discouraged or stigmatized, making it even more difficult to identify and address.

Mosaic Question: What types of harm might be quietly accumulating in your environment right now, and whose perspectives would you need to understand them clearly?

Mosaic in Action: A hospital board is surprised to learn from exit interviews that subtle bias has been causing skilled nurses of color to resign. The issue had never shown up in formal reports, but once identified, the board introduces equity-focused leadership training, reducing turnover.

Hierarchy of Suffering

Definition: The subconscious ranking of certain types of pain, trauma, or hardship as more legitimate, urgent, or worthy of empathy than others.

Business Application: In team settings, this can appear when leadership prioritizes the needs of one group's challenges (e.g., natural disaster recovery) while minimizing another group's ongoing struggles (e.g., chronic discrimination).

Leadership Insight: When leaders break down hierarchies of suffering, they affirm that all forms of harm and hardship deserve acknowledgment and care—without turning empathy into a competition.

Cultural Caution: Cultural narratives often normalize whose suffering "counts" and whose is dismissed. Recognizing these patterns helps prevent unintentional marginalization.

Mosaic Question: Who in your sphere might be experiencing unacknowledged hardship simply because their pain doesn't fit the dominant narrative of what's "serious"?

Mosaic in Action: During a staff wellness initiative, the company initially focuses only on employees affected by a recent flood. A manager then advocates for supporting team members dealing with domestic violence and immigration-related stress, ensuring broader, more inclusive care.

Historical Amnesia

Definition: The collective forgetting, erasure, or sanitization of past events—often to protect dominant narratives or avoid confronting uncomfortable truths.

Business Application: Organizations that ignore their own histories—such as past labor disputes, unfair hiring practices, or harmful community impacts—miss the chance to build genuine trust and accountability.

Leadership Insight: Leaders who incorporate accurate historical context into decision-making help prevent repeating mistakes and foster cultures based on truth-telling and healing.

Cultural Caution: Historical amnesia is often maintained through selective storytelling in education, media, and policy. Restoring the complete record requires humility, openness, and a willingness to challenge familiar narratives.

Mosaic Question: Which parts of your organization's or community's history remain untold, and who benefits from that silence?

Mosaic in Action: A real estate company learns that its early growth was linked to redlining practices. Instead of hiding this fact, the CEO supports affordable housing programs and includes the company's full history in onboarding, showing a commitment to repair and transparency.

Historical Repair

Definition: The intentional process of addressing and repairing historical wrongs—such as colonization, slavery, or systemic discrimination—through restitution, restoration, and policy reform.

Business Application: Organizations can practice historical repair through equitable hiring practices, reparations funding, land acknowledgments, or partnerships that support historically marginalized communities.

Leadership Insight: Leaders who recognize the impact of historical harm and actively work toward repair foster trust and credibility among diverse stakeholders.

Cultural Caution: Symbolic gestures without real change can increase distrust and deepen cynicism.

Mosaic Question: What history is your organization still benefiting from—and what would genuine repair involve?

Mosaic in Action: A university acknowledges that its campus was built on displaced Indigenous land. In addition to issuing a land acknowledgment, it commits to long-term funding for local tribal education programs, scholarships for Indigenous students, and shared governance on land use decisions.

Historical Trauma

Definition: The collective and cumulative emotional and psychological trauma experienced by groups across generations due to historical oppression, colonization, slavery, or genocide.

Business Application: Understanding historical trauma is crucial for creating fair policies across healthcare, education, and workplace inclusion. It guides strategies that acknowledge the intergenerational effects.

Leadership Insight: Leaders who overlook historical trauma risk continuing harm. Those who recognize it promote healing, trust, and systemic repair.

Cultural Caution: Historical trauma presents differently in various cultures. Leaders should avoid broad assumptions and approach each community with humility.

Mosaic Question: How does historical trauma influence the behaviors, resilience, and needs of the communities you serve?

Mosaic in Action: A hospital system trains its staff on the impact of Indigenous historical trauma in healthcare, transforming practices to rebuild trust.

Holistic Inclusion

Definition: An approach to diversity and belonging that addresses structural, emotional, cultural, and interpersonal aspects of inclusion all at once.

Business Application: Holistic inclusion might involve adding mental health resources, flexible work options, cultural awareness training, and fair promotion paths into the organization's culture.

Leadership Insight: Inclusion efforts work best when they focus on the whole person—not just visible demographics or checkbox compliance.

Cultural Caution: Over-focusing on surface-level diversity metrics without fixing underlying structural problems can lead to tokenism.

Mosaic Question: How does your inclusion strategy care for both the visible and hidden parts of people's experiences?

Mosaic in Action: A global company creates leadership training that includes identity reflection, cross-cultural empathy, and personalized career planning. Employees feel more satisfied not just because they see themselves represented, but because their entire selves are acknowledged and valued.

Honor Culture

Definition: A social system where personal or group reputation, respect, and perceived moral standing are valued and often defended through reciprocal loyalty or protective actions.

Business Application: Honor culture can influence how conflicts are resolved, negotiations are conducted, and team dynamics unfold—especially in multicultural or family-run businesses.

Leadership Insight: Leaders working across different cultures need to recognize how honor shapes decision-making, conflict avoidance, or confrontation.

Cultural Caution: Honor-based norms may sustain harmful practices when protecting reputation becomes more important than justice or truth.

Mosaic Question: When has the need to defend your own or your group's reputation influenced your actions—either positively or negatively?

Mosaic in Action: In an international partnership, a U.S.-based executive notices a partner avoiding direct criticism to preserve team honor. The executive adapts by offering private feedback, allowing issues to be addressed without causing public embarrassment.

Host Culture

Definition: The dominant culture of a place that visitors, immigrants, or expatriates enter and adapt to.

Business Application: Understanding host culture norms is crucial for successful relocation, international assignments, and market entry.

Leadership Insight: Leaders must balance integrating into a host culture with honoring their own identity and values.

Cultural Caution: Pressure to assimilate can weaken personal or community identity if adaptation requires conformity without mutual respect.

Mosaic Question: How can you adapt to a host culture without losing your own?

Mosaic in Action: An educator moving to Qatar learns key cultural greetings, participates in local community events, and adjusts classroom practices to match local customs—while still including their own cultural traditions in teaching.

Hostile Architecture

Definition: Hostile architecture involves designing public spaces to discourage certain uses or groups, often targeting unhoused individuals, youth, or marginalized communities. Examples include benches with center bars to prevent lying down, spikes in sheltered areas, or sloped surfaces under bridges.

Business Application: In corporate environments, hostile design can appear in subtle ways, such as policies or layouts that discourage collaboration or restrict accessibility for specific employees. Recognizing this helps leaders determine if their spaces are welcoming or exclusionary.

Leadership Insight: Leaders who overlook how physical spaces subtly communicate values risk alienating those they serve. Architecture can indicate inclusion and care or reinforce inequality and exclusion.

Cultural Caution: What seems like "practical" design in one context might be deeply dehumanizing in another, especially for vulnerable groups.

Mosaic Question: What does your physical or digital environment communicate about who is welcome—and who is not?

Mosaic in Action: A city installs metal dividers on park benches to prevent unhoused individuals from sleeping there. A local business owner, acknowledging the harm, donates comfortable outdoor seating and partners with community groups to offer outreach, transforming the space into a welcoming area for all.

Houselessness

Definition: Houselessness refers to the condition of lacking stable, safe, and adequate housing. Unlike the term "homelessness," it highlights that individuals can feel a sense of home through community or identity, even without a physical dwelling.

Business Application: Employers and institutions may encounter employees, students, or clients facing housing instability. Addressing houselessness in policies—through flexibility, resources, and partnerships—can promote equity and retention.

Leadership Insight: Leaders who see houselessness as more than just a lack of shelter can better develop interventions that respect dignity and autonomy.

Cultural Caution: Avoid assuming that houseless individuals are disconnected from work ethic, community ties, or aspirations.

Mosaic Question: How might your workplace or community initiatives address not only shelter but also belonging and stability?

Mosaic in Action: A university finds several students living in cars. Instead of penalizing them for address discrepancies, leaders establish emergency housing, offer shower access, and connect them with financial aid resources—ensuring their education continues without interruption.

Human-Centered Design (Equity Lens)

Definition: A design and problem-solving approach that focuses on human dignity and lived experience while using an explicit equity lens. It highlights co-creation, empathy, and inclusivity.

Business Application: Organizations use human-centered design in program development, technology, and policy to make sure solutions meet the needs of those most impacted.

Leadership Insight: Human-centered design without equity can worsen inequalities. Leaders must purposefully amplify marginalized voices in the design process.

Cultural Caution: Design practices borrowed from Western frameworks may overlook or misrepresent local needs. Equity-focused design demands cultural humility.

Mosaic Question: Who is at the center — and who is absent — in how your organization creates solutions?

Mosaic in Action: A city planning department involves immigrant residents in co-design workshops to help shape housing policies that reflect cultural realities.

Human Dignity Framework

Definition: The Human Dignity Framework consists of principles or policies that emphasize the inherent worth, autonomy, and rights of every individual in decision-making, governance, and community interactions.

Business Application: Organizations can integrate this framework into hiring practices, conflict resolution, customer service, and product design to promote ethical standards and build trust.

Leadership Insight: Leaders adopting a dignity-first approach shift from transactional interactions to transformational relationships.

Cultural Caution: Implementing dignity frameworks without genuine commitment can result in performative actions that undermine trust.

Mosaic Question: In your leadership decisions, where does dignity appear—and where does it vanish?

Mosaic in Action: A healthcare system adopts a dignity-centered policy that ensures patients are addressed by their preferred names, receive culturally appropriate care, and have their autonomy respected in treatment choices, leading to higher satisfaction and fewer complaints.

Humanizing Leadership

Definition: Humanizing leadership focuses on empathy, trust, and relationship-building alongside achieving performance and results, recognizing the full humanity of both leaders and those they lead.

Business Application: This approach is especially vital during change management, crisis situations, or high-pressure projects, where the risk of dehumanization is greater.

Leadership Insight: Humanizing leadership creates environments where individuals feel valued for who they are, not just their output.

Cultural Caution: Humanizing leadership requires setting boundaries; being empathetic does not mean allowing harmful behavior.

Mosaic Question: What practices make sure the people you lead feel seen, heard, and respected?

Mosaic in Action: During a critical deadline, a project manager notices signs of burnout among the team. Instead of pushing harder, they reschedule deadlines, offer mental health days, and foster open conversations about workload—maintaining both morale and quality.

Humiliation Culture

Definition: An environment where shame, public criticism,

or degradation is used to control people socially or within organizations. Humiliation culture damages dignity and hinders growth.

Business Application: In workplaces, a humiliation culture manifests through public reprimands, performance shaming, or exclusionary practices that harm morale and retention.

Leadership Insight: Leaders who permit humiliation culture normalize harm. Dignity-based leadership, on the other hand, restores respect and psychological safety.

Cultural Caution: In some cultural settings, "saving face" norms might conceal humiliation practices. Leaders must differentiate between accountability and shaming.

Mosaic Question: Does your leadership depend on fear and humiliation — or on respect and dignity?

Mosaic in Action: A retail company moves from public "error callouts" to private coaching sessions, fostering a culture of learning instead of fear.

Humility in Leadership

Definition: A leadership style based on self-awareness, openness to feedback, and acknowledgment of one's limitations, promoting mutual respect between leaders and those they serve.

Business Application: Leaders who demonstrate humility are more likely to foster psychologically safe workplaces, where employees feel appreciated and empowered to share ideas without fear of rejection or retaliation.

Leadership Insight: Humility is not a sign of weakness—it's the confidence to lead without needing to be the smartest or loudest in the room.

Cultural Caution: In some settings, humility might be mistaken for passivity. Clarifying that humility can go hand in hand with decisiveness helps prevent misunderstandings.

Mosaic Question: How does your leadership create space for others' voices without overpowering your own?

Mosaic in Action: During a tense budget meeting, the director admits they don't have all the answers and asks the team to work together to find solutions. This openness changes the tone of the room, encouraging honest discussion and shared ownership of the results.

Hush Culture

Definition: A workplace environment where employees are discouraged, either openly or subtly, from discussing harm, injustice, or misconduct.

Business Application: Hush culture silences discussions about inequity, shielding institutions rather than individuals. It harms morale and weakens accountability.

Leadership Insight: Breaking hush culture involves fostering transparency and valuing honesty over mere compliance.

Cultural Caution: In cultures with high power distance, silence might be seen as a sign of respect. Leaders need to distinguish cultural norms from harmful silence.

Mosaic Question: Where in your organization are people remaining silent out of fear?

Mosaic in Action: After exposing hush culture regarding harassment complaints, a company implemented anonymous reporting systems and publicized follow-up actions.

Hybrid Work Culture Equity

Definition: The intentional design of policies and practices ensuring that employees in both remote and

317

on-site settings have equal access to opportunities, resources, and recognition.

Business Application: From promotions to professional development, leaders must proactively balance benefits to prevent hybrid environments from creating a two-tiered workplace.

Leadership Insight: Equity in hybrid work is not automatic; it requires deliberate structures to avoid favoritism toward the more visible group.

Cultural Caution: Overemphasizing location parity without addressing other inequities (such as pay gaps or bias in assignments) can undermine broader inclusion goals.

Mosaic Question: In your current role, whose contributions are you more likely to notice—those you see in person or those who join from a screen?

Mosaic in Action: A department head rotates meeting leadership between on-site and remote team members, ensuring that decision-making influence is not concentrated in one location.

Hybridity

Definition: The blending or coexistence of different cultural, social, or professional influences, leading to new identities, practices, or expressions.

Business Application: In global markets, hybridity can foster innovation by combining diverse perspectives, methods, and cultural norms into more adaptable strategies.

Leadership Insight: Leaders who embrace hybridity avoid strict definitions and instead create space for multiple truths to exist.

Cultural Caution: Hybridity is sometimes misunderstood as cultural dilution or loss; emphasizing the value of blended perspectives can help change this perception.

Mosaic Question: Where in your leadership do you resist blending, and where could integration produce something more powerful?

Mosaic in Action: A marketing team uses both local customs and global trends to craft a campaign, resulting in a product launch that resonates across cultures without losing authenticity.

Hyper-Compliance Culture

Definition: An organizational environment where strict adherence to rules is prioritized over innovation, flexibility, or critical thinking—often to avoid risk or liability.

Business Application: While compliance is crucial, excessive focus on it can hinder creativity, discourage problem-solving, and lead to disengaged employees.

Leadership Insight: Achieving balance is essential—systems should steer behavior without suppressing initiative.

Cultural Caution: In highly regulated industries, moving away from hyper-compliance requires careful change management to prevent perceptions of negligence.

Mosaic Question: Which rules in your workplace are followed out of fear rather than aligned with shared values?

Mosaic in Action: A nonprofit leader reviews outdated reporting requirements, eliminates unnecessary steps, and empowers staff to dedicate more time to mission-driven work.

Hypervisibility

Definition: The state of being excessively visible or scrutinized—often experienced by individuals from marginalized groups in environments where they are underrepresented.

Business Application: Hypervisibility can lead to increased performance pressure, burnout, and tokenization, even when framed as "opportunity."

Leadership Insight: True inclusion involves distributing attention fairly, ensuring visibility is empowering rather than exploitative.

Cultural Caution: Efforts to "showcase diversity" can unintentionally isolate individuals if they are repeatedly positioned as the symbol of representation.

Mosaic Question: Who in your organization is hypervisible, and what unspoken burdens might they carry because of it?

Mosaic in Action: An executive notices the same employee from a minority group is repeatedly asked to speak at public events. They implement a rotation system, broadening representation and reducing pressure on one individual.

◈ LETTER H CALLOUT

"Healing is not a soft skill — it is a leadership practice that restores people and systems."

Reflection Questions

- Where do you see harm amplified or ignored in your environment?
- How can leaders make space for grief, repair, or justice alongside productivity?
- What cultural traditions of healing could enrich your team or classroom?

Practical Move

Begin a meeting by acknowledging one collective challenge or harm, and invite the group to name a step toward repair before moving on to tasks.

I – Identity, Inclusion, and Internalized Patterns

I explores the deeply personal—and often politicized—territory of cultural leadership who we are, how we are perceived, and what we have learned to silence in order to stay in the room.

Identity is never singular. It is a dynamic mosaic of race, gender, culture, faith, class, ability, language, and lived experience—shaped by shifting contexts and the power dynamics of every space we enter. Inclusion, then, is not just about presence. It is about being seen without distortion, heard without translation, and valued without dilution.

Yet internalized patterns—imposter syndrome, assimilation, self-policing—reside within us as the quiet remnants of dominance. They don't occur by chance; they are learned from systems that reward parts of us while sidelining the whole.

I asks us to pay attention to the subtler forces at work

- The identity affirmed in one setting and erased in another.
- The inclusion that measures itself by numbers instead of lived experience.
- The internalized doubt that echoes from systemic exclusion.
- The survival strategies mistaken for success.

The I terms remind us that identity is fluid and intersectional, changing across different contexts in ways that are both personal and structural. For leaders, facilitators, and organizations, the language of

"I" offers a perspective to understand how policies, norms, "fit," and even silence either cause harm or uphold dignity.

Strategically, I shift the conversation beyond diversity metrics toward relational and narrative accountability. In mentoring, it helps distinguish genuine growth from quiet endurance. In dialogue, it highlights urgent questions Whose voice is missing? Whose story is misnamed? Whose doubt is not theirs alone?

I call on leaders to deepen their tolerance for complexity, their courage to hold tension, and their resolve to create spaces where no one has to fracture themselves to belong. Because the measure of inclusion is not who enters the room—it is who remains whole once they are inside.

I

Identity Agility

Definition: The ability to adjust one's sense of self and role across different cultural, organizational, and social environments without losing core values or authenticity. Identity agility is the third pillar of the Mosaic Intelligence Method™, developed and trademarked by Dr. Karissa Thomas, and it enables leaders to stay both adaptable and grounded in their leadership presence.

Business Application: In a multinational team, a project manager might adapt communication style, leadership tone, or self-disclosure levels based on cultural norms while remaining consistent with professional ethics and project goals. Identity agility allows leaders to succeed across sectors, generations, and changing environments without losing their core identity.

Leadership Insight: Leaders with strong identity agility adapt smoothly in high-pressure moments — whether stepping into a public role, managing a crisis, or bridging generational divides — without seeming inconsistent or inauthentic. Agility here is a strength, not a sign of instability.

Cultural Caution: Agility does not mean erasing or over-bending one's identity to fit in. Over-adjusting can lead to burnout, fragmentation, or perceptions of insincerity. True identity agility balances adaptability with clarity of self.

Mosaic Question: When circumstances change, do you adjust your identity from strength — or do you bend until you lose yourself?

Mosaic in Action: At an international conference, a nonprofit director moderates a panel with speakers from four continents. She adjusts her facilitation style for each — fostering direct debate with some, sharing relational stories with others — while her commitment to equity remains strong. Her flexibility enhances credibility and trust with a diverse audience.

Identity Dissonance

Definition: The tension that occurs when your environment, roles, or external expectations clash with your sense of self. Identity dissonance frequently appears during transitions, cross-cultural experiences, or when values don't align with systems.

Business Application: Identity dissonance can decrease performance and raise turnover if left unaddressed. Leaders who recognize and tackle it in themselves and others build belonging, retention, and resilience in diverse or transitional workplaces.

Leadership Insight: Recognizing dissonance shows maturity, not weakness. Leaders who admit when their identity is strained demonstrate courage and normalize the complexities of growth.

Cultural Caution: In certain contexts, naming identity dissonance might be discouraged or misunderstood. Leaders need to establish safe spaces before encouraging open dialogue about it.

Mosaic Question: When your sense of self conflicts with your environment, do you suppress it — or use it as information for change?

Mosaic in Action: An expatriate teacher in a new country shares her struggles with identity dissonance, leading the school to create support networks for international staff.

Identity Performance

Definition: The conscious or unconscious way of presenting oneself to influence how others see one's identity, skills, or sense of belonging.

Business Application: An employee from a marginalized group may deliberately change language, clothing, or behavior in a corporate setting to be seen as "professional" by dominant standards.

Leadership Insight: Recognizing identity performance in others helps leaders address systemic pressures that make people "code-switch" or hide their true selves to succeed.

Cultural Caution: When ignored, identity performance can strengthen inequalities, creating workplace environments that reward only certain ways of being.

Mosaic Question: Which parts of yourself do you emphasize or hide to succeed in your current environment—and why?

Mosaic in Action: In a boardroom with senior leaders, a young engineer presents with a polished, overly formal style she doesn't usually use with peers. Her manager later checks in and learns she felt pressured to "sound older" to be taken seriously. Together, they plan future presentations that reflect her genuine voice without sacrificing impact.

Identity Safety

Definition: The guarantee that people can freely express and live out their identities without fear of punishment, exclusion, or stereotypes.

Business Application: Identity safety promotes retention and innovation by making sure employees feel safe to be their authentic selves at work.

Leadership Insight: Leaders promote identity safety by shifting from mere tolerance to affirmation, turning identity expression into a source of strength.

Cultural Caution: Identity safety varies across different contexts — what feels supportive in one setting might seem revealing in another. Leaders need to adjust accordingly.

Mosaic Question: Do your people feel safe being completely themselves — or are they still hiding behind masks?

Mosaic in Action: A tech firm created employee resource groups and gained leadership support that enabled staff to openly celebrate cultural and gender identities.

Identity Threat

Definition: A real or perceived challenge to a person's sense of self, belonging, or social worth, often triggered by cues in the environment or interactions with others.

Business Application: During a leadership change, a long-time team member may feel pushed aside when new leaders ignore their institutional knowledge, seeing this as a threat to their professional identity.

Leadership Insight: Effective leaders recognize and reduce identity threats by affirming contributions, clarifying roles, and promoting inclusion during periods of change.

Cultural Caution: Identity threats can be subtle—such as repeated mispronunciations of a name—or structural, like biased promotion practices. Both can weaken trust and performance.

Mosaic Question: When have you felt your identity was threatened at work, and how did you handle it?

Mosaic in Action: A healthcare team reorganizes, moving key responsibilities away from a respected nurse leader without explanation. The director notices her withdrawal from meetings, makes an effort to acknowledge her expertise, and involves her again in decision-making—restoring her sense of value within the team.

Ideological Rigidity

Definition: The unavailability or reluctance to change beliefs, values, or frameworks when faced with new evidence, perspectives, or changing conditions.

Business Application: A department head refuses to implement remote work policies despite clear data showing higher productivity and employee retention in hybrid setups.

Leadership Insight: While it is crucial to stand by core values, too much rigidity can alienate diverse opinions, hinder innovation, and cause conflicts in fast-changing environments.

Cultural Caution: In cross-cultural or intergenerational settings, ideological rigidity often appears as dismissing alternative viewpoints without consideration, reinforcing cultural blind spots.

Mosaic Question: Which deeply held beliefs have you recently re-evaluated, and what led to that reflection?

Mosaic in Action: During a community planning meeting, a senior council member insists on sticking to a zoning model from decades ago despite new environmental data and resident feedback. A facilitator shares case studies from similar towns that adapted successfully, gradually encouraging him to consider a balanced approach that respects tradition while addressing current needs.

Impostor Syndrome

Definition: A persistent internal belief that one's success is unearned or due to luck, often accompanied by fear of being revealed as a fraud despite proof of competence.

Business Application: A newly promoted leader avoids taking on high-visibility projects, fearing they will "mess it up" and prove unworthy of their role, even though their track record shows consistent achievement.

Leadership Insight: Leaders who encourage open talk about self-doubt can lessen its isolating impact and help team members view it as a shared, manageable experience rather than a personal flaw.

Cultural Caution: Impostor syndrome can be worse for people in environments where their identity is underrepresented, making it more difficult to believe that their presence is genuinely appreciated.

Mosaic Question: When have you questioned your right to be in the room, and what helped you remain confident?

Mosaic in Action: A woman of color in a STEM field prepares to give her first conference keynote. Moments before speaking, she doubts her expertise. A colleague quietly reminds her of the groundbreaking research she authored. She delivers confidently, later mentoring others who face similar doubts.

Implicit Bias

Definition: Unconscious attitudes or stereotypes that affect how people perceive, decide, and act toward individuals or groups.

Business Application: During hiring, a manager unintentionally favors candidates with similar educational backgrounds to theirs, which reduces diversity in the applicant pool.

Leadership Insight: Recognizing and mitigating implicit bias requires structured approaches— such as standardized evaluation criteria and diverse interview panels—to ensure fair and equitable results.

Cultural Caution: While everyone has biases, unexamined ones can sustain inequalities and reinforce exclusion in systems that already lack diversity.

Mosaic Question: What patterns do you observe in who you tend to trust, promote, or mentor most often—and why?

Mosaic in Action: A nonprofit director examines promotion data and observes that men have advanced more quickly than women in similar roles. She introduces a blind review process for promotion proposals, resulting in more equitable representation at senior levels within a year.

In-group Bias

Definition: The tendency to favor, trust, or give preferential treatment to people perceived as part of one's own group, often at the expense of fairness toward outsiders.

Business Application: In a global company, a regional manager regularly assigns high-value projects to team members from their home country, unintentionally sidelining equally qualified colleagues in other locations.

Leadership Insight: Leaders who regularly rotate opportunities, seek diverse perspectives, and evaluate outcomes across groups can counteract the limiting effects of in-group bias.

Cultural Caution: In-group bias may seem subtle but has long-lasting effects, such as strengthening power imbalances and weakening trust among those excluded.

Mosaic Question: How could your natural preference for specific people or groups limit the perspectives you consider?

Mosaic in Action: A school principal notices that most leadership positions in school committees are held by longstanding staff from one department. She deliberately opens applications to newer staff and those from different departments, leading to more innovative ideas and better school-wide teamwork.

Incompetent Leadership

Definition: A pattern of leadership characterized by the failure to effectively guide, support, or inspire others. Incompetent leadership can arise from a lack of skill, self-awareness, or accountability, often causing harm to individuals, teams, and organizational culture.

Business Application: Incompetent leadership occurs when managers dodge accountability, fail to communicate effectively, or put ego before results. It damages trust, raises turnover, and undermines organizational strength.

Leadership Insight: Competence is about growth, not perfection. Leaders need to identify their blind spots, ask for feedback, and focus on development. What separates competent leadership from incompetent is the willingness to learn and adapt.

Cultural Caution: What is labeled as incompetence may sometimes reflect cultural misunderstanding, bias, or different leadership norms. Leaders should evaluate whether critiques come from real skill gaps or from resistance to nontraditional leadership styles.

Mosaic Question: How do you react when your leadership isn't effective — with defensiveness or humility and a focus on growth?

Mosaic in Action: After repeated feedback about disengaged staff, a department head begins leadership coaching and reorganizes meetings to focus on listening and transparency, moving from incompetence toward growth.

Inclusion

Definition: The intentional practice of creating environments where all individuals feel valued, respected, and able to fully participate, regardless of their identity or background.

Business Application: A tech startup ensures that product design teams include members from diverse cultural backgrounds, genders, and ability levels to better reflect its customer base.

Leadership Insight: Inclusion is active; it demands ongoing effort to remove barriers, address inequalities, and foster a culture where differences are seen as strengths.

Cultural Caution: Inclusion efforts without structural change risk becoming symbolic—appearing inclusive without tackling deeper systemic inequalities.

Mosaic Question: What specific steps are you taking to ensure every team member has both a voice and influence?

Mosaic in Action: In quarterly meetings, a marketing director notices that only a few voices dominate. She restructures the agenda to include small-group discussions and rotates spokespersons so every team member's perspective reaches the larger group. Engagement and innovation increase across the department.

Inclusion Fatigue

Definition: The exhaustion, frustration, or disengagement that results from ongoing efforts to promote inclusion, often due to slow progress, resistance, or perceived lack of genuine commitment.

Business Application: Diversity committee members start skipping meetings after months of initiatives are stalled by leadership inaction.

Leadership Insight: Leaders can reduce inclusion fatigue by setting realistic goals, communicating progress openly, and recognizing contributors' efforts.

Cultural Caution: Inclusion fatigue often indicates structural issues, not a lack of dedication. Ignoring it risks losing the very people most committed to driving change.

Mosaic Question: What systems or habits in your environment drain energy from inclusion efforts—and how could they be restructured?

Mosaic in Action: In a large nonprofit, staff express burnout over repeated diversity trainings with no policy follow-through. The director responds by implementing measurable hiring equity goals and reporting quarterly progress, restoring momentum and trust in the process.

Inclusive Design

Definition: A design approach that intentionally considers the needs, preferences, and limitations of people with diverse identities, abilities, and experiences, ensuring accessibility and usability for all.

Business Application: A software company develops its app with customizable text sizes, voice navigation, and multiple language options to reach a broader audience and eliminate usage barriers.

Leadership Insight: Leaders who promote inclusive design expand market reach, enhance user satisfaction, and demonstrate that every user's experience is valued.

Cultural Caution: Inclusive design requires early integration in planning, not retrofitting after complaints. Failing to involve diverse stakeholders during design phases can lead to costly fixes and missed opportunities.

Mosaic Question: Whose needs have you unintentionally overlooked in your products, services, or processes?

Mosaic in Action: A university revamps its online learning platform after consulting students with disabilities, multilingual learners, and rural users with limited internet access. The redesign results in higher engagement and improved course completion rates across all student groups.

Inclusive Language

Definition: Communication that avoids words or expressions that exclude, stereotype, or diminish people based on their identity, while actively using words that celebrate diversity and foster belonging.

Business Application: A job posting replaces gendered terms like "salesman" with inclusive alternatives such as "sales representative" to attract a broader pool of applicants.

Leadership Insight: Leaders who use inclusive language demonstrate respect, set a positive organizational tone, and build trust across diverse teams.

Cultural Caution: Inclusion in language goes beyond merely avoiding offense; it involves actively affirming the dignity and identity of others. Over-policing language without encouraging genuine dialogue can hinder learning and trust.

Mosaic Question: Which words or phrases in your daily

communication could be replaced to better promote equity and respect?

Mosaic in Action: A conference organizer replaces "ladies and gentlemen" with "colleagues" when addressing attendees, making gender-diverse participants feel acknowledged and included without singling anyone out.

Inclusive Leadership

Definition: A leadership approach that actively seeks, values, and integrates diverse perspectives into decision-making and organizational culture.

Business Application: A CEO forms cross-functional advisory boards comprising employees from different backgrounds and roles to guide company strategy.

Leadership Insight: Inclusive leaders create environments where diverse viewpoints are heard, respected, and acted upon—enhancing innovation, retention, and trust.

Cultural Caution: Declaring oneself an inclusive leader without changing systems, policies, and behaviors risks tokenism and can damage credibility.

Mosaic Question: How do you ensure that inclusion is embedded

into your leadership decisions, not just your intentions?

Mosaic in Action: A school superintendent hosts community listening sessions in various neighborhoods, providing translation services and childcare so more families can participate in shaping district policies.

Inclusive Procurement

Definition: The deliberate effort to purchase goods and services from diverse and historically marginalized suppliers.

Business Application: Inclusive procurement reallocates economic opportunities, enhances supply chains, and helps organizations meet equity targets.

Leadership Insight: Leaders expand their influence when they see procurement not only as saving costs but also as a tool for systemic equity.

Cultural Caution: Local definitions of "diverse suppliers" differ. Leaders need to tailor inclusivity efforts to their specific context without enforcing uniform standards.

Mosaic Question: Does your supply chain embody your values of equity and inclusion?

Mosaic in Action: A city government established inclusive procurement targets, directing millions to women- and minority-owned businesses.

Indigeneity

Definition: The state or quality of being Indigenous, often linked to ancestral connections to a specific place, community, language, and cultural traditions.

Business Application: A museum consults Indigenous curators and community members to ensure exhibits accurately reflect the histories and identities of the peoples represented.

Leadership Insight: Honoring Indigeneity in decision-making means engaging Indigenous voices directly, respecting sovereignty, and acknowledging the historical and ongoing impacts of colonization.

Cultural Caution: Avoid treating Indigeneity as a monolith; diverse Indigenous nations and communities have distinct histories, governance systems, and traditions.

Mosaic Question: How do you acknowledge and incorporate Indigenous perspectives in your work beyond symbolic gestures?

Mosaic in Action: A city council begins meetings with a land acknowledgment co-written with local Indigenous leaders, followed by concrete commitments such as funding cultural programs and protecting sacred sites.

Indigenous Sovereignty

Definition: The inherent right of Indigenous peoples to govern themselves, control their lands and resources, and maintain their cultural, legal, and political systems without external interference.

Business Application: A renewable energy company consults with tribal governments from the start of a project, respecting their jurisdiction and decision-making authority over proposed developments on tribal land.

Leadership Insight: Respecting Indigenous sovereignty requires more than just consultation — it means honoring decisions, even when they differ from business or governmental interests.

Cultural Caution: Token consultation or moving forward without consent undermines sovereignty and can reinforce historical injustices.

Mosaic Question: In your leadership role, how do you ensure

Indigenous sovereignty is upheld in both principle and practice?

Mosaic in Action: When a developer proposes a tourism project on Indigenous land, the tribal council rejects it due to environmental concerns. The developer respects the decision and instead offers to support a community-led ecotourism initiative.

Information Privilege

Definition: The advantage of having greater access to information, resources, or networks that others may lack, often due to systemic disparities.

Business Application: A senior employee with access to strategic company data can make career moves and investments that newer employees cannot predict.

Leadership Insight: Recognizing information privilege helps leaders intentionally share vital knowledge, enhancing transparency and fairness across teams.

Cultural Caution: Hoarding information—whether intentional or due to neglect—strengthens power imbalances and restricts opportunities for those without the same access.

Mosaic Question: What information do you take for granted that others might not have—and how can you help close that gap?

Mosaic in Action: A university career center notices that high-income students are more likely to hear about internship opportunities through family networks. They create a public, centralized database of internships to ensure equal access for all students.

Inherited Bias

Definition: Prejudices, stereotypes, or assumptions passed down through cultural, familial, or societal conditioning, often absorbed unconsciously from an early age.

Business Application: An employee unconsciously avoids collaborating with colleagues from a certain country because of negative narratives they heard growing up.

Leadership Insight: Addressing inherited bias requires self-reflection, exposure to diverse perspectives, and active unlearning of outdated or harmful beliefs.

Cultural Caution: Inherited biases can persist even in those who value inclusion, surfacing in subtle behaviors unless actively challenged.

Mosaic Question: Which of your earliest learned beliefs about people or groups have you since questioned—and why?

Mosaic in Action: A team leader who grew up hearing gendered assumptions about leadership realizes she assigns technical tasks more often to men. After recognizing the pattern, she intentionally distributes tasks based on skill and interest, not gender.

Inner Clarity

Definition: A grounded understanding of one's internal emotional and mental landscape enables intentional leadership and values-based alignment.

Business Application: Leaders with inner clarity make decisions more confidently and communicate them authentically. Organizations benefit from less conflict and stronger alignment when leaders act from clarity instead of confusion.

Leadership Insight: Clarity acts as an internal compass. Leaders who develop it through reflection and mindfulness provide stability to their teams, even when situations are unclear.

Cultural Caution: Inner clarity can be cultivated in different ways across cultures — through silence,

ritual, meditation, or dialogue. Leaders need to respect various practices for developing clarity.

Mosaic Question: Do you make decisions based on inner clarity or external pressure?

Mosaic in Action: A manager starts each week with ten minutes of reflection before setting priorities, making sure her leadership aligns with both organizational goals and her personal values.

Inner Work

Definition: The personal practice of emotional reflection, healing, and growth that enhances leadership and resilience. Inner work is the foundation for outer impact.

Business Application: Organizations led by individuals dedicated to inner work experience healthier cultures, as leaders manage emotions, prevent projection, and lead with self-awareness.

Leadership Insight: Inner work is a continuous process, not a one-time accomplishment. Leaders who consistently practice it enhance their ability for empathy, resilience, and wise decision-making.

Cultural Caution: Inner work might be undervalued in fast-paced, results-oriented cultures. Leaders should present it as a professional discipline, not a personal indulgence.

Mosaic Question: Do you prioritize inner work — or only expect results from yourself and others?

Mosaic in Action: An executive invests in coaching and reflective journaling during a period of rapid growth, demonstrating how inner work fosters sustainable leadership.

Institutional Betrayal

Definition: Harm caused when an organization fails to prevent or properly respond to misconduct, discrimination, or abuse, especially when the institution has a duty of care.

Business Application: A university dismisses repeated reports of harassment from students, prioritizing the institution's reputation over the safety and well-being of those affected.

Leadership Insight: Recognizing and addressing institutional betrayal involves transparent acknowledgment of harm, accountability measures, and active efforts to rebuild trust.

Cultural Caution: Silence or defensiveness when harm is reported worsens the original wrongdoings and signals to

stakeholders that their safety and dignity are not a priority.

Mosaic Question: How does your organization respond when harm is reported—and does that response strengthen or weaken trust?

Mosaic in Action: A nonprofit is alerted to discriminatory practices within a department. Instead of protecting leadership, the board publicly acknowledges the issue, initiates an independent review, and makes structural changes to prevent it from happening again.

Institutional Courage

Definition: The dedication of an organization to act with integrity, transparency, and accountability, particularly in recognizing and addressing its own shortcomings.

Business Application: A company openly reports on pay equity gaps, develops a clear plan to close them, and updates progress regularly for employees and the public.

Leadership Insight: Institutional courage is cultivated through consistent, values-based actions that prioritize justice and well-being over short-term reputation concerns.

Cultural Caution: Public claims of courage must be supported by measurable results; otherwise, they risk being perceived as performative.

Mosaic Question: What tough truths is your organization willing to confront—and how will you respond?

Mosaic in Action: After an internal audit uncovers systemic bias in hiring, a hospital system shares the findings with staff and patients, allocates funding to bias-reduction training, and revises its recruitment process to ensure fairer representation.

Institutional Racism

Definition: Systemic policies, practices, and cultural norms within institutions that create and sustain racial inequalities, regardless of individual intent.

Business Application: A city's housing policies lead to predominantly white neighborhoods receiving superior public services, schools, and infrastructure compared to communities of color.

Leadership Insight: Dismantling institutional racism requires leaders to analyze policies, distribute resources fairly, and engage directly with affected communities.

Cultural Caution: Focusing only on individual prejudice can hide

the deeper structural changes needed to achieve racial equity.

Mosaic Question: Which institutional practices in your environment might unintentionally uphold racial disparities?

Mosaic in Action: A university reviews its admissions process and finds that legacy preferences overwhelmingly benefit white applicants. The school removes the policy and adopts holistic admissions criteria to increase access for underrepresented students.

Institutional Whiteness

Definition:: The pervasive dominance of whiteness in organizational norms, structures, and expectations, often unnoticed by those who benefit from it.

Business Application: Institutional whiteness influences hiring, promotion, communication styles, and standards of professionalism. Naming it helps organizations redesign systems for real equity.

Leadership Insight:: Leaders who recognize institutional whiteness create space for diverse approaches to leading, learning, and belonging, breaking down exclusionary defaults.

Cultural Caution:: Labeling whiteness as a systemic issue, not just an individual one, helps avoid defensiveness and emphasizes structural change.

Mosaic Question:: Where does whiteness serve as the silent default in your institution?

Mosaic in Action:: A university reviews its "professional dress code," recognizing it was based on Eurocentric standards. By rewriting guidelines to include cultural flexibility, they validate diverse expressions of professionalism.

Instructional Equity

Definition:: The commitment to providing fair access, resources, and outcomes in teaching, training, and professional development.

Business Application: Instructional equity guarantees that learning opportunities are not influenced by race, class, gender, or ability, but are fairly accessible to everyone.

Leadership Insight:: Equitable instruction involves leaders tackling systemic barriers, not merely adjusting content. It requires aligning policies, materials, and support systems.

Cultural Caution:: Equity is different from equality—providing the same resources to everyone may reinforce disadvantages instead of fixing them.

Mosaic Question:: Does your training or teaching provide opportunity fairly—or does it reinforce inequality?

Mosaic in Action:: A leadership program updates its mentorship model to guarantee women and BIPOC participants equal access to senior-level sponsors, impacting career outcomes over the long term.

Instructional Wholeness

Definition:: An approach to learning that combines cognitive, emotional, cultural, and identity aspects, viewing participants as complete beings rather than separate roles.

Business Application: Instructional wholeness fosters engagement by affirming learners' stories, emotions, and cultural frameworks along with skill development.

Leadership Insight:: Whole instruction fosters not only competence but also confidence and a sense of belonging, which builds stronger organizational loyalty.

Cultural Caution:: Wholeness requires resources—without

support, leaders might resort to "holistic" approaches that can become superficial or overwhelming.

Mosaic Question:: Does your instruction respect the entire person—or just the part that aligns with your system?

Mosaic in Action:: A corporate trainer combines reflection, storytelling, and cross-cultural case studies into a technical workshop, ensuring participants leave with both skills and self-awareness.

Intellectual Humility

Definition: Recognizing that your knowledge may be limited and that other perspectives can reveal important truths.

Business Application: A CEO admits uncertainty about an emerging market trend and asks for input from team members at all levels.

Leadership Insight: Leaders who practice intellectual humility promote cultures of learning, innovation, and trust by encouraging open dialogue and feedback.

Cultural Caution: Humility does not mean indecisiveness or lack of expertise; it involves staying open

to correction, growth, and shared wisdom.

Mosaic Question: How do you respond when new information challenges your beliefs or expertise?

Mosaic in Action: A school superintendent suggests a new technology rollout but listens to strong concerns from teachers about its classroom impact. Instead of pushing ahead, she pauses the plan, reviews pilot feedback, and adjusts the strategy with input from educators.

Intercultural Competence

Definition: The ability to effectively and appropriately communicate with people from different cultural backgrounds by recognizing, respecting, and adapting to cultural differences.

Business Application: An international sales team adjusts its negotiation strategies based on the communication styles, decision-making approaches, and values of clients from various countries.

Leadership Insight: Leaders with intercultural competence bridge misunderstandings, build trust across cultures, and promote inclusive collaboration in global or diverse local environments.

Cultural Caution: Believing that awareness alone equals competence can lead to oversimplification; skills must be continuously practiced and improved.

Mosaic Question: How do you modify your approach to connect meaningfully across cultural differences?

Mosaic in Action: A project manager in a multinational company schedules meetings considerate of all time zones, rotates facilitation roles to respect different leadership styles, and adapts materials to be culturally relevant for each team.

Interfaith Fluency

Definition: The ability to understand, respect, and engage positively with people from different religious or spiritual backgrounds without forcing one's own beliefs.

Business Application: A hospital chaplain works effectively with patients of various faiths, making sure spiritual care matches each patient's traditions and needs.

Leadership Insight: Leaders with interfaith fluency can foster environments where people feel safe to share their beliefs, especially in workplaces or communities with diverse religions.

Cultural Caution: Don't reduce interfaith engagement to just recognizing holidays; true fluency involves listening closely and understanding lived practices.

Mosaic Question: How do you create space for religious and spiritual diversity without prioritizing one tradition?

Mosaic in Action: A public school district updates its academic calendar after consulting families from different faith backgrounds, ensuring major religious observances are acknowledged and respected without harming students' academic progress.

Intergenerational Wisdom

Definition: The shared knowledge, insights, and skills exchanged between people of different age groups, leveraging the strengths of each generation.

Business Application: A startup pairs younger tech-savvy employees with experienced professionals in a reverse-mentoring program to exchange digital skills and industry knowledge.

Leadership Insight: Leaders who promote intergenerational wisdom foster innovation, maintain institutional memory, and boost team resilience.

Cultural Caution: Avoid stereotypes that oversimplify generational strengths or weaknesses; wisdom flows both ways.

Mosaic Question: What could you learn—or unlearn—by intentionally exchanging ideas with someone from a different generation?

Mosaic in Action: A nonprofit's leadership team pairs retiring executives with emerging leaders for six months of mutual mentoring, leading to smoother transitions and innovative program updates informed by both legacy and fresh perspectives.

Interpersonal Courage

Definition:: The willingness to engage in difficult, vulnerable, or high-risk conversations that maintain integrity and strengthen relationships at the same time.

Business Application: Interpersonal courage lowers the cost of silence. Teams that practice it identify issues early, stopping conflicts from growing into crises.

Leadership Insight:: Courage in dialogue involves balancing honesty with empathy. It builds trust when leaders demonstrate truth-telling with compassion.

Cultural Caution:: Direct confrontation may be appreciated in some cultures and rejected in others; leaders must adapt courageous acts to the context.

Mosaic Question:: What conversation are you avoiding that could build trust or lead to growth?

Mosaic in Action:: A mid-level manager tells a senior executive that their tone is alienating staff, framing it as concern for both the leader's influence and the team's morale.

Intersectional Leadership

Definition:: A leadership approach that acknowledges overlapping identities (race, gender, class, ability, sexuality, etc.) and adjusts strategies to honor complexity.

Business Application: Intersectional leadership makes sure that initiatives not only include diversity but also tackle complex inequalities—like the specific struggles faced by women of color.

Leadership Insight:: Leaders who think intersectionally avoid one-size-fits-all solutions. They foster innovation by recognizing the unique perspectives at points where identities intersect.

Cultural Caution:: Without depth, intersectionality can become just jargon. Leaders need to link it to real experiences, not only labels.

Mosaic Question:: Do your leadership practices consider how identities overlap, or do they treat people as one-dimensional?

Mosaic in Action:: A global NGO adapts its parental leave policy after feedback from LGBTQ+ staff, recognizing intersecting family structures often overlooked by traditional policies.

Intersectionality

Definition: A framework for understanding how overlapping social identities—such as race, gender, class, sexuality, and ability—interact to create unique experiences of advantage or disadvantage.

Business Application: HR teams analyze pay equity not only by gender but also by the combination of gender and race, revealing disparities that single-category analysis might miss.

Leadership Insight: Using an intersectional lens helps leaders identify subtle barriers and develop solutions that address multiple, interconnected aspects of identity.

Cultural Caution: Ignoring intersectionality can lead to initiatives that benefit some in a marginalized group while neglecting others.

Mosaic Question: Whose voices or needs might be missed if you focus on only one aspect of identity at a time?

Mosaic in Action: A leadership program updates its curriculum after discovering that women of color were underrepresented in participant feedback. By including intersectional case studies and mentorship, participation and satisfaction improve among diverse groups.

Internalized Oppression

Definition: The process where members of marginalized groups absorb and accept negative stereotypes, beliefs, or narratives about themselves, often leading to self-limiting behaviors.

Business Application: An employee from an underrepresented background hesitates to apply for leadership roles, believing they are less qualified than their peers despite having equal credentials.

Leadership Insight: Leaders can help combat internalized oppression by affirming individuals' capabilities, creating fair pathways for advancement, and tackling systemic barriers that reinforce harmful narratives.

Cultural Caution: Internalized oppression stems from external bias systems; focusing only on individual change without addressing these systems limits progress.

Mosaic Question: Which limiting beliefs about your identity might have been influenced by systemic narratives rather than your true experiences?

Mosaic in Action: A community program for women entrepreneurs offers coaching that challenges stereotypes about women in business, resulting in increased confidence and higher rates of new ventures among participants.

Intent vs. Impact

Definition: The idea that the effect of an action or statement on others matters more than the intent behind it when judging harm or misunderstanding.

Business Application: A manager jokes about a stereotype without meaning to offend, but a team member feels hurt and left out. The focus shifts from defending intent to addressing the impact and rebuilding trust.

Leadership Insight: Leaders who emphasize impact over intent create safer, more responsible environments where harm is recognized and handled.

Cultural Caution: Overfocusing on intent can downplay harm, while overfocusing on impact without discussion can hinder learning. Both need to be balanced.

Mosaic Question: How do you handle it when your actions cause a different effect than you planned?

Mosaic in Action: During a client meeting, a consultant makes a comment about cultural customs that unintentionally offends someone. Instead of dismissing it, the consultant apologizes, listens to the concern, and changes their language going forward.

Inward Leadership

Definition: Inward Leadership is about leading from a place of self-awareness, self-regulation, and inner clarity. It focuses on understanding your own emotions, values, and motivations as the foundation for effective outward leadership.

Business Application: Organizations increasingly recognize that leaders who develop inward practices like reflection, mindfulness, or emotional regulation are better prepared to manage stress, make decisions aligned with their values, and build genuine trust. Inward Leadership minimizes reactive choices and boosts resilience in high-pressure situations.

Leadership Insight: Leaders who practice Inward Leadership demonstrate emotional integrity and presence. By recognizing their own triggers and biases, they foster open dialogue and balanced decision-making, establishing a cultural tone of groundedness and self-responsibility.

Cultural Caution: Not all cultures or organizations value introspection. In some settings, focusing on oneself can be wrongly seen as self-centeredness or passivity. Leaders should present inward practices as ways to enhance their service to others and stay aware of cultural differences in leadership expectations.

Mosaic Question: How does nurturing your inner clarity and values influence the way you lead outwardly?

Mosaic in Action: Inward Leadership builds a lasting base for resilience, allowing leaders to connect inner integrity with outward influence.

Invisible Disabilities

Definition: Conditions that are physical, mental, or neurological and are not immediately visible but can limit a person's abilities, requiring understanding and accommodation.

Business Application: An employee with a chronic illness asks for a flexible work schedule to manage symptoms, even though their condition is not outwardly visible.

Leadership Insight: Leaders who recognize and proactively support invisible disabilities promote inclusion, reduce stigma, and improve retention.

Cultural Caution: Assuming someone's health or ability based on appearance can cause exclusion, misunderstanding, or discrimination.

Mosaic Question: How might your workplace or community unintentionally be inaccessible to those with invisible disabilities?

Mosaic in Action: A company updates its leave policy to add flexible sick time, mental health days, and remote work options after employees reveal that current policies don't support those with unseen conditions.

Invisible Labor

Definition: Work that is essential but often goes unnoticed, unpaid, or undervalued, such as providing emotional support, mentoring, or managing behind-the-scenes tasks.

Business Application: A team member routinely organizes events, mentors new staff, and resolves conflicts—efforts that boost morale but aren't counted in performance reviews.

Leadership Insight: Recognizing and valuing invisible labor boosts morale, prevents burnout, and fosters trust within the team.

Cultural Caution: Relying on certain individuals—often women or marginalized groups—to perform invisible labor can reinforce inequality.

Mosaic Question: Who on your team is doing important work that goes unrecognized, and how can you acknowledge it?

Mosaic in Action: Following an internal review, a company includes "team culture contributions" in performance metrics, ensuring that mentoring, community-building, and conflict resolution are considered in promotions and pay decisions.

Invisible Privilege

Definition:: Advantages that individuals or groups have unknowingly, often unseen by beneficiaries but significant to those left out.

Business Application: Recognizing invisible privilege helps leaders create systems that don't unintentionally reinforce inequality—such as assuming all staff can afford unpaid internships.

Leadership Insight:: Leaders who recognize invisible privilege demonstrate humility and build trust among diverse teams.

Cultural Caution:: Discussions about privilege should be approached constructively; otherwise, they might trigger defensiveness instead of reflection.

Mosaic Question:: What privileges influence your leadership that you often overlook?

Mosaic in Action:: A senior executive recognizes that networking events have always been held at costly venues, unintentionally excluding junior staff. They relocate events to accessible locations, increasing participation.

◈ LETTER I CALLOUT

"Identity is never static — it is an evolving story shaped by context, choice, and community."

Reflection Questions

- When have you felt tension between your private and public identities?
- How does inclusion shift when invisible identities are acknowledged?
- What does identity agility look like in cross-cultural teams?

Practical Move

Invite your group to reflect on one aspect of identity that feels important to them today. Normalize that what is named may change tomorrow.

J – Justice, Joy, and
Journeys of Belonging

J challenges us to rethink equity not just as fixing what's broken but as creating something new. It shifts the focus from repairing to imagining what has yet to be built. Justice here is not performative or punitive—it is structural, systemic, and ongoing. Joy is not just a private escape but a form of collective resistance and resilience. And the journeys of belonging require more than just opening doors—they demand unlearning, reimagining, and grounding ourselves in spaces where everyone can thrive.

Too often, the language of equity focuses on urgency and pain, leaving little room for hope. J reminds us that liberation should also include laughter, that healing should involve celebration, and that equity work without joy becomes difficult to sustain.

J asks us to notice the deeper dimensions of this work

- Justice that transforms systems, not just individuals.
- Joy that resists despair and restores energy for change.
- Journeys that require more than entry—they require authenticity and care.
- Belonging that is cultivated through shared humanity, not assimilation.

The J terms challenge us to move beyond guilt, fear, and superficial reforms. They invite a vision of equity rooted in imagination—where justice is a lived experience, where belonging is shared rather than earned, and where leadership is defined by the courage to co-create rather than the power to control.

J encourages leaders to embrace the full emotional spectrum of this work to honor pain without being defined by it, to protect hope without trivializing it, and to build communities where joy is seen not as a luxury but as a necessity for collective growth. Because justice without joy becomes fragile, but together they create the foundation where true belonging can grow and last.

J

Jargon Barriers

Definition: The use of technical, insider, or overly complex language that makes it difficult for those unfamiliar with the terminology to understand or participate.

Business Application: In workplaces, jargon can alienate team members, confuse clients, and create unspoken hierarchies where only those "in the know" can fully participate in decision-making. Eliminating jargon encourages inclusion, improves communication, and speeds up onboarding.

Leadership Insight: Leaders who simplify complex ideas into clear language demonstrate that clarity outweighs status. By making technical or institutional language easier to understand, they eliminate communication barriers that impede progress.

Cultural Caution: What might seem like "everyday" terms in one cultural or professional setting can be confusing or even exclusionary in another. Overusing jargon can unintentionally exclude people from different industries, generations, or language backgrounds.

Mosaic Question: Where could your language unintentionally exclude others, and how might you make it more welcoming by using simpler words?

Mosaic in Action: During a cross-department meeting, an IT manager notices the finance team struggling to understand a presentation loaded with acronyms. She pauses, rephrases it in plain language, and invites questions. The conversation shifts from silence to active participation, revealing ideas that would have otherwise gone unheard.

JEDI (Justice, Equity, Diversity, Inclusion)

Definition: An expanded framework that incorporates justice into equity, diversity, and inclusion initiatives, emphasizing the removal of systemic barriers and promoting restorative change.

Business Application: JEDI principles extend beyond representational diversity by tackling root causes of inequality—such as unfair policies, exclusionary hiring practices, or biased decision-making structures. They help organizations create sustainable, values-driven cultures.

Leadership Insight: Justice is not just the result of equity, diversity, and inclusion; it requires intentional action. Leaders supporting JEDI initiatives must engage in systemic analysis, reallocate resources, and promote cultural healing, not just increase diversity numbers.

Cultural Caution: Without true accountability, JEDI risks being seen as just branding. A public pledge without actual policy changes can lead to distrust and accusations of performative allyship.

Mosaic Question: How can your leadership go beyond inclusion to address the root causes of inequity?

Mosaic in Action: A university expands its DEI office into a JEDI center, adding a justice-focused policy review team. Within a year, outdated disciplinary policies that disproportionately harmed students of color are replaced with restorative practices—improving equity outcomes and campus climate.

Job Fragility

Definition: The vulnerability of a role to removal, restructuring, or devaluation, often caused by budget cuts, political shifts, or organizational instability.

Business Application: Job instability impacts employee morale, retention, and trust. Leaders who proactively communicate about job security—or the lack of it—can reduce speculation and help employees prepare for change.

Leadership Insight: Recognizing job fragility helps leaders determine which roles or functions require strategic safeguarding, clearer career pathways, or cross-training to adapt to change.

Cultural Caution: Job insecurity often unfairly affects roles held by women, minorities, or contingent workers. Overlooking this can deepen inequalities and damage an organization's reputation.

Mosaic Question: Which roles in your organization are the most vulnerable—and what would be needed to solidify them?

Mosaic in Action: During a major budget review, a nonprofit director notices that part-time community liaison roles are the first proposed for cuts. She redefines them as vital trust-building positions, includes them in core program budgets, and ensures they continue despite overall cuts.

Joint Accountability

Definition: A collective responsibility shared by individuals or groups to reach a goal, maintain standards, or produce results—where success or failure impacts everyone equally.

Business Application: Joint accountability promotes stronger collaboration among departments, partners, or stakeholders by ensuring that progress is tracked collectively rather than individually. It is especially effective in cross-sector partnerships where mutual trust and transparency are essential.

Leadership Insight: Leaders who demonstrate joint accountability send a message that "we're in this together," fostering trust, shared responsibility, and a culture of mutual respect. It also means collectively owning mistakes instead of shifting blame to protect reputations.

Cultural Caution: When power is unequal, shared responsibility can mask disparities. Without fair decision-making power, those with less power often carry a heavier burden.

Mosaic Question: How can you ensure accountability is truly shared—and not merely in name?

Mosaic in Action: In a public health initiative, a city government and a nonprofit collaborate to reduce childhood asthma rates. Instead of each organization tracking its own data, they create a shared dashboard, co-own the data, and present the results together to the community.

Journey of Belonging

Definition: The ongoing personal and collective process of creating and maintaining environments where individuals feel accepted, valued, and connected.

Business Application: Organizations that celebrate the journey of belonging understand that inclusion is an ongoing relationship with employees, customers, and communities. This involves recognizing milestones, transitions, and moments when belonging is tested.

Leadership Insight: Belonging is not static—it shifts as people grow, organizations change, and cultural contexts develop. Leaders who understand this view inclusion as an ongoing investment rather than a checklist task.

Cultural Caution:
Overemphasizing "fit" can unintentionally promote conformity, which may diminish authenticity and hinder diversity of thought. The path to belonging should allow space for individuality and healthy differences.

Mosaic Question: How are you fostering a space where the journey of belonging feels both safe and engaging?

Mosaic in Action: A multinational company launches an alumni network for former employees, recognizing that belonging doesn't end after resignation. Former staff become brand ambassadors, mentors, and collaborators, strengthening the organization's sense of community.

Joy as Resistance

Definition: The intentional practice of cultivating joy to strengthen resilience and oppose oppression, hardship, or systemic injustice.

Business Application: In high-stress or unfair environments, encouraging moments of joy—whether through celebration, humor, creativity, or rest—can strengthen teams, foster innovation, and prevent burnout.

Leadership Insight: Joy is not frivolous; it's a leadership strategy.

Leaders who prioritize joy foster cultures where people feel valued beyond productivity, making it harder for harmful systems to erode human dignity.

Cultural Caution: In some environments, joy might be mistaken for a lack of seriousness or unwillingness to address urgency. Leaders must ensure that joy is expressed in ways that respect cultural norms and the importance of the situation.

Mosaic Question: How can you intentionally protect joy as a leadership practice?

Mosaic in Action: In a community enduring ongoing political repression, a local arts collective hosts weekly dance nights. The music and laughter act as both a lifeline and a statement oppression will not steal their joy.

Joy Disruption

Definition: The deliberate or accidental interruption of moments of joy, celebration, or shared positivity—often by adding conflict, negativity, or cynicism.

Business Application: In workplace cultures, joy disruption can occur when a win is immediately followed by criticism, when celebrations are canceled for efficiency, or when leaders downplay achievements to avoid "complacency." Over time, this erodes morale and engagement.

Leadership Insight: Leaders who protect moments of joy send a clear message recognition and celebration matter. Interrupting joy—especially during high-stress times—can accelerate burnout and reduce emotional resilience.

Cultural Caution: In some cultures, humility and restraint are valued more than outward celebration. Leaders must recognize whether joy disruptions stem from cultural norms or unhealthy patterns.

Mosaic Question: How do you protect joy as a shared cultural resource within your team or community?

Mosaic in Action: After a nonprofit team secures a major grant, a senior leader interrupts the celebration to outline the upcoming challenges. Morale drops immediately. Later, the leader adjusts their approach—allowing full recognition of wins before moving on to the next steps—and sees engagement increase.

Joy Equity

Definition: The fair distribution of opportunities for happiness, growth, and celebration among all groups. Joy equity highlights that joy should not be a privilege but a fundamental human right.

Business Application: Organizations that promote joy equity cultivate cultures where recognition, celebration, and creativity are accessible to everyone, not just those in dominant groups.

Leadership Insight: Joy serves as a leadership tool. Leaders who foster joy equity help prevent burnout, boost resilience, and reinforce a sense of belonging.

Cultural Caution: Expressions of joy differ across cultures. Leaders must ensure that "joy practices" do not suppress or ignore cultural ways of expressing joy.

Mosaic Question: Who has access to joy in your leadership spaces — and who is excluded?

Mosaic in Action: A company updates its recognition program to make sure all staff, including frontline workers, are equally acknowledged for their achievements.

Judgment Bias

Definition: A tendency to judge situations, people, or ideas based on personal beliefs, assumptions, or incomplete information, rather than objective evidence or different perspectives.

Business Application: Judgment bias can affect hiring, performance reviews, and decision-making, especially when leaders rely heavily on intuition or first impressions. Reducing it involves using structured evaluation processes and collecting diverse input.

Leadership Insight: Recognizing your own judgment biases is a leadership strength, not a weakness. Leaders who openly challenge their assumptions demonstrate humility and foster trust.

Cultural Caution: Judgment bias is often shaped by culture— what appears "professional" or "credible" in one context may be perceived differently elsewhere. Without awareness, leaders risk unintentionally reinforcing exclusionary norms.

Mosaic Question: How could your initial impressions restrict your perception of someone's potential?

Mosaic in Action: A hiring manager initially dismisses a candidate's unconventional résumé format. After a colleague encourages taking a closer look, the candidate is interviewed and demonstrates exactly the innovative thinking the team needs.

Judgment Drift

Definition: The slow evolution of decision-making standards over time, often influenced by external pressures, the acceptance of shortcuts, or unchecked bias.

Business Application: In organizations, judgment drift can lead to inconsistent policy enforcement, reducing ethical standards or causing unfair treatment of rules.

Leadership Insight: Small compromises, if ignored, can develop into systemic problems. Leaders must regularly revise decision-making frameworks to remain aligned with their core values and ethical commitments.

Cultural Caution: What looks like drift in one culture might be seen as flexible adaptation in another. Leaders must distinguish between healthy change and harmful erosion of standards.

Mosaic Question: How do you know when your standards have shifted—and who helps you notice it?

Mosaic in Action: Over several years, a university gradually relaxes the strictness of its admissions process to meet enrollment targets. When a new dean reviews the history, the trend becomes clear—

and corrective actions are taken to restore balance.

Judicial Inequity

Definition: The unjust treatment of individuals or groups within the legal system, often resulting from systemic bias, resource disparities, or cultural misunderstandings.

Business Application: Organizations operating across different jurisdictions must recognize judicial inequity when managing compliance, dispute resolution, or advocacy efforts. Leaders who assume fairness in the law without acknowledging inequity risk endangering their teams or clients.

Leadership Insight: Ethical leadership understands that "equal under the law" is not always reflected in reality. Leaders can use their influence to promote fairer policies and more just processes.

Cultural Caution: Judicial inequity might worsen for marginalized groups whose cultural norms or languages differ from those of the dominant legal system.

Mosaic Question: How does your organization address inequities within the systems you rely on?

Mosaic in Action: A community housing nonprofit notices that eviction rulings disproportionately affect tenants who speak limited English. They create a legal assistance program that translates proceedings and connects residents with pro bono lawyers—greatly improving case results.

Judicial Privilege

Definition: The advantages certain individuals or groups have within legal and justice systems due to wealth, race, class, or insider access.

Business Application: Awareness of judicial privilege helps leaders in law, compliance, and advocacy address systemic inequities and promote fairer processes.

Leadership Insight: Leaders who acknowledge judicial privilege realize that justice isn't equally accessible. They must leverage their influence to level the playing field.

Cultural Caution: In global contexts, privilege shows up differently. What seems like judicial privilege in one country might be seen as political privilege in another.

Mosaic Question: Who has easier access to justice due to privilege — and who faces obstacles?

Mosaic in Action: A nonprofit legal team advocates for reforms that lower barriers for low-income defendants while ensuring systems are held accountable for bias.

Jurisdictional Bias

Definition: Prejudice or favoritism based on geographic or political boundaries where a decision is made, leading to inconsistent outcomes across regions.

Business Application: In multinational or multi-state operations, jurisdictional bias can influence hiring practices, customer service standards, and product compliance, leading to unequal opportunities and reputational risks.

Leadership Insight: Leaders who anticipate jurisdictional bias develop systems to ensure that location does not determine fairness, opportunity, or service quality.

Cultural Caution: What is considered "fair" or "standard" in one jurisdiction might be discriminatory or exclusionary elsewhere. Leaders must balance local norms with organizational values.

Mosaic Question: How does your place of operation influence who is given the benefit of the doubt?

Mosaic in Action: A tech company discovers that its overseas offices are denying promotions to employees in smaller cities, assuming they lack "big market" readiness. The company updates its promotion criteria to remove location-based assumptions.

Just World Fallacy

Definition: The cognitive bias that believes people get what they deserve and deserve what they get, which leads to victim-blaming and complacency when facing injustice.

Business Application: In the workplace, this bias can justify ignoring inequities—assuming poor outcomes are always due to poor performance rather than systemic barriers.

Leadership Insight: Leaders must acknowledge and address this bias to foster environments where support and opportunity are not determined by pre-existing privilege.

Cultural Caution: The just world fallacy is strongly woven into certain cultural stories, making it difficult to question without careful evidence.

Mosaic Question: How might your policies change if you assumed that systemic barriers—rather than personal failings—are the root of inequity?

Mosaic in Action: A company adjusts its disciplinary process after recognizing that lateness is frequently related to unreliable public transit in low-income neighborhoods.

Justice Benchmarking

Definition: The practice of assessing policies, practices, and outcomes using established standards of equity and justice to find gaps and guide improvements.

Business Application: Justice benchmarking enables organizations to go beyond simple compliance and promote proactive fairness. It can be applied in areas such as pay equity audits, supplier diversity reviews, and community impact assessments.

Leadership Insight: Benchmarking for justice requires both quantitative data and qualitative feedback. Leaders who include lived experiences in the review process gain a more comprehensive understanding of their impact.

Cultural Caution: Standards for "justice" vary across cultures and industries; leaders must select benchmarks that honor both local conditions and universal human rights principles.

Mosaic Question: What if your organization measured justice as rigorously as it measures profit?

Mosaic in Action: A healthcare network examines patient satisfaction data by demographic group to find disparities in treatment times. Using justice benchmarking, they carry out targeted training and staffing changes, resulting in better outcomes overall.

Justice Co-Design

Definition: A collaborative process where communities most affected by inequity are actively involved in shaping policies, systems, or solutions aimed at promoting justice.

Business Application: Co-design makes sure that equity efforts are rooted in real experiences instead of top-down assumptions. Whether in product development, policy making, or service design, it improves relevance and increases adoption.

Leadership Insight: Leaders who adopt co-design shift from being "problem-solvers" to "power-sharers." This not only improves results but also fosters trust and credibility.

Cultural Caution: Tokenized involvement—inviting

marginalized voices without offering real influence—undermines the integrity of co-design.

Mosaic Question: How would your decisions change if the people most affected were also involved as co-creators of the solution?

Mosaic in Action: A city transit authority works with disability advocacy groups to redesign bus routes and stops. Riders with mobility challenges point out overlooked barriers, resulting in increased ridership and better accessibility compliance.

Justice Fatigue

Definition: The fatigue experienced by individuals or organizations engaged in long-term equity, diversity, and justice work, often due to slow progress, systemic resistance, or continuous emotional labor.

Business Application: Justice fatigue can lead to burnout among DEI leaders, employee advocates, and community organizers, hindering progress on change initiatives. Proactive support systems are essential.

Leadership Insight: Leaders should normalize rest, resource allocation, and role rotation to maintain justice-focused initiatives over time.

Cultural Caution: Fatigue should not be confused with apathy; it often signals overexertion in challenging or poorly supported environments.

Mosaic Question: What systems are in place to help your team sustain justice work without sacrificing well-being?

Mosaic in Action: A university DEI committee holds quarterly "pause weeks" where members step back from initiatives to focus on personal well-being and collective reflection.

Justice Framing

Definition: The intentional manner in which leaders communicate issues, solutions, and goals, emphasizing fairness, equity, and systemic responsibility.

Business Application: Effective justice framing can rally stakeholders, attract funding, and create urgency for change without alienating newcomers to the conversation.

Leadership Insight: Leaders skilled in justice framing balance moral clarity with strategic communication, meeting audiences where they are while still driving transformation.

Cultural Caution: Labeling justice solely as "charity" can reinforce power imbalances instead of breaking them down.

Mosaic Question: How does your framing of justice influence who supports or opposes your cause?

Mosaic in Action: A hospital redefines its push for translation services, not as a "courtesy" but as a patient safety essential, securing quick executive approval.

Justice Impact Assessment

Definition: A structured review process that evaluates the potential impacts on equity and justice of a policy, project, or decision before it is implemented.

Business Application: Justice impact assessments help prevent harm by ensuring equity considerations are included from the start, not added after implementation.

Leadership Insight: Leaders who adopt proactive assessments shift from reactive damage control to proactive justice.

Cultural Caution: Impact frameworks should be developed in partnership with affected communities to avoid becoming just symbolic checklists.

Mosaic Question: What justice outcomes will this decision create — and for whom?

Mosaic in Action: Before launching a new data platform, a university conducted a justice impact assessment, identifying risks for marginalized students and adjusting policies accordingly.

Justice Innovation

Definition: The practice of creating new systems, frameworks, and practices that go beyond reform to reimagine justice itself.

Business Application: Justice innovation appears when organizations develop new equity-focused hiring practices, accountability systems, or community partnerships that reshape fairness.

Leadership Insight: Justice innovation demands courage to go beyond incremental steps. Leaders need to envision and create structures that have never been seen before.

Cultural Caution: Innovation can be used as a buzzword. Justice innovation must stay rooted in equity, not just efficiency or appearances.

Mosaic Question: Do you repair old systems — or build new ones for justice?

Mosaic in Action: A city government replaces traditional disciplinary models in schools with restorative justice hubs, decreasing suspensions and fostering trust.

Justice Leakage

Definition: The difference between an organization's declared commitment to justice and how those principles are inconsistently enforced in practice.

Business Application: Leakage can occur when policies appear fair on paper but aren't effective in daily practice—such as selectively enforcing anti-harassment rules.

Leadership Insight: Measuring justice leakage requires both transparency and accountability. Leaders must be prepared to reveal uncomfortable truths.

Cultural Caution: Public displays of diversity initiatives can conceal internal inequalities, risking reputation damage if discrepancies come to light.

Mosaic Question: At what point does your organization's commitment to justice waver under real-world pressure?

Mosaic in Action: A retail chain publicly celebrates Pride Month but doesn't provide benefits for LGBTQ+ employees. Staff organize and advocate for policy changes, closing the gap between their values and actions.

Justice Literacy

Definition: The ability to understand, interpret, and apply principles of justice across personal, organizational, and systemic settings.

Business Application: Justice literacy empowers employees and leaders to recognize inequities, advocate effectively, and create fairer systems. It turns awareness into practical skills.

Leadership Insight: Without literacy, discussions about justice become unclear. Leaders who understand justice literacy can identify issues precisely and mobilize solutions effectively.

Cultural Caution: Justice literacy needs to be taught in context. What justice means in one setting can vary greatly in another.

Mosaic Question: How skilled are you at identifying and tackling injustice in your own environment?

Mosaic in Action: A university incorporates justice literacy training into orientation, providing all students and staff with common language for equity and accountability.

Justice Narratives

Definition: The stories leaders and organizations use to frame justice, inequity, and accountability. Justice narratives shape how people interpret both problems and solutions.

Business Application: Shaping justice narratives helps organizations communicate their commitment to equity authentically and align their brand with their core values.

Leadership Insight: Narratives are just as important as policies. Leaders who effectively tell justice stories inspire action and resilience.

Cultural Caution: Narratives should avoid oversimplification or saviorism. Stories must reflect complexity and focus on those most affected.

Mosaic Question: What justice stories influence your leadership — and whose voices shape them?

Mosaic in Action: An NGO shifts its fundraising campaigns to emphasize community resilience and leadership instead of victimhood, transforming donor and partner engagement.

Justice-Oriented Leadership

Definition: A leadership approach focused on dismantling unfair systems, elevating marginalized voices, and integrating equity into all decision-making.

Business Application: Justice-oriented leaders incorporate equity goals into strategic planning, budget allocation, and performance evaluation—making justice non-negotiable.

Leadership Insight: This type of leadership requires both moral courage and operational discipline; mere intent does not achieve justice.

Cultural Caution: Justice-oriented leadership might challenge deeply rooted norms, demanding persistence and political skill to overcome resistance.

Mosaic Question: How would things change if your leadership decisions were judged mainly by their impact on justice?

Mosaic in Action: A corporate executive updates procurement policy to prioritize vendors from underrepresented groups, directing millions of contracts toward economic equity.

◈ LETTER J CALLOUT

"Justice is not an abstract value — it is the daily design of fair processes and outcomes."

Reflection Questions

- How do jargon and technical language create barriers to justice in your setting?
- Where do you notice justice fatigue in yourself or your peers?
- What does shared accountability for justice look like in practice?

Practical Move

Review one recent policy, project, or assignment. Ask: Who benefited most, who carried the burden, and how could justice be more evenly distributed?

K – Knowledge, Kinship, and the 'Known'

K encourages us to question the foundations of what we consider true, credible, or worth sharing. It asks not only, *What do you know?*—but also, *How did you come to know it?* and *Who was left out along the way?* From the narrow pipelines of formal education to the broad wisdom found in kinship and community, these terms challenge us to expand our understanding of intelligence, expertise, and voice.

In many professional environments, knowledge is measured by degrees, citations, and institutional approval. But what about the stories passed down through generations? The wisdom gained through survival? The brilliance that comes from necessity rather than privilege? K reminds us that when only certain ways of knowing are recognized, entire communities are left out of the conversation.

K asks us to reexamine what we accept as truth

- Knowledge that is credentialed while lived experience is dismissed.
- Kinship that transmits resilience but is overlooked as "informal."
- Narratives that privilege proximity to power over proximity to truth.
- Standards of expertise shaped less by equity than by access.

The importance of the K terms is evident everywhere decisions are made—boardrooms, classrooms, healing spaces, and policy tables.

Who gets to set the agenda? Whose insights are acknowledged? Which voices are considered "professional," and which are quietly left out?

This section reminds us knowledge is never neutral. It is influenced by power, privilege, and access. True equity requires more than simply adding new voices into existing frameworks — it involves reshaping what is considered wisdom.

K calls leaders to expand their view, recognize lived experience as expertise, and question inherited truths. Because cultures of belonging are built not by guarding knowledge, but by allowing wisdom to flow in all directions—top-down, bottom-up, and heart to heart.

K

Karma (Cultural Interpretation)

Definition: A belief rooted in various spiritual and philosophical traditions that actions—good or bad—have future consequences. In leadership contexts, its meaning greatly varies based on cultural interpretation.

Business Application: In multicultural workplaces, different perspectives on karma can influence decision-making, responsibility, and feedback. Some employees may view karma as a personal moral compass, while others see it as a metaphor for systemic cause-and-effect.

Leadership Insight: Leaders who understand the cultural aspects of karma can better grasp how team members view fairness, responsibility, and long-term outcomes.

Cultural Caution: Be careful when using "karma" in international settings. In some cases, it is a sacred term connected to religion; in others, improper use can seem dismissive or superstitious.

Mosaic Question: How does your understanding of cause and effect match or differ from that of the people you lead?

Mosaic in Action: During a cross-cultural training, a manager learns that a team member from India views delayed project results through a karmic lens, leading the manager to adjust how they discuss accountability and timelines.

Keystone Leadership

Definition: A leadership approach focused on stabilizing and preserving the core elements of an organization, similar to how a keystone supports an arch.

Business Application: Keystone leaders strengthen culture, clarify purpose, and maintain trust during transitions or crises. They are often the reason teams remain cohesive despite external pressures.

Leadership Insight: The most effective keystone leaders balance adaptability with consistency, providing both the structure and flexibility teams need to succeed.

Cultural Caution: Keystone leadership is not about doing everything; it's about being intentional in where and how you apply your stabilizing influence.

Mosaic Question: What core cultural or operational "arch" are you holding together, and how visible is that role to your team?

Mosaic in Action: During a merger, a department head maintains open communication, upholds core team rituals, and ensures that shared values continue through structural changes.

Keystone Leadership Behaviors

Definition: Accurate, consistent actions that foster stability and trust within teams, especially during uncertain times.

Business Application: Examples include transparent communication, consistent recognition, active listening, and fair conflict resolution. These behaviors demonstrate dependability and foster psychological safety.

Leadership Insight: Keystone behaviors may seem small, but their collective effect can decide if a team remains united or breaks apart under pressure.

Cultural Caution: Keystone behaviors can vary across cultures; what signals stability in one culture might imply rigidity in another.

Mosaic Question: Which of your daily actions quietly support your team's stability—and which unintentionally weaken it?

Mosaic in Action: A nonprofit leader consistently starts weekly meetings with clear status updates and ends with time for open concerns, fostering team clarity and cohesion during funding uncertainty.

Keyholder Power

Definition: The authority and responsibility assigned to individuals who manage access—whether to information, spaces, systems, or relationships.

Business Application: Keyholder power can be literal (physical access to resources) or symbolic (exclusive access to decision-makers or strategic information). Managing it with integrity builds trust; abusing it damages credibility.

Leadership Insight: Leaders should identify both formal and informal "keyholder" roles within an organization, as these gatekeeping positions can greatly influence equity and inclusion.

Cultural Caution: In some cultures, being a keyholder is seen as an honor; in others, it may cause tension if not paired with transparency and shared responsibility.

Mosaic Question: Who holds the "keys" in your system—and who decides when and how they are used?

Mosaic in Action: A project coordinator with exclusive system access chooses to share credentials with a backup colleague to prevent workflow delays during an unexpected absence.

Kincentric Leadership

Definition: A leadership approach based on kinship values that emphasizes relational accountability, interdependence, and prioritizing the well-being of the group over individual gain.

Business Application: Kincentric leadership builds community organizations, Indigenous businesses, and collaborative teams by focusing on trust, reciprocity, and lasting relationships rather than immediate results.

Leadership Insight: True leadership goes beyond authority to genuinely care for the collective. Leaders who embody kincentric principles foster sustainable and inclusive cultures.

Cultural Caution: Kincentric leadership may be overlooked in competitive or individualistic systems. Leaders need to promote its importance without romanticizing or misusing Indigenous traditions.

Mosaic Question: Do you lead as if your team is family — responsible for their well-being as much as your own?

Mosaic in Action: A tribal council leader organizes decision-making based on kinship obligations, making sure every member's voice influences community priorities.

Kinkeeping

Definition: The often unseen work of maintaining family and social connections, usually through communication, planning get-togethers, and supporting each other.

Business Application: In leadership, kinkeeping involves roles that require ongoing relationship maintenance—such as client retention, community engagement, or alumni networks.

Leadership Insight: Recognizing kinkeeping as a skill shifts it from "unseen labor" to a strategic asset in building loyalty and connection.

Cultural Caution: Kinkeeping is often gendered labor, disproportionately expected of women, which can lead to burnout if overlooked and unsupported.

Mosaic Question: Who keeps your team or network connected, and how are you recognizing or rewarding their efforts?

Mosaic in Action: A community manager notices that a colleague naturally remembers birthdays, checks on sick teammates, and organizes meetups—strengthening bonds that improve retention—leading to the formalization and funding of the role.

Kinship Capital

Definition: The social, emotional, and resource-based value generated by extended family and chosen-family networks.

Business Application: Kinship capital often influences hiring decisions, mentorship opportunities, and support networks in both formal and informal work settings—especially in communities where family connections are crucial for career growth.

Leadership Insight: Leaders who recognize and value the importance of kinship networks can more effectively understand employee loyalty, resource sharing, and nontraditional paths to leadership.

Cultural Caution: In some cultures, kinship ties are embraced and celebrated; in others, perceived nepotism can erode trust. Understanding local norms is essential.

Mosaic Question: How can kinship networks already impact decisions and opportunities within your organization?

Mosaic in Action: A team lead recognizes that a staff member's extended family is an important support system during busy work seasons and adjusts scheduling to ensure family obligations are respected without hindering career growth.

Kinship Systems

Definition: The cultural, legal, and social systems that determine how people are connected through family or chosen relationships.

Business Application: Understanding kinship systems helps leaders manage benefits policies, parental leave, caregiving duties, and community expectations in international workplaces.

Leadership Insight: Leaders who understand kinship systems can develop policies and cultures that support different family definitions—reducing inequities for nontraditional households.

Cultural Caution: Relying on one culture's definition of family can exclude or harm employees from diverse backgrounds. Policies must be inclusive and adaptable.

Mosaic Question: How does your organization's definition of "family" match or differ from the lived experiences of your team members?

Mosaic in Action: A global nonprofit updates its bereavement policy to include leave for the death of a chosen family member, not just legal relatives.

Kinetic Communication

Definition: The deliberate use of body movements, gestures, and spatial positioning to convey meaning and influence perception.

Business Application: In leadership, kinetic communication can reinforce authority, foster approachability, or signal openness during negotiations and presentations.

Leadership Insight: Skilled leaders in kinetic communication understand that body language can often speak louder than words— especially in cross-cultural settings where nonverbal cues are highly important.

Cultural Caution: Gestures and physical distance mean different things across cultures; what signals engagement in one culture may seem intrusive or disrespectful in another.

Mosaic Question: What messages might your movement, posture, and positioning be sending—whether intentional or unintentional?

Mosaic in Action: During a multicultural conference, a facilitator notices that standing too close makes some participants uncomfortable, so they adjust their position to foster a comfortable shared space.

Kinetic Trust

Definition: Trust that is actively built and reinforced through consistent actions, nonverbal cues, and behavioral follow-through rather than through words alone.

Business Application: In high-pressure or multicultural settings, kinetic trust is essential when verbal assurances aren't enough— leaders must show trustworthiness through actions, body language, and tangible decisions.

Leadership Insight: Actions foster credibility; consistent, aligned behaviors create trust that transcends language or cultural differences.

Cultural Caution: In some cultures, visible actions are the main way to show trust; in others, words carry more weight. Mismatches can cause misunderstandings.

Mosaic Question: What do your daily actions subtly reveal about your trustworthiness?

Mosaic in Action: A project manager not only promises transparency—she posts weekly updates, openly answers tough questions, and follows through on commitments, thereby building team trust.

Knowledge Activism

Definition: The deliberate use of knowledge and skills to challenge inequalities, influence policy, and foster systemic reform.

Business Application: Knowledge activists utilize data, lived experience, and cultural insight to influence leadership decisions, resource allocation, and strategic planning.

Leadership Insight: Leaders who promote knowledge activism build cultures where employees feel supported—and safe—when using their expertise to drive change.

Cultural Caution: In some organizational or political environments, speaking truth to power can carry professional risks; leaders must safeguard those who voice uncomfortable truths.

Mosaic Question: Whose expertise could help enhance your systems if it were actively supported?

Mosaic in Action: An HR director uses workforce demographic data to advocate for modifying promotion criteria that disadvantage underrepresented groups, impacting company policy.

Knowledge-Based Exclusion

Definition: The deliberate or accidental exclusion of individuals or groups from opportunities, decision-making, or benefits due to their perceived lack of specific knowledge.

Business Application: Occurs when gatekeeping practices—such as using jargon-heavy language or requiring unnecessary credentials—block access to leadership roles or projects.

Leadership Insight: Excluding people due to assumed knowledge gaps often perpetuates inequality and misses chances for innovation through diverse perspectives.

Cultural Caution: Knowledge hierarchies are shaped by culture and privilege; what is seen as valuable in one setting may be ignored in another.

Mosaic Question: How does your organization decide who "knows enough" to participate—and who has the authority to make that call?

Mosaic in Action: A nonprofit updates its board recruitment process to include community leaders with meaningful lived experience, not just formal education.

Knowledge Commons

Definition: A shared pool of knowledge managed collectively to promote access, collaboration, and stewardship instead of privatization or gatekeeping.

Business Application: Knowledge commons break down silos and prevent inequities caused by knowledge hoarding in organizations.

Leadership Insight: Leaders promote equity by making sure knowledge is accessible to everyone, not limited to a few.

Cultural Caution: Some communities see knowledge as sacred or off-limits. Leaders need to balance transparency with respecting cultural boundaries.

Mosaic Question: How does your organization share knowledge— as a commons or as currency?

Mosaic in Action: An NGO developed open-source toolkits in collaboration with local partners, ensuring collective ownership and continuous adaptation.

Knowledge Decolonization

Definition: The process of dismantling colonial structures that decide which knowledge is valued, shared, or erased. Knowledge decolonization focuses on Indigenous, marginalized, and community-based ways of knowing.

Business Application: Universities, corporations, and nonprofits promote knowledge decolonization by valuing oral histories, local expertise, and cultural practices alongside formal research.

Leadership Insight: Knowledge is power. Leaders who engage in decolonization broaden perspectives, rectify historical erasure, and ensure innovation incorporates diverse voices.

Cultural Caution: Decolonization is not just symbolic inclusion. Using decolonization language without sharing power risks reinforcing existing hierarchies.

Mosaic Question: Whose knowledge has been at the core of your leadership — and whose has been left out?

Mosaic in Action: A development agency redirects research funding to Indigenous-led projects, prioritizing lived experience as well as academic expertise.

Knowledge Equity

Definition: The fair distribution, acknowledgment, and valuation of various types of knowledge—including academic, technical, experiential, and cultural knowledge.

Business Application: Promotes balanced decision-making by integrating multiple knowledge sources into planning, policy, and innovation processes.

Leadership Insight: Leaders who emphasize knowledge equity foster environments where nontraditional expertise is valued just as highly as formal credentials.

Cultural Caution: Ignoring community or cultural knowledge in favor of "expert" opinion can weaken trust and effectiveness in global settings.

Mosaic Question: Which types of knowledge are overrepresented or underrepresented in your decision-making processes?

Mosaic in Action: A health organization collaborates with Indigenous elders and medical researchers to develop care programs together.

Knowledge Erasure

Definition: The systematic ignoring, suppression, or devaluation of specific knowledge forms—often those associated with marginalized identities or cultures.

Business Application: Can happen in research, training, and organizational history when certain voices or narratives are left out of official records.

Leadership Insight: Leaders who recognize knowledge erasure can take action to restore, credit, and preserve lost or overlooked contributions.

Cultural Caution: Reintroducing erased knowledge should be done with respect to the original context, not as a form of tokenism.

Mosaic Question: Whose knowledge is missing from your archives, policies, or stories—and what would be needed to recover it?

Mosaic in Action: A tech company updates its innovation timeline to recognize contributions from women and minority engineers who were previously left out of public histories.

Knowledge Gaps in Leadership

Definition: Gaps in understanding that limit a leader's effectiveness, particularly in cultural, emotional, or contextual areas.

Business Application: Identifying and closing knowledge gaps improves decision-making, crisis management, and innovation.

Leadership Insight: Effective leaders identify their own gaps and actively work to close them through learning, teamwork, and diverse perspectives.

Cultural Caution: In some leadership cultures, admitting a gap might be seen as a weakness; reframing it as a chance for growth is crucial.

Mosaic Question: What are your blind spots—and who can help you recognize what you're missing?

Mosaic in Action: A CEO unfamiliar with accessibility standards hires a disability inclusion consultant to advise on product design and workplace policies.

Knowledge Hierarchies

Definition: Knowledge hierarchies are the implicit or explicit rankings of whose knowledge is considered the most valuable or authoritative within an organization, culture, or system. These hierarchies can be based on formal education, position, cultural norms, or perceived expertise.

Business Application: In the workplace, knowledge hierarchies influence decision-making and innovation. When only senior leaders' ideas are acted upon, valuable insights from frontline employees, community members, or those with lived experience can be ignored—slowing adaptability and obstructing problem-solving.

Leadership Insight: Great leaders flatten knowledge hierarchies without dismantling expertise. They create channels for ideas to flow from all levels, understanding that innovation often comes from unexpected sources.

Cultural Caution: In global or cross-cultural settings, favoring certain academic credentials or communication styles over others can reinforce colonial or class-based biases.

Mosaic Question: Whose knowledge is regarded as the most important in your setting—and who is rarely asked to contribute?

Mosaic in Action: During a product development meeting, the engineering lead pauses the discussion to invite a junior customer service representative to share recurring client feedback. Her insight uncovers a design flaw no one in the room had noticed, saving the company months of costly revisions.

Knowledge Justice

Definition: Fair recognition, inclusion, and sharing of knowledge across communities. Knowledge justice makes sure that marginalized groups' ways of knowing are valued and protected.

Business Application: Organizations promote knowledge justice by recognizing community contributors, protecting intellectual property from exploitation, and providing fair access to information.

Leadership Insight: Without knowledge of justice, innovation turns into extraction. Leaders must align credit, voice, and recognition with fairness.

Cultural Caution: Not all communities share knowledge openly. Leaders need to honor boundaries, consent, and cultural protocols.

Mosaic Question: Does your leadership gather knowledge — or practice justice in how it's distributed and rewarded?

Mosaic in Action: A global nonprofit guarantees Indigenous partners keep ownership and credit for cultural knowledge involved in sustainability projects.

Knowledge Mobilization

Definition: The process of transforming knowledge into action by transferring insights across research, practice, and policy. Knowledge mobilization connects gaps between knowing and doing.

Business Application: Corporations and NGOs utilize knowledge mobilization to convert data into strategy, ensuring evidence informs decisions and drives innovation.

Leadership Insight: Unused knowledge is untapped potential. Leaders who leverage knowledge enable teams to act with purpose and effectiveness.

Cultural Caution: Mobilization should not oversimplify. Removing cultural context from knowledge can lead to misunderstandings.

Mosaic Question: Does your leadership let knowledge sit idle — or turn it into action?

Mosaic in Action: A healthcare coalition converts academic research on mental health into training modules for frontline workers, saving time and lives.

Knowledge Resilience

Definition: Knowledge resilience is the ability of individuals, teams, and systems to sustain, adapt, and reconstruct essential knowledge during disruptions, changes, or losses.

Business Application: This idea is crucial when staff turnover, mergers, or technological changes threaten institutional memory. Documenting processes, promoting cross-training, and encouraging mentorship all enhance knowledge resilience.

Leadership Insight: Leaders who prioritize knowledge resilience ensure that expertise is not confined to just one person's mind. They foster cultures where skills and insights are shared, duplicated, and continually refreshed.

Cultural Caution: Relying too heavily on a single knowledge-keeper—especially in Indigenous or marginalized communities—can pose risks if that person is excluded, silenced, or leaves unexpectedly.

Mosaic Question: If your most experienced team member left tomorrow, how much of their knowledge would still be accessible?

Mosaic in Action: When a nonprofit's veteran grants manager retires, her detailed "knowledge notebook" and recorded training sessions help the new hire step into the role confidently, ensuring funding continuity.

Knowledge-Shaming

Definition: Knowledge-shaming occurs when someone is belittled, dismissed, or excluded for lacking specific information—often reinforcing elitism or gatekeeping.

Business Application: In corporate settings, knowledge-shaming happens when acronyms, technical terms, or insider references are used to belittle colleagues instead of helping them learn.

Leadership Insight: Skilled leaders replace knowledge-shaming with knowledge-sharing. They see gaps as opportunities for growth rather than signs of inadequacy.

Cultural Caution: In diverse teams, assumptions about "common knowledge" can marginalize people from different educational or regional backgrounds.

Mosaic Question: Do you correct others to help them grow or to show that you know more?

Mosaic in Action: A project leader notices that a new hire struggles to understand a conversation packed with technical terms. Instead of skipping past it, she pauses to explain each term and encourages others to do the same—creating a more inclusive and collaborative environment.

Knowledge Stewardship

Definition: Responsible care, protection, and sharing of knowledge as a collective trust rather than private ownership.

Business Application: Organizations practicing knowledge stewardship ensure that institutional memory is preserved, transitions are seamless, and wisdom is shared across generations.

Leadership Insight: Stewardship views knowledge as something to be nurtured and shared, not kept to oneself. Leaders who practice stewardship of knowledge create continuity and resilience.

Cultural Caution: In some communities, stewardship involves

respecting sacred knowledge and boundaries about who can access it.

Mosaic Question: Do you view knowledge as property — or as a trust to manage for others?

Mosaic in Action: A retiring executive shares lessons, mentors successors, and ensures continuity by passing on knowledge instead of withholding it.

Knowledge Sovereignty

Definition: Knowledge sovereignty is the right of communities—particularly Indigenous and historically marginalized groups—to control the collection, ownership, and use of their cultural knowledge and intellectual property.

Business Application: In research and product development, respecting knowledge sovereignty involves obtaining informed consent, ensuring fair benefit-sharing, and safeguarding sensitive information.

Leadership Insight: Leaders who respect knowledge sovereignty build trust and maintain ethical credibility. They recognize that having access to knowledge does not give them the right to use it.

Cultural Caution: Ignoring knowledge sovereignty can result in exploitation and harm—especially when traditional knowledge is commercialized without acknowledgment or compensation.

Mosaic Question: Whose knowledge do you rely on—and on whose conditions?

Mosaic in Action: A tourism company consults with a local Indigenous council before incorporating cultural stories into its marketing, agreeing to share revenue and letting the community approve all materials before publication.

Knowledge Translation

Definition: Knowledge translation involves transforming complex or specialized information into formats that are understandable, accessible, and actionable for different audiences.

Business Application: This skill is vital in healthcare, law, and technical fields where jargon can alienate the public. Clear translation ensures that information leads to informed decision-making.

Leadership Insight: Leaders who excel at translating knowledge bridge experts and non-experts, ensuring insights result in action.

Cultural Caution: Oversimplifying can distort meaning or remove

nuance, while under-simplifying can exclude those without specialized training.

Mosaic Question: Who might be excluded if you only speak in your field's native language or jargon?

Mosaic in Action: A public health director teams up with community artists to turn vaccination data into infographics and street murals, increasing vaccination rates in neighborhoods where government reports are rarely read.

Kuleana (Hawaiian Concept)

Definition: Kuleana is a Hawaiian term that encompasses both the right and the responsibility to act with care, respect, and accountability in one's roles and relationships.

Business Application: In leadership, kuleana means understanding that authority comes with the responsibility to protect and serve—not just to benefit oneself.

Leadership Insight: Leaders embodying kuleana take responsibility for both their successes and failures, acting in ways that foster the collective good.

Cultural Caution: Kuleana has deep roots in Hawaiian culture; using it outside that context should include acknowledgment and respect for its origins and meaning.

Mosaic Question: How do you manage the privileges of your role alongside its responsibilities?

Mosaic in Action: A team leader advocates for fair pay adjustments for her staff, knowing her position gives her both the platform and the responsibility to speak.

◈ LETTER K CALLOUT

"Knowledge is not neutral; it is shaped by who creates it, who controls it, and who is left out."

Reflection Questions

- Whose knowledge is prioritized in your field, syllabus, or workplace?
- Where do you see knowledge erased, dismissed, or devalued?
- How does shared knowledge strengthen leadership?

Practical Move

In your next project or decision, bring in one perspective or source of knowledge that is usually overlooked — and name its value to the group.

L – Language, Labels, and Listening

L takes us to the heart of communication—not just the words we use, but the worlds they build. Language shapes connection, signals safety, and reveals power. It can open doors or close them. It can promote inclusion—or conceal exclusion behind a carefully chosen tone. In every setting, language is more than just words; it is strategy, identity, and survival.

This section examines the emotional and mental effort needed to navigate systems not built for everyone, regardless of their body, background, or beliefs. It highlights the quiet work of code-switching, self-monitoring, and translating lived experiences into terms considered "acceptable." It traces the invisible burden of race, gender, class, accent, ability, and emotion—carried into spaces where only certain voices are recognized as credible.

L asks us to notice what communication conceals as much as what it reveals

- The extra work some must do just to be heard.
- The labels inherited from systems that silence or distort.
- The forms of speech rewarded as "professional" and those dismissed as "disruptive."
- The language never spoken aloud but still powerful enough to shape culture.

From casual conversations to high-stakes decisions, language shapes visibility, voice, and vulnerability. It determines who gets recognized, who gets dismissed, and which truths are allowed to surface.

L calls on leaders to listen beyond words—to question not just what is said, but what is left unsaid, and by whom. Because language is never neutral it can divide belonging or promote healing. The decision is whether we use it to build barriers—or to foster spaces where dignity, trust, and reconnection flourish.

L

Label Fatigue

Definition: The weariness or resistance people feel toward identity-based labels, especially when they oversimplify complex identities or are overused in conversation.

Business Application: In diversity workshops, participants often express frustration at having to constantly define themselves by specific categories instead of being appreciated for their skills or experiences.

Leadership Insight: Leaders can help reduce label fatigue by creating environments where individuals are valued as whole persons, not just as representatives of a category.

Cultural Caution: Ignoring label fatigue entirely can dismiss valid concerns about erasure; instead, find a balance between recognizing identities and allowing self-expression.

Mosaic Question: How can you honor someone's identity without reducing them to a single label?

Mosaic in Action: An organization updates its demographic survey to include an optional narrative section, giving respondents the chance to share their identity details in their own words rather than selecting from preset categories.

Labeling Bias

Definition: The tendency to judge or interpret people's abilities, character, or potential based on the labels assigned to them rather than their actual behavior or merit.

Business Application: A manager assumes that an employee labeled as "junior" cannot lead a project, overlooking their relevant skills.

Leadership Insight: Recognizing labeling bias helps leaders question their assumptions and ensures opportunities are based on ability, not labels.

Cultural Caution: Labels can carry implicit stereotypes that unconsciously influence decision-making, reinforcing inequalities.

Mosaic Question: Which labels in your environment might be quietly shaping decisions without anyone questioning them?

Mosaic in Action: A school district removes "gifted" and "remedial" labels from internal tracking systems and instead uses skill-based assessments to ensure all students can access advanced learning opportunities when they are ready.

Labor Equity

Definition: The fair distribution of work, opportunities, and rewards, ensuring that contributions are acknowledged and compensated fairly across all roles and groups.

Business Application: A nonprofit performs a pay equity audit and adjusts salaries so that employees in similar roles earn equal pay regardless of gender, race, or tenure.

Leadership Insight: Labor equity is maintained through transparent policies, regular audits, and accountability for ensuring fair workloads and rewards.

Cultural Caution: Equity is not about sameness; it considers different needs, contributions, and starting points to achieve fair outcomes.

Mosaic Question: How do you make sure both visible and invisible work are valued equally in your environment?

Mosaic in Action: A company monitors workload distribution by department and finds that some teams, often led by women, have heavier workloads without extra resources. Leadership adjusts staffing and provides more support to fix the inequality.

Land Acknowledgment

Definition: A formal statement that recognizes and respects Indigenous peoples as the traditional stewards of the land where an event, institution, or activity takes place.

Business Application: A university begins every graduation ceremony with a land acknowledgment crafted in consultation with local Indigenous communities.

Leadership Insight: Effective land acknowledgments are connected to ongoing relationships, reparative actions, and support for Indigenous sovereignty — not just ceremonial words.

Cultural Caution: Giving a land acknowledgment without meaningful follow-up risks tokenism and diminishes its purpose.

Mosaic Question: How can your land acknowledgment be paired with lasting, concrete commitments to Indigenous communities?

Mosaic in Action: A city's cultural center partners with the local tribal council to include a land acknowledgment at all public events, while also dedicating part of ticket sales to Indigenous-led educational programs.

Language Access

Definition: Providing communication in multiple languages and formats so individuals can fully understand, participate in, and benefit from services, programs, or information.

Business Application: A hospital offers interpretation services and translated medical forms so patients can make informed decisions about their care.

Leadership Insight: Prioritizing language access ensures fairness in engagement, decision-making, and service delivery, especially in multilingual communities.

Cultural Caution: Offering translation without cultural adaptation can still lead to misunderstandings; access must address both language and context.

Mosaic Question: Who might be excluded from your work because they cannot access information

in a language or format they understand?

Mosaic in Action: A city government launches a public safety campaign in eight languages and provides video content with captions and sign language interpretation, significantly increasing community participation in emergency preparedness events.

Language Colonialism

Definition: The imposition of a dominant language over others, often through historical or ongoing systems of power, leading to the suppression or erasure of Indigenous or minority languages.

Business Application: A school system mandates all instruction to be in the national language, discouraging or prohibiting the use of home languages in the classroom.

Leadership Insight: Leaders who challenge language colonialism create space for linguistic diversity, safeguarding cultural identity and heritage.

Cultural Caution: Ignoring the power dynamics of language risks reinforcing historical oppression and cultural loss.

Mosaic Question: How does language policy in your

environment reinforce or challenge systems of domination?

Mosaic in Action: A nonprofit working with Indigenous youth implements bilingual education programs that value and teach both the community's traditional language and the national language, restoring pride and fluency in younger generations.

Language Justice

Definition: The practice of making sure everyone can communicate, understand, and be understood in the language they are most comfortable with, as a matter of fairness and rights.

Business Application: A community coalition hosts meetings with simultaneous interpretation in participants' preferred languages, ensuring everyone has an equal voice in decision-making.

Leadership Insight: Language justice involves integrating interpretation, translation, and linguistic inclusion into the core structure of events, services, and policies—not treating it as an afterthought.

Cultural Caution: Superficial translation without building cultural trust or recognizing

language power imbalances undercuts justice goals.

Mosaic Question: How can you create processes so that language differences never block participation or leadership?

Mosaic in Action: A housing advocacy group makes sure all tenant meetings are multilingual, providing interpreters and translated materials, and trains bilingual community members as co-facilitators to lead discussions.

Language of Belonging

Definition: Words, phrases, and communication styles that promote inclusion, safety, and value for all participants, fostering a sense of connection and community.

Business Application: An onboarding program greets new employees by sharing stories that highlight diverse voices and explicitly state that every perspective is valued.

Leadership Insight: Leaders who purposefully use a language of belonging impact not only morale but also engagement, retention, and trust.

Cultural Caution: Empty affirmations without follow-up action can weaken trust; belonging must be reinforced through consistent behavior and policies.

Mosaic Question: What words or phrases in your environment make people feel welcome—and which might unintentionally push them away?

Mosaic in Action: A school principal adjusts the wording of policy announcements from "students must" to "our community agrees," emphasizing shared responsibility and encouraging collective ownership of the school culture.

Language Policing

Definition: The act of criticizing, correcting, or restricting someone's language use—often regarding grammar, accent, or word choice— in a way that reinforces power dynamics or marginalizes certain speakers.

Business Application: In a team meeting, a manager repeatedly interrupts a non-native English speaker to correct minor grammar errors instead of focusing on their ideas.

Leadership Insight: Leaders who avoid unnecessary language policing create space for diverse voices and ensure ideas are evaluated on substance, not form.

Cultural Caution: While clarity is important, overemphasis on "correct" language can silence participation and perpetuate bias against linguistic diversity.

Mosaic Question: How might your expectations around "professional" language be limiting who speaks up?

Mosaic in Action: A facilitator in a cross-cultural workshop encourages participants to share ideas in their own words, resisting the urge to correct phrasing. The result is richer, more authentic discussion and greater trust.

Language Privilege

Definition: The unearned advantages granted to speakers of a dominant or "standard" language, often leading to greater opportunities, credibility, and influence.

Business Application: A job candidate who speaks the dominant language without an accent is seen as more competent than equally qualified multilingual candidates with different speech patterns.

Leadership Insight: Recognizing language privilege helps leaders ensure that access, advancement, and influence are not solely dependent on language conformity.

Cultural Caution: Ignoring language privilege perpetuates systems that reward proximity to the dominant culture while marginalizing others.

Mosaic Question: Whose voices are most easily heard and valued in your environment—and how much of that is about language?

Mosaic in Action: A global nonprofit revises its hiring criteria to appreciate multilingual abilities and offers language support in leadership meetings so that English fluency is not a barrier to decision-making.

Latinx

Definition: A gender-neutral term mainly used in the United States to refer to people of Latin American descent, aiming to include all gender identities.

Business Application: An advocacy group uses "Latinx" in public materials to ensure that non-binary and gender-diverse members of the community feel acknowledged.

Leadership Insight: When leaders use identity terms like Latinx, they should understand the cultural and generational differences, as acceptance and usage can vary within communities.

Cultural Caution: Some people see Latinx as linguistically awkward or as an outside imposition; always respect the preference of the individual or group.

Mosaic Question: How do you handle language choices when the terms themselves are debated within the communities they describe?

Mosaic in Action: A community center surveys its members about their preferred identity terms and uses that feedback to guide programming and communication, balancing inclusivity with cultural authenticity.

Lateral Violence

Definition: Harmful behaviors—such as gossip, sabotage, or exclusion—aimed at peers within a marginalized group, often stemming from internalized oppression or competition for scarce resources.

Business Application: In an underrepresented employee network, some members undermine others' credibility instead of supporting their advancement.

Leadership Insight: Combating lateral violence involves strengthening solidarity, addressing systemic shortages, and establishing structures that reward collective success.

Cultural Caution: If external pressures fueling lateral violence aren't addressed, interventions may unfairly blame individuals rather than systems.

Mosaic Question: How can you foster environments where members of marginalized groups view each other as allies rather than competitors?

Mosaic in Action: An Indigenous women's leadership program pairs participants in collaborative projects with shared recognition, replacing competition with mentorship and mutual support.

Leadership Elasticity

Definition: The ability of leaders to stretch and adapt their style, pace, and approach to meet the changing needs of their team, organization, or environment without losing effectiveness.

Business Application: A department head shifts from a directive approach during a crisis to a collaborative style during long-term planning, ensuring both stability and innovation.

Leadership Insight: Elastic leaders maintain clarity of vision while staying flexible in execution,

allowing them to navigate uncertainty without causing instability.

Cultural Caution: Overextending elasticity without clear boundaries can lead to confusion about expectations or weaken consistency.

Mosaic Question: In what situations have you adapted your leadership style most—and what did it cost or gain?

Mosaic in Action: During an unexpected staffing shortage, a school principal temporarily takes on teaching duties, changes meeting formats, and empowers teacher leaders to run committees, maintaining momentum without burning out the team.

Leadership Fragility

Definition: A leader's inability or unwillingness to accept feedback, adapt, or engage with challenges to their authority, often leading to defensiveness or withdrawal.

Business Application: A senior manager reacts to constructive criticism by shutting down discussions and reverting to rigid top-down decision-making.

Leadership Insight: Addressing leadership fragility involves developing self-awareness, resilience, and a mindset that views feedback as a resource rather than a threat.

Cultural Caution: Fragility can increase in environments where leadership is seen as a fixed status instead of a continuous practice.

Mosaic Question: How do you respond—internally and externally—when your leadership decisions are challenged?

Mosaic in Action: After receiving feedback about exclusionary practices in her department, a nonprofit director resists the urge to defend herself, choosing instead to invite a facilitated conversation that results in more inclusive hiring policies.

Leadership from the Middle

Definition:: The practice of shaping culture, leading change, and turning vision into action from a mid-level or non-executive position.

Business Application: Middle leaders connect strategy and practice, shaping policies while representing the realities of frontline staff. They often maintain momentum when executive focus shifts elsewhere.

Leadership Insight:: Leading from the middle requires managing pressures from both sides—balancing accountability to senior leaders while supporting and empowering teams below.

Cultural Caution:: Middle leaders are prone to burnout when given responsibility without authority. Organizations must acknowledge their influence and provide appropriate resources.

Mosaic Question:: How can you lead with courage when you're not at the top or the bottom of the hierarchy?

Mosaic in Action:: A regional manager in a healthcare network implements a peer-learning model across clinics. Without formal authority, she encourages colleagues, enhancing patient outcomes throughout the system.

Leadership in Flux

Definition: A state where leadership roles, priorities, or strategies are changing quickly due to organizational shifts, external pressures, or emerging crises.

Business Application: A company going through a merger experiences leadership in flux as reporting lines, decision-making processes, and strategic goals are redefined.

Leadership Insight: Managing leadership in flux requires transparency, clear communication, and active support for those adjusting to the transition.

Cultural Caution: Extended flux without clear direction can cause instability, erode trust, and lower morale.

Mosaic Question: How do you help others stay grounded when the leadership landscape around them is shifting?

Mosaic in Action: During a government agency restructuring, an interim leader holds weekly Q&A sessions, updates staff on changing decisions, and provides tools for managing uncertainty, easing the stress of constant change.

Leadership Integrity

Definition:: The alignment of a leader's stated values, behaviors, and decisions helps build trust and credibility throughout an organization.

Business Application: Integrity in leadership enhances stakeholder trust, minimizes reputational risk, and fosters cultures where transparency and fairness are the norm.

Leadership Insight:: When actions and words don't match, trust erodes. Leaders who embody their values foster environments where accountability is mutual.

Cultural Caution:: Integrity can show up differently across cultures—what's direct in one setting might be seen as rude in another. Leaders must balance honesty with cultural awareness.

Mosaic Question:: Do your daily choices align with the values you ask others to uphold?

Mosaic in Action:: A corporate leader declines a profitable deal with a supplier discovered to exploit labor. The choice reduces short-term revenue but strengthens long-term trust.

Leadership Resilience

Definition:: The capacity of leaders to maintain clarity, adaptability, and presence during extended stress or crisis.

Business Application: Resilient leaders avoid organizational paralysis by demonstrating calm, channeling energy, and leading teams through disruption.

Leadership Insight:: Resilience is more about rebuilding strength through support networks and adaptive practices than just enduring alone.

Cultural Caution:: Overemphasizing resilience can normalize harmful conditions, causing leaders to silently suffer instead of pushing for systemic change.

Mosaic Question:: How do you restore your strength so your leadership lasts?

Mosaic in Action:: A nonprofit director navigating political unrest implements wellness check-ins for herself and her staff, ensuring emotional reserves are maintained for ongoing advocacy.

Leadership Shadow

Definition: The unspoken influence a leader has on culture, behavior, and morale through their habits, tone, and presence—whether intentional or not.

Business Application: A CEO who regularly arrives late to meetings unintentionally sends the message that punctuality doesn't matter, which impacts the overall organizational culture.

Leadership Insight: Leaders should regularly reflect on their shadow—the silent messages their actions send—and ensure it aligns with their stated values.

Cultural Caution: Ignoring the leadership role can weaken formal policies and damage trust, even when intentions are good.

Mosaic Question: What might your unspoken actions or habits be revealing to others—without you realizing it?

Mosaic in Action: A school superintendent advocates for work-life balance but regularly sends late-night emails. After realizing the conflicting message, she starts scheduling her messages to go out during work hours, reinforcing her stated commitment.

Leadership Sponsorship

Definition: A leadership practice where senior leaders proactively use their influence to open opportunities, advocate for, and promote underrepresented talent.

Business Application: Unlike mentorship, sponsorship entails taking genuine career risks for others. Organizations that formalize sponsorship help close advancement gaps.

Leadership Insight: Leaders who sponsor transition from giving private advice to advocating publicly, increasing equity across pipelines.

Cultural Caution: In some cultures, sponsorship might be seen as favoritism. Leaders need to communicate criteria openly and fairly.

Mosaic Question: Who are you actively sponsoring into rooms they aren't ready to enter alone?

Mosaic in Action: A senior partner risked her reputation to endorse a junior colleague of color for a high-profile client account, boosting his career trajectory.

Learning Agility

Definition: The ability to quickly learn, apply, and adapt knowledge or skills in new and unfamiliar situations.

Business Application: A project manager successfully shifts from managing in-person events to leading a fully virtual conference within weeks, leveraging transferable skills and rapid learning.

Leadership Insight: Leaders with learning agility can navigate complexity, respond to emerging challenges, and foster innovation without becoming overwhelmed by change.

Cultural Caution: High learning agility in some areas can create blind spots in others; overconfidence may lead to underestimating the complexity of certain challenges.

Mosaic Question: How quickly and effectively can you adapt when faced with something you have never done before?

Mosaic in Action: A nonprofit leader with no prior fundraising experience attends a brief intensive course, consults with peers, and

successfully secures major grants within her first quarter in the role.

Learning Disruption

Definition: A major interruption or change in established learning processes, environments, or access to knowledge, often triggered by external events or technological advancements.

Business Application: A school system adjusts to a sudden shift to remote learning by redesigning curriculum and teaching strategies to keep students engaged.

Leadership Insight: Leaders who see learning disruption as an opportunity can reimagine systems to become more equitable, resilient, and relevant.

Cultural Caution: Without careful planning, disruption can worsen existing inequalities, leaving marginalized groups with fewer resources to adapt.

Mosaic Question: How can you ensure that sudden changes in learning environments help, rather than hurt, participants?

Mosaic in Action: A global company uses the switch to hybrid work as a chance to develop a centralized, multilingual e-learning platform, broadening training access for employees in remote locations.

Legacy Privilege

Definition: Benefits inherited from longstanding systems, traditions, or family ties that grant access to opportunities, resources, or status without earning them.

Business Application: A university's legacy admissions policy favors applicants whose parents are alumni, mainly benefiting affluent and historically dominant groups.

Leadership Insight: Recognizing legacy privilege helps leaders develop fairer systems that balance tradition with fairness and access.

Cultural Caution: Challenging legacy privilege can be politically sensitive, but ignoring it continues inequality.

Mosaic Question: What traditions or systems in your area might unintentionally preserve privilege for a few?

Mosaic in Action: A foundation updates its grant criteria to focus on emerging leaders and first-time applicants instead of relying on historical ties that benefit well-connected organizations.

Legacy Systems

Definition: Outdated structures, technologies, or processes that remain within an organization and often hinder efficiency, innovation, or fairness.

Business Application: A hospital still relies on paper-based medical records despite the availability of secure, faster electronic systems, which slows down patient care.

Leadership Insight: Effective leaders recognize when to value a system's history and when to invest in modernization for future needs.

Cultural Caution: Keeping legacy systems out of nostalgia or resistance to change can create operational delays and maintain inequalities embedded in older frameworks.

Mosaic Question: Which of your systems are promoting progress— and which are holding it back?

Mosaic in Action: A municipal government replaces an outdated permitting process with a digital platform, reducing approval times by half and making it easier for residents who previously had to visit city offices.

Legacy Systems Bias

Definition: The inequalities embedded within long-standing structures, policies, or technologies that continue to disadvantage certain groups, even if the original intent was not discriminatory.

Business Application: An old hiring platform automatically filters out applicants without specific degrees, unintentionally excluding skilled candidates from nontraditional educational backgrounds.

Leadership Insight: Leaders must audit and update legacy systems to eliminate hidden barriers and ensure they reflect current values of equity and inclusion.

Cultural Caution: Merely updating technology or procedures without addressing embedded bias simply maintains unfair outcomes behind a modern appearance.

Mosaic Question: Which long-standing systems in your environment might still be quietly reinforcing inequality?

Mosaic in Action: A company replaces its decades-old promotion criteria—heavily based on tenure—with a skills-based assessment, creating new opportunities for younger and more diverse talent.

Legacy Trauma

Definition: The intergenerational transfer of emotional, psychological, and social wounds caused by historical oppression, violence, or displacement.

Business Application: Indigenous employees navigate workplace environments shaped by stereotypes and systemic inequities rooted in colonization, affecting trust and engagement.

Leadership Insight: Addressing legacy trauma in organizations requires creating safe spaces, recognizing historical harm, and supporting healing practices.

Cultural Caution: Do not frame legacy trauma as solely an individual issue; its roots are systemic and collective.

Mosaic Question: How might historical events still influence relationships, trust, and opportunities in your environment today?

Mosaic in Action: A community health program includes culturally specific healing circles for refugees, acknowledging that current challenges are connected to past displacement and conflict.

Liberatory Design

Definition: A design approach that emphasizes equity, inclusion, and freedom from oppression, actively breaking down systemic barriers while creating solutions with—not just for—marginalized communities.

Business Application: A housing nonprofit involves residents in co-developing its redevelopment plans, making sure their priorities influence every step of the process.

Leadership Insight: Liberatory design shifts power toward those most impacted by decisions, ensuring their voices are central in shaping systems and solutions.

Cultural Caution: Without genuine community involvement, "liberatory" efforts risk recreating the very inequalities they seek to eliminate.

Mosaic Question: Who is leading and benefiting from the design decisions in your work—and who is missing from the table?

Mosaic in Action: A school district reimagines its curriculum in partnership with students, families, and community leaders from historically excluded groups, leading to increased engagement and academic success.

Liberatory Leadership

Definition: A leadership style that aims to dismantle systems of oppression, redistribute power, and create environments where everyone can flourish with independence and respect.

Business Application: An executive reorganizes decision-making processes to empower frontline employees with more authority over policies that impact their daily work.

Leadership Insight: Practicing liberatory leadership requires courage to challenge deep-seated norms and a dedication to shared ownership and responsibility.

Cultural Caution: Without structural adjustments, liberatory leadership risks becoming just a personal style rather than fostering organizational change.

Mosaic Question: How do your leadership actions shift power toward those most affected by decisions?

Mosaic in Action: A nonprofit CEO grants budgetary authority to a community advisory board made up of residents served by the organization, ensuring resources go to the priorities they identify.

Liberatory Pedagogy

Definition:: A teaching and leadership approach grounded in justice, aimed at dismantling oppressive systems while promoting critical consciousness and collective empowerment.

Business Application: In corporate training, liberatory pedagogy questions assumptions, amplifies marginalized voices, and helps learners challenge systemic inequities within organizational structures.

Leadership Insight:: Teaching with liberation in mind means viewing learners not as empty vessels but as co-creators of knowledge and change.

Cultural Caution:: Liberatory approaches might face resistance in hierarchical cultures that see questioning as defiance. Leaders need to adapt their delivery without watering down core values.

Mosaic Question:: Do your learning environments reproduce hierarchy or foster liberation?

Mosaic in Action:: A leadership coach redesigns a training program to include storytelling circles, where employees critically reflect on bias in the workplace and collaboratively develop new equity practices.

Liminal Identity

Definition: A sense of self that exists in an in-between space, shaped by multiple cultures, roles, or stages of life, often without full belonging to any one group.

Business Application: A global-minded professional who has lived in multiple countries navigates the advantages and challenges of not fully aligning with a single national culture, using this perspective to bridge communication gaps in international teams.

Leadership Insight: Leaders with liminal identities often excel at managing complexity, understanding multiple perspectives, and adjusting to different environments.

Cultural Caution: While liminal identity can be a strength, it can also cause feelings of invisibility or disconnection if not recognized and appreciated.

Mosaic Question: Where in your life have you navigated between different identities, and how has that influenced your perspective?

Mosaic in Action: A bilingual educator from a diaspora community develops curriculum that integrates perspectives from both her cultural backgrounds, fostering deeper student understanding of global issues.

Linguistic Bias

Definition: The unfair judgment of people based on accent, dialect, or speech patterns rather than their content or competence.

Business Application: Linguistic bias hinders candidates and employees whose communication styles differ from mainstream norms, often restricting their opportunities for advancement.

Leadership Insight: Leaders who tackle linguistic bias broaden access to leadership roles and understand that clarity doesn't mean conformity.

Cultural Caution: Language privilege differs around the world; a dominant dialect in one setting may be marginalized in another.

Mosaic Question: Do you judge communication based on clarity — or on conformity to dominant styles?

Mosaic in Action: The COO of a multinational company separated professionalism metrics from accent, trained managers on linguistic bias, and encouraged communication in multiple styles.

Listening Culture

Definition: An environment where active listening is a core value, integrated into communication, decision-making, and relationship-building processes.

Business Application: A company holds "listening sessions" where employees share feedback directly with leadership, and leaders respond with clear action steps.

Leadership Insight: Leaders who foster a listening culture promote trust, collaboration, and psychological safety, leading to stronger organizational performance.

Cultural Caution: Listening must result in visible change; otherwise, it risks becoming performative and damaging trust.

Mosaic Question: How does your organization show that it values what people share?

Mosaic in Action: A nonprofit experiencing staff turnover holds structured listening forums, implements recurring suggestions on workload balance, and sees retention rates improve significantly within a year.

Listening Exhaustion

Definition: The mental and emotional fatigue that results from sustained or high-intensity listening, especially in roles that demand deep empathy or conflict resolution.

Business Application: A human resources director becomes emotionally drained after weeks of mediating employee disputes without enough time to recover.

Leadership Insight: Leaders need to balance active listening with self-care and boundaries to maintain effectiveness and empathy over time.

Cultural Caution: Ignoring listening exhaustion can cause burnout, lower empathy, and strain relationships.

Mosaic Question: What practices help you recharge your ability to listen deeply?

Mosaic in Action: A school counselor schedules regular peer supervision sessions and rotates caseloads to prevent listening fatigue, ensuring ongoing support for students without sacrificing personal well-being.

Listening Leadership

Definition:: A leadership practice that emphasizes deep listening as the core for decision-making, trust-building, and cultural transformation.

Business Application: Listening leaders uncover hidden issues, foster psychological safety, and diminish costly blind spots that silence often hides.

Leadership Insight:: Listening is not passive; it demands humility, restraint, and the discipline to hear what is uncomfortable without becoming defensive.

Cultural Caution:: Some cultures value vocal authority more than silence; listening leaders might be undervalued unless they present their approach as a deliberate strategy.

Mosaic Question:: Are you listening to respond, or to genuinely understand?

Mosaic in Action:: A school superintendent spends her first 100 days on "listening tours," gathering insights from students, families, and staff. Policies that follow reflect the actual needs of the community, not assumptions from above.

Lived Experience

Definition: Personal knowledge and understanding gained through direct, first-hand involvement in events, identities, or conditions, rather than through theory or observation.

Business Application: A mental health advisory board includes members with lived experience of mental illness to ensure services address real-world needs and barriers.

Leadership Insight: Valuing lived experience enhances decision-making, grounds policies in reality, and fosters trust with the communities served.

Cultural Caution: Tokenizing individuals for their lived experience without giving them influence or authority can be exploitative.

Mosaic Question: How can you incorporate lived experience into decisions without reducing someone to that identity or story?

Mosaic in Action: A city housing task force invites residents who have experienced homelessness to co-design shelter policies, leading to more effective and humane services.

Locational Privilege

Definition: Benefits gained from living in or having access to a specific geographic area, such as proximity to resources, economic opportunities, or political stability.

Business Application: A job candidate in a major city has access to more networking events and industry contacts than equally qualified peers in rural areas.

Leadership Insight: Recognizing locational privilege helps leaders develop systems that provide opportunities and resources beyond the most connected urban centers.

Cultural Caution: Assuming equal access to opportunities without considering geography can reinforce inequalities among urban, suburban, and rural communities.

Mosaic Question: How might your location be providing you with advantages you often take for granted?

Mosaic in Action: A national nonprofit offers its professional development programs both in-person and online, ensuring equal access for staff across all regions.

Loss Visibility

Definition: The degree to which a loss—whether personal, professional, or cultural—is recognized, acknowledged, and supported by others.

Business Application: An employee's grief over the closure of a long-standing community program can be overlooked because it is not seen as a "personal" loss like bereavement.

Leadership Insight: Leaders who enhance loss visibility foster compassionate environments where all types of grief are acknowledged and supported.

Cultural Caution: Downplaying less visible losses can alienate those affected and weaken trust in leadership's empathy.

Mosaic Question: Which losses in your environment might be going unnoticed, and how can they be respected?

Mosaic in Action: A school shows the emotional impact of a program cut by holding a farewell gathering, giving students and staff a chance to share memories and honor the program's contributions.

◈ LETTER L CALLOUT

"Leadership is not a title — it is a practice of influence, integrity, and resilience."

Reflection Questions

- What forms of leadership are often invisible but essential (mentorship, emotional labor, quiet problem-solving)?
- How does fragility undermine leadership in times of stress?
- Which leadership behaviors foster resilience in diverse teams?

Practical Move

Identify one colleague, student, or peer demonstrating quiet leadership. Publicly recognize their contribution so others learn to see leadership beyond titles.

M – Margins, Microaggressions, and Moments of Repair

M guides us to the edges—those overlooked spaces where culture quietly takes shape in whispers, pauses, hallway glances, and unspoken choices. The margins are where identities are misread, where innovation emerges under constraint, and where people navigate systems that were never designed with them in mind. Here, power shifts not only through policy but through relationships—through the subtle dynamics that, over time, shape culture.

From microaggressions that undermine confidence to mirroring that builds connection, from intentional inclusion to missed opportunities for repair, the M terms reveal the landscape of interpersonal equity. Change rarely starts with strategic plans or polished press releases. More often, it begins in micro-moments the glance that welcomes or excludes, the silence that protects or isolates, the acknowledgment that affirms someone's labor and worth.

M asks us to slow down and notice what culture hides in plain sight

- The tone beneath the words.
- The patterns embedded in praise or recognition.
- The assumptions disguised in silence.
- The everyday choices that either fracture or foster trust.

This section reminds us that transformation is not just about structure but also about behavior, emotions, and what it means to be human. Cultures change in how we view the margins—whether we see them as on the edge or as spaces of wisdom, resilience, and leadership.

M urges leaders to practice attunement and presence, recognize microaggressions without dismissing them, and focus on repair that restores dignity. True equity work is not about grand gestures but about consistently showing up in the small moments.

M

Majority Fragility

Definition: Defensive reactions from members of the dominant social group when their privilege, norms, or role in unfair systems are challenged.

Business Application: In a diversity training, participants from the majority group shut down the discussion after being asked to examine their advantages.

Leadership Insight: Leaders can address majority fragility by creating learning environments that are both challenging and supportive, fostering ongoing engagement rather than avoidance.

Cultural Caution: Protecting majority comfort at the cost of truth-telling maintains inequality.

Mosaic Question: How do you react when conversations about equity implicate you or your group in systemic privilege?

Mosaic in Action: During a policy review, a senior leader resists changes to recruitment practices. The facilitator rephrases the conversation around expanding excellence and opportunity, keeping the leader engaged in developing fair solutions.

Marginalization

Definition: The process where individuals or groups are pushed to society's margins, losing access to resources, opportunities, or decision-making power.

Business Application: A company regularly neglects employees from underrepresented backgrounds for promotions, excluding them from strategic discussions.

Leadership Insight: Recognizing marginalization is the first step in reforming systems to promote inclusion and fairness.

Cultural Caution: Marginalization is often systemic and persistent; addressing it requires both policy changes and cultural shifts.

Mosaic Question: Who in your environment has the least influence—and what structures maintain this situation?

Mosaic in Action: A nonprofit notices that younger staff members are excluded from strategic planning. Leadership responds by forming cross-level committees, allowing all staff to participate in shaping organizational goals.

Masculine Norms

Definition: Social expectations and behaviors traditionally linked to masculinity, often regarded as the default standard in workplaces and leadership roles.

Business Application: A performance review system tends to reward assertiveness and competitiveness more than collaboration and emotional intelligence, putting those who lead differently at a disadvantage.

Leadership Insight: Analyzing masculine norms helps leaders diversify what's valued in performance, making room for a broader range of leadership styles.

Cultural Caution: Challenging masculine norms is not about belittling masculinity but about shifting the focus away from it as the only or superior standard.

Mosaic Question: How might unspoken masculine norms influence who is seen as a "natural" leader in your environment?

Mosaic in Action: A tech company updates its leadership competencies to include collaboration, empathy, and community building alongside traditional performance measures.

Maternal Wall Bias

Definition: Discrimination against employees—especially women—based on assumptions about their competence, commitment, or availability after becoming parents.

Business Application: A manager overlooks a new mother for a leadership role, assuming she will not want to travel, without asking her preferences.

Leadership Insight: Combating maternal wall bias involves creating fair policies and ensuring that career advancement is not hindered by parental status.

Cultural Caution: Maternal wall bias can intersect with other biases, increasing inequities for women of color, single mothers, or LGBTQ+ parents.

Mosaic Question: How do you support parenthood without assuming limitations?

Mosaic in Action: A law firm implements flexible scheduling and remote work policies for all staff, normalizing caregiving roles across genders and removing stigma from career growth.

Mattering

Definition: The felt sense that one's presence, contributions, and identity are recognized, valued, and meaningful within a community or organization.

Business Application: Mattering influences retention, engagement, and resilience. Employees who feel invisible tend to disengage or leave more often.

Leadership Insight: Leaders who foster significance do more than recognize performance — they validate identity and importance.

Cultural Caution: Expressions of mattering vary. In collectivist cultures, it often focuses on family or group honor rather than individual recognition.

Mosaic Question: How do you demonstrate to people that they matter beyond their productivity?

Mosaic in Action: A hospital introduced "mattering rounds," during which managers checked in with staff about their contributions and wellbeing, boosting morale.

Media Literacy

Definition: The ability to critically access, evaluate, create, and interpret media messages across various platforms and formats.

Business Application: A marketing department trains staff to identify misinformation and recognize bias in news sources and user-generated content before sharing.

Leadership Insight: Leaders who promote media literacy enhance their teams' capacity to make informed decisions and resist manipulation.

Cultural Caution: Media literacy extends beyond technical skills to include awareness of cultural framing and systemic power in media production.

Mosaic Question: How do you determine whether the media you consume or share is accurate and fair?

Mosaic in Action: A school district incorporates media literacy into the curriculum, teaching students to identify credible sources, analyze perspectives, and produce responsible digital content.

Mediated Identity

Definition: A sense of self shaped or influenced by media portrayals, digital platforms, or public narratives, often blending personal reality with curated representation.

Business Application: an influencer modifies their online persona to align with audience expectations, affecting their self-perception offline.

Leadership Insight: Leaders need to understand how mediated identity can influence team members' self-view, confidence, and professional conduct.

Cultural Caution: Excessive reliance on mediated identity can cause disconnection from one's authentic self and reinforce stereotypes.

Mosaic Question: How much of your identity is influenced by your perception of how others see you online or in media?

Mosaic in Action: A youth leadership program offers workshops on self-presentation and media narratives, helping participants align their digital image with their personal values and real-life experiences.

Mediated Trust

Definition: Trust that is built or maintained through intermediaries, systems, or technology rather than direct personal contact.

Business Application: Remote teams depend on project management tools and transparent digital reporting to foster confidence in each other's contributions.

Leadership Insight: Leaders can enhance mediated trust by ensuring clarity, consistency, and accountability in the systems that support collaboration.

Cultural Caution: Mediated trust can quickly erode if the involved technology or intermediaries are seen as biased or unreliable.

Mosaic Question: What systems or intermediaries influence how trust develops in your work—and how dependable are they?

Mosaic in Action: An international nonprofit sets up shared digital workspaces with defined access levels and regular virtual check-ins, allowing cross-border teams to build trust without frequent in-person meetings.

Meaning-Making

Definition: The process of understanding events, experiences, or information in ways that contribute to personal or shared meaning.

Business Application: After a challenging merger, leadership encourages team discussions to help employees understand the change and unite around common goals.

Leadership Insight: Leaders who support meaning-making help individuals navigate uncertainty, find purpose, and stay engaged.

Cultural Caution: Meaning-making is subjective; leaders should create room for various interpretations instead of enforcing a single narrative.

Mosaic Question: How do you assist yourself or others in finding meaning during moments of change or challenge?

Mosaic in Action: A healthcare team copes with the emotional burden of a tough year by sharing personal stories during a guided session, collectively viewing their work as a testament to resilience and impact.

Memory as Resistance

Definition: The intentional act of preserving and sharing collective or personal memories to challenge dominant narratives, resist erasure, and assert cultural or political identity.

Business Application: A community organization documents the stories of longtime residents to oppose displacement narratives during urban redevelopment.

Leadership Insight: Leaders who honor memory as resistance ensure stories of struggle, resilience, and innovation remain visible and influential in shaping the future.

Cultural Caution: Selectively preserving memories that only support a certain agenda risks replacing one form of erasure with another.

Mosaic Question: Which memories in your community or organization challenge the dominant story—and how are they being protected?

Mosaic in Action: An Indigenous youth center creates an oral history archive of elders' experiences, using the recordings as educational tools in schools and advocacy efforts for land rights.

Memory Politics

Definition: The use of collective memory—what is remembered or forgotten—as a tool to shape identity, policy, or public perception.

Business Application: A government highlights certain historical events during national holidays while leaving others out to promote a specific political narrative.

Leadership Insight: Understanding memory politics helps leaders navigate conflicting histories and craft more inclusive stories that recognize multiple truths.

Cultural Caution: Manipulating memory to serve narrow interests can deepen divisions and damage trust.

Mosaic Question: Whose memories are at the center of the stories your organization shares—and whose are excluded?

Mosaic in Action: A museum updates its exhibits to include marginalized perspectives previously left out of national history, involving community members in curating content.

Mental Health Stigma

Definition: Negative attitudes, beliefs, or discrimination directed toward individuals with mental health conditions, leading to shame, silence, or reduced access to care.

Business Application: Employees may avoid using mental health benefits out of fear that it will harm their career prospects.

Leadership Insight: Leaders can fight mental health stigma by modeling openness, providing resources, and ensuring policies protect confidentiality and prevent discrimination.

Cultural Caution: Awareness campaigns alone are not enough; structural support and an inclusive culture are essential to reduce stigma.

Mosaic Question: How do your workplace norms encourage or discourage open conversations about mental health?

Mosaic in Action: A law firm normalizes mental health days, invites guest speakers to share personal recovery journeys, and sees an increase in employees accessing supportive resources.

Mental Load

Definition: The mental and emotional effort needed to handle and coordinate tasks, responsibilities, and planning, often unevenly borne by women and caregivers.

Business Application: Besides her official job responsibilities, an employee arranges team celebrations, monitors deadlines, and reminds colleagues of tasks — all without acknowledgment or pay.

Leadership Insight: Recognizing and sharing the mental load helps prevent burnout and ensures this unseen work is appreciated.

Cultural Caution: Assuming certain people will take on the mental load because they are "good at it" reinforces gender and role-based inequalities.

Mosaic Question: Who in your environment is quietly managing the burden of keeping things organized and functioning smoothly?

Mosaic in Action: A nonprofit rotates responsibilities for meeting agendas, follow-ups, and logistics among staff members, making the distribution of mental load fairer.

Mentorship Capital

Definition: The total value of guidance, knowledge, and networks gained through mentorship relationships over time.

Business Application: A new entrepreneur accelerates growth by accessing mentors who offer industry expertise and introductions to key partners.

Leadership Insight: Leaders should intentionally develop mentorship capital within their teams to ensure equal access, not just through informal networks.

Cultural Caution: Without deliberate effort, mentorship capital tends to flow to those already advantaged, maintaining inequities.

Mosaic Question: Who in your organization has the most mentorship capital, and who has the least?

Mosaic in Action: A company pairs emerging leaders from underrepresented groups with senior executives, tracking career progress to evaluate impact over time.

Meritocracy Myth

Definition: The misconception that advancement depends only on individual talent and effort, while overlooking systemic inequalities and structural barriers.

Business Application: The myth of meritocracy promotes inequality by blaming individuals for their lack of advancement rather than challenging exclusionary systems.

Leadership Insight: Leaders need to see meritocracy as incomplete and adopt equity strategies that create a fair playing field.

Cultural Caution: Some societies highly value meritocracy as a cultural principle. Leaders should present equity as a way to improve fairness, not diminish effort.

Mosaic Question: Are you still relying on the "hard work alone" narrative — or are you addressing the barriers people encounter?

Mosaic in Action: A company replaced "merit-only" promotion criteria with transparent equity audits, uncovering systemic gaps and rebalancing advancement.

Meta-Bias Awareness

Definition: The ability to recognize and reflect on one's own biases about bias itself, including assumptions about who is or is not biased and how bias operates.

Business Application: A manager assumes that since their team has completed bias training, there is no longer a need to address inequities—overlooking ongoing patterns of favoritism.

Leadership Insight: Meta-bias awareness helps leaders find blind spots in equity work and prevents them from overestimating their objectivity.

Cultural Caution: Believing oneself to be "bias-free" can be more dangerous than admitting and controlling ongoing bias.

Mosaic Question: How could your assumptions about bias influence your actions or inactions in equity work?

Mosaic in Action: An executive team regularly reviews its diversity initiatives for unintended bias, recognizing that their assumptions about "fairness" may still privilege certain groups.

Metronormativity

Definition: The belief that urban life is inherently more progressive, advanced, or desirable than rural life, often leading to the marginalization of rural communities.

Business Application: A national nonprofit focuses its programs in large cities, overlooking the needs and realities of rural populations.

Leadership Insight: Challenging metronormativity involves creating strategies that recognize and include the unique strengths and perspectives of non-urban communities.

Cultural Caution: Assuming rural communities need to "catch up" can reinforce stereotypes and hinder genuine collaboration.

Mosaic Question: How might your work unintentionally prioritize urban experiences over rural ones?

Mosaic in Action: A policy think tank sets up rural advisory boards to ensure legislation recommendations reflect both urban and non-urban perspectives equally.

Microaggressions

Definition: Subtle, often unintended, comments or actions that express bias, stereotypes, or exclusion toward members of marginalized groups.

Business Application: During a meeting, a colleague repeatedly interrupts a woman of color, presuming she has less expertise than others in the room.

Leadership Insight: Leaders must address microaggressions immediately, establish clear standards for respectful communication, and demonstrate inclusive behavior.

Cultural Caution: Dismissing microaggressions as harmless can weaken trust and increase their impact over time.

Mosaic Question: How do you respond when someone points out that your words or actions might have been harmful, even if unintended?

Mosaic in Action: A supervisor notices a team member being overlooked in discussions and intentionally redirects the conversation to make sure their input is heard and appreciated.

Micro-Betrayal

Definition: A subtle act of broken trust, often overlooked but felt deeply. Micro-betrayals can include small dismissals, broken commitments, or breaches of confidentiality that quietly undermine psychological safety.

Business Application: In leadership, micro-betrayals damage credibility and harm team cohesion. Regularly ignoring contributions, canceling commitments without acknowledgment, or failing to keep confidentiality erodes trust over time.

Leadership Insight: Leaders often believe trust is only lost in major scandals, but small betrayals can be just as damaging. Integrity involves honoring both the little promises and the big ones.

Cultural Caution: What feels like betrayal varies across cultures. For some, failing to meet deadlines may signal betrayal; for others, withholding relational acknowledgment is more damaging. Leaders must understand the context.

Mosaic Question: Where might small, unnoticed betrayals be undermining trust in your leadership?

Mosaic in Action: A team member confides in their manager about feeling stressed, only to hear it echoed in a meeting. Though subtle, this micro-betrayal harms trust and decreases morale.

Microrepair

Definition: Small, deliberate actions to repair harm or rebuild trust after a mistake, misunderstanding, or exclusion.

Business Application: After accidentally misgendering a colleague, a manager directly apologizes, uses the correct pronouns moving forward, and implements inclusive practices in team meetings.

Leadership Insight: Microreparations prevent minor damages from worsening and show responsibility in daily interactions.

Cultural Caution: Microrepair is most effective when combined with real reflection and behavioral change, not just superficial gestures.

Mosaic Question: What small actions can you take today to repair harm you've caused, whether intentional or not?

Mosaic in Action: A facilitator mispronounces a participant's name during introductions. They quickly apologize, practice the correct pronunciation, and use it consistently for the rest of the session, reinforcing respect.

Micro-Resistance

Definition: Small, deliberate acts of defiance or disruption against oppressive systems. Micro-resistance allows individuals to assert their agency, even within restrictive structures.

Business Application: Employees engage in micro-resistance by challenging biased jokes, proposing inclusive alternatives, or subtly altering meeting dynamics. These small actions, though minor, build toward systemic change.

Leadership Insight: Leaders who acknowledge and support micro-resistance foster courage and help establish equity. Small actions grow into bigger change when supported from leadership.

Cultural Caution: Micro-resistance might be hidden from outsiders and could pose serious risks in hierarchical cultures. Leaders should support and validate those who practice it.

Mosaic Question: Do you notice—and confirm—the subtle ways your team pushes back against inequity?

Mosaic in Action: An employee consistently makes sure diverse voices are heard during brainstorming by redirecting attention to overlooked colleagues and demonstrating micro-resistance within team culture.

Middle-Person Syndrome

Definition: The stress, frustration, or diminished authority experienced by individuals who act as intermediaries between decision-makers and those carrying out the work.

Business Application: A mid-level manager is tasked with enforcing policies they had no role in creating, which leads to tension with both upper management and their team.

Leadership Insight: Leaders can reduce middle-person syndrome by involving intermediaries in decision-making and giving them clear reasons and authority.

Cultural Caution: Without support, middle-person syndrome can cause burnout, disengagement, and weaken trust at all levels of an organization.

Mosaic Question: How can you empower those in "in-between" roles to lead with clarity and confidence?

Mosaic in Action: An organization redesigns its change management process to include feedback loops from middle managers before finalizing policy changes, increasing buy-in across the company.

Migrant Mindset

Definition: The adaptive, resourceful, and often risk-tolerant outlook developed through experiences of migration, relocation, or navigating new cultural and social systems.

Business Application: A startup founder leverages their migrant mindset to quickly pivot the business model in response to market changes.

Leadership Insight: Valuing the migrant mindset in teams can boost resilience, creativity, and cross-cultural problem-solving.

Cultural Caution: Avoid romanticizing the migrant mindset; migration is often driven by hardship, systemic barriers, and loss.

Mosaic Question: How do the experiences of relocation or cultural transition influence the way you approach challenges?

Mosaic in Action: A healthcare nonprofit hires leaders with lived migration experience to develop outreach strategies for newly arrived communities, enhancing service uptake.

Migration Narratives

Definition: The stories told about migration—by individuals, communities, institutions, or media—that influence public perception, policy, and migrant identity.

Business Application: A documentary film company partners with migrant communities to share personal stories that challenge harmful stereotypes.

Leadership Insight: Leaders who engage with diverse migration narratives can promote more nuanced and compassionate policies.

Cultural Caution: Mainstream narratives can erase the diversity of migrant experiences, reducing them to a single story of struggle or success.

Mosaic Question: Which migration stories are amplified in your environment—and which are left unheard?

Mosaic in Action: A city's welcome program pairs long-term residents with newly arrived families and encourages both to share their migration stories at community events, fostering mutual understanding.

Minoritized Identity

Definition: An identity that is marginalized or holds less power within a specific social, cultural, or institutional setting, regardless of its population size.

Business Application: In a mostly female profession, men may still dominate leadership roles, leaving women with a minoritized identity in decision-making spaces.

Leadership Insight: Recognizing minoritized identities involves addressing structural inequalities rather than assuming inclusion occurs automatically through representation.

Cultural Caution: Minoritization concerns power, not numbers; focusing solely on demographic ratios can hide deeper inequalities.

Mosaic Question: Which identities in your environment are structurally limited in influence or access, and why?

Mosaic in Action: A school board observes that although students of color make up the majority, leadership roles are still mostly held by white individuals. They create leadership pipelines and mentorship programs to correct the imbalance.

Minority Stress

Definition: The chronic stress experienced by marginalized individuals from discrimination, stigma, and exclusion, often worsened by microaggressions and systemic inequity.

Business Application: Minority stress affects productivity, mental health, and retention. Leaders must foster supportive and affirming environments.

Leadership Insight: Recognizing minority stress is essential to equity leadership — silence perpetuates harm.

Cultural Caution: Stressors vary by culture and context. Leaders should avoid broad generalizations and instead seek insights from lived experiences.

Mosaic Question: How does your organization reduce or increase minority stress?

Mosaic in Action: A financial firm implemented wellness programs and affinity groups that directly address stressors reported by LGBTQ+ staff.

Misgendering

Definition: Referring to or addressing someone with language, such as pronouns or titles, that does not match their affirmed gender.

Business Application: A team member is repeatedly called by the wrong pronouns despite sharing their correct ones in introductions and email signatures.

Leadership Insight: Preventing and addressing misgendering requires intentional learning, respectful correction, and systemic support for gender-inclusive practices.

Cultural Caution: Misgendering— whether accidental or intentional— can cause harm, invalidate identity, and erode trust.

Mosaic Question: How do you ensure that your language consistently affirms the identities of the people you work with?

Mosaic in Action: A conference organizer includes pronoun fields on name badges and trains staff to confirm and use correct pronouns, reducing misgendering incidents and fostering an inclusive environment.

Misidentification

Definition: Wrongly categorizing or assuming someone's identity—such as race, ethnicity, nationality, or role—based on appearance, name, accent, or other perceived cues.

413

Business Application: A conference attendee repeatedly mistakes a woman of color for event staff despite her being the keynote speaker.

Leadership Insight: Leaders should address misidentification promptly to affirm the individual's identity and challenge the assumptions that caused the error.

Cultural Caution: Repeated misidentification can lead to feelings of invisibility and exclusion, especially for people in underrepresented groups.

Mosaic Question: What assumptions might you be making about people before learning how they identify themselves?

Mosaic in Action: At a corporate retreat, a facilitator interrupts a conversation to correctly introduce a participant who has been misidentified, affirming her role and expertise in front of the group.

Misogynoir

Definition: The unique combination of racism and sexism faced by Black women, leading to distinct forms of prejudice, stereotyping, and discrimination.

Business Application: A Black woman in leadership is criticized for being "too assertive" in ways that are praised in her non-Black male peers.

Leadership Insight: Addressing misogynoir requires understanding how gender and racial biases reinforce each other, and developing policies that actively oppose both.

Cultural Caution: Not naming misogynoir risks ignoring Black women's unique experiences by grouping them with wider biases.

Mosaic Question: How do your equity strategies tackle the particular challenges faced by Black women?

Mosaic in Action: A media company examines its content for patterns that depict Black women with stereotypes, then adopts new editorial guidelines informed by Black women on staff.

Mixed-Race Identity

Definition: The lived experience of people with heritage from two or more racial backgrounds, often involving navigating multiple cultural worlds.

Business Application: An employee with a mixed-race identity helps bridge cultural misunderstandings among team members by sharing personal insights into various perspectives.

Leadership Insight: Valuing mixed-race identity involves creating environments where complex and fluid self-identifications are respected, without pressuring individuals to "pick a side."

Cultural Caution: Don't assume that mixed-race individuals share a single experience or act as cultural interpreters without their consent.

Mosaic Question: How do you recognize and support the layered experiences of people with mixed heritage?

Mosaic in Action: A museum invites mixed-race artists to curate an exhibit exploring identity fluidity, enabling nuanced narratives to emerge beyond simple category labels.

Mobility Privilege

Definition: The unearned benefit of being able to move freely between locations—locally, nationally, or internationally—without facing significant legal, financial, or safety obstacles.

Business Application: A consultant can easily accept international assignments because of visa-free travel options, whereas colleagues from other countries may encounter extensive restrictions.

Leadership Insight: Recognizing mobility privilege can help leaders create opportunities that address travel barriers, such as offering remote participation or relocation assistance.

Cultural Caution: Assuming everyone has the same ability to move or travel can unintentionally exclude valuable contributors.

Mosaic Question: How might mobility privilege influence who gets access to certain opportunities in your environment?

Mosaic in Action: An international conference offers hybrid attendance options and travel stipends, enabling participation by professionals who face visa or financial barriers.

Model Minority Myth

Definition: A stereotype that depicts a marginalized group—often Asian Americans—as more successful, disciplined, or high-achieving than others, masking the diversity of experiences and systemic inequities.

Business Application: A university ignores the need for financial aid outreach in Asian American communities due to assumptions about universal academic and economic success.

Leadership Insight: Challenging the model minority myth requires recognizing the harm it causes both to the stereotyped group and to other marginalized communities through divisive comparisons.

Cultural Caution: This myth can pressure individuals to meet unrealistic expectations while hiding the barriers they face.

Mosaic Question: What assumptions about achievement or capability might you be making about entire groups without evidence?

Mosaic in Action: A nonprofit working with immigrant youth disaggregates data by ethnicity within Asian American communities, revealing disparities in access to education and adjusting programs accordingly.

Moral Courage

Definition: The willingness to act ethically despite risks, opposition, or fear. Moral courage forms the foundation of principled leadership in challenging situations.

Business Application: Leaders demonstrate moral courage when they stand against discrimination, challenge unethical practices, or protect vulnerable employees — even at personal or professional cost.

Leadership Insight: Moral courage separates obedience from conviction. Leaders who demonstrate it show that values are non-negotiable, even when taking easy shortcuts seems tempting.

Cultural Caution: In some situations, acting with moral courage might be seen as disloyalty to authority. Leaders need to weigh courage against relational and cultural understanding.

Mosaic Question: When confronted with ethical risk, do you prioritize safety — or moral courage?

Mosaic in Action: A department head refuses to alter data under pressure, even knowing it might cost funding, demonstrating moral courage in preserving integrity.

Moral Injury

Definition: The psychological and emotional damage caused when individuals are compelled to act against their core values due to systemic or organizational pressure.

Business Application: Moral injury frequently occurs in fields like healthcare, education, and law enforcement where systemic constraints conflict with ethics.

Leadership Insight: Leaders decrease moral injury by

aligning policies with values and empowering staff to act with integrity.

Cultural Caution: Not all cultures define harm as "injury." Leaders must understand cultural terminology related to moral and spiritual wounds.

Mosaic Question: Where could your systems pressure people to betray their values?

Mosaic in Action: Nurses experienced moral injury due to unsafe patient ratios caused by understaffing. The hospital responded by restructuring staffing and ethics reporting channels.

Moral Licensing

Definition: The tendency to justify questionable behavior based on prior good deeds or actions related to fairness.

Business Application: After hiring one woman for a senior leadership role, an executive resists further diversity initiatives, believing they have already "done enough."

Leadership Insight: Leaders who understand moral licensing realize that equity efforts are ongoing and cannot be balanced out by isolated actions.

Cultural Caution: Moral licensing can subtly hinder progress by framing inclusion as a quota to fulfill rather than a continuous commitment.

Mosaic Question: Where might you be using a past positive action to justify inaction or bias today?

Mosaic in Action: A company that previously donated to social justice causes reviews its hiring data, recognizing that representation gaps still exist and committing to systemic recruitment changes.

Mosaic Identity

Definition: A complex and evolving sense of self composed of intersecting cultural, personal, and social elements that together form a unique whole. Mosaic identity acknowledges that individuals are not defined by a single story but by the layered interaction of many identities. (*A proprietary concept within the Mosaic Intelligence Method™, originated and trademarked by Dr. Karissa Thomas.*)

Business Application: A leader with a mosaic identity can draw on multiple cultural frameworks to navigate global negotiations, build inclusive teams, and approach challenges with empathy and nuanced insight. Organizations that validate mosaic identity strengthen belonging by affirming employees' multidimensional selves.

Leadership Insight: Recognizing mosaic identity in yourself and others fosters greater flexibility, authenticity, and empathy. Leaders who embrace this idea view complexity as a strength rather than a source of fragmentation.

Cultural Caution: Reducing a person's mosaic identity to just one main label — whether cultural, professional, or social — erases important nuance and risks reinforcing stereotypes.

Mosaic Question: How do the various aspects of your identity affect your decisions, leadership, and relationships?

Mosaic in Action: An educator incorporates her heritage languages, academic training, and artistic background into lesson plans, fostering richer and more relatable learning experiences for diverse students.

Mosaic Intelligence Method™

Definition: A proprietary leadership and identity framework developed and trademarked by Dr. Karissa Thomas. Built on three pillars — Emotional Integrity, Cultural Flexibility, and Identity Agility — the Mosaic Intelligence Method™ emphasizes wholeness, adaptability, and relational trust in diverse, high-stakes contexts.

Business Application: Organizations utilize the Mosaic Intelligence Method™ in executive coaching, leadership development, and education to build resilience and promote inclusive cultures. It prepares leaders to handle disruption, cross-cultural complexity, and identity-based challenges with clarity and confidence.

Leadership Insight: Strength in leadership comes from the dynamic balance of integrity, flexibility, and agility, rather than rigid certainty. Leaders who embody the Method foster cultures of trust, belonging, and sustainable performance.

Cultural Caution: The Method must be tailored to sector, culture, and community. Reducing its pillars to checklists risks diluting the framework's depth and transformative potential.

Mosaic Question: Which pillar of the Mosaic Intelligence Method™ — Emotional Integrity, Cultural Flexibility, or Identity Agility — do you rely on most, and which one needs improvement?

Mosaic in Action: An executive team adopts the Mosaic

Intelligence Method™ during annual retreats, using its three pillars as a common language for feedback, resilience, and decision-making across different cultures and generations.

Mosaic Way™

Definition: A leadership and life philosophy developed and trademarked by Dr. Karissa Thomas. The Mosaic Way™ combines emotional integrity, cultural flexibility, and identity agility into daily practices, providing a pathway for leaders and communities to foster trust, belonging, and resilience. At its core, it affirms that we are always in motion — fluid, evolving, and complete in our becoming.

Business Application: The Mosaic Way™ is used in education, corporate leadership, and community development. It guides organizations with a values-based approach that encourages motion and growth, combining human-centered leadership with cultural and emotional intelligence.

Leadership Insight: The Mosaic Way™ emphasizes that wholeness comes not from standing still, but from embracing complexity. Leaders who follow this philosophy see identity and culture as living, shifting mosaics — always changing, yet always complete.

Cultural Caution: The Mosaic Way™ is not a quick fix or checklist. Viewing it as static language or slogans lessens its depth. It must be practiced continuously as movement, relationship, and renewal.

Mosaic Question: How could embracing constant motion — in yourself, your leadership, and your community — foster deeper belonging and resilience?

Mosaic in Action: A cross-sector coalition adopts The Mosaic Way™ as a guiding philosophy, viewing collaboration as a dynamic process. By embracing differences in culture, language, and generations, the group creates bridges that stay flexible, resilient, and unified.

Multicultural Competence

Definition: The ability to effectively engage, communicate, and collaborate with people from different cultural backgrounds, based on knowledge, skills, and self-awareness.

Business Application: A customer service team adapts its approach depending on the cultural norms of politeness and hierarchy in various markets.

Leadership Insight: Leaders with multicultural competence demonstrate respect, curiosity, and adaptability, which enhances cross-cultural trust and collaboration.

Cultural Caution: Competence requires ongoing learning; assuming you've "arrived" can lead to blind spots in rapidly changing cultural environments.

Mosaic Question: How do you intentionally develop skills to engage across cultures?

Mosaic in Action: A nonprofit leader participates in continuous cultural competence training and establishes exchange programs between staff in different regions to foster mutual understanding.

Multilingualism

Definition: The ability to use two or more languages fluently, improving communication, cultural connection, and cognitive flexibility.

Business Application: A multinational company uses employees' multilingual skills to expand market reach and strengthen client relationships.

Leadership Insight: Leaders who value multilingualism foster more inclusive environments and see it as a strategic advantage, not just a personal skill.

Cultural Caution: Not supporting or rewarding multilingual skills can lead to underutilizing important team strengths.

Mosaic Question: How is language diversity recognized and rewarded in your environment?

Mosaic in Action: A hospital employs multilingual staff and offers pay incentives for language proficiency, ensuring patients receive care in their preferred language.

Mutual Accountability

Definition: A shared commitment among individuals or groups to hold each other accountable for actions, decisions, and agreed-upon goals.

Business Application: A cross-departmental team establishes measurable milestones and commits to regular peer check-ins to ensure progress toward a shared initiative.

Leadership Insight: Leaders who promote mutual accountability build cultures where responsibility is shared, decreasing dependence on top-down enforcement.

Cultural Caution: Mutual accountability depends on trust;

without it, it can turn into blame-shifting or avoidance.

Mosaic Question: How do you manage personal responsibility alongside collective ownership in your work?

Mosaic in Action: A nonprofit board establishes a system where all members take turns leading agenda items and handling follow-up actions, emphasizing shared responsibility for outcomes.

Mutual Respect Culture

Definition: An environment where individuals consistently treat each other with dignity, value differences, and engage in constructive dialogue and collaboration.

Business Application: A global company incorporates respect-building practices into team onboarding to ensure members from diverse backgrounds feel valued from day one.

Leadership Insight: Leaders set the tone for a culture of mutual respect by demonstrating attentive listening, fairness, and recognition in all interactions.

Cultural Caution: Respect must be mutual; expecting marginalized groups to accept oppressive behaviors erodes trust.

Mosaic Question: What actions in your environment indicate that respect is a core value, not just a statement?

Mosaic in Action: A community coalition adopts discussion guidelines that emphasize active listening, rotating facilitation, and calling each other in rather than out during disagreements, leading to more productive conversations.

Mutual Vulnerability

Definition: A leadership practice of shared openness that builds trust and connection. Mutual vulnerability enables both leaders and teams to be honest without fear of being exploited.

Business Application: Organizations that encourage mutual vulnerability build cultures where feedback, innovation, and teamwork thrive. When leaders demonstrate vulnerability, teams feel more secure to share genuinely.

Leadership Insight: Vulnerability is mutual. Leaders who only ask for it from others without giving it in return create distrust. Mutuality strengthens connection and maintains collective courage.

Cultural Caution: Some cultures value emotional restraint; open vulnerability can be seen as weakness. Leaders should adjust their vulnerability to fit the cultural context while staying authentic.

Mosaic Question: Do you invite vulnerability from others while safeguarding your own — or do you demonstrate it as a shared practice?

Mosaic in Action: During a leadership retreat, a CEO shares a personal failure and invites others to reflect on their challenges, fostering a culture of mutual vulnerability.

◈ LETTER M CALLOUT

"Marginalization is not a side effect — it is the result of choices about power, voice, and visibility."

Reflection Questions

- Where do you see marginalization operating silently in your community or workplace?
- How does memory — personal or collective — resist marginalization?
- What myths about meritocracy or majority culture reinforce inequity?

Practical Move

In your next group setting, pause to ask whose voices are not present — then take one concrete step to bring those perspectives in.

N – Norms, Naming, and Navigating Tension

N addresses what is often unseen but highly influential the norms that define belonging, the stories that shape perception, and the skills needed to succeed in spaces where not everyone starts from the same position. These terms show how "normal" is built—who sets it, who gains from it, and who must adapt to it, often without noticing.

In many professional settings, unspoken expectations about tone, punctuality, demeanor, or presence are seen as objective standards. However, norms are rarely neutral. They reflect dominant cultural values and histories that exclude those who do not conform. Normativity becomes the unchallenged standard, pushing others to code-switch, self-edit, or hide their true identity to seem "legitimate."

Naming provides a necessary balance. To name exclusion, discomfort, or contradiction is not to incite conflict but to create clarity. Naming makes the implicit explicit, opening space for accountability and cultural repair. However, too often, the person who names the tension is labeled disruptive or unprofessional, while the underlying dynamics stay hidden.

N asks us to notice what remains unspoken but deeply consequential

- The hidden rules that determine legitimacy and belonging.
- The costs of code-switching and self-erasure.
- The stigma placed on those who name what others avoid.

- The quiet labor of navigating tension while preserving integrity.

Navigating tension requires resilience and discernment—the wisdom to know when to speak, when to pause, and how to stay true without becoming the container for others' discomfort. This is the invisible work many carry while leading, collaborating, or simply surviving in systems that were not built for them.

N calls leaders to reexamine norms not as fixed rules but as adaptable pathways that should stay flexible, inclusive, and shared. Because cultures of belonging are not built by punishing truth-telling—they thrive when truth itself becomes a common language for growth and repair.

N

Name-Based Discrimination

Definition: Unfair treatment of individuals based on assumptions or biases associated with their name, often linked to ethnicity, religion, or perceived nationality.

Business Application: A job applicant with a non-Anglicized name receives fewer interview callbacks despite having equal qualifications.

Leadership Insight: Leaders can counter name-based discrimination by implementing anonymized application processes and actively addressing bias in decision-making.

Cultural Caution: Anglicizing or altering names for "ease" without consent can erase cultural identity and perpetuate assimilation pressures.

Mosaic Question: How might biases toward certain names be influencing your perceptions or decisions?

Mosaic in Action: A company removes names from resumes during the initial screening stage, leading to a measurable increase in interviews for candidates from diverse backgrounds.

Naming Injustice

Definition: The act of assigning, altering, or erasing names in ways that misrepresent, devalue, or strip identity from individuals, communities, or places.

Business Application: A development project renames a historic neighborhood for branding purposes, disregarding its cultural and historical significance.

Leadership Insight: Addressing naming injustice requires engaging stakeholders in naming decisions and restoring original or chosen names where possible.

Cultural Caution: Naming is a form of power; altering names without consent can perpetuate colonialism and cultural erasure.

Mosaic Question: Whose right to name or be named is overlooked in your environment?

Mosaic in Action: A school district restores Indigenous place names to campuses and streets after collaboration with local tribal councils, integrating the history into student curriculum.

Naming Practices

Definition: The cultural, familial, or institutional conventions that guide how names are given, used, and recognized.

Business Application: A global company updates its employee directory to allow multiple name formats, including diacritics and order variations, to honor diverse naming practices.

Leadership Insight: Respecting naming practices is a form of cultural competence that reinforces belonging and identity integrity.

Cultural Caution: Standardizing names for administrative convenience can erase important cultural distinctions.

Mosaic Question: How do your systems accommodate or limit the expression of diverse naming traditions?

Mosaic in Action: An international nonprofit trains HR teams on name pronunciation and cultural naming norms, improving relationships with staff and partners worldwide.

Narrative Competence

Definition: The ability to interpret, create, and utilize stories with empathy, accuracy, and cultural sensitivity. Narrative competence enables leaders to hear stories beneath the surface and respond with depth.

Business Application: Leaders utilize narrative skills in conflict resolution, change management, and communication strategies. By identifying themes, silences, and metaphors, they can steer teams through transitions with increased trust.

Leadership Insight: Narrative competence is more than just telling stories; it's about listening to them carefully. Leaders who cultivate this skill gain deeper understanding of identity, culture, and organizational meaning.

Cultural Caution: Narratives don't always follow linear, Western story structures. Leaders should resist the urge to force their own frameworks and instead respect different storytelling styles.

Mosaic Question: Do you listen to stories solely for facts — or for the emotions, silences, and cultural codes within them?

Mosaic in Action: A global health leader interprets patient stories that include ritual, family history, and spirituality — ensuring solutions respect both data and lived experiences.

Narrative Dissonance

Definition: The tension that arises when the dominant narrative about a person, group, or event conflicts with lived experiences or alternative perspectives.

Business Application: An organization's public statement about being inclusive contradicts employee reports of persistent workplace bias.

Leadership Insight: Leaders who acknowledge and address narrative dissonance build credibility and trust by aligning words with reality.

Cultural Caution: Ignoring narrative dissonance can deepen mistrust and disengagement, especially among marginalized groups.

Mosaic Question: Where might there be a gap between the story you tell and the reality people experience?

Mosaic in Action: A city government launches an equity report after community feedback reveals that its "diverse and thriving" branding overlooks ongoing housing discrimination.

Narrative Gaps

Definition: Missing or overlooked perspectives, experiences, or events in the stories told about individuals, communities, or historical moments.

Business Application: A corporate history highlights only the achievements of top executives, omitting the contributions of frontline workers.

Leadership Insight: Leaders who identify and fill narrative gaps create more complete and inclusive accounts that strengthen trust and connection.

Cultural Caution: Filling narrative gaps requires more than adding token references; it must involve meaningful inclusion of missing voices.

Mosaic Question: Which stories in your environment are incomplete, and whose perspectives could help fill the gaps?

Mosaic in Action: A museum revises its exhibit on local industry to include oral histories from immigrant laborers who played a central but previously unrecognized role in its development.

Narrative Identity

Definition: The way people craft and tell their life stories, combining experiences, values, and relationships into a clear sense of self. Narrative identity influences how leaders see themselves and how they present themselves in the world.

Business Application: In organizations, leaders use narrative identity to genuinely connect with teams and stakeholders. A leader who weaves personal story into vision-setting fosters belonging, clarity, and trust.

Leadership Insight: Identity is not fixed but is a story that is told — always being revised as we experience change. Leaders who adopt narrative identity view themselves not as fixed labels, but as ongoing stories that evolve.

Cultural Caution: Narrative identity is influenced by cultural expectations of how stories "should" be told. Leaders must make sure they do not suppress or erase counter-narratives that hold truth and dignity.

Mosaic Question: What story are you sharing about yourself — and who provided you with the language to tell it?

Mosaic in Action: A first-generation college president shares her story of navigating migration and resilience, using it to redefine her institution's commitment to access and equity.

Narrative Justice

Definition: The practice of ensuring that storytelling, history, and representation fairly reflect diverse voices, experiences, and truths, especially those historically marginalized.

Business Application: A publishing house launches an initiative to publish more works by authors from underrepresented backgrounds, reshaping public understanding of history and culture.

Leadership Insight: Narrative justice involves redistributing narrative authority and validating multiple truths, not just supplementing dominant accounts.

Cultural Caution: Without shared authorship, narrative justice efforts can unintentionally replicate existing power imbalances.

Mosaic Question: How do you ensure that storytelling in your environment supports equity rather than reinforcing exclusion?

Mosaic in Action: A documentary team co-produces a film with a refugee community, allowing them to lead the script and creative direction to ensure their story is told authentically.

Narrative Ownership

Definition: The right and ability of individuals or communities to control how their own stories are told, shared, and interpreted.

Business Application: A nonprofit seeks permission from clients before publishing personal stories in marketing materials, allowing them to approve language and framing.

Leadership Insight: Respecting narrative ownership means shifting from extraction to collaboration, letting people speak for themselves wherever possible.

Cultural Caution: Appropriating someone's story without consent or misrepresenting it for strategic purposes can cause lasting harm.

Mosaic Question: Who holds the authority to tell the stories you share—and is that authority theirs by right?

Mosaic in Action: A journalism outlet implements a policy requiring direct collaboration with the subjects of feature pieces, giving them agency over how their experiences are portrayed.

Narrative Power

Definition: The ability to shape perceptions, beliefs, and actions by controlling which stories are told, how they are framed, and who gets to tell them.

Business Application: A national advertising campaign reinforces a brand's values by centering narratives that align with its social impact messaging.

Leadership Insight: Leaders with narrative power can either entrench inequities or drive transformative change depending on whose voices they amplify.

Cultural Caution: Concentrating narrative power in a narrow group risks silencing or distorting the perspectives of others.

Mosaic Question: Who in your environment controls the narratives that define reality—and who is left out of that control?

Mosaic in Action: A grassroots coalition trains community members to share their own stories at city council meetings, shifting public debate and influencing policy decisions.

National Identity

Definition: A shared sense of belonging to a nation, often shaped by common history, culture, language, and symbols.

Business Application: An international marketing team

tailors campaigns to reflect national identity cues, such as cultural holidays and local pride.

Leadership Insight: Leaders can acknowledge national identity while fostering respect for global interconnectedness and diversity within nations.

Cultural Caution: National identity can unify but also exclude those who do not fit the dominant narrative or who hold multiple identities.

Mosaic Question: How does national identity influence who is seen as fully belonging in your environment?

Mosaic in Action: A sports federation highlights athletes from diverse ethnic backgrounds as representatives of the nation, expanding the public image of national identity.

Nationalism Critique

Definition: The examination and questioning of nationalism's impact, particularly when it promotes exclusion, intolerance, or conflict in the name of national unity.

Business Application: A think tank publishes research showing how extreme nationalist policies can harm economic cooperation and minority rights.

Leadership Insight: Critiquing nationalism requires balancing respect for cultural pride with an awareness of its potential to marginalize or divide.

Cultural Caution: Critique can be met with defensiveness; leaders must approach these conversations with evidence, empathy, and clarity.

Mosaic Question: How do you celebrate national pride without reinforcing exclusionary or harmful narratives?

Mosaic in Action: A civic education program teaches students to analyze historical and current examples of nationalism, encouraging critical thinking about inclusion and global responsibility.

Nationality Bias

Definition: Preferential treatment or prejudice toward individuals based on their nationality, often influencing hiring, promotion, or access to resources.

Business Application: A company prioritizes hiring candidates from the same country as its headquarters, despite equally qualified applicants from other nations.

Leadership Insight: Addressing nationality bias involves setting equitable standards and valuing diverse international experience.

Cultural Caution: Nationality bias can intersect with race, language, or immigration status, deepening exclusion.

Mosaic Question: How might nationality be shaping opportunities in your organization, intentionally or unintentionally?

Mosaic in Action: A global nonprofit implements blind resume reviews for international applicants, increasing the number of hires from underrepresented countries.

Nativism

Definition: A political or cultural stance favoring the interests of native-born or established inhabitants over those of immigrants.

Business Application: A local business association lobbies for policies that make it harder for immigrants to start businesses, citing "protection of local culture."

Leadership Insight: Leaders challenging nativism can frame immigration as an asset to economic, cultural, and social vitality.

Cultural Caution: Nativism often draws on fear-based narratives; countering it requires amplifying evidence and stories of mutual benefit.

Mosaic Question: What narratives in your environment reinforce the idea that belonging is limited to certain origins?

Mosaic in Action: A city council launches a campaign celebrating immigrant-owned businesses and their contributions to the local economy, reducing resistance to inclusive policy proposals.

Navigational Labor

Definition: The extra effort required to understand and operate within systems not designed for one's background or identity, often involving translation—literal or cultural—of unwritten rules.

Business Application: First-generation college students spend significant time decoding institutional processes that peers with more familiar backgrounds take for granted.

Leadership Insight: Leaders who reduce navigational labor remove hidden barriers and make systems more accessible for all.

Cultural Caution: Assuming everyone arrives with the same system knowledge ignores the inequitable distribution of access and experience.

Mosaic Question: What hidden rules in your environment make it harder for some people to succeed?

Mosaic in Action: A company creates onboarding guides that explain not just policies but also informal norms, reducing the time it takes new hires from underrepresented backgrounds to feel confident navigating the workplace.

Needs-Based Equity

Definition: The allocation of resources, opportunities, or support based on specific needs rather than providing the same amount to everyone, in order to achieve fair outcomes.

Business Application: A school district directs more funding and tutoring resources to campuses serving historically under-resourced communities.

Leadership Insight: Needs-based equity requires leaders to assess disparities honestly and resist the pressure to equate fairness with sameness.

Cultural Caution: Without transparent criteria, needs-based equity initiatives may be misperceived as favoritism.

Mosaic Question: How do you determine and communicate who gets more resources—and why?

Mosaic in Action: A nonprofit adjusts its grant model so organizations serving marginalized groups receive additional technical assistance, closing capacity gaps over time.

Negotiated Identity

Definition: An identity shaped through ongoing interaction and compromise between personal self-concept and external expectations from social, cultural, or professional environments.

Business Application: An employee adjusts how openly they express their religious identity depending on workplace culture while still maintaining personal integrity.

Leadership Insight: Leaders can create environments where negotiated identity feels like an empowering choice rather than a forced adaptation.

Cultural Caution: Constant negotiation can be exhausting and may signal systemic barriers to authenticity.

Mosaic Question: In what spaces do you feel you must negotiate your identity to be accepted or effective?

Mosaic in Action: A bicultural executive integrates both cultural communication styles in team leadership, gradually influencing company culture to embrace a broader range of expression.

Nepotism

Definition: Favoritism toward relatives or close associates in hiring, promotions, or access to opportunities, regardless of merit.

Business Application: Nepotism damages trust, decreases diversity, and weakens fairness in promotion systems.

Leadership Insight: Equitable leaders create transparent processes to make sure opportunities are earned, not inherited.

Cultural Caution: In some cultures, family loyalty is a core value. Leaders must balance respect for kinship with fairness in institutions.

Mosaic Question: Do your advancement systems reward talent — or proximity to power?

Mosaic in Action: A global company banned nepotism in promotion processes and implemented equity reviews, boosting diversity at leadership levels.

Neocolonialism

Definition: The continued economic, political, or cultural control of formerly colonized nations or peoples by external powers, often through indirect means such as trade, media, or development aid.

Business Application: A multinational corporation extracts resources from a developing country under the guise of "partnership" while keeping profits offshore.

Leadership Insight: Recognizing neocolonial dynamics helps leaders ensure partnerships are mutually beneficial and respect sovereignty.

Cultural Caution: Development work can unintentionally perpetuate neocolonialism if decision-making power remains with outside actors.

Mosaic Question: Whose terms, values, and priorities shape the projects you lead in cross-border or cross-cultural contexts?

Mosaic in Action: An international NGO shifts from importing standardized solutions to funding locally led initiatives, allowing communities to define their own development strategies.

Network Capital

Definition: The value and opportunities gained from one's social and professional networks, including access to information, resources, and influence.

Business Application: A startup founder quickly obtains investors through introductions from former colleagues, leveraging strong network capital.

Leadership Insight: Leaders can increase equity by helping those with limited network capital develop genuine, reciprocal relationships.

Cultural Caution: Network capital often mirrors systemic inequalities, as historically privileged groups tend to have more powerful and extensive networks.

Mosaic Question: Who in your circle has abundant network capital, and who might be left out?

Mosaic in Action: A corporate mentorship program pairs early-career employees from underrepresented backgrounds with senior leaders, intentionally boosting their visibility and access to important networks.

Networked Belonging

Definition: A feeling of inclusion and connection created through overlapping social, cultural, or professional networks, often spanning different communities or geographic areas.

Business Application: A professional association promotes networked belonging by linking members via local chapters, online forums, and international events.

Leadership Insight: Fostering networked belonging can help individuals feel part of multiple, mutually reinforcing communities rather than isolated in one space.

Cultural Caution: Not all networks are equally accessible; leaders must ensure that entry points are open to everyone, not just those already "in the know."

Mosaic Question: How can you deliberately connect people across different networks to enhance belonging?

Mosaic in Action: A nonprofit hosts cross-sector meetups that gather educators, activists, and artists, igniting collaborative projects and a shared community identity.

Neurodiversity

Definition: The idea that neurological differences—such as autism, ADHD, dyslexia, and others—are natural variations of the human brain and should be recognized and respected as forms of diversity.

Business Application: A design firm modifies its workspace with noise-reduction tools and flexible schedules to better support neurodiverse employees.

Leadership Insight: Embracing neurodiversity helps leaders access unique strengths while removing barriers to participation and success.

Cultural Caution: Avoid seeing neurodiversity only as a challenge to "accommodate"; it is also a source of innovation and fresh perspective.

Mosaic Question: How does your environment support and adapt to different ways of thinking and processing information?

Mosaic in Action: A university updates its teaching methods to include multiple learning formats, benefiting both neurodiverse students and the wider student population.

No Flexibility

Definition: A workplace or leadership culture that does not permit adaptation in schedule, method, or approach, often stifling creativity and well-being.

Business Application: Lack of flexibility results in increased burnout, reduced retention, and challenges in attracting diverse talent, particularly caregivers and international workers.

Leadership Insight: Rigid systems show fear instead of strength. Leaders who reject flexibility often damage credibility and hinder innovation.

Cultural Caution: What is "flexible" in one culture (such as remote work or time off) might be viewed as a lack of discipline in another. Leaders need to consider context while ensuring fairness.

Mosaic Question: Where could your rigidity be confused with strength — and what are the consequences?

Mosaic in Action: An insurance company transitioned from rigid office hours to a hybrid work model, increasing productivity and employee satisfaction.

No Growth Opportunities

Definition: A situation where employees or community members have no opportunities for growth, promotion, or valuable skill development.

Business Application: Lack of growth opportunities leads to disengagement, high turnover, and inequity in leadership development. Marginalized employees are particularly affected when access to mentorship and promotions is restricted.

Leadership Insight: Leaders who overlook growth opportunities sacrifice long-term success for short-term stability. Development is a strategy for retention.

Cultural Caution: Growth varies across different contexts — with title changes in one culture and increased responsibility in another. Leaders need to expand their definitions of advancement.

Mosaic Question: How does your culture promote growth — and for whom?

Mosaic in Action: A nonprofit develops leadership programs for staff who have traditionally been excluded from promotions, helping to reduce attrition and increase diversity in leadership.

No Salary Growth

Definition: Lack of financial growth despite ongoing efforts, increased responsibilities, or organizational success.

Business Application: No salary growth indicates inequality when wages stay flat while workloads or profits increase. It reduces motivation, damages trust, and worsens pay gaps.

Leadership Insight: Compensation reflects value. Leaders who do not align salary increases with contribution risk sending a message that loyalty is expendable.

Cultural Caution: Salary discussions face stigma in some cultures but are openly accepted in others. Leaders must handle pay equity with care and fairness.

Mosaic Question: Does your pay structure recognize contribution — or hide inequality?

Mosaic in Action: A tech company uses transparent pay bands and yearly equity reviews to ensure salary increases reflect performance and to minimize hidden wage gaps.

Non-Binary Identity

Definition: A gender identity that doesn't fit exclusively into male or female categories, and may be fluid, multiple, or outside traditional gender frameworks.

Business Application: A company updates HR systems to let employees select non-binary gender markers and use chosen names on all documents.

Leadership Insight: Leaders who respect non-binary identities help foster inclusive environments where gender diversity is normalized.

Cultural Caution: Misrepresenting or erasing non-binary identities can cause harm and sustain exclusion.

Mosaic Question: How are your systems and culture structured to affirm non-binary people's identities?

Mosaic in Action: An event organizer makes sure registration forms include non-binary options and trains staff on gender-inclusive language, creating a visibly welcoming space for all gender identities.

Non-Dominant Culture

Definition: A cultural group within a society that possesses less social, political, or economic power than the dominant culture.

Business Application: In a multinational company based in the U.S., teams from smaller regional offices may represent non-dominant cultures within global decision-making frameworks.

Leadership Insight: Leaders can promote fairness by making sure non-dominant cultures have influence over policies, narratives, and priorities.

Cultural Caution: Simply "including" non-dominant cultures without changing power dynamics can lead to tokenism.

Mosaic Question: How are perspectives from non-dominant cultures influencing—not just appearing in—your work?

Mosaic in Action: A global nonprofit rotates leadership of strategy meetings among regional offices, ensuring that decisions reflect insights from both dominant and non-dominant cultural contexts.

Non-Disclosure Culture

Definition: An environment where individuals feel unable or unwilling to share important information—such as concerns, mistakes, or needs—due to fear of retaliation, stigma, or judgment.

Business Application: Employees avoid reporting safety hazards because past whistleblowers were penalized.

Leadership Insight: Leaders can combat a non-disclosure culture by fostering psychological safety and creating clear, protective reporting channels.

Cultural Caution: Promoting disclosure without addressing why people remain silent can worsen mistrust.

Mosaic Question: What unspoken rules or fears prevent people from sharing openly in your environment?

Mosaic in Action: A healthcare organization introduces anonymous reporting and follow-up protocols by leaders, leading to a significant rise in reported near-misses and safety improvements.

Nonlinear Identity Development

Definition: The idea that identity formation is an ongoing, cyclical process shaped by shifting experiences, contexts, and self-awareness—not a one-time, fixed progression.

Business Application: A professional reshapes their cultural identity after relocating abroad, incorporating new perspectives into their self-concept.

Leadership Insight: Understanding nonlinear identity development enables leaders to better support individuals during transitions without anticipating fixed self-definitions.

Cultural Caution: Assuming identity development follows only a single linear path can dismiss people's lived experiences.

Mosaic Question: How does your environment enable people to reimagine and reshape their identities over time?

Mosaic in Action: A university alumni program updates its records to let graduates change personal information—such as names, pronouns, and cultural affiliations—reflecting ongoing identity development.

Nonverbal Communication

Definition: The transfer of information through body language, facial expressions, tone, gestures, and other nonverbal cues instead of words.

Business Application: A customer service representative keeps an open posture and maintains steady eye contact to show attentiveness and build trust.

Leadership Insight: Leaders who understand nonverbal communication can better interpret unspoken feedback and support their messages with consistent body language.

Cultural Caution: Nonverbal cues can mean different things across cultures; misreading them can cause misunderstandings or offend others.

Mosaic Question: How do you verify your assumptions about the meaning of nonverbal cues in cross-cultural environments?

Mosaic in Action: A cross-cultural training program teaches employees how gestures and eye contact vary around the world, enhancing communication with international clients.

Norm Disruption

Definition: The deliberate or accidental act of challenging established norms, routines, or expectations to create change or encourage reflection.

Business Application: An employee questions the tradition of holding all-staff meetings during standard school pick-up hours, prompting the company to reconsider its schedule.

Leadership Insight: Effective norm disruption can foster innovation and promote equity, but it requires skill to handle resistance.

Cultural Caution: Disrupting norms without a strategy or sensitivity to context can cause backlash and hinder change.

Mosaic Question: Which norms in your environment could be challenged to allow for progress?

Mosaic in Action: A tech firm replaces annual performance reviews with quarterly conversations, enhancing responsiveness and employee development.

Normalization

Definition: The process by which certain ideas, behaviors, or conditions become accepted as standard or "normal" within a society, organization, or culture.

Business Application: Remote work becomes standard after a company adopts it into normal policy, making it a common choice rather than an exception.

Leadership Insight: Leaders should assess what becomes normalized in their environments, as it shapes culture and impacts inclusion.

Cultural Caution: Normalization can strengthen harmful or exclusionary norms if not critically examined.

Mosaic Question: What practices or beliefs in your environment are considered "normal," and who benefits—or is harmed—by them?

Mosaic in Action: A school district standardizes the use of pronouns during introductions, making it a normal part of meetings instead of a special request, which increases comfort for gender-diverse participants.

439

Normative Disruption

Definition: The intentional challenge to dominant social, cultural, or institutional norms that determine what is considered acceptable or "normal," often to address systemic inequalities.

Business Application: A design team introduces non-gendered clothing lines, directly challenging gender norms in the fashion industry.

Leadership Insight: Normative disruption goes beyond minor operational changes to question the core assumptions shaping systems and culture.

Cultural Caution: Because it targets deeply rooted beliefs, normative disruption can trigger strong resistance and requires ongoing commitment.

Mosaic Question: What dominant norms in your environment need to be questioned or dismantled to promote true equity?

Mosaic in Action: A public health campaign uses images of diverse family structures to redefine what "healthy families" look like, increasing representation and acceptance.

Normative Whiteness

Definition: The unspoken assumption that white cultural norms, values, and ways of being are the default or standard used to judge all others.

Business Application: A company's "professional" dress code is based on Eurocentric aesthetics, subtly indicating that other cultural expressions are less acceptable.

Leadership Insight: Leaders who recognize normative whiteness can actively expand definitions of professionalism, excellence, and leadership to genuinely reflect diversity.

Cultural Caution: Not discussing normative whiteness allows inequality to persist and keeps exclusionary standards in place.

Mosaic Question: What unspoken cultural norms influence your environment, and who benefits from them?

Mosaic in Action: An organization updates its branding and marketing materials to include a variety of hairstyles, skin tones, and cultural expressions, challenging the idea of a single "professional" look.

Nostalgic Bias

Definition: The tendency to idealize the past and see it as better than the present, often ignoring historical unfairness or difficulties.

Business Application: A leadership team resists adopting flexible work policies because "things worked just fine" before, ignoring that the old system left out many caregivers.

Leadership Insight: Recognizing nostalgic bias helps leaders avoid holding on to traditions that no longer meet the needs of a changing workforce or society.

Cultural Caution: Nostalgic bias can romanticize past systems that were unfair to certain groups, making it harder to implement equity-focused changes.

Mosaic Question: Which parts of "the way things used to be" are worth keeping, and which should be left behind?

Mosaic in Action: A school district updates long-standing graduation requirements that once limited access for nontraditional students, acknowledging that "tradition" had concealed systemic barriers.

Nuanced Leadership

Definition: A leadership style that embraces complexity, avoids oversimplification, and adapts strategies to consider multiple perspectives and layered realities.

Business Application: A CEO navigates a merger by addressing both operational integration and cultural differences between teams, crafting solutions that benefit both.

Leadership Insight: Nuanced leadership balances decisiveness with curiosity, allowing space for contradictions while still driving progress.

Cultural Caution: Without clear communication, nuanced leadership might be mistaken for indecisiveness or lack of vision.

Mosaic Question: How do you incorporate complexity into decision-making without sacrificing clarity?

Mosaic in Action: A nonprofit director facilitates community discussions that respect conflicting views on a redevelopment project, finding a blended approach that reflects shared priorities.

◈ LETTER N CALLOUT

"Narratives shape power: the stories we tell decide who belongs, who is excluded, and what becomes possible."

Reflection Questions

- What dominant storylines shape your field or team, and who benefits from them?
- How can naming practices reinforce or disrupt bias?
- Where do you see nostalgia or nationalism being used to mask inequity?

Practical Move

Invite a team or class to share one counter-narrative to the "usual story" — and discuss what shifts when that story is centered.

O – Openness, Othering, and Organizational Culture

O prompts us to explore the gap between what organizations claim to value and what people truly experience. It reveals the truths hidden beneath polished statements—"inclusive" slogans, "safe space" declarations, and diversity taglines that promise openness but sometimes result in exclusion masked by civility.

At its best, openness fosters a culture of curiosity, respect, and courageous listening. It enables people to present themselves authentically, not just as they are polished to be. However, too often, openness becomes conditional—only extended to those who conform, agree, or mirror prevailing norms. This selective openness maintains superficial harmony while suppressing dissent, emotional honesty, and cultural differences.

Othering then takes hold, subtly dividing people into insiders and outsiders. It shows up when feedback is filtered through bias, when emotion is labeled as "unprofessional," or when "fit" becomes shorthand for sameness. These dynamics may go unspoken, but their impact is real disengagement, mistrust, burnout, and both literal and emotional resignation.

O asks us to recognize the hidden patterns that define culture

- Who gets interrupted—and who always finishes their thought.
- Whose mistakes are excused—and whose become defining.

- Who is praised as a "natural leader"—and who must prove themselves twice.
- Which voices are protected, and which are silenced to preserve comfort.

Organizational culture is not created by statements alone but through everyday choices of tone, timing, and trust. Culture exists in meetings, mentorship, conflict, and caring. Written values mean little unless they are reflected in action.

O calls on leaders to look beyond statements and ask tougher questions Who benefits from our transparency? Who is shut out by our silence? And what would it take for honesty, dissent, and difference to be valued as essential to growth? Because real openness is not just claimed — it's shown in how we treat each other when agreement is hard.

O

Obligation Culture

Definition: An environment in which individuals feel forced to participate, contribute, or stay involved because of duty, loyalty, or perceived expectations—rather than genuine choice.

Business Application: In workplaces with an obligation culture, employees attend after-hours events out of fear of appearing disengaged, not because they truly want to participate.

Leadership Insight: Leaders should distinguish between voluntary engagement and coerced participation, making sure people feel comfortable saying no without fear of repercussions.

Cultural Caution: Relying too much on obligation can diminish trust and autonomy, leading to burnout and silent resentment.

Mosaic Question: How can you foster conditions where participation is driven by real commitment instead of pressure?

Mosaic in Action: A department head replaces mandatory volunteer weekends with voluntary options and recognizes those who contribute in ways that match their abilities and interests.

Occupational Identity

Definition: The sense of self coming from one's job, trade, or role at work.

Business Application: A nurse might see caregiving as core to their identity, shaping how they interact with patients, colleagues, and challenges.

Leadership Insight: Leaders who understand their teams' occupational identities can link initiatives to personal meaning, boosting buy-in and resilience.

Cultural Caution: Over-identifying with a role can make career changes or organizational shifts feel like threats to self-worth.

Mosaic Question: How much of who you are is connected to what you do?

Mosaic in Action: During an organizational restructure, a leader hosts reflective sessions for employees to explore their strengths beyond job titles, easing the identity shift that comes with change.

Occupational Segregation

Definition: The distribution of workers across and within occupations based on demographic characteristics such as gender, race, ethnicity, or age, often caused by systemic barriers and bias.

Business Application: Women and people of color may be concentrated in support roles, while leadership positions are disproportionately held by men.

Leadership Insight: Tackling occupational segregation requires actively dismantling structural barriers, providing targeted mentorship, and ensuring fair promotion practices.

Cultural Caution: Superficial diversity efforts that ignore underlying segregation can create an illusion of equity without real progress.

Mosaic Question: What patterns in your organization suggest that certain groups are clustered into specific roles?

Mosaic in Action: A company reviews its job categories, identifies disproportionate representation, and develops targeted leadership pipelines to promote equity at senior levels.

Onboarding Culture

Definition: The set of norms, practices, and values communicated to new members when they join an organization, influencing their initial experiences and perceptions.

Business Application: A welcoming onboarding culture might involve mentorship pairings, clear role expectations, and integration into team rituals from the first day.

Leadership Insight: First impressions often shape long-term engagement—leaders who prioritize intentional onboarding foster stronger loyalty and alignment.

Cultural Caution: Poor onboarding can reinforce inequalities if new hires from underrepresented backgrounds are left to navigate unspoken norms alone.

Mosaic Question: How does your onboarding process reflect the values you claim to uphold?

Mosaic in Action: A nonprofit redesigns its onboarding process to include cultural competency training, ensuring every new employee begins with a shared foundation for inclusive collaboration.

Open-Door Policy Myth

Definition: The false belief that simply stating an "open-door policy" automatically encourages accessibility, trust, and open communication—without addressing the cultural or structural barriers that prevent people from speaking up.

Business Application: Leaders may promote their availability, but employees often remain silent due to fear of retaliation, doubts about follow-through, or previous dismissals.

Leadership Insight: An open door means little if the environment discourages honesty. Leaders must actively invite input, show vulnerability, and demonstrate that feedback results in action.

Cultural Caution: Relying solely on this policy without fostering psychological safety can create a false sense of transparency.

Mosaic Question: How do you show—not just say—that your door is genuinely open?

Mosaic in Action: After realizing few employees used her open-door hours, a manager starts scheduling regular one-on-one check-ins and following up on feedback to build real trust.

Opportunity Architecture

Definition: The intentional design of systems, policies, and pathways to ensure fair access to growth, advancement, and meaningful participation.

Business Application: An organization might develop structured mentorship programs, transparent promotion criteria, and targeted outreach to underrepresented groups as part of its opportunity architecture.

Leadership Insight: Leaders are not just gatekeepers of opportunities—they can also be architects who create new doors and redesign existing ones.

Cultural Caution: Even well-designed systems can fail if they are not continually evaluated for unintended bias or shifting barriers.

Mosaic Question: What opportunities in your organization happen by chance, and which ones are intentionally created?

Mosaic in Action: A university revamps its internship placement process to include rural students, offering stipends and remote options to eliminate geographic and financial barriers.

Opportunity Hoarding

Definition: The practice of individuals or groups amassing access, advantages, or resources—often through informal networks—while restricting access for others.

Business Application: Senior staff may keep key client accounts within a small circle, preventing others from gaining experience or visibility.

Leadership Insight: Hoarding opportunities damages team trust and limits organizational growth; leaders must actively share chances for development.

Cultural Caution: Opportunity hoarding often occurs unknowingly, disguised as "rewarding loyalty" or "protecting quality."

Mosaic Question: Who in your sphere has access to high-value assignments—and who never gets a chance?

Mosaic in Action: A law firm rotates lead counsel opportunities among associates instead of reserving them for a few, promoting broader skill development and exposure.

Operational Equity

Definition: Integrating fairness, inclusion, and justice into an organization's daily processes, systems, and decision-making—burs not just in its mission statements.

Business Application: This might include equitable hiring practices, transparent promotion paths, and inclusive procurement procedures embedded in routine operations.

Leadership Insight: Equity becomes sustainable only when it is part of the organization's core practices, not a sporadic or reactionary effort.

Cultural Caution: Operational equity fails when seen as a checklist rather than a continuous practice that requires accountability.

Mosaic Question: How does equity appear in the daily decisions your team makes?

Mosaic in Action: A school district changes budget allocation processes to include community advisory boards, ensuring resources reach historically underfunded schools.

Operational Transparency

Definition: The practice of making organizational processes transparent, understandable, and accountable to stakeholders.

Business Application: Operational transparency fosters trust, decreases rumors, and boosts confidence among customers and employees.

Leadership Insight: Transparent operations demonstrate that leaders have nothing to conceal and are responsible for their decisions.

Cultural Caution: Some cultures expect greater privacy in organizational decision-making. Leaders need to balance transparency with cultural and legal boundaries.

Mosaic Question: How much of your organization's process is transparent — and how much is hidden?

Mosaic in Action: A nonprofit posted its budget and decision-making schedules online, boosting donor confidence and staff support.

Oppression

Definition: A systemic pattern of unfairness, exclusion, and exploitation supported by social, political, and economic structures—often reinforced by cultural stories and institutional practices.

Business Application: In the workplace, oppression appears through wage gaps, biased performance reviews, or exclusion from decision-making roles.

Leadership Insight: Recognizing oppression involves going beyond individual prejudice to tackle the structural forces that sustain it.

Cultural Caution: Trying to "fix" oppression without understanding its historical background risks oversimplifying or ignoring the real experiences of affected groups.

Mosaic Question: What systems around you benefit from keeping certain groups disadvantaged—and how can you help dismantle them?

Mosaic in Action: A nonprofit moves from occasional cultural celebration events to policy advocacy that fights systemic inequalities in housing and education for marginalized communities.

Oppression Fatigue

Definition: The emotional, mental, and physical exhaustion experienced by individuals—often from marginalized groups—due to the constant need to navigate, resist, or educate others about systemic oppression.

Business Application: Employees may suffer burnout from repeated microaggressions, diversity "token" responsibilities, or the burden of advocating for change without enough support.

Leadership Insight: Leaders can lessen oppression fatigue by reallocating the labor of equity work, validating lived experiences, and making organizational change a shared responsibility.

Cultural Caution: Dismissing or minimizing fatigue as "oversensitivity" worsens harm and deepens inequalities.

Mosaic Question: Who in your organization bears the heaviest burden of explaining or challenging injustice—and how can you support them?

Mosaic in Action: A company rotates diversity training facilitation among trained staff from various backgrounds instead of always relying on employees from marginalized identities.

Oppression Literacy

Definition: The ability to recognize, understand, and respond to systemic and structural oppression. Oppression literacy extends beyond awareness to give leaders practical tools for action.

Business Application: Organizations use oppression literacy to create equitable policies, trainings, and interventions that break down exclusionary practices.

Leadership Insight: Leaders with oppression literacy can differentiate between personal bias and systemic injustice, enabling them to focus change where it is most effective.

Cultural Caution: Oppression manifests in various ways within societies. Literacy demands humility to understand context-specific histories and realities.

Mosaic Question: Do you understand the difference between personal prejudice and systemic oppression in your leadership choices?

Mosaic in Action: A leadership team updates hiring policies after discovering how systemic credential barriers disproportionately exclude candidates from marginalized communities.

Oral Tradition

Definition: The cultural practice of passing knowledge, history, values, and identity through spoken word, storytelling, song, and performance across generations.

Business Application: Oral traditions can be incorporated into leadership development, onboarding, and team culture-building by capturing and sharing origin stories, lessons, and values.

Leadership Insight: Respect for oral tradition involves valuing storytelling as a legitimate and powerful form of knowledge, not just a supplement to written records.

Cultural Caution: Misappropriating or commodifying oral traditions without respecting their origins and custodians risks cultural theft and distortion.

Mosaic Question: What knowledge in your community is at risk of being lost if it is not spoken and shared?

Mosaic in Action: An Indigenous-owned consulting firm begins meetings with brief cultural narratives that connect current projects to ancestral values and practices.

Organizational Accountability

Definition: A system of transparency and accountability within organizations where leaders and institutions are held responsible for equity, culture, and ethical practices.

Business Application: Organizational accountability appears in regular equity audits, transparent pay scales, and published progress on inclusion goals.

Leadership Insight: Accountability fosters trust. Leaders who invite scrutiny show that integrity is more important than appearances.

Cultural Caution: Accountability might face resistance in cultures with hierarchies or high power distance. Leaders must adjust their approaches while upholding core principles.

Mosaic Question: Does your organization really practice accountability — or just talk about it?

Mosaic in Action: A nonprofit board releases yearly diversity metrics along with financial reports, incorporating equity into its accountability framework.

Organizational Belonging

Definition: A lasting sense of inclusion, trust, and value experienced by individuals within a workplace or institution, based on genuine relationships and fair systems.

Business Application: Strong organizational belonging is associated with higher retention, engagement, and innovation. It is developed through inclusive policies, leadership example, and shared decision-making.

Leadership Insight: Belonging is not created through perks or slogans but through consistent alignment between declared values and everyday experiences.

Cultural Caution: Overemphasizing "fitting in" can pressure individuals to conform at the cost of their true identity.

Mosaic Question: How does your organization actively make space for people to show up fully as themselves?

Mosaic in Action: A global tech company creates mentorship programs pairing employees from different regions and cultural backgrounds, encouraging connections beyond immediate teams.

Organizational Culture

Definition: The shared values, norms, beliefs, and practices that influence how people within an organization interact, make decisions, and interpret success.

Business Application: Organizational culture affects hiring, leadership styles, communication norms, and how well an organization adapts to change.

Leadership Insight: Healthy cultures are intentionally cultivated; unhealthy ones continue by default. Leaders establish the tone through what they prioritize and reward.

Cultural Caution: Believing that culture is fixed ignores its ability to change through intentional efforts and inclusive leadership.

Mosaic Question: What unspoken rules influence behavior in your organization, and do they match your stated mission?

Mosaic in Action: A nonprofit moves from hierarchical approval processes to collaborative decision-making, boosting transparency and trust across teams.

Organizational Gaslighting

Definition: A pattern where an organization dismisses, distorts, or denies valid concerns or experiences, causing individuals to doubt their perceptions or reality.

Business Application: This can happen during performance reviews, grievance procedures, or diversity initiatives, where feedback is invalidated or reframed to protect the organization.

Leadership Insight: Combating organizational gaslighting requires transparent communication, accountability, and genuine responsiveness to concerns.

Cultural Caution: Downplaying or reframing harm damages trust more quickly than the original problem and can result in long-term reputational harm.

Mosaic Question: How does your organization react when someone raises a difficult truth?

Mosaic in Action: An employee reports discriminatory behavior, and instead of minimizing it, leadership promptly investigates, shares findings, and enforces policy changes.

Organizational Gatekeeping

Definition: The act of controlling or restricting access to opportunities, resources, or decision-making processes within an organization—often influenced by bias, hierarchy, or politics.

Business Application: Gatekeeping can be seen in selective promotion criteria, limited networks, or requiring unnecessary credentials that exclude capable candidates.

Leadership Insight: True leadership broadens access and helps more people contribute meaningfully, rather than safeguarding power for a few.

Cultural Caution: Gatekeeping disguised as "maintaining standards" often protects privilege rather than genuine quality or integrity.

Mosaic Question: Who decides who gets access—and what criteria do they use?

Mosaic in Action: A professional association updates its membership requirements to acknowledge lived experience alongside formal qualifications, diversifying its leadership pipeline.

Organizational Justice

Definition: The sense of fairness in organizational procedures, results, and interpersonal interactions.

Business Application: High organizational justice boosts trust, engagement, and loyalty, while low justice raises turnover and conflict.

Leadership Insight: Leaders promote justice by guaranteeing fairness in decision-making, openness in communication, and equality in resource allocation.

Cultural Caution: Justice expectations differ across cultures. Leaders need to adjust fairness practices to fit local norms.

Mosaic Question: Do your justice systems make people feel safe, seen, and fairly treated?

Mosaic in Action: An agency implemented participatory evaluation methods, making sure staff could contribute to fairness assessments.

Organizational Learning

Definition: The process through which organizations adapt, grow, and transform by reflecting on experiences, mistakes, and successes.

Business Application: Organizational learning helps companies enhance culture, foster innovation, and respond effectively to complex challenges.

Leadership Insight: Leaders who promote organizational learning encourage reflection, feedback, and adaptation. They view mistakes not as failures but as chances to grow.

Cultural Caution: Some organizational cultures prioritize efficiency over learning. Without intentional effort, learning may be undervalued or rushed.

Mosaic Question: Does your organization punish mistakes — or learn from them?

Mosaic in Action: A global firm forms learning circles after project failures, turning setbacks into systemic improvements.

Organizational Norms

Definition: Unwritten rules, behaviors, and expectations that influence how members of an organization act, interact, and make decisions.

Business Application: Organizational norms shape communication styles, decision-making speed, meeting etiquette, and responses to conflict or change.

Leadership Insight: Norms often have a greater impact than formal policies—leaders must demonstrate and support the ones they want to flourish.

Cultural Caution: Unexamined norms can uphold exclusion, especially when they mirror the preferences of the dominant group instead of collective consensus.

Mosaic Question: Which norms in your organization promote equity and belonging—and which ones quietly undermine them?

Mosaic in Action: A leadership team replaces the norm of "speaking up only when spoken to" with organized open forums, ensuring diverse voices are heard in decision-making.

Organizational Resilience Mapping

Definition: A strategic process for identifying strengths, vulnerabilities, and adaptive capacities within an organization to prepare for and recover from disruption.

Business Application: Resilience mapping supports organizations in risk management, change initiatives, and crisis response by helping them allocate resources and develop recovery strategies.

Leadership Insight: Resilience is developed before disruptions—mapping offers a guide for action when the unexpected happens.

Cultural Caution: Focusing solely on operational resilience while neglecting relational or cultural resilience makes the organization vulnerable to internal failure.

Mosaic Question: How prepared is your organization to handle both external shocks and internal cultural challenges?

Mosaic in Action: A healthcare nonprofit performs yearly resilience mapping, focusing on staff wellbeing, to improve crisis preparedness without lowering morale.

Organizational Silence

Definition: A culture where employees withhold ideas, concerns, or dissent because they fear retaliation, futility, or exclusion.

Business Application: Organizational silence suppresses innovation and creates blind spots for risk management and equity. Breaking silence requires psychological safety.

Leadership Insight: Leaders must actively encourage and safeguard voices. Silence isn't neutrality — it's a sign of fear and mistrust.

Cultural Caution: In certain cultures, silence signifies respect. Leaders need to distinguish between cultural communication customs and toxic silence.

Mosaic Question: Is silence in your organization a choice — or a way to survive?

Mosaic in Action: An engineering team establishes anonymous feedback channels after recognizing employees' fear of speaking up during safety reviews.

Organizational Trauma

Definition: Collective psychological and cultural harm experienced by an organization's members after a significant event, pattern of harm, or extended stress.

Business Application: Common after layoffs, scandals, leadership abuses, or ongoing crises, organizational trauma can diminish trust, engagement, and performance.

Leadership Insight: Healing organizational trauma requires transparent leadership, restorative practices, and a deliberate effort to rebuild trust.

Cultural Caution: Ignoring the emotional impact of organizational events risks normalizing dysfunction and losing top talent.

Mosaic Question: What harm has your organization not yet acknowledged — and what healing is still needed?

Mosaic in Action: After a major restructuring, leadership conducts facilitated listening sessions, implements staff-led policy reforms, and invests in team rebuilding.

Optics Culture

Definition: An organizational environment where appearances of inclusion, progress, or accountability are prioritized over genuine systemic change.

Business Application: Leaders might display diversity in marketing materials while neglecting pay inequities or retention issues.

Leadership Insight: Optics-focused strategies may protect reputation temporarily but can damage credibility if actions don't align with appearances.

Cultural Caution: Symbolic gestures without real substance can alienate the communities the organization aims to engage.

Mosaic Question: How do you make sure your organization's image truly reflects reality rather than just covering it up?

Mosaic in Action: After hosting a prominent diversity event, a company reviews its leadership diversity and invests in internal equity efforts before the next public campaign.

Othering

Definition: The process of perceiving or portraying individuals or groups as fundamentally different, inferior, or outside the accepted "us."

Business Application: Othering often appears in hiring, promotions, and project assignments, affecting who is included or excluded from influence.

Leadership Insight: Inclusive leadership actively interrupts othering by affirming shared humanity and creating space for difference without hierarchy.

Cultural Caution: Well-intentioned diversity efforts can still other people when they highlight them only as "representatives" of their group.

Mosaic Question: Where in your workplace might difference be turned into distance?

Mosaic in Action: In a global company, leaders replace token "diversity panels" with cross-cultural project teams where collaboration—not identity labels—drives interaction.

Outcome Equity

Definition: Fairness in the results or impacts of a policy, decision, or process, ensuring that all groups benefit equally, not just in opportunity but in measurable outcomes.

Business Application: Organizations use outcome equity metrics to evaluate whether diversity and inclusion initiatives generate real benefits across all demographics.

Leadership Insight: Measuring equity involves more than tracking participation; it requires assessing how results are distributed.

Cultural Caution: Focusing only on equal inputs without tackling systemic barriers can lead to unfair outcomes, even with fair processes.

Mosaic Question: Whose results are you measuring—and do they reflect the full scope of equity?

Mosaic in Action: A company reviews promotion data and finds that, although all groups have equal access to leadership training, promotion rates are lower for women of color, prompting the implementation of a targeted mentorship program.

Outgroup Bias

Definition: The tendency to see individuals outside one's perceived group less favorably, often leading to mistrust, stereotyping, or exclusion.

Business Application: Outgroup bias can damage collaboration in cross-departmental teams, global partnerships, and client relationships.

Leadership Insight: Leaders need to deliberately build trust across group boundaries to counteract bias and promote cooperation.

Cultural Caution: Even unconscious outgroup bias can cause subtle but lasting harm to morale, innovation, and retention.

Mosaic Question: Which groups are most likely to be viewed as "them" in your workplace—and how can you include them as part of "us"?

Mosaic in Action: A tech company pairs engineers from different regions on innovation projects, breaking down outgroup perceptions through shared success.

Outsider Within

Definition: A person who belongs to an organization or group but remains socially or culturally marginalized within it, often navigating dual identities.

Business Application: Outsider within experiences can provide valuable perspectives but also cause emotional and mental strain.

Leadership Insight: These individuals can act as bridges between different viewpoints if given support, but without recognition and a sense of belonging, they risk burnout.

Cultural Caution: Assuming someone is fully included because of their position or tenure can overlook the subtle exclusions they face every day.

Mosaic Question: Who in your organization is present but not fully accepted—and what would true inclusion look like for them?

Mosaic in Action: An executive coach works with a mid-level manager who feels excluded from informal leadership networks

despite years of service, helping them build strategic alliances.

Outsourcing Diversity

Definition: Relying on external consultants, programs, or hires to meet diversity goals without embedding inclusion and equity into the organization's culture.

Business Application: While experts can offer valuable insights, lasting change requires internal ownership of diversity initiatives.

Leadership Insight: True diversity work is not a one-time event—it's an ingrained practice that leaders must demonstrate and uphold.

Cultural Caution: Outsourcing diversity efforts without internal accountability may give the illusion of progress while systemic issues remain unaddressed.

Mosaic Question: Are your diversity efforts something you do—or something you embody?

Mosaic in Action: A company shifts from annual DEI workshops conducted by outside firms to continuous, leader-driven equity councils that influence everyday decisions.

Outrage Fatigue

Definition: Emotional exhaustion caused by ongoing exposure to injustice, crises, or societal conflicts, which diminishes the ability to respond effectively.

Business Application: In organizations, outrage fatigue can result in disengagement from key causes or initiatives if employees feel overwhelmed by constant demands to act.

Leadership Insight: Leaders can help prevent outrage fatigue by managing communication frequency, focusing on priority areas, and providing resources for recovery.

Cultural Caution: Ignoring outrage fatigue may cause important social issues to lose momentum—not because they are resolved, but because people feel emotionally drained.

Mosaic Question: How can you sustain attention on injustice without exhausting your capacity to act?

Mosaic in Action: A nonprofit moves from constant crisis alerts to a quarterly action plan, enabling staff and volunteers to balance advocacy with rest.

Over-Identification

Definition: Becoming so aligned with a person, role, or group that personal boundaries blur and objectivity is compromised.

Business Application: Over-identification can lead leaders to avoid necessary feedback, make biased decisions, or carry emotional burdens that should be shared.

Leadership Insight: Empathy is powerful but needs to be balanced with perspective to prevent enabling unhealthy dynamics.

Cultural Caution: Over-identifying with a marginalized group one is not part of can unintentionally center your experience instead of theirs.

Mosaic Question: Where might your empathy be shifting into over-identification—and what boundaries could help restore balance?

Mosaic in Action: A manager working closely with a struggling team member realizes they have absorbed the employee's stress and begins directing them toward professional support.

Overcompensation

Definition: Excessive effort to fix perceived flaws, disadvantages, or mistakes, often leading to imbalance or inauthentic behavior.

Business Application: In the workplace, overcompensation can look like overworking, excessive self-promotion, or overemphasizing a single skill to hide perceived weaknesses.

Leadership Insight: While trying to improve is healthy, overcompensation can create pressure that damages trust and teamwork.

Cultural Caution: Overcompensating in cross-cultural settings can result in performative inclusion rather than building genuine relationships.

Mosaic Question: Where might your drive for excellence border on overcompensation—and what would balance look like?

Mosaic in Action: After being told she lacked "executive presence," a director overcompensates with formal, scripted interactions—until feedback helps her adopt a more authentic leadership style.

Overtalking

Definition: Dominating conversations to the extent that others' contributions are minimized, interrupted, or silenced.

Business Application: Over-talking in meetings suppresses collaboration, discourages diverse perspectives, and can harm team morale.

Leadership Insight: Effective leaders intentionally create space for others to speak, especially those whose voices are less often heard.

Cultural Caution: In some cultures, silence is a sign of respect or reflection—not a lack of ideas. Over-talking can unintentionally violate these norms.

Mosaic Question: Who in your conversations is being overshadowed, and how can you make space for their voice?

Mosaic in Action: A project leader notices they're answering every question in a client meeting; they start redirecting responses to junior team members to highlight their expertise.

Overwork Culture

Definition: An organizational norm that promotes excessive work hours, self-sacrifice, and productivity at the expense of health, equity, and sustainability.

Business Application: Overwork culture causes burnout, unfair workloads, and talent drain. Tackling it boosts retention and innovation.

Leadership Insight: Leaders who model balance challenge overwork culture and create healthier, more sustainable performance environments.

Cultural Caution: In some industries or cultures, overwork is praised. Leaders need to carefully change values without dismissing strongly held norms.

Mosaic Question: Does your organization encourage overwork — or sustainable excellence?

Mosaic in Action: A law firm updates performance metrics to focus on impact and innovation instead of just billable hours, lowering overwork pressures.

Ownership vs. Access

Definition: The difference between having full control over a resource or decision (ownership) and merely having permission to use or be involved in it (access).

Business Application: Equity efforts must consider both—providing access without ownership can lead to dependency and limit influence.

Leadership Insight: True empowerment involves not only creating opportunities but also transferring decision-making authority and control of resources.

Cultural Caution: Offering symbolic access without genuine ownership can cause mistrust and disengagement.

Mosaic Question: Are you giving others real ownership—or just temporary access?

Mosaic in Action: A community program moves from providing local leaders with access to meeting space to giving them co-ownership of the facility, fostering long-term influence and investment.

◈ LETTER O CALLOUT

"Organizations are living systems; their culture is revealed in what is rewarded, ignored, or silenced."

Reflection Questions

- What signals tell you an organization values equity — or just optics?
- How do silence and gatekeeping shape organizational norms?
- Where is accountability strongest or weakest in your setting?

Practical Move

Map one recurring organizational practice (onboarding, evaluation, meetings). Identify where equity is reinforced — and where silence or avoidance holds sway.

P – Power, Privilege, and Psychological Safety

P represents the forces that shape outcomes long before a decision is made or a voice is raised. Power influences who is heard, who is believed, and who can stay whole in systems built more for speed than for care. Privilege affects how feedback is received, how leadership is judged, and how mistakes are interpreted—either as forgivable growth or as defining flaws. And psychological safety, often mistaken for comfort, is the foundation of equity, innovation, and sustainable performance.

This section offers language to analyze the structures of influence and exclusion. It asks Who has decision-making power? Who is accepted without question? And how does proximity to dominant norms—whether in race, gender, accent, or education—distort perceptions of credibility, opportunity, and belonging?

P asks us to surface the unspoken calculations many professionals carry

- How much of myself can I share without facing consequences?
- Will honesty be seen as courage—or punished as defiance?
- Whose "professionalism" is rewarded, and whose authenticity is penalized?
- Who enjoys psychological safety as a given, and who must earn it at great cost?

The P terms reveal the hidden rules behind performance, the coded expectations of "presence," and the narrow scripts of legitimacy that demand conformity rather than authenticity. They demonstrate how unchecked power sustains harm and how privilege determines not only who advances but also whose humanity is maintained in the process.

Leading with integrity involves more than just making inclusion statements. It requires rebalancing attention, resources, and safety. It means using power not to protect oneself from harm but to dismantle it, and ensuring psychological safety is a right for everyone—not a privilege for just a few.

P urges leaders to address how power and privilege operate quietly—and to commit to creating cultures where safety is a fundamental, not conditional. Because true leadership is about protecting wholeness, not just maintaining control.

P

Parental Bias

Definition: The unfair treatment of caregivers, especially parents, rooted in assumptions about their availability, dedication, or productivity.

Business Application: Parental bias sidelines employees, often women, from promotions or high-visibility projects, maintaining inequality.

Leadership Insight: Leaders combat bias by viewing caregiving as a strength instead of a liability and creating fair policies.

Cultural Caution: Expectations regarding caregiving vary worldwide. Leaders should refrain from applying Western-centered standards to family roles.

Mosaic Question: Do you assume caregivers are less committed — or have different resources?

Mosaic in Action: A consulting firm revised its promotion processes after discovering that parents were often overlooked for stretch assignments.

Passing

Definition: Presenting oneself in a way that conceals or downplays an aspect of identity to avoid discrimination or gain acceptance.

Business Application: In professional settings, passing can occur when employees hide a disability, ethnicity, religion, or sexual orientation to fit perceived norms.

Leadership Insight: Leaders who foster psychologically safe environments reduce the pressure for individuals to pass, encouraging authentic contributions.

Cultural Caution: Passing may be a survival tactic, but it can also negatively impact mental health and community bonds.

Mosaic Question: Which parts of yourself—or others—are being hidden to meet expectations?

Mosaic in Action: An employee who previously avoided mentioning their same-sex partner begins openly sharing personal updates after their workplace adopts inclusive policies.

Paternalism

Definition: When authority figures restrict the autonomy of others because they believe it is for their own good.

Business Application: In organizations, paternalism may show up as leadership making unilateral decisions "for the team's benefit" without real input.

Leadership Insight: Protecting people from risk shouldn't mean taking away their agency; collaborative decision-making fosters trust.

Cultural Caution: Paternalism often sustains unequal power dynamics, especially across cultural, gender, or socioeconomic lines.

Mosaic Question: Are you making choices for others that they could—and should—make for themselves?

Mosaic in Action: A manager pre-approves all professional development opportunities for their team "to avoid overload," until feedback leads to a shift toward self-selection.

Patriarchy

Definition: A system of social structures and practices where men hold primary power, influencing institutions, culture, and resources.

Business Application: Patriarchal norms can restrict leadership chances for women and non-binary people, impacting hiring, pay, and promotion.

Leadership Insight: Tackling patriarchy in the workplace involves challenging both structural barriers and everyday cultural beliefs.

Cultural Caution: Patriarchy varies across different cultural contexts—solutions should be adapted rather than copied exactly.

Mosaic Question: Where do patriarchal assumptions appear in your systems—and how can they be broken down?

Mosaic in Action: A company reviews its promotion practices and notices women are often passed over for senior technical roles; it then introduces transparent, bias-aware criteria.

Pay Equity

Definition: Ensuring fair, transparent, and proportionate compensation for work performed, regardless of gender, race, or other identity factors.

Business Application: Pay equity audits help organizations identify and fix systemic disparities in salary, bonuses, and benefits.

Leadership Insight: Committing to pay equity is not just about compliance—it's about building credibility and keeping diverse talent.

Cultural Caution: Pay equity efforts must consider intersectional disparities; addressing gender without addressing race can leave inequities unaddressed.

Mosaic Question: Who in your organization is doing the same work for less pay—and why?

Mosaic in Action: After a pay audit finds disparities, a nonprofit adjusts salaries and releases annual transparency reports.

Pay Transparency

Definition: The transparent sharing of salary ranges, pay structures, and compensation decisions to decrease disparities and foster trust.

Business Application: Pay transparency helps reduce gender and racial wage gaps, improves retention, and promotes fairness in hiring and promotions.

Leadership Insight: Leaders who embrace pay transparency demonstrate confidence in fair practices and a dedication to accountability.

Cultural Caution: In some cultures, talking about pay is taboo.

Leaders need to adjust strategies to respect the context while making sure things are fair.

Mosaic Question: What would your workplace be like if everyone understood how pay is decided?

Mosaic in Action: A tech company started publishing salary bands internally, which resulted in a noticeable decrease in wage gaps across genders.

Performative Allyship

Definition: Publicly showing support for marginalized groups without engaging in meaningful, ongoing efforts to address inequalities.

Business Application: Examples include companies posting solidarity messages during heritage months but neglecting to address internal biases or unfair practices.

Leadership Insight: Genuine allyship is demonstrated through consistent, behind-the-scenes actions, not just visible statements.

Cultural Caution: Performative acts can damage trust and harm the very communities they claim to support.

Mosaic Question: How do your actions match your stated values—and who would agree with that assessment?

Mosaic in Action: An organization moves from issuing generic diversity statements to funding employee-led inclusion initiatives and measuring their impact.

Perfectionism Culture

Definition: A workplace or social environment that rewards flawless performance and punishes mistakes, often hindering creativity and risk-taking.

Business Application: In high-stakes industries, perfectionism culture can cause burnout, slow innovation, and lead to fear-based decision-making.

Leadership Insight: Leaders who normalize learning from mistakes promote growth, resilience, and adaptive problem-solving.

Cultural Caution: Perfectionism may stem from cultural stories about worth and respectability—addressing it requires exploring these deeper causes.

Mosaic Question: How does your workplace handle mistakes—and what does that say about its values?

Mosaic in Action: A tech team leader starts "failure showcases," where teams share lessons from unsuccessful projects to reduce fear of risk.

Perspective-Taking

Definition: The ability to see a situation from another person's cultural, emotional, or experiential point of view.

Business Application: Perspective-taking enhances cross-functional teamwork, especially in diverse teams or global collaborations.

Leadership Insight: Leaders who regularly practice perspective-taking make fairer and more empathetic decisions.

Cultural Caution: True perspective-taking requires humility—it's not about assuming you fully understand someone else's experience, but about staying open to correction.

Mosaic Question: Whose perspective is missing from your current decision—and how can you include it?

Mosaic in Action: During a policy review, a manager asks for feedback from employees in multiple countries to better understand cultural influences.

Pipeline Problem Myth

Definition: The false narrative that underrepresentation stems from a lack of qualified diverse candidates, rather than systemic exclusion in hiring and advancement.

Business Application: Believing in the pipeline myth excuses organizations from accountability for inequality, instead blaming candidates rather than systems.

Leadership Insight: Equitable leaders address barriers in recruitment, promotion, and culture instead of just using "pipeline" rhetoric to excuse inequity.

Cultural Caution: Pipeline myths vary, such as gender in tech or caste in South Asia. Leaders must adapt responses to local contexts.

Mosaic Question: Do you blame the pipeline — or evaluate your practices?

Mosaic in Action: A corporation partnered with historically Black colleges and women-in-STEM groups, disproving its "pipeline problem" excuse.

Platform Equity

Definition: Ensuring fair access to opportunities for visibility, voice, and influence within an organization or community.

Business Application: In meetings, platform equity involves deliberately creating space for those

whose voices are often marginalized or overlooked.

Leadership Insight: Leaders who redistribute airtime and visibility promote innovation and inclusion.

Cultural Caution: Equity is not about sameness—some individuals may require more intentional amplification to reach balance.

Mosaic Question: Who consistently has the microphone in your space—and who never gets the chance?

Mosaic in Action: At a conference, organizers set quotas for diverse panel representation and train moderators to prevent a few voices from dominating the panel.

Pluralism

Definition: An approach within society or organizations that actively values and maintains diverse cultural, religious, and ideological viewpoints.

Business Application: Pluralistic workplaces develop policies, benefits, and communication strategies that reflect multiple traditions and perspectives, preventing any single group's norms from dominating.

Leadership Insight: Leaders in pluralistic settings must manage complexity without defaulting to the comfort or convenience of the majority.

Cultural Caution: Pluralism is more than mere representation—it demands equitable participation and shared influence.

Mosaic Question: In your sphere of influence, is diversity only visible on paper, or does it influence decision-making in practice?

Mosaic in Action: A school board invites leaders from different faith communities to collaboratively create an inclusive holiday calendar that balances community needs with commitments to equity.

Policy Capture

Definition:: When public policy or institutional regulations are influenced more by corporate or special interests than by the needs of the broader community.

Business Application: Policy capture erodes trust and can reinforce inequalities, particularly in sectors like healthcare, education, or finance where lobbying influence distorts results.

Leadership Insight:: Leaders who recognize and oppose policy capture promote transparency and focus on decisions that benefit people over profit.

Cultural Caution:: In some situations, questioning policy influence can be politically risky; leaders need to balance bravery with strategy.

Mosaic Question:: Who gains the most from the policies shaping your industry—and who is excluded?

Mosaic in Action:: A city council reviews zoning laws influenced by developers and revises them to focus on affordable housing, restoring fairness to the policy process.

Politeness Culture

Definition: A social or workplace environment where civility is prioritized over addressing real issues or conflicts.

Business Application: While politeness can promote surface harmony, it may also prevent necessary conversations about inequality or misconduct.

Leadership Insight: Effective leaders understand when to set aside politeness in favor of honest dialogue.

Cultural Caution: In some cultures, indirectness is respectful; in others, it can be seen as avoidance or insincerity.

Mosaic Question: How often do you choose "being nice" over being honest—and at whose expense?

Mosaic in Action: A nonprofit replaces its unwritten "don't rock the boat" mindset with facilitated dialogue training to address tensions effectively.

Positionality

Definition: The awareness of how one's social, cultural, and professional positions affect perception, privilege, and interactions.

Business Application: Understanding positionality helps leaders see how their identity and role influence their access to resources and decision-making power.

Leadership Insight: Leaders who acknowledge their positionality build trust by recognizing both their influence and their blind spots.

Cultural Caution: Positionality is fluid—it changes depending on context, culture, and the identities of those involved.

Mosaic Question: How does your position help you see some things clearly while making others invisible?

Mosaic in Action: A CEO leading a diversity effort shares their own journey of privilege and learning before inviting employee stories.

Postcolonial Lens

Definition: A way of examining systems, narratives, and relationships that considers the lasting effects of colonial history and power structures.

Business Application: Using a postcolonial lens in global operations can uncover hidden inequities in supply chains, partnerships, and branding.

Leadership Insight: Leaders applying this lens avoid repeating extractive practices by prioritizing mutual benefit and cultural respect.

Cultural Caution: A postcolonial lens demands deep humility—good intentions alone cannot undo centuries of structural harm.

Mosaic Question: Whose history is missing from the stories your organization tells—and who benefits from that omission?

Mosaic in Action: A tourism company redesigns its marketing to recognize Indigenous histories of the lands it promotes, collaborating with local communities for co-authored narratives.

Post-Traumatic Growth (Organizational)

Definition:: The process through which individuals and organizations discover resilience, innovation, and renewed purpose after facing crisis or trauma.

Business Application: Organizations that deliberately process trauma—such as layoffs, disasters, or scandals—can develop stronger cultures and more adaptable systems.

Leadership Insight:: Growth after trauma requires leaders to view hardship as both a loss and a learning opportunity, honoring pain while pointing toward possibility.

Cultural Caution:: Not all trauma leads to growth; forcing "positivity" can suppress grief and cause more harm. Growth needs to be natural and genuine.

Mosaic Question:: What strength or clarity did your team gain after the disruption?

Mosaic in Action:: A nonprofit impacted by a financial scandal rebuilds trust by adopting new transparency practices and involving staff in rewriting its values, leading to renewed commitment.

Power Dynamics

Definition: The changing patterns of influence, control, and authority within relationships, teams, or systems.

Business Application: Understanding power dynamics helps leaders anticipate resistance, distribute resources fairly, and correct imbalances that hinder collaboration.

Leadership Insight: Leaders who can identify and name existing power flows—both formal and informal—are better equipped to create equity.

Cultural Caution: Power manifests differently across cultures; a behavior seen as assertive in one context might be perceived as overstepping in another.

Mosaic Question: Who holds influence in your environment without an official title—and how does that impact outcomes?

Mosaic in Action: A project manager notices a veteran staffer's informal influence and deliberately involves them to advocate for a new initiative.

Power Literacy

Definition: The skill to recognize, interpret, and navigate how power functions in different settings.

Business Application: Power-literate teams can challenge unfair systems, advocate effectively, and decide when to push forward, collaborate, or hold back.

Leadership Insight: Without power literacy, leaders might unintentionally strengthen the hierarchies they aim to dismantle.

Cultural Caution: Discussions about power can trigger defensiveness—approach them with clarity, evidence, and emotional intelligence.

Mosaic Question: When you think about power, do you see it only as control—or also as a shared resource?

Mosaic in Action: An executive team receives training on structural power, revealing how decision-making processes marginalize certain departments.

Power Over vs. Power With

Definition: Two contrasting leadership paradigms: power over involves control and dominance, while power with promotes collaboration, shared agency, and collective strength.

Business Application: Switching from power over to power with fosters inclusive cultures, breaks down hierarchies, and elevates marginalized voices.

Leadership Insight: Leaders increase their impact when they share power instead of hoarding it, turning authority into teamwork.

Cultural Caution: In high power-distance cultures, "power with" might seem unfamiliar or even intimidating. Leaders need to find a balance between collaboration and cultural expectations.

Mosaic Question: Do you lead by dominating or by partnering?

Mosaic in Action: A school superintendent replaced top-down mandates with shared decision-making councils, boosting buy-in and enhancing outcomes.

Power Sharing

Definition: The intentional redistribution of decision-making authority and resources to include more voices in shaping outcomes.

Business Application: Power sharing can boost innovation, trust, and retention by making team members feel genuinely invested in results.

Leadership Insight: Sharing power doesn't mean giving up responsibility; it means expanding ownership.

Cultural Caution: Power sharing demands follow-through; inviting input without acting on it erodes trust faster than exclusion.

Mosaic Question: Who could make better decisions if given the same access you have?

Mosaic in Action: A school district shifts budget decisions from central office administrators to a council that includes teachers, parents, and students.

Predictive Leadership

Definition: A leadership style that predicts future trends, challenges, and opportunities by using data, pattern recognition, and foresight.

Business Application: Predictive leaders combine analytics with human insight to adjust strategies before crises occur.

Leadership Insight: Anticipation is not about guessing; it's about preparing for multiple possible futures.

Cultural Caution: Predictive tools can reflect cultural and historical biases; ensure they are complemented with diverse perspectives.

Mosaic Question: What future patterns are already evident in your organization's current behaviors?

Mosaic in Action: A nonprofit monitors early changes in donor engagement and adjusts its outreach strategy months before funding gaps develop.

Prejudice

Definition: A preconceived opinion or judgment about a person or group, often negative, formed without enough knowledge or facts.

Business Application: Prejudice in hiring, promotion, or team assignments can restrict talent pipelines and hinder diversity goals.

Leadership Insight: Recognizing and confronting prejudice openly is crucial for building cultures where merit and potential—rather than bias—shape opportunities.

Cultural Caution: Prejudice can be obvious or subtle; both damage trust and can reinforce systemic inequalities.

Mosaic Question: What assumptions do you hold about others before they even speak?

Mosaic in Action: A manager notices themselves making a quick judgment based on an applicant's accent and decides to review resumes without identifiers before interviews.

Privilege

Definition: Unearned advantages or access granted to individuals or groups based on identity factors such as race, gender, class, or ability.

Business Application: Recognizing privilege helps leaders identify where processes or systems unintentionally favor some while disadvantaging others.

Leadership Insight: Awareness of one's privilege is a starting point for equitable leadership, not an endpoint.

Cultural Caution: Privilege conversations can trigger defensiveness; frame them as opportunities for shared responsibility and change.

Mosaic Question: Where do you have access others do not—and what can you do with it?

Mosaic in Action: A senior executive uses their influence to ensure junior staff from underrepresented backgrounds are invited to high-profile client meetings.

Privilege Erosion

Definition: The perceived or actual reduction of benefits previously enjoyed by individuals or groups, often due to a shift toward greater equity or inclusion.

Business Application: Leaders should anticipate and manage resistance from those who see equity initiatives as losses rather than shared benefits.

Leadership Insight: Addressing privilege erosion involves reframing equity as a positive outcome, not a zero-sum situation.

Cultural Caution: Perceptions of erosion can be just as impactful as real loss; both can cause backlash if ignored.

Mosaic Question: How can you help others view inclusion as an expansion rather than a threat?

Mosaic in Action: After adopting a fairer bonus system, a company hosts open forums to address concerns from employees accustomed to disproportionate rewards.

Privilege Fragility

Definition: Discomfort, defensiveness, or denial expressed when individuals with privilege are confronted with evidence of systemic inequities.

Business Application: Fragility can undermine diversity efforts if not anticipated; leaders must foster conditions for constructive discomfort.

Leadership Insight: Privilege fragility is not a moral failing—it is a developmental challenge that can be guided toward awareness and action.

Cultural Caution: Avoid shaming; instead, combine accountability with opportunities for growth and contribution.

Mosaic Question: How do you respond when your advantage is pointed out?

Mosaic in Action: During a leadership retreat, a participant reacts defensively to discussions of gender pay gaps; the facilitator employs structured dialogue to transform defensiveness into inquiry.

Professional Burnout

Definition:: A condition of ongoing physical, emotional, and mental exhaustion caused by long-term workplace stress, often related to systemic issues.

Business Application: Burnout lowers productivity, raises healthcare costs, and accelerates turnover, creating a human and organizational crisis.

Leadership Insight:: Burnout reflects broken systems, not broken individuals. Leaders who address root causes—such as workload, culture, and recognition—develop healthier and more sustainable organizations.

Cultural Caution:: In cultures that celebrate overwork, burnout might be mistaken for weakness rather than symptoms of systemic failure.

Mosaic Question:: Does your workplace view burnout as a personal failure or a team warning?

Mosaic in Action:: A hospital system redesigns schedules to decrease double shifts and include mental health days, reducing turnover and increasing morale.

Professional Fragmentation

Definition:: The fragmentation of one's professional identity, values, or roles caused by conflicting demands, cultural pressures, or organizational misalignment.

Business Application: Fragmentation decreases effectiveness and morale when professionals feel they need to hide or compartmentalize essential parts of themselves.

Leadership Insight:: Addressing fragmentation requires leaders to foster cultures where integrity is valued and authenticity is recognized.

Cultural Caution:: Fragmentation can be protective in certain environments where revealing identity or beliefs is risky. Leaders should not require vulnerability without ensuring safety.

Mosaic Question:: Where are professionals in your system required to fragment themselves to belong?

Mosaic in Action:: An educator hides her bilingual identity in meetings to "fit in." A new leader promotes linguistic diversity, enabling her to bring her whole self to work.

Professional Isolation

Definition:: The exclusion of individuals—often those who are underrepresented in race, gender, or role—from informal networks and mentorship opportunities that promote advancement.

Business Application: Isolation hinders career progress and sustains inequality, as access to opportunities is often linked to unseen networks.

Leadership Insight:: Leaders must actively break down isolation by creating mentoring programs, inclusive networks, and sponsorship channels.

Cultural Caution:: Isolation can show up subtly—through missing invitations, unnoticed collaborations, or silence in decision-making rooms. Leaders need to learn to recognize these signs.

Mosaic Question:: Who in your workplace is regularly excluded from informal influence networks?

Mosaic in Action:: A law firm implements structured mentorship programs that pair junior associates from marginalized backgrounds with senior partners, breaking patterns of exclusion.

Pronoun Respect

Definition: The deliberate use of a person's self-identified pronouns to recognize, affirm, and include them.

Business Application: Consistently respecting pronouns in meetings, email signatures, and documentation promotes psychological safety and reduces workplace exclusion.

Leadership Insight: Pronoun respect is a simple yet powerful leadership practice that shows belonging and trust.

Cultural Caution: Avoid performative gestures—respect for pronouns must be paired with a truly inclusive culture for LGBTQ+ employees.

Mosaic Question: How do your daily communication habits affirm or overlook people's identities?

Mosaic in Action: A project lead includes pronouns when introducing themselves in cross-team meetings, creating a respectful tone from the outset.

Protected Class

Definition: A group of people legally protected from discrimination based on specific characteristics like race, religion, gender, age, or disability, as defined by law.

Business Application: Understanding protected classes helps leaders comply with anti-discrimination laws and actively promote fairness.

Leadership Insight: Compliance is the minimum—true leaders aim to uphold people's dignity beyond just legal obligations.

Cultural Caution: Laws differ across countries and regions; global leaders need to navigate multiple legal and cultural frameworks thoughtfully.

Mosaic Question: How do you promote protection and inclusion for everyone—regardless of legal requirements?

Mosaic in Action: An international company updates its anti-harassment policy to include protections not required in every region where it operates.

Proximity Bias

Definition: Favoring individuals who are physically closer or more visible to leaders, often disadvantaging remote or less visible employees.

Business Application: Proximity bias can cause unfairness in promotions, recognition, and project opportunities.

Leadership Insight: Good leaders actively counter proximity bias by providing equal access to mentorship, feedback, and decision-making.

Cultural Caution: In global or hybrid teams, proximity bias can unintentionally emphasize geographic, cultural, or class differences.

Mosaic Question: Who gets your attention most often—and why?

Mosaic in Action: A manager changes one-on-one meeting schedules to ensure remote staff have equal face time and input on key initiatives.

Pseudoinclusion

Definition: The appearance of inclusion without meaningful changes to systems, policies, or power dynamics—often symbolic rather than substantive.

Business Application: Pseudoinclusion can erode trust if employees see diversity statements without structural follow-through.

Leadership Insight: Genuine inclusion changes how decisions are made, not just how they are promoted.

Cultural Caution: Token representation without real influence can harm the communities inclusion aims to serve.

Mosaic Question: Does your inclusion effort improve the experiences of marginalized people—or just improve appearances?

Mosaic in Action: A company features diverse faces in promotional materials but, after feedback, revamps its promotion process to address pay gaps and bias.

Public Mourning

Definition: The collective expression of grief in shared or visible spaces, often following a public tragedy or the loss of a well-known person.

Business Application: Organizations may participate in public mourning through statements, observances, or policy changes, showing empathy and shared humanity.

Leadership Insight: Recognizing collective grief can build trust and connection, especially when silence might seem dismissive.

Cultural Caution: Different cultures express grief in unique ways; do not assume one mourning method fits all.

Mosaic Question: How does your leadership create space for grief without taking advantage of it?

Mosaic in Action: After a tragic local event, a community organization cancels its celebratory event and redirects funds to relief efforts while providing counseling to staff.

Public Trust Capital

Definition: The amount of credibility, goodwill, and confidence a leader or organization has in the eyes of the public, built through consistent transparency and ethical conduct.

Business Application: High public trust capital helps

organizations handle crises with less damage to their reputation and more support from stakeholders.

Leadership Insight: Public trust is earned gradually through reliability and can be lost quickly through dishonesty or neglect.

Cultural Caution: In some cultures, public trust depends more on community relationships than on formal credentials or branding.

Mosaic Question: What consistent actions strengthen the trust others have in you?

Mosaic in Action: A nonprofit provides detailed, accessible financial reports each year, leading to increased donor retention even during economic downturns.

Punishment Culture

Definition: An environment where mistakes are met with punishment instead of opportunities to learn, creating fear and stifling innovation.

Business Application: Punishment cultures often lead to lower morale, higher turnover, and less creative problem-solving.

Leadership Insight: Leaders who replace punishment with accountability and growth-focused feedback build resilience and adaptability.

Cultural Caution: In high power-distance cultures, shifting away from punishment may require intentional trust-building and policy changes.

Mosaic Question: Do people in your organization feel safe enough to take risks?

Mosaic in Action: A team replaces public reprimands with private "lessons learned" sessions, leading to better collaboration and fewer repeated mistakes.

Purpose-Driven Leadership

Definition: A leadership approach rooted in a clear mission and values, guiding decisions and actions toward a significant, larger goal.

Business Application: Purpose-driven leaders align team priorities with the organizational mission, inspiring dedication and loyalty.

Leadership Insight: Purpose acts as a compass that helps leaders stay steady during uncertainty and change.

Cultural Caution: While purpose is universal, its expression must honor local values, histories, and cultural narratives.

Mosaic Question: How do your everyday actions reflect the purpose you claim to serve?

Mosaic in Action: A healthcare leader bases every strategic decision on the organization's stated mission—improving patient dignity—leading to service innovations that surpass competitors.

Purposewashing

Definition: The act of publicly promoting a socially conscious mission or set of values while failing to truly incorporate them into organizational practices.

Business Application: Companies that purposewash may launch prominent campaigns about sustainability or equity without making internal changes to support those goals.

Leadership Insight: Purpose that exists only in marketing damages trust and can backfire when employees or stakeholders reveal the gap between words and actions.

Cultural Caution: In global settings, superficial claims of purpose can seem exploitative, especially in communities historically harmed by extractive or performative practices.

Mosaic Question: How accurately do your internal realities reflect your public commitments?

Mosaic in Action: A retail brand is criticized when its "women's empowerment" campaign is linked to labor violations in factories employing underpaid women.

Pushback Fatigue

Definition: The emotional and mental tiredness that happens when people or groups face ongoing resistance to necessary change or advocacy efforts.

Business Application: Leaders and advocates can experience pushback fatigue when dealing with deeply rooted systems, which can lead to burnout or withdrawal from the effort.

Leadership Insight: Recognizing and addressing pushback fatigue helps maintain momentum by balancing rest, support, and strategic planning.

Cultural Caution: In some cultural contexts, resistance to change may be seen as "tradition," requiring careful approaches that honor heritage while encouraging progress.

Mosaic Question: What strategies help you maintain your energy when change encounters constant resistance?

Mosaic in Action: A diversity officer takes a sabbatical after years of defending inclusive hiring policies against internal opposition, returning with renewed energy and new tactics.

Purity Politics

Definition: A strict adherence to ideological or moral standards that results in excluding or silencing those who do not fully meet every criterion.

Business Application: In workplaces, purity politics can break bonds and hinder progress by dismissing valuable contributions that are not perfect.

Leadership Insight: Effective leaders find a balance between maintaining high standards and accepting the imperfect realities of human growth and teamwork.

Cultural Caution: The idea of "purity" varies widely across cultures, and what is considered principled in one culture may be seen as exclusionary in another.

Mosaic Question: Where might your dedication to values unknowingly prevent open dialogue or progress?

Mosaic in Action: An activist group loses members when it demands unanimous agreement on every issue before taking collective action.

Psychological Contract

Definition: The unspoken set of expectations between employer and employee beyond the official job description, including fairness, trust, and reciprocity.

Business Application: When psychological contracts are broken — through layoffs, inequity, or broken promises — engagement and trust break down.

Leadership Insight: Leaders must honor both implicit and explicit agreements to sustain credibility and foster a sense of belonging.

Cultural Caution: Expectations vary across cultures — loyalty might be transactional in some cultures and not in others. Leaders need to clarify and align them.

Mosaic Question: What promises — spoken or unspoken — influence how your team perceives you?

Mosaic in Action: An NGO leader recognized unmet expectations during a restructuring and held restorative dialogues to rebuild trust.

Psychological Flexibility

Definition:: The ability to adjust thoughts, feelings, and actions to meet changing needs while remaining true to core values.

Business Application: Flexible leaders lower stress and boost performance by helping teams adapt without losing focus or identity.

Leadership Insight:: Resilience builds through flexibility—rigid leaders might survive a single crisis, but adaptable leaders thrive through many.

Cultural Caution:: Flexibility should not be mistaken for passivity; adapting does not mean giving up boundaries or values.

Mosaic Question:: How fast can you adapt without losing yourself?

Mosaic in Action:: A startup CEO shifts business strategy after the market collapse, inviting staff to collaborate on new priorities. Flexibility grounded in shared values helps prevent panic.

Psychological Safety

Definition: A shared belief that individuals can speak up, take risks, and admit mistakes without fear of punishment or humiliation.

Business Application: Teams with high psychological safety tend to innovate more, resolve conflicts effectively, and learn faster from failures.

Leadership Insight: Leaders promote psychological safety by demonstrating vulnerability, listening attentively, and responding to challenges without defensiveness.

Cultural Caution: Expressions of safety differ; in some cultures, open disagreement may seem unsafe unless trust has been established through relationships and time.

Mosaic Question: How do people in your circle know it's safe to speak their truth?

Mosaic in Action: A project manager openly admits a miscalculation during a team meeting, prompting a problem-solving discussion rather than assigning blame.

◈ LETTER P CALLOUT

"Power is never neutral — it is either shared, hoarded, or reshaped."

Reflection Questions

- How does paternalism or patriarchy appear in your environment?
- When has performative allyship undermined trust in your team or class?
- What does purpose-driven leadership look like in practice, beyond slogans?

Practical Move

In your next project or meeting, identify one decision point. Ask explicitly: Who holds the power here, and how can it be shared more equitably?

Q – Questions, Quotas, and Quiet Resistance

Q ventures into the corridors of transformation—where curiosity, interruption, and unseen defiance influence more than we often realize. This letter reminds us that questioning, when guided by courage and purpose, becomes a powerful tool for disruption and redesign. Too often, institutions see curiosity as a threat and questioning as deviation. But the right question at the right time can shake a system more profoundly than any policy. Questions reveal what lies beneath the surface the assumptions we inherit, the patterns we normalize, and the standards we never thought to challenge.

Q also reaffirms the importance of quotas. Often misunderstood as lowering standards, quotas are actually structural tools to restore access and visibility after long periods of exclusion. They don't reduce excellence—they address inequality. Quotas challenge the myth of meritocracy by exposing where bias has influenced progress. Their goal is not just numbers, but also storytelling redefining who belongs, who leads, and who is considered "enough."

And then there is quiet resistance—the strategic, silent refusal of those who no longer feel safe to speak. It shows up as disengagement, coded language, withdrawal, or the decision not to push too far. It's not indifference but a way to survive, born from exhaustion and judgment in cultures where confrontation is punished and naming harm has consequences. Leaders often overlook it, yet quiet resistance is a warning trust has broken, and a sense of belonging is fading.

Q asks us to notice the subtle but powerful ways influence takes shape

- The questions left unasked because the culture punishes inquiry.
- The quotas distorted as weakness instead of understood as recalibration.
- The quiet resistance mistaken for apathy rather than resilience.
- The voices repeatedly asked to justify their presence while others move unquestioned.

From queer inclusion to systemic equity, from unspoken questions to misunderstood resistance, Q shows how marginalization quietly yet strongly continues.

Q urges leaders to deepen their listening to see questions as opportunities, quotas as promises, and silence as information. Because real leadership doesn't fear asking, misrepresent fairness, or ignore resistance—it learns to see all as ways to change.

Q

Qualitative Inclusion Metrics

Definition: Measures that assess inclusion based on lived experiences, perceptions, and stories rather than only numerical data.

Business Application: Employee listening sessions, focus groups, and open-ended survey responses help identify patterns of exclusion or belonging that quantitative surveys might miss.

Leadership Insight: Numbers alone cannot fully show whether people feel safe, respected, or valued. Leaders who include qualitative measures gain a deeper understanding of organizational culture.

Cultural Caution: Qualitative insights require careful interpretation—while one person's experience can highlight issues, patterns only form when diverse voices are heard.

Mosaic Question: What stories or lived experiences within your organization go unnoticed in your dashboards?

Mosaic in Action: A company adds narrative interviews to yearly diversity data, discovering that women of color often feel left out of informal decision-making spaces despite formal policy inclusion.

Qualitative Insight

Definition: Knowledge gained from non-numerical data—such as observations, interviews, stories, and context—that enriches decision-making.

Business Application: In product development, qualitative insights from customer conversations can reveal unmet needs that quantitative data might overlook.

Leadership Insight: Leaders who focus on qualitative insight can make decisions based on human experience rather than just statistical trends.

Cultural Caution: Relying solely on qualitative insight without additional evidence may lead to a distorted view influenced by louder voices.

Mosaic Question: How do you balance human stories with measurable results?

Mosaic in Action: A leadership team updates workplace layout plans based on qualitative feedback from employees, emphasizing the need for quieter, culturally sensitive spaces for prayer and focus.

Qualitative Risk

Definition: Non-numerical risks that stem from cultural, ethical, or reputational factors, often ignored by typical risk assessments.

Business Application: A marketing campaign might meet compliance standards but pose qualitative risks if it offends certain cultural groups.

Leadership Insight: Leaders who recognize qualitative risks are better equipped to prevent public backlash, internal morale problems, or ethical breaches.

Cultural Caution: Qualitative risks can be subjective—seek diverse perspectives to prevent bias when assessing potential harm.

Mosaic Question: What risks are present in the emotional or cultural aspects of your decision, even if they don't show up in a spreadsheet?

Mosaic in Action: Before launching a new brand name, a global company consults local cultural advisors to avoid a term

that translates into an offensive phrase in one language.

Quantified Bias

Definition: The measurable expression of bias through data, algorithms, or statistical patterns.

Business Application: Reviewing hiring algorithms for disproportionate rejection rates of candidates from certain demographics can reveal quantifiable bias.

Leadership Insight: Quantifying bias allows leaders to set specific improvement goals and track progress over time.

Cultural Caution: Numbers may confirm bias, but they don't explain its roots—quantitative data must be combined with qualitative understanding to promote change.

Mosaic Question: What measurable disparities are present in your systems—and what steps will you take once you identify them?

Mosaic in Action: A talent acquisition team discovers their screening software rejects 30 percent more resumes from applicants with non-Western names. They update the algorithm and review processes to eliminate the discrepancy.

Quantum Leadership

Definition: A leadership approach that applies principles from quantum physics—such as interconnectedness, uncertainty, and nonlinearity—to handle complexity.

Business Application: Leaders practicing quantum leadership embrace dynamic networks, emergent strategies, and adaptive responses rather than rigid plans.

Leadership Insight: In a world where small actions can cause ripple effects, quantum leaders balance vision with agility, recognizing that influence flows in multiple directions.

Cultural Caution: Quantum metaphors can be powerful, but avoid using them superficially— base the approach on real, inclusive leadership practices.

Mosaic Question: Where in your leadership do you need to trade control for connection?

Mosaic in Action: A global nonprofit leader enables regional teams to adjust strategies instantly during a crisis, delivering solutions more quickly than a centralized command can.

Quantum Leadership Thinking

Definition: The mindset that supports quantum leadership, focusing on fluidity, possibility, and interconnected problem-solving.

Business Application: In innovation labs, quantum leadership thinking encourages cross-disciplinary teams to explore multiple solutions at once instead of sticking to a single path.

Leadership Insight: Leaders who think in quantum terms can hold paradoxes, adapt quickly to change, and recognize patterns that are invisible in linear thinking.

Cultural Caution: Without clear communication, quantum thinking can be mistaken for a lack of direction—make the invisible connections visible to others.

Mosaic Question: How can you create space for multiple truths to influence one decision?

Mosaic in Action: A CEO frames a merger not as a zero-sum win/lose but as an ecosystem merger where both organizations' strengths create new, unexpected value chains.

Queer Inclusion

Definition: Creating environments where people of diverse sexual orientations, gender identities, and expressions are welcomed, respected, and valued.

Business Application: Policies that go beyond non-discrimination—such as inclusive benefits, gender-neutral facilities, and recognition of chosen families—signal genuine queer inclusion.

Leadership Insight: Inclusion means shifting from just tolerance to active support, making sure queer voices influence decisions, culture, and policy.

Cultural Caution: Avoid assuming a single "queer perspective"—LGBTQ+ identities are diverse and intersectional.

Mosaic Question: How are queer perspectives shaping—not just reflected in—your organization's future?

Mosaic in Action: An HR department updates parental leave policies to be inclusive of all family structures after consulting with LGBTQ+ employee resource groups.

Queer Joy

Definition: Celebrating LGBTQ+ existence, resilience, and creativity through visibility, art, and community connection.

Business Application: Highlighting queer joy in marketing, events, and workplace culture shifts the narrative from struggle to thriving and authenticity.

Leadership Insight: Joy acts as a form of resistance—leaders who promote it affirm dignity and belonging, even in tough times.

Cultural Caution: Ensure celebrations are genuine—authentic representation includes queer communities in planning and leadership.

Mosaic Question: How does your leadership create space for marginalized communities to flourish, not just survive?

Mosaic in Action: A museum co-curates an exhibition with queer artists focused on joy, beauty, and everyday life, rather than only on oppression.

Queer Leadership

Definition: A leadership approach influenced by queer experiences of resilience, fluidity, and nonconformity. Queer leadership questions dominant models by emphasizing authenticity, intersectionality, and collective care.

Business Application:
Organizations gain from queer leadership through innovation, flexibility, and equity-focused viewpoints that challenge strict hierarchies.

Leadership Insight: Queer leadership broadens opportunities for everyone by showing that effective leadership doesn't have to follow mainstream norms.

Cultural Caution: Queer leadership should not be tokenized or limited to identity. It is about action, not just representation.

Mosaic Question: What could leadership look like if queerness were regarded as an asset instead of a risk?

Mosaic in Action: A queer executive leads an innovation hub where fluid identity is valued as a strength, fostering a culture of creativity and trust.

Queerphobia

Definition: Prejudice, discrimination, or hostility toward LGBTQ+ individuals, identities, or expressions.

Business Application:
Queerphobia can manifest as discrimination in hiring, biased promotion practices, exclusion from leadership roles, or hostile workplace environments.

Leadership Insight: Recognizing and addressing queerphobia is essential for building trust— remaining silent or avoiding the issue often signals complicity.

Cultural Caution: Queerphobia can be obvious or subtle; microaggressions, erasure, and tokenism are just as damaging.

Mosaic Question: What systems in your workplace unintentionally promote queerphobia?

Mosaic in Action: A retail company revises its dress code after discovering it unfairly targets non-binary employees' clothing choices.

Queer Visibility

Definition: Being openly and authentically queer in leadership, organizational, or community settings involves visibility, which brings both power and vulnerability.

Business Application: Queer visibility influences hiring, retention, and workplace culture. Organizations that promote visibility help create belonging and lessen fear.

Leadership Insight: Visibility equals leadership. When queer leaders show their true selves, they increase representation and make authenticity normal for others.

Cultural Caution: In some situations, queer visibility may pose risks or cause harm. Leaders must weigh safety against advocacy.

Mosaic Question: What parts of your organization create a safe or unsafe space for queer visibility?

Mosaic in Action: A nonprofit CEO consistently uses pronouns and commits to LGBTQ+ equity in all public messages, demonstrating genuine authenticity.

Queering Leadership

Definition: A key approach to challenging traditional, heteronormative, and hierarchical leadership models by using queer theory and lived experience.

Business Application: Queering leadership fosters more inclusive workplaces by challenging assumptions about authority, structure, and identity.

Leadership Insight: Queering leadership involves rethinking it — breaking free from strict binaries and creating space for fluid, relational, and co-created forms of power.

Cultural Caution: Queering leadership should not be seen as "anti-leadership." It's about broadening models, not rejecting leadership entirely.

Mosaic Question: What assumptions about leadership could you "queer" to create space for new possibilities?

Mosaic in Action: A university leadership program redefines authority as shared, adaptable, and specific to context, drawing on queer theory principles.

Questioning Culture

Definition: An environment that encourages curiosity, dissent, and exploration of ideas without fear of retaliation.

Business Application: Promoting questioning boosts innovation, risk management, and employee engagement.

Leadership Insight: Leaders who foster a questioning culture balance inquiry with psychological safety, ensuring all voices—especially dissenting ones—are valued.

Cultural Caution: Without boundaries, questioning can be misused to undermine authority or harass marginalized voices.

Mosaic Question: How can you ensure curiosity strengthens rather than divides your team?

Mosaic in Action: A school district invites teachers to challenge new curriculum changes during open forums, leading to better resources for diverse classrooms.

Questioning Leadership

Definition: A leadership style based on curiosity, reflection, and inquiry instead of strict control. Questioning leadership focuses on dialogue and exploration.

Business Application: Organizations with questioning leaders promote innovation, psychological safety, and ongoing learning.

Leadership Insight: Strong leaders don't just give answers — they ask better questions. Questioning leadership turns uncertainty into opportunity.

Cultural Caution: In certain environments, questioning authority is discouraged. Leaders need to balance inquiry with cultural expectations.

Mosaic Question: Do you ask questions to challenge, listen, or control?

Mosaic in Action: A healthcare leader starts each strategy meeting with an open question: "What are we missing?" encouraging everyone to contribute their ideas.

Quota Fatigue

Definition: Burnout or resistance resulting from attempting to meet diversity, equity, or inclusion targets without implementing meaningful structural changes.

Business Application: Setting quotas without transforming the culture can result in token hires, increased turnover, and decreased trust in leadership.

Leadership Insight: Representation goals should be integrated with policies, mentoring, and clear advancement pathways to foster lasting equity.

Cultural Caution: Don't view quotas as charity or just compliance; they should reflect organizational values and mission.

Mosaic Question: How can you ensure diversity goals lead to opportunities instead of obstacles?

Mosaic in Action: A healthcare company aligns its hiring goals with leadership development programs for underrepresented staff, leading to lasting change.

Quiet Algorithmic Bias

Definition: Bias embedded in AI or automated systems that operate invisibly, shaping decisions without transparency.

Business Application: Quiet algorithmic bias can affect hiring, promotions, credit scoring, and content moderation—often reinforcing inequalities.

Leadership Insight: Leaders must require algorithm audits, diverse data sets, and human oversight to prevent hidden discrimination.

Cultural Caution: Over-reliance on "neutral" algorithms can hide deep structural inequalities—bias in, bias out.

Mosaic Question: Where in your systems might hidden code be rewriting fairness?

Mosaic in Action: A city government updates its housing application algorithm after discovering it unfairly rejects applications from immigrant families.

Quiet Bias

Definition: Subtle biases or stereotypes that influence decisions and interactions without overt acknowledgment.

Business Application: Quiet bias can affect hiring, promotions, and daily workplace interactions, often going unnoticed by formal policies.

Leadership Insight: Leaders who educate themselves and their teams to recognize quiet bias can help

prevent exclusion before it becomes embedded in the culture.

Cultural Caution: Quiet bias thrives in environments where people believe they are "objective." Self-awareness is the key to counteracting it.

Mosaic Question: What assumptions do you hold that influence your choices without realizing?

Mosaic in Action: A project manager notices she consistently assigns detail-heavy work to women on her team. She changes her process to rotate assignments, revealing new strengths across the group.

Quiet Influence

Definition: The ability to influence outcomes, decisions, or culture without explicit authority or visibility.

Business Application: Quiet influencers can act as the culture carriers of an organization, spreading ideas through relationships rather than titles.

Leadership Insight: Recognizing and engaging quiet influencers strengthens change efforts by tapping into trust networks.

Cultural Caution: Quiet influence can be used for both inclusion and exclusion—leaders must understand its direction.

Mosaic Question: Who shapes the culture here, and how do they do it without a microphone?

Mosaic in Action: An administrative assistant quietly ensures that meeting agendas include time for staff from underrepresented departments to present updates, gradually increasing visibility.

Quiet Leadership

Definition: A leadership style that focuses on listening, observing, and thoughtful action rather than constant visibility or talking.

Business Application: Quiet leaders can help stabilize teams during uncertain times by offering calm guidance and clear direction without unnecessary fuss.

Leadership Insight: Quiet leadership is not passive; it's a strategic presence that leverages timing and trust to increase impact.

Cultural Caution: In high-pressure or competitive environments, quiet leaders need to ensure their contributions are visible to avoid being overlooked.

Mosaic Question: How can saying less help you lead more effectively?

Mosaic in Action: A department head spends the first month simply listening to her new team before making changes, building credibility and trust that support later reforms.

Quiet Quitting

Definition: When employees limit discretionary effort, they meet only the minimum expectations of their role without openly quitting.

Business Application: Quiet quitting often indicates burnout, disengagement, or a misalignment between employee values and workplace culture.

Leadership Insight: Addressing quiet quitting involves tackling root causes—recognition, workload balance, and opportunities for growth—not just enforcing compliance.

Cultural Caution: Labeling employees as "quiet quitters" without understanding the context can deepen their alienation.

Mosaic Question: How can you reconnect with someone who's emotionally disengaged without judgment?

Mosaic in Action: After an employee starts doing only the bare minimum, their manager has a career development conversation, which leads to a role change that boosts their motivation.

Quiet Resistance

Definition: Subtle, often unnoticed acts of opposition to unfair or oppressive systems. Quiet resistance involves small daily actions that challenge harmful norms.

Business Application: Employees resist quietly by withholding labor from unjust systems, subtly supporting marginalized colleagues, or bending rules to promote fairness.

Leadership Insight: Quiet resistance indicates that formal systems are failing. Wise leaders listen for it and address the underlying causes.

Cultural Caution: Silent resistance might go unnoticed by those in power. Leaders should not mistake it for apathy.

Mosaic Question: Where in your organization might quiet resistance already be occurring — and what is it revealing to you?

Mosaic in Action: Teachers in a strict district quietly modify lesson plans to incorporate cultural histories that are erased by the official curriculum, resisting exclusion through their daily practices.

◈ LETTER Q CALLOUT

"Questions are not weaknesses — they are the starting point of transformation."

Reflection Questions

- What kinds of questions are encouraged in your space, and which are avoided?
- How does queerness expand our understanding of inclusion and visibility?
- Where might quotas or quiet resistance mask deeper equity challenges?

Practical Move

Begin your next discussion by asking a "why" or "what if" question — one that shifts the focus from assumptions to possibility.

R – Representation, Repair, and Relational Leadership

R starts with language that goes beyond appearances, beyond intentions, and into responsibility. These terms remind us that equity is not maintained by surface-level gestures but by daily practices that transform culture. Representation is not just about who is in the room; it is about who has authority, whose voice shapes decisions, and whose presence leads to meaningful change. Without power and safety, representation risks becoming tokenism dressed up as progress.

R also emphasizes the importance of repair. In cultures where harm has become normalized—through exclusion, neglect, or bias—repair is not optional. It is a leadership duty. And it involves more than just apologies. Repair requires acknowledgment, redress, process, and transformation. It is how trust is restored and how systems become sustainable.

At its core, relational leadership is an approach founded on humility, presence, and mutual respect. It acknowledges the humanity behind policies, the emotions behind data, and the relationships that foster real change. It is not just performative but genuinely responsive. It asks not only how you lead but how your leadership resonates.

R asks us to confront what often gets minimized

- Representation without voice or power becomes tokenism.
- Repair without systems change becomes performance.

- Relational leadership without humility becomes control.
- Resilience without recognition becomes exploitation.

From racialized trauma to resilience fatigue, R holds space for the burdens carried by those who continue to show up despite being overlooked. It affirms that representation without safety is not inclusion, that repair without accountability is not justice, and that relational leadership is not soft; it is strategic and transformative.

R urges leaders to shift from focusing on performance to being present, from avoiding issues to repairing them, and from relying on authority to building relationships. Because equity is not a feeling—it is a function. Repair is not a single moment—it is a continuous process. And genuine leadership listens before it leads.

R

Race-Evasiveness

Definition: The intentional avoidance of discussing race or acknowledging racism, often framed as focusing on "common humanity" to avoid discomfort.

Business Application: In organizations, race-evasiveness can show up during hiring, promotion, or performance reviews, where systemic inequities are downplayed or ignored.

Leadership Insight: Leaders who dodge race-related conversations miss chances to address disparities and model honest, inclusive engagement.

Cultural Caution: In some cultural settings, talking about race directly may be taboo; however, silence can worsen harm and misunderstanding.

Mosaic Question: What truths are you avoiding by trying to keep the peace?

Mosaic in Action: A manager avoids addressing racial disparities in a team's pay structure to "avoid tension," which ends up increasing mistrust among staff.

Racial Battle Fatigue

Definition: The ongoing emotional, psychological, and physical strain experienced by people of color due to persistent racial microaggressions, discrimination, or systemic inequalities.

Business Application: Employees suffering from racial battle fatigue may face burnout, reduced productivity, or withdrawal from workplace involvement.

Leadership Insight: Leaders who recognize and address the realities of racial battle fatigue contribute to building more sustainable and equitable workplaces.

Cultural Caution: Although the term originated in U.S. contexts, similar issues occur worldwide wherever racialized groups experience ongoing bias and marginalization.

Mosaic Question: How does your leadership consider the long-term impact of racial inequity on individuals and teams?

Mosaic in Action: An educator of color leaves the profession after years of being the only advocate for students' racial concerns without institutional support.

Racial Literacy

Definition: The ability to recognize, understand, and respond to how race and racism influence individual and group experiences.

Business Application: Racial literacy helps leaders identify inequalities, challenge bias, and have constructive, informed conversations.

Leadership Insight: Developing racial literacy is a continuous process that requires humility, active learning, and engagement with diverse perspectives.

Cultural Caution: Racial ideas and histories vary across countries, making it essential to learn what is relevant locally for effective cross-cultural understanding.

Mosaic Question: How well do you understand the racial realities affecting your organization and community?

Mosaic in Action: A department head starts a monthly reading group focused on racial equity, using case studies relevant to both local and global contexts.

Radical Empathy

Definition: A deliberate effort to understand and empathize with another person's lived experience—especially when it challenges one's own perspective—and to respond based on that understanding.

Business Application: Radical empathy in leadership changes workplace culture by strengthening trust and fostering genuine collaboration.

Leadership Insight: Radical empathy demands both emotional openness and the bravery to take actions that eliminate harm.

Cultural Caution: In some cultures, empathy is shown through actions rather than words; leaders should adjust their approach accordingly.

Mosaic Question: Where might empathy call you not just to feel, but to take a risk?

Mosaic in Action: A CEO changes company policy after listening to and walking through the daily challenges faced by frontline employees.

Radical Hospitality

Definition: An intentional and proactive welcome that exceeds basic politeness, creating environments where people feel truly valued, safe, and seen.

Business Application: Radical hospitality can enhance client experiences, recruitment, and workplace culture by fostering genuine belonging.

Leadership Insight: This is not about convenience—it's about making systemic, policy, and norm changes to promote true inclusivity.

Cultural Caution: What seems hospitable in one culture could be intrusive in another; leaders should adapt their approaches with cultural sensitivity.

Mosaic Question: How can your welcome communicate more than just tolerance—show real care?

Mosaic in Action: A conference organizer makes sure to plan for dietary, mobility, prayer, and childcare needs of all attendees ahead of time.

Rainbow Washing

Definition: The superficial use of LGBTQIA+ symbols or messaging to signal inclusion without taking meaningful actions to support the community.

Business Application: Companies may change logos or run Pride campaigns without addressing discriminatory policies or workplace bias.

Leadership Insight: Symbolic gestures need to be accompanied by real change for trust and credibility to be maintained.

Cultural Caution: In some regions, overt displays of LGBTQIA+ support might require careful strategies to protect employees and community members.

Mosaic Question: Is your public show of solidarity supported by genuine commitment?

Mosaic in Action: A retailer launches Pride merchandise but is criticized for donating to politicians who support anti-LGBTQIA+ legislation.

Reclamation

Definition: The act of reclaiming control, ownership, or meaning—often related to land, culture, language, or identity—that was previously taken or suppressed.

Business Application: Reclamation appears in branding, workplace representation, and community engagement, especially when historically excluded groups lead the narrative.

Leadership Insight: Supporting reclamation efforts can build trust and repair past harm when approached with humility and collaboration.

Cultural Caution: Leaders should avoid using reclamation efforts for marketing purposes without genuine alignment and accountability.

Mosaic Question: Whose voice or heritage in your community needs reclamation?

Mosaic in Action: An Indigenous-led design team reintroduces traditional motifs into a corporate project, ensuring royalties go directly to their community.

Reconciliation Work

Definition:: Processes of relational and systemic healing that address harm through truth-telling, acknowledgment, and reparative action.

Business Application: In workplaces, reconciliation efforts help rebuild trust following discrimination, organizational betrayal, or cultural exclusion.

Leadership Insight:: True reconciliation demands both symbolic acknowledgment and structural change; lacking either fosters cynicism.

Cultural Caution:: Reconciliation should be led by the community;

imposing it from above risks repeating the harm it aims to fix.

Mosaic Question:: Where does reconciliation need to happen in your system, and who should be responsible for leading it?

Mosaic in Action:: A university involves Indigenous elders to jointly develop land acknowledgment practices along with systemic changes in hiring, curriculum, and funding.

Redlining (Legacy)

Definition: A discriminatory practice—historically seen in housing and lending—that systematically denied services to residents in certain areas based on race or ethnicity, resulting in long-term socioeconomic effects.

Business Application: The legacy of redlining continues to affect wealth disparities, resource allocation, and access to opportunities, shaping corporate responsibility and community engagement.

Leadership Insight: Addressing these systemic inequalities is vital for fair growth and inclusive hiring practices.

Cultural Caution: Although the term originates in the U.S., similar exclusionary zoning and financial practices are present worldwide under different names.

Mosaic Question: How might your organization's operations inadvertently perpetuate historical inequities?

Mosaic in Action: A company analyzes its supplier network and finds most vendors are concentrated in historically privileged areas, prompting efforts to connect with underrepresented communities.

Redistributive Justice

Definition:: A justice framework that aims to address structural inequalities by reallocating resources, opportunities, and power.

Business Application: Organizations practicing redistributive justice focus on fair pay, resource distribution, and support for historically marginalized groups.

Leadership Insight:: Redistribution is not charity; it is accountability for systemic imbalance.

Cultural Caution:: Redistribution can trigger resistance from those who view equity as a loss. Leaders must present it as collective progress.

Mosaic Question:: How do you make sure resources go to those who have been historically denied them?

Mosaic in Action:: A foundation shifts its funding priorities to grassroots organizations led by people of color, redistributing millions to historically underfunded communities.

Reflexivity

Definition: The ongoing process of critically examining one's own beliefs, biases, and actions, and understanding how they influence perceptions and behavior.

Business Application: Reflexivity helps leaders recognize how personal assumptions affect hiring, conflict resolution, and strategic planning.

Leadership Insight: Reflexive leaders are better at adapting, building trust, and avoiding blind spots in decision-making.

Cultural Caution: Reflexivity requires humility and openness— being defensive can prevent meaningful change.

Mosaic Question: How often do you evaluate the perspective through which you lead?

Mosaic in Action: A senior manager reviews a failed project and realizes their bias toward "fast talkers" caused them to overlook quieter—but more prepared—team members.

Refugee Experience

Definition: The real-life experiences of people who are forced to leave their home countries because of conflict, persecution, or disaster, often involving loss, displacement, and rebuilding their identity in a new setting.

Business Application: Recognizing refugee experiences helps create inclusive hiring, training, and community programs that appreciate their unique skills and challenges.

Leadership Insight: Refugees bring resilience and adaptability—qualities often overlooked if organizations focus only on "gaps" in formal credentials.

Cultural Caution: Do not view refugee experiences merely as deficits or charity cases; instead, respect their agency, dignity, and professional abilities.

Mosaic Question: How does your workplace accommodate displaced voices?

Mosaic in Action: A city-based nonprofit collaborates with refugee entrepreneurs to develop small business incubators, allowing their cultural knowledge to enhance local markets.

Reframing

Definition: The practice of changing perspective to view a situation, challenge, or conflict in a more positive or opportunity-focused way.

Business Application: Leaders use reframing to reduce conflict, encourage innovation, and re-engage teams during change processes.

Leadership Insight: Reframing is not about ignoring problems; it's about expanding options and finding solutions that may be hidden by rigid viewpoints.

Cultural Caution: Make sure reframing doesn't dismiss real experiences; "positive spin" without recognizing harm can seem invalidating.

Mosaic Question: What challenge could be seen in a new light to turn it into an opportunity?

Mosaic in Action: During budget cuts, a department head reframes restrictions as a chance to streamline processes and cross-train staff, leading to better collaboration.

Reentry Shock

Definition: The disorientation and emotional adjustment challenges that happen when returning to a familiar environment after being away for a while—often following work abroad, deployment, or an extended absence.

Business Application: Organizations with international staff or rotational assignments can ease reentry shock through structured reintegration programs.

Leadership Insight: Returning employees might face reverse culture shock; leaders should provide opportunities for them to share insights without dismissing their perspective as "out of touch."

Cultural Caution: Reentry shock can also happen after returning from crisis assignments or high-intensity roles—assuming a smooth transition can hurt retention.

Mosaic Question: How do you welcome back those whose experiences have changed them?

Mosaic in Action: After a humanitarian mission, a project lead struggles with the pace of corporate work. Their supervisor offers flexible scheduling and a debrief session to incorporate lessons learned into team practices.

Regulation

Definition: The ability to effectively manage one's emotional responses, especially in difficult situations. Regulation fosters connection, calmness, and deliberate decision-making.

Business Application: Leaders who practice regulation prevent reactive outbursts, de-escalate conflict, and maintain trust under pressure. Teams benefit when regulation becomes part of the culture — meetings are more steady, feedback is more constructive, and crises are handled with clarity.

Leadership Insight: Regulation is not about suppression. It's about recognizing emotions, naming them, and selecting responses that match your values instead of reacting impulsively.

Cultural Caution: Expectations for emotional regulation vary across cultures. What is considered calm in one setting might be seen as detached or cold in another. Leaders need to adjust their regulation to fit cultural and relational norms.

Mosaic Question: When tension escalates, do you suppress emotion or manage it with integrity?

Mosaic in Action: A hospital director observes increasing panic during an emergency drill. By speaking slowly and acknowledging the fear, she demonstrates self-control and brings back group focus.

Relational Accountability

Definition: The responsibility to honor and uphold trust, commitments, and respect in relationships, recognizing the interdependence among people and communities.

Business Application: Relational accountability promotes reliability in partnerships, mentorship, and team collaboration, ensuring commitments are honored even under pressure.

Leadership Insight: Leaders who demonstrate accountability in relationships inspire loyalty and minimize conflict through consistent follow-through.

Cultural Caution: In collectivist or Indigenous contexts, relational accountability goes beyond individuals to include the well-being of the community—reducing it to mere transactional exchanges can cause harm.

Mosaic Question: How do you ensure your commitments are perceived as reliable rather than just spoken?

Mosaic in Action: A project leader delays a product launch to honor commitments made to a partner organization regarding cultural review, thereby maintaining trust over short-term profit.

Relational Culture

Definition: An organizational or community environment where connection, trust, and mutual care are prioritized alongside goals and outcomes.

Business Application: Relational cultures often lead to higher employee engagement and retention, as people feel valued beyond just their output.

Leadership Insight: A relational culture is developed intentionally—leaders must balance empathy with clear accountability structures.

Cultural Caution: Relational culture can unintentionally exclude those unfamiliar with its norms if onboarding fails to make expectations clear.

Mosaic Question: What does your workplace prioritize more—relationships or results?

Mosaic in Action: A tech startup holds regular "story circles" where team members share personal updates, strengthening collaboration across departments.

Relational Intelligence

Definition: The ability to understand, navigate, and improve interpersonal relationships through empathy, trust-building, and adaptable communication.

Business Application: Relational intelligence is vital for leaders managing cross-functional teams, client relationships, or culturally diverse groups.

Leadership Insight: Unlike technical skills, relational intelligence grows over time—leaders who develop it establish lasting influence.

Cultural Caution: Ideas about "good relationships" differ across cultures; adjusting relational strategies is essential for global success.

Mosaic Question: How do you modify your relational approach for different contexts and cultures?

Mosaic in Action: A regional director changes feedback styles when working with international teams, balancing directness with relational harmony norms.

Relational Leadership

Definition:: A leadership style that focuses on trust, empathy, and genuine connection instead of hierarchy, authority, or control.

Business Application: Relational leadership promotes cultures of belonging, enhances collaboration, and cuts turnover by prioritizing people over process.

Leadership Insight:: Influence becomes stronger when leaders focus on connection; authority without relationship seldom maintains trust.

Cultural Caution:: Relational styles might be underestimated in highly hierarchical cultures, where authority is seen as strength.

Mosaic Question:: Do you depend more on authority or relationships to influence people?

Mosaic in Action:: A senior leader replaces rigid performance reviews with dialogue-based check-ins, fostering trust and increasing team motivation.

Relational Safety

Definition: The interpersonal layer of psychological safety, where trust, respect, and empathy create an environment where feedback, collaboration, and disagreement are safe.

Business Application: Relational safety fosters team cohesion and encourages honest dialogue in high-stakes or cross-cultural environments.

Leadership Insight: Leaders demonstrate relational safety by listening intently, responding empathetically, and respecting vulnerability.

Cultural Caution: Relational safety cues differ across cultures — eye contact, tone, or silence can have different meanings.

Mosaic Question: Do your relationships foster honesty — or create guardedness?

Mosaic in Action: A manager normalized feedback by sharing her own mistakes, allowing staff to speak openly.

Relational Trust

Definition:: The mutual confidence among colleagues that intentions are good and commitments will be honored.

Business Application: Relational trust fuels collaboration, knowledge sharing, and innovation—without it, teams fall apart into silos and suspicion.

Leadership Insight:: Trust is built through consistency, empathy, and transparency; it can't be demanded.

Cultural Caution:: Trust-building behaviors vary—direct

communication can foster trust in one culture but harm it in another.

Mosaic Question:: How do you actively build trust with those you lead?

Mosaic in Action:: A principal builds relational trust by consistently keeping promises, openly admitting mistakes, and involving staff in decision-making.

Religious Literacy

Definition: Knowledge of various religious beliefs, practices, and histories to promote respectful and informed engagement.

Business Application: Religious literacy aids in preventing discrimination, promotes inclusive policies, and encourages stronger cross-cultural business relationships.

Leadership Insight: Leaders with religious literacy can confidently and sensitively handle faith-related accommodations, holidays, and ethical issues.

Cultural Caution: Religious literacy is different from religious advocacy—leaders need to combine understanding with neutrality in diverse environments.

Mosaic Question: How does your leadership address the spiritual aspects of diversity?

Mosaic in Action: A multinational company adjusts meeting schedules to avoid major religious observances for its global teams, increasing participation and boosting morale.

Remote Inclusion

Definition: The deliberate practice of making sure that individuals working remotely are equally engaged, valued, and provided with opportunities for contribution and advancement.

Business Application: Remote inclusion strategies—such as fair access to information, facilitating virtual meetings, and flexible schedules—help distributed teams stay connected and perform well.

Leadership Insight: Without intentional inclusion, remote staff can become invisible in decision-making and career growth.

Cultural Caution: Not all employees have the same access to stable internet, quiet workspaces, or equipment—assuming everyone has a level playing field can worsen inequalities.

Mosaic Question: How do you make remote team members feel recognized and integral to the work?

Mosaic in Action: A global nonprofit rotates meeting times across time zones and uses collaborative digital tools so all staff can contribute meaningfully.

Reparative Practice

Definition: Actions taken to repair harm, rebuild trust, and restore relationships after mistakes, inequalities, or injustices have happened.

Business Application: Reparative practices may include public acknowledgments, policy updates, restitution, and process redesign to prevent future issues.

Leadership Insight: Repairing harm boosts credibility—avoiding it damages trust, even when good intentions exist.

Cultural Caution: True repair involves engaging those harmed to define what repair looks like; imposing a solution without consultation can worsen the damage.

Mosaic Question: When harm occurs under your leadership, how do you incorporate repair into the culture, not just address the crisis?

Mosaic in Action: After a discriminatory incident at a conference, organizers involve affected participants in co-creating new inclusion protocols for future events.

Reparations (Organizational)

Definition: Institutional efforts to recognize and address past harms—often systemic or historical—through concrete actions, policy changes, and resource distribution.

Business Application: Organizations may offer scholarships, targeted hiring, debt forgiveness, or community investment as responses to their histories of exclusion or exploitation.

Leadership Insight: Organizational reparations serve as a form of strategic integrity—aligning stated values with actions and accountability.

Cultural Caution: Symbolic gestures without tangible results may be seen as performative; transparency about scope, limitations, and commitments is crucial.

Mosaic Question: How might your organization's history call for investment in a fairer future?

Mosaic in Action: A university creates a long-term fund for the descendants of communities displaced during campus expansion decades ago.

Repair

Definition: The process of restoring emotional trust after a rupture involves acknowledgment, accountability, and reconnecting. Repair turns conflict into an opportunity for a closer relationship.

Business Application: Workplaces that promote repair foster resilience. Leaders who address mistakes such as missed deadlines, harmful comments, or broken commitments help prevent long-term disengagement and restore credibility.

Leadership Insight: Conflict is unavoidable; disconnection is not. Leaders who embrace a repair model of humility and courage demonstrate that mistakes can serve as turning points instead of endings.

Cultural Caution: Repair practices vary across cultures. In some, a direct apology is essential; in others, repair is demonstrated through changed behavior, symbolic gestures, or shared rituals.

Mosaic Question: When trust breaks down, do you ignore it — or embrace repairing it as a leadership move?

Mosaic in Action: After publicly cutting off a colleague during a meeting, a manager follows up with an apology and invites the colleague's input first in the next session, restoring respect and trust.

Repair Culture

Definition:: An organizational norm that emphasizes repairing harm, relationships, and systems instead of hiding mistakes or blaming others.

Business Application: Repair culture lowers conflict costs and enhances reputations, especially after public mistakes or internal failures.

Leadership Insight:: Repair requires humility. Leaders who normalize apology and making amends foster cultures of resilience and integrity.

Cultural Caution:: In certain situations, apologies are seen as a sign of weakness. Framing making amends as a display of strength encourages acceptance.

Mosaic Question:: Does your culture hide mistakes or use them to build trust through repair?

Mosaic in Action:: After a flawed product launch, a company issues a transparent public apology, fixes the problem, and emphasizes customer feedback in the redesign process.

Representation

Definition: The presence and visibility of diverse identities, perspectives, and experiences in decision-making spaces, leadership roles, and cultural narratives.

Business Application: Diverse representation enhances innovation, problem-solving, and market reach by reflecting the realities of various stakeholders.

Leadership Insight:
Representation is not just about numbers — it's about meaningful participation and influence in shaping outcomes.

Cultural Caution: Tokenizing individuals to meet diversity optics without granting them real power undermines trust and damages morale.

Mosaic Question: In your leadership context, who is visible — and who is missing from the table?

Mosaic in Action: A design firm diversifies its leadership board and grants decision-making authority to members with lived experience in the markets they serve.

Representation Without Belonging

Definition: The existence of individuals from underrepresented groups without true inclusion, influence, or cultural acceptance.

Business Application: Organizations might appear diverse through images, marketing, or staffing, but fail to foster environments where those individuals can truly thrive.

Leadership Insight: Representation without belonging can lead to higher turnover and increased disillusionment, as people see a gap between the public image and their actual experiences.

Cultural Caution: Publicly displaying diversity while neglecting internal exclusionary practices risks damaging reputation and causing employee disengagement.

Mosaic Question: How does your leadership ensure that representation is accompanied by influence and genuine inclusion?

Mosaic in Action: A media company moves from merely hiring diverse talent for visibility to redesigning editorial processes so those voices influence story directions and company priorities.

Resilience Fatigue

Definition: The exhaustion that happens when individuals or groups are repeatedly expected to adapt, recover, and endure without relief or systemic change.

Business Application: Constant demands for resilience without fixing underlying issues—such as toxic work environments or unfair structures—lead to burnout and turnover.

Leadership Insight: Resilience is limited; leaders must balance building capacity with addressing the systemic causes of ongoing stress.

Cultural Caution: Praising resilience can unintentionally romanticize struggle and normalize conditions that need improvement.

Mosaic Question: Are you celebrating resilience while neglecting to remove the obstacles that require it?

Mosaic in Action: A school district moves from resilience training for teachers to systemic workload reforms, mental health support, and policy changes that reduce chronic stress.

Resilient Leadership

Definition:: A leadership approach that maintains clarity, flexibility, and steady presence during long-term stress or disruption.

Business Application: Resilient leadership stops organizational paralysis, leading teams through uncertainty with confidence and care.

Leadership Insight:: Resilience relies on support networks and recovery practices, not silent endurance.

Cultural Caution::
Overemphasizing resilience without tackling systemic issues risks making exploitation seem normal.

Mosaic Question:: Do you view resilience as a collective strength or as individual suffering?

Mosaic in Action:: A nonprofit director navigates political unrest by exemplifying transparency, fostering collective problem-solving spaces, and ensuring staff well-being.

Resistance Culture

Definition: A collective mindset or set of practices that actively challenges, disrupts, or subverts dominant systems, norms, or power structures.

Business Application: Resistance culture can be used to drive organizational change, innovation, and advocacy—especially in response to unfair policies.

Leadership Insight: Recognizing resistance as a form of engagement can help leaders direct it into positive reform rather than suppress it.

Cultural Caution: Resistance without a plan can tire out participants or cause punitive backlash; leaders need to consider timing, allies, and protective measures.

Mosaic Question: When resistance appears in your organization, do you shut it down—or listen for the truths it reveals?

Mosaic in Action: Employees oppose a biased evaluation system, leading leadership to redesign it with input from diverse staff.

Respectability Politics

Definition: Social and cultural expectations that marginalized individuals conform to dominant norms of appearance, behavior, or language to gain acceptance or opportunity.

Business Application: While adhering to respectability norms may provide short-term access, it often reinforces exclusionary standards and hinders genuine expression.

Leadership Insight: Leaders who oppose respectability politics can foster cultures where authenticity is prioritized over conformity.

Cultural Caution: Promoting conformity to dominant norms as a requirement for opportunity can sustain systemic bias and undermine trust.

Mosaic Question: What norms in your environment favor assimilation over authenticity—and who determines them?

Mosaic in Action: A corporate leader redefines "professionalism" in dress code policy to include cultural attire, hairstyles, and expressions of identity.

Cultural Caution: Confusing equality with equity can reinforce existing disparities by overlooking differences in starting points and systemic challenges.

Mosaic Question: Do your resource choices respond to actual needs or merely to appearances?

Mosaic in Action: A university assigns additional teaching assistants and technology grants to departments with a higher number of first-generation students, helping to improve retention rates.

Resource Equity

Definition: The fair and strategic distribution of resources—such as time, funding, staff, and opportunities—based on need and potential impact, rather than on equal sharing.

Business Application: Leaders dedicated to resource equity focus on supporting teams or individuals who face greater systemic barriers, ensuring everyone has the resources they need to succeed.

Leadership Insight: Achieving equity requires intentional redistribution, which can be uncomfortable but ultimately results in stronger collective outcomes.

Resource Guarding

Definition: The tendency of leaders or teams to hoard information, opportunities, or authority to safeguard their power.

Business Application: Resource guarding hinders collaboration, innovation, and equity by limiting access to growth.

Leadership Insight: Equitable leaders increase access to resources instead of limiting it, boosting capacity and fostering a sense of belonging.

Cultural Caution: In some settings, scarcity leads to real guarding. Leaders need to tell apart protective need from exclusionary control.

Mosaic Question: Where are resources being protected — and who is losing access because of it?

Mosaic in Action: An executive team rotated high-profile assignments rather than reserving them for insiders, expanding leadership pipelines.

Rest Culture

Definition: An organizational and cultural dedication to valuing rest, recovery, and balance as vital to performance and well-being.

Business Application: Companies that support breaks, vacations, and flexible schedules often experience higher creativity, productivity, and retention.

Leadership Insight: Leaders set the tone by modeling rest themselves, signaling that restoration is a strategic asset rather than a sign of weakness.

Cultural Caution: Celebrating rest only in words while rewarding overwork damages trust and promotes burnout culture.

Mosaic Question: How does your leadership safeguard — not just allow — rest?

Mosaic in Action: A nonprofit closes for one week each quarter, ensuring all employees disconnect and come back refreshed without fear of falling behind.

Restorative Justice Culture

Definition: An organizational approach that focuses on repairing harm, rebuilding trust, and restoring relationships instead of punishment and exclusion.

Business Application: This culture promotes dialogue, accountability, and collaborative problem-solving after conflict or misconduct, fostering deeper understanding and systemic improvement.

Leadership Insight: Restorative justice shifts the focus from "who's to blame" to "what needs repair," promoting resilience and cohesion in diverse teams.

Cultural Caution: Without proper training, restorative practices can be misused, seeming superficial or reducing the significance of harm.

Mosaic Question: When harm occurs in your space, do you punish, ignore, or repair?

Mosaic in Action: After a public workplace conflict, a facilitated conversation between the parties results in policy changes and renewed collaboration.

Restorative Leadership

Definition: A leadership style focused on repairing trust, healing relationships, and rebuilding systems after harm or disruption.

Business Application: Restorative leaders prioritize long-term relational health, guiding teams through repair processes that address both emotional and structural needs.

Leadership Insight: In high-stakes environments, restorative leadership can turn crises into opportunities for growth and cultural renewal.

Cultural Caution: Excessive focus on restoration without accountability can allow repeated harm; balance care with consequences.

Mosaic Question: When trust is broken, do you move on quickly— or take the time to repair what was lost?

Mosaic in Action: A CEO publicly acknowledges organizational harm during a restructuring, invites feedback from affected employees, and implements reforms based on their input.

Restorative Practice

Definition:: A framework for accountability and community-building that emphasizes repairing relationships, healing harm, and fostering inclusive dialogue.

Business Application: Restorative practices reduce conflict escalation, strengthen workplace culture, and provide alternatives to punitive discipline.

Leadership Insight:: Leaders who integrate restorative approaches model accountability as repair, not punishment, creating more resilient teams.

Cultural Caution:: Restorative practices must be authentic; using them as "soft punishment" without real repair undermines credibility.

Mosaic Question:: Do your systems repair harm or simply redistribute blame?

Mosaic in Action:: A school shifts from suspension policies to restorative circles, where students, teachers, and families collaborate to repair harm and rebuild trust.

Retaliation Culture

Definition: An environment where speaking up results in punishment, exclusion, or covert career sabotage.

Business Application: Retaliation culture suppresses misconduct reports and weakens whistleblower protections. It shields institutions instead of individuals.

Leadership Insight: Leaders dedicated to equity must dismantle the retaliation culture by ensuring protections and rewarding honesty.

Cultural Caution: In certain situations, loyalty is confused with silence. Leaders need to clearly demonstrate that accountability is a form of loyalty.

Mosaic Question: Do people feel safer remaining silent than telling the truth?

Mosaic in Action: After receiving retaliation complaints, an organization implemented anti-retaliation policies with external oversight.

Reversible Decision-Making

Definition: A decision-making approach where choices can be revisited, adjusted, or undone with minimal cost or disruption if circumstances change.

Business Application: Leaders utilize reversible decisions in pilot programs, iterative design, and adaptive strategies, enabling teams to respond swiftly to new information.

Leadership Insight: Recognizing which decisions are reversible helps prevent over-deliberation, accelerates innovation, and reduces fear of failure.

Cultural Caution: Treating high-stakes, irreversible choices as "testable" can undermine trust and introduce unnecessary risk.

Mosaic Question: Which of your current decisions could be approached as experiments rather than final decisions?

Mosaic in Action: A marketing team tests a new campaign in one region before scaling to a nationwide rollout, making adjustments based on feedback.

Rhetorical Inclusion

Definition: The use of inclusive language and statements without ensuring that actions and systems uphold these values.

Business Application: Organizations relying on rhetorical inclusion may post diversity statements while maintaining exclusive hiring practices or unfair policies.

Leadership Insight: Words set expectations—if not supported by action, they can increase cynicism and weaken credibility.

Cultural Caution: Public commitments without systemic change might be seen as tokenism or "virtue signaling."

Mosaic Question: Where do your words about inclusion surpass your actions?

Mosaic in Action: A company that publicly celebrates International Women's Day but has no women in senior leadership reviews its promotion criteria and adjusts its hiring practices.

Rhythms of Work

Definition: The natural cycles of energy, focus, and productivity that influence how individuals and teams perform over time.

Business Application: Leaders who understand and align workflows with team rhythms can boost output, prevent burnout, and promote sustainable productivity.

Leadership Insight: Effective leaders balance periods of high effort with recovery time, respecting both individual and collective energy patterns.

Cultural Caution: Applying uniform rhythms across diverse teams may overlook cultural, time zone, and neurodiversity needs.

Mosaic Question: Does your team's schedule reflect human energy patterns or just the clock?

Mosaic in Action: A global team adopts staggered deadlines and meeting-free afternoons, leading to higher-quality work and fewer stress-related absences.

Role Clarity

Definition: A clear definition of responsibilities, expectations, and decision-making authority within teams or organizations.

Business Application: Lack of role clarity drives conflict, duplication, and inequity. Clear roles promote fairness and efficiency.

Leadership Insight: Leaders promote stability and fairness by making roles clear, open, and flexible.

Cultural Caution: Cultures differ in their tolerance for ambiguity. Leaders must find a balance between clarity and flexibility.

Mosaic Question: Do your people clearly understand what is expected of them?

Mosaic in Action: A nonprofit decreased staff burnout by clarifying decision-making authority and documenting responsibilities.

Role-Model Gap

Definition: The disconnect between the leadership a group hopes to see and the representation or behaviors they actually experience.

Business Application: Addressing the role-model gap involves proactively developing and promoting diverse leaders who embody organizational values.

Leadership Insight: Representation without authenticity fails; genuine role models inspire because they mirror lived integrity and achievable paths.

Cultural Caution: Token appointments without real authority or influence reinforce the idea of a symbolic rather than genuine presence.

Mosaic Question: Who in your organization genuinely exemplifies the future you're creating—and who is absent from that vision?

Mosaic in Action: A company pairs emerging leaders from underrepresented backgrounds with high-visibility projects and decision-making authority, bridging the gap between aspiration and reality.

Root Cause Leadership

Definition: A leadership approach that tackles systemic and underlying issues instead of just addressing surface symptoms or quick fixes.

Business Application: Root cause leaders focus on diagnosing structural problems—such as unfair processes or outdated incentives—before implementing solutions.

Leadership Insight: Addressing problems at their source results in lasting change and minimizes the chances of crises repeating.

Cultural Caution: Leaders might face resistance when root causes involve deep-rooted power structures or long-standing norms.

Mosaic Question: Are you solving what's urgent, or what's truly foundational?

Mosaic in Action: Rather than adding wellness perks to combat burnout, a company reorganizes workloads, adjusts staffing ratios, and trains managers in sustainable scheduling.

◈ LETTER R CALLOUT

"Resilience is not endurance; it is the capacity to recover, adapt, and renew with others."

Reflection Questions

- When does resilience become fatigue, and how can leaders notice the difference?
- How does relational trust strengthen resilience across teams or communities?
- What role does reconciliation or repair play in your context?

Practical Move

Close your week by naming one resilience practice that helped you — then share it with a peer to normalize talking about recovery, not just output.

S – Silence, Safety, and Systemic Awareness

S reveals what is often hidden in plain sight. It does not focus on the loudest policies or most visible actions, but on the quieter forces that shape culture, belonging, and power long before words are spoken.

Silence, in this context, is never neutral. It can be wisdom or erasure, a trauma-informed pause or an institutional habit of avoidance. Sometimes, silence functions as a protective strategy—used to preserve dignity, manage risk, or conserve energy. Other times, it becomes a form of complicity—perpetuating harm by refusing to acknowledge it.

Safety, too, is never the same for everyone. What feels like psychological safety for one person may seem like emotional risk to another. Safety is relational, influenced by identity, history, and lived experience. A room can be polite yet feel unsafe. A meeting can be quiet but still exclusionary. True safety is not the absence of conflict but the presence of trust, voice, and humanity.

Systemic awareness, the third pillar, urges us to recognize how hidden hierarchies and unspoken rules impact outcomes within organizations and communities. It teaches us to observe systems in action—even when no one is deliberately discriminating. From "neutral" hiring practices that favor conformity to standardized language that suppresses cultural expression, systemic inequities often lie beneath the language of fairness.

S asks us to confront the subtler dynamics that sustain inequity

- Silence used as protection versus silence used as avoidance.
- Safety defined by dominant comfort rather than collective trust.
- Standardization presented as neutrality while reinforcing exclusion.
- Systems that reproduce inequality even under the banner of inclusion.

S challenges us to listen differently Who is asked to speak? Who is punished for staying silent—or for daring to use their voice? Whose sense of safety shapes the room, and whose discomfort is ignored?

S is a call to courage. Systems do not change on their own—people change them. The words we choose, the silences we break, and the structures we question determine whether we reinforce the status quo or disrupt it.

S calls leaders to move from focusing on appearances to genuine awareness, from superficial inclusion to structural strength, and from silence that shields power to silence that safeguards people. Because true leadership is judged not by how quietly you keep things comfortable, but by how boldly you drive change.

S

Safe Space vs Brave Space

Definition: A framework for dialogue that contrasts "safe spaces"—where individuals expect comfort and protection from harm—with "brave spaces," where discomfort is recognized as a driver for growth and deeper understanding.

Business Application: In diversity training, leaders may shift from promising "safe spaces" to creating "brave spaces" that foster honest, sometimes challenging conversations without fear of punishment.

Leadership Insight: Both safe and brave spaces need intentional facilitation, clear agreements, and trust-building—safety without bravery can hinder progress, while bravery without safety can cause harm.

Cultural Caution: What feels "brave" for one person can be very unsafe for another; leaders must understand power dynamics when setting up these spaces.

Mosaic Question: In your team's conversations, are you prioritizing comfort or encouraging courage?

Mosaic in Action: A nonprofit's leadership retreat begins with community agreements on respectful engagement, followed by guided discussions on racial equity that go beyond polite consensus into honest truth-telling.

Saviorism

Definition: A mindset or behavior where individuals or groups try to "rescue" others, often from a position of privilege, without emphasizing the agency, voice, or leadership of those directly affected.

Business Application: In corporate social responsibility efforts, saviorism occurs when companies implement solutions for marginalized communities without consulting or collaborating with them.

Leadership Insight: Real impact requires partnership, co-creation, and humility—not a hero story that makes the helper the focus.

Cultural Caution: Saviorism can reinforce stereotypes of incompetence or dependence, which weakens the very empowerment it claims to promote.

Mosaic Question: Are you helping in a way that keeps you in the spotlight—or that directs attention to others?

Mosaic in Action: An international aid organization moves from delivering pre-made aid packages to funding and training local leaders to develop their own recovery plans.

Scarcity Mindset

Definition: A belief that resources, opportunities, or recognition are scarce, leading to competition, gatekeeping, and fear of losing out.

Business Application: A scarcity mindset damages collaboration, weakens equity efforts, and creates division among employees instead of fostering shared success.

Leadership Insight: Leaders who move from scarcity to abundance foster inclusive cultures where opportunities grow instead of shrink.

Cultural Caution: In situations of real scarcity (funding, jobs), leaders must balance optimism with recognition of constraints.

Mosaic Question: Does your leadership model promote scarcity — or foster abundance?

Mosaic in Action: A nonprofit shifted from competitive grant seeking to shared funding coalitions, broadening impact and partnerships.

Segregated Systems

Definition: Structures or processes that, whether intentionally or unintentionally, divide people based on race, class, gender, ability, or other identity markers, thereby limiting fair access to resources, opportunities, or influence.

Business Application: Segregated systems can exist in education (tracking), housing (zoning), and corporate promotion pathways when advancement is limited to specific groups.

Leadership Insight: Equity-minded leaders analyze systems for both obvious and hidden segregation and work to redesign them for complete inclusion.

Cultural Caution: Segregation is often upheld by "neutral" policies that seem fair but sustain historic inequalities.

Mosaic Question: Where in your organization do "separate paths" result in unequal outcomes?

Mosaic in Action: A school district evaluates gifted program enrollment and adjusts criteria to incorporate broader measures of potential, leading to increased representation across various demographics.

Self-Awareness

Definition: The ability to recognize and understand your own emotional states, motivations, and behaviors. Self-awareness is the foundation of all emotional growth and leadership integrity.

Business Application: Leaders with self-awareness make better decisions, communicate more clearly, and adapt with humility. Organizations benefit when leaders understand their strengths, blind spots, and emotional effects on others.

Leadership Insight: Without self-awareness, no other leadership skill can be sustained. It is the mirror leaders must confront before guiding others.

Cultural Caution: Different cultures influence self-disclosure, either encouraging or discouraging it. Leaders must demonstrate self-awareness in ways that fit the context while staying authentic.

Mosaic Question: Do you really understand how your emotions and actions impact others?

Mosaic in Action: A director notices his stress is affecting

meetings. He pauses, acknowledges it to the team, and resets, demonstrating humility and emotional growth.

Self-Determination

Definition: The right and ability of individuals or communities to make choices about their own lives, resources, and futures without outside control or coercion.

Business Application: Supporting self-determination involves leaders helping team members set goals, shape processes, and define success in ways that match their values and strengths.

Leadership Insight: Empowerment feels empty if it lacks true decision-making power and respect for independence.

Cultural Caution: Forcing "best practices" from outside sources can weaken self-determination, even with good intentions.

Mosaic Question: Are you encouraging people to make decisions—or just to carry out yours?

Mosaic in Action: A community development project transitions from donor-led planning to resident-led councils that control funding priorities and project timelines.

Self-Leadership

Definition: The ability to guide, regulate, and align oneself emotionally and behaviorally, especially when external guidance is not available. Self-leadership combines independence with responsibility.

Business Application: Organizations succeed when individuals practice self-leadership — managing priorities, controlling stress, and staying aligned with the mission without constant oversight. It minimizes micromanagement and fosters resilience.

Leadership Insight: Self-leadership comes before leading others. Leaders who can't guide themselves may cause chaos or dependency within teams.

Cultural Caution: In some situations, self-leadership might be misunderstood as individualism. Leaders need to balance self-leadership with relational and cultural interdependence.

Mosaic Question: When no one is guiding you, can you still lead clearly?

Mosaic in Action: An emerging leader practices daily reflection to align values and actions, maintaining resilience without relying on external validation.

Sense of Belonging

Definition: The emotional feeling of being accepted, valued, and connected within a group, organization, or community.

Business Application: Organizations can cultivate a sense of belonging by implementing inclusive policies, acknowledging diverse contributions, and providing equitable access to opportunities.

Leadership Insight: Belonging is not just about showing up—it's about being recognized, heard, and appreciated for who you truly are.

Cultural Caution: Trying to foster belonging can fail if it requires conformity or suppresses individual identity.

Mosaic Question: What signals—verbal or nonverbal—does your environment send about who really belongs?

Mosaic in Action: A tech company updates its onboarding process to match new hires with mentors from similar cultural backgrounds, leading to higher retention and engagement rates.

Shadow Inclusion

Definition: A superficial look of inclusion that conceals underlying exclusionary practices or inequities.

Business Application: A company might showcase diversity in marketing while decision-making remains concentrated among a homogeneous leadership team.

Leadership Insight: True inclusion is gauged by influence, decision-making power, and respect—not just by representation.

Cultural Caution: Shadow inclusion can deepen mistrust, especially among marginalized groups who see the gap between appearance and reality.

Mosaic Question: Who seems to be included in your space—and who truly influences its direction?

Mosaic in Action: After promoting several women to mid-level management, an organization reviews its leadership pipeline and finds no women prepared for executive roles, prompting a change in mentorship strategies.

Shame Resilience

Definition: The ability to face shame without being paralyzed, to process it with self-compassion, and to work toward repair and growth.

Business Application: Shame resilience helps leaders and teams bounce back after mistakes, transforming failures into chances to learn.

Leadership Insight: Leaders with shame resilience demonstrate humility, which enhances psychological safety.

Cultural Caution: Shame functions differently in various cultures — collective versus individual. Leaders need to respond with cultural sensitivity.

Mosaic Question: Do you demonstrate resilience in the face of shame — or do you avoid it?

Mosaic in Action: After a public misstep, a leader acknowledged the mistake, apologized, and invited collaboration to create new norms, rebuilding trust.

Shared Language

Definition: A set of terms, concepts, and expressions understood and used consistently by members of a group to promote clarity, alignment, and connection.

Business Application: Developing shared language around values, goals, and equity commitments can improve communication and strengthen culture.

Leadership Insight: Shared language is a bridge for collaboration, but it must be regularly refreshed to reflect changing understanding.

Cultural Caution: Using shared language without shared meaning can create false consensus and slow progress.

Mosaic Question: Does your team's language reflect actual experiences—or just aspirational slogans?

Mosaic in Action: A nonprofit adopts consistent terminology for describing its equity goals, training all staff to use the same terms in meetings, reports, and external communications.

Silencing

Definition: The act—whether intentional or unintentional—of suppressing, dismissing, or ignoring someone's voice, perspective, or contributions.

Business Application: Silencing can happen in meetings when leaders interrupt certain participants more often than others or dismiss input without considering it.

Leadership Insight: Creating space for all voices is not passive; it requires active facilitation and accountability.

Cultural Caution: Silencing frequently impacts marginalized voices more heavily, reinforcing systemic inequalities.

Mosaic Question: Whose voice is missing in your discussions—and why?

Mosaic in Action: During a strategy meeting, a project leader notices that junior staff members stay quiet. They intentionally pause the conversation, invite input, and implement several suggestions, boosting overall team engagement.

Social Capital

Definition: The value gained from relationships, networks, and shared norms that foster trust, cooperation, and mutual support within and across groups.

Business Application: Leaders can use social capital to speed up change initiatives, promote cross-department collaboration, and improve problem-solving.

Leadership Insight: Social capital is built through consistent reciprocity, integrity, and genuine investment in others — not through quick networking gains.

Cultural Caution: Social capital can become exclusive if it depends on closed networks or favors those with preexisting privilege.

Mosaic Question: Who in your organization holds influence without formal authority, and how do they utilize it?

Mosaic in Action: A mid-level manager develops strong connections across teams, enabling them to quickly mobilize resources during a crisis — earning credibility beyond their official role.

Social Construct

Definition: An idea, category, or perception that is formed and upheld through collective agreement within a society or culture.

Business Application: Recognizing that norms around professionalism, leadership, or competence are socially constructed can lead to more inclusive definitions and practices.

Leadership Insight: Naming a concept as a social construct enables leaders to question and reshape it to promote more equitable outcomes.

Cultural Caution: Dismissing something as "just a social construct" can downplay its real-life impact on people dealing with it every day.

Mosaic Question: Which of your organization's "givens" are truly human-made rules that can be changed?

Mosaic in Action: A company revises its dress code after realizing it was based on Western corporate standards, updating it to be culturally inclusive without losing professionalism.

Social Debt

Definition: The ongoing obligation people feel because of favors, support, or opportunities others have given them without immediate return.

Business Application: Social debt can influence career choices, loyalty, and workplace interactions—sometimes causing unfair expectations or exploitation.

Leadership Insight: Leaders need to be aware of how unspoken debts can shape decisions and create power imbalances.

Cultural Caution: In collectivist cultures, social debt is often a valued part of mutual obligation, but it can also hide coercion.

Mosaic Question: How does the feeling of "owing" someone impact your willingness to be honest or challenge decisions?

Mosaic in Action: A team member consistently takes on extra tasks to "repay" a manager who supported them early in their career—until the organization steps in to balance the workload.

Social Grief

Definition: Collective mourning experienced by a community, nation, or group in response to shared loss, injustice, or disruption.

Business Application: Recognizing social grief in the workplace after major public events can foster empathy, solidarity, and trust.

Leadership Insight: Leaders who acknowledge and create space for grief—without rushing productivity—strengthen community resilience.

Cultural Caution: Trying to "move on" too quickly can increase alienation for those still going through loss.

Mosaic Question: How does your organization respond when there's grief outside your walls?

Mosaic in Action: After a major local tragedy, a company offers optional discussion groups and flexible schedules to support employees' emotional needs.

Social Imagination

Definition:: The ability to imagine different social realities beyond existing systems of inequality or restriction.

Business Application: Social imagination fuels innovation in organizations, enabling teams to rethink policies, practices, and cultures that no longer promote equity or sustainability.

Leadership Insight:: Leaders who cultivate social imagination inspire others to see not only what is, but what could be.

Cultural Caution:: Vision without follow-through risks becoming performative; imagination must be connected to practical action.

Mosaic Question:: What opportunities for justice or inclusion can you envision that haven't been created yet?

Mosaic in Action:: A city council involves youth in imagining climate-friendly public spaces. Their ideas influence zoning plans, incorporating parks and community gardens into redevelopment.

Social Intelligence

Definition: The skill of navigating interpersonal relationships with awareness, empathy, and emotional clarity. Social intelligence is the counterpart to emotional intelligence.

Business Application: Leaders who have social intelligence excel in collaboration, negotiation, and team building. They interpret cues accurately, adjust communication across differences, and build trust effectively.

Leadership Insight: Social intelligence is more than charm — it involves listening, attuning, and responding in ways that respect dignity and build connection.

Cultural Caution: Social cues differ across cultures. What signals warmth in one context (like direct eye contact or casual tone) might seem inappropriate in another.

Mosaic Question: Do you approach relationships for efficiency — or with the insight that fosters trust?

Mosaic in Action: A project manager observes tension among cross-cultural team members. By clarifying her intent and validating each voice, she restores collaboration and minimizes misunderstandings.

Social Location

Definition: The mix of social identities and positions—such as race, gender, class, ability, and geography—that influence how someone experiences and is seen by others.

Business Application: Knowing about social location helps leaders understand how personal and systemic factors affect decision-making, access to resources, and how people interact at work.

Leadership Insight: Leaders who think about their own social location as well as others' can better address bias, earn trust, and create fair systems.

Cultural Caution: Focusing too much on social location without recognizing individual differences can make people feel reduced to a list of identities.

Mosaic Question: How does your social location shape your view of conflict or opportunity?

Mosaic in Action: A senior leader reflects on how being a first-generation college graduate influences their mentorship style, giving targeted support to employees with similar backgrounds.

Social Reproduction

Definition: The processes through which social structures, norms, and inequalities are passed down across generations.

Business Application: Organizations may unconsciously perpetuate social reproduction by hiring from the same schools, valuing similar career paths, or promoting within homogeneous networks.

Leadership Insight: Disrupting social reproduction requires deliberate changes to hiring practices, leadership development, and cultural norms.

Cultural Caution: Efforts to uphold "tradition" can unintentionally reinforce inequity if they ignore which traditions are being preserved.

Mosaic Question: What systems in your organization pass privilege or disadvantage from one generation to the next?

Mosaic in Action: A nonprofit changes its internship program from unpaid to paid, breaking a cycle that favored applicants with financial means.

Socioeconomic Identity

Definition: An individual's self-concept and social standing are shaped by economic class, income, education, occupation, and other indicators of social status.

Business Application: Recognizing socioeconomic identity can help create more inclusive benefits packages, professional development

opportunities, and communication strategies.

Leadership Insight: Leaders who understand the importance of socioeconomic identity can help connect employees with different lived experiences.

Cultural Caution: Assuming class homogeneity can alienate employees and ignore barriers faced by people from working-class or economically marginalized backgrounds.

Mosaic Question: How does your socioeconomic background shape your leadership style and how you allocate resources?

Mosaic in Action: A CEO who grew up in a rural, low-income community advocates for tuition assistance programs to help employees pursue further education.

Solidarity Economy

Definition:: An economic model focused on cooperation, mutual aid, and shared ownership instead of competition and exploitation.

Business Application: Organizations aligned with solidarity economies focus on collective benefit—through worker cooperatives, ethical supply chains, or community reinvestment.

Leadership Insight:: Leaders in solidarity frameworks redefine success from profit maximization to shared resilience and equity.

Cultural Caution:: Solidarity economies might be dismissed as "utopian" in capitalist settings; leaders need to show they are practically viable.

Mosaic Question:: How does your economic model promote extraction or foster solidarity?

Mosaic in Action:: A local cooperative reinvests profits into housing, education, and healthcare for its members, fostering long-term community stability.

Solidarity Practice

Definition: Actions that demonstrate consistent, committed support for others—especially those from marginalized or underrepresented groups—based on shared values and mutual accountability.

Business Application: Practicing solidarity can strengthen partnerships, improve retention, and align organizational behavior with stated diversity goals.

Leadership Insight: Solidarity is not performative allyship; it demands ongoing action, taking risks, and the willingness to redistribute resources or influence.

Cultural Caution: Declaring solidarity without concrete follow-through can damage credibility and trust.

Mosaic Question: What risks are you willing to take to stand with others during challenging times?

Mosaic in Action: When a partner organization faces public backlash for advocating equity, a corporate leader issues a joint statement of support and commits funding to the cause.

Spiritual Identity

Definition: The sense of self shaped by spiritual or religious beliefs, practices, and affiliations, which can influence values, behaviors, and worldviews.

Business Application: Recognizing spiritual identity helps leaders develop inclusive policies around holidays, dress codes, and work schedules, promoting respect for diverse expressions of faith and meaning.

Leadership Insight: Leaders who acknowledge spiritual identity can better support overall well-being and recognize sources of resilience within their teams.

Cultural Caution: Assuming someone's spirituality—or lack thereof—based on appearance, cultural background, or stereotypes can lead to alienation and exclusion.

Mosaic Question: How does your spiritual identity influence how you lead, handle conflict, or define success?

Mosaic in Action: A team leader adjusts a project schedule to let members observe religious fasting, ensuring no one feels pressured to choose between work and faith.

Spiritual Leadership

Definition:: A leadership approach rooted in meaning, purpose, and values that go beyond personal ambition, often inspired by spiritual or moral traditions.

Business Application: Spiritual leadership promotes cultures of integrity and belonging by grounding work in core values beyond metrics or profit.

Leadership Insight:: When leaders combine spirituality with humility, they create environments where people align personal purpose with the organizational mission.

Cultural Caution:: Spiritual leadership should avoid enforcing a single belief system; inclusivity means allowing space for various ways of expressing meaning.

Mosaic Question:: What core values or purposes influence your leadership choices?

Mosaic in Action:: A hospital director starts team meetings with reflections on dignity and compassion, aligning daily work with the mission of patient care.

Sponsorship Culture

Definition: An organizational system in which sponsorship—leaders leveraging their influence to support others—is embedded, expected, and measured.

Business Application: Sponsorship culture ensures underrepresented employees aren't left to rely on luck or favoritism for advancement.

Leadership Insight: Leaders build equity through intentional and structured sponsorship, not randomly or sporadically.

Cultural Caution: In some areas, sponsorship is confused with nepotism. Leaders need to differentiate equity-focused sponsorship from favoritism.

Mosaic Question: Is sponsorship within your organization random — or a cultural norm?

Mosaic in Action: A consulting firm integrated sponsorship metrics into performance evaluations, holding leaders responsible for promoting diverse talent.

Stereotype Threat

Definition: The danger of confirming negative stereotypes about a social group, which can harm performance, confidence, and participation.

Business Application: Recognizing stereotype threat helps leaders create fair evaluation systems and foster psychologically safe workplaces for all employees.

Leadership Insight: By removing cues that trigger stereotype threat, leaders can unlock the potential of individuals who might otherwise underperform due to external pressures.

Cultural Caution: Do not frame stereotype threat as a personal weakness—it is a systemic problem that needs structural solutions.

Mosaic Question: What unspoken expectations in your environment could cause stereotype threat for certain groups?

Mosaic in Action: A manager adjusts presentation norms to promote multiple ways of contributing, reducing performance anxiety for those from underrepresented backgrounds.

Status Threat

Definition: The perceived decline in social standing, recognition, or influence when equity and inclusion alter traditional power dynamics.

Business Application: Status threats frequently drive backlash against DEI initiatives and inclusion efforts, especially among dominant groups.

Leadership Insight: Recognizing status threat while framing equity as a group benefit helps leaders handle resistance.

Cultural Caution: Expressions of status and hierarchy vary across cultures. Leaders should present equity in ways that match cultural values.

Mosaic Question: How do you encourage people to view equity as growth, not a loss?

Mosaic in Action: During pay equity reform, a leader stressed that closing gaps builds trust for everyone, reducing resistance.

Storytelling as Resistance

Definition: The deliberate use of personal or collective stories to challenge dominant narratives, disrupt injustice, and affirm marginalized identities.

Business Application: Using storytelling as resistance in training, marketing, or team-building can highlight diverse perspectives and promote cultural change.

Leadership Insight: Leaders who emphasize this type of storytelling show that dissent and lived experience are vital for organizational growth and innovation.

Cultural Caution: Using resistance stories for branding without backing the underlying movements can harm trust and authenticity.

Mosaic Question: Whose stories are missing from your organization's narrative—and what change might their inclusion bring?

Mosaic in Action: An employee resource group shares members' migration stories during an all-staff meeting, sparking new policy discussions about supporting immigrant employees.

Stagnant Leadership

Definition: A leadership style characterized by resistance to growth, innovation, or change. Stagnant leadership constrains organizational flexibility and hinders teams from achieving new levels of potential.

Business Application: In stagnant leadership cultures, outdated policies, rigid hierarchies, or unexamined traditions hinder progress. The result is declining morale, high turnover, and decreased competitiveness.

Leadership Insight: Leaders who cease learning set limits for everyone they lead. Ongoing self-reflection and adaptation are the cures for stagnation.

Cultural Caution: In certain cases, stability is valued and confused with strength. Leaders must tell the difference between offering steadiness and resisting essential growth.

Mosaic Question: Which aspect of your leadership has stalled, and what is it costing your team?

Mosaic in Action: A CEO stuck on outdated sales strategies ignored changing market trends until staff pushed for innovation. When leadership finally adapted, morale and performance rebounded.

Structural Competency

Definition: The ability to identify and address social, economic, and political systems that influence health, opportunities, and inequality.

Business Application: Leaders with this skill can develop strategies that target systemic issues rather than just individual problems.

Leadership Insight: This skill helps leaders connect daily decisions—such as resource distribution or service provision—to larger structural effects.

Cultural Caution: Only focusing on individual behavior without considering structural factors can lead to blaming those most impacted by inequality.

Mosaic Question: What structural barriers are affecting the patterns in your organization or community?

Mosaic in Action: A healthcare administrator notices transportation issues as a barrier to care and partners with a local ride-share service to increase patient access.

Structural Racism

Definition:: The embedding of racial inequities in laws, policies, institutions, and cultural norms creates systemic advantages for some and disadvantages for others.

Business Application: Structural racism accounts for disparities in housing, healthcare, education, and employment. Identifying it enables leaders to tackle inequities at their source.

Leadership Insight:: Leaders who focus solely on interpersonal bias but overlook structural racism perpetuate inequality. Lasting change demands systemic action.

Cultural Caution:: Some contexts deny the existence of structural racism; leaders must combine evidence with dialogue to promote understanding.

Mosaic Question:: Where do workplace structures unintentionally reproduce racial inequity?

Mosaic in Action:: A bank updates lending practices after data reveal racial disparities in loan approvals, adding accountability measures to combat structural bias.

Structural Violence

Definition: Systemic harm resulting from social, economic, and political structures that disadvantage specific groups over time.

Business Application: Structural violence appears through unequal access to healthcare, education, and leadership opportunities. Leaders must acknowledge their responsibility in dismantling it.

Leadership Insight: Leaders who focus only on interpersonal conflict overlook the deeper structural forces that cause inequality.

Cultural Caution: Structural violence manifests in various forms worldwide (e.g., caste, colonization, racial inequity). Leaders must consider the context.

Mosaic Question: What structural damages does your leadership cause — even unintentionally?

Mosaic in Action: A university tackled structural violence by removing legacy admissions and boosting equity for first-generation students.

Stunted Leadership

Definition: Leadership that lacks proper development, mentoring, or preparation — leaving leaders unprepared to manage complexity, equity, or adaptive challenges.

Business Application: Stunted leadership often emerges when individuals are promoted based on technical skills but are not provided with leadership training. Teams under such leaders face confusion, mismanagement, and limited opportunities for growth.

Leadership Insight: A leader can only guide others as far as they've gone themselves. Investing in leadership development ensures

leaders are prepared to foster growth in others.

Cultural Caution: In some organizations, rapid promotions without proper development are celebrated. Without training or mentoring, however, these leaders risk causing long-term damage to culture and trust.

Mosaic Question: Are you investing in your leadership development, or expecting others to follow where you haven't been?

Mosaic in Action: A new director, promoted for her technical expertise, enrolled in leadership coaching to improve her emotional and cultural intelligence, enhancing her ability to lead her team effectively.

Subtle Bias

Definition: Indirect, often unintentional prejudices or attitudes that influence interactions, decisions, and perceptions without overt hostility.

Business Application: Recognizing subtle bias helps leaders improve hiring, evaluation, and promotion processes to promote fairness and inclusion.

Leadership Insight: Addressing subtle bias requires self-awareness and the willingness to examine ingrained habits that may exclude or undervalue others.

Cultural Caution: Subtle bias can be more harmful than overt discrimination because it is harder to identify, name, and address—yet it accumulates over time.

Mosaic Question: Where might subtle bias be shaping your assumptions or decisions without you realizing?

Mosaic in Action: During a meeting, a project manager notices they consistently direct technical questions to male engineers and intentionally starts engaging female team members equally.

Super-Diversity

Definition: A term describing complex, multilayered diversity that extends beyond ethnicity to include factors such as migration history, legal status, language, faith, and education.

Business Application: Understanding super-diversity helps organizations design products, services, and communications that address the detailed needs of diverse communities.

Leadership Insight: Leaders who embrace super-diversity move past one-dimensional diversity metrics,

creating policies and programs that reflect actual-world complexity.

Cultural Caution: Treating all diversity the same or oversimplifying differences into a single category risks erasing important nuances that shape experiences and inclusion.

Mosaic Question: How might super-diversity within your team impact communication, problem-solving, and innovation?

Mosaic in Action: A city council adjusts community outreach strategies for neighborhoods where residents differ not only in ethnicity but also in language, migration background, and socioeconomic status.

Suppressive Leadership

Definition: A destructive leadership style where leaders intentionally hinder the progress, voice, or growth of others to maintain control or dominance.

Business Application: Suppressive leadership appears in practices like gatekeeping promotions, silencing dissent, or withholding resources. It fosters inequity, damages trust, and pushes talent away.

Leadership Insight: True leadership fosters growth; oppressive leadership hoards power.

Leaders who suppress others show fear and insecurity instead of strength.

Cultural Caution: In hierarchical or high power-distance cultures, suppression may be normalized or concealed as "discipline." Leaders must differentiate cultural respect for authority from abusive control.

Mosaic Question: Where might you be unknowingly suppressing others to protect your position?

Mosaic in Action: An executive prevented junior staff from attending client meetings to maintain control of information. After intervention, the company adopted inclusive practices that provided opportunities across different levels.

Symbolic Inclusion

Definition: The presence of diversity or representation that lacks real influence, voice, or decision-making power for marginalized individuals.

Business Application: Leaders must evaluate whether diversity initiatives truly empower or merely serve as symbolism to improve optics without altering power structures.

Leadership Insight: Genuine inclusion involves integrating marginalized voices into meaningful roles, not just displaying them in marketing materials or ceremonial positions.

Cultural Caution: Symbolic inclusion can backfire by increasing cynicism and mistrust among those it claims to represent.

Mosaic Question: Are your inclusion efforts creating actual opportunities for influence, or are they just ticking a box?

Mosaic in Action: A nonprofit's advisory board includes community members only in name until the director updates bylaws to give them equal voting rights.

Systemic Fatigue

Definition:: The exhaustion that builds up from dealing with unfair, bureaucratic, or unjust systems over time.

Business Application: Systemic fatigue presents as disengagement from DEI initiatives, mistrust of institutions, and turnover among underrepresented staff.

Leadership Insight:: Fatigue indicates that systems, not people, need fixing. Leaders must create equity initiatives that are sustainable, well-funded, and restorative.

Cultural Caution:: Labeling fatigue as laziness or apathy only causes harm and dismisses valid criticism.

Mosaic Question:: Where has systemic fatigue diminished trust in your institution—and how can you rebuild it?

Mosaic in Action:: After years of ineffective DEI committees, a company reallocates funds, sets measurable goals, and shares responsibility, reducing fatigue and rebuilding trust.

Systemic Oppression

Definition: The institutionalized and structural systems of disadvantage and privilege that sustain inequality across social, economic, and political domains.

Business Application: Recognizing systemic oppression enables leaders to develop strategies that target root causes of inequity rather than just surface solutions.

Leadership Insight: Lasting change happens when leaders work to dismantle policies, norms, and structures that cause harm.

Cultural Caution: Only focusing on individual behavior while ignoring systemic forces can continue cycles of inequality.

Mosaic Question: Which systems within your sphere of influence reinforce inequities, and how can you start to dismantle them?

Mosaic in Action: A school district reviews disciplinary policies and removes zero-tolerance rules that unfairly affect students of color.

Systemic Privilege

Definition: The unearned advantages and benefits given to certain groups through established social, economic, and political systems.

Business Application: Recognizing systemic privilege helps leaders create policies that address inherited advantages and increase access to resources for underrepresented groups.

Leadership Insight: Leaders need to examine how they benefit from systemic privilege to genuinely work toward removing inequalities.

Cultural Caution: Privilege is often unseen by those who have it, so acknowledgment and accountability are crucial for meaningful progress.

Mosaic Question: In what ways might you be benefiting from systemic privilege while others face exclusion?

Mosaic in Action: A hiring manager understands that their preference for "top schools" unintentionally disadvantages first-generation graduates from lesser-known universities and then adjusts the recruitment process.

Systemic Resilience

Definition:: The capacity of systems—whether organizational, cultural, or societal—to adapt, recover, and thrive under stress without collapsing.

Business Application: Systemic resilience is developed through redundancy, adaptability, and equity, ensuring continuation during crises.

Leadership Insight:: Resilient systems aren't inflexible—they bend under pressure while safeguarding the most vulnerable.

Cultural Caution:: Over-celebrating resilience can excuse harmful structures by expecting communities to endlessly endure.

Mosaic Question:: Does your system bend and adapt under pressure—or does it break?

Mosaic in Action:: A global nonprofit decentralizes decision-making across regions, enabling local leaders to respond quickly to crises while staying aligned with the shared mission.

Systems Healing

Definition: The process of repairing and transforming systems that have caused harm, focusing on restoration, equity, and long-term resilience.

Business Application: Systems healing emphasizes structural changes that prevent harm from happening again while rebuilding trust among stakeholders.

Leadership Insight: True healing involves both recognizing past harms and making ongoing investments in structural changes.

Cultural Caution: Systems healing cannot be rushed; rushing for quick "closure" often skips the deeper repairs needed.

Mosaic Question: What would it look like to shift from merely fixing broken systems to genuinely healing them?

Mosaic in Action: After identifying discriminatory practices in lending, a bank partners with affected communities to redesign its approval process and support local businesses.

Systems Literacy

Definition: The ability to understand, analyze, and navigate the interconnected structures and processes that influence outcomes in organizations and society.

Business Application: Leaders with systems literacy can spot leverage points for change, predict unintended consequences, and align decisions with long-term goals.

Leadership Insight: Systems literacy enables leaders to go beyond quick fixes and develop strategies that change entire ecosystems.

Cultural Caution: Without systems literacy, well-meaning interventions can worsen the very problems they aim to fix.

Mosaic Question: How could a deeper understanding of systemic relationships alter your approach to solving challenges?

Mosaic in Action: A public health leader identifies how housing policy, food access, and transportation affect community health outcomes, then collaborates across sectors to address these issues.

Business Application: Sustainable inclusion aligns diversity initiatives with business goals, embedding them into leadership development, policies, and daily activities.

Leadership Insight: Inclusion becomes sustainable when it is measured, supported, and championed at all levels—not viewed as a temporary project.

Cultural Caution: Without planning for sustainability, inclusion progress can reverse if funding, leadership, or public interest declines.

Mosaic Question: How will you ensure that today's inclusion efforts stay effective five or ten years from now?

Mosaic in Action: A tech company creates mentorship and sponsorship programs with clear accountability metrics, guaranteeing ongoing representation in leadership roles for decades.

Sustainable Inclusion

Definition: The continuous integration of inclusive practices into an organization's core operations, culture, and strategy, ensuring they last over time.

◈ LETTER S CALLOUT

"Systems do not fail accidentally — they fail in ways that mirror their design."

Reflection Questions

- How does silence sustain inequity in your environment?
- What signs of solidarity do you notice when people resist exclusion?
- Where does systemic fatigue appear in your team or classroom?

Practical Move

Pick one system you interact with daily (grading, hiring, feedback). Identify one way it advantages some and disadvantages others — and raise that insight in dialogue.

T – Tone, Tokenism, and Truth-Telling

T is the language of impact—how we choose words, how we deliver them, and the emotional responses they evoke. Tone is not just a stylistic choice; it reflects power, intent, and identity. In culturally diverse settings, tone signals whether someone belongs or is excluded. What sounds "measured" to one listener might seem "patronizing" to another. What reads as "assertive" from one voice might be seen as "aggressive" in another. Tone is rarely neutral—it is influenced by who is speaking, how others perceive them, and the systems that establish legitimacy.

Tokenism occurs when representation is symbolic instead of systemic—when individuals are invited for appearances but denied genuine influence. It is the display of inclusion without actually sharing power. Tokenism forces people to "represent" entire groups while taking authority away from them to influence outcomes. The result is reduced authenticity, broken trust, and visibility without a voice.

Truth-telling involves revealing what others avoid. In equity work, it's not a disturbance to progress—it is progress. Too often, environments prioritize comfort over clarity, shielding status instead of promoting accountability. Those most affected are branded "divisive" when they speak up, while silence is seen as professionalism. Truth-telling is not an attack—it is a step toward repair. But for it to be sustainable, it must be protected culturally, not just driven by individual courage.

T asks us to pay attention to what lies beneath communication

- Tone that carries hidden codes of power, legitimacy, or dismissal.
- Tokenism that performs diversity while withholding authority.
- Truth-telling reframed as disruption instead of recognized as courage.
- Trust that is fractured when voices are policed instead of heard.

The T terms remind us that language is more than words—it's about impact. Tone is never neutral. Tokenism is never harmless. And truth-telling is never optional if equity is the goal.

T calls on leaders to shift from policing voices to protecting them, from symbolic gestures to systemic inclusion, and from avoiding hard truths to embracing them as the foundation of trust. Because leadership is not measured by how smooth things sound, but by how courageously truth is spoken and received.

T

Taboo

Definition: A socially or culturally forbidden action, discussion, or behavior, often regulated through informal norms or official sanctions.

Business Application: Recognizing taboos helps leaders handle sensitive topics carefully, avoiding alienating stakeholders, while also knowing when and how to challenge harmful silences.

Leadership Insight: Leaders who understand taboos can strategically decide when to honor boundaries and when to push them for necessary change.

Cultural Caution: What is taboo in one culture may be neutral or even encouraged in another; cross-cultural awareness is crucial.

Mosaic Question: Which unspoken rules influence your environment — and do they promote or hinder progress?

Mosaic in Action: A global manager learns that discussing salary is taboo in one office but openly discussed in another, so they adjust their communication approach accordingly.

Tactical Empathy

Definition: The intentional and strategic use of empathy to build trust, understand perspectives, and influence outcomes in high-stakes situations.

Business Application: Tactical empathy enables negotiators, mediators, and leaders to anticipate needs and address unspoken concerns without manipulation.

Leadership Insight: When applied ethically, tactical empathy shifts power dynamics from adversarial to collaborative.

Cultural Caution: Overusing or feigning empathy can damage credibility and harm relationships if seen as insincere.

Mosaic Question: How can you use empathy not just to understand, but to strategically foster cooperation?

Mosaic in Action: During a conflict over resource allocation, a department head actively reflects the other team's frustrations before proposing a solution—resulting in a faster, mutually beneficial agreement.

Team Equity

Definition: The fair and inclusive distribution of opportunities, resources, recognition, and decision-making authority within a team.

Business Application: Prioritizing team equity boosts retention, morale, and performance by making sure contributions are valued and advancement is accessible to all team members.

Leadership Insight: Leaders who demonstrate equitable practices promote fairness among peers and work to eliminate favoritism.

Cultural Caution: Equality and equity are different—treating everyone the same can reinforce existing inequalities.

Mosaic Question: Where might unequal access to voice, credit, or growth opportunities be present within your team?

Mosaic in Action: A project manager alternates high-visibility presentation duties among all team members instead of always assigning them to the same few individuals.

Techno-solutionism

Definition: The idea that technology alone can resolve complex social, cultural, or organizational issues.

Business Application: Techno-solutionism fuels superficial DEI efforts, like algorithmic hiring tools that reproduce bias rather than eliminate it.

Leadership Insight: Leaders must avoid relying on tools alone for equity and instead combine technology with human-centered strategies.

Cultural Caution: Some communities might oppose or distrust tech solutions because of past experiences with surveillance or exploitation.

Mosaic Question: Do you trust technology to "fix" inequity — or people to lead it?

Mosaic in Action: A corporation enhanced AI resume screening with human reviewers to promote fairness in candidate selection.

Temporal Culture

Definition: The shared attitudes, norms, and practices a group has about time—such as punctuality, scheduling, and work pace.

Business Application: Understanding temporal culture helps leaders establish realistic timelines, coordinate across different time zones, and minimize friction in global teams.

Leadership Insight: Time is not just a resource—it's a cultural lens that influences how people perceive urgency, deadlines, and long-term planning.

Cultural Caution: Imposing a single temporal norm, such as strict punctuality or quick turnaround, without adaptation can lead to tension and misunderstandings in multicultural environments.

Mosaic Question: How does your relationship with time align or conflict with those you work with?

Mosaic in Action: In a partnership between a U.S. company and a Latin American supplier, leaders modify project timelines to respect cultural differences in pace and process.

Territorial Acknowledgment

Definition: A formal or informal recognition of the Indigenous peoples who have historically inhabited and cared for the land where an event, organization, or activity takes place.

Business Application: Territorial acknowledgments can serve as an entry point for organizations to build deeper relationships, support reconciliation, and provide tangible support for Indigenous communities.

Leadership Insight: Acknowledgment without ongoing action risks being superficial; effective leaders follow acknowledgment with policies, resources, or partnership commitments.

Cultural Caution: Ensure accuracy and consult local Indigenous leaders or knowledge keepers—misrepresentation or generic language can cause harm.

Mosaic Question: What commitments follow your acknowledgment of the land and its history?

Mosaic in Action: At the opening of a leadership summit, the host organization acknowledges the Indigenous nation whose land they occupy and announces a new scholarship fund for Indigenous students.

Textured Identity

Definition: An identity formed by various layered influences like culture, heritage, geography, class, and personal experiences, often resisting easy categorization.

Business Application: Recognizing textured identities helps leaders avoid one-dimensional assumptions and create more inclusive policies and experiences.

Leadership Insight: Leaders who embrace the complexity of textured identities create environments where people can fully express their authentic selves without oversimplifying their stories.

Cultural Caution: Respect the complexities of identity instead of forcing individuals to "simplify" it for your understanding; honor the layers, even if they challenge tidy categories.

Mosaic Question: Where in your leadership do you allow space for the complexity of others' stories?

Mosaic in Action: A marketing director works with employees from diverse backgrounds to develop a campaign that showcases layered cultural influences instead of relying on stereotypes.

Third Culture Kid (TCK)

Definition: An individual who spends much of their developmental years outside their parents' culture, blending aspects of their birth culture(s) with those of the host culture(s).

Business Application: TCKs often possess high adaptability, cross-cultural skills, and a global

perspective—valuable assets in international organizations and diverse teams.

Leadership Insight: While TCKs may be adept at navigating differences, they can also face identity confusion and feelings of rootlessness; leaders should provide anchors of belonging.

Cultural Caution: Don't assume all TCKs share the same experiences or that their cross-cultural skills eliminate the need for support.

Mosaic Question: How can you identify and utilize the global perspectives that TCKs offer without neglecting their need for stability?

Mosaic in Action: A company hires a TCK for an international client relations position, pairing them with a mentor to help navigate the internal corporate culture.

Threshold Conversations

Definition: Dialogues that happen at crucial moments of change, decision, or entering a new phase— often shaping the tone, trust, and path of what follows.

Business Application: Leaders who approach threshold conversations intentionally can strengthen alignment, build trust, and prevent miscommunication during transitions.

Leadership Insight: These moments provide opportunities to set expectations, clarify values, and establish psychological safety before moving forward.

Cultural Caution: In some cultures, threshold conversations may be indirect or symbolic; using a direct style might miss important cues.

Mosaic Question: What key conversations mark the thresholds in your work—and how do you prepare for them?

Mosaic in Action: Before a merger, two department heads hold a threshold conversation to acknowledge uncertainties, share non-negotiables, and commit to transparent updates.

Threshold Fatigue

Definition: Emotional or mental exhaustion resulting from repeatedly facing major transitions or change points that demand increased attention, adaptation, and emotional effort.

Business Application: Teams experiencing frequent restructuring, leadership changes, or policy updates may have a reduced ability to fully engage with each new initiative.

Leadership Insight: Recognizing threshold fatigue helps leaders pace change, allow recovery time, and focus on stability when possible.

Cultural Caution: In environments with high change, understand that people may need more than just procedural updates—consider the human impact of constant transition.

Mosaic Question: How are you incorporating rest and recovery during periods of frequent change?

Mosaic in Action: After several reorganizations, a department leader delays launching a new strategic plan in favor of holding sessions to rebuild trust and morale.

Time Privilege

Definition: Unequal access to discretionary time due to socioeconomic status, job role, caregiving responsibilities, or systemic inequities.

Business Application: Leaders with more flexible schedules often underestimate the barriers faced by those with rigid or multiple-shift schedules.

Leadership Insight: Time is a resource; equitable leadership requires considering who can afford to attend events, training, or networking outside of normal hours.

Cultural Caution: Avoid assuming that being "always available" is a sign of commitment—it may simply reflect privilege.

Mosaic Question: Whose voices and contributions might be missing because they lack the same control over their time?

Mosaic in Action: A nonprofit adjusts its staff meeting times to accommodate both night-shift workers and caregivers, boosting attendance and engagement.

Time Sovereignty

Definition: The ability to control, prioritize, and protect one's own time in line with personal values, needs, and goals.

Business Application: Promoting time sovereignty helps prevent burnout, enhances focus, and encourages a culture of respecting boundaries.

Leadership Insight: Leaders who demonstrate and safeguard time sovereignty show that rest and focused work are as important as responsiveness.

Cultural Caution: In cultures where long hours are viewed as a sign of loyalty, supporting time sovereignty may require deliberate cultural changes.

Mosaic Question: How can you build systems that let people own their time without facing penalties?

Mosaic in Action: A project manager starts "focus hours" with no scheduled meetings, allowing team members to work uninterrupted.

Tokenism

Definition: The practice of making a superficial or symbolic effort to include underrepresented individuals without addressing deeper systemic inequalities.

Business Application: Tokenism weakens genuine inclusion by prioritizing appearance over meaningful structural change.

Leadership Insight: True inclusion involves valuing individuals for their skills and perspectives, not just their identity category.

Cultural Caution: Tokenism can place excessive pressure on individuals to represent an entire group, which reinforces stereotypes.

Mosaic Question: Are your diversity initiatives fostering real belonging or merely meeting an appearance quota?

Mosaic in Action: A company shifts from a one-time diversity hire approach to a comprehensive program of recruitment, mentorship, and leadership development.

Tolerance vs Transformation

Definition: The difference between passively accepting diversity (tolerance) and actively reshaping systems to create equity and belonging (transformation).

Business Application: Organizations that stop at tolerance risk maintaining the status quo rather than dismantling systemic barriers.

Leadership Insight: Transformation requires courageous policy changes, cultural shifts, and accountability measures beyond surface-level inclusion.

Cultural Caution: Tolerance may seem positive, but it often reinforces power imbalances by framing acceptance as a favor rather than a right.

Mosaic Question: Are you simply making room at the table, or are you rebuilding the table entirely?

Mosaic in Action: A school district moves from "celebrating diversity week" to redesigning curriculum with multiple cultural perspectives year-round.

Tonal Shifts

Definition: Changes in the emotional or communicative tone of a person, group, or organization, often indicating shifts in mood, power, or intent.

Business Application: Leaders who notice tonal shifts in meetings or communications can step in early to preserve trust and alignment.

Leadership Insight: Paying attention to tonal shifts involves active listening, cultural awareness, and sensitivity to unspoken cues.

Cultural Caution: What might seem like a small tonal change in one culture can signal serious disapproval or disengagement in another.

Mosaic Question: What tonal changes have you observed recently, and what might they indicate beneath the surface?

Mosaic in Action: During a tense negotiation, a team leader senses the shift from collaborative to defensive language and pauses to reset expectations.

Tone Policing

Definition: Critiquing the emotional tone of a message— especially from marginalized voices—rather than engaging with the substance of the message itself.

Business Application: Tone policing can undermine psychological safety, reduce trust, and silence important perspectives in the workplace.

Leadership Insight: Leaders need to separate emotional expression from the validity of the concern being raised.

Cultural Caution: In multicultural teams, differences in communication style can be misunderstood as aggression, disrespect, or unprofessionalism.

Mosaic Question: Are you focusing on how something is said rather than what is being said?

Mosaic in Action: In a staff meeting, an employee expresses frustration about a policy. Instead of criticizing their tone, the manager acknowledges the concern and guides the conversation toward solutions.

Toxic Leadership

Definition: A destructive leadership style marked by manipulation, abuse of power, or self-interest that harms team well-being and organizational health.

Business Application: Toxic leadership leads to higher turnover, disengagement, and burnout. Recognizing and addressing toxic behaviors is essential for creating resilient and sustainable workplaces.

Leadership Insight: Toxic leadership prospers in silence. Leaders need to find the courage to identify and challenge toxicity, replacing it with accountability and restorative practices.

Cultural Caution: Behaviors labeled "toxic" in one situation (e.g., aggressive confrontation) may be accepted in another. Leaders need to distinguish between cultural differences and harmful actions.

Mosaic Question: Do you accept toxic behaviors for results — or do you stand up to them to protect others?

Mosaic in Action: A board steps in to remove a high-performing yet abusive manager, emphasizing organizational culture over short-term profits.

Tradition vs. Transformation

Definition: The tension between maintaining established cultural or organizational practices and adapting to meet changing needs and values.

Business Application: Leaders must identify when tradition enhances identity and when it restricts progress.

Leadership Insight: Balancing respect for tradition with the bravery to innovate is essential for staying relevant and building trust.

Cultural Caution: In some cultures, changing tradition might be seen as disrespectful; transformation efforts need to be approached carefully.

Mosaic Question: Which traditions are worth keeping, and which should be transformed to meet today's realities?

Mosaic in Action: A nonprofit updates its annual gala to include community storytelling and local vendors, preserving its history while broadening its impact.

Trans Inclusion

Definition: The deliberate effort to foster environments where transgender and gender-diverse individuals are respected, affirmed, and fully integrated into all aspects of society or an organization.

Business Application: Trans inclusion policies might include hiring practices, healthcare benefits, restroom access, pronoun use, and anti-discrimination measures— demonstrating a commitment to equity and retention.

Leadership Insight: Leaders who actively normalize gender diversity through language, policy, and representation help create safer spaces for authenticity, innovation, and belonging.

Cultural Caution: Trans inclusion strategies should be adapted to fit the legal, cultural, and safety contexts of different regions— applying them globally without local adjustments can put people at risk.

Mosaic Question: How do your systems support trans identities not only through policies but also in daily practices?

Mosaic in Action: A multinational company creates an employee resource group for gender-diverse staff, updates internal systems to include chosen names, and provides trans-affirming health coverage worldwide.

Transformational Leadership

Definition: A leadership style that encourages and inspires people to go beyond expectations by promoting vision, innovation, and personal development.

Business Application: Transformational leaders foster cultural change, boost engagement, and build resilience during organizational transitions.

Leadership Insight: This approach relies on trust, authenticity, and the leader's ability to link personal purpose with organizational objectives.

Cultural Caution: Without cultural awareness, transformational efforts may unintentionally enforce values that clash with local or community norms.

Mosaic Question: How do you inspire people to transform themselves and the systems they influence?

Mosaic in Action: A CEO facing industry disruption unites employees around a shared vision and invests in professional growth to address new challenges.

Transformative Justice

Definition: A framework for addressing harm that aims to repair relationships, address root causes, and change the conditions that enabled the harm.

Business Application: In workplaces, transformative justice can guide conflict resolution processes that focus on healing, accountability, and cultural change.

Leadership Insight: It shifts the focus from punishment to prevention, fostering environments where harm is less likely to happen again.

Cultural Caution: Implementing transformative justice without community input risks recreating power imbalances it aims to eliminate.

Mosaic Question: How can your response to harm reshape the system that allowed it to happen?

Mosaic in Action: After a harassment incident, an organization uses facilitated dialogue and structural policy changes instead of just issuing formal warnings.

Transgenerational Resilience

Definition: The ability for strength, adaptability, and thriving to be passed down through generations, often in response to adversity.

Business Application: Organizations led by communities with histories of displacement, colonization, or systemic oppression often inherit survival skills and cultural wisdom that enhance innovation and solidarity.

Leadership Insight: Recognizing and honoring inherited resilience shifts the narrative from deficit-based to strength-based leadership, unlocking untapped potential.

Cultural Caution: Celebrating resilience should not be used to justify ongoing inequity or to minimize the need for systemic change.

Mosaic Question: What forms of resilience have you inherited, and how are you passing them on?

Mosaic in Action: A community-led nonprofit develops programs rooted in intergenerational knowledge, blending ancestral farming techniques with modern sustainability practices.

Transgenerational Trauma

Definition: The psychological and physiological effects of trauma passed from one generation to the next through stories, behaviors, biology, and social conditions.

Business Application: In the workplace, unaddressed transgenerational trauma can affect communication styles, trust, and conflict, especially in diverse teams.

Leadership Insight: Trauma-aware leaders recognize that performance issues or interpersonal conflicts may stem from historical and family backgrounds, not just individual actions.

Cultural Caution: Addressing trauma without cultural sensitivity risks retraumatization; solutions should be co-created and implemented carefully.

Mosaic Question: How does history influence your leadership—and how can healing become part of your impact?

Mosaic in Action: A school district serving refugee populations combines trauma-informed counseling with culturally responsive curricula to support students and families.

Transitional Leadership

Definition: A leadership approach dedicated to guiding teams and organizations during times of change, uncertainty, or interim leadership. Transitional leaders stabilize, prepare, and lay the groundwork for long-term direction.

Business Application: Transitional leadership is essential during mergers, successions, or crisis recovery. It maintains continuity, alleviates anxiety, and builds trust until permanent structures are established.

Leadership Insight: Transitional leaders balance stability and change. They create space for uncertainty while conveying hope and possibility.

Cultural Caution: Different cultures react to transitions in different ways. Some prioritize consistency; others look for significant change. Leaders need to understand the context to prevent additional disruptions.

Mosaic Question: Do you see leadership transitions as gaps to endure — or as opportunities to intentionally reset?

Mosaic in Action: An interim nonprofit director concentrates on listening sessions and boosting morale before transferring leadership to a long-term successor.

Translation Fatigue

Definition: The exhaustion that results from repeatedly adapting language, tone, or cultural references to ensure understanding.

Business Application: Employees in multicultural teams often carry an unseen burden of continuous translation—both linguistic and cultural—that affects productivity.

Leadership Insight: Recognizing and sharing this workload helps prevent burnout and promotes fairness in cross-cultural communication.

Cultural Caution: Ignoring translation fatigue can lead to disengagement among those needed to bridge cultural or language gaps.

Mosaic Question: Who takes on the most translation work in your environment, and how can you distribute that responsibility?

Mosaic in Action: A bilingual project manager's translation role is formalized within her job description, along with additional compensation and support.

Translation Loss

Definition: The subtle or significant meaning lost when ideas are translated across languages or cultural contexts.

Business Application: Translation loss misunderstandings can disrupt negotiations, marketing, or team alignment.

Leadership Insight: Effective leaders confirm understanding through conversation, not just literal translation.

Cultural Caution: Direct translations can remove nuance, humor, or cultural meaning, which can cause misunderstanding.

Mosaic Question: What meaning might have been lost between what you said and what others heard?

Mosaic in Action: An international campaign customizes key messages with local input to maintain the intended emotional impact.

Translation Privilege

Definition: The advantage held by individuals whose language or cultural background is dominant, making it easier for others to understand them.

Business Application: Translation privilege often gives certain employees more influence because their communication is considered the default.

Leadership Insight: To address translation privilege, organizations should develop systems that value multiple communication styles and languages equally.

Cultural Caution: Assuming everyone shares the same cultural references can reinforce exclusion and limit diverse perspectives.

Mosaic Question: In whose language or cultural context are your decisions and communications centered?

Mosaic in Action: A global company rotates meeting facilitation across different languages to ensure decision-making is not always based on English norms.

Transparency Culture

Definition: An organizational environment where openness, honesty, and clarity are integral to communication and decision-making. A culture of transparency prioritizes trust and accountability over secrecy.

Business Application: Companies that foster a transparency culture share both successes and setbacks. Leaders explain the reasons behind decisions, which helps reduce speculation and disengagement.

Leadership Insight: Transparency is not oversharing; it's maintaining consistent clarity. Leaders who foster a transparency culture build credibility, even in tough situations.

Cultural Caution: Transparency might clash with norms that prioritize hierarchy or discretion. Leaders need to balance openness with respect for cultural expectations.

Mosaic Question: Do people in your organization trust the process, or do they fill gaps with speculation?

Mosaic in Action: A CEO shares decision rationales in staff newsletters, making sure employees understand not just *what* decisions were made but *why*.

Trauma-Informed

Definition: An approach that acknowledges the widespread impact of trauma and aims to prevent re-traumatization by promoting safety, trust, and empowerment. Being trauma-informed involves incorporating an understanding of trauma's effects into policies, practices, and relationships.

Business Application: Trauma-informed workplaces foster environments where employees feel safe, valued, and supported. This involves adjusting HR processes, leadership training, and wellness programs to recognize and reduce the impact of trauma.

Leadership Insight: Trauma-informed leaders look beyond behavior to underlying experiences. They respond with empathy and accountability, which helps reduce harm and build resilience.

Cultural Caution: Not all cultures define or express trauma the same way. Leaders must avoid imposing Western trauma frameworks without respecting local understandings of suffering and healing.

Mosaic Question: Do your systems and relationships unintentionally cause re-traumatization — or do they create space for healing?

Mosaic in Action: A school district updates disciplinary policies to include trauma-informed practices,

moving from punishment to relational support for students.

Trauma-Informed Leadership

Definition: An approach to leadership based on understanding the prevalence and effects of trauma, with the goal of creating safety, trust, and empowerment for everyone involved.

Business Application: Trauma-informed leaders develop policies and environments that minimize re-traumatization, emphasize psychological safety, and promote recovery.

Leadership Insight: This style of leadership fosters resilience and retention by focusing on empathy without compromising accountability or excellence.

Cultural Caution: Focusing too much on trauma without providing solutions can foster a culture of learned helplessness; leaders need to balance validation with opportunities for agency.

Mosaic Question: How can you lead in a way that restores safety and dignity to those who have experienced harm?

Mosaic in Action: A nonprofit director implements flexible schedules, peer support groups, and training for managers to identify trauma responses in staff and clients.

Trauma-Informed Practice

Definition: An approach to service delivery or interaction that recognizes signs of trauma, integrates that knowledge into practices, and actively works to prevent re-traumatization.

Business Application: This practice applies across sectors—healthcare, education, law enforcement, and corporate HR—ensuring interactions are based on safety, trust, and empowerment.

Leadership Insight: Incorporating trauma-informed principles into daily operations creates environments where people feel seen, respected, and capable of growth.

Cultural Caution: Trauma-informed work must consider cultural understandings of harm, healing, and resilience; applying a single model can undermine trust.

Mosaic Question: How does your work environment demonstrate emotional safety to those who enter?

Mosaic in Action: A hospital redesigns patient intake procedures to allow survivors of violence to select their care provider's gender and control the pace of questioning.

Trauma-Informed Systems

Definition: Organizations and institutions built with trauma-informed principles integrated into their structures, policies, and culture. These systems go beyond individual practices to achieve institutional transformation.

Business Application: Trauma-informed systems address equity gaps by ensuring that hiring, evaluation, and accountability processes minimize harm. Healthcare, education, and corporate sectors are increasingly adopting systemic trauma awareness.

Leadership Insight: Systemic change requires leaders to go beyond just personal awareness. Trauma-informed systems establish conditions where healing and resilience become standard, not rare.

Cultural Caution: Systems may resist change if trauma is seen as personal weakness rather than a systemic issue. Leaders must reframe trauma as a collective and systemic concern.

Mosaic Question: Does your institution function as a trauma-informed system — or does it rely on individuals to do the work?

Mosaic in Action: A hospital integrates trauma-informed design into its patient care approach, ensuring staff training, physical environments, and protocols all promote dignity and safety.

Trauma Stewardship

Definition: The practice of caring for oneself and others while engaged in work involving trauma exposure, ensuring sustainability and resilience.

Business Application: Trauma stewardship helps staff in healthcare, education, and humanitarian aid avoid burnout and secondary trauma.

Leadership Insight: Leaders who practice trauma stewardship promote rest, reflection, and resilience-building in high-stakes work.

Cultural Caution: Approaches to trauma differ. Some cultures focus on collective rituals, while others emphasize private processing. Leaders must adjust their strategies.

Mosaic Question: How can you protect yourself and others while leading through trauma?

Mosaic in Action: An NGO implemented reflection circles and

peer-support systems for frontline disaster relief workers.

Tribalism

Definition: A strong loyalty to one's own social group, often accompanied by distrust or hostility toward outsiders, which can influence identity and decision-making.

Business Application: In organizations, tribalism can manifest as departmental silos, "us versus them" thinking, or resistance to collaborating with external partners—hindering innovation and adaptability.

Leadership Insight: Leaders should promote the positive aspects of group loyalty (such as solidarity and shared purpose) while working to eliminate exclusionary behaviors that undermine trust and diversity.

Cultural Caution: In some contexts, "tribal" refers to actual Indigenous or ethnic communities with rich cultural heritages; avoid using the term metaphorically without recognizing its original meaning.

Mosaic Question: Where does your loyalty strengthen unity, and where might it restrict your openness to others?

Mosaic in Action: A CEO notices rivalry between regional offices and forms cross-location project teams to build trust and develop a shared identity.

Trust-Building

Definition: The ongoing process of building credibility, trustworthiness, and psychological safety in relationships. Trust-building is the foundation of effective collaboration and leadership.

Business Application: Building trust enhances engagement, innovation, and conflict resolution. Leaders who focus on trust-building lower turnover and promote long-term loyalty.

Leadership Insight: Trust is not a one-time achievement but a daily practice. Leaders who focus on small acts of trust-building maintain credibility through change and stress.

Cultural Caution: Trust-building practices differ. In some cultures, trust is based on personal relationships; in others, it relies on competence or dependability. Leaders need to adjust their methods.

Mosaic Question: Which leadership practices actively foster trust — and which silently undermine it?

Mosaic in Action: A project leader provides tough feedback privately while praising strengths publicly, strengthening both accountability and trust.

Trust Culture

Definition: An organizational environment where reliability, transparency, and mutual respect are actively fostered, allowing people to feel safe in taking risks and sharing ideas.

Business Application: A trust culture enhances collaboration, lowers turnover, and accelerates decision-making because people spend less time managing fear or protecting themselves.

Leadership Insight: Trust develops from consistent actions over time; it is earned gradually and lost quickly. Leaders must demonstrate the behaviors they want to see, especially during high-pressure moments.

Cultural Caution: Trust-building practices differ around the world; what indicates reliability in one culture may seem evasive or aggressive in another.

Mosaic Question: What do people in your team trust you to always do—and what do they quietly doubt?

Mosaic in Action: A department head shares quarterly decision rationales with their team, even when outcomes are unpopular, showing a commitment to transparency.

Trust Repair

Definition: The intentional process of restoring credibility and reliability after a breach of trust, whether between individuals, teams, or entire organizations.

Business Application: Trust repair may include public acknowledgment of harm, policy adjustments, compensation, and consistent demonstration of new behaviors over time.

Leadership Insight: Repair requires overcommunication, humility, and ongoing effort; words alone rarely rebuild broken trust.

Cultural Caution: The timeline and approach for trust repair differ across cultures; in some contexts, a public apology is crucial, while in others, discreet restitution is more effective.

Mosaic Question: What would it take for those you've lost trust with to believe in you again?

Mosaic in Action: After a failed product launch harms client relationships, a company creates a recovery plan with transparent updates, direct outreach, and service guarantees.

Trust Resilience

Definition: The ability of relationships, teams, or organizations to maintain or regain trust after facing challenges, conflicts, or setbacks.

Business Application: In unpredictable markets or high-pressure situations, trust resilience helps teams navigate uncertainty without resorting to suspicion or disengagement. It maintains ongoing collaboration even when mistakes happen.

Leadership Insight: Trust resilience is developed through consistent reliability before a crisis occurs. Leaders with a history of fairness, transparency, and follow-through find it easier to restore trust when it is tested.

Cultural Caution: The way people define "trust" and "resilience" varies across cultures; actions that show recovery in one context may not rebuild confidence in another.

Mosaic Question: When trust has been tested, what actions indicate that the relationship can withstand the challenge?

Mosaic in Action: A project team misses a key deadline, but because the leader has fostered a culture of mutual accountability, stakeholders agree on a revised plan without blaming each other.

Trust Tax

Definition: The extra burden on marginalized employees to constantly prove credibility, competence, or belonging.

Business Application: The trust tax saps energy, hampers progress, and sustains inequality within organizations.

Leadership Insight: Leaders should reduce unnecessary scrutiny and create systems that foster equitable trust.

Cultural Caution: Trust functions differently across cultures — in some, it is given collectively, while in others, it is granted individually.

Mosaic Question: Who in your organization is paying a higher trust tax — and for what reason?

Mosaic in Action: After staff complained about inconsistent scrutiny, the company overhauled its evaluation systems to eliminate double standards in performance reviews.

Trustworthy Leadership

Definition: Leadership based on integrity, transparency, and consistency between words and actions, building confidence among stakeholders.

Business Application: Trustworthy leaders attract and keep talent, foster loyalty, and motivate discretionary effort because people feel secure in their guidance.

Leadership Insight: Trustworthiness is earned through consistent behavior, not titles or credentials. Leaders who admit mistakes and take corrective steps are seen as more credible than those who avoid accountability.

Cultural Caution: What is seen as trustworthy leadership in one culture (e.g., bold decision-making) might be seen as reckless or domineering in another.

Mosaic Question: How do people know they can rely on you— especially when the outcome is uncertain?

Mosaic in Action: A regional director discusses both the risks and benefits of an expansion plan, inviting team input before making final decisions, which builds confidence in their leadership.

Truth and Reconciliation

Definition: A structured process for addressing historical or systemic harm, recognizing its impact, and working toward collective healing and restorative justice.

Business Application: In corporate or institutional settings, truth and reconciliation initiatives may address past discrimination, inequitable policies, or environmental harm, fostering long-term legitimacy and stakeholder trust.

Leadership Insight: Leaders involved in reconciliation must be ready for discomfort, long timelines, and the fact that truth-telling doesn't ensure immediate forgiveness.

Cultural Caution: Using the language of "truth and reconciliation" without a real commitment to follow through risks worsening mistrust and doing more harm.

Mosaic Question: What truth needs to be spoken before reconciliation can start?

Mosaic in Action: A university commissions an independent review of its role in historic land dispossession and then collaborates with affected Indigenous communities to develop reparative programs.

Truth-Telling Culture

Definition: A workplace or community norm where honesty is valued and encouraged, even when the truth challenges authority or disrupts comfort.

Business Application: A truth-telling culture promotes innovation by enabling people to bring up problems early, reducing costly mistakes and damage to reputation.

Leadership Insight: Leaders need to differentiate between constructive truth-telling and unfiltered venting; the former bolsters the culture, while the latter can weaken it if not managed.

Cultural Caution: In some societies, direct truth-telling might clash with norms of harmony or face-saving; adjust your approach to fit the cultural setting without compromising integrity.

Mosaic Question: How do you create space for hard truths without punishing those who voice them?

Mosaic in Action: An nonprofit uses an anonymous feedback system and hosts quarterly "courageous conversation" sessions to openly discuss concerns.

Tuning Bias

Definition: The unconscious tendency to selectively focus on, amplify, or dismiss information based on preconceived expectations, preferences, or stereotypes.

Business Application: In hiring, performance reviews, and decision-making, tuning bias can cause overlooking important insights or undervaluing contributions from certain individuals or groups.

Leadership Insight: Effective leaders intentionally broaden their perspective by seeking disconfirming evidence and diversifying their sources of information.

Cultural Caution: Tuning bias often overlaps with cultural bias; leaders should be aware of how their mental "filters" may unconsciously favor specific communication styles, accents, or approaches.

Mosaic Question: What perspectives might you be unknowingly tuning out—and at what cost?

Mosaic in Action: During a design review, a manager realizes they've been prioritizing feedback from senior engineers and overlooking junior team members, whose ideas later prove critical to the project's success.

Tuning In

Definition: The intentional practice of giving full, present attention to people, situations, or environmental cues to accurately understand needs and dynamics.

Business Application: Tuning in enhances communication, improves conflict resolution, and helps leaders anticipate issues before they escalate.

Leadership Insight: Tuning in involves slowing down and noticing not just what is said, but how it's said—tone, timing, and unspoken signals often provide the most insight.

Cultural Caution: The cues people use to signal meaning vary widely across cultures; for example, silence may indicate disagreement in one context and agreement in another.

Mosaic Question: When was the last time you truly heard beyond the words?

Mosaic in Action: A facilitator observes that two team members are unusually quiet during a strategy session, pauses the discussion, and invites their input—unlocking a perspective that shifts the group's direction.

Turnkey Inclusion

Definition: A fully developed, ready-to-implement set of practices, policies, or systems designed to seamlessly embed inclusion into an organization's daily operations.

Business Application: Turnkey inclusion initiatives ease the load on internal teams by providing ready-to-use frameworks for equitable hiring, onboarding, training, and culture-building.

Leadership Insight: While turnkey solutions enable quick implementation, leaders must adapt them to their organization's unique context; inclusion that feels "off the shelf" without genuine integration risks tokenism.

Cultural Caution: Pre-packaged inclusion programs need to be tailored to reflect local cultures, legal requirements, and community histories to avoid a one-size-fits-all approach.

Mosaic Question: How can ready-made tools be customized so they reflect your culture's reality rather than an outsider's template?

Mosaic in Action: A mid-sized company adopts a turnkey diversity training program but enhances it with local employee-led storytelling sessions to ensure cultural relevance and authenticity.

◇ LETTER T CALLOUT

"Trust is the currency of leadership — once broken, it cannot simply be demanded back."

Reflection Questions

- How does tone policing or toxic leadership erode trust where you work or study?
- When has transparency restored confidence in a decision or leader?
- How do trauma-informed practices shift how teams respond to stress?

Practical Move

At the close of your next meeting, ask participants one trust-building question: *What helped you feel safe here, and what could improve next time?*

U – Unconscious Bias, Unspoken Norms, and Unearned Advantage

U guides us into the unseen structures of inequality—the embedded cues, silent scripts, and hidden frameworks that shape belonging before anyone speaks. These forces often go unnamed, yet they determine whose voices are trusted, whose leadership is recognized, and whose differences are quietly managed instead of celebrated.

Unconscious bias resides in the automatic assumptions we make about others based on race, gender, age, accent, disability, or perceived "fit." These judgments may not always be malicious, but they are always impactful. They influence hiring decisions, mentoring opportunities, perceptions of professionalism, and the definition of leadership potential.

Unspoken norms serve as invisible guidelines that determine how people are expected to speak, act, or succeed. They often come across as "common sense" or "professionalism," but they are rooted in dominant cultural expectations. These norms reward conformity and punish authenticity—leaving those who resist them labeled as "unfit" or "difficult."

Unearned advantage points out the privileges given just for fitting in with dominant norms. Being seen as competent, receiving the benefit of the doubt, or being listened to without interruption might seem normal to those who have these advantages, but they come at a cost to others who are struggling in systems never made for them.

U asks us to recognize the cumulative toll of these dynamics

- The constant decoding of unspoken expectations.
- The emotional exhaustion of translating difference into "acceptability."
- The inequities that persist even under inclusive mission statements.
- The gaps between intention and impact in DEI strategies.

U reminds us that transformation starts with self-awareness, not strategy. It encourages leaders to evaluate whether norms preserve sameness under the guise of cohesion, whether power is held mostly by those aligned with the dominant culture, and whether policies that claim to promote inclusion are actually enacted in practice.

U calls leaders to lead with discernment—to question assumptions, challenge hidden rules, and redistribute unearned advantages. Because equity is not only about who enters the room, but about whose truth is safe, whose needs are supported, and whose differences are honored without condition.

U

Ubuntu Leadership

Definition: A leadership philosophy based on the African idea of Ubuntu — "I am because we are." Ubuntu leadership focuses on interconnectedness, compassion, and shared responsibility rather than individual success.

Business Application: Organizations practicing Ubuntu leadership prioritize shared success, community well-being, and inclusive decision-making. It enhances loyalty, collaboration, and trust across diverse teams.

Leadership Insight: Ubuntu leadership redefines power as relational, not hierarchical. Genuine authority comes from empowering others rather than focusing on oneself.

Cultural Caution: Ubuntu is a concept rooted in African culture with profound significance. Using it without understanding its context can lead to appropriation. Leaders should respect its origins and recognize its cultural background.

Mosaic Question: How might your leadership change if you measured success not by "I" but by "we"?

Mosaic in Action: A community health initiative adopts Ubuntu leadership principles, making sure strategy meetings start by asking, "How will this decision affect the whole?"

Unacknowledged Grief

Definition: Emotional pain and loss that are felt but not openly recognized, validated, or processed, often because they are considered inappropriate, inconvenient, or invisible by societal standards.

Business Application: In the workplace, unacknowledged grief can show up as disengagement, conflict, or sudden turnover— especially after organizational changes like layoffs, leadership shifts, or cultural transformations.

Leadership Insight: Leaders who acknowledge and create space for grief help rebuild trust, boost morale, and foster a sense of belonging. Recognition doesn't mean fixing the loss; it starts with being seen and showing empathy.

Cultural Caution: Some cultures expect grief to be private; others see public acknowledgment as crucial for healing. Leaders should approach with cultural awareness and avoid forcing a single grieving style.

Mosaic Question: What losses—personal or shared—might be influencing the unspoken dynamics within your team right now?

Mosaic in Action: Following a community tragedy, a school principal takes a quiet moment of reflection at the start of the day, acknowledging the shared loss without pressuring anyone to speak.

Unapologetic Leadership

Definition: Leading with clear conviction, authenticity, and alignment to values—without diluting decisions to appease discomfort—while maintaining respect and openness to dialogue.

Business Application: Unapologetic leaders exemplify clarity and courage, attracting individuals who resonate with the mission and preventing mission drift caused by over-accommodation.

Leadership Insight: Being unapologetic does not mean being inflexible or dismissive; it involves making decisions rooted in purpose, considering diverse perspectives, and acting with integrity.

Cultural Caution: In some settings, assertive leadership may be misunderstood as arrogance or authoritarianism, especially across different cultural or gender expectations. Adjusting tone and approach is crucial.

Mosaic Question: When have you watered down a decision to avoid discomfort—and what might have been different if you had stood firmly in your values?

Mosaic in Action: A nonprofit director declines funding from a source that conflicts with the organization's mission, explaining the decision openly to staff and stakeholders despite potential backlash.

Unconscious Bias

Definition: Automatic, unexamined attitudes or stereotypes that influence perception, decision-making, and behavior without conscious awareness.

Business Application: Unconscious bias affects hiring, promotions, client relationships, and crisis response—often interfering with diversity and inclusion efforts despite formal commitments.

Leadership Insight: Awareness is the first step, but implementing structural safeguards—like standardized evaluation criteria or blind recruitment methods—is necessary to address these hidden biases.

Cultural Caution: Biases are culture-specific; a stereotype in one setting might not exist in another, and new biases can develop during cross-cultural interactions.

Mosaic Question: Which assumptions do you rarely question—and how might they be influencing your decisions without your awareness?

Mosaic in Action: A hiring manager notices their shortlisting process favors candidates from a particular university and adopts blind résumé reviews to broaden the applicant pool.

Unconscious Compliance

Definition: The unintentional acceptance of rules, norms, or systems without questioning their fairness, relevance, or alignment with one's values.

Business Application: Organizations succeed when compliance is conscious and intentional, not automatic. Unquestioned adherence can sustain outdated practices, inequalities, and inefficiencies.

Leadership Insight: Leaders need to differentiate between essential compliance for safety or ethics and inherited procedures that no longer support the mission. Promoting thoughtful questioning encourages innovation and accountability.

Cultural Caution: In cultures with high power distance, challenging compliance can be risky; in others, it may be expected. Leaders must balance cultural norms with the need for principled change.

Mosaic Question: Where in your work are you following rules that no longer make sense—and what is the cost of doing so?

Mosaic in Action: During a policy review, a new team lead questions a long-standing approval process that delays project launches, realizing it exists only because "we've always done it this way."

Unconscious Gatekeeping

Definition: The unintentional limiting of access, opportunities, or resources by individuals or systems, often based on unexamined assumptions about who is "ready," "qualified," or "a good fit."

Business Application: Managers might unknowingly withhold stretch assignments from team members based on perceived readiness, which can reinforce inequalities and hinder talent growth.

Leadership Insight: Genuine inclusion requires leaders to actively review decision points for bias—both in formal policies and informal choices—so that opportunities are fairly distributed.

Cultural Caution: Standards for readiness or fit are often culturally built and may favor dominant norms. Without cultural awareness, gatekeeping can unintentionally exclude high-potential contributors.

Mosaic Question: What opportunities might you be unknowingly closing off—and for whom?

Mosaic in Action: A senior editor notices only writers with specific stylistic backgrounds are chosen for lead articles. She adjusts the process to incorporate diverse voices and perspectives, expanding the publication's reach.

Unconventional Leadership

Definition: A leadership style that breaks away from traditional norms, structures, or expectations, often combining creativity, authenticity, and flexible problem-solving.

Business Application: Unconventional leaders can challenge stagnant processes, inspire innovation, and engage teams or audiences in new, unexpected ways that standard strategies might miss.

Leadership Insight: While unconventional methods can lead to breakthroughs, leaders need to ground them in clear values and goals to ensure they are seen as purposeful rather than unpredictable.

Cultural Caution: In some environments, breaking from tradition is celebrated; in others, it can cause mistrust or resistance. Recognizing the culture's openness to change is important.

Mosaic Question: Where might an unexpected approach create opportunities your usual methods can't reach?

Mosaic in Action: A department head replaces formal weekly meetings with walking one-on-ones, boosting morale, open communication, and creative problem-solving.

Underrepresentation

Definition: The inadequate presence or participation of specific groups in roles of influence, decision-making, or visibility compared to their share in the overall population.

Business Application: Underrepresentation affects innovation, cultural understanding, and market expansion by restricting the variety of perspectives that inform strategies and decisions.

Leadership Insight: Tackling underrepresentation requires more than just recruitment—it also involves retaining talent, promoting advancement, and fostering environments where underrepresented individuals can succeed.

Cultural Caution: Efforts to combat underrepresentation must steer clear of tokenism, ensuring that inclusion is genuine and not merely symbolic.

Mosaic Question: Who is absent from the table—and in what ways does their absence influence the conversation and outcomes?

Mosaic in Action: A technology company observes a shortage of women in senior engineering roles and implements mentorship and sponsorship programs that result in clear increases in promotions.

Undermining

Definition: Actions or words that weaken someone's credibility, authority, or confidence—whether intentional or unintentional—often in subtle, indirect ways.

Business Application: Undermining behavior can damage team trust, slow decision-making, and create hostile work environments, even when it's disguised as "just being realistic" or "offering feedback."

Leadership Insight: Leaders must model and promote constructive communication, addressing undermining behavior early to protect psychological safety and team cohesion.

Cultural Caution: In some cultures, indirect criticism is common; in others, it may be seen as passive-aggressive or disloyal. Leaders need to carefully consider intent versus impact.

Mosaic Question: Where might you be unintentionally weakening someone's position instead of strengthening the team's collective strength?

Mosaic in Action: A project manager realizes their casual jokes about a colleague's inexperience are discouraging participation and harming that colleague's influence. They apologize and start highlighting that colleague's contributions in meetings.

Unearned Advantage

Definition: Benefits, privileges, or opportunities given to individuals or groups because of systemic factors like race, gender, socioeconomic status, or geographic location—rather than individual effort or merit.

Business Application: Unearned advantages can impact hiring, promotions, and access to resources, shaping workplace demographics and power dynamics unintentionally.

Leadership Insight: Recognizing unearned advantage is not about undermining individual success; it's about understanding systemic patterns that influence results and working to create a fairer playing field.

Cultural Caution: Discussions about unearned advantage can trigger defensiveness if they are framed as personal blame. Rooting these conversations in systemic context helps keep them constructive.

Mosaic Question: Which of your advantages stem from systems you didn't build—and how can you leverage them to broaden opportunities for others?

Mosaic in Action: A senior leader recognizes that her career growth was supported by informal networks she didn't have to pursue. She starts a structured mentorship program so others without that access can also benefit.

Unexamined Tradition

Definition: A custom, ritual, or practice that is maintained over time without critically assessing its current relevance, inclusivity, or impact.

Business Application: Many organizational norms—such as strict dress codes or hierarchical meeting structures—are legacies of the past that may now obstruct innovation or inclusion.

Leadership Insight: Effective leaders respect valuable traditions while questioning those that no longer serve their people, goals, or changing circumstances.

Cultural Caution: Challenging tradition without cultural sensitivity can be perceived as disrespect or arrogance; framing the discussion as evolution rather than erasure fosters trust.

Mosaic Question: Which traditions in your environment deserve renewal—and which should be let go?

Mosaic in Action: A university stops hosting its annual "Founders' Day" under its original name after students reveal the founders' involvement in exclusionary practices. The event is repositioned to honor a more inclusive legacy.

Unfiltered Feedback

Definition: Honest, straightforward input given without softening, sugarcoating, or filtering for politeness—sometimes helpful for clarity, sometimes harmful if not careful.

Business Application: Unfiltered feedback can speed up problem-solving and build trust when shared constructively, but it can harm relationships if seen as harsh or dismissive.

Leadership Insight: Leaders must set the right tone for feedback that is both honest and caring, making sure clarity doesn't come at the expense of dignity.

Cultural Caution: Communication styles differ; what feels like directness in one culture might seem rude or aggressive in another.

Mosaic Question: How can you tell the whole truth in a way that strengthens rather than breaks connection?

Mosaic in Action: During a design review, a team leader offers honest but respectful feedback, clearly explaining why a concept doesn't work and immediately offering suggestions for improvement—leading to a better final product.

Unheard Voices

Definition: Perspectives, experiences, or ideas that remain overlooked or dismissed, often because of power dynamics, bias, or lack of representation.

Business Application: Unheard voices restrict innovation, problem-solving, and decision-making quality by limiting the variety of insights leaders consider.

Leadership Insight: Leaders must establish structures that actively invite, amplify, and act on perspectives that are not usually elevated in current systems.

Cultural Caution: Simply inviting voices into the room is not enough; without follow-through, this can lead to tokenism or damage trust.

Mosaic Question: Who is speaking but not being heard in your organization or community?

Mosaic in Action: During a strategy meeting, a junior staff member's suggestion is overlooked until a senior manager revisits it, credits the original speaker, and incorporates the idea into the final plan.

Unintentional Exclusion

Definition: The unknowing overlooking or Marginalization of individuals or groups due to unconscious bias, habitual practices, or systemic blind spots.

Business Application: Unintentional exclusion can happen in meeting scheduling that overlooks time zones, policies that fail to consider cultural holidays, or product designs that assume a single type of user.

Leadership Insight: Good intentions do not ensure inclusion. Leaders must actively review systems, language, and environments to find where exclusion occurs automatically.

Cultural Caution: Labeling exclusion as "unintentional" should not be used to lessen its impact; harm happens regardless of motive.

Mosaic Question: Where might your processes unintentionally exclude people—and how will you remove those gaps?

Mosaic in Action: A tech company recognizes their new app lacks accessibility features for visually impaired users. Instead of treating it as a minor oversight, they invest in redesigning it and involve disability advocates to guide the process.

Unintended Consequences

Definition: Outcomes — often harmful — that happen when policies, practices, or interventions produce results not originally planned or foreseen.

Business Application: In DEI efforts, unintended consequences could include overloading marginalized staff with committee work or unintentionally reinforcing exclusion through poorly designed mentorship programs.

Leadership Insight: Leaders who anticipate unintended consequences enhance resilience. Incorporating feedback loops and humility helps prevent harm.

Cultural Caution: What is unintended in one context can be highly predictable in another. Leaders need to listen to historically marginalized voices to prevent making the same mistakes.

Mosaic Question: What unintended consequences might your leadership decisions cause — and who could end up bearing the cost?

Mosaic in Action: A company launches a women's leadership program but makes adjustments after feedback shows it unintentionally excluded nonbinary employees.

Unlearning

Definition: The deliberate process of releasing outdated knowledge, beliefs, or habits that no longer contribute to personal growth, equity, or collective progress.

Business Application: Organizations undergoing cultural transformation often require employees to unlearn legacy procedures, language norms, or hierarchical mindsets that conflict with new practices values.

Leadership Insight: Unlearning is not a passive loss of knowledge but an active skill that makes room for more relevant, inclusive, and effective practices.

Cultural Caution: Unlearning can be uncomfortable, especially when old habits are linked to identity or perceived expertise; leaders should accompany it with support and dialogue.

Mosaic Question: What do you need to let go of to lead more clearly and effectively?

Mosaic in Action: A manager trained in top-down command styles learns to step back, facilitate collaboration, and share decision-making power with the team, boosting morale and innovation.

Unmotivated Engagement

Definition: The state where individuals engage in organizational or cultural activities with little energy, effort, or purpose — often just being present without genuine connection.

Business Application: Unmotivated engagement appears in staff meetings, diversity initiatives, or team projects where people are present but disengaged. It indicates deeper cultural problems like burnout, lack of trust, or unclear purpose.

Leadership Insight: True engagement requires meaning. Leaders must go beyond participation metrics and foster environments where people are driven by values, belonging, and shared vision.

Cultural Caution: In some cultures, quiet or passive presence might not indicate disengagement but represent a different form of respect. Leaders should differentiate cultural styles of engagement from true withdrawal.

Mosaic Question: Are your teams showing up with confidence — or with intention?

Mosaic in Action: A school district switches from mandatory DEI training to voluntary affinity groups and dialogue sessions, turning unmotivated participation into genuine engagement.

Unpaid Emotional Labor

Definition: The unseen, unpaid effort of managing others' feelings, maintaining harmony, or providing emotional support in professional or personal settings.

Business Application: Employees—often women, people of color, or those in marginalized roles—may be expected to resolve conflicts, mentor struggling peers, or ease tensions without formal recognition or compensation.

Leadership Insight: Leaders should ensure that emotional labor is valued, fairly shared, and, when possible, formally recognized or rewarded.

Cultural Caution: Believing that certain groups are "naturally better" at emotional work reinforces stereotypes and can cause burnout.

Mosaic Question: Who is silently bearing the emotional burden in your workplace, and how can you help share or support it?

Mosaic in Action: In a nonprofit, one staff member is always the go-to for comforting upset clients. The leadership team begins rotating this role and adds emotional support duties to job descriptions with extra pay.

Unrecorded Contribution

Definition: Work, ideas, or support that significantly influence outcomes but are not formally recognized in records, reports, or credits.

Business Application: Unrecorded contributions can distort performance metrics, hinder career growth, and diminish trust within teams—especially when credit consistently goes to the most visible voices.

Leadership Insight: Effective leaders monitor both visible results and behind-the-scenes efforts, ensuring recognition extends beyond those with the loudest presence or highest rank.

Cultural Caution: In some cultures, humility and collective credit are important, but in global workplaces, not documenting contributions can unintentionally put individuals at a disadvantage.

Mosaic Question: Who helped make your last success possible, and have they been properly recognized?

Mosaic in Action: During an annual award ceremony, a CEO publicly acknowledges the administrative staff whose coordination enabled a high-profile project, adding their names to the official project credits.

Unrecognized Expertise

Definition: The skills, knowledge, or problem-solving abilities someone possesses that go unnoticed, undervalued, or are dismissed within a specific setting.

Business Application: Unrecognized expertise can happen when an employee's qualifications are ignored because they don't follow traditional credentialing paths, belong to an underrepresented group, or work outside visible leadership channels.

Leadership Insight: Leaders who actively uncover hidden expertise improve decision-making, innovation, and team morale. This involves listening beyond formal résumés and observing performance in real situations.

Cultural Caution: In some cultures, modesty or indirect self-promotion is common; without deliberate recognition efforts, these individuals may be consistently underestimated.

Mosaic Question: Who in your circle knows more than you've ever asked them to share?

Mosaic in Action: A school administrator finds out that a janitor has advanced carpentry skills. Instead of outsourcing a major repair, they hire him for the project—saving money and increasing respect in the workplace.

Uncredited Policy Editor

Definition:: A person who significantly influences policies, frameworks, or official documents but does not receive recognition or authorship.

Business Application: Many policies bear the fingerprints of administrative staff, consultants, or marginalized colleagues whose unseen edits influence outcomes. Recognizing their role enhances equity and transparency.

Leadership Insight:: Leaders who properly credit contributors build trust and avoid erasure. Recognition confirms that intellectual labor is valued, not exploited.

Cultural Caution:: In some organizational cultures, ghost-editing is accepted. Calling it out questions power hierarchies but may face resistance from those who benefit from remaining unseen.

Mosaic Question:: Whose fingerprints are on the policies in your workplace, and do they get credit?

Mosaic in Action:: A junior staff member rewrites key sections of a diversity policy to include measurable equity benchmarks. Although the final policy is launched under an executive's name, the team later recognizes her contribution during an internal acknowledgment ceremony.

Unseen Identities

Definition: Aspects of identity — such as chronic illness, neurodiversity, sexuality, or invisible disabilities — that influence lived experience but are not always visible to others.

Business Application: Recognizing unseen identities enables organizations to create policies and cultures that extend beyond visible diversity indicators.

Leadership Insight: Inclusive leaders create space for unseen identities by avoiding assumptions and fostering cultures where disclosure isn't necessary for respect.

Cultural Caution: Not all unseen identities should be "made visible." Respecting choice and privacy is essential for inclusion.

Mosaic Question: What hidden identities could be present in your team — and how do you lead with awareness of them?

Mosaic in Action: A manager implements flexible work policies that assist employees managing chronic illnesses, even when those needs are not disclosed.

Unseen Labor

Definition: Essential work that sustains systems, relationships, and outcomes but remains invisible because it occurs behind the scenes or is not officially measured.

Business Application: From maintaining community trust to organizing team resources, unseen labor often determines success but is left out of job descriptions, performance reviews, and budgets.

Leadership Insight: Recognizing unseen labor—by naming it, compensating it, and distributing it fairly—helps prevent burnout and improves retention.

Cultural Caution: In many environments, unseen labor disproportionately falls on women, minorities, or junior staff, reinforcing inequalities and hindering career advancement.

Mosaic Question: What work is holding your system together that no one is tracking?

Mosaic in Action: During a leadership retreat, participants list all the tasks that keep the organization running. They realize some employees are carrying an unspoken workload—and immediately reallocate resources to support them.

Unshared Consequences

Definition: A situation where the negative consequences of decisions mostly affect those without the power to decide, while those in charge stay protected from the results.

Business Application: Unshared consequences emerge when executives create strategies that burden frontline workers or when policies put risk on marginalized groups without accountability at the top.

Leadership Insight: True equity involves sharing not just power but also the consequences. Leaders who bear the costs with their teams foster trust and moral authority.

Cultural Caution: In individualistic cultures, consequences are often passed down the hierarchy. In collectivist cultures, shared accountability might be expected but not always evenly enforced. Leaders must understand both patterns.

Mosaic Question: When your organization makes decisions, who

bears the consequences — and who escapes them?

Mosaic in Action: During an economic downturn, a CEO cuts their own salary and executive bonuses along with staff pay adjustments, making sure the consequences are shared rather than outsourced.

Unshared Power

Definition: The concentration of decision-making power in the hands of a few, leaving others without influence or participation. Unshared power shows unfair systems where leadership claims inclusion but withholds true authority.

Business Application: Unshared power appears in executive teams, boards, or leadership councils that make decisions without significant staff or community involvement. It causes blind spots, reduces buy-in, and damages trust.

Leadership Insight: Equitable leadership isn't just about consultation — it's about sharing real power. Leaders who distribute decision-making authority foster innovation, accountability, and belonging.

Cultural Caution: In some high power-distance cultures, concentrated authority is accepted as normal. Moving away from unshared power needs sensitivity, dialogue, and approaches suited to the specific context.

Mosaic Question: Who in your organization holds the most power — and who should be invited to share it?

Mosaic in Action: A university dean reorganizes hiring committees to include faculty, staff, and students, shifting from centralized power to shared governance.

Unspoken Norms

Definition: The unwritten rules, habits, and expectations that influence how people behave, communicate, and make decisions within a group.

Business Application: Unspoken norms can guide meeting etiquette, decision-making speed, or who feels entitled to speak—often stronger than any formal policy.

Leadership Insight: Bringing unspoken norms to light and discussing them helps leaders align practices with values, avoid misunderstandings, and foster cultures rooted in equity and trust.

Cultural Caution: In cross-cultural settings, unspoken norms can be easily misinterpreted; what is considered "normal" in one

environment might be exclusionary in another.

Mosaic Question: Which of your team's "rules" are only in people's heads, and who do they unintentionally disadvantage?

Mosaic in Action: A new hire stays quiet in meetings because the unspoken norm is to avoid challenging senior staff. Once this is recognized and addressed, contributions across all levels increase significantly.

Unstated Expectations

Definition: Unstated assumptions about performance, behavior, or priorities that are still used to evaluate others.

Business Application: Unstated expectations often lead to conflict and reduce productivity— employees are criticized for not meeting a standard they were never informed of.

Leadership Insight: Clear communication turns hidden expectations into shared commitments, lowering frustration and turnover.

Cultural Caution: Different cultural and professional backgrounds shape how people interpret "obvious" expectations; explicit communication bridges those gaps.

Mosaic Question: What do you expect everyone to naturally understand— and how will you communicate it clearly?

Mosaic in Action: A nonprofit leader notices that staff are expected to answer emails after hours despite no policy stating this. They establish a "no after-hours email" rule to prevent burnout and clarify boundaries.

Unrealistic Expectation

Definition: The enforcement of standards or demands that are unfairly high, unrealistic, or out of context, causing stress, inequality, and disappointment.

Business Application: Unrealistic expectations show up in performance reviews, workloads, or leadership pipelines that assume unlimited capacity while overlooking systemic barriers.

Leadership Insight: Setting the bar high isn't the same as making it impossible. Wise leaders match ambition with resources, clarity, and compassion.

Cultural Caution: Expectations vary across cultures — what seems unrealistic in one setting may be normal in another. Leaders need to set standards with fairness and awareness.

Mosaic Question: Do the expectations you set foster growth — or lead to burnout?

Mosaic in Action: A nonprofit updates its evaluation system after discovering staff were penalized for goals based on 60-hour work weeks, moving toward sustainable benchmarks.

Universal Design

Definition: The creation of products, environments, and systems that are accessible and usable by people of all abilities, ages, and backgrounds without the need for adaptation.

Business Application: Organizations applying universal design principles expand their market reach, enhance user satisfaction, and show their commitment to inclusivity.

Leadership Insight: Leaders who incorporate universal design into planning from the beginning reduce retrofitting costs and prevent unintentionally excluding stakeholders.

Cultural Caution: While universal design strives to be inclusive, "universal" assumptions must still be tested across diverse cultural and contextual needs.

Mosaic Question: How can your design or decision-making process be reimagined so it works for everyone the first time?

Mosaic in Action: A conference organizer chooses a venue with ramps, adjustable lighting, multilingual signage, and flexible seating to ensure accessibility for all attendees.

Untapped Potential

Definition: The skills, talents, or capacities that remain underdeveloped or unused within an individual, team, or system.

Business Application: Untapped potential can be a strategic advantage if recognized and nurtured; otherwise, it results in missed opportunities for innovation, productivity, and retention.

Leadership Insight: Leaders who invest in developing hidden strengths often see benefits in loyalty, creative problem-solving, and organizational resilience.

Cultural Caution: In some cultures, self-promotion is discouraged, making it more difficult for individuals to showcase their potential without intentional outreach from leadership.

Mosaic Question: Who on your team has room for growth—and what's preventing them from stepping into it?

Mosaic in Action: A customer service rep is invited to lead a new training initiative after a manager notices their natural skill in conflict resolution, revealing leadership talent that had gone unrecognized.

Untold Stories

Definition: Personal or collective stories that remain silenced, erased, or unacknowledged within organizations or cultures.

Business Application: Sharing untold stories enriches organizational culture by uncovering histories and viewpoints that contest mainstream narratives.

Leadership Insight: Leaders who create space for untold stories unlock innovation and build trust. Storytelling fosters belonging.

Cultural Caution: Not every story needs to be pushed into visibility. Leaders should let stories be told with agency and consent.

Mosaic Question: What stories in your organization are still untold — and what potential could they have?

Mosaic in Action: An equity audit involves collecting oral histories from long-tenured employees, revealing hidden organizational truths that inform future strategy.

Untraceable Harm

Definition: Damage or injury that cannot be directly traced to a specific cause, often because it develops over time, is spread out, or affects the body systemically.

Business Application: In organizations, untraceable harm can stem from biased processes, toxic microcultures, or fragmented communication patterns that gradually weaken trust and performance without a specific incident to identify.

Leadership Insight: Naming and addressing harm that is not tied to a single moment requires emotional intelligence, pattern recognition, and a commitment to healing instead of blame.

Cultural Caution: In cross-cultural settings, subtle harm can arise from small, repeated cultural slights or exclusions that seem harmless alone but have a serious cumulative effect.

Mosaic Question: What issues in your system are dismissed as "just the way things are" but might actually be remnants of unseen harm?

Mosaic in Action: A manager notices a steady decline in employee engagement. After focus groups, it becomes clear that years of dismissive comments from leadership—not a single incident—have led to quiet resignation.

Untranslatable Words

Definition: Words or phrases in one language that carry cultural meanings, emotions, or concepts so specific they cannot be fully expressed in another language.

Business Application: Recognizing untranslatable words can help teams understand cultural nuances and prevent oversimplifying ideas in global communication, training, and branding.

Leadership Insight: Leaders who take time to understand the essence behind untranslatable words foster deeper cross-cultural relationships and more inclusive decision-making.

Cultural Caution: Translating such terms literally without context can remove their meaning or cause cultural misunderstandings.

Mosaic Question: Which words at your workplace hold more meaning than their literal translation can ever express?

Mosaic in Action: A global team incorporates the Portuguese word saudade—a deep, nostalgic longing—into their wellness check-ins, enhancing emotional expression among colleagues from different countries.

Unwritten Histories

Definition: Stories, experiences, and contributions that remain undocumented in official records, often because of marginalization, censorship, or oversight.

Business Application: Including unwritten histories in organizational storytelling, archives, and training enhances understanding, promotes inclusion, and corrects incomplete narratives.

Leadership Insight: Leaders who seek out unwritten histories challenge dominant stories, giving visibility and dignity to those whose contributions shaped outcomes from the shadows.

Cultural Caution: Revisiting unwritten histories can bring up discomfort, contested memories, or political tensions; approach these with cultural sensitivity and a willingness to listen.

Mosaic Question: Which parts of your organization's story have never

been told—and who has the right to tell them?

Mosaic in Action: A museum's exhibit on local industry features oral histories from immigrant workers whose labor was erased from the city's economic archives, changing the public's understanding of the community's past.

Unyielding Standards

Definition: Expectations or requirements that stay fixed, no matter how the context, needs, or challenges change.

Business Application: In high-stakes industries, unyielding standards can guarantee quality and safety, but they can also cause inflexibility that blocking adaptation and innovation.

Leadership Insight: Effective leaders know when to maintain important standards and when to modify them to respect human realities, changing markets, or cultural differences.

Cultural Caution: What is seen as "non-negotiable" in one culture might be viewed as rigidity or arrogance in another; finding a balance between firmness and flexibility is essential.

Mosaic Question: Which of your standards safeguard excellence—

and which might be preventing necessary change?

Mosaic in Action: A nonprofit keeps strict financial transparency requirements but adjusts its reporting format so community partners with limited internet access can still participate.

Upstander

Definition: A person who actively intervenes or speaks out against injustice, discrimination, or harm instead of being a passive bystander.

Business Application: Creating a culture of upstanders enhances ethical decision-making, encourages accountability, and shows that harmful behaviors are not acceptable.

Leadership Insight: Leaders can demonstrate upstander behavior by using their influence to address wrongdoing, even if it's uncomfortable or unpopular.

Cultural Caution: In some environments, public confrontation might be seen as disrespectful or disruptive; promote culturally sensitive ways of intervening.

Mosaic Question: When was the last time you saw something wrong — and what did you do?

Mosaic in Action: During a virtual meeting, a team member interrupts

a colleague's dismissive comments about a junior employee and shifts the conversation to acknowledge her idea.

Uplift Strategy

Definition: A conscious approach to empower individuals, communities, or groups through focused investment, mentorship, opportunities, or visibility.

Business Application: Companies adopt uplift strategies to promote underrepresented talent, enhance community impact, and boost brand trust via equity-centered initiatives.

Leadership Insight: Leaders practicing uplift don't just offer help—they create systems that make progress sustainable rather than occasional.

Cultural Caution: If used selectively or performatively, uplift strategies can foster dependence or suggest favoritism; transparency in choosing who to support is crucial.

Mosaic Question: Who in your circle could reach higher if given the right opportunity—and how can you eliminate obstacles in their way?

Mosaic in Action: A senior engineer mentors junior colleagues from underrepresented backgrounds, pairing them with high-visibility projects that lead to promotions within a year.

Upstream Accountability

Definition: The duty of leaders or policymakers to tackle the root causes of harm or failure before they impact others downstream.

Business Application: Organizations that practice upstream accountability focus on prevention—addressing flawed processes or policies before they lead to crises, complaints, or inequities.

Leadership Insight: True accountability is not about fixing problems after they happen—it's about creating conditions where harm never occurs.

Cultural Caution: In some hierarchical cultures, questioning upstream decisions might be seen as insubordination; establish safe channels for raising systemic concerns.

Mosaic Question: Where in your system do issues keep recurring—and what root cause are you sidestepping?

Mosaic in Action: A school district updates its curriculum development process to address biases before lesson plans are implemented in classrooms, preventing discriminatory content from being taught.

Upward Assimilation

Definition: The process where individuals from marginalized or minority groups adopt the norms, values, and behaviors of a dominant group to gain access, recognition, or advancement.

Business Application: While upward assimilation can create opportunities, it may also force individuals to hide parts of their identity, resulting in long-term disengagement or burnout.

Leadership Insight: Leaders who prioritize authenticity over conformity create room for people to grow without losing their cultural or personal identity.

Cultural Caution: Upward assimilation can reinforce inequalities by suggesting that the dominant group's norms are superior; oppose this by appreciating different types of excellence.

Mosaic Question: What opportunities in your organization compel people to "fit in" at the cost of being themselves?

Mosaic in Action: A talented employee changes her communication style to align with senior executives. A new director adjusts evaluation criteria to appreciate her unique approach, opening opportunities for her leadership.

Urban Bias

Definition: The tendency to prioritize urban perspectives, resources, and needs over those of rural or remote areas.

Business Application: Urban bias can influence hiring, funding, and service delivery, often overlooking rural talent pools, markets, and innovation potential.

Leadership Insight: Combating urban bias requires intentional outreach and policy efforts that recognize the unique strengths and challenges of rural areas.

Cultural Caution: Overemphasizing urban norms can alienate rural communities, fostering perceptions of elitism or neglect.

Mosaic Question: Which of your decisions unintentionally prioritize urban concerns—and what rural perspectives are missing from the discussion?

Mosaic in Action: A health agency expands its telemedicine network after realizing rural patients face long travel times for basic care.

Urgency Culture

Definition: A workplace environment where speed and constant responsiveness are prioritized over careful planning, rest, and long-term sustainability.

Business Application: While urgency can help achieve results in crises, over time it reduces quality, decision-making, and employee well-being.

Leadership Insight: Leaders need to distinguish between genuine urgency and manufactured urgency, ensuring that speed serves the purpose rather than becoming the norm.

Cultural Caution: In cultures that value reflection or consensus, urgency culture might be viewed as reckless or disrespectful.

Mosaic Question: How often is your sense of urgency driven by real need—and how often by habit or pressure?

Mosaic in Action: A nonprofit director pauses a rushed funding proposal to include staff input, leading to a more strategic and successful grant application.

User Bias

Definition: The influence of one's own preferences, experiences, and assumptions when designing, testing, or evaluating products, services, or systems.

Business Application: User bias can lead to products that cater to a small segment but fail to meet the needs of the broader, intended audience.

Leadership Insight: Leaders can reduce user bias by involving diverse stakeholders early and throughout the design process.

Cultural Caution: Assuming your primary user shares your cultural, economic, or physical background can result in exclusionary design.

Mosaic Question: Who is missing from your "user" definition—and how is their absence affecting your outcomes?

Mosaic in Action: A software team broadens beta testing to include users from multiple countries and accessibility needs, revealing design flaws that would have otherwise gone unnoticed.

◈ LETTER U CALLOUT

"Urgency without equity creates burnout; urgency with equity creates momentum."

Reflection Questions

- Where do urgency cultures push speed over fairness in your environment?
- How do unseen or unpaid forms of labor show up in your team?
- Which unspoken norms shape whose voices carry weight?

Practical Move

Pause before your next decision. Ask: *Is this urgent because it truly matters — or because we are avoiding deeper structural repair?*

V – Voice, Visibility, and Values in Action

V does not whisper—it resists, reveals, and recalibrates. It explores the dynamics of voice equity, visibility politics, and the uncomfortable space between stated values and actual behavior. It exposes the emotional calculation behind speaking out, the pressure of constant performance when hyper-visible, and the quiet exhaustion of carrying community hopes without institutional support.

Voice is not just the ability to speak—it's the freedom to be heard without fear of punishment. For some, voice opens opportunities; for others, it comes with risks. Visibility is also not automatically empowering. It can be strategic, symbolic, or selectively given. Without true agency, visibility turns people into spectacle. Without support, agency can lead to burnout.

V also explores how values are often performative—embedded in mission statements but missing in hiring, pay equity, and crisis response. It critiques "vulnerability culture," where authenticity is demanded from the marginalized while comfort is maintained for those in power. It urges leaders to rethink validation—when it becomes the currency of belonging—and visibility—when it serves optics instead of opportunity.

V asks us to recognize the contradictions that fracture trust

- Voice without protection becomes performance.
- Visibility without influence becomes vulnerability.
- Values without embodiment become branding.
- Vulnerability demanded unequally becomes exploitation.

From voicelessness in team meetings to values betrayed in strategy rooms, V highlights the dissonance between what organizations claim and what they deliver. It asks Whose story only gets airtime when it is convenient? Who must share pain to be believed? And what do our most visible actions reveal about what we truly value?

V calls on leaders to reflect on whether their equity work amplifies voices or suppresses them, whether visibility truly empowers or merely entertains, and if their values are upheld beyond words. Leadership is not determined by how many statements are made, but by the consistency of its actions when the stakes are highest.

V

Validation Seeking

Definition: Validation seeking is the repeated desire for outside approval to verify one's worth, choices, or performance.

Business Application: In leadership, excessive validation seeking can cause decision paralysis, overreliance on approval from superiors, and vulnerability to flattery or groupthink.

Leadership Insight: Leaders who foster internal validation—grounding their decisions in values and vision—are more capable of handling criticism and ambiguity.

Cultural Caution: In some cultures, seeking approval is linked to respect and building relationships rather than insecurity. Misunderstanding this dynamic can cause unnecessary tension.

Mosaic Question: Do you need others to recognize your worth before you take action?

Mosaic in Action: A department head moves from repeated "Does this look right?" check-ins to sharing confident drafts and asking for specific feedback, which helps build trust in their judgment.

Value-Based Decision Making

Definition: Value-based decision making involves guiding choices based on core ethical principles and organizational values instead of convenience, cost, or short-term benefits.

Business Application: This approach fosters trust with stakeholders, enhances brand integrity, and can support navigating complex situations where the "right" choice is not immediately clear.

Leadership Insight: Leaders who clearly state the values guiding a decision promote transparency, foster accountability, and enhance team cohesion under pressure.

Cultural Caution: In multicultural settings, leaders must understand that the same expressed value— such as "loyalty" or "fairness"—can be interpreted differently based on cultural context.

Mosaic Question: When making a tough decision, can you clearly link it to your values?

Mosaic in Action: A CEO refuses to work with a supplier

that breaches labor standards, even though it would reduce costs, reaffirming the company's commitment to human rights.

Value Chain Equity

Definition: Value chain equity means fairness in how benefits, resources, and risks are shared across all steps of production and delivery.

Business Application: Organizations that audit their value chains for inequity—such as labor exploitation, environmental harm, or disproportionate risk—can align their operations with ethical principles and brand commitments.

Leadership Insight: Equitable value chains demand leaders to look beyond profit margins and understand the lived realities of suppliers, workers, and communities.

Cultural Caution: Applying a single standard for equity without considering local economic and cultural contexts can lead to new imbalances.

Mosaic Question: Who gains the most from your organization's value chain — and who incurs the hidden costs?

Mosaic in Action: A coffee company revises supplier contracts to ensure living wages and environmental safeguards, boosting both product quality and supplier loyalty.

Value Congruence

Definition: Alignment between an individual's values and the organization's communicated and practiced values fosters coherence, trust, and motivation.

Business Application: High value congruence decreases turnover and ethical drift, enhances decision-making under pressure, and boosts engagement because people find purpose in their work.

Leadership Insight: It's not enough to publish values—leaders must put them into action through budgets, incentives, hiring, and promotions so daily behaviors align with the banner.

Cultural Caution: Values are influenced by culture. Find common principles (e.g., dignity, fairness) while avoiding imposing one group's norms as "universal."

Mosaic Question: Where do your policies and behaviors differ from the values you claim?

Mosaic in Action: A product team declines a lucrative data deal that conflicts with the company's privacy commitments and documents the decision as a values case study for future choices.

Value Drift

Definition: Value drift is the slow loss of an individual's or organization's core principles caused by external pressures, incentives, or complacency.

Business Application: This can occur when companies prioritize short-term profits over long-term mission alignment, damaging trust with stakeholders.

Leadership Insight: Leaders who consistently revisit and reaffirm core values build organizational resilience against market or political shifts.

Cultural Caution: In global contexts, perceived "drift" might actually be necessary adaptation to local values—discernment is essential.

Mosaic Question: How have your values shifted over the past five years—and was it deliberate?

Mosaic in Action: A nonprofit reaffirms its original mission after realizing that its recent campaigns shifted focus from community needs to appeasing donors.

Value Signaling

Definition: Value signaling is the act of publicly showing support for a principle, cause, or moral stance—often without taking meaningful action to back it up.

Business Application: While signaling can increase awareness, overdoing it without follow-up damages credibility and fosters skepticism.

Leadership Insight: Authentic leaders make sure that public statements are supported by clear actions and responsibility.

Cultural Caution: In some communities, signaling is a form of collective solidarity and should not be dismissed as merely performative without further investigation.

Mosaic Question: Do your actions match your declarations—or do they end at just the statement?

Mosaic in Action: After publicly endorsing climate action, a logistics company invests in electric fleet vehicles and carbon offset programs, aligning its actions with its words.

Values-Based Leadership

Definition: A leadership model that bases decisions and actions on clearly defined personal and organizational values, ensuring consistency and integrity across different contexts.

Business Application: Values-based leadership aligns mission with action. Organizations following this approach build trust by making decisions based on ethics instead of convenience.

Leadership Insight: Leaders who act based on values inspire trust, even during uncertain times. Their consistency serves as a stabilizing force.

Cultural Caution: Values vary across cultures. Leaders need to determine if they are using universal principles or those specific to a particular culture.

Mosaic Question: Do your daily leadership decisions reflect your values — or your pressures?

Mosaic in Action: A healthcare director refuses to reduce patient care programs despite financial pressure, emphasizing organizational values of equity and compassion.

Values Dissonance

Definition: Values dissonance happens when personal or organizational actions conflict with stated beliefs or principles, causing

internal tension, lowering morale, and damaging trust.

Business Application: If employees feel pressured to compromise their values to achieve organizational goals, disengagement and turnover often occur.

Leadership Insight: Leaders should regularly verify alignment between policy, practice, and principles—especially during times of rapid change or crisis.

Cultural Caution: In some cultures, harmony and group cohesion might be prioritized over directly addressing values misalignment, requiring more nuanced approaches to resolution.

Mosaic Question: Where in your work have you felt pressured to compromise your values—and how did you respond?

Mosaic in Action: A project manager raises concerns when marketing campaigns overstate product benefits, leading the company to revise materials and restore customer trust.

Values in Conflict

Definition: Values in conflict describe situations where two or more equally important principles oppose each other, making decision-making complex and often emotionally charged.

Business Application: Examples include balancing transparency with confidentiality, or innovation with safety. Leaders must navigate these tensions with clarity and fairness.

Leadership Insight: Addressing value conflicts openly—calling out both sides and recognizing their importance—can turn divisive moments into trust-building opportunities.

Cultural Caution: What looks like a values conflict in one culture might be viewed as a natural priority hierarchy in another, requiring leaders to adjust their resolution approaches.

Mosaic Question: When two core values you hold are in conflict, which one do you prioritize—and why?

Mosaic in Action: A nonprofit leader balances donor transparency with staff privacy by developing a reporting system that safeguards individual confidentiality while fulfilling disclosure requirements.

Vantage Bias

Definition: Vantage bias happens when individuals or groups interpret information mainly through their own position, status, or privilege, which results in biased conclusions and decision-making.

Business Application: This can occur in leadership when executives assume their access to resources or networks is shared by all employees, creating blind spots in strategy and policy development.

Leadership Insight: Recognizing vantage bias involves actively seeking perspectives from various levels of the organization, especially those most affected by decisions.

Cultural Caution: In global or cross-cultural settings, vantage bias can lead leaders to misunderstand challenges faced by colleagues working in vastly different economic, political, or social environments.

Mosaic Question: How could your current position be influencing— and possibly restricting—the way you view this situation?

Mosaic in Action: A senior leader reviews employee feedback anonymously and finds that what seemed like "lack of ambition" was actually frustration over inaccessible career development pathways.

Vicarious Resilience

Definition: Vicarious resilience is the positive psychological effect that results from observing others' strength, recovery, or growth in the face of adversity.

Business Application: In sectors like healthcare, education, and social work, vicarious resilience can maintain professionals' motivation, even when their roles involve ongoing exposure to hardship.

Leadership Insight: Leaders who emphasize stories of resilience within teams can foster shared hope and strengthen a culture of perseverance.

Cultural Caution: The meaning of resilience differs across cultures; what is considered "overcoming" in one context might be viewed as "enduring with dignity" in another.

Mosaic Question: Whose resilience has influenced how you handle your own challenges?

Mosaic in Action: A disaster response coordinator discusses community-led rebuilding efforts with their team, inspiring renewed commitment after months of exhausting relief work.

Vicarious Trauma

Definition: Vicarious trauma describes the emotional aftermath and mental changes that happen from repeatedly witnessing others' traumatic experiences.

Business Application: This is common in professions involving direct support, crisis intervention, or conflict resolution, and it can lead to burnout if not addressed.

Leadership Insight: Leaders must normalize conversations about mental health, provide regular debriefing opportunities, and ensure staff in high-exposure roles have access to professional support.

Cultural Caution: Cultural norms may prevent open discussions of trauma, so leaders must introduce care practices that honor local customs.

Mosaic Question: How do you acknowledge others' stories without taking them on as your own?

Mosaic in Action: A school counselor, after months of listening to students' crisis disclosures, goes on scheduled reflective retreats to process emotions and stay professionally clear.

Victim Blaming

Definition: Victim blaming happens when responsibility for harm is shifted from the perpetrator to the person who experienced the harm, often reinforcing systemic injustice.

Business Application: In workplace investigations, victim blaming can appear subtly—like questioning why someone "didn't speak up sooner"—and can discourage future reports.

Leadership Insight: Leaders must model language and processes that focus on accountability, fairness, and dignity, avoiding assumptions about the behavior or credibility of the harmed party.

Cultural Caution: Victim blaming is often deeply embedded in societal stories, especially in environments influenced by strict gender roles or power hierarchies.

Mosaic Question: When hearing someone's story of harm, are you trying to understand or to doubt?

Mosaic in Action: A company updates its harassment investigation protocols to eliminate subjective credibility assessments and instead concentrate on evidence and policy violations.

Viewpoint Diversity

Definition: Viewpoint diversity is the deliberate inclusion of different perspectives, experiences, and interpretations in decision-making, problem-solving, and dialogue.

Business Application: Organizations that encourage viewpoint diversity are better able to innovate and foresee challenges,

as they examine multiple perspectives before settling on strategies.

Leadership Insight: True viewpoint diversity requires more than just inviting a range of voices—it involves fostering an environment where dissenting opinions are appreciated, not punished.

Cultural Caution: In some cultures, openly challenging group consensus might be viewed as disrespectful. Leaders need to adapt facilitation styles to promote contribution without causing cultural offense.

Mosaic Question: When was the last time you changed your mind due to a perspective you initially resisted?

Mosaic in Action: A product design team includes frontline staff and community members in brainstorming sessions, revealing needs that executives had overlooked.

Virtual Inclusion

Definition: Virtual inclusion guarantees that individuals participating remotely in meetings, projects, or communities have equal access, visibility, and influence compared to in-person participants.

Business Application: This is essential in hybrid workplaces, where remote workers may be excluded from informal conversations or decision-making moments that happen in physical offices.

Leadership Insight: Virtual inclusion is not just about "adding a Zoom link"—it demands intentional facilitation, equal speaking chances, and careful use of technology.

Cultural Caution: Time zone differences, internet reliability, and cultural communication norms all affect how virtual inclusion is experienced.

Mosaic Question: Are your virtual team members as engaged in the conversation as those in the room?

Mosaic in Action: A manager alternates meeting facilitation between in-person and remote team members, ensuring that the agenda control is shared equally.

performing employees who prefer asynchronous communication or face technical or environmental constraints that restrict continuous online engagement.

Leadership Insight: Leaders should prioritize results and impact over visibility metrics such as online presence or how often they attend meetings.

Cultural Caution: In collectivist cultures, the absence of constant presence might be understood differently than in individualist cultures, where autonomy is appreciated.

Mosaic Question: Are you equating constant online visibility with competence or commitment?

Mosaic in Action: A project lead shifts performance reviews from activity logs to evaluations based on deliverables, reducing bias against employees who perform better offline.

Virtual Presence Bias

Definition: Virtual presence bias happens when people's contributions are judged—or their credibility is perceived—based on how often and in what way they appear in virtual spaces.

Business Application: This bias can cause overlooking high-

Virtual Presence Gap

Definition: The virtual presence gap describes the disparities in influence, contribution, and visibility between individuals who are regularly seen in virtual settings and those who are not.

Business Application: The gap can lead to unbalanced decision-making power, where those who are regularly on camera or in meetings informally dominate the conversation.

Leadership Insight: To close the gap, leaders must proactively seek input from those with less visibility and offer alternative ways to contribute beyond live sessions.

Cultural Caution: Some cultures see constant camera use as intrusive or unwanted, so it's important to balance capturing moments with respecting personal boundaries.

Mosaic Question: Who is often left out of the virtual "spotlight," and how can you include them?

Mosaic in Action: A team uses a rotating "insight board" where all members post weekly updates visible to everyone in the organization, ensuring contributions are acknowledged regardless of meeting attendance.

Visibility Fatigue

Definition: Visibility fatigue is the exhaustion caused by being constantly required to be "seen" in physical, digital, or public spaces—often as a representative of a group or identity rather than as an individual.

Business Application: This can happen when a few employees

from underrepresented groups are repeatedly asked to serve on panels, committees, or diversity initiatives, draining their time and energy from other priorities.

Leadership Insight: Leaders must balance recognition with rest, ensuring visibility is empowering rather than depleting, and that it is shared fairly among team members.

Cultural Caution: In some cultural settings, public recognition can be uncomfortable or even unsafe, especially for individuals with marginalized identities.

Mosaic Question: Whose visibility is being celebrated—and at what expense to them?

Mosaic in Action: A company rotates public-facing duties among staff to decrease burnout among frequently spotlighted employees.

Visibility Gap

Definition: The visibility gap describes differences in recognition, acknowledgment, or access to influence among individuals or groups within an organization or society.

Business Application: Employees in high-profile roles or projects might get more career advancement opportunities, while equally talented individuals in less visible positions are overlooked.

Leadership Insight: Closing the visibility gap involves creating intentional pathways for recognition, especially for behind-the-scenes contributors whose work is essential but less visible.

Cultural Caution: In collectivist cultures, individual recognition might not be as highly valued, but visibility still influences access to resources and opportunities.

Mosaic Question: Who is making impactful work that remains unknown outside their close circle?

Mosaic in Action: A manager introduces a "hidden heroes" feature in the company newsletter to showcase contributions from staff in non-public roles.

Visibility Politics

Definition: Visibility politics involves the strategic use of public presence, identity, or representation to shape perception, acquire power, or promote social or organizational change.

Business Application: Leaders might intentionally present themselves—or others—as the public face of an initiative to influence stories or communicate values to stakeholders.

Leadership Insight: While visibility can be a powerful tool for influence, it must be used ethically to prevent tokenism or exploitation.

Cultural Caution: In some cases, visibility politics can put individuals at risk of unwanted scrutiny or backlash, especially when related to identity-based advocacy.

Mosaic Question: Is visibility in this situation a true platform or just for show?

Mosaic in Action: An organization empowers frontline workers to lead media interviews about service improvements, giving authentic voice to those directly involved.

Vision Drift

Definition: Vision drift happens when an organization or leader slowly moves away from their original mission or purpose—sometimes unintentionally—because of changing priorities, external pressures, or leadership changes.

Business Application: Without regular alignment checks, vision drift can weaken brand identity, employee morale, and stakeholder trust.

Leadership Insight: Periodically reviewing core values and vision statements ensures that daily actions stay aligned with the organization's true purpose.

Cultural Caution: In global contexts, vision drift can also result from adopting practices or narratives that unintentionally align more with dominant cultures than with the original, inclusive purpose.

Mosaic Question: Has your mission changed in ways your team and stakeholders still see as genuine?

Mosaic in Action: A nonprofit holds an annual "mission audit" where staff and community members assess whether programs still align with the founding vision.

Vision Integrity

Definition: Vision integrity is the consistency between an organization's stated mission and its actual decisions, actions, and culture over time.

Business Application: Companies with strong vision integrity attract loyal stakeholders because they consistently act in ways that reflect their declared purpose, even when under pressure.

Leadership Insight: Leaders must safeguard vision integrity by embedding it into policies,

daily operations, and performance metrics—not just promotional language.

Cultural Caution: In cross-cultural settings, vision statements can unintentionally adopt the values of dominant groups; protecting integrity means ensuring inclusivity remains central.

Mosaic Question: Where does your current reality reinforce—or quietly contradict—your vision?

Mosaic in Action: A global nonprofit rejects a lucrative sponsorship that conflicts with its environmental mission, preserving stakeholder trust.

Visionary Leadership

Definition: A leadership style characterized by foresight, creativity, and the ability to motivate others toward a daring, future-focused vision.

Business Application: Visionary leaders shape organizations by foreseeing future challenges, developing innovative strategies, and bringing diverse groups together around a shared purpose.

Leadership Insight: Visionary leadership is not just about envisioning the future — it's about inspiring people to believe in and create it together.

Cultural Caution: A powerful vision without inclusion can turn authoritarian. True vision needs to be co-created and flexible.

Mosaic Question: Does your vision encourage others to see themselves in the future you're creating?

Mosaic in Action: A social entrepreneur unites global partners around a vision of universal digital access, igniting innovation across industries.

Virtue Signaling (Critical View)

Definition: Making public statements or gestures about ethics, justice, or equity without any actual action or structural change.

Business Application: Virtue signaling shows up in corporate DEI statements that lack real investment or public campaigns that dodge addressing internal inequities.

Leadership Insight: Leaders need to recognize the difference between communication and transformation. Virtue signaling damages credibility, while genuine commitment fosters trust.

Cultural Caution: Public declarations matter in some cultures; silence can also be harmful. The key is alignment between words and actions.

Mosaic Question: Do your equity commitments appear in policy and practice — or only in statements?

Mosaic in Action: A company replaces symbolic diversity messaging with transparent pay equity audits and responsible change.

Vocational Identity

Definition: Vocational identity is the internalized sense of self shaped by one's profession, work values, and career path.

Business Application: A strong vocational identity can guide ethical decision-making, increase resilience, and align personal purpose with organizational goals.

Leadership Insight: When a leader's vocational identity becomes too rigid, they risk burnout or resistance to necessary role changes; flexibility ensures longevity.

Cultural Caution: In collectivist cultures, vocational identity may be linked to family or community expectations, influencing career choices and self-definition.

Mosaic Question: How much of who you are is defined by what you do?

Mosaic in Action: A long-time educator moves into policy work and redefines their vocational identity from "teacher" to "advocate for equitable learning systems," maintaining purpose while shifting roles.

Voice Amplification

Definition: Voice amplification is the deliberate act of raising and broadening the reach of someone else's perspective, especially those who have been historically marginalized or ignored.

Business Application: Leaders amplify voices by giving credit, quoting team members in prominent forums, or making sure meeting contributions are documented and acted upon.

Leadership Insight: Amplification is not about speaking for someone, but about creating conditions where their words reach farther and their influence expands.

Cultural Caution: Amplifying voices without permission—or altering the message to fit a dominant narrative—can lead to exploitation rather than empowerment.

Mosaic Question: Whose voice could change the conversation if it reached the right ears?

Mosaic in Action: During a strategy session, an executive mentions a junior analyst's data insight, making sure it is included in the final presentation to the board.

Voice as Currency

Definition: Voice as currency recognizes that the ability to speak, be heard, and influence decisions is a form of power that can be traded, shared, or withheld.

Business Application: In negotiations, public forums, or team decisions, those with more speaking opportunities often gain greater influence over outcomes.

Leadership Insight: Leaders can use their "voice capital" to create space for others, redistributing influence to achieve more balanced decision-making.

Cultural Caution: In hierarchical or collectivist cultures, speaking out may carry social risks; the value of "voice" depends on the context.

Mosaic Question: How are you using your voice — and whose voice are you investing in?

Mosaic in Action: A manager gives up their conference speaking slot to a team member whose lived experience enhances the session's credibility.

Voice Climate

Definition: The collective perception of whether it is safe and worthwhile to speak up in an organization.

Business Application: A positive voice climate encourages innovation, accountability, and retention. A negative one fosters silence and mistrust.

Leadership Insight: Leaders cultivate strong voice climates by responding to feedback with openness, not defensiveness.

Cultural Caution: In hierarchical contexts, voicing concerns may conflict with respect norms. Leaders must signal that voice is valued.

Mosaic Question: Does your organization reward voice — or punish it?

Mosaic in Action: After introducing regular feedback forums with transparent follow-up, a corporation saw a surge in employee-led innovations.

Voice Equity

Definition: Voice equity guarantees all individuals have equal opportunities to speak, be heard, and influence decisions—regardless of role, identity, or power status.

Business Application: Establishing voice equity may involve structured turn-taking, anonymous idea submissions, or fair facilitation during meetings.

Leadership Insight: Equity in voice results in more diverse ideas, improved problem-solving, and greater team engagement, as contributions represent a wider range of perspectives.

Cultural Caution: True equity extends beyond "letting everyone talk"—it requires confronting the unspoken hierarchies that influence which inputs are acted upon.

Mosaic Question: Whose ideas are consistently recognized, and whose seem to be overlooked?

Mosaic in Action: A project leader initiates an "idea rotation" policy in meetings, ensuring everyone's input is considered before proceeding.

Voice Fatigue

Definition: The fatigue felt when people, often from marginalized groups, are repeatedly asked to speak, explain, or represent their identity in organizational or cultural spaces.

Business Application: Voice fatigue can weaken DEI efforts if the same individuals are repeatedly asked to educate or advocate without institutional backing.

Leadership Insight: Inclusive leaders broaden whose voices are heard and create structures where marginalized employees are not overwhelmed.

Cultural Caution: Not all silence indicates disengagement; sometimes it results from fatigue due to overexposure. Leaders must learn to listen without extracting.

Mosaic Question: Who in your organization might be experiencing voice fatigue — and how can you help them?

Mosaic in Action: An equity task force rotates facilitators and develops external partnerships, easing the workload on underrepresented staff.

Voice Privilege

Definition: Voice privilege is the unearned advantage of being easily heard, respected, and influential in decision-making spaces because of identity, role, or perceived credibility.

Business Application: Those with voice privilege often dominate meetings or set agendas without realizing others must work harder to get heard. Leaders can review discussions to ensure everyone's contributions are balanced.

Leadership Insight: Recognizing voice privilege is the first step toward using it to create space for those whose perspectives are usually sidelined.

Cultural Caution: In some cultures, showing deference to authority can hide voice privilege; power dynamics may be reinforced through silence rather than direct exclusion.

Mosaic Question: Where might your voice carry further simply because of who you are—and how will you use that influence?

Mosaic in Action: A senior manager uses their credibility to reframe a junior colleague's overlooked idea, giving it the attention it deserved initially.

Voice Suppression

Definition: Voice suppression is the intentional or unintentional silencing of individuals or groups, preventing them from contributing or influencing decisions.

Business Application: Suppression can show up as talking over others, penalizing dissent, ignoring contributions, or excluding key stakeholders from meetings.

Leadership Insight: A culture that tolerates voice suppression will eventually lose innovation and trust, as silenced team members disengage or leave.

Cultural Caution: In some settings, silence may be mistaken for agreement; leaders need to distinguish between respectful listening and imposed quiet.

Mosaic Question: Whose silence in your environment reflects safety—and whose reflects suppression?

Mosaic in Action: In a policy discussion, staff members from underrepresented groups are consistently passed over. A department head notices and implements structured speaking rounds to ensure equity.

Voice Tokenism

Definition: Voice tokenism occurs when a marginalized individual is given a platform or invited to speak, but only to fulfill diversity optics—without real influence over outcomes.

Business Application: This can look like including one woman on a panel, one person of color on a hiring committee, or one youth representative on a board without empowering them to shape decisions.

Leadership Insight: Tokenism erodes trust; leaders must ensure that representation is paired with actual authority, resources, and decision-making power.

Cultural Caution: In some communities, token voices may be pressured to conform to the dominant narrative, which limits genuine contribution.

Mosaic Question: Is representation in your organization accompanied by influence—or merely visibility?

Mosaic in Action: A nonprofit invites an Indigenous leader to join a project steering group but also ensures they serve as co-chair and help guide key funding decisions.

Voluntary Silence

Definition: A conscious decision to stay silent as a way of resilience, reflection, or quiet resistance in situations where speaking could be unsafe or unhelpful.

Business Application: Voluntary silence helps employees conserve energy, prevent tokenization, and show their agency without speaking.

Leadership Insight: Wise leaders value silence as a form of communication. Voluntary silence can convey dignity, set boundaries, or serve as a subtle protest.

Cultural Caution: In some cultures, silence is a sign of respect; in others, it may be mistaken for disengagement. Leaders need to interpret silence carefully.

Mosaic Question: When have you opted for silence — and what strength or safety did it provide you?

Mosaic in Action: An employee silently refuses to take part in a performative DEI campaign, signaling opposition to superficial organizational gestures.

Voluntourism

Definition: Voluntourism is the practice of combining tourism with short-term volunteer work, often in communities facing economic or social challenges. While meant to help, it can put traveler experience above sustainable, community-led solutions.

Business Application: Nonprofits and companies organizing voluntourism trips can unintentionally create dependency or displace local workers if they do not focus on capacity-building and long-term partnerships.

Leadership Insight: Ethical leaders make sure that any volunteer effort is based on local priorities, skills transfer, and genuine collaboration—not just charity optics.

Cultural Caution: In some areas, voluntourism has

reinforced stereotypes of "saving" communities instead of empowering them, which can damage dignity and agency.

Mosaic Question: If you were part of the host community, would you see the help as empowering—or just performative?

Mosaic in Action: An international company shifts from sending employees on week-long build projects to funding and mentoring local entrepreneurs all year, fostering lasting economic growth.

Vulnerability Culture

Definition: Vulnerability culture is the shared norm within a group or organization that values openness, emotional honesty, and the sharing of struggles without fear of judgment or penalty.

Business Application: Teams that embrace vulnerability culture can address mistakes more quickly, innovate more effectively, and build stronger trust.

Leadership Insight: Leaders set the example by modeling appropriate vulnerability—sharing challenges without overburdening or oversharing—and responding supportively to others' disclosures.

Cultural Caution: In some cultures, showing vulnerability may be perceived as a sign of weakness, making it important to build trust gradually and respectfully.

Mosaic Question: Do people in your organization feel safe enough to speak honestly about struggles as well as successes?

Mosaic in Action: A department head begins team meetings by sharing a professional challenge they're facing and inviting input to solve it, fostering openness within the group.

Vulnerability Tax

Definition: The vulnerability tax is the additional emotional or professional cost that individuals—often from marginalized groups—pay when sharing their struggles, traumas, or challenges in spaces that may not fully support or protect them.

Business Application: This tax can occur when employees must repeatedly educate others on diversity issues, share personal hardships to justify accommodations, or prove their need for resources.

Leadership Insight: Leaders can lessen the vulnerability tax by actively listening, documenting needs so stories don't have to be repeated, and providing proactive resources.

Cultural Caution: In some settings, those who share vulnerabilities risk professional retaliation, stalled advancement, or subtle exclusion.

Mosaic Question: Who is bearing the highest cost for honesty in your organization—and how can you ease that burden?

Mosaic in Action: A Black woman executive notices she's consistently asked to recount personal experiences of bias during DEI sessions. She advocates for the company to hire external facilitators and create a storytelling archive to prevent retraumatization.

◈ LETTER V CALLOUT

"Values are revealed not in words but in trade-offs: what we protect, what we sacrifice, and what we ignore."

Reflection Questions

- When have you seen value drift in your organization or classroom?
- How do virtue signaling or visibility gaps distort authentic values?
- Which values guide you when equity and efficiency seem in conflict?

Practical Move

Write down your top three professional or academic values. Share them with a peer and ask: *Where do you see me living these out? Where do I fall short?*

W – Whiteness, Witnessing, and Worldviews

W directly confronts systems—naming what is often unspoken but deeply felt. It reveals how whiteness, more than a racial identity, functions as an invisible cultural standard. It shapes language, leadership, professionalism, and even emotional expression. What is labeled "neutral" in many settings is rarely neutral at all—it is often white, Western, male, able-bodied, and heteronormative. Against this standard, other identities are measured, misunderstood, or marginalized.

This section examines how symbolic harm and systemic bias become part of everyday practices who is labeled "difficult," how conflicts are handled, and which communication styles are considered "professional." Terms like white adjacency and woke fatigue reveal how dominant norms continue to exist even in spaces that call themselves inclusive. Whiteness here is not just an identity—it is infrastructure, a cultural organizing principle that must be named to be dismantled.

But W also expands the scope. It introduces witnessing culture—teams trained to listen without centering themselves, to hold space without overshadowing others. It elevates wisdom traditions as valid frameworks for leadership—not just heritage to honor, but knowledge to use. And it moves equity work beyond symbolic gestures toward transformation that is systemic, lasting, and genuine.

W asks us to examine the unseen foundations of our cultures

- Whiteness positioned as the silent "neutral" against which others are measured.
- Workplace norms that disguise bias as professionalism.
- The exhaustion of woke fatigue in spaces that resist accountability.
- The opportunity of witnessing and wisdom traditions to expand belonging.

Every organization has a worldview—whether explicitly expressed or subtly reinforced. The more important question is whose worldview is at the core, and what are the costs involved?

W calls leaders to name whiteness without hesitation, to expand worldviews without fear, and to embrace wisdom that disrupts sameness. Because equity is not about uniformity—it is about truth, acknowledgment, and growth. Cultures thrive not when everyone conforms, but when no one must sacrifice their dignity to belong.

W

Wage Disparity

Definition: Wage disparity describes the ongoing pay differences between individuals or groups doing similar work, often affected by factors like gender, race, industry, location, or employment status.

Business Application: Wage disparities can damage trust, reduce retention, and pose legal risks. Organizations that regularly review pay structures and communicate transparently are better equipped to attract and keep top talent.

Leadership Insight: Leaders committed to equity view compensation as a reflection of values, not merely market rates. Addressing wage disparities shows integrity and a readiness to challenge systemic bias.

Cultural Caution: Wage disparities might stem from historical inequalities and be kept in place by cultural norms that undervalue certain types of work—especially care, creative, or community roles.

Mosaic Question: How does your organization justify its pay differences, and does that reasoning hold up under ethical and cultural scrutiny?

Mosaic in Action: A tech startup performs a pay equity review and finds that women earn 12 percent less than men in similar roles. The leadership team adjusts salaries and publishes the results to hold themselves publicly accountable.

Wage Transparency

Definition: Openly disclose salary ranges, pay structures, and criteria used in compensation decisions to reduce inequalities and build trust.

Business Application: Publishing bands on postings and internally, tying raises to clear criteria, and running regular pay audits helps reduce gender and racial wage gaps and boosts retention.

Leadership Insight: Opacity conceals bias. Leaders who normalize transparent policies and reasoning demonstrate confidence in fairness and encourage accountability.

Cultural Caution: Discussing pay is taboo in some settings and regulated in others. Balance transparency with privacy laws, local customs, and employee consent—without sacrificing fairness.

Mosaic Question: If everyone understood the ranges and rules behind pay, would they trust the system?

Mosaic in Action: An organization publishes salary ranges for all roles, reviews pay equity annually, and makes one-time adjustments to address unexplained disparities.

Weaponized Civility

Definition: Weaponized civility is when politeness, tone policing, or social etiquette are used to silence, undermine, or delegitimize someone's message—especially when that message challenges authority.

Business Application: In corporate environments, weaponized civility often shows up in feedback about "tone" instead of content, especially toward women, people of color, or individuals from non-dominant cultures.

Leadership Insight: Leaders must differentiate between genuine respect and civility used as a control tactic. True inclusion involves making space for discomfort when confronting inequity.

Cultural Caution: Many cultures prioritize harmony over confrontation; in these settings, weaponized civility can be especially dangerous because it disguises cultural agreement while suppressing dissent.

Mosaic Question: Are you more concerned with how feedback is delivered or whether it conveys something you need to hear?

Mosaic in Action: During a meeting on workplace equity, a manager interrupts an employee's valid critique to comment on their "negative tone." The facilitator redirects, ensuring the original concern is addressed rather than dismissed.

Welfare Colonialism

Definition: Welfare colonialism refers to systems where outside powers supply resources or services to marginalized communities in ways that sustain dependency, weaken local autonomy, and reinforce systemic control.

Business Application: In development, philanthropy, or corporate social responsibility, welfare colonialism happens when aid is designed without community-led decision-making, often displacing local solutions.

Leadership Insight: Ethical leaders shift from dependency models to empowerment models, ensuring resources enhance capacity rather than exert control.

Cultural Caution: What can be seen as "help" may cause harm if it sidelines Indigenous or local knowledge, or if aid is pulled back as a way to manipulate politically.

Mosaic Question: Are your interventions meant to transfer power—or to keep it in your control?

Mosaic in Action: A government program provides food to a rural community but bans traditional farming practices. Years later, when funding stops, the community faces food insecurity because its local food systems were dismantled.

Wellness Colonialism

Definition: Wellness Colonialism involves the seizure, commercialization, and control of healing and well-being practices by dominant groups without respecting their origins. It shows how industries often exploit Indigenous or marginalized knowledge systems while erasing their cultural significance and context.

Business Application: In organizational settings, wellness programs can unintentionally reinforce colonial patterns by focusing only on surface-level perks—like yoga classes or mindfulness apps—while overlooking systemic issues such as racism, inequality, or workplace exploitation. Leaders who understand this dynamic can create wellness strategies that are culturally rooted, inclusive, and truly address employees' real needs.

Leadership Insight: Leaders who oppose wellness colonialism exemplify integrity by creating programs that honor cultural roots and prioritize employee voices. By moving beyond simple perks, they foster practices that strengthen resilience, celebrate community traditions, and tackle structural barriers to well-being.

Cultural Caution: A one-size-fits-all approach to wellness risks marginalizing groups whose traditions fall outside mainstream frameworks. Without recognition, credit, or compensation, organizations can perpetuate cultural erasure under the facade of "wellness." Leaders must stay alert about which practices are showcased and which are left unseen.

Mosaic Question: How can wellness initiatives embody cultural authenticity while tackling the root causes of stress and burnout?

Mosaic in Action: Conduct a wellness audit with employees from diverse backgrounds. Identify practices that may be misused or not aligned, and collaboratively redesign one initiative—ensuring cultural acknowledgment, fair representation, and equitable access for everyone.

Wellbeing Capital

Definition: Wellbeing capital is the total worth of physical, emotional, and social health resources within an individual, team, or organization that support sustained performance and resilience.

Business Application: Companies that invest in wellbeing capital—through flexible work, mental health resources, and supportive culture—reduce burnout and improve retention.

Leadership Insight: Wellbeing is not just a perk; it drives productivity and innovation. Leaders who build wellbeing capital experience higher engagement and more creative problem-solving.

Cultural Caution: Wellbeing initiatives that overlook cultural differences in rest, health, or work-life balance may fall short or cause inequities in access.

Mosaic Question: Does your organization track wellbeing as carefully as it tracks profit?

Mosaic in Action: A multinational firm implements paid community service days, counseling support,

and cross-cultural wellness programs, leading to lower absenteeism and increased employee satisfaction across regions.

Western-Centric Thinking

Definition: Western-centric thinking emphasizes Western norms, histories, and frameworks as the default or superior way to understand the world—often marginalizing other knowledge systems and ways of knowing.

Business Application: In global business strategy, Western-centric thinking can lead to products, marketing, and policies that do not connect with non-Western markets, causing missed opportunities and reputational damage.

Leadership Insight: Leaders committed to global understanding actively seek out and incorporate multiple ways of knowing, recognizing that innovation often happens where different perspectives meet.

Cultural Caution: Western-centric approaches can unintentionally erase or undervalue the lived experiences of colleagues from other cultural backgrounds, restricting organizational learning.

Mosaic Question: Whose knowledge and worldview

influence how you define "best practice"?

Mosaic in Action: A multinational company creates a leadership competency model based solely on U.S. management literature. After seeing low adoption in Asia and Africa, the company works with regional leaders to develop a revised model that reflects local leadership values and decision-making styles.

White Comfort

Definition: The tendency to prioritize white individuals' emotional comfort over open conversations about racism, equity, or systemic harm.

Business Application: White comfort emerges when organizations water down DEI training or avoid naming racism to prevent white defensiveness. It sustains inequity by prioritizing feelings over meaningful change.

Leadership Insight: True leadership isn't about comfort; it's about courage. Leaders who challenge white comfort foster genuine equity and trust.

Cultural Caution: In some cultures, discomfort is regarded as disrespect; leaders need to balance honesty with cultural sensitivity. Avoiding discomfort entirely sustains the status quo.

Mosaic Question: Do you prioritize comfort, or seek change?

Mosaic in Action: A company commits to anti-racism language in its equity training despite initial pushback from white staff, prioritizing integrity over comfort.

White Fragility

Definition: White fragility describes the defensive reactions—such as anger, withdrawal, denial, or guilt—that some White individuals show when faced with discussions about race, racism, or privilege. These responses aim to protect their comfort and uphold racial hierarchies.

Business Application: In workplace diversity initiatives, White fragility can hinder conversations and training by shifting attention from systemic inequities to personal feelings, thus delaying progress toward inclusion.

Leadership Insight: Strong leaders understand and accept discomfort as a natural part of growth, fostering environments where defensiveness can give way to curiosity and accountability.

Cultural Caution: When fragility is not addressed, it emphasizes patterns where marginalized coworkers bear the burden of educating or placating those in power.

Mosaic Question: How do you react when your worldview is questioned—and what does that response reveal about your leadership?

Mosaic in Action: During a racial equity meeting, a White executive becomes defensive after a colleague points out a biased hiring trend. The facilitator calmly redirects the conversation toward systemic solutions, demonstrating how discomfort can be turned into constructive action.

White Institutional Presence

Definition: The way whiteness functions as the unstated standard in institutions—shaping ideas of "professionalism," communication, aesthetics, and authority—often making other cultures seem like deviations that need correction.

Business Application: It manifests in accent and dialect bias, hair and dress codes, meeting norms, "standard English" expectations, and evaluation rubrics that favor behaviors aligned with white-coded standards.

Leadership Insight: Leaders de-center whiteness by collaboratively establishing standards that distinguish

excellence from cultural conformity (e.g., clarity over accent, outcomes over style) and by updating policies that reinforce exclusion.

Cultural Caution: Focus on systems, not shaming individuals. Outside the U.S., "whiteness as default" is understood differently; identify the dominant-culture presence relevant to the local context.

Mosaic Question: Which of your "neutral" norms truly reflect a dominant culture standard—and who bears the cost?

Mosaic in Action: A COO updates performance criteria to distinguish "professionalism" from accent and style, trains managers on linguistic bias, and establishes clear-language meetings where diverse speech styles are accepted.

White Saviorism

Definition: White saviorism refers to the paternalistic attitudes and actions of White individuals or organizations who see themselves as rescuers of non-White people, often emphasizing their own narrative of kindness over the communities' own autonomy.

Business Application: In international development or corporate philanthropy, white saviorism can appear when leaders create solutions without genuine collaboration, unintentionally reinforcing dependency and erasing local expertise.

Leadership Insight: Inclusive leadership focuses on local voices, ensuring those directly affected are the ones designing and deciding on their own solutions.

Cultural Caution: Even well-meaning actions can reinforce colonial power structures if they focus on the helper's identity and story more than the community's independence.

Mosaic Question: Who controls the story you're sharing — your organization or the people you say you serve?

Mosaic in Action: A nonprofit's marketing campaign initially features only images of White volunteers helping children of color. After an internal review, the nonprofit shifts to emphasizing community leaders, highlighting their expertise and leadership in driving change.

White Silence

Definition: White Silence refers to the choice of white individuals or groups to stay silent in the face of racism, inequality, or exclusion. While often seen as avoidance, silence can also stem from fear of saying the wrong thing, feeling unsafe, or uncertainty about how to respond.

Business Application: In organizational settings, white silence occurs during meetings when biased remarks go unchallenged or when leaders avoid confronting systemic inequities. It damages trust and continues to harm, sending a message to marginalized colleagues that their concerns are unimportant or unsafe to express.

Leadership Insight: Silence equals complicity when injustice is visible. Leaders must understand that inaction reinforces exclusion and damages credibility. Creating space for courageous conversations and equipping teams with language and tools for intervention helps transform silence into accountability.

Cultural Caution: Not all silence is meant to be harmful. In some cultural settings, silence can indicate politeness, respect, or uncertainty. Leaders should set clear standards that differentiate respectful pauses from avoidance, fostering fair dialogue while respecting cultural differences.

Mosaic Question: When bias occurs, are you holding back out of fear or stepping forward with courage?

Mosaic in Action: A model for speaking up against bias. A leader who interrupts a biased comment during a hiring panel not only breaks the silence but also shows accountability, setting a new standard for the team.

White-Passing Privilege

Definition: White-passing privilege describes the social and systemic benefits given to individuals of non-White heritage who are perceived as White, often leading to less exposure to racial discrimination.

Business Application: In hiring or promotion, White-passing privilege can affect perceptions of "fit," resulting in unfair advantages over visibly marginalized colleagues.

Leadership Insight: Leaders who understand this dynamic can better evaluate diversity data, recognizing that paper representation doesn't always match lived experience.

Cultural Caution: White-passing individuals might experience specific identity conflicts, balancing the advantage of passing with the disconnect from their cultural roots.

Mosaic Question: Does your definition of diversity include both visible and invisible aspects of identity?

Mosaic in Action: A biracial employee who is often assumed to be White notices they are invited to client meetings more often than visibly Black colleagues. Recognizing this, they use their position to advocate for fair inclusion in high-visibility opportunities.

Whitewashing

Definition: Whitewashing is the practice of downplaying, erasing, or modifying the contributions, histories, or representations of non-White people to focus on White narratives or aesthetics.

Business Application: In media, marketing, and product development, whitewashing can appear in casting, branding, or historical retellings that strip away cultural specificity to appeal to a perceived White mainstream.

Leadership Insight: Leaders must stay alert in protecting the authenticity of representation, making sure that diverse contributions are recognized and maintained.

Cultural Caution: Whitewashing not only distorts history but also reduces opportunities for communities whose stories and images are erased or diluted.

Mosaic Question: Are you sharing the complete story—or only the version that aligns with the dominant culture?

Mosaic in Action: A film adaptation of a historical novel replaces characters of color with White actors. Public backlash prompts the production team to consult cultural historians and recast roles to reflect authentic representation.

Whiteness as Normativity

Definition: Whiteness as normativity refers to positioning White cultural values, behaviors, and aesthetics as the default or "normal" standard against which all other racial and cultural identities are compared, judged, or measured.

Business Application: In recruitment, product design, and policy creation, Whiteness as normativity can lead to practices that unintentionally prioritize White experiences, making other cultural perspectives seem "deviant" or "special interest."

Leadership Insight: Leaders who challenge traditional Whiteness actively work to broaden organizational definitions of professionalism, competence, and excellence to embrace diverse cultural expressions.

Cultural Caution: Treating Whiteness as the unspoken baseline not only reinforces exclusion but also limits creativity, problem-solving, and market potential.

Mosaic Question: How often do your policies and standards reflect only one cultural perspective—and what could expand if multiple perspectives influenced the norm?

Mosaic in Action: An organization's dress code bans natural Black hairstyles under the guise of "professionalism." After an employee raises the issue, leadership revises the policy to allow culturally significant hairstyles, recognizing that professionalism is not culture-specific.

Whisper Network

Definition: Informal communication channels — often used among women or marginalized groups — to share warnings, survival tactics, or reputation information in unsafe cultures.

Business Application: Whisper networks develop in workplaces where formal channels for accountability break down. While they offer protection, they also indicate a lack of trust in leadership.

Leadership Insight: Wise leaders understand why whisper networks form. Rebuilding trust needs openness, responsibility, and genuine safety.

Cultural Caution: In certain situations, whisper networks might be dismissed as gossip. Leaders need to differentiate between harmful rumors and helpful truth-sharing.

Mosaic Question: If whisper networks are part of your culture, what does that say about safety and trust?

Mosaic in Action: After discovering that staff depend on whisper networks to report harassment concerns, an organization establishes independent reporting channels and enhances accountability.

Whistleblower Culture

Definition: Whistleblower culture refers to an environment where individuals feel empowered and protected when reporting misconduct, corruption, or ethical violations without fear of retaliation.

Business Application: A robust whistleblower culture enhances organizational integrity, decreases legal risk, and demonstrates a commitment to transparency, making the organization more appealing to ethical talent and partners.

Leadership Insight: Leaders promote a whistleblower culture by establishing clear reporting channels, guaranteeing anonymity, and responding quickly to credible reports.

Cultural Caution: In organizations where whistleblowing is stigmatized or punished, misconduct often becomes systemic, resulting in a loss of trust both internally and publicly.

Mosaic Question: Does your culture encourage speaking up or staying silent?

Mosaic in Action: An employee reports financial irregularities anonymously. The leadership team initiates a third-party investigation, shares the findings transparently, and tightens oversight procedures—demonstrating that speaking up is encouraged and protected.

Wholeness

Definition: A state of integration where values, emotions, and actions align into a coherent sense of self. Wholeness resists fragmentation and affirms that leaders can embody complexity without losing authenticity.

Business Application:
Organizations that promote
wholeness encourage employees
to bring their authentic selves
to work. Leaders who embody
wholeness lower burnout, build
belonging, and maintain resilience
by refusing to separate identity
from professional performance.

Leadership Insight: Wholeness is
not about being perfect but about
being integrated. Leaders who seek
wholeness accept contradictions,
welcome growth, and lead
from a position of authentic
groundedness.

Cultural Caution: The pursuit of
wholeness must respect cultural
differences. In some contexts,
wholeness is shown through
community, ritual, or spiritual
practice rather than personal
reflection.

Mosaic Question: What parts of
yourself are you breaking apart to
lead — and what would wholeness
look like instead?

Mosaic in Action: A senior leader,
once pressured to hide parts of
her identity, starts incorporating
her cultural heritage into her
leadership. This integration boosts
her credibility and sets an example
of authenticity for her team.

Wisdom Economy

Definition: The wisdom
economy describes a societal and
organizational shift that emphasizes
the use of deep knowledge, lived
experience, and a long-term
perspective over speed, volume, or
solely data-driven decision-making.

Business Application: In a
wisdom economy framework,
organizations value elder expertise,
cross-generational mentorship, and
reflective practices as key assets for
innovation and resilience.

Leadership Insight: Leaders
thriving in a wisdom economy
foster environments where
decisions are guided not only by
analytics but also by historical
insight, ethical reflection, and
cultural intelligence.

Cultural Caution:
Overemphasizing novelty while
dismissing institutional or cultural
memory can lead to repeating
past mistakes in the name of
"innovation."

Mosaic Question: Are your
strategies guided by urgency or by a
mix of insight and foresight?

Mosaic in Action: A tech startup
connects senior retired engineers
with young developers to solve
complex sustainability challenges.
This blend of historical engineering
expertise and new technologies

results in groundbreaking solutions more quickly than expected.

Wisdom Justice

Definition: Wisdom justice combines the principles of fairness, equity, and accountability with the discernment and humility gained through lived experience and deep reflection.

Business Application: In leadership, wisdom and justice guide decision-making that is not only legally compliant but also morally sound, balancing the letter of the law with the spirit of community care.

Leadership Insight: Leaders practicing wisdom and justice consider the long-term effects of their actions on all stakeholders, prioritizing relationship maintenance alongside systemic fairness.

Cultural Caution: When justice is sought without wisdom, it risks becoming reactionary, punitive, or disconnected from the complexities of human experience.

Mosaic Question: How can your approach to justice create room for compassion while maintaining accountability?

Mosaic in Action: During a workplace dispute, leadership opts

for a restorative justice approach—bringing together the impacted parties, acknowledging harm, and co-creating an action plan—rather than defaulting to termination.

Wisdom Leadership

Definition: A leadership approach based on discernment, humility, and ethical clarity, focusing on long-term flourishing rather than short-term gains.

Business Application: Wisdom-based leadership guides organizations through complexity by considering not just profits but also human dignity, cultural equity, and future impact.

Leadership Insight: Knowledge informs, but wisdom transforms. Leaders with wise leadership incorporate experience, ethics, and empathy into every decision.

Cultural Caution: Wisdom can be defined differently across cultures. Leaders must avoid applying one cultural view of "wisdom" as universal.

Mosaic Question: Do you lead solely from expertise — or from wisdom that respects humanity?

Mosaic in Action: An executive halts a lucrative contract after evaluating its negative impact on the community, demonstrating wise leadership by aligning actions with values.

Wisdom Traditions

Definition: Wisdom traditions are cultural, philosophical, and spiritual knowledge systems that have been handed down through generations, providing moral guidance, ethical principles, and ways of living that support both individuals and communities.

Business Application: Incorporating wisdom traditions into organizational strategy can encourage values-based decision-making, improve cultural respect, and support intergenerational learning in leadership development programs.

Leadership Insight: Leaders who respect wisdom traditions draw from various sources of knowledge—combining ancient insights with modern innovation to tackle complex challenges.

Cultural Caution: Taking elements from wisdom traditions without understanding their cultural roots risks turning them into trends or losing their sacred meaning.

Mosaic Question: Which lasting lessons from history could influence your leadership today?

Mosaic in Action: A global NGO adopts principles from Indigenous land stewardship traditions to guide its sustainability policies, ensuring environmental decisions align with community values and long-term ecological care.

Witness Fatigue

Definition: Witness fatigue happens when individuals or communities become emotionally drained from repeatedly seeing injustice, violence, or systemic harm—whether in person or through media exposure.

Business Application: In workplace settings, witness fatigue can lessen empathy, decrease involvement in diversity efforts, and foster a sense of hopelessness regarding systemic change.

Leadership Insight: Leaders can help manage witness fatigue by controlling exposure to traumatic content, providing mental health resources, and establishing structured chances for collective healing.

Cultural Caution: Expecting marginalized employees to constantly educate others about injustices can increase witness fatigue and add to emotional labor.

Mosaic Question: Are you prompting others to observe pain without providing a way to heal?

Mosaic in Action: A nonprofit dedicated to anti-violence work holds regular debriefing and support sessions for staff exposed to challenging cases, helping prevent burnout and maintain long-term dedication.

Witnessing Culture

Definition: Witnessing culture is the shared expectation that members of a community, workplace, or society will actively observe, document, and speak out against injustice or harm.

Business Application: Embedding a witnessing culture in organizations encourages employees to report misconduct, uphold ethical standards, and act as allies during moments of crisis.

Leadership Insight: Leaders influence the witnessing culture by demonstrating intervention, safeguarding whistleblowers, and honoring those who take ethical stands.

Cultural Caution: A witnessing culture without follow-through can foster cynicism, as people become skeptical when observation doesn't result in tangible change.

Mosaic Question: When you see harm happen, does your culture speak up or stay silent?

Mosaic in Action: When a team member witnesses discriminatory remarks in a meeting, the company responds with mediation, training, and updated anti-bias policies— showing that witnessing incidents leads to accountability.

Woke Backlash

Definition: Woke backlash refers to the political, social, or organizational response against diversity, equity, and inclusion efforts—often seen as resistance to "overcorrection" or "political correctness."

Business Application: Organizations facing woke backlash might see funding cut, policies reversed, or leaders challenged for promoting equity-focused initiatives.

Leadership Insight: Effective leaders prepare for woke backlash by building coalitions, grounding initiatives in clear values, and clearly communicating the long-term business and human benefits of equity.

Cultural Caution: Backtracking on equity commitments to quell backlash can erode trust, harm brand reputation, and send a message to marginalized communities that inclusion is conditional.

Mosaic Question: How will you respond when your commitment to equity is challenged—not just praised?

Mosaic in Action: A school district faces political pressure to remove its ethnic studies program. Instead of eliminating it, leaders involve parents, teachers, and students in discussions, reaffirming the program's importance in promoting critical thinking and cultural understanding.

Wounded Leadership

Definition: Wounded leadership describes how unresolved personal pain in leaders influences their leadership style, decisions, and relationships.

Business Application: While vulnerability can foster trust, unaddressed wounds may lead to defensiveness, micromanagement, or punitive cultures.

Leadership Insight: Leaders who include self-reflection and healing in their development can transform personal struggles into sources of wisdom and empathy.

Cultural Caution: Romanticizing wounded leadership without accountability risks normalizing harm to teams and continuing cycles of trauma.

Mosaic Question: How might your unhealed experiences be shaping your leadership—both positively and negatively?

Mosaic in Action: A nonprofit executive takes a sabbatical to recover from trauma and returns with new policies to support mental health for all staff.

Work Ethic Bias

Definition: Work ethic bias happens when individuals or groups are judged—either positively or negatively—based on perceived adherence to specific cultural or generational standards of productivity, punctuality, and commitment.

Business Application: This bias can affect hiring, promotions, and performance reviews, often favoring those whose work styles align with dominant cultural expectations rather than actual performance or results.

Leadership Insight: Leaders who understand work ethic bias recognize that high performance can appear differently across cultures, time zones, and individual work styles.

Cultural Caution: Equating long hours with dedication or assuming flexible schedules indicate laziness

632

can overlook talent and deepen inequalities.

Mosaic Question: Are you prioritizing visible effort over real impact?

Mosaic in Action: A company moves from monitoring employee "desk time" to assessing outcomes, enabling various work styles without docking productivity.

Workforce Equity Design

Definition: Workforce equity design is the strategic process of integrating fairness, representation, and inclusion into every stage of the employee experience—from recruitment to retirement.

Business Application: This approach aligns hiring, promotion, pay, and policy structures with measurable equity goals, supported by data analysis and community feedback.

Leadership Insight: Leaders who commit to equity design shift from reactive diversity initiatives to proactive systems that remove barriers before they appear.

Cultural Caution: Treating equity as a one-time effort rather than an ongoing design principle risks superficial compliance without genuine change.

Mosaic Question: How does your workforce structure ensure equity is inevitable rather than optional?

Mosaic in Action: A healthcare system applies equity design to revamp pay scales, mentorship programs, and promotion criteria, leading to a 35 percent rise in leadership roles for underrepresented employees.

Workforce Fragmentation

Definition: Workforce fragmentation happens when employees or teams work in isolated silos, usually because of structural, cultural, or technological gaps.

Business Application: It can arise in global organizations, hybrid workplaces, or after mergers, causing misaligned goals, communication issues, and duplicated efforts.

Leadership Insight: Leaders who intentionally address fragmentation—by promoting shared language, interdepartmental initiatives, and cultural connections—set the stage for innovation and trust.

Cultural Caution: Ignoring fragmentation can worsen inequities, as marginalized employees are often left out of informal networks where influence flows.

Mosaic Question: Where in your organization do people work side by side but never actually collaborate?

Mosaic in Action: A multinational engineering company launches a cross-region mentorship program to bridge gaps between its headquarters and offshore teams, enhancing retention and collaboration.

Workplace Assimilation

Definition: Workplace assimilation is the often unspoken process through which employees are pressured to conform to dominant cultural norms, values, and behaviors in order to be accepted or succeed.

Business Application: Assimilation pressures can undermine authenticity, decrease employee engagement, and increase attrition, especially among those from marginalized backgrounds.

Leadership Insight: Inclusive leaders create space for diverse communication styles, problem-solving methods, and cultural expressions instead of demanding conformity.

Cultural Caution: Prioritizing "culture fit" over "culture add" can sustain exclusionary practices and hinder organizational innovation.

Mosaic Question: What unintentional expectations are you asking people to leave at the door?

Mosaic in Action: A law firm updates its dress code and meeting etiquette to support cultural attire and diverse communication styles, lowering turnover among underrepresented employees.

Workplace Belonging

Definition: Workplace belonging is the sense of being accepted, valued, and able to contribute authentically within a professional environment.

Business Application: Fostering a sense of belonging can boost retention, teamwork, and innovation, directly affecting both morale and profits.

Leadership Insight: Belonging is created through trust, shared purpose, and psychological safety— not just by inclusion policies or onboarding rituals.

Cultural Caution: Confusing superficial inclusion (such as holiday potlucks) with true belonging risks tokenizing employees instead of empowering them.

Mosaic Question: How do members of your organization know they genuinely belong?

Mosaic in Action: A healthcare organization implements peer mentoring programs that connect employees across departments, leading to increased engagement and cross-team trust.

Workplace Emotional Tax

Definition: Workplace emotional tax is the increased mental and emotional stress faced by employees—often from underrepresented groups—due to dealing with bias, exclusion, or the need to code-switch at work.

Business Application: Emotional tax can cause burnout, lower performance, and increase attrition, which undermines diversity and inclusion efforts.

Leadership Insight: Leaders who actively address emotional tax lower turnover and build resilience by encouraging open dialogue and providing targeted support.

Cultural Caution: Ignoring emotional labor continues systemic harm, even in workplaces that outwardly seem diverse.

Mosaic Question: What unspoken emotional sacrifices are your team members making to succeed here?

Mosaic in Action: A tech company establishes a confidential support group for employees experiencing microaggressions, along with

leadership accountability measures to drive systemic change.

Workplace Restoration

Definition: Workplace restoration refers to the intentional process of rebuilding trust, culture, and operational health after a period of conflict, crisis, or organizational harm.

Business Application: Restoration efforts can address incidents such as leadership misconduct, layoffs, public controversies, or toxic workplace cultures. They often involve structured listening sessions, policy updates, and culture-renewal initiatives.

Leadership Insight: Effective leaders view restoration as a long-term investment in stability and morale—not as a quick fix or PR stunt. Transparency, consistency, and accountability are crucial.

Cultural Caution: Avoiding deep restoration work in favor of superficial changes can foster cynicism, damage credibility, and speed up talent loss.

Mosaic Question: How do you rebuild trust after a breach—and how do you demonstrate that it's genuine?

Mosaic in Action: After a high-profile discrimination lawsuit, a nonprofit launches a multi-year cultural renewal plan that features community-led policy reviews and quarterly accountability reports.

Workplace Surveillance

Definition: Workplace surveillance involves monitoring employees' activities, behaviors, or communications, often using technology like keystroke trackers, location tracking, or video recording.

Business Application: While some surveillance is used for safety or compliance, excessive monitoring can break trust, hinder creativity, and lead to burnout.

Leadership Insight: Leaders who balance security needs with employee autonomy create environments where people feel respected rather than controlled.

Cultural Caution: Surveillance disproportionately impacts remote, gig, and frontline workers, and can reinforce existing inequities when monitoring is applied inconsistently.

Mosaic Question: Is your monitoring policy safeguarding your people—or surveillance them?

Mosaic in Action: A global retailer replaces productivity-tracking software with team-based accountability measures, resulting

in increased morale and improved customer service ratings.

Workplace Wholeness

Definition: A workplace culture that encourages individuals to be authentic, blending personal and professional identities without fear of punishment or division.

Business Application: Workplace wholeness boosts retention and innovation by lowering emotional tax, assimilation pressure, and identity suppression.

Leadership Insight: Wholeness requires leaders to embrace complexity — valuing people as multidimensional beings, not only employees.

Cultural Caution: What feels like wholeness in one culture may seem like overexposure in another. Leaders must permit individuals to choose how much they share.

Mosaic Question: Does your workplace require hiding parts of people — or encourage them to bring their whole selves?

Mosaic in Action: A global company updates policies to support gender expression, religious practices, and family responsibilities, promoting inclusiveness in the workplace.

World-Building Language

Definition: World-building language refers to the purposeful use of narratives, metaphors, and terms that shape the shared reality of an organization or movement.

Business Application: This language influences culture, reinforces values, and can unify diverse teams by creating a collective vision that feels tangible and authentic.

Leadership Insight: Skilled leaders recognize that every policy, slogan, and story contributes to a cultural "map" that employees navigate daily.

Cultural Caution: Exclusive or jargon-heavy world-building can alienate stakeholders and restrict who feels included in the vision.

Mosaic Question: What kind of "world" does your language invite people into—and who feels excluded from its gates?

Mosaic in Action: A social enterprise shifts its mission from "fighting poverty" to "building prosperity ecosystems," inspiring collaborative, long-term engagement across partners.

Worldview Conflict

Definition: Worldview conflict occurs when core belief systems— religious, cultural, political, or philosophical—clash in ways that affect relationships, decision-making, or policy.

Business Application: In diverse organizations, such conflicts may appear in discussions about ethical practices, social causes, or workplace norms.

Leadership Insight: Managing worldview conflict requires emotional literacy, cultural adaptability, and the skill to focus on shared goals without dismissing differences.

Cultural Caution: Pushing for consensus on deeply held beliefs can create resentment; effective dialogue provides space for disagreement while fostering mutual respect.

Mosaic Question: How do you lead when the "right" path depends on the perspective through which it's viewed?

Mosaic in Action: A city council adopts structured dialogue circles to address tensions between environmental priorities and economic growth agendas.

◈ LETTER W CALLOUT

"Whiteness and workplace culture intertwine — until named, the defaults remain invisible but powerful."

Reflection Questions

- How do practices like white silence or white comfort shape group dynamics?
- Where does wellness culture reinforce privilege rather than healing?
- What "unwritten rules" about professionalism exist in your environment?

Practical Move

In your next team or class discussion, name one hidden norm (dress, tone, timing). Ask openly: *Who does this serve? Who does it silence?*

X – Xenophobia, Xenocentrism, and the Edges of Belonging

X marks the crossing—the moment when differences become visible and belonging feels conditional. Though few terms start here, they carry disproportionate weight in shaping how inclusion, identity, and recognition develop across cultures and systems.

Xenophobia is more than just personal bias. It is a systemic fear, rejection, or devaluation of those seen as foreigners — expressed through language, skin color, accent, clothing, or even body language. It doesn't only show up in border policies or news stories; it also exists in hiring choices, leadership assumptions, and subtle messages that quietly determine who is accepted and who is excluded.

Xenocentrism, more subtle yet equally harmful, idealizes the "foreign" at the expense of one's own culture or community. In global organizations, it can appear as prioritizing overseas models over local expertise. In daily interactions, it can manifest as admiring an accent or style without understanding the complexity of the culture it reflects. What seems like admiration turns into erasure when it reduces depth to novelty.

Together, these forces shape the emotional foundation of belonging. They determine who is trusted without question, who must overperform to be accepted, and whose discomfort is considered minor. They establish whose ideas are seen as valuable and whose culture is regarded as the standard.

X asks us to confront the crossings where bias and hierarchy emerge

- Xenophobia that normalizes exclusion under the guise of neutrality.
- Xenocentrism that romanticizes difference while dismissing homegrown wisdom.
- The conditional belonging that forces some to prove worth repeatedly.
- The systemic cues that signal who is "inside" and who remains "other."

X is more than just a letter; it is a signal—a prompt to scrutinize the boundaries we set within our teams, systems, and stories. It serves as a reminder that equity cannot thrive alongside conditional belonging.

X urges leaders to recognize how exclusion often hides behind "fit" or "fairness," and to replace these patterns with practices that turn difference into a bridge. Because true leadership is not proven by how it manages sameness but by how it expands the circle where difference is seen, valued,, and upheld.

X

X-Change Leadership

Definition: A leadership style based on cross-experience exchange, where leaders and teams purposefully swap perspectives, roles, or environments to broaden empathy and improve problem-solving skills.

Business Application: Organizations implement X-change leadership through mentorship programs, job shadowing, and cross-department rotations to break down silos and encourage innovation.

Leadership Insight: The most influential leaders don't just share information—they exchange contexts, generating insights that resonate because they are experienced firsthand, not just communicated.

Cultural Caution: Exchanges that ignore power imbalances risk becoming tokenistic, strengthening rather than challenging inequities.

Mosaic Question: How often do you genuinely swap perspectives rather than simply sharing your own?

Mosaic in Action: A CEO spends a week working alongside the customer service team, returning to strategy meetings with fresh insights that influence the company to prioritize customer retention.

X-Factor Bias

Definition: The tendency to overvalue certain charismatic or intangible qualities—like charm, presence, or image—when making hiring, promotion, or leadership decisions.

Business Application: In recruitment, X-factor bias can lead to favoring "likable" candidates over those with proven skills and long-term potential.

Leadership Insight: While charisma can inspire, bias toward it often hides systemic favoritism and overlooks the power of quieter, steadier leadership styles.

Cultural Caution: What's considered an "X-factor" varies by culture; assuming universal agreement risks privileging dominant cultural aesthetics.

Mosaic Question: Are you rewarding real impact, or the performance of it?

Mosaic in Action: A board chooses a less flashy candidate for a leadership role after reviewing data showing their department's higher retention, innovation, and morale under their guidance.

X-Leadership (Experimental Leadership)

Definition: A future-focused leadership model that values experimentation, adaptability, and risk-taking over strict adherence to tradition. X-Leadership excels in uncertain, rapidly changing environments.

Business Application: Organizations practicing X-Leadership utilize pilot projects, iterative learning, and rapid prototyping to remain adaptable to cultural, technological, and global changes.

Leadership Insight: Great leaders are not just guardians of stability but creators of innovation. X-Leadership shows that failure can be a teacher, not a threat.

Cultural Caution: In cultures that value hierarchy or predictability, experimental leadership may seem reckless. Leaders need to balance innovation with building trust within the culture.

Mosaic Question: Do you play it safe in leadership — or make room to experiment and adapt?

Mosaic in Action: A healthcare executive conducts small-scale innovation sprints before implementing system-wide rollouts, enabling safe testing and quick learning.

X-Reality Leadership

Definition: A leadership approach that combines physical, virtual, and augmented realities, guiding teams to adapt across blended and immersive work environments.

Business Application: As workplaces incorporate AR/VR, leaders skilled in X-reality develop protocols for collaboration, safety, and ethical tech use that respect both human connection and digital innovation.

Leadership Insight: Leading in X-reality involves balancing innovation with humanity— ensuring the tech serves people, not the other way around.

Cultural Caution: Not all employees have equal access to immersive tech, and cultural norms regarding privacy, embodiment, and interaction differ widely.

Mosaic Question: How do you lead when the boundaries between "real" and "virtual" are blurred?

Mosaic in Action: A global design firm runs hybrid brainstorming sessions where on-site staff use physical whiteboards, while remote staff collaborate through a shared VR environment, ensuring equal voice in the creative process.

Xenocentrism

Definition: A preference for ideas, products, or cultural norms from outside one's own society, often involving undervaluing local or native traditions.

Business Application: Global teams may adopt foreign management models or branding styles without tailoring them to the local context, risking cultural disconnect with employees or customers.

Leadership Insight: Valuing other cultures can inspire innovation, but unchecked xenocentrism can damage cultural identity and weaken trust from those who feel their heritage is overlooked.

Cultural Caution: Romanticizing other cultures without proper understanding can lead to cultural missteps, reinforce stereotypes, or ignore systemic inequalities.

Mosaic Question: How can you incorporate the best aspects of other cultures while respecting your own?

Mosaic in Action: A startup founder, initially captivated by Silicon Valley's fast-growth mindset, adjusts their approach after employees request work practices based on local cultural rhythms and community values.

Xenodialogue

Definition: Xenodialogue is the practice of engaging in dialogue across deep differences with those seen as strangers or outsiders. It emphasizes humility, openness, and building relationships.

Business Application: Organizations utilize xenodialogue in cross-cultural partnerships, conflict resolution, and stakeholder engagement to foster trust and minimize division.

Leadership Insight: True leadership involves listening to voices beyond your usual circle. Xenodialogue turns strangers into partners.

Cultural Caution: In some situations, starting conversations with outsiders might be viewed as disloyalty or risk. Leaders need to assess relational and cultural factors carefully.

Mosaic Question: Who do you avoid engaging in dialogue with — and what might change if you leaned in?

Mosaic in Action: A city leader hosts xenodialogue sessions between immigrant residents and long-time citizens to foster mutual understanding.

Xenoinclusion

Definition: The deliberate act of inviting and including individuals or groups seen as outsiders or foreigners into organizational, cultural, or community life.

Business Application: Xenoinclusion helps global organizations bridge gaps, enhance cross-border collaboration, and foster innovation by valuing diverse perspectives.

Leadership Insight: Inclusion is most tested when differences feel unfamiliar. Leaders who practice xenoinclusion broaden the circle of belonging.

Cultural Caution: Xenoinclusion should not be mistaken for assimilation. It involves maintaining the integrity of new members while fostering mutual connections.

Mosaic Question: Who in your organization still feels like an "outsider"— and what would true inclusion look like?

Mosaic in Action: An international NGO develops programs for refugee staff that promote xenoinclusion, offering mentorship and leadership opportunities.

Xenophobia

Definition: Fear, distrust, or prejudice toward people perceived as foreign or different, often rooted in historical, political, or economic concerns.

Business Application: Xenophobia can hinder global collaboration, creating obstacles in cross-border negotiations, hiring, and team integration.

Leadership Insight: Leaders who confront xenophobia directly— through education, dialogue, and policy—can transform team culture to prioritize safety and inclusion.

Cultural Caution: Addressing xenophobia requires more than superficial training; it needs ongoing structural and relational changes.

Mosaic Question: What biases might you hold against people whose culture or origin differs from your own?

Mosaic in Action: A multinational company adopts anonymous reporting and accountability procedures after realizing that casual jokes about "outsiders" were undermining trust and productivity.

Xenoresistance

Definition: The subtle or obvious opposition to outsiders, foreigners, or external cultural influences. Xenoresistance appears in workplace mergers, cross-cultural teams, and communities experiencing demographic shifts.

Business Application: Recognizing xenoresistance helps leaders anticipate tension during globalization, immigration shifts, or organizational change.

Leadership Insight: Resistance often indicates fear or a loss of control. Leaders who confront xenoresistance head-on open up opportunities for adaptation instead of provoking backlash.

Cultural Caution: Labeling resistance as xenophobia might oversimplify complex dynamics. Leaders need to examine if resistance is based on identity, fear, or systemic inequality.

Mosaic Question: Where is xenoresistance appearing in your team or organization, and what does it uncover?

Mosaic in Action: During a corporate merger, leaders observe xenoresistance in cross-border teams and develop cultural exchange programs to foster trust.

Xenotranslation

Definition: The practice of translating language, ideas, or cultural references between groups with significant cultural differences, going beyond literal meaning to preserve intent, context, and emotional resonance.

Business Application: In cross-cultural marketing, xenotranslation ensures campaigns connect authentically, avoiding cultural misinterpretations.

Leadership Insight: True leadership in diverse settings means not just speaking someone's language but translating ideas so they land as intended within their cultural framework.

Cultural Caution: Over-simplifying or "domesticating" cultural expressions during translation can strip away essential meaning and identity.

Mosaic Question: How do you ensure your message resonates across cultural lines without losing its original essence?

Mosaic in Action: During an international summit, a facilitator adapts an English metaphor into a locally relevant folk saying, preserving its humor and impact for all attendees.

◈ LETTER X CALLOUT

"Exchanges across difference are not experiments — they are opportunities to expand what leadership can mean."

Reflection Questions

- What fears surface in cross-cultural dialogue or xenodialogue?
- How does xenophobia resist inclusion in subtle ways?
- Where can experimental leadership practices create safety instead of risk?

Practical Move

Pair with someone outside your usual circle. Exchange one story of navigating difference, and note what leadership insight emerges from that dialogue.

Y – Youth, Yearning, and Yet-to-Be-Seen Voices

Y embodies the energy of becoming—the rise of potential, the quiet growth of leadership, and the tension between visibility and trust. It represents those who are often called the future but rarely receive support in the present. Youth here is not just about age but about stage—characterized by newness, questions, and the search for belonging.

In many systems, youth is both celebrated and overlooked. Young professionals are highlighted in recruitment campaigns but left out of real decision-making. Their creativity is praised in theory but questioned in strategic discussions. Those still finding their voice are often asked to show confidence they haven't been given the safety or space to develop.

Y also embodies yearning—the desire to matter, grow, and contribute in spaces that offer feedback without dismissal, guidance without condescension, and opportunity without tokenism. It includes the yet-to-be voices of people at any stage of life who are stepping into new roles, claiming new identities, or daring to lead in unfamiliar territory.

Y asks us to notice the hidden hierarchies of credibility

- Youth praised for innovation but sidelined in influence.
- The pressure to overperform just to be taken seriously.
- The silencing of yet-to-be voices who fear mistakes more than they trust support.

- The failure of mentorship when it seeks to mold rather than empower.

Y reminds us that the future does not come fully formed. It develops through voices still learning to speak in rooms not built for them.

Y urges leaders to move beyond symbolic encouragement toward structural empowerment to mentor by witnessing instead of controlling, to create spaces where new voices are nurtured rather than tested, and to see yearning not as immaturity but as the raw material of transformation. Because cultures do not evolve by protecting hierarchy—they grow when they invest in the voices still emerging.

Y

Yardstick Bias

Definition: The tendency to judge different cultures, practices, or identities by a dominant "standard" or norm — often unconsciously using one culture as the benchmark for all others.

Business Application: Organizations fall into yardstick bias when they judge leadership, communication, or success only by Western, male, or majority-culture standards.

Leadership Insight: Leaders who recognize yardstick bias expand their evaluative perspective, valuing multiple approaches instead of relying solely on one "correct" model.

Cultural Caution: Yardstick bias can silently undermine entire communities. Leaders must ensure they are not reinforcing hierarchy under the pretense of evaluation.

Mosaic Question: What "yardstick" are you using to measure leadership, and who does it exclude?

Mosaic in Action: A global company adapts performance reviews to consider different communication styles, minimizing bias toward extroverted, Westernized norms.

Yearning for Belonging

Definition: A deep, often unspoken desire to be accepted, valued, and included within a group, culture, or community.

Business Application: This yearning influences employee engagement and retention; when unmet, it can cause disengagement or turnover.

Leadership Insight: Leaders who recognize and foster a sense of belonging tap into a powerful source of motivation and loyalty.

Cultural Caution: Belonging should not demand conformity that eliminates individuality—true belonging respects differences.

Mosaic Question: Where in your organization do people still feel like outsiders, and why?

Mosaic in Action: A team leader implements a rotating "origin story" segment in staff meetings where members share parts of their personal journeys, enhancing mutual understanding.

Yes-Culture

Definition: An organizational environment where people agree with authority or group consensus, often at the expense of critical thinking or dissent.

Business Application: While fostering harmony, yes-culture can lead to groupthink and missed opportunities for innovation.

Leadership Insight: Healthy leadership encourages constructive disagreement and questions, not just compliance.

Cultural Caution: In cultures with high respect for hierarchy, countering yes-culture requires explicit permission for alternative viewpoints.

Mosaic Question: How do you signal that dissent is welcome—and safe—in your environment?

Mosaic in Action: A CEO institutes a "red team" protocol for major initiatives, assigning staff to challenge assumptions before decisions are finalized.

Yes-Man Syndrome

Definition: A pattern where subordinates avoid dissent, and leaders either unconsciously or intentionally surround themselves with agreement, thereby limiting critical feedback.

Business Application: Yes-man syndrome fosters groupthink, hinders innovation, and stops organizations from spotting risks or blind spots.

Leadership Insight: Leaders who appreciate dissent and open dialogue sidestep the trap of yes-man syndrome and promote better decision-making.

Cultural Caution: In some high power-distance cultures, disagreement is often discouraged. Leaders need to establish culturally appropriate ways for dissent.

Mosaic Question: Do people in your organization feel comfortable saying no to you?

Mosaic in Action: A CEO implements "red team" reviews to challenge strategic decisions, ensuring that disagreement is valued as part of planning.

Yet-to-Be-Seen Voices

Definition: Individuals or groups whose perspectives, knowledge, or leadership have not yet been acknowledged, invited, or valued in decision-making spaces. These voices represent untapped potential for innovation, belonging, and cultural alignment.

Business Application: Identifying and elevating voices that haven't been heard yet helps organizations unlock new solutions, expand relevance, and build trust. It ensures that leadership decisions mirror lived realities beyond the dominant perspectives.

Leadership Insight: Inclusive leadership is characterized not only by who is present at the table but also by who is absent. Leaders who intentionally open doors for unheard voices show vision, courage, and integrity.

Cultural Caution: Inviting voices without genuine follow-through can do more harm than silence. Tokenism, performative gestures, or superficial listening worsen exclusion instead of fixing it.

Mosaic Question: Which voices are you still not listening to — and what barriers are preventing you from hearing them?

Mosaic in Action: A policy team establishes anonymous feedback channels and targeted listening sessions, providing space for historically silenced staff to share insights that influence strategic priorities.

Yielding Culture

Definition: An environment in an organization or community where deference, compliance, or passivity become the norm, often at the expense of equity and innovation.

Business Application: A yielding culture results in suppressed dissent, silenced voices, and decreased accountability. It might be seen as harmony, but it is actually a form of avoidance.

Leadership Insight: A yielding culture flourishes when leaders suppress risk-taking. Challenging this requires demonstrating courage and accepting healthy tension.

Cultural Caution: What appears to be yielding in one culture might actually be a sign of respect or deference in another. Leaders need to understand the intent before making judgments.

Mosaic Question: Is your culture genuinely collaborative — or merely compliant?

Mosaic in Action: A nonprofit moves from top-down decision-making to shared governance, promoting staff to express disagreement constructively.

Yielding Leadership

Definition: A leadership style that willingly steps back to let others lead, often to empower emerging voices or adapt to the situation.

Business Application: Yielding leadership can foster growth, trust, and shared ownership of outcomes.

Leadership Insight: Stepping aside strategically is not a sign of weakness—it's a form of influence that expands leadership capacity.

Cultural Caution: Yielding without clear intent can seem like disengagement; clarity of purpose is important.

Mosaic Question: When is your leadership most effective by creating space for someone else?

Mosaic in Action: A project director hands over a high-visibility client meeting to a junior team member, staying present to support but letting them take the lead.

Yielding Norms

Definition: Workplace or cultural rules that are flexible and can be adapted to suit changing needs, contexts, or participants.

Business Application: Yielding norms enable organizations to stay responsive in dynamic environments, fostering innovation and inclusion.

Leadership Insight: Leaders must find a balance between adaptability and the stability that makes people feel secure.

Cultural Caution: Too much flexibility can lead to confusion or perceptions of unfairness; transparency about why norms shift is essential.

Mosaic Question: Which of your norms could bend without damaging your culture?

Mosaic in Action: A nonprofit relaxes its strict work-from-office policy during a local transit strike, boosting trust and productivity.

Yoked Identity

Definition: When a person's identity is tied—by perception or assignment—to a group, role, or label, often without their consent.

Business Application: Yoked identities can hinder advancement or affect how contributions are valued.

Leadership Insight: Breaking the "yoke" involves both setting personal boundaries and changing systemic perceptions.

Cultural Caution: Yoking can reinforce stereotypes and reduce individuality, even when framed positively.

Mosaic Question: Who's being defined for in your space, and how can you help free it?

Mosaic in Action: A Latina engineer is repeatedly selected for diversity panels instead of technical projects; her manager redirects requests to ensure her expertise is recognized beyond just representation.

Young Leader Syndrome

Definition: The tendency to underestimate or overly scrutinize leaders because of their age, regardless of their competence.

Business Application: This bias can hinder organizational progress by sidelining capable emerging leaders.

Leadership Insight: Age does not determine ability; mentorship combined with opportunity can boost impact.

Cultural Caution: In cultures with strong age-based hierarchies, this bias might require systemic re-education.

Mosaic Question: Are you assessing leadership based on results and integrity—or on assumptions about age?

Mosaic in Action: A tech startup's board appoints a 26-year-old COO and pairs them with a veteran advisor, leading to record-breaking growth within a year.

Youth-Centered Equity Design

Definition: An approach to program or policy development that emphasizes the lived experiences and needs of young people from the beginning.

Business Application: This method results in more relevant services, increased engagement, and lasting impact in youth-focused projects.

Leadership Insight: Designing with youth, rather than just for them, builds trust and leads to better solutions.

Cultural Caution: Token youth involvement without real decision-making power diminishes authenticity.

Mosaic Question: How often are youth voices the architects, not just the audience, of your initiatives?

Mosaic in Action: A city council's youth climate committee is given direct control over the budget for selected environmental projects.

Youth Equity Gap

Definition: The gap in resources, opportunities, and influence given to young people compared to older populations.

Business Application: Closing this gap is crucial for developing future-ready workforces and communities.

Leadership Insight: Equity is as much generation-based as it is cultural or racial; ignoring youth access sustains systemic imbalance.

Cultural Caution: Efforts to "empower youth" without tackling structural barriers can become symbolic rather than truly transformative.

Mosaic Question: What barriers prevent young people from fully contributing to your organization's mission?

Mosaic in Action: A professional association removes "years of experience" as a requirement for board positions, opening doors for talented early-career leaders.

Youth-Led Leadership

Definition: An approach that views young people not only as participants but also as decision-makers and leaders with genuine influence and agency.

Business Application: Youth-led leadership guarantees programs, policies, and initiatives are guided directly by the voices and expertise of young people.

Leadership Insight: Investing in youth-led leadership enhances innovation, grounds strategies in emerging realities, and creates sustainable pipelines of leaders.

Cultural Caution: Some societies undervalue youth voices. Leaders must guard against tokenizing young people and instead create genuine pathways to authority.

Mosaic Question: Do you give youth a seat at the table — or a voice in shaping it?

Mosaic in Action: A climate coalition transitions from "youth engagement" to youth-led councils, empowering young leaders to set agendas and priorities.

Youth Tokenism

Definition: Including a small number of young people in leadership or decision-making roles solely for symbolic representation.

Business Application: Tokenism damages trust and diminishes the perceived legitimacy of youth contributions.

Leadership Insight: Genuine inclusion involves responsibility, authority, and the ability to influence outcomes.

Cultural Caution: Tokenism can reinforce stereotypes about youth being inexperienced or only novel, rather than capable.

Mosaic Question: Are youth in your space influencers or just photo opportunities?

Mosaic in Action: A nonprofit moves from having a single "youth representative" role to a co-leadership model where young and older leaders share equal voting power.

Youthful Insight

Definition: The new perspectives, adaptability, and creativity that younger individuals contribute to problem-solving.

Business Application: Harnessing youthful insight can ignite innovation and challenge longstanding patterns.

Leadership Insight: Valuing the contributions of youth equally with those of experienced professionals fosters a balance between expertise and fresh ideas.

Cultural Caution: Romanticizing youthful energy without recognizing skill and knowledge can lead to condescension.

Mosaic Question: How do you capture and incorporate youthful insight into strategic planning?

Mosaic in Action: A manufacturing company invites high school interns to redesign product packaging, leading to a design that wins industry awards.

◆ LETTER Y CALLOUT

"Youth voices do not signal inexperience; they remind us of futures not yet foreclosed."

Reflection Questions

- Where in your space are young or emerging leaders undervalued?
- How do 'yes-culture' dynamics undermine authenticity?
- What does yearning for belonging look like in younger generations?

Practical Move

Invite a younger colleague or student to share their perspective on a current challenge. Act on one idea they raise, signaling that their voice shapes outcomes.

Z – Zoom Fatigue, Zones of Identity, and the Zeitgeist of Now

Z is both a closure and a crossing—an ending, yes, but also an invitation into the urgency of now. In a world moving at relentless speed, Z roots us in the emotional fabric of the present a time characterized by digital intensity, identity fluidity, and the increasing demand for meaning, presence, and cultural clarity.

Zoom fatigue is more than just screen fatigue. It emphasizes the emotional toll of being present without truly being seen—of interpreting micro-reactions through pixels and performing connection without the grounding of shared space. It shows how digital work can increase invisibility, widen inequalities, and amplify the emotional labor of those already facing bias.

Zones of identity represent the fluid, liminal spaces where who we are shifts depending on context. In hybrid and remote environments, people switch between roles, codes, and cultural expressions—sometimes freeing, sometimes confusing. These zones serve as a reminder that identity is not fixed but constantly negotiated between self and system, context and connection.

The zeitgeist of now names the cultural atmosphere of this moment collective burnout, cross-generational friction, racial and geopolitical reckonings, and the collapse of outdated leadership norms. In such a climate, leadership cannot remain performative. It must be grounded, present, and responsive.

Z asks us to notice the defining forces of our moment

- Digital fatigue that diminishes presence and deepens inequity.
- Identity zones that demand flexibility and cultural safety.
- A zeitgeist pressing leaders to release outdated norms.
- The urgency of recalibrating not just what we say, but how we truly show up.

Z may be the last letter of the alphabet, but it also represents a threshold. It urges leaders to embrace humility and humanity, recognizing that communication is no longer solely verbal but also emotional, visual, digital, and deeply contextual.

Z challenges us to lead not just with speed, but with presence—creating cultures that value both efficiency and soul. Because this list's end is not closure, but a new beginning a fresh way of leading, listening, and belonging in real time.

Z

Zero Visibility Roles

Definition: Roles within an organization that involve significant responsibility but receive little recognition, visibility, or public acknowledgment, often leading to the undervaluing of the people in these positions.

Business Application: Many administrative, support, and operational roles fall into this category—such as data analysts, lab technicians, and behind-the-scenes coordinators—whose work directly impacts outcomes but is rarely mentioned in reports or press releases.

Leadership Insight: Leaders who neglect these roles risk losing essential talent and damaging morale. Recognizing and publicly appreciating invisible work not only enhances retention but also builds trust.

Cultural Caution: In some cultures, humility and low-profile work are appreciated; in others, lack of recognition might be perceived as dismissal. Leaders need to handle recognition practices with cultural sensitivity.

Mosaic Question: Who on your team keeps the system running quietly—and how can you spotlight their contributions without tokenizing them?

Mosaic in Action: A university's event planning team is seldom acknowledged during commencement ceremonies. A new dean invites the team on stage at the end to thank them publicly, shifting how faculty and students perceive their contribution.

Zero-Visibility Leadership

Definition: Leadership practiced in situations where decision-making and influence occur without public recognition, often because the work is behind the scenes or politically sensitive.

Business Application: Crisis negotiators, internal change managers, or conflict mediators frequently lead without public acknowledgment. Their efforts shape outcomes, but their names might never appear in a press release.

Leadership Insight: Genuine leadership is not about seeking applause. Influencing others without public praise fosters resilience, patience, and a focus on impact instead of ego.

Cultural Caution: In organizations that overly value public visibility, leaders who operate without visibility may be seen as less important or powerful, which can unintentionally weaken their ability to influence.

Mosaic Question: Can you stay steady in your leadership when no one realizes it's you keeping the structure intact?

Mosaic in Action: During a corporate merger, an HR manager quietly mediates between warring department heads. No one outside the leadership team knows, but the merger succeeds with minimal attrition because of her work.

Zero-Sum Mindset

Definition: A belief that resources, opportunities, or recognition are limited—meaning one person's gain is another's loss.

Business Application: In competitive industries or tight budgets, this mindset can create silos, hoarding of resources, and internal rivalries that damage the organization's overall potential.

Leadership Insight: Leaders who replace zero-sum thinking with

abundance mindsets promote collaboration and long-term innovation, even when resources are scarce.

Cultural Caution: In some situations, resource scarcity is a real challenge, not just a mindset. Leaders need to be sensitive to the fears and pressures that drive zero-sum thinking.

Mosaic Question: Where might a win-win solution be found in a space you've always seen as either/or?

Mosaic in Action: In a nonprofit with limited grant funding, two program managers initially compete for resources. The director encourages them to co-develop a joint proposal that wins a larger grant than either could have secured alone.

Zero-Tolerance Policy (Critical View)

Definition: A strict rule or enforcement policy that offers no flexibility in responding to violations. In discussions about equity and leadership, zero-tolerance policies are criticized for affecting marginalized groups unfairly and not addressing the underlying causes.

Business Application: Organizations often implement

zero-tolerance policies for harassment or misconduct, but without nuance, they risk fostering fear instead of accountability.

Leadership Insight: Accountability isn't the same as inflexibility. Leaders need to differentiate between high standards and rigid policies that can cause unintended harm.

Cultural Caution: In certain situations, "zero-tolerance" is viewed as essential for safety (for example, violence prevention). Leaders must balance consistency with fairness.

Mosaic Question: Does your leadership apply strict rules, or does it act with fairness and understanding?

Mosaic in Action: A school district replaces its zero-tolerance discipline policy with restorative practices, which lowers suspensions and builds community trust.

Zonal Leadership

Definition: A leadership approach that recognizes and adapts to the specific needs, resources, and challenges of different geographic, cultural, or organizational zones.

Business Application: International NGOs and regional corporations use zonal leadership to delegate decision-making authority to local leaders while aligning with a shared global strategy.

Leadership Insight: Leaders who understand zonal differences avoid "one-size-fits-all" directives, instead developing frameworks flexible enough to accommodate unique local realities.

Cultural Caution: Assuming uniformity across zones can lead to mistrust, inefficiency, and cultural mistakes—especially in cross-border operations.

Mosaic Question: How do your leadership strategies change when the context shifts?

Mosaic in Action: A humanitarian organization coordinates disaster response differently in coastal, rural, and urban zones— prioritizing local partnerships and resource flows based on each community's realities.

Zone of Cultural Safety

Definition: An environment where individuals from diverse cultural backgrounds feel respected, heard, and protected from discrimination or cultural harm.

Business Application: Hospitals, schools, and multinational corporations often implement cultural safety frameworks to ensure that policies, language, and behaviors do not undermine the identity or dignity of staff and clients.

Leadership Insight: Cultural safety goes beyond inclusion—it actively prevents harm by integrating protective measures into organizational systems, not just through interpersonal interactions.

Cultural Caution: What feels "safe" for one culture may feel performative or insufficient for another. Leaders must seek feedback from the communities they aim to serve.

Mosaic Question: How are you actively reducing the risk of cultural harm in your leadership spaces?

Mosaic in Action: In a healthcare clinic serving Indigenous communities, leadership invites Elders to review patient intake forms. The revised forms respect traditional naming structures and minimize culturally unsafe questioning.

Zone of Ethical Innovation

Definition: The intentional space where creativity and experimentation occur within clear ethical boundaries, ensuring innovation benefits people without causing harm.

Business Application: Tech companies use this zone to test AI models or new products in a controlled way, balancing innovation speed with ethical safeguards like bias testing and community consultation.

Leadership Insight: True innovation requires boundaries—without them, leaders risk creating solutions that solve one problem but create another.

Cultural Caution: Ethical standards vary across cultures and industries; leaders must clarify which values guide innovation in their context and ensure they are not exporting harm.

Mosaic Question: Are your innovations protecting as much as they are advancing?

Mosaic in Action: A design team developing a new payment app partners with disability advocates to ensure accessibility features are embedded before launch, rather than treated as an afterthought.

Zones of Belonging

Definition: Layers or levels of inclusion, trust, and psychological safety that individuals experience within a group or organization.

Business Application: Leaders can use zones of belonging to evaluate where employees feel fully included, partially accepted, or entirely excluded.

Leadership Insight: Belonging exists on a spectrum, not as a simple yes or no. Leaders need to understand this range and work to foster deeper inclusion.

Cultural Caution: Belonging varies across cultures. What seems like inclusion in one group might feel like tokenism in another.

Mosaic Question: Where in your organization are people "on the edge" of belonging — and what would help them feel more included?

Mosaic in Action: A global corporation identifies zones by department and applies customized inclusion strategies for underrepresented staff.

Zones of Identity™

Definition: A branded framework created by Dr. Karissa Thomas that charts the changing areas where identity is expressed, negotiated, and transformed. It emphasizes how people move between authenticity, adaptation, and alignment.

Business Application: Organizations can utilize Zones of Identity™ to more effectively

assist employees in managing cultural shifts, career changes, or generational differences.

Leadership Insight: Identity is fluid. Leaders who grasp the layers of identity develop more adaptable, compassionate strategies for diversity and progress.

Cultural Caution: Misusing or oversimplifying the Zones of Identity™ risks turning it into mere labels. It needs to be applied with nuance and depth.

Mosaic Question: Which identity zone do you occupy during moments of challenge — and what changes when you feel fully seen?

Mosaic in Action: A leadership retreat presents the Zones of Identity™ framework, guiding participants to reflect on how their identities shift between personal and professional realms.

Zones of Proximal Identity

Definition: The range between one's current self-understanding and the next stage of identity development, similar to the educational concept of the zone of proximal development.

Business Application: In leadership growth, recognizing employees' proximal identity zones helps customize mentorship, stretch assignments, and succession planning.

Leadership Insight: Growth occurs at the edge of comfort. Leaders who effectively work within these zones create environments where individuals feel both challenged and supported in evolving their identities.

Cultural Caution: Overstepping this zone can cause identity shock or burnout, especially for those navigating marginalized identities in dominant culture spaces.

Mosaic Question: Whose identity growth could you support by providing the right balance of challenge and safety?

Mosaic in Action: A mid-level manager from a rural background is mentored into a global leadership role. The mentor introduces international project work gradually, aligning each assignment with the manager's developing professional identity.

Zones of Tolerance

Definition: The level of stress, conflict, or discomfort an individual or group can tolerate before performance, safety, or trust deteriorates.

Business Application: Leaders utilize zones of tolerance to assess organizational resilience and develop interventions that ensure teams stay within a healthy adaptive range.

Leadership Insight: Growth demands discomfort, but excessive stress leads to collapse. Skilled leaders understand how to balance challenge with support.

Cultural Caution: Tolerance levels vary across different cultures and individuals. Leaders should not assume that what "tolerance" looks like is the same everywhere.

Mosaic Question: Is your team growing healthily or being pushed beyond its limits?

Mosaic in Action: A healthcare team monitors stress levels during crisis response, rotating shifts to maintain staff within sustainable tolerance zones.

Zoom Fatigue (Cultural Variant)

Definition: The exhaustion caused by prolonged video conferencing, intensified by cross-cultural communication stress, different time zones, and technology gaps.

Business Application: Global teams working virtually need guidelines for meeting length, camera use, and culturally inclusive participation to lessen burnout.

Leadership Insight: Zoom fatigue is not just mental fatigue—it's also cultural fatigue, as non-native speakers and marginalized employees often use extra energy to "perform" on camera.

Cultural Caution: Some cultures prefer formal video presence, while others favor audio-only or asynchronous communication. Ignoring these norms can damage trust.

Mosaic Question: Are your virtual meeting practices sustainable for all the cultural groups you lead?

Mosaic in Action: An international project team rotates meeting times to share the inconvenience across time zones and adopts a "camera-optional" policy, boosting participation and cutting fatigue.

Zoom Inclusion

Definition: Intentionally practice creating belonging and equity in virtual and hybrid spaces, making sure all participants are seen, heard, and valued.

Business Application: Zoom inclusion involves creating meetings with accessibility features, fair speaking opportunities, and awareness of digital fatigue.

Leadership Insight: Digital tools can either reinforce exclusion or promote inclusion. Leaders who practice Zoom inclusion build spaces that break down borders and barriers.

Cultural Caution: Not all participants have equal access to technology, bandwidth, or quiet workspaces. Leaders must adjust expectations with fairness in mind.

Mosaic Question: How inclusive are your virtual spaces — and who is excluded from the conversation?

Mosaic in Action: A global nonprofit incorporates multilingual captions, flexible meeting schedules, and rotating facilitation roles to promote Zoom inclusion across regions.

Zoom Privilege

Definition: The benefit possessed by individuals or organizations with dependable internet, private work areas, and technology access that enable smooth video conferencing.

Business Application: In hybrid workplaces, leaders must address disparities in remote work setups to ensure that those without Zoom privileges are not excluded from decision-making or career opportunities.

Leadership Insight: Access to technology creates a power dynamic—those who have it can dominate virtual spaces, leaving others unheard.

Cultural Caution: Assuming everyone can "just hop on Zoom" overlooks the realities of infrastructure, cost, and home environments in different regions or socioeconomic groups.

Mosaic Question: Whose voice might you be missing because they can't—or choose not to—be on video?

Mosaic in Action: A consulting firm adds phone dial-in and asynchronous feedback channels to all meetings, ensuring fair input from team members with limited internet bandwidth.

◈ LETTER Z CALLOUT

"Zero-sum thinking shrinks possibility; equity expands it."

Reflection Questions

- Where do zero-tolerance policies reinforce compliance over growth?
- How do zones of safety and belonging shift power dynamics?
- What does zoom fatigue reveal about inclusion in digital spaces?

Practical Move

In your next online or in-person session, set one ground rule that promotes safety and inclusion — and explain why it matters for collective growth.

TRAINING COMPANION TOOLS

Quick Reference A–Z Term List

This section provides a quick alphabetical index of the glossary terms. It is meant for rapid reference during trainings, coaching sessions, or strategic planning discussions. Use this list to find key concepts easily. For a complete understanding—including definitions, leadership uses, cultural cautions, and Mosaic Question™ prompts—refer back to the full entry in the main glossary.

Letter	Terms
A	Accountability, Allyship, Assimilation, Authenticity
B	Bias, Belonging, Burnout, Boundaries
C	Code-Switching, Cognitive Dissonance, Cultural Competence, Cultural Fluency, Cultural Humility
D	Disruption, Disparity, Dissonance
E	Equity, Emotional Labor, Erasure
F	Fragility, Feedback Fatigue, Foundational Values
G	Gaslighting, Gatekeeping, Generational Intelligence
H	Hair Politics, Healing Justice, Heritage Language, Hidden Curriculum, Historical Repair
I	Inclusion Fatigue, Identity Agility, Implicit Bias
J	Justice-Oriented Leadership, Joy as Resistance
K	Knowledge Gaps, Kinship Bias

Letter	Terms
L	Listening Culture, Lived Experience, Language Dominance
M	Microaggressions, Mirror Work, Mosaic Intelligence
N	Narrative Power, Naming Discomfort, Norm Shifting
O	Othering, Organizational Trust, Outsider Within
P	Power Literacy, Psychological Safety, Performative Allyship
Q	Quiet Disengagement, Questioning the Norm
R	Representation, Restorative Leadership, Respectability Politics
S	Silence in Systems, Stereotype Threat, Storytelling as Strategy
T	Tone Policing, Tokenism, Trust Leakage
U	Unconscious Bias, Unspoken Rules, Underrepresentation
V	Voice, Visibility, Validation-Seeking, Values in Action
W	Whiteness, Worldviews, Workplace Culture, Witnessing
X	Xenophobia, Xenocentrism, X-Factor Bias
Y	Youth, Yearning, Yet-to-Be-Seen Voices
Z	Zoom Fatigue, Zones of Identity, Zeitgeist of Now

Acronym Index

360 Feedback – A performance review method where input is gathered from supervisors, peers, and subordinates to provide a full-circle perspective on leadership and work style

AI – Artificial Intelligence

CEO – Chief Executive Officer

COO – Chief Operating Officer

CQ – Cultural Intelligence

CRT – Critical Race Theory

CWS – Critical Whiteness Studies

DEI – Diversity, Equity, and Inclusion

ERG – Employee Resource Group

ESG – Environmental, Social, and Governance

EQ – Emotional Intelligence

GM – General Manager

HR – Human Resources

JEDI – Justice, Equity, Diversity, Inclusion

KPI – Key Performance Indicator

LGBTQ+ – Lesbian, Gay, Bisexual, Transgender, Queer/Questioning, and others

NGO – Non-Governmental Organization

OKRs – Objectives and Key Results

PR – Public Relations

Q&A – Questions and Answers

RACI – Responsible, Accountable, Consulted, Informed

ROI – Return on Investment

TCK – Third Culture Kid

VP – Vice President

How to Use This Glossary
For Training, Coaching, and Strategic Culture Work

The Mosaic Way™ Field Glossary is more than just a list of terms—it's a practical tool for transformation. It aims to help leaders, facilitators, educators, and teams move from awareness to action by identifying unspoken dynamics, uncovering hidden cultural codes, and creating shared language for belonging. Each entry is designed for real-world use, providing definitions, leadership insights, cultural cautions, and Mosaic Questions™ to encourage deeper dialogue.

This glossary can be integrated into leadership programs, onboarding processes, DEI initiatives, coaching engagements, facilitation sessions, and organizational policy reform. Below are ways to bring the glossary to life in different contexts.

In Leadership Coaching

- Use glossary terms to identify and name the emotional and cultural factors driving performance challenges, disengagement, or conflict.
- Invite leaders to highlight entries that align with their current growth edges or recent challenges.
- Introduce lesser-known concepts such as **trust leakage**, **x-factor bias**, or **emotional taxation** to expand reflection and insight.
- Use Mosaic Questions™ from relevant entries to help reframe resistance, clarify values, and explore the impact of leadership choices.

When to use

- Preparing for high-stakes or emotionally intense conversations
- Addressing avoidance of feedback or unhealthy power dynamics
- Providing coaching for burnout recovery, reducing turnover, or repairing company culture

In DEI, HR, or Organizational Strategy

- Choose a "term of the week" to feature in newsletters, internal chats, or learning sessions.
- Embed glossary terms into policies, performance evaluations, and onboarding materials.
- Conduct culture audits using entries such as **psychological safety**, **invisible labor**, or **representation gap**.
- Update leadership competency models with language that integrates identity awareness, emotional clarity, and cultural nuance.
- Link DEI metrics to glossary language to measure progress beyond optics or compliance.

When to use

- Designing inclusive leadership frameworks
- Rewriting hiring, onboarding, and conflict resolution protocols
- Facilitating cross-functional strategy meetings or culture alignment sessions

In Facilitation, Retreats, and Team Reflection

- Have each participant select a term that resonates and share why it matters to them.
- Use related clusters of terms—such as **burnout, belonging**, and **boundaries**—to anchor retreat or workshop discussions.
- Incorporate Mosaic Questions™ into listening circles, restorative practices, and post-conflict debriefs.
- Create a visual "glossary wall" for teams to track which terms they are adopting in daily practice.

- Use culturally layered entries like **code-switching**, **tone policing**, or **zones of identity** to spark empathy across generational, racial, and neurodiverse lines.

When to use

- Hosting all-staff or cross-team retreats
- Leading trust-building after organizational change, crisis, or merger
- Supporting emotional recovery after extended stress cycles

Tips for Meaningful Use

- **Avoid weaponizing language.** Use glossary terms to build shared understanding—not as labels or tools for shaming.
- **Let discomfort lead to discovery.** Tension around a term can signal an important growth opportunity.
- **Revisit entries often.** As language evolves, terms may gain new relevance over time.
- **Encourage shared ownership.** Ask *How can this glossary become part of our daily leadership language, not just a book on a shelf?*

Reflection Questions for Teams & Leaders

Turning Language into Leadership Practice

The Mosaic Way™ Field Glossary is more than just a reference—it's a reflection, a guide, and a catalyst. Language influences culture, and culture influences how we lead, include, listen, and decide. These questions are created to help you and your team understand the terms not only intellectually but also emotionally and relationally.

Whether you're leading a team retreat, guiding a strategic reset, or reflecting on your growth as a leader, use these prompts to

- Spark deeper dialogue
- Build trust across differences
- Translate insight into practice
- Name what's been unspoken
- Restore clarity where confusion or conflict has taken root

You can use them for personal journaling, coaching sessions, team debriefs, or as discussion starters for culture-shifting meetings.

Reflection Prompts

1. Which term from the glossary resonated most with you, and what personal or professional moment did it remind you of?
2. Which experience provided you with words for something you previously couldn't describe?
3. Where in your organization is language used to preserve power rather than distribute it?
4. Which term challenged your leadership style—and how can you embrace that discomfort rather than rush past it?
5. Which Mosaic Question™ resonated with you— and what deeper truth might it be prompting you to explore?
6. What are the risks of leaving certain words, dynamics, or identities unnamed in your workplace?
7. Where is emotional labor being overlooked—and how can you spread recognition and responsibility?
8. How could your leadership change if you focused on the Mosaic Intelligence pillars Emotional Integrity, Cultural Fluency, and Identity Agility?
9. Which glossary term do you wish had been included during your onboarding, training, or early career discussions?
10. How will you hold yourself—and your team—responsible for not just understanding these terms but also applying them clearly, carefully, and consistently?

11. How does your current communication style embody the values of inclusion, trust, and emotional clarity?
12. What's one question, term, or insight you want to bring up in your next meeting, hiring process, training session, or policy review?

Sample Dialogues and Discussion Starters

1. Navigating Burnout and Boundaries

Context A team member is showing signs of emotional fatigue.
Manager

"I've noticed how much you've been carrying lately. The term burnout came up in a leadership conversation I had yesterday, and it made me wonder—have we unintentionally created a culture where rest feels out of reach? Let's talk honestly about your bandwidth and how we can adjust expectations without guilt."

2. Addressing Representation Without Tokenism

Context A company highlights a single team member's identity but hasn't addressed structural gaps.

Team Lead

"I want to name something I'm reflecting on. While it's great that we celebrated your story in the newsletter, I realize we haven't backed that up with systemic change. The term representation really stuck with me. I'd love to hear your honest thoughts—do you feel truly supported, or spotlighted without support?"

3. Repairing a Harmful Comment

Context A colleague made a culturally insensitive remark.
Colleague

"I've been sitting with something I said the other day. I read the entry on microaggressions in the glossary, and I recognize how my comment may have landed. I want to take responsibility and better understand the impact. Would you be open to talking about how that moment felt for you?"

4. Reframing Feedback Avoidance
Context A leader is struggling to give feedback across lines of difference. Coach

"I hear that you want to be respectful—but avoiding feedback can actually deepen the gap. Let's explore the glossary terms feedback and emotional labor. How can you give feedback in a way that honors both clarity and care?"

5. Exploring Cultural Identity on a Team Retreat
Context A diverse team is engaging in reflective work. Facilitator

"Today, we'll be working with the term code-switching. Think about a time when you had to adjust how you spoke, moved, or presented yourself just to feel safe or accepted at work. What did that moment cost you—and what would true inclusion have looked like instead?"

6. Building Shared Vocabulary After Conflict
Context A cross-functional team recently experienced tension. Team Lead

"We've had some hard moments lately, and I want us to move through—not around—the discomfort. I found a term in the glossary called trust leakage. It describes what happens when small moments of inconsistency chip away at psychological safety. Can we name where trust may have been impacted, and what repair might look like?"

7. Naming Invisible Labor in Project Planning
Context A woman of color consistently does unseen relational work on her team.

Colleague or Manager

"I want to bring something into the open. As I read the term invisible labor, I realized how often you've been the one to smooth things over, keep communication flowing, or check in on morale—and how rarely that's acknowledged. How can we share this load more equitably moving forward?"

Group Exercises and Culture-Building Prompts

The following exercises help teams shift from conceptual understanding to practical alignment. Each prompt is based on the three pillars of the Mosaic Intelligence Method™—**emotional integrity, cultural fluency,** and **identity agility**—and aims to encourage dialogue, build trust, and generate actionable insights. All can be customized for in-person or virtual sessions, whether for large groups or small teams.

1. Glossary Wall Terms That Shape Us

Purpose: Build shared vocabulary and self-awareness.

Instructions

- Give each participant 3–5 glossary terms on individual cards, or allow them to select their own from the glossary.
- Have them silently choose one that resonates most with their lived or work experience.
- On a sticky note or virtual board, write
  ○ **Why this term matters**
  ○ **Where they've seen it show up** (positively or negatively)
- Create a visual "glossary wall" with all responses.
- **Debrief**: What patterns emerged? Which terms feel overlooked in your current culture?

2. Mosaic Match-Up Connecting Terms to Real Scenarios

Purpose: Strengthen the link between glossary concepts and real-world situations.

Instructions

- Prepare 10 real or fictional workplace scenarios (e.g., a team conflict, a misstep in a DEI initiative, a leadership transition).
- In groups of 2–4, have participants match each scenario with 1–2 glossary terms.
- Ask *Why did you choose those terms? What leadership response would align with the Mosaic Way™?*
- Optional Rotate groups so each set interprets different scenarios.

3. Cultural Fluency Roundtable

Purpose: Explore how identity and communication intersect in daily work life.

Instructions

- Divide participants into small groups.
- Pose the question *When have you had to explain, minimize, or adjust part of your identity at work?*
- After sharing, assign glossary terms such as *code-switching, tone policing,* or *emotional taxation.*
- Ask Which term best describes your experience? How could your workplace reduce this burden?

4. The Discomfort Audit

Purpose: Normalize constructive discomfort as a driver for growth.

Instructions

- Ask each person to choose one glossary term that makes them uncomfortable or unsure.
- In pairs or small groups, discuss
  - What about this term brings discomfort?
  - Could that discomfort point to a learning edge or blind spot?
  - What's one action that would move you toward greater understanding or accountability?
- Reinforce that discomfort is not failure—it's valuable feedback.

5. Vision Mapping with the Pillars

Purpose: Connect everyday behaviors to the Mosaic Intelligence Method™ pillars.

Instructions

- Create three boards labeled *Emotional Integrity*, *Cultural Fluency*, *Identity Agility*.
- Have team members brainstorm behaviors, systems, or language that would bring each pillar to life in your organization.
- Use prompts such as
  - "What does emotional integrity look like in how we handle mistakes?"
  - "Where does cultural fluency show up in our team dynamics?"

- ○ "How do we show—or fail to show—identity agility in hiring, mentoring, or conflict resolution?"
- Use the collected insights to co-create a shared vision statement or team commitment charter.

Mosaic Method Pillars Overview:
Emotional Integrity. Cultural Fluency. Identity Agility.

The Mosaic Intelligence Method™ is built on three interconnected pillars that support humane, responsive, and inclusive leadership. Together, they provide a foundation for transforming individual behavior, organizational culture, and collective impact.

Each glossary entry in this book links to one or more of these pillars—helping leaders, educators, and changemakers shift from reactive habits to intentional, mindful leadership practices.

Emotional Integrity

Definition

The ability to recognize, manage, and align your emotional reactions with your values—even when under pressure.

In Practice

Leaders with emotional integrity don't just manage emotions—they honor them. They listen deeply, repair harm when it occurs, and lead from presence rather than performance. This includes the courage to name discomfort, embrace vulnerability, and stay accountable when emotions run high.

Look for terms such as

psychological safety, emotional labor, trust leakage, tone escalation, repair culture.

Cultural Fluency

Definition

The ability to navigate, respect, and respond to cultural differences with curiosity, clarity, and care.

In Practice

Cultural fluency goes beyond just being competent. It's not only about understanding other groups—it's about adjusting how we lead, communicate, and make decisions to respect different lived experiences. Fluent leaders recognize coded norms, challenge bias, and use inclusive language across race, gender, ability, class, and generation.

Look for terms such as

code-switching, cultural taxation, representation gap, tone policing, and assimilation fatigue.

Identity Agility

Definition

The ability to understand, accept, and adapt to changing identities—yours and others'—without stereotyping or oversimplifying.

In Practice

Identity agility involves understanding that people are constantly evolving. Agile leaders shift perspectives, navigate across generational or neurodiverse boundaries, and adapt to social contexts without losing authenticity. They address complex identities with flexibility rather than fear.

Look for terms such as

generational misreading, zones of identity, intersectional fatigue, naming dynamics, stereotype pressure.

The Whole Mosaic

These three pillars are not just ideals—they are active practices. Use them as your internal compass while you navigate the glossary, and as an external perspective to assess how your culture manifests in moments of pressure, power, and possibility.

CONCLUSION
From Language to Leadership

This glossary may have started as a list of terms—but it was never only about vocabulary. It was about voice. Values. A shared vision for leadership that respects difference, promotes dignity, and mends what hierarchy and history have too often harmed.

Throughout these pages, you've encountered words that express what is often felt but rarely spoken—the hidden currents of power, the quiet weight of silence, the coded language of exclusion, and the emotional framework of genuine belonging. You've seen how bias can hide behind neutrality, how culture influences not only what we say but how we say it—and who we believe. You've explored how identity doesn't just inform communication—it changes it.

But knowing the language is only the beginning. Naming is not the same as living. Awareness is not the same as action. The real work of The Mosaic Way™ begins when we bring these terms into our meetings, policies, hiring practices, mentorship relationships, team dynamics, and moments of tension. It starts when we stop using language to protect comfort—and begin using it to expand capacity. Capacity for justice, for relationship, and for sustainable change.

Leadership today is not about having all the answers; it's about asking better questions. It involves noticing what's missing, holding complexity without reducing it to clichés, and having the courage to sit with discomfort instead of seeking control. It's about developing emotional intelligence to recognize when we've caused harm and cultural intelligence to repair it. It also means making room for voices that differ from our own and creating systems that do more than just demonstrate inclusion—they actively practice it.

It's about moving from transactional engagement to relational leadership—where people are not just managed, but truly seen, heard, and respected.

Let this glossary be more than just a reference. Make it a living practice—a shared language for brave conversations, evolving teams, and workplaces where humanity is not just a footnote but the foundation. Whether you're reshaping culture, healing from institutional harm, mentoring the next generation, or redefining how you show up—these words can support your journey. But it's your presence, integrity, and courage that truly carry the meaning forward.

Speak clearly. Listen openly. Lead by creating space for others' truths because they do exist. *The Mosaic Way*™ doesn't stop here. It continues in every hallway conversation, hiring decision, apology, policy update, classroom exchange, and courageous question that brings us closer to shared understanding.

Language can divide, but it can also heal, connect, and inspire new possibilities. Let this be the start of that reimagining.

AUTHOR'S CLOSING NOTE

The Language We Carry Forward

When I first started this glossary, I wasn't just collecting terms—I was addressing a deeper need. The need for language that can embrace complexity. That can validate the unspoken. That can be used in real time by real people facing real tension.

Throughout this journey, I've listened to exhausted professionals, brilliant leaders, under-recognized innovators, and emerging voices—all searching for words to match their experiences. These realities weren't always reflected in textbooks. They lived in meeting rooms, on Zoom calls, in classroom silences, in hiring bias, in policy gaps, and in all the in-between places where identity and power collide.

This glossary is not a conclusion—it's a continuation. It's part of a living, breathing framework the Mosaic Intelligence Method™. This method was developed not just from theory, but from lived experience—witnessing the quiet unraveling of belonging, the moments of cultural misalignment left unaddressed, and the emotional courage required to keep leading through it all.

My hope is that this glossary has provided you with more than just words. I trust it has offered validation, clarity, and guidance. That it has helped you feel less isolated in the in-betweens. That it has inspired better questions. And that it has reminded you leadership is not about perfection—it's about presence.

Whether you are a coach, a team leader, a DEI strategist, an educator, or someone who simply wants to improve how you treat others—

this language is now part of your toolkit. Use it thoughtfully. Use it courageously.

As we move forward, may we remember

- That language shapes not just how we describe the world, but how we lead within it.
- That every glossary term is also a decision point.
- And that our capacity to grow depends on our willingness to name what we once avoided.

Thank you for doing this work—whether quietly or publicly, personally or institutionally. You are contributing to a movement aimed at making leadership more honest, communication more humane, and culture more whole.

I'll see you in the next conversation.

— Dr. Karissa Thomas

Founder, The Mosaic Way™

ABOUT THE AUTHOR

Dr. Karissa Thomas is an award-winning author, educator, and leadership strategist whose work integrates emotional intelligence, cultural insight, and identity-focused communication. With over twenty years of experience in education, corporate leadership, and the insurance industry, her approach blends research-based insight with practical application.

Her doctoral research centered on identity conflict and belonging in cross-cultural professional settings, and she has since created the Mosaic Intelligence Method™—a transformative framework for leading with emotional integrity, cultural flexibility, and identity agility.

Dr. Thomas has spoken to thousands through keynotes, courses, and trainings, helping leaders navigate complex dynamics with clarity, courage, and care. Her work is based on the strong belief that language can either harm or heal—and that leadership begins with the words we choose, the stories we honor, and the systems we are willing to change.

For more information, visit **www.mosaicintelligencemethod.com**.

Journal Pages
for Self and Team Insight

_____

_____

_____

_____

_____

_____

_____

_____

_____

_____

_____

_____

_____

_____

_____

_____

_____

_____

www.ingramcontent.com/pod-product-compliance
Lightning Source LLC
Chambersburg PA
CBHW052014030426

42335CB00026B/3138